W9-BNS-814

QUALITY PLANNING AND ANALYSIS
From Product Development through Use

McGraw-Hill Series in Industrial Engineering and Management Science

Consulting Editors

Kenneth E. Case
Department of Industrial Engineering and Management
Oklahoma State University
Philip M. Wolfe
Department of Industrial and Management Systems Engineering
Arizona State University

Barish and Kaplan: *Economic Analysis: For Engineering and Managerial Decision Making*

Bedworth, Henderson, and Wolfe: *Computer-Integrated Design and Manufacturing*

Black: *The Design of the Factory with a Future*

Blank: *Statistical Procedures for Engineering, Management, and Science*

Denton: *Safety Management: Improving Performance*

Dervitsiotis: *Operations Management*

Hicks: *Introduction to Industrial Engineering and Management Science*

Huchingson: *New Horizons for Human Factors in Design*

Juran and Gryna: *Quality Planning and Analysis: From Product Development through Use*

Law and Kelton: *Simulation Modeling and Analysis*

Leherer: *White-Collar Productivity*

Moen, Noland, and Provost: *Improving Quality through Planned Experimentation*

Niebel, Draper, and Wysk: *Modern Manufacturing Process Engineering*

Polk: *Methods Analysis and Work Measurement*

Riggs and West: *Engineering Economics*

Riggs and West: *Essentials of Engineering Economics*

Taguchi, Elsayed, and Hsiang: *Quality Engineering in Production Systems*

Wu and Coppins: *Linear Programming and Extensions*

QUALITY PLANNING AND ANALYSIS

From Product Development through Use

Third Edition
prepared by Frank M. Gryna

J. M. Juran
Chairman Emeritus
Juran Institute, Inc.

Frank M. Gryna
Director, Center for Quality
University of Tampa

McGraw-Hill, Inc.
New York   St. Louis   San Francisco   Auckland   Bogotá   Caracas
Lisbon   London   Madrid   Mexico   Milan   Montreal   New Delhi
Paris   San Juan   Singapore   Sydney   Tokyo   Toronto

This book was set in Times Roman.
The editors were Eric M. Munson, Margery Luhrs, and John M. Morriss;
the production supervisor was Louise Karam.
The cover was designed by Joan Greenfield.
R. R. Donnelley & Sons Company was printer and binder.

QUALITY PLANNING AND ANALYSIS
From Product Development through Use

1 2 3 4 5 6 7 8 9 0 DOC DOC 9 0 9 8 7 6 5 4 3 2

ISBN 0-07-033183-9

Library of Congress Cataloging-in-Publication Data

Juran, J. M. (Joseph M.), (date).
    Quality planning and analysis: from product development through
use / J.M. Juran, Frank M. Gryna. — 3rd ed.
        p.   cm. — (McGraw-Hill series in industrial engineering and
management science)
    "Third edition prepared by Frank M. Gryna."
    Includes bibliographical references and index.
    ISBN 0-07-033183-9
    1. Quality control.   2. Quality assurance.   I. Gryna, Frank M.
II. Title.   III. Series.
TS156.J86   1993
    658.5'62—dc20   92-37795

ABOUT THE AUTHORS

J. M. Juran, Chairman Emeritus, Juran Institute, has since 1924 pursued a varied career in management as an engineer, industrial executive, government administrator, university professor, impartial labor arbitrator, corporate director, and management consultant. This career has been marked by a search for the underlying principles which are common to all managerial activity. Applied to the specialty of management for quality, this search has produced the leading international reference literature and the leading international training courses, training books, and videocassettes:

- *Juran's Quality Control Handbook* (fourth edition, 1988) is the international standard reference work on the subject.
- *Making Quality Happen: Upper Management's Role* (fifth edition, 1988) is the pioneering training manual dealing with the strategies needed to attain and hold quality leadership, the roles of upper managers in leading their companies to that goal, and the means to be used by upper managers to supply that leadership. This manual has been edited and published in book form by The Free Press (Macmillan) under the title *Juran on Leadership for Quality*.
- *Juran on Quality Improvement* (1981) is a series of 16 videocassettes plus related training manuals on the subject of annual quality improvement and cost reduction.
- *Planning for Quality* (second edition, 1990) is the notes for the course which provide managers with a structured approach to company-wide quality planning. The bound version has been published by The Free Press under the title *Juran on Planning for Quality*.
- *Quality Planning and Analysis* (with F. M. Gryna) third edition, 1993.
- *Juran on Quality Planning* is a series of videocassettes plus training manuals on the subject of quality planning.

In the field of general management, Dr. Juran's book *Managerial Breakthrough* generalizes the principles of creating beneficial change (breakthrough) and of preventing adverse change (control). The book *The Corporate Director* (with J. K. Louden) generalizes the work of the Board of Directors.

Collectively these and other publications have been translated into sixteen languages: Chinese, Danish, Finnish, French, German, Hungarian, Italian, Japanese, Korean, Polish, Portuguese, Rumanian, Russian, Serbo-Croatian, Spanish, and Swedish.

A holder of degrees in engineering and law, Dr. Juran maintains an active schedule as author and international lecturer, while serving various industrial companies, governmental agencies, and other institutions as a consultant. His honors include over thirty medals, fellowships, honorary memberships, etc., awarded by professional and honor societies in twelve countries. The most recent of these include membership in the National Academy of Engineering and the Order of the Sacred Treasure awarded by the Emperor of Japan for ". . . the development of Quality Control in Japan and the facilitation of U.S. and Japanese friendship."

Frank M. Gryna is Director of the Center for Quality and Professor of Business Administration at the University of Tampa. From 1982 to 1991, he was with the Juran Institute, as Senior Vice-President. Prior to 1982, Dr. Gryna was based at Bradley University, where he taught industrial engineering and also served as Acting Dean of the College of Engineering and Technology. He is now Distinguished Professor of Industrial Engineering Emeritus. In addition, he is a consultant for various companies on the managerial and statistical aspects of quality and reliability programs, from initial design through field use.

Dr. Gryna also served in the U.S. Army Signal Corps Engineering Labs and at the Esso Research and Engineering Company. At the Space Systems Division of the Martin Company, he was Manager of Reliability and Quality Assurance.

He coauthored *Quality Planning and Analysis* with J. M. Juran and was Associate Editor of the second, third and fourth editions of the *Quality Control Handbook*. His research project, *Quality Circles,* received the Book of the Year Award sponsored by various publishers and the Institute of Industrial Engineers. He has received recognitions as a Fellow of the American Society for Quality Control, a Fellow of the Institute of Industrial Engineers, a Certified Quality Engineer, a Certified Reliability Engineer, and a Professional Engineer (Quality Engineering). He has been the recipient of various awards, including the E. L. Grant Award of the ASQC, Engineer of the Year Award of the Peoria Engineering Council, teaching and professional excellence awards from Bradley University, and the Award of Excellence of the Quality Control and Reliability Engineering Division of the Institute of Industrial Engineers. Dr. Gryna is also the recipient of the Ott Foundation Award, presented by the Metropolitan Chapter of the American Society for Quality Control.

CONTENTS

20 Marketing, Field Performance, and Customer Service

21 Marketing, Field Performance, and Customer Service—Statistical Tools

22 Administrative and Support Operations

PREFACE

This is a textbook about achieving customer satisfaction. Not just about meeting specifications, not just about statistical process control, but a textbook about—to use an old-fashioned word—quality.

Meeting the quality needs of society requires an active role by all the major activities of an organization. Marketing Research must discover the quality needs of the users; Product Development must create designs responsive to these needs; Manufacturing and Operations Planning must devise processes capable of executing the product designs; Production and Operations must regulate these processes to achieve the desired qualities; Purchasing must obtain adequate materials; Inspection and Test must prove the adequacy of the product through simulated use; Marketing must sell the product for the proper application; and Customer Service must observe the usage, remedy failures, and report on opportunities for improvement. In addition, the administrative and support activities must meet the needs of their customers, both internal and external.

The quality subactivities present in each of these major activities are themselves collectively a major activity which has become known as the "quality function." It may be defined as that collection of activities, no matter where performed, through which the company achieves customer satisfaction. The outlines of this quality function have been emerging clearly. It has now become evident that, in common with other major company functions, successful conduct of the quality function demands much specialized knowledge and many specialized tools, as well as trained specialists to use these tools and apply this knowledge. This book rejects the concept that the control of quality is primarily a matter of statistical techniques. Instead, it develops the viewpoint that product and service quality requires managerial, technological, and statistical concepts throughout all the major functions of an organization. Some of this will seem like strong medicine; it is.

Since the publication of the second edition in 1980, we have seen an explosion of new concepts. This third edition explains concepts such as strategic quality management, competitive benchmarking, quality function deployment, self-managing teams, employee empowerment, zone control charts, box-and-whisker plots, and more—many more. Also, we recognize and discuss the great strides that have been made in applying concepts in service industries.

With material on a broad subject such as product quality, topics can be presented in several sequences. The sequence selected for this book takes the viewpoint that the practitioner is often faced with the urgent task of solving the quality problem of current products. An equally important task is proper planning for quality of future products. This latter task must sometimes wait until the most urgent problems are solved. The foregoing priorities have guided the sequence of topics in this book.

A brief Chapter 1 has important definitions and concepts, including distinctions between manufacturing and service industries; Chapter 2 presents a four-step assessment process to help an organization determine where it stands on quality today; Chapters 3–5 explain some structure in the form of three quality processes; in Chapters 6–8, we speak about strategy, organization, and culture. The remainder of the book presents the elements of a broad process covering the collection of activities through which we achieve customer satisfaction. For many of these activities, the operative phrase is *prevention of quality problems*.

Throughout the book, chapters on statistical concepts have been included, as needed, to supplement the managerial concepts. However, the only mathematical background assumed for the book is college algebra, and there is no attempt to provide a state of advanced knowledge in statistical methodology. There are many excellent books that cover the statistical aspects in greater depth.

Readers may wish to rearrange the sequence of chapters to meet their specific needs.

All chapters include problems. These problems are so structured as to reflect the "real" world "outside" rather than the more limited world of the classroom. Such problems require the student to face the realities which confront managers, designers, engineers, marketers, inspectors, users, and others involved in the quality function. Students must make assumptions, estimate economics, reach conclusions from incomplete facts, and otherwise adapt themselves to the imperfect world of the practitioner. An *Instructor's Manual* provides solutions, additional questions, case examples, and enlargements of selected figures for preparing transparencies.

Appendix I contains sample questions from former ASQC Quality Engineer and Reliability Engineer certification examinations. These questions and the associated answers are reprinted with permission from *Quality Progress,* February 1976, August 1978, September 1980, and July 1984.

We also draw attention to the relationship of *Quality Planning and*

Analysis and *Juran's Quality Control Handbook,* fourth edition (J. M. Juran, editor-in-chief, and Frank M. Gryna, associate editor, McGraw-Hill Book Company, New York, 1988). The handbook is a reference compendium which, through broad sale in the English language plus translation into other languages, has become the standard international reference work on the subject. In preparing *Quality Planning and Analysis,* we have introduced frequent references to the handbook (as well as to other sources) where space limitations placed restriction on detail.

Many organizations have kindly given us permission to reprint material from their publications. We particularly note the helping hands of the American Society for Quality Control, the Juran Institute, Inc., and McGraw-Hill, Inc. We are grateful to the literary executor of the late Sir Ronald A. Fisher, F.R.S., to Dr. Frank Yates, F.R.S., and to Longman Group Ltd., London, for permission to reprint Table III from their book *Statistical Tables for Biological, Agricultural and Medical Research* (fourth edition, 1974). We also appreciate the cooperation of the Ford Motor Company in enabling us to use some material from their Reliability Methods Modules.

Leonard A. Seder deserves special mention for his contribution of a case problem on quality costs. In addition, his many contributions to quality methodology have been reflected in this book.

This third edition was prepared by Frank M. Gryna. The content draws upon the concepts of previous editions. Many of these concepts were originally proposed by J. M. Juran as part of his pioneering work in the field of quality management.

The late 1980s saw the emergence of a remarkable focus and action on quality. We need to make this continue—with emphasis on action.

ACKNOWLEDGMENTS

Many people deserve to be recognized. I particularly want to thank the reviewers of the manuscript. Their efforts—a labor of love under tight deadlines—provided me with extremely useful comments. These reviewers were: Sant Arora, University of Minnesota; Albert B. Bishop, Ohio State University; R. J. Buhman, University of Nebraska; Kenneth E. Case, Oklahoma State University; James P. Gilbert, University of Georgia; Lynwood A. Johnson, Georgia Institute of Technology; Thomas A. Little, San Jose University; Cecil R. Peterson, GMI Engineering and Management Institute; C. B. Rogers, M. J. Steinberg, and Gary Wasserman, Wayne State University.

Dean Ronald L. Vaughn provided me with the time and support that brought this edition to completion.

Then there was the host of people that I called upon for input and advice. My son, Derek S. Gryna, provided help on many topics. My colleagues at Bradley University, Juran Institute, and The University of Tampa, as well as the many quality practitioners, were also generous with their time. To cite a few of many: Roger Berger, Kenneth Case, Gordon Couturier, Douglas Ekings, Joseph Emanuel, Al Endres, Robert Hoogstoel, K. S. Krishnamoorthi, Bennie Pandorf, John Ramberg, James Riley, Jr., Lennart Sandholm, Judith Schalick, Mary Jane Schenck and Roy Stringfellow.

Where would authors be without the help of those who sit at a typewriter or a personal computer? This burden was carried by my wife, Dee, and Brenda Woodard with the help of Laura Molina.

In creating a book, the greatest burden is on the shoulders of the family of an author. A book often—indeed always—interferes with family life. Throughout all of my career, my wife, Dee, has amazed me with her patience and support. I'll try my best to replace the lost evenings and weekends.

Frank M. Gryna

CHAPTER

1

BASIC CONCEPTS

1.1 QUALITY—A LOOK AT HISTORY

Listen to the president of a specialty casting manufacturing company: "Our scrap and rework costs this year were five times our profit. Because of those costs, we have had to increase our selling price and we subsequently lost market share. Quality is no longer a technical issue; it is a business issue."

Does this company have a marginal quality reputation in the marketplace? No. Customers rate it as having the best quality available. But the old approach of inspection has failed it—and it has embarked on a new approach.

Our forefathers knew—as we know—that quality is important. Metrology, specifications, inspection—all go back many centuries before the Christian era.

Then came the twentieth century. The pace quickened with a lengthy procession of "new" activities and ideas launched under a bewildering array of names: quality control, quality planning, continuous quality improvement, defect prevention, statistical process control, reliability engineering, quality cost analysis, zero defects, total quality control, supplier certification, quality circles, quality audit, quality assurance, quality function deployment, Taguchi methods, competitive benchmarking. This book will discuss these concepts.

1

Following World War II, two major forces emerged that have had a profound impact on quality.

The first force was the Japanese revolution in quality. Prior to World War II, many Japanese products were perceived, throughout the world, to be poor in quality. To help sell their products in international markets, the Japanese took some revolutionary steps to improve quality:

1. The upper managers personally took charge of leading the revolution.
2. All levels and functions received training in the quality disciplines.
3. Quality improvement projects were undertaken on a continuing basis—at a revolutionary pace.

The Japanese success has been almost legendary.

The second major force was the prominence of product quality in the public mind. Several trends converged to highlight this prominence: product liability cases, concern about the environment, some major disasters and near disasters, pressure by consumer organizations, and the awareness of the role of quality in trade, weapons, and other areas of international competition.

These two major forces, combined with others, have resulted (for many companies) in a changing set of business conditions that are enmeshed with the quality parameter.

1.2 QUALITY—THE CHANGING BUSINESS CONDITIONS

The forces identified above have resulted in quality becoming a cardinal priority for most organizations. This reality has evolved through a number of changing business conditions. These include:

1. *Competition.* In the past, higher quality usually meant the need to pay a higher price. Today, customers can obtain high quality and low prices simultaneously. Thus, it is not sufficient to have a "good quality image." If the internal costs of achieving that image (sorting inspection, rework, scrap) are high, a company will lose sales because of the higher prices needed to cover these costs of poor quality.
2. *Changing customer.* Some companies are now entering industrial or consumer markets for the first time. For example, a manufacturer of small agricultural tractors for the individual farmer is now making engine blocks for a major automotive manufacturer. That automotive customer not only commands priority based on volume but is more demanding about the "quality system."
3. *Changing product mix.* For example, a computer manufacturer has shifted from primarily low-volume, high-price mix to a mix that includes high volume and low price. These new product lines have resulted in a need to reduce the internal costs of poor quality.

4. *Product complexity.* As systems have become more complex, the reliability requirements for suppliers of components have become more stringent.

5. *Higher levels of customer expectation.* Higher expectations, spawned by competition, take many forms. One example is lower variability around a target value on a product characteristic even though all product meets the specification limits. Another form of higher expectation is improved quality of service both before and after the sale.

The business conditions of yesteryear made it feasible to rely on simpler approaches to quality, e.g., product inspection to control quality and incorporation of the internal costs of poor quality into the selling price. In fairness to past leadership, such approaches worked admirably for many companies under past conditions. But will they work under current conditions? No. Today's ever-changing business conditions require new approaches if companies are to survive in competitive world markets.

Before learning these new approaches, we need to define some terms.

1.3 "QUALITY" DEFINED

The dictionary has many definitions of "quality." A short definition that has achieved acceptance is: *Quality is customer satisfaction.* "Fitness for use" is an alternative short definition.

Although such a brief definition has a focus, it must be developed further to provide a basis for action.

Unfolding the definition starts with defining the word "customer." A customer is anyone who is impacted by the product or process:

1. *External customers* include not only ultimate users but also intermediate processors, as well as merchants. Other customers are not purchasers but have some connection to the product, e.g., government regulatory bodies.

2. *Internal customers* include not only other divisions of a company that are provided with components for an assembly but others that are affected, e.g., a Purchasing Department that receives an engineering specification for a procurement.

A "product" is the output of any process. Three categories can be identified:

1. *Goods:* e.g., automobiles, circuit boards, reagent chemicals.

2. *Software:* e.g., a computer program, a report, an instruction.

3. *Service:* e.g., banking, insurance, transportation. Service also includes support activities within companies, e.g., employee benefits, plant maintenance, secretarial support.

Throughout this book, "product" means goods, software, or services.

Next, we need to define "customer satisfaction." This is achieved through two components: product features and freedom from deficiencies. Examples of the main categories of these components are shown in Table 1.1 for manufacturing and service industries. We see dramatic differences within manufacturing industries (assembly versus chemicals) and within services (restaurants versus banking).

A closer examination of the two components reveals further insights:

1. *Product features* have a major effect on *sales income* (through market share, premium prices, etc.). In many industries, the total external customer population can be segmented by the level or "grade" of quality desired. Thus the spectrum of customers leads to a demand for luxury hotels and budget hotels; to a demand for refrigerators with many special features as well as for those with basic cooling capabilities. Product features refer to the *quality of design*. Increasing the quality of the design generally leads to *higher* costs.

2. *Freedom from deficiencies* has a major effect on *costs* through reduction in scrap, rework, complaints, and other results of deficiencies. "Deficiencies"

TABLE 1.1
Two components of quality

Manufacturing industries	Service industries
Product features	
Performance	Accuracy
Reliability	Timeliness
Durability	Completeness
Ease of use	Friendliness and courtesy
Serviceability	Anticipating customer needs
Esthetics	Knowledge of server
Availability of options and expandability	Esthetics
	Reputation
Reputation	
Freedom from deficiencies	
Product free of defects and errors at delivery, during use, and during servicing	Service free of errors during original and future service transactions
Sales, billing, and other business processes free of errors	Sales, billing, and other business processes free of errors

are stated in different units, e.g., errors, defects, failures, off-specification. Freedom from deficiencies refers to *quality of conformance*. Increasing the quality of conformance usually results in *lower* costs. In addition, higher conformance means fewer complaints and therefore increased customer satisfaction.

How product features and freedom from deficiencies interrelate and lead to higher profits is shown in Figure 1.1.

To summarize, quality means external and internal customer satisfaction. Product features and freedom from deficiencies are the main determinants of satisfaction. For example, an external customer of an automobile desires certain performance features along with a record of few defects and breakdowns. The Manufacturing Department as an internal customer of the Product Development Department wants an engineering specification that is producible in the shop and is free of errors or omissions. Both of these customers want "the right product right."

1.4   THE QUALITY FUNCTION

Attainment of quality requires the performance of a wide variety of identifiable activities or quality tasks. Obvious examples are the study of customers' quality needs, design review, product tests, and field complaint analysis. In a tiny enterprise these tasks (sometimes called work elements) may all be performed by a few persons. As the enterprise grows, however, specific tasks may become so time-consuming that we must create specialized departments to perform them. Corporations have created departments such as product design, manufacture, inspection and testing, etc., which are essential to launching any new or changed product. These functions follow a relatively unvarying sequence of events (see the spiral in Figure 1.2). In addition to the main "line"

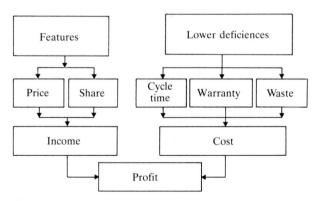

FIGURE 1.1
Quality, market share, and ROI. (*From Juran Institute, Inc., 1990.*)

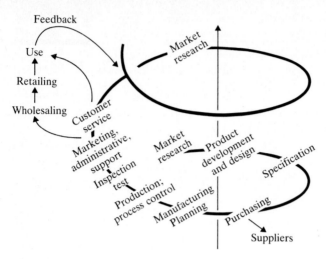

FIGURE 1.2
Spiral of progress in quality.

activities in the spiral, we need many administrative and support activities such as finance, human resources, warehousing, and data processing.

It is evident from the spiral that many activities and tasks must be performed to attain fitness for use. Some of these are performed within manufacturing or service companies. Others are performed elsewhere, e.g., by suppliers, merchants, regulators, etc. It is convenient to have a shorthand name for this collection of activities, and the term "quality function" is used for this purpose. Quality function is the entire collection of activities through which we achieve fitness for use, no matter where these activities are performed.

Some practitioners look upon the spiral or the quality function as a system, i.e., a network of activities or subsystems. Some of these subsystems correspond to segments of the spiral. Others, although not shown on the spiral, are nevertheless present and active, e.g., data processing, standardization. These subsystems, when well designed and coordinated, become a unified system which carries out the intended quality objectives.

The traditional scope of quality activities is undergoing a radical and exciting change from the historical emphasis on quality of physical products in manufacturing industries ("little Q") to what is now emerging as the application of quality concepts to all products, all functional activities, and all industries ("big Q"). Table 1.2 summarizes this change in scope.

Table 1.3 illustrates this enlarged scope based on the triple role concept. Under this concept, all jobs encompass three roles for the jobholder: the customer who receives inputs of information and physical goods; the processor who converts these inputs into products (outputs); the supplier who delivers the resulting products to customers.

TABLE 1.2
Little Q and big Q

Topic	Content of little Q	Content of big Q
Products	Manufactured goods	All products, goods, and services, whether for sale or not
Processes	Processes directly related to manufacture of goods	All processes; manufacturing support; business, etc.
Industries	Manufacturing	All industries; manufacturing; service, government, etc., whether for profit or not

Table 1.3 provides a few examples of activities in each of the three roles for a finance function and for a product development function. Figure 1.3 shows how one organization, AT&T Paradyne, identifies the actions to be taken in each of these three roles to pursue continuous improvement.

1.5   MANAGING FOR QUALITY

Quality management is the process of identifying and administering the activities needed to achieve the quality objectives of an organization. One useful way to illustrate the basic elements of quality management is to draw a parallel to a well-established function, namely finance (Juran, 1986).

TABLE 1.3
Examples of triple roles of customer/user, processor, and supplier

Customer/user	Processor	Supplier
Finance (financial data) function		
Receive basic data from various sources	Establish data processing system	Publish reports
Receive feedback from published reports	Process data into summaries	Disseminate to internal and external customers
	Analyze data, prepare reports	
Product development function		
Receive information on customer needs	Create concepts for new products	Provide specifications to manufacturing departments
Receive data on field performance	Develop design of products	Provide specifications and other requirements to purchasing department
	Plan and conduct prototype tests	

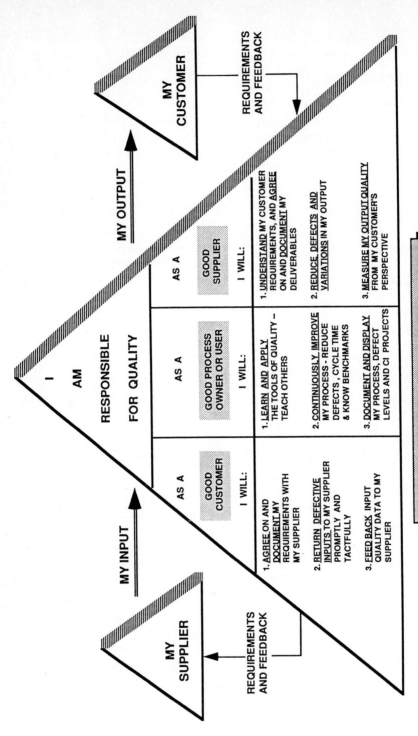

FIGURE 1.3
AT&T Paradyne: Continuous improvement practices. (*From AT&T Paradyne Continuous Improvement Leadership Team.*)

Financial management is accomplished by the use of three managerial processes: planning, control, and improvement. Some key elements of these three processes are shown in Table 1.4. The same three processes apply to quality. The three financial processes provide a methodical approach to addressing finance; the three quality processes provide a methodical approach to addressing quality. Of particular importance is that each of the three quality processes can be further defined in a universal sequence of activities. Table 1.5 summarizes these sequences. Later chapters will develop further detail for these "road maps."

The three processes of the quality trilogy are interrelated. Figure 1.4 shows the interrelationship as applied to one of the two components of the quality definition, freedom from deficiencies. This figure is of uncommon importance. For example, note the graphic distinction between the noisy *sporadic* quality problem and the muted *chronic* waste. The sporadic problem is detected and acted upon by the process of *quality control*. The chronic problem requires a different process, namely, *quality improvement*. Such chronic problems are traceable to an inadequate *quality planning* process. Later chapters will develop these concepts in more detail.

For the trilogy of quality processes to be a successful framework for

TABLE 1.4
Financial processes

Process	Some elements
Financial planning	Budgeting
Financial control	Expense measurement
Financial improvement	Cost reduction

TABLE 1.5
Universal processes for managing quality

Quality planning	Quality control	Quality improvement
Establish quality goals	Choose control subjects	Prove the need
Identify customers	Choose units of measure	Identify projects
Discover customer needs	Set goals	Organize project teams
Develop product features	Create a sensor	Diagnose the causes
Develop process features	Measure actual performance	Provide remedies, prove that the remedies are effective
Establish process controls, transfer to operations	Interpret the difference	Deal with resistance to change
	Take action on the difference	Control to hold the gains

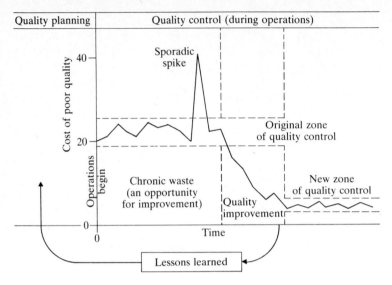

FIGURE 1.4
The Juran Trilogy diagram. (*From Juran, 1986.*)

achieving quality objectives, it is necessary that the processes rest on a foundation of inspirational leadership and environment and practices strongly supportive to quality. Without such a quality "culture," the trilogy of quality processes cannot be fully effective. These elements have an impact on people at *all* levels. Again, later chapters will provide additional explanation.

1.6   QUALITY, COSTS, AND SCHEDULES

Does an emphasis on quality have a positive or negative impact on costs and schedules? The three parameters should be mutually compatible; realistically, they may be either supportive or opposing forces.

An emphasis on quality can be supportive by identifying and eliminating the causes of errors and rework, thereby reducing costs and making more units of product available for meeting delivery schedules. A misguided quality effort, on the other hand, can cause both cost and schedule problems by designing in unnecessary product features, by specifying unrealistic tolerances, and by condoning perfectionism in inspection.

An overemphasis on costs and delivery schedules can have a deadly impact on quality by failing to provide sufficient time and resources to achieve good quality and by decisions to ship product of marginal quality in order to meet a delivery schedule or avoid the costs of rework.

In an end-of-chapter problem, the reader will be asked to calculate the benefits that a quality improvement program contributes to cost savings, delivery schedules, and productivity.

1.7 QUALITY DISCIPLINES AND OTHER DISCIPLINES

This book will discuss the concepts, tools, techniques, etc., essential to modern competition in quality. "Quality disciplines" is the term used to denote the body of quality-related knowledge. Originally this knowledge was applied to the quality of manufacturing processes for physical goods (little Q). As the scope of quality activities has expanded to all processes—and to both external and internal customers—knowledge from other disciplines has proved to be useful. The contributions of other disciplines are sometimes unique and sometimes overlap with quality disciplines. A summary of the contributions of other disciplines is shown in Table 1.6. People concerned with quality management must draw upon the contributions of all disciplines. Potential applications will be identified throughout this book.

1.8 PERSPECTIVE ON QUALITY— INTERNAL VERSUS EXTERNAL

As a preview of the rest of this book, Table 1.7 shows two views of quality: the conventional internal view still followed by many organizations and the

TABLE 1.6
Contributions of various disciplines

Discipline	Example of contribution
Finance	Measuring the cost of poor quality
Industrial engineering	Design of integrated systems, measurement, problem solving, work analysis
Marketing research	Competitive standing on quality; understand customer desires
Operations management	Management of integrated systems
Operations research	Analyzing product design alternatives for optimization
Organizational behavior	Understanding quality culture; making teams effective
Organizational effectiveness	Satisfying the needs of both internal and external customers
Strategic planning	Quality as a means of achieving a unique competitive advantage
Systems engineering	Translating customer needs into product features and process features
Value engineering	Analysis of essential functions needed by customer

TABLE 1.7
Two views of quality

Internal view	External view
Compare product to specification	Compare product to competition and to the best
Get product accepted at inspection	Provide satisfaction over product life
Prevent plant and field defects	Meet customer needs on goods and services
Concentrate on manufacturing	Cover all functions
Use internal quality measures	Use customer-based quality measures
View quality as a technical issue	View quality as a business issue
Efforts coordinated by quality manager	Efforts directed by upper management

Source: Juran Institute, Inc. (1990).

modern external view that many other organizations have found to be imperative for survival. Stay tuned for some obvious and some more subtle aspects of the entries in this table.

The recent emphasis on customer satisfaction, broad application of quality concepts, and participation of all employees has given rise to a new title—Total Quality Management (TQM). TQM is the system of activities directed at achieving delighted customers, empowered employees, higher revenues, and lower costs. That system will unfold throughout this book.

SUMMARY

- Quality is customer satisfaction.
- Quality has two components: product features and freedom from deficiencies.
- Product features affect sales income.
- Freedom from deficiencies affects costs.
- Attainment of quality requires activities in all functions of an organization.
- Traditional quality activities have concentrated on manufacturing ("little Q"); modern quality activities encompass all activities ("big Q").
- All jobs have three roles: customer, processor, supplier.
- We can identify three quality processes: quality planning, quality control, quality improvement. Each process has a defined list of steps.
- Sporadic and chronic quality problems require different approaches.
- Quality, costs, and schedules can be mutually compatible.

- Quality management draws upon the knowledge of many other disciplines.
- Both internal and external views of quality are essential.
- Total Quality Management (TQM) is the system of activities directed at achieving delighted customers, empowered employees, higher revenues, and lower costs.

PROBLEMS

Note: This book has an Instructor's Manual with additional teaching materials.

1.1. For customer satisfaction, computer software must not only be free of errors or "bugs," but must also have the necessary product features. List some important features of a word processing software package.

1.2. Quality has been defined as customer satisfaction (or "fitness for use"). Quality may also be defined as "conformance to specification." In theory, creating the proper specifications and then manufacturing product that conforms to those specifications should lead to customer satisfaction. Alas, life isn't that simple. Consider these four situations for a product:

- Conforms to specifications; is competitive on fitness
- Conforms to specifications; is not competitive on fitness
- Does not conform to specifications; is competitive on fitness
- Does not conform to specifications; is not competitive on fitness

Which two of these four situations are theoretically not plausible, but in practice do occur (and cause much confusion and concern)? Can you cite any examples?

1.3. Select one functional department in a manufacturing or service organization, such as the Product Development Department.
   (a) For the selected department, list two internal customers. For example, the Manufacturing Department is a likely internal customer of Product Development.
   (b) For each internal customer, describe in one sentence a likely requirement of that customer that the supplier department must meet.
   (c) Propose a measurement which might be used to quantify how well the requirement is being met.

1.4. For each 100 units of product manufactured, a certain process yields 85 conforming units, 5 that must be scrapped, and 10 that must be reprocessed. Each unit scrapped results in a $50 loss; each reprocessed unit requires 0.5 hours' extra processing time. The resource time of producing the original 100 units is 20 hours.
   (a) Calculate the scrap cost, reprocessing time, and productivity per hour. Productivity should be calculated in terms of conforming units per hour of resource input.
   (b) A quality improvement program has recently been successfully introduced. For each 100 units manufactured, the process now yields 95 conforming units, 1 to be scrapped, and 4 for reprocessing. Repeat the calculations of paragraph (a). What are the quantitative benefits of the quality effort to costs, to delivery schedules, and to productivity?

REFERENCES

Juran, J. M. (1986). "The Quality Trilogy," *Quality Progress*, August, pp. 19–24.
Juran Institute, Inc. (1990). "Management of Quality-Manufacturing," course notes, Wilton, Connecticut.

SUPPLEMENTARY READING

History of quality: *Juran's Quality Control Handbook*, 4th ed. (QCH4), McGraw-Hill Book Company, New York, 1988, pp. 35G.1–35G.7.
    Juran, J. M. "China's Ancient History of Managing for Quality," *Quality Progress*, July 1990, pp. 31–35.

Quality defined: QCH4, pp. 2.2–2.4.

Fitness for use: QCH4, pp. 2.8–2.11.

Approaches of different experts: Lowe, Theodore A. and Joseph M. Mazzeo. "Lessons Learned from the Masters—Experiences in Applying the Principles of Deming, Juran, and Crosby," *ASQC Quality Congress Transactions,* Milwaukee, 1988, pp. 397–402.

Quality and other disciplines: Golomski, William A. "Social Science Aspects of Quality," *Proceedings of Conference on Quality in the Year 2000,* Rochester Institute of Technology, June 10, 1992, Rochester, N.Y.

CHAPTER

2

COMPANYWIDE ASSESSMENT OF QUALITY

2.1 WHY ASSESSMENT?

In recent decades, the quality movement has been bombarded by a never-ending procession of new techniques with promises of near miracles. There have been successes; there have been failures. A formal assessment of quality provides a starting point by providing an understanding of (1) the size of the quality issue and (2) the areas demanding attention. A feet-on-the-ground strategy can then be developed.

"Quality assessment" will be the term used to describe a companywide review of the status of quality.

Assessment of quality comprises four elements:

1. Cost of poor quality
2. Standing in the marketplace
3. Quality culture in the organization
4. Operation of the company quality system

Other elements may be added as required by circumstances. An annual or biannual assessment is usually warranted.

We will start with the assessment of the cost of poor quality.

2.2 COST OF POOR QUALITY

All organizations make use of the concept of identifying the costs needed to carry out the various functions—product development, marketing, personnel, production, etc. Until the 1950s this concept had not been extended to the quality function, except for the departmental activities of inspection and testing. There were, of course, many other quality-related costs, but they were scattered among various accounts, especially "overhead."

During the 1950s the concept of "quality costs" emerged. Different people assigned different meanings to the term. Some people equated quality costs with the costs of *attaining* quality; some people equated the term with the extra costs incurred due to poor quality. In this book the emphasis will be on the cost of poor quality. This component of assessment will prove to be important in reducing costs.

2.3 CATEGORIES OF QUALITY COST

Many companies summarize these costs into four broad categories. These categories and examples of typical subcategories are discussed below. (A source that includes details of these four categories is ASQC, 1986. A source that applies these same categories to a service industry, banking, is Aubrey and Zimbler, 1982.)

Internal Failure Costs

These are costs associated with defects (errors, nonconformance, etc.) that are found prior to transfer of the product to the customer. They are costs that would disappear if no defects existed in the product before shipment. Examples of subcategories are:

Scrap: the labor, material, and (usually) overhead on defective products that cannot economically be repaired. The titles are numerous—scrap, spoilage, defectives, waste, etc.

Rework: the cost of correcting defectives to make them conform to specifications

Failure analysis: costs of analyzing nonconforming product to determine causes

Scrap and rework supplies: costs of scrap and rework due to nonconforming product received from suppliers

One hundred percent sorting inspection: costs of finding defective units in product lots which contain unacceptably high levels of defectives

Reinspection and retesting: costs of reinspection and retesting of products that have undergone rework or other revision

Avoidable process losses: costs of losses that occur even with conforming product—for example, overfill of containers (going to customers) due to excessive variability in filling and measuring equipment

Downgrading: the difference between the normal selling price and the reduced price due to quality reasons

External Failure Costs

These are costs associated with defects that are found after product is shipped to the customer. These costs would also disappear if there were no defects. Examples are:

Warranty charges: costs involved in replacing or making repairs to products that are still within the warranty period

Complaint adjustment: costs of investigation and adjustment of justified complaints attributable to defective product or installation

Returned material: costs associated with receipt and replacement of defective product received from the field

Allowances: costs of concessions made to customers due to substandard product being accepted by the customer as is or to conforming product that does not meet fitness-for-use specifications.

Appraisal Costs

These are the costs incurred in determining the degree of conformance to quality requirements. Examples are:

Incoming inspection and testing: costs of determining the quality of purchased product, whether by inspection on receipt, by inspection at the source, or by surveillance

In-process inspection and testing: costs of in-process evaluation of conformance to requirements

Final inspection and testing: costs of evaluation of conformance to requirements for product acceptance

Product quality audits: costs of performing quality audits on in-process or finished products

Maintaining accuracy of testing equipment: costs of keeping measuring instruments and equipment in calibration

Inspection and testing of materials and services: costs of material and suppliers in inspection and testing work (e.g., X-ray film) and services (e.g., electric power) where significant

Evaluation of stock: costs of testing products in field storage or in stock to evaluate degradation

In collecting appraisal costs, what is decisive is the kind of work done and not the department name (the work may be done by chemists in the laboratory, by sorters in Production, by testers in Inspection, or by an external firm engaged for the purpose of testing).

Prevention Costs

These are costs incurred in keeping failure and appraisal costs to a minimum. Examples are:

Quality planning: the broad array of activities which collectively create the overall quality plan and the numerous specialized plans; also, the preparation of procedures needed to communicate these plans to all concerned

New-product review: costs of reliability engineering and other quality-related activities associated with the launching of new designs

Process control: costs of in-process inspection and testing to determine the status of the process rather than product acceptance)

Quality audits: costs of evaluating the execution of activities in the overall quality plan

Supplier quality evaluation: costs of evaluating supplier quality activities prior to supplier selection, auditing the activities during the contract, and carrying out associated efforts with suppliers

Training: costs of preparing and conducting quality-related training programs (as in the case of appraisal costs, some of this work may be done by personnel who are not on the payroll of the Quality Department; the decisive criterion is again the type of work, not the name of the department performing the work)

An example of a study for a tire manufacturer is shown in Table 2.1. This example resulted in some conclusions that are typical of these studies:

- The total of almost $900,000 per year is large.
- Most (79.1 percent) of the total is concentrated in failure costs, specifically in "waste scrap" and consumer adjustments.
- Failure costs are about five times the appraisal costs.
- A small amount (4.3 percent) is spent on prevention.
- There are some consequences of poor quality that could not be conveniently quantified, e.g., "customer ill will" and "customer policy adjustment." However, these factors are listed as a reminder of their existence.

As a result of this study, management decided to increase the budget for prevention activities. Three engineers were assigned to identify and pursue specific quality improvement projects.

Strictly defined, the cost of poor quality is the sum of the internal and

TABLE 2.1
Annual quality cost—tire manufacturer

Cost of quality failures—losses		
Defective stock	$ 3,276	0.37%
Repairs to product	73,229	8.31
Collect scrap	2,288	0.26
Waste—scrap	187,428	21.26
Consumer adjustments	408,200	46.31
Downgrading products	22,838	2.59
Customer ill will	Not counted	
Customer policy adjustment	Not counted	
Total	$697,259	79.10%
Cost of appraisal		
Incoming inspection	$ 32,655	2.68
Inspection 1	32,582	3.70
Inspection 2	25,200	2.86
Spot-check inspection	65,910	7.37
Total	$147,347	16.61%
Cost of prevention		
Local plant quality		
Control engineering	7,848	0.89
Corporate quality		
Control engineering	30,000	3.40
Total	$ 37,848	4.29%
Grand total	$882,454	100.00%

external failure costs categories. This assumes that those elements of appraisal costs—e.g., 100 percent sorting inspection—necessitated by inadequate processes are classified under internal failures. Some practitioners use the term "cost of quality" for the four broad categories.

As the detailed categories of the cost of poor quality are identified, there are some that will be controversial. Much of the controversy centers around the assertion that these are not quality-related costs but costs that are part of normal operating expenses, and therefore they should not be included. One example is the inclusion of overhead on top of direct labor and material of scrap and rework (see QCH4, p. 4.9–4.12, for elaboration). A useful guide is to ask: "Suppose all defects disappeared. Would the cost in question also disappear?" A "yes" answer means that the cost is associated with quality problems and should therefore be included. A "no" answer means that the category should not be included in the cost of poor quality.

2.4 OBJECTIVES OF EVALUATION

Companies estimate quality costs for several reasons:

1. Quantifying the size of the quality problem in the language of money improves communication between middle managers and upper managers.

In some companies the need to improve communication on quality-related matters has been so acute as to become a major objective for embarking on a study of the costs of poor quality. Some managers say, "We don't need to spend time to translate the defects into dollars. We realize that quality is important, and we already know what the major problems are." But typically, when a study is done, these managers are surprised by two results. First, the quality costs turn out to be much higher than they had thought—in many industries in excess of 20 percent of sales. Second, while the distribution of the quality costs confirms some of the known problem areas, it also reveals other problem areas that had not previously been recognized.

2. Major opportunities for cost reduction can be identified. Costs of poor quality do not exist as a homogeneous mass. Instead, they are the total of specific segments, each traceable to some specific cause. These segments are unequal in size, and a relative few of the segments account for the bulk of the costs. A major by-product of evaluation of costs of poor quality is identification of these vital few segments. We will cover this in Chapter 3 under "The Pareto Principle."

3. Opportunities for reducing customer dissatisfaction and associated threats to product salability can be identified. Some costs of poor quality are the result of product failures which take place after sale. In part, these costs are paid by the manufacturer in the form of warranty charges, claims, etc. But whether the costs are paid by the manufacturer or not, the failures add to customers' costs because of downtime and other forms of disturbance. Analysis of the manufacturer's costs, supplemented by marketing research into customers' costs of poor quality, can identify the vital few areas of high costs. These areas then lead to problem identification.

2.5 RELATING THE GRAND TOTAL TO BUSINESS MEASURES

Interpretation of the total is aided by relating total quality costs to other figures with which managers are familiar. The relationships which have the greatest impact on upper management are:

- Quality costs as a percentage of sales
- Quality costs compared to profit
- Quality costs per share of common stock outstanding
- Quality costs as a percentage of cost of goods sold
- Quality costs as a percentage of total manufacturing costs
- Effect of quality costs on the break-even point

While money is the universal language of upper management, there are additional ways to convey significance to these managers.

Two universal languages are spoken in the company. At the "bottom" the language is that of objects and deeds: square meters of floor space, schedules in tons per week, rejection rates of X percent. At the "top" the language is that of money: sales, profit, taxes, investment. Middle managers and technical specialists must therefore be "bilingual."

In one company which was preoccupied with meeting delivery schedules, quality costs were translated into equivalent added production. Since this coincided with the managers' chief current goals, their attention was aroused. In another company, the total quality costs of $76 million per year for the company were shown to be equivalent to the cost of running one company plant employing 2900 people, occupying 1.1 million square feet of space, and requiring $6 million of in-process inventory. These three figures in turn meant the equivalent of one of their company's major plants making 100 percent defective work every working day of the year. And this company is the quality leader in its industry!

A computer manufacturer translated the annual cost of poor quality into these terms:

- 25 percent of manufacturing assets
- 25 percent of people
- 40 percent of space
- 70 percent of inventory

For example, 25 percent of the people were primarily spending time on finding and correcting defective product.

2.6 ANALYSIS OF QUALITY COSTS

Additional useful comparisons can be derived from the interrelationships among the subtotals of the quality costs in the major categories. In many companies, appraisal costs have been budgeted and hence have long been a subject of discussion. However, the typical quality cost study will show that the previously underemphasized failure costs are several times the appraisal costs. This comes as a surprise to most managers and forces them to reconsider their emphasis.

In like manner, when managers discover that the prevention costs are pitifully low in relation to the total, their instinctive reaction is to look more attentively at the possibilities of increasing preventive efforts. The relationship between internal failure costs and external failure costs is likewise significant. The former generally point to a need for programs involving manufacturing planning and production, whereas the latter generally point to a need for programs involving product design and field service.

An example, using data for 8 months, is shown in Table 2.2. Here, for each product, the failure costs are over 80 percent of the total—at least six

TABLE 2.2
Quality cost statement by product line

	Product A	Product B	Product C
Prevention, $	5,698	1,569	1,908
Appraisal, $	37,676	10,384	9,206
Internal failures, $	119,107	60,876	63,523
External failures, $	133,168	12,625	15,755
Grant total, $	295,649	85,454	90,392
Shipments, $	8,165,000	1,750,000	840,000
Ratio—quality cost to shipments, %	3.62	4.88	10.76
Number of machines,	71	14	14
Total quality cost per machine, $	4,165	6,104	6,456

times the appraisal costs—and prevention costs are less than 2 percent of the total. The implications are clear:

- To achieve any significant cost reduction, failure costs must be attacked first. This will have more impact than reducing inspection (appraisal) costs.
- An increase in prevention costs could reap a return in terms of lower failure costs.
- The largest opportunity for cost reduction is with product A. Note that using "quality cost to shipments" and "total quality cost per machine" results in highlighting product C. This is because of the product mix.
- Product A generates scrap and rework internally, but there are also external field problems. For products B and C the problem centers more on internal scrap and rework.

Hidden Quality Costs

There are also costs incurred that may result in understating the costs of poor quality. These "hidden" costs include:

1. Potential lost sales. One attempt to partially measure this hidden cost is to estimate the percentage of signed orders that are canceled and convert this percentage to sales dollars. The cancellations, although due to many possible reasons including quality, are a reflection of less-than-satisfactory performance. See also Section 21.3 for another approach.
2. Costs of redesign due to quality reasons.
3. Costs of changing manufacturing processes due to inability to meet quality requirements.
4. Costs of software changes due to quality reasons.

5. Costs included in standards because history shows that a certain level of defects is inevitable and allowances should be included in standards. In such cases, the alarm signals ring only when the standard value is exceeded. However, even when operating within those standards, such costs should be a part of the cost of poor quality. They represent opportunities for improvement.

6. Extra manufacturing costs due to defects. These include additional costs for space, inventory charges, and overtime.

7. Scrap not reported. This may mean scrap that is never reported because of fear of reprisals, or scrap that is charged to a general ledger account without an identification as scrap.

8. Excess process costs for acceptable product. For example, a process for filling packages with a dry soap mix meets requirements for label weight on the contents. However, the process aim is set above label weight to account for the variability in the filling process. If the variability is large, the aim must be set far enough above the minimum to accommodate the variability. A reduction in variability could mean that the aim could be set closer to the minimum, thus reducing the average amount of overfill.

Obvious costs of poor quality are the tip of the iceberg. Figure 2.1 illustrates both the obvious and hidden costs of a manufacturing company.

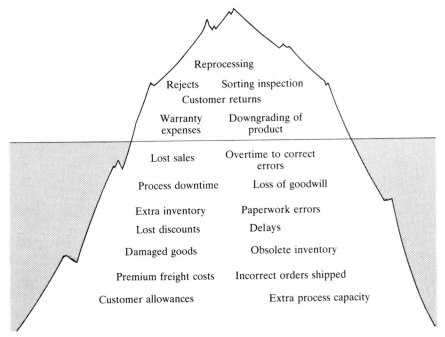

FIGURE 2.1
Hidden costs of poor quality.

Discovering the Optimum

When cost summaries on quality are first presented to managers, one of the usual questions is "What are the right costs?" The managers are looking for a standard ("par") against which to compare their actual costs so that they can make a judgment on whether there is a need for action.

Unfortunately, few credible data are available. Companies almost never publish such data. Attempts to conduct research on these costs have encountered several obstacles (see "Quality Cost Survey," 1980; Gilmore, 1983). First, the cost data are confidential. Also, some companies include unavoidable manufacturing waste as a part of the cost of poor quality, while other companies do not; some companies add overhead to the direct cost of labor and material on scrap and rework, while other companies do not. The wide ranges in published examples are a grim reminder of the risk in comparing quality costs in one company with so called industry averages. Three conclusions do stand out: The total costs are higher for complex industries, failure costs are the largest percentage of the total, and prevention costs are a small percentage of the total.

Having stated these cautions, we can cite some numbers. For manufacturing organizations, the annual cost of poor quality is about 15 percent of sales income, varying from about 5 percent to 35 percent depending on product complexity. For service organizations, the average is about 30 percent of operating expenses, varying from 25 percent to 40 percent depending on service complexity.

2.7 ECONOMIC MODELS OF QUALITY OF CONFORMANCE

The study of the distribution of quality costs over the major categories can be further explored using models as shown in Figure 2.2a and b.

Each model shows three curves:

1. *Failure costs.* These equal zero when the product is 100 percent good, and rise to infinity when the product is 100 percent defective. (Note that the vertical scale is cost per good unit of product. At 100 percent defective, the number of good units is zero, and hence the cost per good unit is infinity.)
2. *Costs of appraisal plus prevention.* These costs are zero at 100 percent defective and rise as perfection is approached. However, the amount of rise differs for the two models.
3. *The sum of curves 1 and 2.* This third curve is marked "total" and represents the total cost of quality per good unit of product.

The model in Figure 2.2a represents the conditions which prevailed widely during much of the twentieth century. "Appraisal plus prevention"

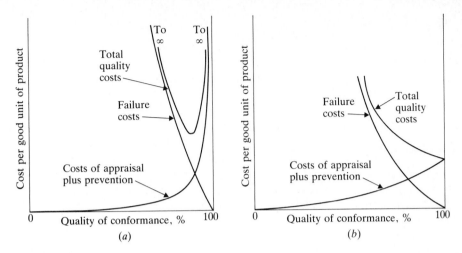

FIGURE 2.2
Model for optimum quality costs: (*a*) Traditional processes. (*b*) Emerging processes. (*From QCH*4. p. 4.19.)

consisted of much appraisal and little prevention. Moreover, most appraisal was carried out by fallible human beings, who are unable to maintain attention 100 percent of the time, are unable to exert muscular energy 100 percent of the time, etc. This human fallibility effectively limits the efforts to attain perfection at finite costs. Hence the model shows the curve "costs of appraisal plus prevention" rising to infinity as perfection is approached. In consequence the "total cost" curve also rises to infinity.

The model in Figure 2.1*b* represents conditions as they evolved in the late twentieth century. Priorities on prevention became higher. New technology reduced the inherent failure rates of materials and products. Robotics and other forms of automation reduced human error during production. Automated inspection and testing reduced the human error of appraisal. (Automated processes do not have lapses in attention, do not get tired, etc.) Collectively these developments have resulted in an ability to achieve perfection at a finite cost.

While perfection is a goal for the long run, it does not follow that perfection is the most economical goal for the short run, or for every situation. In Figure 2.2*a* the total cost curve reaches a minimum at a level short of perfection. Figure 2.3 shows this total cost curve in more detail.

Figure 2.3 divides the total quality cost curve of Figure 2.2*a* into three zones. The zone a company is in can usually be identified from the prevailing ratios of the quality costs in the principal categories, as follows:

ZONE OF IMPROVEMENT PROJECTS. This is the left-hand portion of Figure 2.3. The distinguishing features are that failure costs constitute more than 70

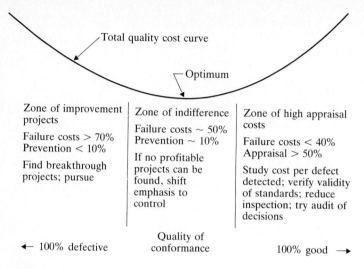

Zone of improvement projects	Zone of indifference	Zone of high appraisal costs
Failure costs > 70% Prevention < 10%	Failure costs ~ 50% Prevention ~ 10%	Failure costs < 40% Appraisal > 50%
Find breakthrough projects; pursue	If no profitable projects can be found, shift emphasis to control	Study cost per defect detected; verify validity of standards; reduce inspection; try audit of decisions

← 100% defective   Quality of conformance   100% good →

FIGURE 2.3
Optimum segment of quality cost model.

percent of the total quality costs, while prevention costs are less than 10 percent of the total. In such cases, there are opportunities for reducing total quality costs by improving the quality of conformance. The approach is to identify specific improvement projects and pursue them to improve the quality of conformance, thereby reducing the costs of poor quality, especially the failure costs.

ZONE OF HIGH APPRAISAL COSTS. This is the right-hand portion of Figure 2.3. It is usually characterized by the fact that appraisal costs exceed failure costs. In such cases there are also opportunities to reduce costs. This may be done in ways such as:

- Comparing the cost of detecting defects to the damage done if they are not detected. For example, a company had long engaged in detailed inspection for quality characteristic X. The detailed inspection had been started at a time when defect X was widespread. Over the years, the process had been improved to a point where defect X was now a rare occurrence—only 15 defects per million parts. However, the detailed inspection went on and on. A study showed that it was costing the company about $2.80 to find each of the defects, yet the sales price of the product was about 5 cents.
- Reviewing the quality standards to see if they are realistic in relation to fitness for use.
- Seeing if it is feasible to reduce the amount of inspection through sampling based on knowledge of process capability and order of manufacture.

• Seeing if it is feasible to avoid duplication of inspection through auditing of decisions.

ZONE OF INDIFFERENCE. This is the central area of Figure 2.3. In this zone, the failure costs are usually about half of the quality costs while prevention costs are about 10 percent of the quality costs. In the indifference zone, the optimum has been reached in terms of worthwhile quality improvement projects to pursue. Continuous improvement is always desirable, but the projects are competing against other worthwhile projects, projects which are not yet at optimum levels.

Several concepts need to be stressed in relation to Figures 2.2 and 2.3.

• The models are conceptual and illustrate the importance of an optimum value of quality of conformance for many industries. In practice, data are not available to construct such curves.
• Improving the quality of conformance results in a reduction of total costs over most of the horizontal spectrum. This is contrary to the belief that higher "quality" results in higher costs.
• A reduction in cost can be achieved by moving toward the optimum from either the zone of improvement projects or the zone of high appraisal costs.
• Companies which have not yet engaged extensively in quality improvement are likely to find their processes mainly in the improvement zone. For such companies, the main opportunities for cost reduction are through projects for improving conformance.
• The hidden costs of poor quality (see above under "Hidden Quality Costs") are not included in the model. If the data were available, the effect would be to move the optimum toward 100 percent conformance. We should therefore strive for continuous improvement.

Additional circumstances, discussed below, also have an impact on the cost balance.

2.8 COST BALANCE DIFFERENT IN CERTAIN CIRCUMSTANCES

The models shown in Figures 2.2a and 2.3 apply to a wide variety of industries. However, there are exceptions:

1. Industries producing goods that have a critical impact on human safety: Examples include generation of nuclear power or manufacture of pharmaceuticals. Such industries are subject to social pressures to achieve perfect quality at almost any cost.

2. Highly automated industries: Here, it is often possible to achieve a low level of defects by proper planning of the manufacturing process to ensure that processes are capable of meeting specifications. In addition, automated inspection often makes it economically feasible to perform 100 percent inspection to find all the defects.
3. Companies selling to affluent clients: These customers are often willing to pay a premium price for perfect quality to avoid even a small risk of a defect.
4. Companies striving to optimize the user's cost: The models depicted in Figure 2.2a and b show the concept of an optimum from the viewpoint of the producer. When the user's costs due to product failure are added to such models, the optimum point moves toward perfection. The same result occurs if lost sales income to the manufacturer is included in the failure costs.

These conditions provide us with additional incentives to pursue continuous quality improvement. The reason is that the added sales value of perfect product more than offsets the added cost of attaining 100 percent conformance. This has already approached realization in products such as electric refrigerators and color television sets. The prospect is that the trend to 100 percent conformance will extend to more and more products of greater and greater complexity.

Next, we move to another element of assessment.

2.9 STANDING IN THE MARKETPLACE

Estimating the cost of poor quality is an essential part of the assessment. But it is not enough. We also need to understand where the company stands on quality in the marketplace, relative to the competition. This component of assessment will prove to be important in increasing sales income.

Similar to the assessment of the cost of poor quality, the market study (1) gives a snapshot of standing relative to competition and (2) identifies opportunities and threats.

The approach must be based on a marketing research study. Such studies should be planned not by any one department but by a team involving members from Marketing, Product Development, Quality, Manufacturing, and other areas as needed. This team must agree beforehand on what questions need to be answered by the field study. The types of questions which should be considered are: (1) What is the relative importance of various product qualities as seen by the user? (2) For each of the key qualities, how does our product compare with competitors' products, as seen by the users?

Chapter 11, "Understanding Customer Needs," includes some follow-up questions.

Answers to such questions must be based on input from *customers.* Opinions of company personnel, no matter how extensive the experience base, cannot and should not substitute for the voice of the customer.

Examples of Field Studies

The first example comes from a manufacturer of health products. A multiattribute study was conducted in which customers were asked to consider several product attributes and indicate both their relative importance and a competitive rating. The results for one product are shown in Table 2.3. Note that an overall score is obtained for each manufacturer by multiplying the relative importance by the score for that attribute and then adding these results.

In another example, a manufacturer of equipment was experiencing a decline in market share. Complaints about quality led to a proposal to "beef up the inspection." Discussions within the company revealed uncertainty about the nature of the complaints, so it was decided to conduct a field study to learn more about customer views. A team was formed to plan and conduct the study. Visits were made to about 50 customers.

In one part of the study, six attributes were identified and customers were asked to rate the company as superior, competitive, or inferior to competition on each of the attributes (see Table 2.4). The results were a surprise. The equipment problems were confirmed, but the study revealed the presence of both design and manufacturing causes. Also, documentation and field repair service were identified as weak areas; these were surprises to the company involved. Dramatic action was taken. A broad approach to quality was created, starting with the initial design and continuing throughout the spiral of all activities affecting fitness for use. This was in stark contrast to the original proposal of adding inspectors. The study required about 7 worker-months of

TABLE 2.3
Multiattribute study

Attribute	Relative importance, %	Company X		Competitor A		Competitor B	
		Rating	Weighted rating	Rating	Weighted rating	Rating	Weighted rating
Safety	28	6	168	5	140	4.5	126
Performance	20	6	120	7	140	6.5	130
Quality	20	6	120	7	140	4	80
Field service	12	4	48	8	96	5	60
Ease of use	8	4	32	6	48	5	40
Company image	8	8	64	4	32	4	32
Plant service	4	7.5	30	7.5	30	5	20
Total			582		626		488

TABLE 2.4
Heavy equipment case

	Comparison to competition, %		
Attribute	Superior	Competitive	Inferior
Analysis of customer needs			
Preparation of quality requirements and purchase order			
Preparation of specifications and technical documentation			
Quality of equipment			
Quality and availability of spare parts			
Quality of field repair service			

Source: Private communication.

effort, including planning, customer visits, analysis of results, and preparation of a report—a small price to pay to develop a proper strategy.

Many organizations in service industries have extensive experience in marketing research. For example, one bank periodically conducts marketing research as part of a quality system. This research probes 20 attributes of banking service by asking consumers about the relative importance of attributes and consumer degree of satisfaction. Table 2.5 shows the format of the summarized results.

Let's generalize from these examples. First, all of them involved a study of customers who were experienced in using the product. Also, the studies

TABLE 2.5
Marketing research at a bank

Satisfaction with . . .	Very satisfied, %	Sample Size	Important and low in satisfaction, %	Important and high in satisfaction, %
1. Greeting you with a smile				
8. Processing transactions without error				
14. Easy to read and understand bank statements				
20. Prompt follow-up to questions and problems				

identified specific attributes leading to customer satisfaction, quantified their relative importance, and then determined ratings for each of those attributes.

A full picture of a company's standing in the marketplace involves more than a multiattributes study. NCR (Willets, 1989) provides an example of a comprehensive approach. Formal questioning is conducted at four levels of customers:

1. Those who approve the purchase, e.g., a senior executive
2. Those who influence the decision, e.g., a technical executive
3. Those who sign the purchase order, e.g., a buyer
4. Those who are users, e.g., a store manager who uses an NCR computer.

In addition, other information is collected on a continuous basis through 11 means including analysis of sales trends, analysis of complaints, and customer focus groups.

Many of the concepts presented above for external customers can be adapted and applied to internal customers. Stevens (1987) describes the application to internal customers of departments such as Central Engineering and Central Quality Assurance.

The next element of assessment is culture.

2.10 COMPANY CULTURE ON QUALITY

Employees in an organization have opinions, beliefs, traditions, and practices concerning quality. We will call this the company quality culture. Gaining an understanding of this culture should be part of a company assessment of quality.

Formal approaches to assessing the quality culture are still evolving, but two can be identified, i.e., focused discussions with groups of employees and the use of written questionnaires. With either of these approaches assessment of the quality culture can be done separately or as part of a larger survey of attitudes on many matters.

An example from the health care products industry illustrates the use of the discussion group approach (Hulse, 1983). A "round table" of 15 individuals was formed to discuss the state of quality affairs in the company. It included an inspection supervisor, several engineering managers, a plant manager, a production manager, a vice president of manufacturing, a director of marketing, a director of quality assurance, and several other members involved in quality assurance activity. The meeting was held for three days at a rural retreat.

To give some structure and direction, a series of topical graphs was used. The graphs were designed to evoke personal opinion and observations about the perceptions of the attendees and other people in their work units. Three areas were addressed by the graphs:

1. Attitudes, perceptions, and activity within the company. One example was the attitude toward product quality as seen at three levels—senior management, line management, and production workers. Another example explored the company quality mission: Does the company have one? If so, what is it? Do the employees perceive a quality mission?
2. Perceived user attitudes about the quality of products. Examples of issues discussed were market share losses and customer complaints as an indication of user attitudes.
3. Understanding the tools of quality. Examples of issues discussed were understanding and degree of application of process control concepts, statistical engineering tools, and product sampling practices.

At the final stages of the conference, three independent working groups were formed to achieve a commonality of opinions and perceptions. The groups were given a statement concerning shortcomings in companies in the form of practices that lead to falling behind the competition in quality. Group discussions (lasting about 3 hours) were directed to confirm or deny the accuracy of the statement. The full round table then discussed the group reports.

The approach used generated a positive and critical analysis of quality affairs, "very probably to a level of constructive analysis unprecedented in nature in our organization."

Asking employees to answer a questionnaire provides another approach for the company quality culture. An example from a manufacturing company (Ryan and Wong, 1984) consisted of 14 questions. Three of the questions, and some surprising answers, were:

"Do you feel that you understand what good quality is? Please write what you feel is management's attitude toward quality." The answers were summarized in a word: hostile.

"Have you ever been told to go ahead with a defective job because of production schedules?" About 52 percent of the respondents said "Yes."

"Mark three areas which you feel cause the most defects." Many of the responses to the questionnaire were a sobering revelation to management.

In another example, a service organization studied the quality culture through a questionnaire consisting of these six questions:

• To what degree are you familiar with the company's emphasis on Quality?
• To what degree do you agree with the statement, "My manager's actions and attitude convince me that Quality is important"?

- To what degree do you understand the Quality measurements used in your department?
- Everything considered, how do you rate your department on providing high quality service and outputs?
- To what degree do you think your achievement of quality standards affects your performance evaluation?
- Have you worked in a Quality Circle, Quality Improvement Project, or Quality Improvement Team in the last twelve months?

Rather than a brief list of questions, some organizations find it valuable to employ an extensive array. One organization uses 56 questions to explore eight areas: overall product quality, conformance to requirements, equipment, supplier quality, management commitment, work group performance, employee participation, and training. In another organization, 82 questions are posed to evaluate 18 factors that collectively address the quality culture.

Understanding a company's quality culture is important for assessment. Gaining that understanding has risks. The reader will be asked to examine those risks in an end-of-chapter problem.

2.11 ASSESSMENT OF CURRENT QUALITY ACTIVITIES

The fourth element of assessment is the evaluation of current quality-related activities in the organization. Such an evaluation could cover a wide range of both scope (global to a few activities) and examination (cursory to detailed). Our discussion concentrates on a companywide examination in sufficient depth to meet the needs of the overall quality assessment. Chapter 24 will address assessment of current activities in further detail.

We start with assessment questions that address companywide issues of quality management. Questions in this category include:

- Have quality objectives been established?
- Have quality objectives been linked to business objectives?
- Are policies and plans such that, if followed, quality will be competitive in the marketplace?
- Is the approach to quality led by line management rather than staff?
- Does it cover all processes (big Q)?
- Is the organizational machinery in place to identify and pursue opportunities for increasing sales income and for reducing costs of poor quality?
- Is there an effective system for providing early warning of potential quality problems?

In addition, there are questions relating to functional areas. The following are common to *all* functional areas:

- What measures are used to judge output quality?
- What is the company's performance, as reflected in these measures?
- Have the resources spent in detecting and correcting quality-related problems been estimated?
- To what extent are quality-related responsibilities understood by the personnel?
- To what extent have personnel been trained in the quality disciplines?
- To what extent has the capability of key processes been quantified?
- Does the data system meet the needs of personnel?

Questions unique to *specific* functional areas are discussed in QCH4, pages 9.18–9.20.

A more detailed companywide assessment makes use of established criteria. An example is the criteria used in connection with the Malcolm Baldrige National Quality Award. This award is presented annually in the United States. A maximum of two organizations in each of three categories (manufacturing, service, and small businesses) may be selected each year. An exhaustive evaluation is based on submitted written materials followed by site visits to qualifying organizations. The examination categories and points assigned are listed in Table 2.6. Note the heavy emphasis on quality results and customer satisfaction. The Baldrige Award recognizes organizations which have achieved the highest levels of quality.

A government agency reviewed 20 companies that were among the highest-scoring applicants for the Baldrige Award in 1988 and 1989 (U.S. General Accounting Office, 1991). Three key conclusions:

1. In nearly all cases, companies achieved improvements in employee relations, productivity, customer satisfaction, market share, and profitability.
2. Six common features contributed to the improved performance: customer focus, senior management leadership, employee involvement and empowerment, an open corporate culture, fact-based decision making, and partnership with suppliers.
3. The companies required an average of about $2\frac{1}{2}$ years to realize the initial benefits.

The report makes excellent reading.

An international effort to identify the key elements of a quality system for manufactured products has resulted in a series of quality standards.

These standards have been developed by the International Standards Organization (ISO) and are known as the ISO 9000 series quality standards. Table 2.7 lists the documents involved. (In the United States, the standards are

TABLE 2.6
Malcolm Baldrige National Quality Award 1992 Examination Items

Categories/items	Maximum points
Leadership	90
Senior executive leadership	
Management for quality	
Public responsibility	
Information and analysis	80
Scope and management of quality and performance data and information	
Competitive comparisons and benchmarks	
Analysis and uses of company-level data	
Strategic quality planning	60
Strategic quality and company performance planning process	
Quality and performance plans	
Human resource development and management	150
Human resource management	
Employee involvement	
Employee education and training	
Employee performance and recognition	
Employee well-being and morale	
Management of process quality	140
Design and introduction of quality products and services	
Process management—product and service production and delivery processes	
Process management—business processes and support services	
Supplier quality	
Quality assessment	
Quality and operational results	180
Product and service quality results	
Company operational results	
Business process and support service results	
Supplier quality results	
Customer focus and satisfaction	300
Customer relationship management	
Commitment to customers	
Customer satisfaction determination	
Customer satisfaction results	
Customer satisfaction comparison	
Future requirements and expectation of customers	
Total points	1000

Source: Application guidelines—Malcolm Baldrige National Quality Award, 1992.

TABLE 2.7
ISO 9000 series quality standards

ISO	ANSI/ASOC	Scope
9000	Q90—1987	Selection of documents
9001	Q91—1987	Design, development, production, installation, and servicing
9002	Q92—1987	Production and installation
9003	Q93—1987	Final inspection and test
9004	Q94—1987	Quality management and system elements

published by the American National Standards Institute and the American Society for Quality Control.) In some countries, these standards are being used to certify that an organization meets the minimum criteria for a quality system as defined by the standards. Evaluation for such formal certification is made by an independent organization. Purchasers of products can require that potential suppliers be certified to the appropriate ISO criteria as a prerequisite to receiving a contract. Organizations will find that it is important to achieve ISO 9000 certification to meet both domestic and international competition.

Further elaboration on the assessment of activities within a quality system can be found in Chapter 24, "Quality Assurance," and also in QCH4, Section 9, "Quality Assurance."

SUMMARY

- All organizations periodically need a companywide assessment of quality.
- Quality assessment comprises four elements:

   Cost of poor quality
   Standing in the marketplace
   Quality culture
   Operation of the quality system

- The Malcolm Baldrige National Quality Award provides criteria to identify organizations which have achieved the highest levels of quality. This is an award that recognizes superior achievement.
- The ISO 9000 standards provide minimum criteria for a quality system. These documents provide some assurance to potential customers that an organization certified as meeting the standard does have an adequate quality system.

PROBLEMS

2.1. The Federated Screw Company manufactures a wide variety of made-to-order screws for industrial companies. The designs are usually supplied by customers. Total manufacturing payroll is 260 people with sales of about $8 million. Operations are relatively simple but geared to high-volume production. Wire in rolls is fed at high speeds to heading machines, where the contour of the screw is formed. Pointers and slotters perform secondary operations. The thread-rolling operation completes the screw configuration. Heat treatment, plating, and sometimes baking are the final steps and are performed by an outside contractor located nearby.

You have been asked to prepare a quality cost summary for the company and have made the following notes:

- The Quality Control Department is primarily a Final Inspection Department (eight inspectors), which also inspects the incoming wire. Patrol inspection is performed in the Heading Room by checking the first and last pieces of each run. The Quality Control Department also handles the checking and setting of all ring, snap, and plus gages used by themselves and production personnel. An inspector's salary is approximately $24,000 per year.

- Quality during manufacture is the responsibility of the operator setup teams assigned to batteries of about four machines each. It is difficult to estimate how much of their time is spent checking setups or checking the running of the machines, so you have not tried to do this as yet. Production has two sorting inspectors, each earning $18,000, who sort lots rejected by Final Inspection.

- The Engineering Department prepares quotations, designs tools, plans the routing of jobs, and establishes quality requirements, working from customers' prints. They also do troubleshooting, at a cost of about $20,000 a year. Another $16,000 is spent in previewing customers' prints to identify critical dimensions, trying to get such items changed by the customer, and interpreting customers' quality requirements into specifications for use by Federated inspectors and manufacturing personnel.

- Records of scrap, rework, and customer returns are meager, but you have been able to piece together a certain amount of information from records and estimates:

    Scrap from Final Inspection rejections and customer returns amounted to 438,000 and 667,000 pieces, respectively, for the last two months.

    Customer returns requiring rework average about 1 million pieces per month.

    Scrap generated during production is believed to be about half of the total floor scrap (the rest not being quality related) of 30,000 lb per month.

    Final Inspection rejects an average of 400,000 reworkable pieces per month. These are items that can be flat-rolled or rerolled.

- Rough cost figures have been obtained from the accountants, who say that scrap items can be figured at $12.00 per thousand pieces, floor scrap at $800 per thousand pounds, reworking of customer returns at $4.00 per thousand pieces, and flat-rolling or rerolling at $1.20 per thousand pieces. All of these figures are supposed to include factory overhead.

Prepare a quality cost summary on an annual basis. (This example was adapted from one originally prepared by L. A. Seder.)

2.2. Review the explanation of the marketing research study depicted in Table 2.4. What additional question would have been useful to ask during the study?

2.3. Information on the present quality culture in an organization is an important input to assessment. Asking employees their opinions about the quality culture incurs some risks. State two such risks.

2.4. In a survey used to learn about the quality culture in an organization, employees are asked questions that relate to three levels—upper management, their own manager, and the people in their work group. For each of these levels, state two questions that would identify employee perceptions about the quality culture.

2.5. When consumers eat at a fine restaurant, they expect excellent food and service. Research has identified seven features of restaurant service. What are these service features?

REFERENCES

ASQC (1986). *Principles of Quality Costs,* American Society for Quality Control, Milwaukee.

Aubrey, C. A. III, and D. A. Zimbler (1982). "A Banking Quality Cost Model: Its Uses and Results," *ASQC Quality Congress Transactions,* Milwaukee, pp. 195–201.

Gilmore, Harold L. (1983). "Consumer Product Quality Control Costs Revisited," *Quality Progress,* April, pp. 28–32.

Hulse, James W. (1983). "The Technique of Conducting a State of Quality Affairs Roundtable Conference to Ascertain the Employees' Perception of Quality," *Juran Report Number Two,* Juran Institute, Inc., Wilton, Connecticut, pp. 132–135.

"Quality Cost Survey" (1980). *Quality,* July, pp. 16–17.

Ryan, H. N., and H. Y. S. Wong (1984). "Breaking Down the Barrier," *Quality,* April, pp. 40–41.

Stevens, Eric R. (1987). "Implementing an Internal Customer Satisfaction Improvement Process," *Juran Report Number Eight,* Juran Institute, Inc., Wilton, Connecticut, pp. 140–145.

U.S. General Accounting Office (1991). "Management Practices: U.S. Companies Improve Performance Through Quality Efforts," P.O. Box 6015, Gaithersburg, MD 20877.

Willets, Gary G. (1989). "Internal and External Measures of Customer Satisfaction," *Customer Satisfaction Measurement Conference Notes,* American Society for Quality Control and American Marketing Association, Atlanta.

SUPPLEMENTARY READING

Quality costs: QCH4, Section 4.

Schneiderman, Arthur M. (1986). "Optimum Quality Costs and Zero Defects: Are They Contradictory Concepts?" *Quality Progress,* November, pp. 28–31.

Juran, J. M. (1987). "Letter to Editors," *Quality Progress,* April, pp. 7, 9.

Reeve, James M. (1991). "Variation and the Cost of Quality," *Quality Engineering,* vol. 4, no. 1, pp. 41–55.

Standing in the marketplace: QCH4, pp. 12.1–12.20

Company quality culture: QCH4, pp. 10.17–10.21

Assessment of current quality activities: QCH4, pp. 9.18–9.20
> *ISO 9000–9004 Quality Standards (ANSI/ASQC Q90–Q94),* ASQC, Milwaukee.
> *Application Guidelines—Malcolm Baldrige National Quality Award,* National Institute of Standards and Technology, Gaithersburg, MD 20899.

CHAPTER
3

QUALITY IMPROVEMENT AND COST REDUCTION

3.1 SPORADIC AND CHRONIC QUALITY PROBLEMS

Of the trilogy of quality processes (see Section 1.5., "Managing for Quality"), the process of quality improvement plays a dominant role in reducing costs.

The costs associated with poor quality are due to both *sporadic* and *chronic* quality problems (see Figure 3.1). A sporadic problem is a sudden, adverse change in the status quo, which requires remedy through *restoring* the status quo (e.g., changing a depleted reagent chemical). A chronic problem is a long-standing adverse situation, which requires remedy through *changing* the status quo (e.g., revising an unrealistic specification).

"Continuous improvement" (called Kaizen by the Japanese) has acquired a broad meaning, i.e., enduring efforts to act upon both chronic and sporadic problems and to make refinements to processes. For chronic problems, it means achieving better and better levels of performance each year; for sporadic problems, it means taking corrective action on periodic problems; for process refinements, it means taking such action as reducing variation around a target value.

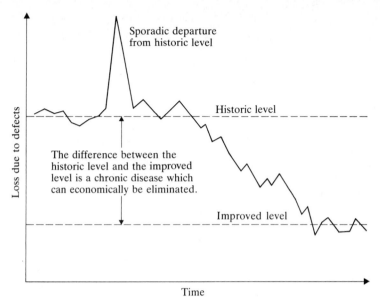

FIGURE 3.1
Sporadic and chronic quality problems.

The distinction between chronic and sporadic problems is important for two reasons:

1. The approach to solving sporadic problems differs from that to solving chronic problems. Sporadic problems are attacked by the control process defined and developed in Chapter 5. Chronic problems use the improvement process discussed in this chapter.
2. Sporadic problems are dramatic (e.g., an irate customer reacting to a shipment of bad parts) and must receive immediate attention. Chronic problems are not dramatic because they occur for a long time (e.g., 2 percent scrap has been typical for the past five years), are often difficult to solve, and are accepted as inevitable. The danger is that the fire fighting on sporadic problems may take continuing priority over efforts to achieve the larger savings that are possible, i.e., on chronic problems.

Addressing chronic quality problems achieves a breakthrough to an improved level of quality (Figure 1.3). This is best achieved by the "project-by-project" approach.

3.2 PROJECT-BY-PROJECT APPROACH

The most effective approach to improvement is "project by project." Here, a project is a chronic, quality-related problem which has been chosen for solution.

The sequence of steps listed in Table 1.5 provides for (1) setting up the project approach and (2) executing the individual projects. Setting up the approach comprises three main steps:

- Proving the need
- Identifying projects
- Organizing project teams

Carrying out each project involves:

- Verifying the project need and mission
- Diagnosing the causes
- Providing a remedy and proving its effectiveness
- Dealing with resistance to change
- Instituting controls to hold the gains

Improvement results on specific projects are limited only by our imagination. We need to question all traditions and assumptions about work activities and also aim for large improvements. Some people call this "reengineering the work" (see Hammer, 1990).

To provide perspective on individual projects, we first present a summarized example. Discussion of the steps in the improvement process then follows.

3.3 EXAMPLE OF A PROJECT

The problem (Betker, 1983) concerns the soldering process used at the GTE Corporation in the manufacture of printed circuit boards (PCBs). A typical PCB has 1700 solder connections. Any defective solder connection can cause testing problems or performance and reliability problems for the customer. We will trace the steps of the improvement sequence for an individual project.

Verify the Project Need and Mission

Over 15 percent of observations exceeded control limits and a large number of solder connections required "touch-up." The project team's mission was to reduce the number of defective solder connections.

Diagnose the Causes

A team of people, not from one department but from several cross-functional departments, was set up to guide the project and do the diagnosis. Figure 3.2 (a "Pareto diagram") depicts the distribution of symptoms by type of solder defect. Data on the defects were analyzed and theories were offered on the causes of the defects. Figure 3.3 is a cause-and-effect diagram summarizing the

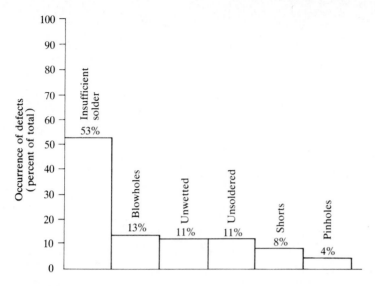

FIGURE 3.2
Solder defect types, Pareto analysis. (*From Betker, 1983.*)

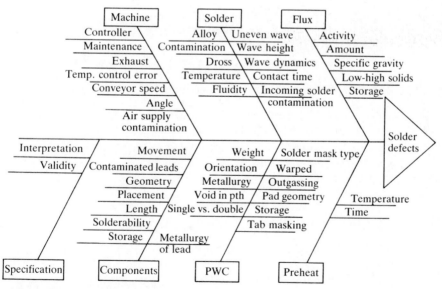

FIGURE 3.3
Ishikawa cause-and-effect diagram. (*From Betker, 1983.*)

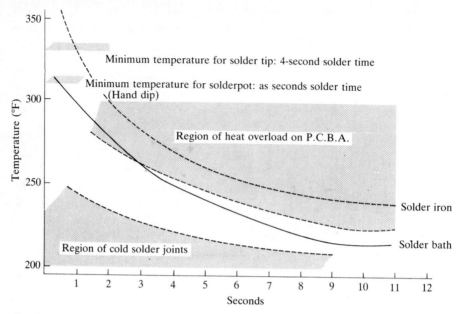

FIGURE 3.4
Temperature/time relationship when flow or dip soldering is applied. (*From Betker, 1983.*)

theories. These theories were grouped into three categories, thereby allowing a checklist to be developed that was used by supervisors and the control inspector to evaluate the theories. After additional data collection and analysis, low solder temperature was found to be the main cause of defects. Figure 3.4 shows a part of the analysis.

Provide a Remedy and Prove Its Effectiveness

Data and further analysis revealed that, for ideal soldering conditions, either the temperature of the solder should be raised or the conveyor speed of the wave soldering machine should be reduced. These were remedies to remove the cause. A trial was conducted using a higher temperature. This resulted in an improvement in solder defects without any adverse effects.

Deal with Resistance to Change

From the start of the project, a manufacturing engineer on the team argued that the cause was outside the control of the machine. The diagnosis explained above convinced him otherwise. But he felt that raising the temperature would result in "reflow of tin under the solder mask, thereby causing solder shorts and peeling of the solder mask." This belief, based on a trial conducted 10 years earlier on other equipment, had been expressed so often that it was no longer questioned. The proof of the remedy step overcame this resistance.

Institute Controls to Hold the Gains

The defect level was reduced by 62 percent and the out-of-control points on statistical control charts were eliminated. To assure that the improved level was maintained, the process was monitored. Not only was the improved level maintained but the elimination of the dominant cause (low temperature) unmasked other causes. Performance has been improved to the point that the hand solder touch-up operation may be eliminated.

This example provides an overview of the entire breakthrough sequence in manufacturing. Chapter 22 illustrates the breakthrough sequence for administrative and support activities. Next we examine the three steps for setting up the project-by-project approach.

3.4 PROVE THE NEED

This step consists of convincing the appropriate level of management that the quality issue is significant enough to require a new approach. Such justification starts with a companywide improvement effort but also applies to individual projects.

Chronic problems often require substantial time and resources for investigation, and thus the need must be justified. If solutions were easy, the problems would not be chronic.

To gain management approval for a new approach to quality:

1. Collect factual information to show the size of the quality problem. Experience shows that studies on the costs of poor quality and on competitive standing in the marketplace are convincing methods (see Chapter 2).
2. Show the benefits possible from an improvement program and use this to justify the resources requested for the program. This might take the form of percentage return on investment, time required to pay back the investment through savings, or other measures. Even when there is agreement on the importance of a problem, it is still helpful to quantify the size of the quality loss and the potential savings, because they can justify a sufficient investment to solve the problem.

The Several Languages of Management

To establish proof of the need, different "languages" may be required for different levels of management. For upper management, the language of money works best; for lower levels, other languages are effective. Table 3.1 shows examples of statements in money and other languages.

TABLE 3.1
Languages of management

Money (annual cost of poor quality)

24% of sales revenue
15% of manufacturing cost
13 cents per share of common stock
$7.5 million per year for scrap and rework compared to a profit of $1.5 million per year
$176 million per year
40% of the operating cost of a department

Other languages

The equivalent of one plant in the company making 100% defective work all year
32% of engineering resources spent in finding and correcting design weaknesses
25% of manufacturing capacity devoted to correcting quality problems
13% of sales orders canceled
70% of inventory carried attributed to poor quality levels
25% of manufacturing personnel assigned to correcting quality problems

Use of a Bellwether Project

An even more effective way to achieve a breakthrough in the attitude of management is to couple the study on the cost of poor quality with a case example of a successful quality improvement project within the company. This is illustrated in the approach taken by the ABC electronics company.

The estimated cost of poor quality was $200 million per year and a notorious quality problem was scrap for a certain major electronic component. This scrap ran to about $9 million per year. The principal defect type was defect X, and it was costing about $3 million per year ("proof of the need" for eliminating defect X).

The company took on a project to reduce the incidence of defect X. The project was a stunning success. The cost of defect X was cut from $3 million to $1 million—an annual profit improvement of $2 million. An investment of about $250,000 was needed.

Then followed an exciting extrapolation and contrast. It was estimated that extension of the improvement to the entire $200 million cost of poor quality could cut the total in half—thus creating a profit improvement of $100 million annually.

The defect X project proved to the ABC company managers that they could get a big return on investment by improving quality. This in-house project was more convincing to results-oriented managers than any number of lectures, books, or success stories about other companies.

But proof of the need is also important for *each* project for two reasons: (1) to confirm that the project is significant enough to justify spending the time to do diagnosis and (2) to show the potential benefits. For example, the monthly closing of the books in an accounting function incurred a 2.5 percent error rate. This translated into about 5000 miscodes per day during the closing period. Those miscodes resulted in large failure costs, high overtime, and low morale. Such information gave the impetus for an improvement study that resulted in an 80 percent reduction in miscodes, elimination of most of the overtime, and a great improvement in morale (*Fortune*, 1985).

3.5 IDENTIFY PROJECTS

Breakthrough is achieved project by project. Project identification consists of nominating, screening, and selecting projects.

Nomination for Projects

Nominations come from several sources:

- Analysis of data on the cost of poor quality, quality standing in the marketplace, or other forms of assessment (see Chapter 2)
- Analysis of other field intelligence, e.g., inputs from Sales, Customer Service, and other personnel
- Goal-setting processes, e.g., the annual budget, management by objectives
- All levels of management and the work force
- Developments arising from the impact of product quality on society, e.g., government regulation, growth of product liability lawsuits

A data analysis tool for generating project nominations is the Pareto principle.

The Pareto Principle

As applied to the cost of poor quality, the Pareto principle states that a few contributors to the cost are responsible for the bulk of the cost. These vital few contributors need to be identified so that quality improvement resources can be concentrated in those areas.

A study of quality-related costs at a paper mill showed a total of $9.07 million (Table 3.2a). The category called "broke" (paper mill jargon for paper so defective that it is returned to the beater for reprocessing) amounts to $5.56 million, or 61 percent of the quality costs. Clearly, there will be no major reduction in these costs unless there is a successful attack on the broke—which is where the loss of money is concentrated.

In that paper mill, 53 types of paper are made. When the broke is allocated among the various types of paper, the Pareto principle is again in evidence (Table 3.2b). Six of the product types account for $4.48 million, which is 80 percent of the $5.56 million. There will be no major improvement

TABLE 3.2a
Pareto analysis by accounts—quality losses in a paper mill

Accounting category	Annual quality loss,* $ thousands	Total quality loss, %	
		This category	Cumulative
"Broke"	5560	61	61
Customer claim	1220	14	75
Odd lot	780	9	84
High material cost	670	7	91
Downtime	370	4	95
Excess inspection	280	3	98
High testing cost	190	2	100
Total	9070		

* Adjusted for estimated inflation since time of original study.

TABLE 3.2b
Pareto analysis by products—"broke" losses in a paper mill

Product type	Annual "broke" loss,* $ thousands	"Broke" loss, %	"Broke" loss, cumulative %
A	1320	24	24
B	960	17	41
C	720	13	54
D	680	12	66
E	470	8	74
F	330 (4480)	6	80
47 other types	1080	20	100
Total 53 types	5560	100	

* Adjusted for estimated inflation since time of original study.

TABLE 3.2c
Matrix of quality costs*

Type	Trim, $ thousands	Visual defects, † $ thousands	Caliper, $ thousands	Tear, $ thousands	Porosity, $ thousands	All other causes, $ thousands	Total, $ thousands
A	270	94	None‡	162	430	364	1320
B	120	33	None‡	612	58	137	960
C	95	78	380	31	74	62	720
D	82	103	None‡	90	297	108	680
E	54	108	None‡	246	None‡	62	470
F	51	49	39	16	33	142	330
Total	672	465	419	1157	892	875	4480

* Adjusted for estimated inflation since time of original study.

† Slime spots, holes, wrinkles, etc.

‡ Not a specified requirement for this type.

in broke unless there is a successful attack on these six types of paper. Studying 12 percent (6 types out of 53) of the problem results in attacking 80 percent of the broke.

Finally, it is helpful to look at what kinds of defects are being encountered in these six types of paper, and how much the associated costs for broke are. The matrix of Table 3.2c shows this analysis. There are numerous defect types, but five dominate. In addition, the cost figures in the table also follow the Pareto principle. The largest number is $612,000 for tear on paper type B, then comes $430,000 for porosity on A, and so on. Such analysis would be helpful in nominating projects for cost reduction.

Establishing Priorities for Projects

Typically, project nominations are reviewed by middle management and recommendations are then made to upper management for final approval.

The review varies from an analysis of the project scope and potential benefit to a formal examination of several factors to help set priorities. For example, Berry (1988) explains how the Colonial Penn Insurance Company screens potential projects by asking six questions: Can we impact? Can we analyze? Are data available? Are they measurable? What areas are affected? What is the level of control?

Hartman (1983) describes an approach at AT&T that makes use of a "Pareto Priority Index" (PPI) to evaluate each project. The index is:

$$PPI = \frac{Savings \times probability\ of\ success}{Cost \times time\ to\ completion\ (years)}$$

Table 3.3 shows the application of this index to five potential projects. High PPI values suggest high priority. Note how the ranking of projects A and C is affected when the criterion is changed from cost savings alone to the index covering the four factors.

The result of the review by middle management is a recommended list of projects. Typically, one responsibility of an upper management quality council is reviewing the recommendations or creating the organizational machinery for review and final approval.

TABLE 3.3
Ranking by use of Pareto Priority Index (PPI)

Project	Savings, $ thousands	Probability	Cost, $ thousands	Time, years	PPI
A	100	0.7	10.0	2.0	3.5
B	50	0.7	2.0	1.0	17.5
C	30	0.8	1.6	0.25	60.0
D	10	0.9	0.5	0.50	36.0
E	1.5	0.6	1.0	0.10	9.0

Selection of Initial Projects

"The first project should be a winner." A successful project is a form of evidence to the project team members that the improvement process does lead to useful results. Ideally:

- The project should deal with a chronic problem—one which has been awaiting solution for a long time.
- The project should be feasible, i.e., have a good likelihood of being brought to a successful conclusion within about six months.
- The project should be significant. The end results should be sufficiently useful to merit attention and recognition.
- The results should be measurable in money as well as in technological terms.
- The project should serve as a learning experience for the process of problem solving.

Problem and Mission Statement

A problem statement identifies a visible deficiency in a planned outcome, e.g., "During the past year, 7 percent of invoices sent to customers included errors." A problem statement should never imply a cause or a solution or affix blame.

A mission statement is based upon the problem statement but provides direction to the project team. If possible, a goal or other measure of project completion and a target date should be defined. For example, the team is asked to reduce the error rate in invoices to 2 percent or less within the next 6 months.

3.6   ORGANIZE PROJECT TEAMS

A project team usually consists of about six to eight persons who are drawn from multiple departments and assigned to address the selected problem. Their job is to bring the project to a successful conclusion as defined in the mission statement for the project.

The team meets periodically and members serve part time in addition to performing their regular functional responsibilities. When the project is finished, the team disbands.

The project team consists of a leader, a secretary, and other team members. (Consulting specialists from disciplines such as accounting, software, metallurgy, etc., are invited to meetings when needed.)

PROJECT TEAM LEADER. The project team leader steers the team in its responsibility of carrying out the project. Successful leadership requires knowledge of the project area and skills in getting team members from several functional areas to work as a team. It is often useful for the team leader to come from the organizational unit most impacted by the problem.

PROJECT SECRETARY. Each team requires a project secretary to handle documentation: agendas, minutes, reports, etc. The secretary should be a member of the project team.

PROJECT TEAM MEMBERS. Team membership draws upon all of the skills and knowledge necessary for the project. For chronic problems, the teams are usually cross-functional and consist of middle management, professional, and work force personnel. Surprisingly, some projects are relatively easy and can be handled with a minimum of skills and knowledge. (Such projects are often the result of a previous lack of a project approach.) Other projects are complex and require more depth in team membership, perhaps even including consulting specialists from within the company.

Supplementing the formal team membership is a "facilitator." Many companies have adopted the concept of using a facilitator to help project teams carry out their first project. Although not a member of the team, the facilitator can play an important role. The role of the facilitator consists of any or all of the following:

- Explaining the company's approach to quality improvement and how it differs from prior efforts at quality improvement
- Providing assistance in team building
- Assisting in the training of project teams
- Assisting the project team leader to solve human relations problems among team members
- Helping the team avoid a poor choice of project
- Reporting progress on projects to management
- Revitalizing a stalled project

PROJECT TEAMS: INTRADEPARTMENTAL AND INTERDEPART-MENTAL. The vital few chronic problems usually cut across department lines and require cross-functional "project teams." Other chronic problems are centered within one department. Some of these problems can be solved by individuals, but many call for departmental teams called "Quality Circles" or "employee involvement groups," which we will discuss in Chapter 7.

While both types of teams are essential, there are important differences between the two (see Table 3.4).

A companywide effort on improvement involves many teams (and other individual activities). This, in turn, requires setting up the machinery to select problems and then form, train, monitor and provide time and recognition for

TABLE 3.4
Comparison: quality circles and project teams

Feature	Quality circles	Project teams
Scope of project	Within a single department	Multidepartmental
Size of project	One of the useful many	One of the vital few
Members come from	A single department	Multiple departments
Basis of membership	Voluntary	Mandatory
Composition of membership	Work force	Mostly middle management and specialists
Continuity	Circle remains intact, project after project	Team is ad hoc, disbands after project is completed

these teams. A companywide Quality Council usually has this responsibility, as will be discussed in Chapter 7.

3.7   EXPERIENCES WITH THE PROJECT-BY-PROJECT APPROACH

Experiences in both manufacturing and service industries have led to encouraging conclusions:

- Large cost reductions and improved quality to customers have been achieved. For each dollar invested in improvement activity, the return is between 5 and 10 dollars.
- Investment required for improvement has been modest and *not* capital intensive. Most of the investment is in the time of people doing diagnosis for the projects.
- Most projects can be completed in 6 months if the scope in the mission statement is carefully defined.
- The key chronic quality-related problems cut across departments and thereby require cross-functional project teams.

An increasing number of companies have reported the completion of over a thousand projects during a period of about 4 years. Today's competitive business conditions dictate such a revolutionary rate of improvement to replace the evolutionary rate of the past.

3.8   BREAKTHROUGH SEQUENCE FOR AN INDIVIDUAL PROJECT

Individual projects are selected, a problem and mission statement is prepared, and a project team is organized for each project. The team should then follow a sequence of steps to solve the problem. The following sequence has a good track record.

3.9 VERIFY THE PROJECT NEED AND MISSION

Presumably, a project has been selected because it is "important." It is useful, however, to verify the size of the problem *in numbers*. This serves two purposes: (1) assure that the time to be spent by the project team is justified and (2) help to overcome resistance to accepting and implementing a remedy. Verifying the need for an individual project makes use of the same type of information discussed above under "Prove the Need." It is also essential that the *scope* of the project be reviewed after the team has met once or twice, to be sure that the mission assigned to the team can be accomplished within, say, about 6 months. Otherwise, the project should be divided into several projects. Failure is likely if a project stretches out like a freight train.

3.10 DIAGNOSE THE CAUSES

Diagnosis is the process of studying the symptoms of a problem and determining their cause(s). The beginning of diagnosis is collecting data on the symptoms; the end is agreement on the causes.

Many managers harbor deep-seated beliefs that most defects are caused during manufacture and specifically are due to worker errors, i.e., that defects are mainly worker-controllable. The facts seldom bear this out, but the belief persists. To deal with such deep-seated beliefs, it can be useful to conduct studies to separate defects into broad categories of responsibility. Such studies include:

1. A study to determine the origin of the defects in the design, manufacture, etc. Such a study to determine the distribution of causes over functional areas often has some surprising results. In a classic study, Greenidge (1953) examined 850 failures of electronic products supplied by a number of companies. The results showed that 43 percent of the failures were caused by the product design, 30 percent by field operation conditions, 20 percent by manufacturing, and the remaining 7 percent by miscellaneous causes. For products of moderately high technology, it is not unusual for about 40 percent of field problems to be traceable to the product design.

2. A study to determine whether defects are primarily management-controllable or worker-controllable ("management" here includes not only people in supervisory positions but also others who influence quality, e.g., design engineers, process engineers, buyers, etc.). In general, defects are more than 80 percent management-controllable and less than 20 percent worker-controllable. Some authors use the term "system-controllable" for "management-controllable."

Such broad studies provide important guidance for improvement.

Some relevant definitions are:

A *defect* is any nonfulfillment of intended usage requirements, e.g., oversize, low mean time between failures, illegible invoice. A defect can also go by other names, e.g., error, discrepancy, nonconformance.

A *symptom* is an observable phenomenon arising from and accompanying a defect. Sometimes, but not always, the same word is used both as a defect description and as a symptom description, e.g., "open circuit." More usually, a defect will have multiple symptoms; e.g., "insufficient torque" may include the symptoms of vibration, overheating, erratic function, etc.

A *theory* is an unproved assertion as to reasons for the existence of defects and symptoms. Usually, several theories are advanced to explain the presence of the observed phenomena.

A *cause* is a proven reason for the existence of the defect. Often, there are multiple causes, in which case they follow the Pareto principle, i.e., the vital few causes will dominate all the rest.

A *remedy* is a change that can successfully eliminate or neutralize a cause of defects.

Two journeys are required for quality improvement: the diagnostic journey from symptom to cause, and the remedial journey from cause to remedy. This distinction is critical. To illustrate, three supervisors were faced with a problem of burrs on screws at the final assembly of kitchen stoves. In their haste to act, they skipped the diagnostic journey and concluded that better screws were needed (a remedy). Fortunately, a diagnostician interceded. He pointed out that three separate assembly lines were feeding product into one inspection station, and he suggested that the data be segregated by assembly line. The data revealed that the burrs occurred only on line 3. Further diagnosis based on data led to agreement that the true cause was an improperly trained assembler. Then the remedy came easily.

The diagnostic journey consists of:

1. Study of the symptoms surrounding the defects to serve as a basis for theorizing about causes
2. Theorizing on the causes of these symptoms
3. Data collection and analysis to test the theories and thereby determine the causes

Many analysis techniques are available to assist in these three steps. Some are illustrated in the following pages. A compilation with examples is provided in QCH4, Section 22. This compilation includes the "Magnificent Seven" tools: control chart, checksheet, histogram, Pareto diagram, cause-and-effect diagram, scatterplot, and flowchart. Additional tools continually emerge.

Evidence of defects and errors comes in two forms:

1. Words used in written documentation or oral comments describing the problem
2. "Autopsies" conducted to measure and examine the defects

Description of Symptoms

Understanding of symptoms is often hindered because some key word or phrase has multiple meanings.

In one example, a Pareto analysis of inspection data in a wire mill indicated a high percentage of defects due to "contamination." Various remedies were tried to prevent the contamination. All were unsuccessful. In desperation, the investigators spoke with the inspectors to learn more about the contamination. The inspectors explained that there were 12 defect categories on the inspection form. If the observed defect did not fit any of the categories, they would report the defect as "contamination."

Imprecise wording also occurs due to use of generic terminology. For example, a software problem is described in a discrepancy report as a "coding error." Such a description is useless for analysis because there are many types of coding errors, e.g., undefined variables, violation of language rules, and violation of programming standards.

A way out of such semantic tangles is to think through the meanings of the words used, reach an agreement, and record the agreement in the form of a glossary. Once published, the glossary simplifies the subsequent analysis.

Quantification of Symptoms

The frequency and intensity of symptoms are of great significance in pointing to directions for analysis. The Pareto principle, when applied to records of past performance, can help to quantify the symptom pattern. Figure 3.5 displays a Pareto diagram for deficiencies in the handling of classified information at the Honeywell Corporation. Seven categories of symptoms were identified, e.g., "container improperly secured" and "unattended material." The Pareto principle applies to several levels of diagnosis: finding the vital few defects, finding the vital few symptoms of a defect, and finding the vital few causes of one symptom.

Formulation of Theories

The process consists of three steps: generation of theories, arrangement of theories, and choice of theories to be tested.

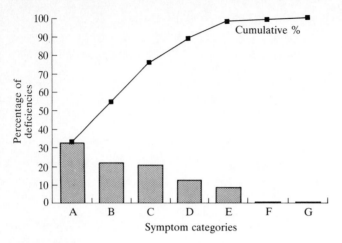

FIGURE 3.5
Pareto analysis of security violations. (*From Parvey, 1990.*)

GENERATION OF THEORIES. The best sources of theories are the line managers, the technologists, the line supervisors, and the work force. A systematic way to generate theories is the brainstorming technique. Persons who are potential contributors are assembled for the purpose of generating theories. Creative thinking is encouraged by asking each person, in turn, to propose a theory. No criticism or discussion of ideas is allowed, and all ideas are recorded. The end result is a list of theories which, after the brainstorming session is completed, are critically reviewed.

A useful supplement to the brainstorming technique is "storyboarding." Each theory proposed is recorded on an index card. The cards are arranged on a board to form a visual display of the theories. Storyboarding provides a visual system for organizing theories and planning subsequent evaluation of these theories.

ARRANGEMENT OF THEORIES. Normally, the list of theories should be extensive, 20 or more. As the list grows in size, it is essential to create an orderly arrangement. Such order helps us to understand the interrelationships among theories and to plan for testing of the theories. Table 3.5 shows a tabular arrangement of theories contributing to low yield of a process making fine powder chemicals. The theories consist of major variables and contributing subvariables. A second method, which is highly effective, is a graphical arrangement called the Ishikawa cause-and-effect (or "fishbone") diagram. Figure 3.6 shows such a diagram, which presents the same information as is listed in Table 3.5. QCH4, pages 22.39–22.40, discusses other methods of arranging theories.

CHOOSING THEORIES TO BE TESTED. After the theories are arranged in an orderly fashion, priorities must be established for testing the theories. In

TABLE 3.5
Orderly arrangement of theories

Raw material
  Shortage of weight
  Method of discharge

Catalyzer
  Types
  Quantity
  Quality

Reaction
  Solution and concentration
  B solution temperature
  Solution and pouring speed
  pH
  Stirrer, rpm
  Time

Crystallization
  Temperature
  Time
  Concentration
  Mother crystal
    Weight
    Size

Moisture content
  Charging speed of wet powder
  Dryer, rpm
  Temperature
    Stream pressure
    Steam flow

Overweight of package
  Type of balance
  Accuracy of balance
  Maintenance of balance
  Method of weighing
  Operator

Transportation
  Road
  Cover
  Spill
  Container

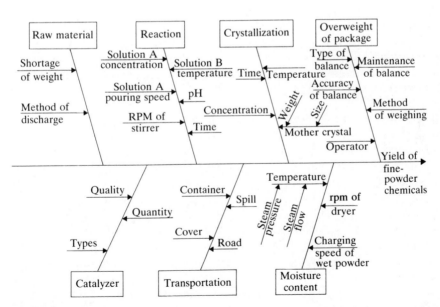

FIGURE 3.6
Ishikawa cause-and-effect diagram.

practice, the improvement team reaches a consensus on the "most likely" theory for testing. Whether to test just one theory at a time, one group of interrelated theories at a time, or all theories simultaneously requires a judgment based on the experience and creativity of the team.

We proceed next to the test of theories—first, management-controllable, then worker-controllable.

Test of Theories of Management-Controllable Problems

Numerous diagnostic methods have been created to test theories. Some are illustrated below; others abound in the literature.

PRODUCT AND PROCESS DISSECTION. Some products are produced by a "procession" type of process, i.e., a series of sequential operations. At the end of the series, the product is found to be defective, but it is not known which operation did the damage. In some of these cases, it is feasible to dissect the process, i.e., make measurements at intermediate steps in the process to discover at which step the defect appears. Such a discovery can drastically reduce the subsequent effort in testing theories.

FLOW DIAGRAM. Dissection of a process is aided by constructing a flow diagram (recent jargon is "process map") showing the various steps in the process. Engle and Ball (1986) explain the role of a flow diagram in reducing the time required for handling special customer orders. Thus we have a process—a cycle of steps to handle special customer orders—and we need to reduce the process cycle time. A quality improvement team discovered that no one was able to describe the special order process. To understand the process they were trying to improve, the team created a flow diagram. Examples of several types of diagrams for understanding a process are given in Section 16.2, "Initial Planning for Quality."

PROCESS CAPABILITY ANALYSIS. One of the theories most widely encountered is "The process can't hold the tolerances." To test this theory, measurements from the process must be taken and analyzed to determine the amount of variability inherent in the process. This variability is then compared to the specification limits. Those steps are performed in a "process capability" study (see Section 17.8, "Process Capability").

STREAM-TO-STREAM ANALYSIS. In order to meet production volume requirements, several sources of production ("streams") are often necessary. Streams take the form of different machines, operators, shifts, suppliers, etc. Although the streams may seem to be identical, the resulting products may not be. Stream-to-stream analysis consists of recording and examining data separately for each stream.

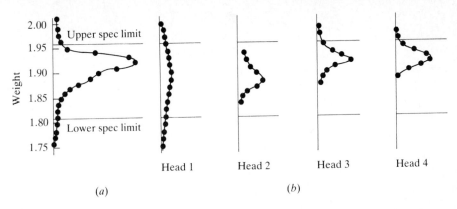

FIGURE 3.7
Distribution of glass bead weights: (*a*) sum of four heads, (*b*) weight distribution on each of the four heads. (*From QCH4*, p. *22.42.*)

An example (Payne, 1984) comes from a glass tube cutting machine. Glass tubing was cut into small glass rings. The weight of the rings was the critical element in determining the properties of the finished glass product. A sample of data (Figure 3.7*a*) apparently confirmed a theory that the machine was not functioning correctly. However, the machine contained four heads. Data collected separately from each head (stream) revealed that there was nothing wrong with heads 2, 3, 4—except for a need to recenter their position (Figure 3.7*b*). There was, however, something wrong with head 1. Ultimately, the remedy was proper maintenance of the machine rather than a redesign of the machine, as had originally been contemplated based on Figure 3.7*a*.

TIME-TO-TIME ANALYSIS. Time-to-time analyses include: (1) a simple plot of data on a time scale; (2) analysis of the time between abnormalities or problems; (3) analysis of the rate of change, or "drift," of a characteristic; and (4) the use of cumulative data techniques with respect to time. Examples are given below.

In one example, field failures of oil coolers were assumed to be due to manufacturing. A parade of remedies (skipping the journey from symptom to cause) resulted in zero improvement. An engineer decided to plot the frequency of failures by month of the year, and this led to an important discovery. Of 70 failures over a 9-month period, 44 occurred during January, February, and March. These facts shifted the search to other causes such as winter climatic conditions. Subsequent diagnosis revealed the cause to be in design rather than manufacturing.

In analyzing time-to-time variations, the length of time between abnormalities can be a major clue to the cause. In a textile carding operation, there was a cyclic rise and fall in yarn weights, the cycle being about 12 minutes in

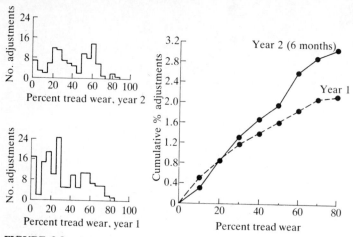

FIGURE 3.8
Comparison of histograms and cumulative plots. (*From QCH*4, p. *22.44.*)

length. The reaction of the production superintendent was immediate: "The only thing we do every 12 minutes or so is to stuff that feed box."

Within many streams, there is a time-to-time "drift"; e.g., the processing solution gradually becomes more dilute, the tools gradually wear, the worker becomes fatigued. Such drifts can often be quantified to determine the magnitude of the effect.

Cumulative data plots can help to discover differences that are hidden when the data are in noncumulative form. Figure 3.8 compares histograms (noncumulative) and cumulative plots for data from 2 separate years. A difference in adjustments for year 1 versus year 2 is apparent from the cumulative plot but is hidden in the histogram.

Control charts are a powerful diagnostic tool. Data are plotted chronologically, and the chart then shows whether the variability from sample to sample is due to chance or assignable causes of variation. Detection of assignable causes of variation can be the link to discovering the cause of a problem. Chapter 17, "Statistical Process Control," explains the concept.

ANALYSIS OF PIECE-PART VARIATION. Some products exhibit several types of variation, e.g., piece-to-piece, within-piece, and time-to-time. The multivari chart is a clever tool for analyzing such variation. In this chart, a vertical line depicts the range of variation within a single piece of product. Figure 3.9 depicts three different examples of the relationship of product variation to tolerance limits. The left-hand case is one in which the within-piece variation alone is too great in relation to the tolerance. Hence, no solution is possible unless within-piece variation is reduced. The middle example is a case in which within-piece variation is comfortable, occupying

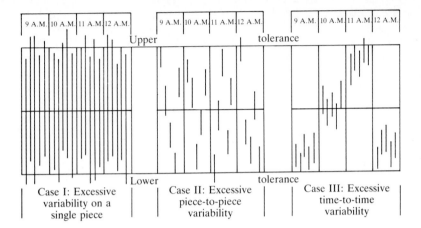

FIGURE 3.9
Multivari chart.

only about 20 percent of the tolerance. The problem, then, is piece-to-piece variation. In the right-hand example, the problem is excess time-to-time variability.

DEFECT-CONCENTRATION ANALYSIS. A different form of piece-to-piece variation is the defect-concentration study used for attribute types of defects. The purpose is to discover whether defects are located in the same physical area. The technique has long been used by shop personnel when they observe that all pieces are defective and in precisely the same way. However, when the defects are intermittent or become evident only in later departments, the analysis can be beyond the unaided memory of the shop personnel.

For example, a problem of pitted castings was analyzed by dividing the castings into 12 zones and tallying up the number of pits in each zone over many units of product. The concentration at the gates (through which the metal flows) became evident, as did areas which were free of pits (Figure 3.10).

ASSOCIATION SEARCHES. Sometimes diagnosis can be advanced by analyzing data relating symptoms of the problem to some theory of causation, pinpointing process, tools, workers, or design. Possible relationships can be examined using various statistical tools such as correlation and matrixes.

Correlation. In this approach, data are plotted that relate the incidence of symptoms of the problem to values of a potential causal variable.

In one case, the symptom was yarn breakage on weaving machines. One theory was "handling damages to the board bobbin" (the spinning mill supplied the yarn reeled onto a board bobbin). A plot of the amount of

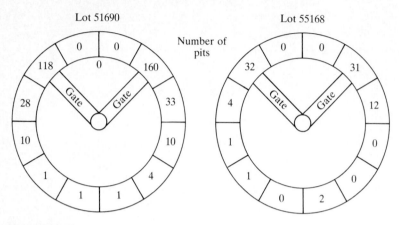

FIGURE 3.10
Concentration of pits in cast rings.

damage versus the number of yarn breakages clearly revealed a relationship between reels with heavy damage and subsequent yarn breakage. Further investigation showed that the corrugated paperboard plates used to protect the bobbins were inadequate. An investment of a few hundred dollars yielded a savings of $10,000 per year, an amount heretofore lost because of yarn breakages (Bergstrom, 1985).

Matrix. In this approach, past or current data are collected on two or more variables of a problem and summarized in a table to see if any pattern exists. In a study involving 23 types of torque tubes, the symptom was dynamic unbalance. One theory was that a swaging operation was a dominant cause. Table 3.6 tabulates the percentage of defective pieces (dynamic unbalance)

TABLE 3.6
Test of theories by ranking

Type	Defective, %	Swaged (marked ×)	Type	Defective, %	Swaged (marked ×)
A	52.3	×	M	19.2	×
B	36.7	×	N	18.0	×
C	30.8	×	O	17.3	
D	29.9	×	P	16.9	×
E	25.3	×	Q	15.8	
F	23.3	×	R	15.3	
G	23.1	×	S	14.9	
H	22.5		T	14.7	
I	21.8	×	U	14.2	
J	21.7	×	V	13.5	
K	20.7	×	W	12.3	
L	20.3				

and also shows if swaging was part of the process. The result was dramatic—the worst seven types of tubes were all swaged; the best seven were all unswaged. This partially confirmed that swaging was a dominant cause. Later analysis revealed an inadequate specification on an important coaxial dimension.

Later in this chapter, the matrix technique for analyzing problems in insurance contracts is illustrated.

TEST OF THEORIES BY COLLECTION OF NEW DATA. In some cases, discovery of causes requires careful examination of additional stages in the process. This "cutting of new windows" can take several forms:

1. *Measurement at intermediate stages of a single operation.* An example concerned a defect known as "voids" in welded joints of pressure vessels. Initial diagnosis established six sources of variation: operator, time-to-time, joint-to-joint, layer-to-layer, within layers, and within one welding "bead." Available past data permitted analysis of the first two sources as possible causes of voids. The remaining three could not be analyzed since the critical X-ray test was performed only when a joint was completely finished. The answer was to "cut a new window" by making an X ray after each of the several beads needed to make a joint. The data established that the main variable was within-bead variation and that the problem was concentrated at the start of the bead.

   An example from a human resources process concerns the time required for hiring new engineers. Measurements taken at six steps in the hiring process formed the basis for a diagnosis of excessive time taken to hire engineers.

2. *Measurement following noncontrolled operations.* Here, diagnosis includes the collection of additional information at individual steps in a process. Marquez (1985) describes the diagnosis of excessive shutdown time for removing a hot mold from a molding machine. The process of shutdown was divided into 11 steps, and measurements were taken to estimate the time required for each step. Two of the 11 steps accounted for 62 percent of the shutdown time. This Pareto effect was important in further diagnosis.

3. *Measurement of additional or related properties of the product or process.* Diagnosis sometimes requires measurements of characteristics other than those for which the specification is not being met. In the manufacture of phonograph records, the symptom was a high percentage of records with surface defects. Automatic timers controlled the pressing cycle. Diagnosis revealed that the times for various steps should not be fixed but should be determined based on additional measurements taken periodically. The remedy was to monitor pressure, temperature, viscosity, and other factors. An on-line computer evaluates these data for each disk and decides on the

optimum molding conditions. Only then, and no sooner, does the press create the product.

4. *Study of worker methods.* In some situations, there are consistent differences in the defect levels coming from various workers. Month after month, some workers produce more "good" product than others. In such situations, there must be a cause for this consistent difference in observed performance. Diagnosis of problems related to human performance is discussed later in this section.

TEST OF THEORIES THROUGH EXPERIMENTS. Experiments in the laboratory or outside world may be necessary to determine and analyze the dominant causes of a quality problem. Four types of diagnostic experiments are summarized in Table 3.7.

Experiments for evaluating one or two suspected variables ("factors") are sometimes called "rifle shot experiments." The purpose is to test a theory that a suspected variable is a major cause of a problem.

In the exploratory experiment, the dominant variables are not known but must be pursued by a formal experiment. This is called an unbridled experiment.

A well-organized exploratory experiment has a high probability of identifying the dominant causes of variability. However, there is a risk of overloading the experimental plan with too much detail. A check on overextension of the experiment is to require that the analyst prepare a written plan for review. This written plan must define:

1. The characteristics of material, process, environment, and product to be observed

TABLE 3.7
Types of diagnostic experiments

Type of experiment	Purpose and approach
Evaluating suspected dominant variables	Evaluate changes in values of a variable by dividing a lot into several parts and processing each portion at some different value, e.g., temperature.
Exploratory experiments to determine dominant variables	Statistically plan an experiment in which a number of characteristics are carefully varied in a manner to yield data for quantifying each dominant variable and the interactions among variables.
Production experiments (evolutionary operation)	Make small changes in selected variables of a process and evaluate the effect to find the optimum combination of variables.
Simulation	Use the computer to study the variability of several dependent variables which interact to yield a final result.

2. The control of these characteristics during the experiment; a characteristic may be:

   (*a*) Allowed to vary as it will and measured as is

   (*b*) Held at a standard value

   (*c*) Deliberately randomized

   (*d*) Deliberately varied, in several classes or treatments

3. The means of measurement to be used (if different from standard practice)

   If the plan shows that the experiment may be overloaded, a "dry run" in the form of a small-scale experiment is in order. A review of the dry-run experiment can then help decide the final plan.

Production experiments. Experimentation is often regarded as an activity that can be performed only under laboratory conditions. To achieve maximum performance from some manufacturing processes, however, the effect of key process variables on process yield or product properties must be demonstrated under shop conditions. Laboratory experimentation to evaluate these variables does not always yield conclusions that are completely applicable to shop conditions. When justified, a "pilot plant" may be set up to evaluate process variables. However, the final determination of the effect of process variables must often be done during the regular production run by informally observing results and making changes if these are deemed necessary. Thus, informal experimentation *does* take place on the manufacturing floor.

   To systematize informal experimentation and provide a methodical approach for process improvement, G.E.P. Box developed a technique known as "evolutionary operations" (EVOP). EVOP is based on the concept that every manufactured lot has information to contribute about the effects of process variables on a quality characteristic. Although such variables could be analyzed by an experimental design, EVOP introduces *small* changes into these variables according to a planned pattern of changes. These changes are small enough to avoid nonconformance but large enough to gradually establish (1) what variables are important and (2) the optimum process values for these variables. Although this approach is slower than a formal experimental design, results are achieved in a production environment without the additional costs of a special experiment.

   The steps are:

1. Select two or three independent process variables which are likely to influence quality. For example, time and temperature were selected as variables affecting the yield of a chemical process.

2. Change these steps according to a plan (see Figure 3.11). This diagram shows the *plan,* not any data. For example, a reference run was made with the production process set to run at 130°C for three and a half hours. The

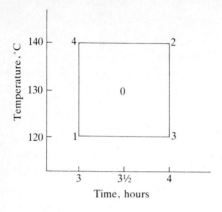

FIGURE 3.11
An EVOP plan. Numbers are in run order. "0" is the reference run.

next batch (point one in Figure 3.11) was run at 120°C for three hours. The first *cycle* contains five runs, one at each condition. Samples were taken from each batch and analyses were made.

3. After the second repetition of the plan (cycle 2) and each succeeding cycle, calculate the effects (see QCH4, page 26.31).
4. When one or more of the effects is significant, change the midpoints of the variables and perhaps their ranges.
5. After eight cycles, if no variable has been shown to be effective, change the ranges or select new variables.
6. Continue moving the midpoint of the EVOP plan and adjust the ranges as necessary.
7. When a maximum has been obtained, or the rate of gain is too slow, drop the current variables from the plan and run a new plan with different variables.

   EVOP is a highly structured form of production experimentation. Ott and Schilling (1990) present a variety of practical design and analysis techniques for solving production quality problems.

Simulation experiments. From the field of operations research comes a technique called *simulation* that can be useful in analyzing quality problems. Simulation provides a method of studying the effect of a number of variables on a final quality characteristic—but all of this is done on paper without conducting experiments! A simulation study requires the following inputs:

1. Definition of the output variable(s).
2. Definition of the input variable(s).
3. Description of the complete system relating the input and output variables.
4. Data on the distribution of each input variable; thus variability is accepted as inherent in the process.

In simulation, a system model is developed and translated into a computer program. This program not only defines the relationship between input and output variables but makes provision for storing the distribution of each input variable. The computer then selects values at random from each input distribution and combines these values, using the relationship defined, to generate a simulated value of the output variable. Each repetition of this process results in a simulated output result. These can then be formed into a frequency distribution. The payoff is to make *changes* in the input variables or the relationships, run another simulation, and observe the effect of the change. Thus the significance of variables can be evaluated on paper, providing one more way of evaluating theories on causes of problems.

Simulation has been applied to many quality problems, including interacting tolerances, circuit design, and reliability.

Test of Theories of Worker-Controllable Problems

Diagnosis of human errors reveals that there are "multiple species" of error. To illustrate these species, Table 3.8 shows the distribution of 80 errors made by six office workers engaged in preparing insurance policy contracts.

There were 29 types of errors, and they follow the Pareto principle. Notice the data for error type 3. There were 19 of these, and worker *B* made 16 of the 19. The table also shows the rest of the work done by worker *B*. Except for error type 3, *B* made few errors. There is nothing basically wrong with the job specification or the method, since the other five workers had little or no trouble with error type 3. There is nothing basically wrong with worker

TABLE 3.8
Matrix of errors by insurance policy writers

Error type	Policy writer						Total
	A	B	C	D	E	F	
1	0	0	1	0	2	1	4
2	1	0	0	0	1	0	2
3	0	⑯	1	0	2	0	⑲
4	0	0	0	0	1	0	1
5	2	1	3	1	4	2	⑬
6	0	0	0	0	3	0	3
⋮							
27							
28							
29							
Total	6	⑳	8	3	㊱	7	80

B except for defect type 3. It follows that worker *B* and no one else is misinterpreting some instruction, resulting in that cluster of 16 errors of type 3.

Error type 5 is of a different species. There is a cluster of 13 of these, and all the workers made this error, more or less uniformly. This suggests some difference in approach between all the workers on the one hand and the inspector on the other. Such a difference is usually of management-controllable origin, but the reality can soon be established by interviews with the respective employees.

Notice also the column of numbers associated with worker *E*. The total is 36 errors, the largest cluster in the table. Worker *E* made nearly half the errors for the entire team, and that worker made them in virtually all error categories. Why did worker *E* make so many errors? It might be any of a variety of reasons, e.g., inadequate training, lack of capacity to do such exacting work, etc. Further study is needed, but it might be easier to go from symptom directly to remedy—find a less demanding job for that worker.

Thus, this one table shows the presence of multiple species of worker error. The remedy is not as simplistic as "motivate the worker." Understanding these species through diagnosis is important in identifying causes. The great majority of worker errors fall into one of three categories: inadvertent, technique, and conscious. Table 3.9 shows the interrelationship among the

TABLE 3.9
Interrelationship among error pattern, likely subspecies of worker error, and likely solution

Pattern disclosed by analysis of worker error	Likely subspecies of error causing this pattern	Likely solution
On certain defects, no one is error-prone; defect pattern is random.	Errors are due to inadvertence.	Error-proof the process.
On certain defects, some workers are consistently error-prone while others are consistently "good."	Errors are due to lack of technique (ability, knowhow, etc.). Lack of technique may take the form of secret ignorance. Technique may consist of known knack or of secret knowledge.	Discovery and propagation of knack. Discovery and elimination of secret ignorance.
Some workers are consistently error-prone over a wide range of defects.	There are several potential causes: Conscious failure to comply with standards Inherent incapacity to perform this task Lack of training	Solution follows the cause: Increase motivation Transfer worker Supply training
On certain defects, all workers are error-prone.	Errors are management-controllable.	Meet the criteria for self-control.

error pattern, the likely subcategory, and the likely remedies. The three categories are examined below.

INADVERTENT ERRORS. Inadvertent errors are those which workers are unable to avoid because of human inability to maintain attention. Centuries of experience have demonstrated that human beings are simply unable to maintain continual attention.

The usual examples involve a component omitted from an assembly or a process adjustment that is set incorrectly. Unusual examples also occur. Some stockbrokerage companies maintain a special account to cover expenses in connection with errors made in trading stock, e.g., purchase of the wrong stock because of a similarity in the acronyms used to identify companies. In the athletic arena, a football game may be lost because, on a key play near the end of the game, a player mistakenly hears a play called as "green" instead of "three." He misses his defensive assignment, and the opposing team scores a touchdown.

Diagnosis to identify errors as inadvertent is aided by understanding their distinguishing features. They are:

• Unintentional. The worker does not want to make errors.
• Unwitting. At the time of making an error, the worker is unaware of having made it.
• Unpredictable. There is nothing systematic as to when an error will be made, what type of error will be made, or which worker will make the error. As a consequence of this unpredictability, the error pattern exhibits randomness. *A set of data which shows a random pattern of worker error suggests that the errors are inadvertent.* The randomness of the data may apply to the types of errors, to the persons who make errors, and to the times when the errors are made.

Remedies for inadvertent errors involve two approaches:

1. Reducing the extent of dependence on human attention. The tools used here are all of the error-proofing type: fail-safe designs, validation of processes, countdowns, redundant verifications, cutoffs, interlocks, alarm signals, automation, robots. Large reductions in errors can result from the use of bar codes to help identify items.
2. Making it easier for human beings to remain attentive. Examples of remedies are reorganization of work to reduce fatigue and monotony, job rotation, and use of sense multipliers, templates, masks, and overlays.

TECHNIQUE ERRORS. These errors arise because the worker lacks some essential technique, skill, or knowledge needed to prevent the error from happening. Diagnosis to identify errors due to technique is aided by understanding their features. They are:

- *Unintentional.* The worker does not want to make errors.
- *Specific.* Technique errors are unique to certain defect types—those types for which the missing technique is essential.
- *Consistent.* Workers who lack the essential technique consistently make more defects than workers who possess the technique. This consistency is readily evident from data on worker errors.
- *Unavoidable.* The inferior workers are unable to match the performance of the superior workers because they do not know "what to do differently."

Discovery of the existence of technique errors makes use of the diagnostic tools for worker errors, as illustrated here in the assembly of shotguns.

The gun assembly case. Guns were assembled by 22 skilled craft workers, each of whom assembled a complete gun from bits and pieces. After a safety test, about 10 percent of the guns could not be opened up to remove the spent cartridge—a defect known as "open hard after fire." For such defects, it was necessary to disassemble the gun and then reassemble it, which required about 2 hours per defective gun—a significant waste.

After an agony of fruitless discussion, it was clear that the missing element was factual information. Data already in the files by assembler and time were collected and arranged in a matrix (Table 3.10). Some helpful information became evident:

1. There was a wide month-to-month *departmental* variation in the defect rate, ranging from a low of 1.8 percent in January to a high of 22.6 percent in February. Since all workers seemed to be affected, this variation must have had its cause outside of the department. (Subsequent analysis confirmed this.)
2. The ratio of the five best performances to the five worst showed *a stunning consistency.* In each of the 6 months, the five worst performances add up to an error rate which is at least ten times as great as the sum of the five best performances. There must be a reason for such a consistent difference, and it can be found by studying work methods—the techniques used by the respective workers.

The knack. The study of work methods showed that the superior performers used a file to cut down one of the dimensions on a complex component; the inferior performers did not file that component. This filing constituted a "knack"—a small difference in method which accounts for a large difference in

TABLE 3.10
Matrix analysis

Assembly operator rank	Nov.	Dec.	Jan.	Feb.	Mar.	Apr.	Total
1	4	1	0	0	0	0	5
2	1	2	0	5	1	0	9
3	3	1	0	3	0	3	10
4	1	1	0	2	2	4	10
5	0	1	0	10	2	1	14
6	2	1	0	2	2	15	22
⋮							
17	18	8	3	37	9	23	98
18	16	17	0	22	36	11	102
19	27	13	4	62	4	14	124
20	6	5	2	61	22	29	125
21	39	10	2	45	20	14	130
22	26	17	4	75	31	35	188
Total	234	146	34	496	239	241	1390
% defective	10.6	6.6	1.8	22.6	10.9	11.0	10.5
5 best	9	6	0	20	5	8	48
5 worst	114	62	12	265	113	103	669
Ratio	13	10	∞	13	23	13	14

results. (Until the diagnosis was made, the superior assemblers had not realized that filing greatly reduced the incidence of defects.)

Usually the difference in worker performance is traceable to some superior knack used by the successful performers to benefit the product. In the case of the gun assemblers, the knack consisted of filing one component. In some cases, however, the difference in worker performance is due to unwitting *damage* done to the product by the inferior performers.

There is a useful rule for predicting whether the difference in worker performance is due to a beneficial knack or to a negative knack. Who are in the minority? If the superior performers are in the minority, the difference is probably due to a beneficial knack. If the inferior performers are in the minority, the difference in performance is probably due to a negative knack.

Summary of technique errors. The sequence of events to identify, analyze, and remedy technique errors is:

1. For the defect types under study, create and collect data which can disclose any significant worker-to-worker differences.
2. Analyze the data on a time-to-time basis to discover whether consistency is present.

3. Identify the consistently best and consistently worst performers.
4. Study the work methods used by the best and worst performers to identify their differences in technique.
5. Study these differences further so as to discover the beneficial knack which produces superior results or the negative knack which is damaging the product.
6. Bring everyone up to the level of the best through appropriate remedial action such as:
   (*a*) Training inferior performers in use of the knack or in avoidance of damage.
   (*b*) Changing the technology so that the process embodies the knack.
   (*c*) Error-proofing the process in ways which require use of the knack or which prohibit the technique which is damaging to the product.

CONSCIOUS ERRORS. Diagnosis to identify errors as conscious is aided by understanding their features. They are:

- *Witting.* At the time of making an error, the worker is aware of it.
- *Intentional.* The error is the result of a deliberate intention on the part of the worker.
- *Persistent.* The worker who makes the error usually intends to keep it up.

The outward evidence of conscious errors is likewise unique. Whereas inadvertent errors exhibit randomness, conscious errors exhibit consistency, i.e., some workers consistently make more errors than others. However, whereas technique errors are typically restricted to those defect types which require some special knack, conscious errors tend to cover a wider spectrum of defect types. Knowing these types is helpful in diagnosing errors as conscious.

Management-initiated conscious errors. Many "conscious" errors are management initiated. The most common examples arise from the multiple standards which all managers must meet—cost, delivery, and productivity, as well as quality. Because of changes in the marketplace, managers keep shifting their priorities; e.g., in a seller's market, delivery schedules will prevail over some quality standards. The pressures on the managers are then transmitted to the work force and can result in conscious violation of one standard in order to meet another.

Worker-initiated conscious errors. Some conscious errors are worker initiated. Workers may have real or fancied grievances against the boss or the company. They get their revenge by not meeting standards. A few become rebels against the whole social system, and they use sabotage to show their resentment. Some of the instances encountered are so obviously antisocial that no one—not the fellow employees, not the union—will defend the actions.

Some conscious errors *seem* to be worker initiated but have their origin in inadequate communication by management. For example, three product batches fail to conform to quality characteristic X. In each case, the inspector places a hold on the batch. In each case, the Material Review Board concludes that the batch is fit for use and releases it for delivery. However, neither the production worker nor the inspector is told why. Not knowing the reason, these workers may conclude that characteristic X is unimportant. That sets the stage for unauthorized actions.

Remedies for conscious errors. Generally, the remedies listed here emphasize securing changes in behavior without making any special effort to secure a change in attitude. Either way, the approach is oriented primarily to the persons rather than to the "system"—the managerial or technological aspects of the job. Possible remedies include:

- Explaining the impact of the error on internal or external customers
- Establishing individual accountability
- Providing a balance between productivity and quality
- Conducting periodic audits
- Providing reminders to workers about specific defects
- Improving communication between management and workers on quality issues
- Creating competition and incentives
- Error-proofing the operation
- Reassigning the work

For elaboration on these remedies, see QCH4, pages 22.60–22.61.

Next, we consider the development of remedies in general for both management-controllable and worker-controllable problems.

3.11 PROVIDE A REMEDY AND PROVE ITS EFFECTIVENESS

Following diagnosis to determine the cause, the next step in the breakthrough process is to choose a remedy.

Choice of Alternatives

The diagnostic journey may lead to a wide variety of dominant causes of the symptoms: weakness in the design, inadequacy in a process, etc. Remedial action responds to the findings of the diagnosis. An essential criterion is that both company costs and customer costs be optimized.

In quantifying company costs, the cost impact for each alternative should be calculated on a companywide basis. Included should be the impact on the cost of poor quality, materials usage, facilities usage, energy consumption, etc. The project team, rather than any one department, is best suited to make this evaluation.

Similarly, the impact on customers' costs and well-being should be evaluated for each alternative remedy. Of particular concern is a remedy that results in perfectionism, i.e., adding cost without adding value.

Rare but Critical Defects

Some defects or errors occur at a low frequency but have a serious effect when they do occur. These "rare but critical" defects demand a special approach. Such approaches include increased design margins (e.g., designing for higher stress levels than expected), increased severity of test conditions, significantly lower variability than allowed by specifications, automated 100 percent inspection, and redundant 100 percent inspection. For elaboration, see QCH4, page 22.63.

Proving Effectiveness of the Remedy

Before a remedy is finally adopted, it must be proven effective. Two steps are involved:

1. Preliminary evaluation of the remedy under conditions that simulate the real world. Such evaluation can make use of a "paper" reliability prediction, a dry run in a pilot plant, or the testing of a prototype unit. But these preliminary evaluations have assumptions that are never fully met, e.g., the prototype unit is assumed to be made under typical manufacturing conditions, when actually it is made in the engineering model shop.
2. Final evaluation under real-world conditions. There is no substitute for testing the remedies in the real world. If the remedy is a design change on a component, the final evaluation must be a test of the redesigned component operating in the complete system under field conditions; if the remedy is a change in a manufacturing procedure, the new procedure must be tried under typical (not ideal) factory conditions; if the remedy is a change in a maintenance procedure, the effectiveness must be demonstrated in the field environment by personnel with representative skill levels.

Finally, after a remedy is proven effective, an issue of communication remains. A remedy on one project may also apply to similar problems elsewhere in an organization. It is useful, therefore, to communicate the remedy to (1) others who may face similar problems and (2) those responsible for planning future products and processes. In one approach, the remedy is entered into a data base that can easily be examined by means of key words.

3.12 DEAL WITH RESISTANCE
TO CHANGE

Various objections to the remedy may be voiced by different parties, e.g., through delaying tactics or outright rejection of the remedy by a manager, the work force, or the union. "Resistance to change" is the usual name. Change consists of two parts: (1) a technological change; (2) a social consequence of the technological change.

People often voice objections to technological change, although the true reason for their objection is the social effect. Thus, those proposing the change can be misled by the objections stated. For example, an industrial engineer once proposed a change in work method that involved moving the storage of finished parts from a specific machine to a central storage area. The engineer was confused by the affected worker's resistance to the new method. The method seemed to benefit all parties concerned, but the worker argued that it "would not work." The supervisor was perceptive enough to know the true reason for resistance—the worker's production was superb, and many people stopped at his machine to admire and compliment him. Who would want to give up that pleasure? To cite another example, some design engineers resist the use of computer-aided design (CAD), claiming that the technology is not as effective as design analysis by a human being. The real reason, for some older designers, may include the fear of having difficulty adapting to CAD. To achieve change, we must:

- Be aware that we are dealing with a pattern of human habits, beliefs, and traditions (culture) that may differ from our own
- Discover just what will be the social effects of the proposed technological changes

Based on the scars of experience, some rules can be identified for introducing change.

Rules of the Road for Introducing Change

Important among these are:

- *Provide for participation.* This is the single most important rule for introducing change. To do it effectively means that those who are likely to be affected by the change should be members of the project team in order to participate in both diagnosis and remedy. Lack of participation leads to resentment, which can harden into a rock of resistance.
- *Establish the need for the change.* This should be done in terms that are important to the people involved rather than on the basis of the logic of the change.

- *Provide enough time.* How long does it take the members of a culture to accept a change? They must take enough time to evaluate the impact of the change and find an accommodation with the advocates of the change. Providing enough time takes various forms:
  - (*a*) *Starting small.* Conducting a small-scale tryout before going "all out" reduces the risks for the advocates as well as for the members of the culture.
  - (*b*) *Avoiding surprises.* A major benefit of the cultural pattern is its predictability. A surprise is a shock to this predictability and a disturber of the peace.
  - (*c*) *Choosing the right year.* There are right and wrong years—even decades—for a change.
- *Keeping the proposals free of excess baggage.* Avoid cluttering the proposals with extraneous matters not closely concerned with getting results. The risk is that debate will get off the main subject and onto side issues.
- *Working with the recognized leadership of the culture.* The culture is best understood by its members. They have their own leadership, and this is often informal. Convincing the leadership is a significant step in getting the change accepted.
- *Treating people with dignity.* The classic example is that of the relay assemblers in the "Hawthorne experiments." Their productivity kept rising, under good illumination or poor, because in the laboratory they were being treated with dignity.
- *Reversing the positions.* Ask the question: What position would I take if I were a member of the culture? It is even useful to get into role playing to stimulate understanding of the other person's position.
- *Dealing directly with the resistance.* There are many ways of dealing directly with resistance to change:
  - (*a*) Trying a program of persuasion
  - (*b*) Offering a quid pro quo—something for something
  - (*c*) Changing the proposals to meet specific objections
  - (*d*) Changing the social climate in ways which will make the change more acceptable.
  - (*e*) Forgetting it; there are cases in which the correct alternative is to drop the proposal

Dealing with resistance to change will always be an art. There are, however, some approaches that provide a methodical way of (1) understanding the impact of change and (2) resolving differences among the parties involved. One approach to understanding the impact is to identify the restraining forces and the driving forces for change ("force field analysis"). Another approach to resolving differences focuses on having the parties clearly state their positions to identify the exact areas of disagreement (see QCH4, pages 22.39 and 22.68, for elaboration).

3.13 INSTITUTE CONTROLS TO HOLD THE GAINS

The final step in the breakthrough sequence is holding the gains so that the benefits of the breakthrough will continue on and on. Three steps are essential:

1. Providing the operating forces with a process capable of holding the gains under operating conditions. Sometimes this involves minimal change; other times, the process change may be complex.

   To the extent which is economic, the process changes should be designed to be *irreversible*. For example, changing from hand insertion of components for printed circuit boards to automatic insertion by programmed tape rolls illustrates an irreversible remedy. In wave soldering, a remedy which requires a different specific gravity for a flux could be reversible because contamination or other factors may result in a flux having a specific gravity that was previously unacceptable.

2. Establishing operating procedures and training the operating forces to use the new procedures and to meet the standards. In conducting this training, it is helpful to make use of information collected during diagnosis to help explain the reasons for the change.

3. Providing a systematic means for holding the gains—the process of *control*. Control during operations is done through use of a feedback loop—a measurement of actual performance, comparison with the standard of performance, and action on the difference. Elaboration of the concept of control is discussed in Chapter 5, "Control of Quality"; Chapter 17, "Statistical Process Control," explains a collection of statistical process control techniques useful in detecting out-of-control conditions. Chapter 16 describes process audits as a means of verifying the presence of the required process conditions and other remedial steps.

SUMMARY

- The quality improvement process addresses *chronic* quality problems.
- The project-by-project approach uses a sequence of steps to solve chronic quality problems.
- "Proving the need" helps to convince management that the quality issue needs a new approach.
- "Identifying projects" consists of nominating, screening, and selecting projects.
- "Organizing project teams" involves forming teams of people from multiple departments.

- "Verifying the project need and mission" confirms the importance and scope of the project.
- "Diagnosing the causes" quantifies the symptoms and formulates and tests theories until the causes of the problem are determined.
- "Providing a remedy and proving its effectiveness" supplies the necessary action to remove the cause.
- "Dealing with resistance to change" focuses on the obstacles to implementing the remedies.
- "Instituting controls to hold the gains" ensures that the benefits from the project will continue in the future.

PROBLEMS

3.1. Selwitchka (1980) presents data on 10 types of errors using two measures—frequency and cost:

Type of error	Frequency	Cost ($, DM)
A	960	20,000
B	870	28,460
C	420	375,000
D	210	42,000
E	180	124,300
F	180	9,000
G	60	77,800
H	60	12,125
I	30	9,000
J	30	9,125

Note that the first two columns present a Pareto analysis based on frequency of occurrence. Prepare a second Pareto table based on cost. Comment on the ranking of errors using frequency versus the ranking based on cost.

3.2. Unplanned shutdowns of reactors have been a chronic problem. After much discussion, the consensus—called the "wisdom"—identified "cylinder changes" and "human error" as the primary causes. A diagnostic approach based on facts was instituted. Here are data on the causes of previous shutdowns:

Cause	Frequency
Cylinder changes	21
Human error	16
Hot melt system	65
Initiator system	25
Interlock malfunction	19
Other	23
	169

(*a*) Convert the above data into a Pareto table having three columns: cause, frequency, and percentage of total frequency.

(*b*) Calculate the cumulative frequencies for the table in part (*a*).

(*c*) Calculate the percentage cumulative frequencies. Make a Pareto diagram by plotting percentage cumulative frequency versus causes.

(*d*) Comment about the "wisdom" versus the facts.

3.3. In diagnosing causes, it is helpful to ask "why" not once but several times. Imai (1986) attributes the following example on a machine stoppage to Taiichi Ohno:

Question 1:	Why did the machine stop?
Answer 1:	Because the fuse blew due to an overload.
Question 2:	Why was there an overload?
Answer 2:	Because the bearing lubrication was inadequate.
Question 3:	Why was the lubrication inadequate?
Answer 3:	Because the lubrication pump was not functioning right.
Question 4:	Why wasn't the lubricating pump working right?
Answer 4:	Because the pump axle was worn out.
Question 5:	Why was it worn out?
Answer 5:	Because sludge got in.

What is the benefit of repeating "why"? Can you cite a similar example from your own experience?

3.4. Draw an Ishikawa diagram for one of the following: (*a*) the quality level of a specific activity at a university, bank, or automobile repair shop; (*b*) the quality level of *one* important characteristic of a product at a local plant. Base the diagram on discussions with the organization involved.

3.5. The following data summarize the total number of defects for each worker at a company over the past six months:

Worker	Number of defects	Worker	Number of defects
A	46	H	9
B	22	I	130
C	64	J	10
D	5	K	125
E	65	L	39
F	79	M	26
G	188	N	94

A quality cost study indicates that the cost of these defects is excessive. There is much discussion about the type of quality improvement program. Analysis indicates that the manufacturing equipment is adequate, the specifications are clear, and workers are given periodic information about their quality record. What do you suggest as the next step?

3.6. An engineer in a research organization has twice proposed that the department be authorized to conduct a research project. The project involves a redesign of a component to reduce the frequency of failures. The research approach has been meticulously defined by the engineer and verified as valid by an outside expert. Management has not authorized the project because "other projects seem more important." What further action should the engineer consider?

3.7. A company that manufactures small household appliances has experienced high scrap and rework for several years. The total cost of the scrap and rework was recently estimated on an annual basis. The number shocked top management. Discussions by the management team degenerated into arguments. Finally, top management proposed that all departments reduce scrap and rework costs by 20 percent in the coming year. Comment on this proposal.

3.8. A small steel manufacturing firm has had a chronic problem of scrap and rework in the wire mill. The costs involved have reached a level where they are a major factor in the profits of the division. All levels of personnel in the wire mill are aware of the problem, and there is agreement on the vital few product lines that account for most of the problem. However, no reduction in scrap and rework costs has been achieved. What do you propose as a next step?

3.9. The medical profession makes the journey from symptom to cause and cause to remedy for medical problems of human beings. Compare this with the task of diagnosing quality problems of physical products. If possible, speak with a physician to learn the diagnostic approach used in medicine.

3.10. From your experience, recall a chronic quality-related problem that was acted upon by an organization. Critique the approach for handling the problem in terms of the use—or nonuse—of the steps in the breakthrough sequence.

3.11. Select one chronic quality-related problem in your organization.

(*a*) Write a brief problem statement.

(*b*) Write a mission statement for a quality improvement team.

(*c*) What data could be collected to show proof of the need to address the problem?

(*d*) What departments should be represented on the team?

(*e*) State one or more symptoms of the problem.

(*f*) State at least three theories on the cause(s).

(*g*) Select one theory. What data or other information is needed to test the theory?

(*h*) Assume the data show that your selected theory is the true cause. State a remedy to remove the cause.

(*i*) What forms of resistance to the proposed remedy are you likely to encounter, and how will you deal with this resistance to change?

(*j*) What methods should be instituted to hold the gains?

REFERENCES

Bergstrom, Sigvard (1985). "Quality by Problem-Solving Groups," Proceedings EOQC Conference, vol. 2, pp. 327–333.

Berry, Thomas H. (1988). "Introducing Total Quality Management in a Financial Services Organization," *Impro 88,* Juran Institute, Inc., Wilton, Connecticut, pp. 8C13–8C22.

Betker, Harry A. (1983). "Quality Improvement Program: Reducing Solder Defects on Printed Circuit Board Assemblies," *Juran Report Number Two,* Juran Institute, Inc., Wilton, Connecticut, pp. 53–58.

Engle, David, and David Ball (1986). "Improving Customer Service for Special Orders," *Juran Report Number Six,* Juran Institute, Inc., Wilton, Connecticut, pp. 106–110.

Fortune (1985). "The Renaissance of American Quality," October 14.

Greenidge, R. M. C. (1953). "The Case of Reliability versus Defective Components, et al.," *Electronic Applications Reliability Review,* no. 1, p.12.

Hammer, Michael (1990). "Reengineering Work: Don't Automate, Obliterate," *Harvard Business Review,* July/August, pp. 104–112.

Hartman, Bob (1983). "Implementing Quality Improvement," *Juran Report Number Two,* pp. 124–131.

Imai, Masaaki (1986). Kaizen, Random House Business Division, New York, p. 50.

Marquez, Manuel (1985). "Quality Improvement at Challenger Caribbean Corporation," *Juran Report Number Four,* pp. 52–56.

Ott, E. R., and E. G. Schilling (1990). *Process Quality Control*, 2nd ed., McGraw-Hill, Inc., New York.

Parvey, Dale E. (1990). "The Juran Improvement Methodology Applied to Information Security Systems," *Impro 90,* Juran Institute, Inc., Wilton, Connecticut, pp. 4B–1 to 4B–17.

Payne, B. J. (1984). "Statistical Techniques in the Management of Quality Improvement," *International Journal of Quality and Reliability Management,* vol. 1, no. 3, pp. 24–35.

Selwitchka, R. (1980). "The Priority List on Measures for Reducing Quality Related Costs," *EOQC Quality,* vol. 24, no. 5, pp. 3–7.

SUPPLEMENTARY READING

Quality improvement, general: QCH4, Section 22, and applications in Sections 28–33.

Breakthrough and control: Juran, J. M. (1964). *Managerial Breakthrough*, McGraw-Hill, Inc., New York.

Nadler, Gerald and Shozo Hibino (1990). "Breakthrough Thinking," Prima Publishing and Communications, Rocklin, California.

Data analysis and other diagnostic techniques:
Tukey, John W. (1977). *Exploratory Data Analysis*, Addison-Wesley Publishing Company, Inc., Reading, Mass.

Mizuno, Shigeru (1988). *Management for Quality Improvement*, Productivity Press, Cambridge, Mass.

CHAPTER
4

QUALITY PLANNING AND SALES INCOME

4.1 CONTRIBUTION OF QUALITY TO SALES INCOME

In defining quality for goods and services, two components have been identified: product features and freedom from deficiencies (Figure 1.1). Although both of these components are essential to generating sales, in general the product features component is more dominant. This chapter discusses the implication of quality on sales income and then provides an overview of an approach to providing the product features necessary to meet sales goals. Chapter 11, "Understanding Customer Needs," and Chapter 12, "Designing for Quality," provide further elaboration.

For profit-making organizations, the contribution of quality to sales income occurs through several means:

- Increasing market share
- Securing premium prices
- Achieving economics of scale through increased production
- Achieving unique competitive advantages that cement brand loyalties

For both profit and nonprofit organizations, quality is synonymous with providing satisfaction to customers, both internal and external. For most organizations, satisfaction must be viewed relative to the competition's and thus goes far beyond the document called a "specification."

4.2 QUALITY AND FINANCIAL PERFORMANCE

Understanding the affect of quality on sales and financial performance can be aided by looking at some valuable research efforts. This research is based on a data base known as Profit Impact of Market Strategies (PIMS). The PIMS program aims at determining how key dimensions of strategy affect profitability and growth. Over 450 companies from a wide variety of manufacturing and service industries have contributed data.

Analysis of the PIMS data has led to important conclusions that center on quality relative to the competition's. Assessment of relative quality involves the use of multiattribute comparisons (see Section 2.9 "Standing in the Marketplace"). A key conclusion is this: In the long run, the most important single factor affecting business performance is quality relative to the competition's. Market share and profitability measure the business performance. Table 4.1 is based on PIMS data. Note that businesses having both a larger market share and better quality earn returns much higher than businesses with a smaller market share and inferior quality. Further, although quality and market share are correlated, each has a strong separate relationship to profitability. Figure 4.1 shows the relationship of quality to profitability (return on sales or return on investment).

Of course, the greater profitability could be due to either higher prices or lower costs. But analysis of the PIMS data sheds some additional light. Quality affects relative price, but separate from quality, market share has little effect on price. The quality/price relationship is shown in Table 4.2. Superiority in quality commands a premium price.

According to other PIMS data, relative quality has little effect on cost. Apparently, this is because the savings from efforts to reduce scrap and rework

TABLE 4.1
Quality and market share both drive marketability

Relative quality percentile	Relative market share		
	Below 25%	25–59%	60% and above
Below 33%	7	14	21
33–66%	13	20	27
67% and above	20	29	38

Source: Buzzell and Gale (1987).

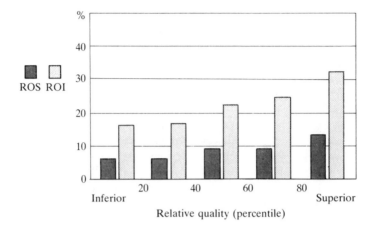

FIGURE 4.1.
Relative quality boosts rates of return. (*From Buzzell and Gale, 1987.*)

(deficiencies) are offset by the increased costs for product attributes (features) that sell the product.

4.3 QUALITY LEADERSHIP AND BUSINESS STRATEGY

The importance of quality to profitability as established by the PIMS (and other) studies makes it clear that business strategy development must place a high priority on quality. Executives understand this. Miller and Roth (1988) conducted an annual survey of 207 executives in manufacturing industries in North America. They were asked to indicate the relative importance of eleven capabilities for competing through 1992. The results in order of rank are presented in Table 4.3. Quality was first. Also, for each industry group, quality was viewed as the most critical variable for success in the marketplace. When the top 10 action programs were summarized, the quality theme ran strongly through each of the industry groups. Note also in Table 4.3 that not one but

TABLE 4.2
Quality and price

Relative quality	Relative price
Lowest	100
Commodity	102
Average	104
Better	106
Best	108

Source: Gale and Klavans (1985).

TABLE 4.3
Key competitive capabilities

Consistent quality
Dependable delivery
High-performance products
Fast deliveries
Offer low prices
Introduce new products/design changes quickly
Offer a broad product line
Advertise/promote effectively
Broad distribution
Rapid volume change
After-sales service

Source: Miller and Roth (1988).

several of the 11 attributes represent quality in the broad sense (big Q in Chapter 1).

Competitive Benchmarking

A benchmark is a point of reference by which performance is judged or measured. For quality, possible benchmarks go from the traditional to the unusual:

- The specification
- Customer desires
- Competition
- Best in our industry
- Best in any industry

For survival in the marketplace, the traditional benchmark (the product specification) must be supplemented by measuring quality relative to competition; for quality leadership the benchmark must be the "best." Xerox, for examples, defines competitive benchmarking as "the continuous process of measuring our products, services and practices against our toughest competitors or those companies renowned as leaders." Thus a benchmark for a photocopier product would be the best competitor in the photocopier industry; a benchmark for the Xerox system of packing warehouse orders might be the performance of a company in any industry, e.g., a mail order firm selling consumer products. The initial benchmarking steps are:

1. Determining the characteristics to be benchmarked
2. Determining the organizations from which data will be collected

3. Collecting and analyzing the data

4. Determining the "best in class"

Strategic plans are then developed to develop or adapt the "best practices." Such strategies are, of course, directed at both retaining present customers and generating new ones. This approach will be illustrated later in this chapter.

The full process of competitive benchmarking as an approach to achieving quality leadership is discussed in Chapter 6.

4.4 IMPACT OF QUALITY ON LOST SALES

Sometimes the evidence of the importance of quality to retaining present customers is dramatic. Manufacturer B of household appliances had a leadership position for two of the four models of a product (see Table 4.4). Over a 4-year period leadership was lost even though the company was competitive on product features, price, and delivery dates. It was not competitive, however, on field failures and warranty costs. The president had to personally lead the development and execution of a strategy to reduce the failures and warranty costs. He was successful.

Sometimes the sales lost because of poor quality can be quantified. Two manufacturers of washing machines were compared. One measure used was the percentage of present customers who would not purchase the same brand again. For brand A, only 1.1 percent said they would not purchase it again; for brand B, 10.5 percent declined to purchase it again. For brand B, the overwhelming reason was "poor quality." When the 10.5 percent was translated to the total present customer population for brand B, it was concluded that an additional sales income of $5 million would be needed to make up the profit in the lost replacement sales. In a case involving an industrial product, a survey was made of present customers who were buying the product made by one manufacturer. Some of those customers had purchased a different brand. One-third of these former customers said the primary reason was poor quality. These lost sales due to poor quality amounted to $1.3 billion in sales income (and 2000 jobs).

TABLE 4.4
Change in suppliers of product

Model	1979	1980	1981	1982
High price	A	C	C	C
Middle price	B	B	C	C
Low price	C	C	C	C
Special model	B	B	B	C

Note: A, B, and C indicate suppliers.

TABLE 4.5
Satisfaction and sales

Customer view of quality	Who will recommend supplier, % (GTE)	Very willing to repurchase, % (AT&T)
Excellent	96	92
Good	76	63
Fair	35	18
Poor	3	0

Source: Bultmann (1989); Scanlan (1989).

These examples are presented not only to emphasize the importance of quality, but to urge that the effect of marginal quality be estimated in terms of lost sales income. Such measurement can help to focus business strategies on quality and stimulate action at all levels.

4.5   LEVEL OF SATISFACTION TO RETAIN PRESENT CUSTOMERS

Sometimes acceptable levels of customer satisfaction with the product still result in a significant loss of new sales. Table 4.5 presents two examples from the service industry. Note that even when the customer view of quality is "good," a quarter or more of the present customers may not return.

Another dimension of this phenomenon is the level of customer satisfaction with the handling of their complaints. Table 4.6 shows the percentage of customers who intend to purchase a product or service again,

TABLE 4.6
Brand loyalty

	Completely satisfied complaint, %	Response acceptable, %	Dissatisfied complaint, %
Financial service	73	45	17
Automotive service	71	54	22
	Complaint satisfactorily resolved, %		Complaint unsatisfactorily resolved, %
Large Durable Good	80		40

Source: Tarp (1986).

based on their level of satisfaction with the resolution of their complaints. Complaints which are resolved with less-than-complete satisfaction will result in significant lost sales. Note that even with complete satisfaction, some customers will not return. More on this subject in Chapter 20.

4.6 PLANNING FOR PRODUCT QUALITY TO GENERATE SALES INCOME

A starting point for planning quality for individual products is the definition of quality provided in Chapter 1. The components of the definition—product features and freedom from deficiencies—can be expanded into the major areas that must be addressed to achieve customer satisfaction. Table 1.1 lists some major subcategories of the two components. Note that these subcategories go far beyond the specification of a physical product.

In designing a specific product or service, the detailed characteristics supporting the subcategories must be identified, planned for, and executed. For example, Ford identified 429 characteristics for the Taurus model car; GTE identified 31 characteristics for a telecommunications service. Clearly customer input must be taken into account when defining specific characteristics. That input takes the form of not only identifying the characteristics but also clarifying the importance of each, and finally providing a status in the current marketplace relative to competition. (This was introduced in Section 2.9, "Standing in the Marketplace." More later in Chapter 11, "Understanding Customer Needs.")

This emphasis on understanding customer needs as a prerequisite to meeting sales goals addresses the reality that warehouses are filled with products that meet specifications and are competitively priced but *don't satisfy customers' needs* as well as a competitor's product. Examples from a spectrum of industries provide reasons why sales are lost to competition (Table 4.7). Note that some of the examples involve increased satisfaction for the ultimate user (e.g., the driver of an automobile); other examples involve increased satisfaction for an intermediate user (e.g., the processor of photographic film). In recent years, lower variability around a target value within a set of specification limits has become increasingly important to customers who do further processing of a product.

4.7 SPECTRUM OF CUSTOMERS

For both consumer and industrial products and for both physical goods and services, the variety of customers forms a wide spectrum. Some companies choose to address one part of the spectrum, while other companies pursue

TABLE 4.7
Hidden customer needs

Product	Hidden customer need satisfied by a competitor
Abrasive cloth	Lower internal cost of polishing parts due to better durability of cloth
Automobile	Less effort in closing door, better "sound" when door closes
Dishwasher	Sense of greater durability due to heavier parts making up the appliance
Software	Understandable owner's manual
Fibers	Lower number of breaks in processing fibers
Tire valve	Higher productivity when tire manufacturer uses valve in a vulcanizing operation
Photographic film	Fewer process adjustments when processing film due to lower variability
Commodity product	Delivery of orders within 24 hours rather than the 48-hour standard requirement
Home mortgage application	Decision in shorter time than that of competition

several types of customers. For purposes of planning for quality, we will identify three types of customers:

1. Those who emphasize initial purchase price as equal to or more important than quality
2. Those who evaluate alternative products on both initial price and quality simultaneously
3. Those who place emphasis on obtaining "the best"

Table 4.8 links these three categories with a translation into desires on product features and freedom from deficiencies.

All three categories need to be satisfied in the marketplace. In consumer products particularly, some customers change categories over a lifetime, e.g., some young couples with growing children change from "economy minded" to "value minded."

4.8 LIFE CYCLE COSTS

For simple consumable products like food or transportation, the purchase price is also the cost of using the product. As products grow in complexity and as the length of use increases, the purchase price must also increase to include operational, maintenance, and other special costs. For some products, the after-sale costs can easily exceed the original purchase price.

TABLE 4.8
Categories of customer emphasis as related to quality

Emphasis	Product features	Freedom from deficiencies
Initial economy	Willing to forego some features Like "do-it-yourself" features and add options later Will tolerate a relatively short product life	Will tolerate some product deficiencies at delivery and during use Will tolerate some deficiencies in service before and after purchase
Value	Willing to make trade-offs between quality and price Features must be justified by benefits and related price	Warranty provisions can be important Concerned abut operating and repair costs
The "best"	Desire many convenience features Emphasis on luxury, esthetics, brand image Desire high level of performance from product and from all personnel	Greatly annoyed at deficiencies and associated inconveniences Demand complete and timely response to all problems

A life cycle cost can be defined as the total cost to the user of purchasing, using, and maintaining a product over its life. A study of all of the cost elements can lead to a redesign of a product that could result in a significantly lower life cycle cost, perhaps at the expense of a small increase in the original price. This presents a marketing opportunity to provide a product that will result in savings over the life of the product to potential customers. These customers are urged to make purchasing decisions by comparing life cycle costs for competing products. But the initial purchase price may be higher and marketing people may find it more difficult to sell the product to potential

TABLE 4.9
Life cycle costs: Consumer products

Product	Ratio, life cycle cost to original price
Room air conditioner	3.3
Dishwasher	2.5
Freezer	4.8
Range, electric	4.4
Range, gas	1.9
Refrigerator	3.5
TV (black and white)	2.5
TV (color)	1.9
Washing machine	3.6

TABLE 4.10
Annual quality cost of foundry equipment

	11 shell core makers	12 induction furnaces
Repairs	$16,000	$ 70,000
Effectiveness loss	25,000	90,000
Lost income	8,000	50,000
Extra capacity	2,500	8,000
Preventive maintenance	8,000	20,000
Total	$59,500	$238,000
Initial investment	$70,000	$700,000

customers whose first priority is initial price. Table 4.9 shows the ratio of life cycle costs to original price for various consumer products.

An associated concept, user failure cost, calculates the cost to the user of failures over the product life. Table 4.10 shows an example of annual failure-related costs (Gryna, 1977).

The life cycle cost concept is fundamentally sound in logic, but has achieved slow progress in implementation. Two reasons for the slow pace of adoption predominate. First, it is difficult to estimate the future costs of operation and maintenance. A greater obstacle, however, is the cultural resistance of purchasing managers, marketing people, and product designers. The skills, habits, and practices of these people have long been built around the concept of the original purchase price being of primary importance (see QCH4, pages 3.20–3.27, for further elaboration).

4.9 ACHIEVING A QUALITY SUPERIORITY FOR A PRODUCT

Differences in quality can be translated into either a higher market share or a premium price. The benefit to the manufacturer depends on the nature of the difference and on who is the user. It is useful to categorize the differences as an aid to developing quality superiority for new or modified products. Some categories of quality differences are:

1. *Differences that are obvious to the user.* Products or services which possess a desirable feature which is lacking in competing products will command a premium price (or a higher market share if the price is competitive). Two of the many examples are appliances with automatic features that simplify housework and services which provide overnight delivery.
2. *Differences that are translatable into user economics.* Some products look alike but are different in operating, maintenance, or other costs. Fuel

economy of automobiles is an example of a difference that has become a competitive issue. The concept of life cycle costs (see above) is a formal way of providing evidence to the user of a quality superiority in the language of cost.

3. *Differences that are minor but demonstrable.* Sometimes a small but demonstrable superiority can be a forceful selling tool. A manufacturer of antifriction bearings showed that the bearings were more precise than the competition's. The competing products were entirely fit for use, so no price differential was feasible. But the fact of greater precision was emphasized and resulted in an increased market share. In a case of candy-coated chocolates, the "superiority" was the lack of chocolate smudge marks on consumers' hands—a minor quality but one that is demonstrable on television.

4. *Differences that are accepted on faith.* Sometimes a quality difference cannot easily be verified by a buyer, but a demonstration by the manufacturer can persuade the buyer to accept the difference as true. A manufacturer of electric razors employed an independent test laboratory to conduct tests. Consumers shaved themselves with two competing razors. The contents of the razors after shaving were weighed precisely. Of course, the contents of the sponsoring company's razor weighed more than the competition's.

Achieving quality superiority requires understanding customers' needs in depth and then translating those needs into a specification and a resulting physical product or service. The elements involved are discussed in the following chapters. At this point, however, it is well to emphasize that the search for quality differences may be the means of achieving a unique competitive advantage in the marketplace. Basic to the effort is observing customer use of the product and then searching for unique product features or characteristics that can increase customer satisfaction. This approach of "stapling ourselves to the product" must, of course, be continuous because the competition is not standing still either. Table 4.7 lists examples of hidden customer needs that can be identified and steps that can be taken to satisfy those needs and thereby increase sales income.

4.10 A ROAD MAP FOR PLANNING OF PRODUCTS FOR SALABILITY

The quality planning road map (see Table 1.5) presents a framework for the planning of new products or product revisions. Juran (1988) provides an extensive discussion of the steps.

The road map is presented in more detail in Figure 4.2. Discussion of the steps will unfold in later chapters. It is useful, however, to present an overview now in the form of an example that illustrates many of the steps along the road map. Our example is based on the planning work done for the Ford Motor Company's Taurus model automobile (Veraldi, 1985).

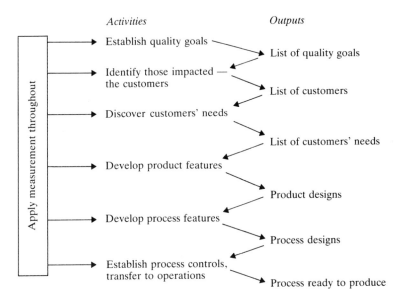

FIGURE 4.2.
Quality planning road map. (*From Juran, 1990.*)

In the early 1980s, Ford began the initial planning for a new front-wheel-drive midsize car. The business environment included some ominous elements: strong foreign competition, decreasing market share, and a projection of greatly increased fuel prices. Ford concluded that a new approach to designing the model was essential. Basic to the new approach was "customer satisfaction" with the objective being that the Taurus would be the best car in its class. This "best in class" focus spawned some unusual approaches to planning. One of the breaks with tradition was the organization of the planning for the Taurus. Historically, new cars were designed using the traditional organizational structure (Figure 4.3*a*). With such a structure, the main activities were executed *sequentially*, e.g., Planning studied customer desires and then presented the results to Design; Design performed its tasks and handed the results to Engineering; Engineering created the detailed specifications; and the results were then given to Manufacturing. Unfortunately, the sequential approach results in a minimum of communication between the departments as the planning proceeds—each department hands its output "over the wall" to the next department. This lack of communication often leads to problems for the next internal customer department. Under Taurus, activities were organized as a team (Figure 4.3*b*) from the beginning of the project. Thus, for example, Manufacturing worked *simultaneously* with Design and Engineering before the detailed specifications were finalized. This provided an opportunity to address producibility issues during the preparation of the specifications.

We will now refer to the steps in Figure 4.2 to explain how the Taurus

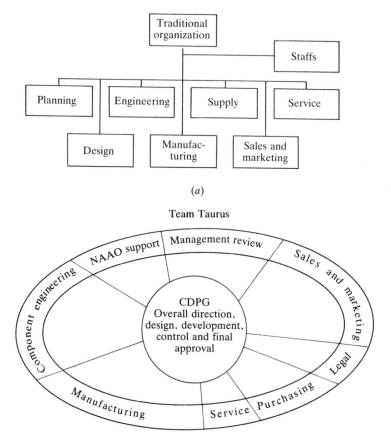

FIGURE 4.3.
(*a*) Traditional organization. (*b*) Organization for Taurus. (*From Juran, 1990.*)

program proceeded. As a homework problem, the reader will be asked to provide further illustrations.

1. *Establish quality goals.* The quality goal was for the Taurus to be "best in class."

2. *Identify those impacted—the customers.* Some customers were obvious; others were not. A few examples:

Company function	Customer
Sales	Consumer
Legal	U.S. Department of Transportation (DOT)
Parts manufacturing	Assembly plant

(Note that the customers are both external and internal.)

3. *Discover customers' need*

Customer	Need
Consumer	Effective heater
DOT	Hi-mount brake light
Assembly plant	Ease of assembly

These needs were detailed by conducting extensive marketing research and obtaining the input of technical experts. The inputs obtained were discussed as part of the joint planning by all functions. Now the needs had to be translated from the customer's language to "Taurus language." For example:

Need	Translation
Effective heater	Time to reach a required temperature
Ease of assembly	Reduction in the number of parts

4. *Develop product features.* This step made use of the marketing research to provide Product Development with detailed guidelines for 429 product features that were important to achieving high product salability. These guidelines then became the basis of specific design projects. Two examples of these features were the amount of effort required to raise the hood of the car and the level of wind noise. For each of these features, a means of measurement was defined, competitive data were obtained, and a numerical goal was set. For example, the effort required to raise the hood was measured in pounds by a spring scale. Competitive data showed that the best competitor had a design requiring 9 pounds of effort. For Taurus, a goal of 8 pounds was set; the final design exceeded the goal by requiring only 7 pounds. Taurus achieved best in class for 80 percent of the product features. Certain other product features were also incorporated even though they were not directly related to product salability, e.g., the high mounting of the brake light, a feature that was desired by the DOT.

5. *Develop process features.* The simultaneous approach to activities provided the Assembly Plant with the opportunity to identify specific manufacturing issues to be addressed during design and manufacturing planning. The Assembly Plant listed 1400 issues ranging from a desire to have an automated body side assembly to having an annual assembly plant shutdown for vacation. Much effort to achieve process capability and to optimize the processes was also part of the planning. The result of all this was a set of process plans that were ready at the start of production.

6. *Establish process controls, transfer to operations.* As these plans were put into production, the coordination among all functions continued and resulted in final refinements to the product and process design.

Several of the steps in quality planning involve the translation and deployment of customer needs into product features, process features, and process control features. This process is called Quality Function Deployment (QFD). The deployment process is discussed in Chapters 11 and 12.

SUMMARY

- Businesses having larger market share and better quality earn returns much higher than their competitors'. Quality and market share each has a strong separate relationship to profitability.
- Competitive benchmarking is the continuous process of measuring products, services, and practices against those of the toughest competitors or leading companies.
- Quality can be the decisive factor in lost sales, and sometimes its impact can be quantified.
- Customer complaints resolved with less-than-complete customer satisfaction will result in significant lost sales.
- Planning for product quality must be based on meeting customer needs, not just meeting product specification.
- In-depth marketing research can identify suddenly arising customer needs.
- Planning for quality must recognize a spectrum of customers with different needs.
- For some products, we need to plan for perfection; for other products, we need to plan for value.
- We define life cycle cost as the total cost to the user of purchasing, using, and maintaining a product over its life.
- Quality superiority can be translated into a higher market share or a premium price.
- Quality planning for a new product or product revision follows these steps: establish quality goals, identify all customers, discover customers' needs, develop product features, develop process features, establish process control controls, and transfer the plans to operations. The measurement process must be applied during all of the steps.

PROBLEMS

4.1. In the explanation of the Taurus case, examples were given to illustrate each step in the planning road map, e.g., for "Identify Customers," three customers were listed.

 For each of the steps in the planning road map, state two examples in addition to those provided in the case. The examples may apply to any product or service.

4.2. For a consumer or industrial physical product, make a quality comparison of three brands at the low, medium, and high price levels. The comparison should list differences in product features and freedom from deficiencies.

4.3. For a consumer or industrial service, make a quality comparison as described in problem 2.

REFERENCES

Bultmann, Charles (1989). "How to Define Customer Needs and Expectations: An Overview," *Customer Satisfaction Measurement Conference Notes,* American Marketing Association and ASQC, February 26, 28. The written paper was "New Ways of Understanding Customers' Service Needs" by Tom F. Gillett.

Buzzell, Robert D., and Bradley T. Gale (1987). *The PIMS Principles: Linking Strategy to Performance.* The Free Press, Macmillan, New York, reprinted with permission.

Gale, Bradley T., and Richard Klavans (1985). "Formulating A Quality Improvement Strategy," *Journal of Business Strategy,* Winter, pp. 21–32, Warren, Gorham, and Lamont, used with permission.

Gryna, Frank M. (1977). "Quality Costs: User vs Manufacturer," *Quality Progress,* June, pp. 10–15.

Juran, J. M. (1988). *Juran on Planning for Quality,* The Free Press, New York.

Juran, J. M., *et al.* (1990). "Planning for Quality" Course Notes, 2nd ed., Juran Institute, Inc., Wilton, Connecticut.

Miller, Jeffrey G., and Aleda V. Roth (1988). "Manufacturing Strategies," *Operations Management Review,* Fall 1987 and Winter 1988, pp. 8–20.

Scanlan, Phillip M. (1989). "Integrating Quality and Customer Satisfaction Measurement," *Customer Satisfaction Measurement Conference Notes,* American Management Association and ASQC, February, pp. 26–28.

TARP (1986). "Consumer Complaint Handling in America: An Update Study," part II, pp. 46–47, Technical Assistance Research Programs Institute, Washington, D.C.

Veraldi, L. C. (1985). "The Team Taurus Story," MIT Conference Paper, August, p. 22, Center for Advanced Engineering Study, MIT, Cambridge, Massachusetts.

SUPPLEMENTARY READING

Quality and income: QCH4, Section 3.

Quality and profitability: Buzzell and Gale (1987), Chapter 6.

CHAPTER
5

CONTROL
OF QUALITY

5.1 DEFINITION OF CONTROL

As used in this book, "control" refers to the process employed in order to meet standards. This consists of observing actual performance, comparing this performance with some standard, and then taking action if the observed performance is significantly different from the standard.

The control process is in the nature of a feedback loop (Figure 5.1). Control involves a universal sequence of steps as follows:

1. Choosing the control subject: i.e., choosing what we intend to regulate
2. Choosing a unit of measure
3. Setting a goal for the control subject
4. Creating a sensor which can measure the control subject in terms of the unit of measure
5. Measuring actual performance
6. Interpreting the difference between actual performance and the goal
7. Taking action (if any) on the difference.

The foregoing sequence of steps is universal, i.e., it applies to cost control, inventory control, quality control, etc.

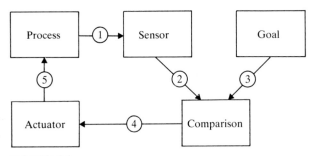

FIGURE 5.1
The feedback loop.

The reader is cautioned about the different meanings given to the word "control" throughout the world. In many European countries, control is often used in the narrower sense of inspection. Some Japanese authors refer to on-line and off-line quality control. These terms refer, respectively, to activities performed during production and prior to production (see Taguchi, 1978).

Control, one of the trilogy of quality processes, is largely directed at meeting goals and preventing adverse change, i.e., holding the status quo. This is in contrast to "improvement," which focuses on creating change, i.e., changing the status quo. The control process addresses sporadic quality problems; the improvement process addresses chronic problems.

Central to the process of quality control is the act of quality measurement: "What gets measured, gets done." Measurement is basic for all three of the quality processes: for quality control, measurement provides feedback and early warnings of problems; for quality planning, measurement quantifies customer needs and product and process capabilities; for quality improvement, measurement can motivate people, prioritize improvement opportunities, and help in diagnosing causes. This chapter presents concepts underlying quality measurement; later chapters present examples of quality measurement at both the operational and executive levels.

5.2 SELF-CONTROL

Ideally, quality planning for any task should put the employee into a state of self-control. When work is organized in a way which enables a person to have full mastery over the attainment of planned results, that person is said to be in a state of self-control and can therefore be held responsible for the results. Self-control is a universal concept, applicable to a general manager responsible for running a company division at a profit, a plant manager responsible for meeting the various goals set for that plant, a technician running a chemical reactor, or a bank teller serving customers.

To be in a state of self-control, people must be provided with:

1. Knowledge of what they are supposed to do, e.g., the budgeted profit, the schedule, and the specification.
2. Knowledge of their performance, e.g., the actual profit, the delivery rate, the extent of conformance to specification (this is quality measurement).
3. Means of regulating performance in the event that they fail to meet the goals. These means must always include both the authority to regulate and the ability to regulate by varying either (a) the process under the person's authority, or (b) the person's own conduct.

If all the foregoing parameters have been met, the person is said to be in a state of self-control and can properly be held responsible for any deficiencies in performance. If any parameter has not been met, the person is not in a state of self-control and, to the extent of the deficiency, cannot properly be held responsible.

In practice, these three criteria are not fully met. For example, some specifications may be vague or disregarded (the first criterion); feedback of data may be insufficient, often vague, or too late (the second criterion); people may not be provided with the knowledge and process adjustment mechanisms to correct a process (the third criterion). Thus, if we have a quality problem and we fail to meet any of the three criteria, the problem is "management-controllable" (or "system-controllable"); if we have a quality problem and if all three criteria are fully met, the problem is "worker-controllable." The concept of self-control will be applied in detail in later chapters to product development, manufacturing, and administrative and support activities.

Classical control and self-control are complementary (Table 5.1). An important difference, however, involves timing. Classical control takes place *during* the execution of a task; self-control provides useful criteria for evaluating plans *before* a task is executed.

Kondo (1988, p. 35F.11) submits that there is a relationship among the control process, the "plan, do, check, act" cycle, and the concept of self-control. Figure 5.2a depicts the plan, do, check, act cycle which cor-

TABLE 5.1
Classical control and self-control

Classical control	Self-control
Standard or goal	Knowledge of what people are supposed to do
Measurement	Knowledge of performance
Action on the difference	Means of regulating a process
Primary emphasis during execution	Primary emphasis before execution

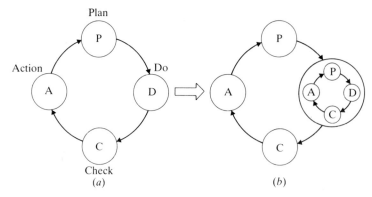

FIGURE 5.2
Deming's cycle. (*From QCH4, p. 35.11*)

responds to the main elements of the feedback loop (Figure 5.1) of the control process. Kondo observes that individual worker performance during the "do" step is also composed of a plan, do, check, act cycle (Figure 5.2b). The extent to which the task of the worker is adequately planned reflects the degree to which the worker is placed in a state of self-control. The plan, do, check, act cycle, often called the "Deming cycle," is described in Gitlow *et al.* (1989). (In this cycle, the term "study" is sometimes used instead of "check.")

Be aware that another concept, "self-inspection," is *not* the same as self-control. Self-inspection addresses the examination of the product; self-control addresses the process of accomplishing a task. Self-inspection is discussed in Chapter 16.

We now proceed with an examination of the steps in the control sequence.

5.3 THE CONTROL SUBJECT FOR QUALITY

Control subjects for quality exist in large numbers. At the technological level, each division of a product—components, units, subsystems, and systems—has quality characteristics. Processing conditions (e.g. time cycle, temperature) and processing facilities also have quality characteristics. In addition, input materials and services have quality characteristics. Still more quality control subjects are imposed by external forces: clients, government regulations, and standardization bodies.

Beyond technological quality control subjects are managerial quality control subjects. These are mainly the performance goals for organization units and the associated managers. Managerial goals extend to nontechnological matters such as customer relations, financial trends (e.g., progress in reducing the cost of poor quality), employee relations, and community relations.

To identify and choose quality control subjects, several principles apply:

1. Quality control subjects should be customer oriented. Paramount are the external customers, who affect sales income; equally important are internal customers, who affect internal costs. Table 5.2 shows examples of quality control subjects from different organizations. Later in this chapter, we will specify these categories further by defining the units of measure.
2. Quality control subjects should be inclusive enough to evaluate current organizational performance. However, they should also provide early warning of potential problems.
3. Quality control subjects should recognize both components of the definition of quality, i.e., freedom from deficiencies and product features. The number of errors per thousand lines of computer code (KLOC) is important, but the fact that there are zero errors does not mean that a customer will be satisfied with the software.
4. Potential quality control subjects can be identified by obtaining ideas from both customers and employees. Customers can be asked "How do you evaluate the product or service that you receive from me?" A focus group of customers can provide valuable responses. Again, we are addressing both external and internal customers. All employees are sources of ideas, but employees who have direct contact with external customers can be a fertile source of imaginative ideas on quality control subjects.
5. Quality control subjects must be viewed by those who will be measured as valid, appropriate, and easy to understand when translated into numbers. These are nice notions, surely. But in the real world they can be pretty elusive.

TABLE 5.2
Control subject categories

Electronics manufacturer	A bank
Document quality	Operations
Software quality	Retail banking
Hardware quality	Commercial banking
Process quality	Credit card and ATM cards
System quality	Financial and investments
	Human resources
	Information services
	Administrative

5.4 UNITS OF MEASURE

In order to quantify, it is necessary to create a system of measurement consisting of:

- *A unit of measure:* a defined amount of some quality feature which permits evaluation of that feature in numbers
- *A sensor:* a method or instrument which can carry out the evaluation and state the findings in numbers in terms of the unit of measure.

Units of measure for product and process performance are usually expressed in technological terms; for example, fuel efficiency is measured in terms of distance traveled per volume of fuel; timeliness of service is expressed in minutes (hours, days, etc.) required to provide service.

Units of measure for product deficiencies usually take the form of a fraction:

$$\frac{\text{Number of occurrences}}{\text{Opportunity for occurrence}}$$

The numerator may be in such terms as defects per million, number of field failures, or cost of warranty charges. The denominator may be in such terms as number of units produced, dollar volume of sales, number of units in service, or length of time in service.

Units of measure for product features are more difficult to create. The number and variety of these features may be large. Sometimes inventing a new unit of measure is a fascinating technical challenge. In one example, a manufacturer of a newly developed polystyrene product had to invent a unit of measure and a sensor to evaluate an important product feature. It was then possible to measure that feature both of the product and of competitors' products before releasing the product for manufacture. In another case, the process of harvesting peas in the field required the development of a unit of measure for tenderness and the invention of a "tenderometer" gauge. A numerical scale was created and measurements were taken in the field to determine when the peas were ready for harvesting.

Table 5.3 shows examples of units of measure for a manufacturing organization and for a service organization. It should be noted that for many service industries, the *time* taken to deliver a service to an external customer is the decisive unit of measure.

Often a number of important product features exist. To develop an overall unit of measure, we can identify the important product features and then define the relative importance of each feature. In subsequent measurement, each feature receives a score. The overall measure is calculated as the weighted average of the scores for all features. This approach is illustrated in Table 2.6. In using such an approach for periodic or continuous measurement, some cautions should be cited (Early, 1989). First, the relative importance of

TABLE 5.3
Units of measure—examples

Electronics manufacturer	A bank

Document quality
  Defects per thousand formatted
  output pages
	Operations
	
	  $\dfrac{\text{Number of statements mailed late}}{\text{Total number of statements processed}}$

Software quality
  Defects corrected per thousand
  noncomment source statements
	Retail banking
	
	  $\dfrac{\text{Number of teller entry errors}}{\text{Total number of teller entries}}$

Hardware quality
  Field removal rate
	Commercial banking
	
	  $\dfrac{\text{Loan payments posted incorrectly}}{\text{Total loan payments}}$

Process quality
  Functional yields
	Credit card and ATM cards
	
	  $\dfrac{\text{Number of mispostings}}{\text{Total number of transactions}}$

System quality
  Total outages
	Financial/investments
	
	  $\dfrac{\text{Number of trading corrections}}{\text{Number of trades made}}$

	Human resources $\dfrac{\text{Requisitions not filled in 30 days}}{\text{Total number of requisitions}}$
	Information services $\dfrac{\text{Customer information system (CIS) downtime}}{\text{Total CIS time}}$
	Administrative $\dfrac{\text{Number of work orders not completed within 10 days}}{\text{Number of work orders completed}}$

each feature is not precise and may change greatly over time. Second, improvement in certain features can result in an improved overall measure but can hide a deterioration in one feature that has great importance.

5.5 SETTING A GOAL FOR THE CONTROL SUBJECT

Each control subject must have a quality goal, i.e., be aimed at a quality target. Table 5.4 shows examples of control subjects and associated goals for a variety of control subjects ranging from those for products, processes, and

TABLE 5.4
Control subjects and goals

Control subject	Goals
Reliability of product	Minimum of 5000 hours mean time between failures
Solder temperature of wave soldering process	500°F
Departmental error rate	Maximum of 2 per 1000 documents
Quality standing in the marketplace	At least equal in quality to competitors *A* and *B*

departments to that of an entire organization. This chapter concentrates on goals at operational levels; Section 6.5, "Quality Goals," discusses overall company quality goals.

To set operational quality goals, certain criteria must be met. The goals should be:

- *Legitimate:* have official status
- *Measurable:* numbers aid clarity
- *Attainable:* with a reasonable effort
- *Equitable:* for all individuals at the same level

In setting quality goals, several bases are available—the history of previous performance, engineering studies, and the competitive marketplace. Later chapters in this book provide illustrations and methods. The "deployment" of company quality goals to operational goals is discussed in Section 6.5 under "Deployment of Goals."

5.6 THE SENSOR

Most sensors are designed to provide information in terms of units of measure. For operational control subjects, the sensors are usually technological instruments or human beings employed as instruments (e.g., inspectors, auditors); for managerial subjects, the sensors are data systems.

There has been a continuing trend toward providing sensors with additional functions of the feedback loop: data recording, data processing, comparison of performance with standards, and initiating corrective action in the process.

Despite the large number of control subjects, relatively few human beings are needed to carry out the control process. Imagine a pyramid of control subjects: A few vital controls are carried out by supervisors and managers; another segment is carried out by the work force; the remaining majority of control subjects is handled by nonhuman means (stable processes, automated processes, servomechanisms).

Clearly, sensors must be economic and easy to use. In addition, as sensors provide data which in turn can lead to critical decisions on products and processes, they must be both accurate and precise. The meaning, measurement, and impact of accuracy and precision are discussed in Chapter 18.

5.7 MEASURING ACTUAL PERFORMANCE

In organizing for control, it is useful to establish a limited number of control stations for measurement. Each such control station is then given the responsibility for carrying out the steps of the feedback loop for a selected list of control subjects. A review of numerous control stations discloses that they are usually located at one of several principal junctures:

- At changes of jurisdiction, e.g., where products are moved between companies or between major departments
- Before embarking on an irreversible path, e.g., setup approval before production
- After creation of a critical quality
- At dominant process variables, e.g., the "vital few"
- At natural "windows," for economical control

The choice of control stations is aided by preparation of a flow diagram which shows the progression of events through which the product is produced.

It is essential to measure both the quality of the output going to the external customer ("final yield") and the quality at earlier points in the process, including the "first-time yield."

In Figure 5.3, 100 units of input enter a process. After operations A, B, and C, an inspection is conducted; 87 acceptable units continue on to operation D, 8 units are reprocessed at previous operations, and 5 units are discarded. The first-time yield is thus 87 percent. After operations D and E, a second inspection is conducted; 82 acceptable units (of the 87) are available for delivery, 2 units are reprocessed, and 3 units are discarded. Assuming that all reprocessed units are acceptable, the final yield is 92 (82 + 8 + 2), or 92 percent of the original input. Note how the measurement of yield at several places highlights several opportunities for improvement. This concept applies to both manufacturing and nonmanufacturing processes. Don't let different terminology (e.g., inspection versus checking) obscure the concept. For example, in a software development organization, the average number of software errors was about two errors per thousand lines of code, just before delivery to the customer. The average level of errors, however, when measured earlier in the

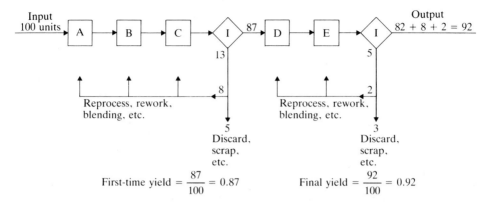

First-time yield $= \dfrac{87}{100} = 0.87$ Final yield $= \dfrac{92}{100} = 0.92$

A, B, C, D, E: operations or tasks
I: inspections, checks, reviews

FIGURE 5.3
First-time yield and final yield (A, B, C, D, E = operations or tasks; I = inspections, checks, reviews).

development process, was 50 errors per thousand lines of code. Huge resources were needed to screen out these errors. Ironically, the head of the organization was unaware of this first-time yield until it was revealed by a consultant.

For each control station, it is necessary to define the work to be done: which control subjects are to be measured, goals and standards to be met, procedures, instruments to be used, the data to be recorded, and the decisions to be made including the criteria and responsibility for making each decision.

The "flag diagram" (Figure 5.4) is an innovative illustration of how measurement can be combined with control subjects for tracking improvement. This diagram makes use of measurement data in combination with the Pareto concept and the cause-and-effect diagram (both previously discussed in Chapter 3).

The overall control subject (reduction of machining time) is divided into five major subjects, e.g., improving machining procedure. Each major subject is then further divided into secondary subjects, e.g., improving operation. Goals for each subject are shown as dotted lines on the charts and then performance is plotted on the same charts. The diagrams become a basis for review by the responsible manager and for action if there is a significant deviation from a goal.

5.8 INTERPRETING THE DIFFERENCE BETWEEN ACTUAL PERFORMANCE AND THE GOAL

This phase of the control process consists of comparing the measurement to the goal and deciding if any difference is significant enough to justify action.

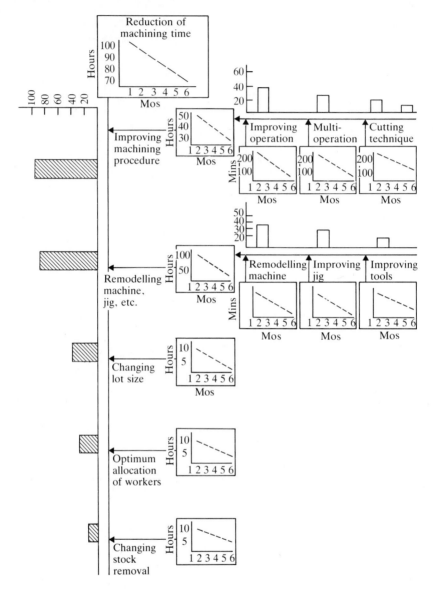

FIGURE 5.4
An example of a "flag diagram." (*Adapted from Kondo, 1988, p. 35F.14.*)

Statistical Significance

An observed difference between performance and a goal can be the result of (1) a real difference due to some cause, or (2) an apparent difference arising from random variation. Further, differences between a measurement and a goal should not be viewed individually. Knowing the pattern of differences over time is essential to drawing correct conclusions. In Figure 5.5, the

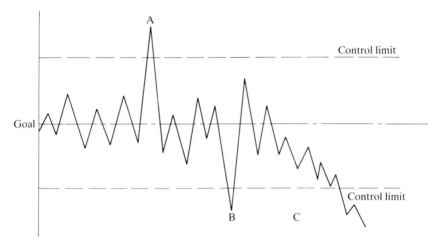

FIGURE 5.5
Control chart.

measurements at *A* and *B* and the trend at *C* represent real ("statistically significant") differences from the goal; the other measurements are due to random variation. Figure 5.5 is a statistical control chart—one of the elegant statistical tools used to evaluate statistical significance.

A control chart is a graphic comparison of process performance data to computed "control limits" drawn as limit lines on the chart. The process performance data usually consist of groups of measurements ("rational subgroups") selected in regular sequence of production.

A prime use of the control chart is to detect assignable causes of variation in the process. The term "assignable causes" has a special meaning, and it is essential to understand this meaning in order to understand the control chart concept (see Table 5.5).

Process variations are traceable to two kinds of causes: (1) random, i.e., due solely to chance, and (2) assignable, i.e., due to specific "special" causes. Ideally, only random (also called "common") causes should be present in a process. A process that is operating without assignable causes of variation is said to be "in a state of statistical control," which is usually abbreviated to "in control."

The control chart distinguishes between random and assignable causes of variation through its choice of control limits. These are calculated from the laws of probability in such a way that highly improbable random variations are presumed to be due not to random causes, but to assignable causes. When the actual variation exceeds the control limits, it is a signal that assignable causes entered the process and the process should be investigated. Variation within the control limits means that only random causes are present.

The important advantages of statistical control and the methodology of

TABLE 5.5
Distinction between random and assignable causes of variation

Random (common) causes	Assignable (special) causes
Description	
Consists of many individual causes.	Consists of one or just a few individual causes.
Any one random cause results in a minute amount of variation (but many random causes act together to yield a substantial total).	Any one assignable cause can result in a large amount of variation.
Examples are human variation in setting control dials; slight vibration in machines; slight variation in raw material.	Examples are operator blunder, a faulty setup, or a batch of defective raw material.
Interpretation	
Random variation cannot economically be eliminated from a process.	Assignable variation can be detected; action to eliminate the causes is usually economically justified.
An observation within the control limits of random variation means the process should not be adjusted.	An observation beyond control limits means the process should be investigated and corrected.
With only random variation, the process is sufficiently stable to use sampling procedures to predict the quality of total production or make process optimization studies.	With assignable variation present, the process is not sufficiently stable to use sampling procedures for prediction.

constructing and interpreting control charts are given in Chapter 17, 'Statistical Process Control.''

The control chart not only evaluates statistical significance but also provides an early warning of problems that could have major economic significance.

Economic Significance

The fact that a difference between a measurement and a goal is statistically significant does not mean that corrective action will be taken. In some companies the differences, often in the form of nonconformance, are so numerous that it is necessary to establish priorities for action based on economic significance and related parameters. In situations where nonconformance is great, it is customary to document the cases and create machinery to make decisions. We will elaborate on this in Chapter 18.

5.9 TAKING ACTION ON THE DIFFERENCE

In the closing step of the feedback loop, action is taken to restore the process to a state of meeting the goal. Action may be needed for three different types of conditions:

1. *Elimination of chronic sources of deficiency.* The feedback loop is not a suitable means of dealing with such chronic problems. Instead, the quality improvement process described in Chapter 3 should be employed.
2. *Elimination of sporadic sources of deficiency.* The feedback loop is well designed for this purpose. In such sporadic cases, the cardinal issue is what changes caused the sporadic difference to arise. Discovery of those changes, plus action to restore control, can usually be carried out by the local operating supervision using troubleshooting procedures (see below).
3. *Continuous process regulation to minimize variation* (see below).

Troubleshooting

Troubleshooting (fire fighting) is diagnostic and remedial action applied to sporadic (not chronic) troubles. Ineffective troubleshooting can result in failure to hold the gains. The same two "journeys" (diagnostic and remedial) are needed, but each is much simpler than for chronic troubles. Sporadic trouble is the result of some adverse change, so the diagnostic journey is one of discovering what the adverse change was. The remedial journey removes the discovered adverse change so as to restore the status quo.

Structured Procedure for Troubleshooting

The Monsanto Corporation (undated) describes a step-by-step approach to finding the cause of deviations between expected and actual performance. This approach first describes the deviation and searches for possible causes, and then determines the true cause. Seven steps are involved:

1. *State the deviation.* Questions are posed to identify a single effect and a single object or group of related objects. What object (or group of related objects) is involved? What is the effect? Does anyone know the cause of this deviation?
2. *Specify the deviation.* The nature of the deviation is described in terms of what is involved with the deviation and what is not involved. Questions about the deviation involve what, where, when, and how much. Analyzing the "is not involved" column can greatly reduce the number of possible causes.
3. *Identify the unique characteristics of the deviation.* This is done through the use of a matrix (Figure 5.6).

	Is involved	Is not involved	Unique characteristics of "is involved"	Changes
What?				
Where?				
When?				
How much?				

FIGURE 5.6
Deviation analysis. (*From QCH4, p. 22.71.*)

4. *Search for changes.* The matrix is used and the question is asked, "What, if anything, has changed in, around or about this unique characteristic?" Answers are listed under "Changes."
5. *Develop possible causes.* For each change, the question is asked, "How could this change have caused the deviation?"
6. *Test the possible causes against the specification.* Compare each possible cause to the information in the "Is involved" and "Is not involved" descriptions and see if the cause is consistent with the information.
7. *Verify the cause.* Attempt to reproduce the deviation using the most probable cause, or eliminate the deviation by correcting the most probable cause.

Operating personnel can be trained to use this type of approach to do their own troubleshooting. An elaboration of this approach is presented by Kepner and Tregoe (1981).

5.10 CONTINUOUS PROCESS REGULATION

Operating forces (i.e., people operating the process) crave an effective way of continuously regulating the process to minimize deviations from a goal. To provide effective regulating mechanisms, the following principles are helpful:

- Each product characteristic (quality control subject) result should be linked to one or a few process variables.
- Means should be provided for convenient adjustment of the setting for the process variables.
- There should be a predictable, precise relationship between the amount of change in the setting of a process variable and the resulting amount of effect on the product characteristic.

In practice, unfortunately, knowledge of the true relationships between process variables and product results is often weak. These matters are discussed further in Section 16.2, "Review of Process Design."

The elements of the feedback loop discussed in this chapter are universal. Not only do the concepts apply to both manufacturing and service industries, they apply to both executive and operational activities within all industries.

SUMMARY

- Control is the process we employ in order to meet standards.
- Control involves a universal sequence of steps: choosing the control subject, choosing a unit of measure, setting a goal, creating a sensor, measuring performance, interpreting the difference between actual performance and the goal, and taking action on the difference. Measurement is a quiet source of action.
- Self-control involves three elements: People must have knowledge of what they are supposed to do, knowledge of their performance, and means of regulating their performance.
- Troubleshooting is diagnostic and remedial action applied to sporadic troubles.

PROBLEMS

5.1. Select a specific task which you have regularly performed for an organization. For this task, evaluate the degree to which the three criteria for self-control are met.

5.2. Interview someone who regularly performs a specific task for an organization. Explain the three criteria of self-control to that person and document the degree to which the criteria are met, as viewed by the person performing the task.

5.3. Place yourself in the role of a customer for any product—a good or a service. Identify at least four quality control subjects related to quality that are of importance to you as a customer and that the supplier should measure. For each quality control subject, propose a unit of measure.

5.4. Place yourself in the role of upper management for any organization producing goods or service. Identify at least four quality control subjects related to quality that are of importance to internal organizational performance and that the organization should measure. For each quality control subject, propose a unit of measure.

5.5. Select one process consisting of a series of tasks within an organization. Identify the location and data that are collected on quality-related control subjects throughout the process.

5.6. Interview someone who regularly performs a manufacturing task which includes taking periodic measurements on a product or process characteristic and making a comparison to a specification. Determine how the person makes each of two decisions:

   (a) How large a deviation of a measurement from a specification is permitted before the person takes action to adjust the process?

   (b) If a process adjustment is needed, what *amount* of adjustment is made?

REFERENCES

Early, John F. (1989). "Strategies for Measuring Service Quality," *ASQC Quality Congress Transactions*, Milwaukee pp. 2–9.

Gitlow, Howard, Shelly Gitlow, Alan Oppenheim, and Rosa Oppenheim (1989). *Tools and Methods for the Improvement of Quality*, Homewood, Illinois, pp. 18–24, 159–162.

Kepner, Charles H., and Benjamin B. Tregoe (1981). *The New Rational Manager*, Princeton Research Press, Princeton, N.J.

Kondo, Yoshio (1988). "Quality in Japan," QCH4, Section 35F.

Monsanto Company (undated). "Managerial Analytics Pocket Manual," Monsanto Company, St. Louis, Missouri.

Taguchi, G. (1978). "Off-Line and On-Line Quality Control Systems," International Conference on Quality Control, Japanese Union of Scientists and Engineers, Tokyo, pp. B4–1 to B4–5.

SUPPLEMENTARY READING

Executive reports on quality: QCH4, pp. 8.8–8.20.

Control processes: Juran, J. M. (1964). *Managerial Breakthrough*, McGraw-Hill, Inc. New York, 1964, Chapters 12–20.

Quality goals and objectives: QCH4, pp. 5.15–5.18.

Measurement: Juran, J. M. (1988). *Juran on Planning for Quality*, Chapters 5, 6.

Sink, D. Scott (1991). "The Role of Measurement in Achieving World Class Quality and Productivity Management," *Industrial Engineering*, June, pp. 23–29.

CHAPTER

6

STRATEGIC QUALITY MANAGEMENT

6.1 ELEMENTS OF STRATEGIC MANAGEMENT

Strategic quality management (SQM) is the process of establishing long-range quality goals and defining the approach to meeting those goals. SQM is developed, implemented, and led by upper management.

We will examine the basic elements of a strategic plan and then address how the quality parameter can be integrated. The following elements provide a widely accepted framework:

- Define the mission of our organization
- Analyze the opportunities and threats
- Analyze our strengths and weaknesses
- Identify and evaluate alternative strategies
- Select a strategy
- Develop goals
- Prepare detailed short range plans
- Translate plans into budgets
- Monitor performance

Typically, the plan covers a 5-year span in broad terms, with the first year in more detail.

Below *et al.* (1987) and Thompson *et al.* (1990) are helpful references that elaborate on the general concept of strategic planning. Delaplane (1987) discusses integrating quality into strategic planning in a manufacturing organization.

Specific approaches to strategic quality management are still evolving, but several elements have emerged as basic:

1. A focus on customer needs. This focus covers strengths, weaknesses, opportunities, and threats—in the language of strategic management, a "SWOT analysis." If a significant difference exists, then specific goals and actions must be identified—call it a "gap analysis." Sometimes the focus on customer needs gives birth to a quality strategy which leads to a unique competitive advantage.
2. Leadership by upper management to develop quality goals and strategies.
3. Translation of strategies into annual business plans.
4. Implementation of actions by line departments instead of relying on a Quality Department.

These elements will be illustrated by three examples described below.

6.2 INTEGRATING QUALITY INTO STRATEGIC MANAGEMENT

One of the authors has adapted the basic elements of strategic planning to incorporate the quality parameter. In the model below, the steps will be illustrated by a case from General Electric (Utzig, 1980). Thus, the model is really a generalization of the case. The model is applied to a specific product or product line, product X:

In the example, General Electric was the minimum-unit-cost producer but the company was losing market share.

Step 1: What are the financial goals for product X?

The short-range financial goal was a return on investment of at least 25 percent; the 5-year goal on cumulative net income was $120 million.

Step 2: What is our present quality goal with respect to competition?

The goal was to be equal to competitors A and B.

Step 3: What are the key quality factors that influence the purchasing decision of potential customers?

Marketing research determined that the factors, for product X, were reliability, efficient performance, durability, ease of inspection and maintenance, ease of wiring and installation, and product service.

TABLE 6.1
Customer-based measurements

Product attributes	Mean importance rating	Competitor performance ratings		
		GE	A	B
Reliable operation	9.7	8.1	9.3	9.1
Efficient performance	9.5	8.3	9.4	9.0
Durability/life	9.3	8.4	9.5	8.9
Easy to inspect and maintain	8.7	8.1	9.0	8.6
Easy to wire and install	8.8	8.3	9.2	8.8
Product service	8.8	8.9	9.4	9.2

Step 4: How do we compare to competition on each of the key factors?

The surprising result is shown in Table 6.1. Note that GE was rated lowest on each of the six factors. Of course, the results were not believed—until the study was done three times. Can't you just hear the criticisms of the study?

Step 5: Does anyone have a unique competitive advantage on quality?

Table 6.1 shows that competitor *A* was best on all six factors.

Step 6: What are the internal results on quality?

Failure costs were low and complaints were low. Thus, a traditional cost-of-poor-quality study would *not* have identified the seriousness of the problem.

Step 7: What are alternative quality goals with respect to competition?

Several alternatives were examined by studying the benefits and costs. It was decided that the present goal (to be equal in quality to competitors *A* and *B*) was to be retained.

Step 8: For the chosen goal, what departmental goals are needed to achieve the changes of level in the key factors?

New departmental goals were needed in the Design, Manufacturing, Service, and Quality Assurance departments.

Step 9: What departmental plans must be developed?

The goals were translated into specifics such as strengthening the magnetic structure to improve reliability, providing more uniform heat treatment, instituting a special training program for service technicians, and performing additional life testing on the product.

Step 10: What resources are required?

After the usual give-and-take of negotiation, appropriate resources were assigned.

Note that the driving force in this model (step 1) was a profit goal, not a quality goal. The competitive analysis, when viewed in light of the profit goal and regaining market share, was decisive in changing priorities and assigning the necessary resources. Business planning, involving steps 8, 9, and 10, glued the quality strategy into place. All of this led to a successful result.

In a different approach, the business management team for a process industry product decided to integrate quality issues into its regular strategic planning process. The corporation had a structured process for strategic planning which the business unit was required to apply to its products.

In this process, a 5-year strategic plan was developed in broad terms with the first year specified in more detail. The process was repeated annually.

The members of the business team first learned some modern concepts of quality management. They participated in an off-site workshop in which specific concepts were presented and immediately discussed to decide the relevance to the product involved. Examples of these concepts included quality factors influencing purchasing decisions, extra costs associated with poor quality, marketing research for quality, quality goals, quality processes, etc.

Potential issues were nominated and assignments made for team members to perform further study and report back. After discussion, four quality-related issues were identified as worthy of inclusion in the overall strategic planning exercise. For example, one issue was that future product planning should place more stress on value (the combination of quality and price) rather than on quality alone. This issue had important implications on sales income.

In an approach at Carolina Power and Light, middle managers were the source of input in developing a strategy (Allen and Bailes, 1988). A series of meetings was held to identify critical issues which were obstacles to quality. More than 100 issues were identified. These were reduced to 22 issues, e.g., enhanced leadership, direction and control by senior management. Next, further meetings took place to develop goals to address the 22 issues. The result was 297 goals, e.g., sense of unity of purpose, visible commitment to corporate mission and beliefs. Finally, the goals were grouped into four "macrostrategies": communications, changing the culture and management style, recognition and reward, and education and training. For each of these four strategies, brainstorming was employed to identify action items. Action items, providing a framework for each strategy, then led to the development of a 5-year plan for quality.

Increasingly, organizations are finding that although upper management leadership is essential, the development of strategy should involve both "top down" and "bottom up" viewpoints. For elaboration, see Jarvis (1988).

We will now examine elements of the management cycle that develop *and* implement strategies for quality.

6.3 QUALITY AND THE MANAGEMENT CYCLE

The classic management cycle has its roots in the work of Henri Fayol, a French industrialist who was active through about 1920. Fayol proposed that the elements of management consist of five functions: planning, organizing, commanding, coordinating, and controlling. The discussion below covers some elements of planning as applied to quality; subsequent elements of the management cycle are addressed in other chapters.

As applied to quality, elements of the management cycle include:

- Quality policies
- Quality goals
- Deployment of goals
- Plans to meet goals
- Organizational structure
- Resources
- Measurement feedback
- Review of progress
- Rewards based on performance against goals
- Training

The Japanese use an approach called *"hoshin* planning," which is built around the management cycle of plan, execute, and audit (or plan, do, check, act). Key aspects of *hoshin* planning include a focus on the planning process, company targets known by all employees, individual initiative, self-audit, and documentation and communication. See King (1989) and Brunetti (1986) for elaboration.

6.4 QUALITY POLICIES

A policy is a broad guide to action. It is a statement of principles. A policy differs from a procedure, which details how a given activity is to be accomplished. Thus a quality policy might state that quality costs will be measured. The corresponding procedure would describe how the costs are to be measured.

The subject matter of quality policies must be tailormade for each company. However, some matters are fundamental and should be considered by any company which is about to prepare written quality policy. These fundamental topics include:

- What level of clientele constitutes the company's market? (This bears directly on choice of quality of design or grade.)
- Is the company to strive for quality leadership, competitiveness, or adequacy?
- Is the company selling standard products, or is it selling a service in which the product is one of the ingredients of sale? (This affects the emphasis on conformance to specifications versus fitness for use.)

- Is the company to market its products on the basis of high reliability at higher initial price or lower reliability at lower initial price?
- Should the effort be to optimize users' costs or manufacturers' costs?
- Should the "abilities" (reliability, maintainability, etc.) be quantified?
- Should the company rely for its controls on systems or on people?
- Should quality planning be done by staff or line people?
- Should the supplier be put onto the team?
- Should top management actively participate in quality planning and assurance, or should it delegate this to someone else?

As the company grows to an extent which involves it in multiple markets and products, it becomes evident that no one set of quality policies can fit all company activities. This problem is solved by creating several levels of quality policy, e.g., a corporate policy and divisional policies. The corporate policy applies companywide. It lists the subjects that are to be contained in the policies created by each division. Such subjects might include preparation of a formal quality program, publishing of a quality manual that includes responsibilities, procedures, etc., and provision for audit to determine the extent to which plans are adequate and are being followed. Policies can also be created for programmed activities such as reliability or for activities within functional departments.

Some organizations find it valuable to develop a "vision statement." Often, such a statement is a collection of quality policies. Table 6.2 lists possible elements to address in a vision statement.

TABLE 6.2
Possible elements of a vision statement on quality

Definition of quality
Quality linked to business goals
Scope of quality effort—"big Q"
Goals—long range, short range
Focus on customers—internal and external
Involvement of all employees
Impact on job security
Implementation by the line organization
Leadership by upper management

Example of Quality Policies

Policies do not have to be vague. They can be specific enough to provide useful guidance. Here are two dramatic examples:

One computer manufacturer: A new product must perform better than the product it replaces and better than the competition's and this must be the case at the time of the first regular customer shipment.

Another computer manufacturer: In selecting suppliers, decision makers are responsible for choosing the best source even if this means internal sources are not selected. (This rescinded a previous policy which placed a priority on buying from "sister divisions.")

The following corporate quality policies were prepared for discussion at a health products company.

1. At both the corporate and plant levels, the Quality Control Department shall be independent of the production function.
2. The company shall place a new product on the market only if its overall quality is superior to the competition's.
3. All tasks necessary to achieve superior quality shall be taken, but each task shall be evaluated to assure that the investment has a tangible effect on quality.
4. Specific quality responsibilities for all company areas including top management shall be defined in writing.
5. Quality activities shall emphasize the prevention of quality problems rather than only detection and correction.
6. Quality and reliability shall be defined and measured in quantitative terms.
7. All quality parameters and tests shall reflect customer needs, usage conditions, and regulatory requirements.
8. Total company costs associated with achieving quality objectives shall be periodically measured.
9. Technical assistance shall be provided to suppliers to improve their quality control programs.
10. Each quality task responsibility defined for a functional department shall have a written procedure describing how the task will be performed.
11. The company shall propose to regulating agencies or other organizations any additions or changes to industry practice that will ensure a minimum acceptable quality of products.
12. Each year, quality objectives shall be defined for corporate, division, and plant activities and shall include both product objectives and objectives on tasks in the company quality program.
13. All levels of management shall have a defined quality motivation program for the employees in their department.

These policies were prepared to provide guidelines for (1) planning the overall quality program and (2) defining the action to be taken in situations for which personnel had requested guidance.

Policies may also be needed within a functional department. For example, policies for use within a quality department might include statements such as:

1. The amount of inspection of incoming parts and materials shall be based on criticality and a quantitative analysis of supplier history.
2. The evaluation of new products for release to production shall include an analysis of data for compliance to performance requirements and shall also include an evaluation of overall fitness for use, including reliability, maintainability, and ease of user operation.
3. The evaluation of new products for compliance to performance requirements shall be made to defined numerical limits of performance.
4. Suppliers shall be supplied with a written statement of all quality requirements before a contract is signed.
5. Burn-in testing is not a cost-effective method of eliminating failures and shall be used only on the first units of a new product type (or a major modification of an existing product) in order to get rapid knowledge of problems.

Note that these examples of policies state (1) a principle to be followed or (2) *what* is to be done but not *how* it is to be done. The "how" is described in a procedure. Often it is best to have a policy instead of a procedure in order to provide needed flexibility for different situations.

A sensitive policy issue may arise as the result of improvement projects that reduce rework or reprocessing to correct errors. Those people who have been doing the rework wonder: What will happen to me if this work is no longer necessary? This apprehension should be faced head on and a policy formulated. Several alternatives are possible:

- Guarantee that no employee will lose employment as a result of the quality effort. A small number of companies have issued such a policy statement.
- Rely on resignations and retirements as a source of new jobs for those whose jobs have been eliminated. Retrain those impacted to qualify for the new jobs.
- Reassign impacted employees to other areas which do have openings. This can include creating positions for additional quality improvement work.
- Offer early retirement.
- If all else fails, offer termination assistance to locate jobs in other companies.

Planning for this situation in advance can often lead to creative solutions.

One of the most critical and difficult policy issues of a companywide nature is the need for early and thorough cooperation among the marketing, product development, and manufacturing functions ("tear down the walls"). For a blow-by-blow case history in which development time was reduced from 3 years to 1 year, see Kleinfield (1990).

6.5 QUALITY GOALS

A goal (or objective) is a statement of the desired result to be achieved within a specified time—an aimed-at target. These goals then form the basis of detailed planning of activities. Tactical goals are short range (say, 1 year); strategic goals are long range (say, 5 years). The concept of management by objectives is widespread. Under this concept, managers participate in establishing objectives, which are then reduced to writing and become the basis of planning for results.

Goals may be created for breakthrough or control. There are many reasons why companies create goals for breakthrough:

1. They wish to attain or hold quality leadership.
2. They have identified opportunities to improve income through superior fitness for use.
3. They are losing market share through lack of competitiveness.
4. They have too many field troubles—failures, complaints, returns—and wish to reduce these as well as to cut the external costs resulting from guarantee charges, investigation expense, product discounts, etc.
5. They have identified some projects which offer internal cost reduction opportunities, e.g., improvement of process yields or reduction of scrap, rework, inspection, or testing.
6. They have a poor image with customers, suppliers, the public, or other groups of outsiders.

Goals for breakthrough are not limited to "hardware" or to matters that can be counted, e.g., income, cost. Goals for breakthrough can include projects such as a reliability training program for designers, a supplier rating plan, a complaint investigation manual, a reorganization of the quality control staff, or a new executive report on quality.

Some examples of corporate quality goals prepared for a health products company for the coming year were:

1. Quality costs for the company shall be reduced by _____ percent.
2. The material loss for the company shall not exceed _____.
3. The average leakage rate for _____ product shall be reduced to _____.
4. The company shall have _____ Certified Quality Engineers.

5. Quality costs shall be determined for at least one product.
6. A specific in-process quality data analysis technique shall be developed and implemented for at least one product.
7. Numerical reliability and maintainability objectives shall be defined for at least one product.
8. A procedure that assures that all corporate product specifications are reviewed by the plants before plant production planning starts shall be implemented.
9. A procedure that assures that all specifications for suppliers are agreed to by the supplier before finalization of the purchasing contract shall be implemented.
10. A quality procedures manual shall be developed.
11. The president or senior vice president shall make at least _____ visits to customers to review product quality.

Other examples of overall quality goals are:

- Create the Taurus/Sable car model at a level of quality which is "best in class."
- Reduce by 50 percent the time required to resolve customer complaints.
- Increase the percentage of research results that become incorporated into products by _____ percent.

Note that these statements include a quantification in either terms of a product characteristic or a date (the end of the calendar year). These cover both product characteristics and tasks in the overall company quality program. Quality goals can also be created for individual departments.

Managers have many reasons for avoiding breakthrough. In such cases, the goals are to hold the status quo, i.e., maintain control at present levels. The more usual reasons for choosing control are that:

- The managers believe that improvement is uneconomic: i.e., the cost of trying for breakthrough would not be recovered.
- Present performance is competitive. Many managers regard "the market" as a sound standard since it embodies the breakthrough efforts of competitors.
- There are few alarm signals—e.g., few complaints or internal flare-ups—to suggest the need for breakthrough.
- There is need for breakthrough, but it is not timely to undertake it because (a) there has been no agreement on the specific projects to be tackled or (b) the climate for quality breakthrough is unfavorable (e.g., too many other programs going; some key manager is not convinced; the breakthrough would require risky technological research).

The more usual goals for control include: holding materials, processes, and products to specification; holding field failures, complaints, returns, and other external performance measures to current levels; holding costs of inspection, test, scrap, rework, and other internal costs to current levels; holding gains achieved by recent breakthrough projects.

Formulation of Quality Goals

Quality goals can be identified from a variety of inputs, such as the following:

- Pareto analysis (see Chapter 3) of repetitive external alarm signals (field failures, complaints, returns, etc.)
- Pareto analysis of repetitive internal alarm signals (scrap, rework, sorting, 100 percent test, etc.)
- Proposals from key insiders—managers, supervisors, professionals, union shop stewards
- Proposals from suggestion schemes
- Field study of users' needs, costs
- Data on performance of products versus competitors' (from users and from laboratory tests)
- Comments of key people outside the company (customers, vendors, journalists, critics)
- Findings and comments of government regulators, independent laboratories, reformers

Analysis of these inputs requires, as in formulating policies, a mechanism that gives managers the opportunity to participate in setting goals without the burden of performing the detailed staff work. Quality engineers and other staff specialists are assigned the job of analyzing the available inputs and of creating any essential missing inputs. These analyses point to potential projects which are then proposed. The proposals are reviewed by managers at progressively higher organizational levels. At each level there is summary and consolidation until the corporate level is reached. The foregoing process is similar to that used in preparing the annual financial budget.

The process employed at a chemical plant of Union Carbide to set annual goals is shown in Figure 6.1. Note that this approach includes a vision, a strategy (long range) and tactical plans (short range).

Several alternative criteria may be used to define quality goals: historical performance, engineering analysis, or competition in the marketplace. Companies aspiring to excellence often set goals which go beyond those which are clearly attainable. These are "stretch goals." All goals—but particularly stretch goals—require a thorough follow-through of goal deployment and assignment of resources.

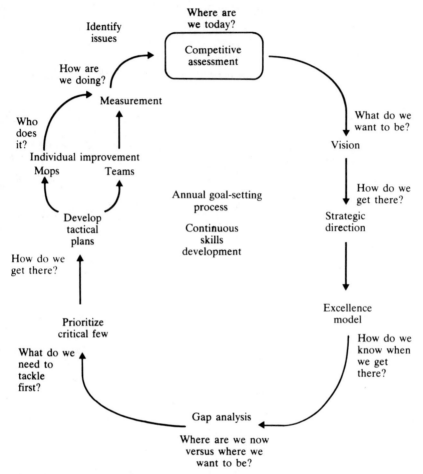

FIGURE 6.1
Annual goal-setting process. (*From Perry, 1989.*)

An extension of the marketplace approach is benchmarking, in which the performance of the best organization (competitor or not) is used as the standard.

Competitive Benchmarking

Competitive analysis is one of the distinguishing features of modern strategic quality management. Some organizations have built their SQM approach around such competitive analysis—they then call the overall approach "competitive benchmarking."

A "benchmark" is simply a reference point which is used as a standard of comparison for actual performance. Table 6.3 lists typical benchmarks.

TABLE 6.3
Benchmarks

The specification
Customer desires
Competition
Best in our industry
Best in any industry

Unfortunately, adherence to a specification may be woefully insufficient to generate sales. Also note that some of the other benchmarks listed in Table 6.3 go beyond competition. In this context, competition means other organizations that compete to sell, for example, office reproduction equipment. But a benchmark organization may be "best in our industry" or "best in any industry." For example, the Xerox Corporation used IBM and Kodak (direct competitors on some products) as benchmark organizations to evaluate many Xerox operations. But for warehousing and distribution activities, Xerox chose as a benchmark the L. L. Bean Company, a catalog sales distributor of clothing and other consumer products. Benchmarks serve not only as a standard of comparison but as a means of self-evaluation and subsequent improvement. The concept of searching for the "best" performer in *any* industry is a valuable contribution of the benchmarking approach.

Competitive benchmarking involves the following steps:

1. Determining the characteristics to be benchmarked
2. Determining which organizations will serve as benchmarks
3. Collecting data
4. Determining best in class
5. Analyzing a company's status versus best in class
6. Setting goals and integrating them into overall business planning
7. Developing strategies and action plans including milestones
8. Tracking progress against milestones

Bemowski (1991) describes the benchmarking processes applied by Alcoa and AT&T. Camp (1989) provides a complete discussion of benchmarking.

Deployment of Goals

Broad goals do not lead directly to results; they must first be "deployed." Such deployment consists of:

• Division and subdivision of the goals until specific deeds to be done are identified.

- Allocation of responsibility for doing these deeds
- Provision of the needed resources

    Such deployment involves communication both up and down the hierarchy. Corporate quality goals may be proposed at the top. The lower levels then identify the deeds which, if done, will collectively meet the goals. The lower levels also submit the bill: To perform these deeds, we need the

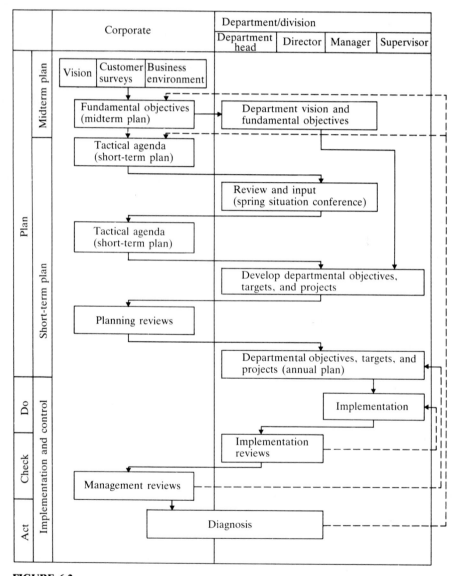

FIGURE 6.2
Policy deployment process. (*From Brunetti, 1986.*)

following resources. The subsequent negotiations then arrive at an optimum which balances the value of meeting the goals against the cost of doing so. Figure 6.2 summarizes this approach as practiced at Florida Power and Light. Note that quality projects are built into the annual business plan.

In another example, Banc One requires branch banks to develop an annual quality plan that deploys corporate strategy into quality goals covering five subject areas:

- Leadership
- Human resource utilization
- Information and analysis
- Quality assurance of products and services
- Customer satisfaction

To illustrate, under "leadership" separate goals are set for the number of Quality Councils, the number of managers and officers attending quality training, the time that will be devoted to quality by the CEO, COO, CQO (Chief Quality Officer), and department heads, the number of people attending quarterly quality conferences, and the total direct expense of quality activities. Aubrey (1989) describes the role of this approach at Banc One.

The reader should also review the approach taken in the initial planning for the Taurus automobile (see Chapter 4). Starting with a goal to be "world class," the goal was deployed into 429 specific design goals. The result was one of the most successful new-car introductions in modern American automotive history.

6.6 RESOURCES FOR QUALITY ACTIVITIES

The modern approach to quality requires an investment of time and resources throughout the entire organization—for many people, the price is about 10 percent of their time. In the *long run*, this investment yields time savings that then become available for quality activities or other activities; in the *short run*, the investment of resources can be a problem.

Upper management has the key role in providing resources for quality activities. One alternative is to add resources, but in highly competitive times this may not be feasible. Often, time and resources can be found only by changing the priorities of both line and staff work units. This means that some work must be eliminated or delayed in order to make personnel available for the quality activities.

People who are assigned to quality teams should be aware of the amount of time that will be required while they are on a team. If time is a problem, they should be encouraged to propose changes in their other priorities (before the team activity starts). Resources for project teams will be made available only if the pilot teams demonstrate benefits by achieving tangible results; thus the importance of nurturing those pilot teams to yield results. As a track record builds up for successful teams, the resource issue becomes less of a problem. One outcome can be for the annual budgeting process of an organization to include a list of proposed projects and necessary resources on the agenda for discussion.

6.7 TRAINING FOR QUALITY

One of the essential ingredients of a broad-scope quality program is an extensive amount of training. Table 6.4 identifies constituencies and subject matter.

Experience in training has identified the reasons why some training programs fail:

- *Failure to provide training at the time it will be used.* In too many cases, training is given to a large number of personnel who have little or no opportunity to use it until many months later (if ever). A much better approach schedules training for each group at the time it is needed—"just in time" training.

TABLE 6.4
Who needs to be trained in what

Subject matter	Top management	Quality managers	Other middle managers	Specialists	Facilitators	Work force
Quality awareness	X		X	X	X	X
Basic concepts	X	X	X	X	X	X
Strategic quality management	X	X				
Personal roles	X	X	X	X	X	X
Three quality processes	X	X	X	X	X	
Problem-solving methods		X	X	X	X	X
Basic statistics	X	X	X	X	X	X
Advanced statistics		X		X		
Quality in functional areas		X	X	X		
Motivation for quality	X	X	X		X	

- *Lack of participation by line managers in designing training.* Without this participation, training is often technique oriented rather than problem and results oriented.
- *Reliance on the lecture method of training.* Particularly in the industrial world, training must be highly interactive, that is, it must enable a trainee to *apply* the concepts during the training process.
- *Poor communication during training.* The technology of quality, particularly statistical methodology, can be mystifying to some people. Many benefits are possible if we emphasize simple language and graphical techniques.

Training programs are a failure if they do not result in a change in behavior. Applying these lessons can help to prevent such failures.

6.8 IMPLEMENTING TOTAL QUALITY

Translating the elements of the management cycle for quality into reality can be addressed in five phases: decide, prepare, start, expand, and integrate.

Decide

In the *decide* phase, we face the question "Do we need a different approach to quality?" Often, driving forces such as competitive pressures, customer dissatisfaction, and excessive costs of poor quality lead to a conclusion that the current quality system needs to be changed. This phase also examines some alternative approaches: statistical process control, quality circles, benchmarking, additional inspection—the list goes on and on.

Prepare

In the *prepare* phase, training is given to upper managers and selected middle managers who then apply the training to develop initial goals, plans, and some assignments. The elements of this phase are shown in Figure 6.3.

Start

The *start* phase includes more training, pilot quality projects, and revision and expansion of various management systems to implement and sustain the new approach to quality (see Figure 6.4). Of cardinal importance are the pilot projects—a road map for these is shown in Figure 6.5. The success of these projects broadcasts a message to many in the organization who are watching with a "wait and see" attitude; any failures in pilot projects teach us lessons for the next phase.

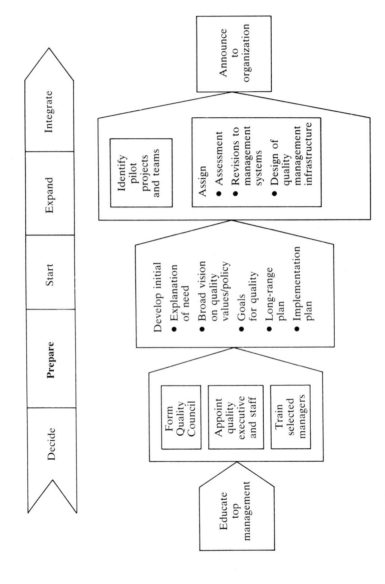

FIGURE 6.3
Prepare phase. (*From Juran Institute, Inc., 1991.*)

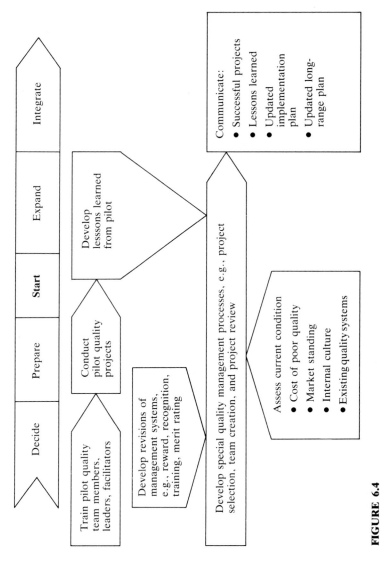

FIGURE 6.4
Start phase. (*From Juran Institute, Inc., 1991.*)

Decide · Prepare · **Start** · Expand · Integrate

Train pilot quality team members, leaders, facilitators

Conduct pilot quality projects

Develop lessons learned from pilot

Develop revisions of management systems, e.g., reward, recognition, training, merit rating

Develop special quality management processes, e.g., project selection, team creation, and project review

Assess current condition
- Cost of poor quality
- Market standing
- Internal culture
- Existing quality systems

Communicate:
- Successful projects
- Lessons learned
- Updated implementation plan
- Updated long-range plan

133

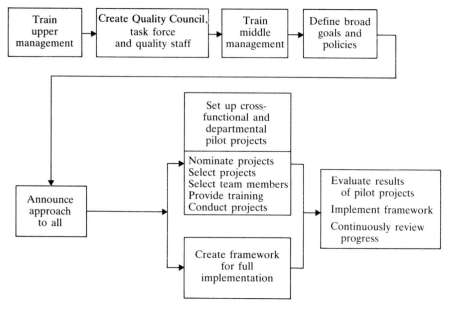

FIGURE 6.5
Pilot phase. (*From Juran Institute, Inc., 1991.*)

Expand

In the *expand* phase, the new approach is unfolded to other organizational units by setting up teams, measurement systems, individual quality initiatives, and additional training.

Integrate

Integrate is the ultimate phase, when quality becomes a way of life. Strategic goals are finalized and deployed to various levels; people are trained to participate on teams and to carry out individual quality roles; key business processes are identified and analyzed; assessments, reviews, and audits are in place. In summary, quality is no longer a "program"; it is now a part of business planning.

How long will all of this take? Tangible, measurable results will start to appear after about a year, but the heaven of quality truly being a way of life requires about six years. In most organizations, the phases follow a fairly predictable calendar (Figure 6.6).

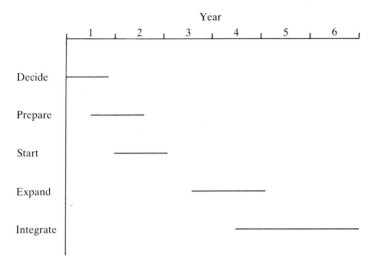

FIGURE 6.6
Timing of phases.

6.9 OBSTACLES TO ACHIEVING SUCCESSFUL SQM

The reasons for failure are many, but seven stand out as important:

1. *Lack of leadership by upper management.* Without this leadership, SQM is likely to be doomed. Some in upper management may be "committed," but lack of *evidence* of this commitment has a damaging result on the rest of the organization. Chapter 7, "Organization for Quality," discusses the leadership role of upper management.

2. *Lack of an infrastructure for quality.* With other major activities, management has successfully delegated responsibility but only after evolving mechanisms that include clear goals, plans, organizational mechanisms for carrying out the plans, budgets, and provision for recognition and rewards. In contrast, these same elements are usually vague or are missing with respect to quality.

3. *Failure to understand the skepticism about the "new quality program."* Many people have seen previous programs on quality quietly sink into oblivion. Unfortunately, the skepticism is not vocalized. The result is that management fails to present a convincing case of (a) "proof of the need" for the quality effort, and (b) their determination to make the effort a success.

4. *An assumption by management that the exhortation approach will work.* This approach involves a strong presentation on proof of the need (i.e.,

convincing everyone about the seriousness of the quality problem) coupled with relying principally on motivational techniques to inspire everyone to do better.

5. *Failure to "start small" and learn from pilot activities.* Sometimes, in a haste to achieve sizable results rapidly, the small pilot phase is omitted; instead, massive training takes place with the expectation that the troops can then simultaneously advance on all fronts. This doesn't work. A much better alternative uses a small number of pilot projects, with the scope of each project carefully defined so that completion is likely within six months. Perhaps the most common error in quality projects is failure to limit their scope to a digestible bite. People quickly grow tired of projects that seem to take forever.

6. *Reliance on specific techniques as the primary means of achieving quality goals.* Examples of such techniques are statistical process control, quality cost, quality circles, quality function deployment, etc. All of these are valuable and often necessary, but they are techniques that address only specific parts of the problem.

7. *Underestimating the time and resources required.* About 10 percent of the time of upper and middle management and professional specialists is required to achieve breakthroughs in quality. Typically, this time must be found without adding personnel. Thus priorities must be changed, i.e., other activities must be delayed or eliminated.

Organizations embarking on a significant new effort on quality are well advised to seek out the advice of other organizations and particularly to learn about their reasons for failure.

Endres (1990) provides examples of lessons learned from successes and failures during three phases of implementing quality improvement.

SUMMARY

- Strategic quality management (SQM) is the process of establishing long-range quality goals and defining the approach to meeting those goals.
- Upper management develops and implements SQM.
- Approaches to SQM have some common elements: a focus on customer needs, upper management leadership, integrating quality strategies into business plans, and implementation by line departments.
- A policy is a broad guide to action.
- A goal is a statement of the desired result to be achieved within a specified time.
- Competitive benchmarking identifies key quality characteristics and uses other leading organizations as reference points in order to develop goals and strategies.

- We "deploy" quality goals by dividing them into specific deeds, allocating responsibility, and providing resources.
- Implementing a quality strategy involves five phases: decide, prepare, start, expand, and integrate.

PROBLEMS

6.1. Select one improvement program that you have observed in an organization. The program of improvement may focus on quality, safety, absenteeism, costs, or other matters. With respect to implementing the program, what were its strengths? What were the weaknesses in implementing? What recommendations would you make to implement an improvement program in the future?

6.2. Propose a list of five quality policies for a specific organization, e.g., your company, a supermarket.

6.3. Propose a list of five quality goals for a specific organization, e.g., your company, a supermarket.

6.4. Many organizations have a general statement called a "quality policy." Often this is vague and states that the organization will supply the customer with "high quality." Obtain an example of such a statement and explain how it could be made more specific.

6.5. Refer to the list of 13 quality policies under "Example of Quality Policies" in Section 6.4. Comment on the extent to which each of the policies applies to a specific organization.

6.6. The chapter mentioned a bank that requires branch banks to develop an annual quality plan that deploys corporate strategy into quality goals for five subject areas. One of the areas is "Human Resource Utilization." Propose four goals to support this area.

6.7. Four months ago, an organization decided that it needed a new approach to quality. One of the steps taken was the establishment of quality goals. As part of a "50 percent in 5" focus, each department now has a goal of reducing the cost of poor quality by 50 percent in 5 years. Comment on this approach.

REFERENCES

Allen, Roger L. and C. V. Bailes (1988). "Managing the Startup of a Corporate Quality Improvement Effort—Translating Corporate Strategies into Field Operations." *Impro Conference Proceedings,* Juran Institute, Inc., Wilton, Connecticut, pp. 6A–13 to 6A–18.

Aubrey, Charles A. II (1989). "Continuous Improvement to Meet Customer Needs," *ASQC Quality Congress Transactions,* Milwaukee, pp. 600–606.

Below, Patrick J., George L. Morrissey, and Betty L. Acomb (1987). *The Executive Guide to Strategic Planning,* Jossey-Bass, San Francisco.

Bemowski, Karen (1991). "The Benchmarking Bandwagon," *Quality Progress,* January, pp. 19–24.

Brunetti, Wayne (1986). "Policy Deployment—A Corporate Roadmap," *Juran Report Number Eight,* Juran Institute, Inc., Wilton, Connecticut, pp. 20–29.

Camp, Robert C. (1989). *Benchmarking: The Search for Industry's Best Practices That Lead to Superior Performance,* ASQC Quality Press, Milwaukee.

Delaplane, Gary W. (1987). "Integrating Quality Into Strategic Planning," *Impro Conference Proceedings,* Juran Institute, Inc., Wilton, Connecticut, pp. 4B–21 to 4B–29.

Endres, Al C. (1990). "Managing the Three Phases of Quality Improvement," *ASQC Quality Congress Transactions,* Milwaukee, pp. 139–145.

Jarvis, John E. F. (1988). "Making It Happen—Vision, Leadership and Strategy for the Vital Few," *Impro Conference Proceedings,* Juran Institute, Inc., Wilton, Connecticut, pp. 2–21 to 2–29.

King, Robert E. (1989). "Hoshin Planning, the Foundation of Total Quality Management," *ASQC Quality Congress Transactions,* Milwaukee, pp. 476–480.

Kleinfield, N. R. (1990). "How Strykeforce Beat the Clock," *The New York Times,* March 25, pp. 3–1, 3–6.

Perry, Ann C. (1989). "From Teams to Total Quality," *Impro Conference Proceedings,* Juran Institute, Inc., Wilton, Connecticut, pp. 3A-7–3A-16.

Thompson, Arthur A., and A. J. Strickland (1990). *Strategic Management,* 5th ed., Richard D. Irwin, Homewood, Illinois.

Utzig, Lawrence (1980). "Quality Reputation—A Precious Asset," *ASQC Technical Conference Transactions,* Milwaukee, pp. 145–154.

SUPPLEMENTARY READING

Saraph, Jayant, P. George Benson, and Roger C. Schroeder (1989). "An Instrument for Measuring the Critical Factors of Quality Management," *Decision Sciences Journal,* vol. 20, no. 4, pp. 810-829.

CHAPTER
7

ORGANIZATION
FOR
QUALITY

7.1 EVOLUTION OF ORGANIZATION FOR QUALITY

Many organizations, particularly in manufacturing industries, have focused quality-related activities in a "Quality Department." Over the decades, the names and the scope of activities have changed—inspection, statistical quality control, quality control, reliability engineering, total quality control, quality assurance, total quality management.

During the 1980s in the United States, there emerged four major trends in organizing for quality:

1. Quality management tasks were assigned (or transferred) to functional line departments rather than the quality departments. For example, process capability studies were transferred from a Quality Department to a Process Engineering Department.

2. The scope of quality management was broadened from operations only (little Q) to all activities (big Q) and from external customers to external and internal customers. Most organizations now train personnel in the functional departments in the tools of quality management and make them responsible for implementing modern concepts of quality.

3. A major expansion occurred in the use of quality teams (see below).
4. Authority to make decisions was delegated to lower levels (see Section 7.9, "Self-Managing Teams").

These trends led to new approaches to organizing and coordinating quality activities.

7.2 COORDINATION OF QUALITY ACTIVITIES

The approach used to coordinate quality activities throughout an organization takes two major forms:

1. Coordination for *control* is achieved by the regular line and staff departments, primarily through employment of formal procedures and use of the feedback loop. Feedback loops take such forms as audit of execution versus plans, sampling to evaluate process and product quality, control charts, reports on quality, etc.
2. Coordination for *creating change* is achieved primarily through the use of quality project teams and other organizational forms for creating change.

Coordination for control is often the focus of a Quality Department; sometimes, such a focus is so preoccupying that the quality department is unable to make major strides in coordination for change. As a result, some "parallel organizations" for creating change have evolved.

Parallel Organizations for Creating Change

All organizations are engaged in creating beneficial change as well as preventing adverse change ("control"). Much of the work of creating change consists of processing small, similar changes. An example is the continuing introduction into the product line of new products consisting of new colors, sizes, shapes, and whatever. Coordination for this level of change can often be handled by carefully prepared procedures. "Maintenance organizations" can handle this type of activity.

For nonroutine, unusual programs of change, it is usually necessary to create new organizational forms. These new forms are called "parallel organizations." Here, "parallel" means that these organizational forms exist in addition to and simultaneously with the regular "line" organization.

Kanter (1983) effectively makes the point for parallel organizations as an important approach to innovation. Her comments apply full force to innovation in quality. As applied to quality, "maintenance" refers to the activities to achieve (primarily) conformance to specifications and procedures; "parallel" refers to improvement activities to change the level of quality.

Examples of parallel organizations for achieving change in quality are Quality Councils (see below), quality improvement project teams (see Section 3.6, "Organize Project Teams"), Quality Circles (see below), and business process teams (see Section 22.5, "Business Process Quality Management"). Parallel organizations may be permanent or ad hoc (a business process team versus a quality improvement team) and may be mandatory or voluntary (a Quality Council versus a Quality Circle). Dronkers (1987) discusses parallel and traditional organizations for quality. An early form of a parallel organization for product reliability is described by Gryna (1960).

QCH4, pages 7.21–7.25, elaborates on the subject of coordination of the quality function.

7.3 TOMORROW—A COMPANY WITHOUT WALLS

Most organizations organize around functional departments having a well-defined management hierarchy. Under the business conditions of the past, the concept has worked well; under today's business conditions, the concept does not work well.

Organizing by functional departments has certain advantages—clear responsibilities, efficiency of activities within a function, etc. But the organizational form also creates "walls" between the departments. These walls—sometimes visible, sometimes invisible—often cause serious communication barriers. The outcome can be efficient operations *within* each department but with a less-than-optimum result delivered to external (and internal) customers.

A common, repeated scenario is the following sequence: First, the Marketing Department determines the customer needs and transmits these to Product Development; Development then designs a product and hands the design to Manufacturing; etc. The joke is that Development "tosses the design over the wall" to Manufacturing. The implication is that each department performs its work with little or no regard to the impact of its output on the subsequent departments in the process. Experience suggests that these departmental barriers result in (1) extra internal costs and (2) longer time taken to complete the overall task. One measure of these costs and time is the number of avoidable design changes due to inadequate functional performance and difficulty of manufacturing, servicing, repairing, or operating a product. Such changes have been tolerated as part of the industrial fabric, but competitive pressures are causing companies to try new approaches such as the parallel type of organization.

Kilmann (1989) predicts that the future will bring a new "network" type of organization without walls. Among the characteristics are:

1. A small staff, at the hub, is responsible for strategic and management focus. It will control assets, set priorities and standards, and motivate the rest of the organization.

2. The people in the hub will be located together physically. These people will be connected electronically to those who are outside the hub.
3. At the hub, the traditional functional division of labor will be replaced by a division of knowledge, i.e., categories such as setting goals, identifying customer needs, etc. The traditional management hierarchy will be replaced by people at the hub who have the information needed to address these categories.

In designing and manufacturing the Taurus automobile, the organization was changed from a traditional to a hub type of organization (Figure 4.4). The future is certain to see new organizational forms in many organizations.

7.4   ROLE OF UPPER MANAGEMENT

Of all the ingredients for successfully achieving quality superiority, one stands out above all: active leadership by upper management. Commitment to quality is assumed, but it is not enough.
Certain roles can be identified:

- Establish and serve on a Quality Council (see below).
- Establish quality policies (see Chapter 6).
- Establish and deploy quality goals (see Chapter 6).
- Provide the resources.
- Provide problem-oriented training (see Chapter 6).
- Serve on upper management quality improvement teams which address chronic problems of an upper management nature (see Chapter 8).
- Stimulate improvement (see Chapter 8).
- Provide for reward and recognition (see Chapter 8).

In brief, upper management develops the strategy for quality and assures its implementation through personal leadership.
One effective example is the action taken by the head of a manufacturing division. He personally chairs an annual meeting at which improvement projects are proposed and discussed. By the end of the meeting, a list of approved projects for the coming year is finalized and responsibility and resources assigned for each project.
Unfortunately, there is a price to be paid for this active leadership. That price is time—usually about 10 percent of the time of upper management.
Waite (1989) identifies three "natural phases" of a quality effort and describes the role of upper management in each phase. The three phases are "euphoria" (initial problems are being solved), "slow down" (tougher problems require more time), and "settling in" (making the improvement process a permanent part of the company).

Quality Council

A Quality Council is a group of upper managers who develop the quality strategy and guide and support their implementation. Councils may be established at several levels—corporate, division, plant. For any level, membership consists of upper managers—both line and staff. The chairperson is the manager having overall responsibility and authority for that level, e.g., the president for the Corporate Council and the division and plant managers for their levels. One member of the council is the quality director whose role in the company is discussed below.

Each council should prepare a mission statement which includes responsibilities such as:

- Formulating quality policy
- Estimating major dimensions of the quality problem
- Establishing an infrastructure including Quality Councils, project system, assignment of roles and responsibilities, etc.
- Planning for training for all levels
- Establishing support for teams
- Providing for coordination
- Establishing new measures for progress review
- Revising the merit rating approach
- Designing a plan for recognition
- Establishing a plan for publicity of quality-related activities

Upper managers often ask: Isn't the Quality Council identical in membership to the regular top management team? Usually, yes. If so, instead of having a separate council, why not add quality issues to the agenda of the periodic upper management meetings? Eventually (when quality has become "a way of life"), the two can be combined, *but not at the start.* The seriousness and complexity of the quality issues require a focus that is best achieved by meetings that address quality alone.

As a council works on its various activities, it often designates one or more full-time staff people to assist the council by preparing draft recommendations for council review. In another approach, several council members serve on ad hoc task forces to investigate various issues for the council.

7.5 ROLE OF MIDDLE MANAGEMENT

Middle managers, supervisors, professional specialists, and the work force are the people who execute the quality strategy developed by upper management.

The roles of middle managers, supervisors, and specialists include:

- Nominating quality problems for solutions
- Serving as leaders of various types of quality teams
- Serving as members of quality teams
- Serving on task forces to assist the Quality Council in developing elements of the quality strategy
- Leading the quality activities within their own area by demonstrating a personal commitment and encouraging their employees
- Identifying customers and suppliers and meeting with them to discover and address their needs

Increasingly, middle managers are asked to serve as team leaders as a continuing part of their job. For many of them, their role as a team leader requires special managerial skills. For a manager of a department directing the people in that department, a traditional hierarchical approach is common. The leader of a cross-functional quality improvement team faces several challenges, e.g., the leader usually has no hierarchical authority over anyone on the team because they come from other departments, and team members serve part time and have priorities back in their home department. The success of a team leader depends on technical competence, ability to get people to work together as a team, and a personal sense of responsibility for arriving at a solution to the assigned problem. All this calls for quite an array of talents and a willingness to assume responsibility. For some middle managers, the required change in managerial style is too much of a burden; for others, the role presents an opportunity. Dietch et al. (1989) identified and studied 15 characteristics of team leaders at the Southern California Edison Company. The research concluded that team leaders (as compared to team members) have a higher tolerance for handling setbacks, believe that they have great influence over what happens to them, exhibit a greater tolerance for ambiguity, are more flexible, and are more curious (see Section 8.4, "Provide Evidence of Management Leadership").

7.6 ROLE OF THE WORK FORCE

By work force, we mean all employees except those in management and the professional specialists.

Recall that most quality problems are management- or system-controllable. This means that management must (1) direct the steps necessary to identify and remove the causes of quality problems (see Chapter 3) and (2) provide the system that places workers in a state of self-control (see Section

5.2, "Self-Control"). Both inputs from and cooperation by the work force are essential. The roles of the work force include:

- Nominating quality problems for solution
- Serving as members of various types of quality teams
- Identifying elements of their own jobs that do not meet the three criteria of self-control
- Becoming knowledgeable as to the needs of their customers

At last we are starting to tap the potential of the work force by using its experience, training, and knowledge. One plant manager says this: "No one knows a workplace and a radius of twenty feet around it better than the worker." Quality goals cannot be achieved unless we use the hands and the heads of the work force. Period. Some of the work force roles on teams are discussed below.

7.7 ROLE OF TEAMS

The "organization of the future" will be influenced by the interaction of two systems that are present in all organizations: the technical system (equipment, procedures, etc.) and the social system (people, roles, etc.); thus the name "sociotechnical systems" (STS).

Much of the research on sociotechnical systems has concentrated on designing new ways of organizing work, particularly at the work force level. Team concepts play an important role in these new approaches. Some organizations now report that, within a given year, 40 percent of their people participate on a team; some organizations have a goal of 80 percent. A summary of the most common types of quality teams is given in Table 7.1. Quality project teams are discussed in Section 3.6, "Organize Project Teams"; business management quality teams are described in Chapter 22; Quality Circles and self-managing teams are discussed in Sections 7.8 and 7.9.

Aubrey and D. Gryna (1991) describe the experiences of more than one thousand quality teams during 4 years at 75 banking affiliates of Banc One. This effort yielded significant results: $18 million in cost savings and revenue enhancement; a 10 to 15 percent improvement in customer satisfaction rating; and a 5/10 percent reduction in costs, defects, and lost customers. On some teams, membership was assigned; on other teams, membership was voluntary. A summary of some of the results of an organizational nature is given in Table 7.2. The focus is to improve customer satisfaction, reduce cost and increase revenue, and improve communication between front-line employees and management.

Next, we examine two types of work force teams: Quality Circles and self-managing teams.

TABLE 7.1
Summary of types of quality teams

	Quality project team	Quality Circle	Business process quality team	Self-managing team
Purpose	Solve cross-functional quality problems	Solve problems within a department	Plan, control, and improve the quality of a key cross-functional process	Plan, execute, and control work to achieve a defined output
Membership	Combination of managers, professionals, and work force from multiple departments	Primarily work force from one department	Primarily managers and professionals from multiple departments	Primarily work force from one work area
Basis of and size of membership	Mandatory; 4–8 members	Voluntary; 6–12 members	Mandatory; 4–6 members	Mandatory; all members in the work area (6–18)
Continuity	Team disbands after project is completed	Team remains intact, project after project	Permanent	Permanent
Other names	Quality improvement team	Employee involvement group	Business process management team; process team	Self-supervising team; semiautonomous team

TABLE 7.2
Observations on organization of quality teams at a bank

Feature	Results of research
Team size	Average of 7 members, with a range of 2–11
Project selection	75% by management, 15% by Quality Council, 10% by individual team
Average savings related to project selection	Projects selected by management or the Quality Council achieved savings about twice as high as projects selected by the team
Project duration	Average of 3 months; 24 worker-hours per team member (excluding time spent outside team meetings)
Factors to maximize team success	Ideal team size of 4–5 employees; 75% officer/staff level, 25% nonexempt employees; members selected by management; project selected by management or Quality Council; project duration of 3–4 months with weekly 90-minute team meetings.

7.8 QUALITY CIRCLES

One organizational mechanism for worker participation in quality is the Quality Circle. (Workers can also participate on other types of teams, see Table 7.1.) A Quality Circle is a group of work force–level people, usually from within one department, who volunteer to meet weekly (on company time) to address quality problems that occur within their department. Quality Circle members select the problems and are given training in problem-solving techniques.

Where the introduction of Quality Circles is carefully planned and where the company environment is supportive, they are highly successful. The benefits fall into two categories: measurable savings and improvement in the attitudes and behavior of people.

Quality Circles pursue two types of problems: those concerned with the personal well-being of the worker and those concerned with the well-being of the company. Workers' problems are those of their environment, e.g., reducing the amount of "junk food" in vending machines, eliminating a draft in a work area, designing special work tables for worker convenience. These "frustration"-type problems are important to the work force and therefore are frequently selected as early problems to address. Many of these problems can be solved in a short time with little or no investment. But management must be prepared to pay some dues by permitting workers to spend time on such frustration problems. Later, as Quality Circles start to address company problems, the focus is on products and processes. The benefits are improved quality for both internal and external customers and monetary savings. Savings on these types of Quality Circle projects typically range from $5,000 to $25,000 per year with a benefit-to-cost ratio of at least four to one.

Perhaps the most important benefit of Quality Circles is their effect on people's attitudes and behavior. The enthusiastic reactions of workers, sometimes streaked with emotion, are based on their personal involvement in solving problems. Beneficial effects fall into three categories (Gryna, 1981):

1. Quality Circles' effects on individuals' characteristics

Quality Circles enable the individual to improve personal capabilities. Many Quality Circle members spoke of the benefits gained from group participation and learning specific problem-solving tools. One worker felt he had developed a better relationship with his wife as a result of his participation in a Quality Circle, because the circle had improved his ability to interact with others.

Quality Circles increase the individual's self-respect. At Woodward Governor, a worker spoke highly of Quality Circles because "the little guy can get in on things."

Quality Circles help workers change certain personality characteristics. Almost every organization reported at least one case of an extremely shy person who had become more outgoing through participation in Quality Circles. Circles help workers develop the potential to become the supervisors of the future.

2. Quality Circles' effects on individuals' relations with others

Quality Circles increase the respect of the supervisor for the workers. "As a result of circles, I find that I talk more with workers on the line."

Quality Circles increase workers' understanding of the difficulties faced by supervisors. As a result of problem selection, solving, and implementation, circle members become aware for the first time of the supervisor's many burdens and demands on her or his time.

Quality Circles increase management's respect for workers. "Some of the presentations by circles have been better than those of my staff people."

3. Quality Circles' effects on workers and their attitudes toward the company

Quality Circles change some workers' negative attitudes. At one company, a worker stated, "I always had a chip on my shoulder around here because I didn't think the company cared about the worker. As a result of some circle projects, I've got a lot better attitude."

Quality Circles reduce conflict stemming from the working environment. The removal of these frustrations not only eliminates sources of conflicts, but workers' involvement in the removal process encourages them to think that they can deal with other frustrations as well.

Quality Circles help workers to understand better the reasons why many problems cannot be solved quickly. For instance, certain process changes at the Henry, Illinois, facility of the BF Goodrich Chemical Group required approval of the Chemical Group technical function. Workers at the plant could understand the need for this and have subsequently learned why this approval process required some time because of many other process changes being considered.

Quality Circles instill in the worker a better understanding of the importance of product quality. At Keystone Consolidated Industries, a Quality Circle was started in the wire mill. At an early meeting, the circle was given the results of a study that showed the dollars per year that were being lost due to poor quality. At the next meeting, a worker voluntarily showed some calculations he had made that indicated that the dollar value of the scrap he was personally producing was more than his salary.

With all the potential benefits of Quality Circles, their success rate has been mixed. Baker (1988) provides some perceptive recommendations for management to support and sustain Quality Circles. These are:

1. Recognizing and rewarding (not necessarily monetarily) workers' efforts, even if recommendations are not adopted. Giving workers increased

discretion and self-control to act on their own recommendations is an excellent reward.

2. Offering monetary rewards through the suggestion program (which may have to be modified to accommodate joint submission by circle members).

3. Providing sufficient training to expand worker skills to take on more complex projects.

4. Establishing a system for circles to expand into cross-functional teams when it appears to be a logical step. Circles may become 'fatigued' when they feel they have accomplished about all they can by themselves and see the need to work with their internal suppliers and customers.

5. Training of middle managers in circle tools and techniques so they can ask their subordinates the 'right questions' and not be 'outsiders.' These tools are also useful for the managers' own processes.

6. Addressing middle management resistance when diagnosed. Typically, management is concerned about a loss of authority and control.

7. Measuring effectiveness by focusing on the quality of the process—e.g., the training, the group discussion process, the interpersonal relationships, supervisory leadership style—rather than outcomes (e.g., reduction of scrap and costs). If the process is right, the outcomes will be also and that will reinforce employee involvement, as well as management commitment."

Every organization must provide for the participation of the work force in solving quality problems. One approach makes use of Quality Circles. A more revolutionary approach involves self-managing teams.

7.9 SELF-MANAGING TEAMS

We define a self-managing team as a group of people who work together continuously and who plan, execute, and control their work to achieve a defined output. That definition starkly contrasts with the traditional Taylor system of work design. Basic to the Taylor system is the division of an overall task into narrow, specialized subtasks which are assigned to individuals by a supervisor. That supervisor then coordinates and controls the execution and handles the general supervision of the workers.

In contrast, here are two examples of self-managing work teams:

• In an electronics plant, an assembly team handles all aspects of a customer order: It receives the order, prepares the components, assembles and solders circuit boards, tests the boards, ships the boards, monitors inventory levels, and processes all paperwork.

• At an insurance company (the Aid Association for Lutherans), work was originally organized into three areas—life insurance, health insurance, and support services such as billing. Under the new organizational design, teams of 20 to 30 employees perform all of the 167 tasks that formerly were split among the three functional sections. Now field agents deal solely with one team. The result is a shorter processing time for cases (*Business Week*, 1988).

The contrasting features of the traditional organization of the work force and self-managing teams are shown in Table 7.3. The difference is revolutionary. Workers are empowered to make certain decisions previously reserved for a supervisor.

The advantages of these teams include improvements in productivity, quality, customer satisfaction, and cost, as well as commitment of personnel. For example, a reduction of 30 percent in total production costs and turnover and absence rates of only 1/2 percent a year are now reported. Further, one layer of management can often be removed, thereby providing resources for quality improvement and quality planning projects.

Lawler (1986) provides a good perspective in terms of benefits and problems (see an adaptation in Table 7.4).

TABLE 7.3
Comparison of organizational forms

Feature	Traditional organization	Self-managing team
Scope of work	Each individual is responsible for a narrow scope	Team is responsible for a broad scope
Job categories for personnel	Many narrow categories	A few broad categories
Organizing, scheduling and assigning work	Primarily by supervisor or staff	Primarily by team
Measuring and taking corrective action	Primarily by supervisor or staff	Primarily by team
Training provided	Training for task assigned to individual	Extensive training for multiple tasks plus interpersonal skill training
Opportunity for job rotation	Minimum	High because of extensive training
Reward system	Related to job, individual performance, and seniority	Related to team performance and scope of skills acquired by individual
Handling of personnel issues	Primarily by supervisory personnel or staff	Many issues handled by team
Sharing of business information	Limited to nonconfidential information	Open sharing of all information

TABLE 7.4
Self-managing teams

Benefits	Problems
Improvement in work methods	Salary costs go up
Helpful in recruiting	Training costs go up
Staffing flexibility	Personnel needed for training
Improvement in quality	Unmet expectations may occur
Output may improve	Resistance by middle management
Staff support reduced	Resistance by staff groups
Supervision reduced	Conflict between participants and nonparticipants
Improved decision making	Time lost in team meetings

Source: Adapted from Lawler (1986).

Clearly, the implementation of such a fascinating but radical approach will be like walking through a mine field. Some key steps involved are:

1. Upper management commitment to undertake the approach and to accept some unknown risks.
2. In-depth orientation and participation of upper management, middle management, specialists, work force, and union officers.
3. Analysis of production work flow to define logical segments for teams.
4. Definition of skills required, levels of skills, and requirements for certification.
5. Formation of teams and training for teams and individuals.
6. Development of production goals for teams and provision for continuous feedback of information to teams. Such feedback must have the content and timeliness needed to control the process.
7. Changes to the compensation system to reflect the additional skills acquired by individuals.
8. Actions to develop trust between management and the work force, e.g., the sharing of financial and other sensitive information on company performance.
9. An implementation plan spanning about three years and starting slowly, with a few pilot teams.

The single most important—and most difficult—issue is how to guide middle management through the transition to this team concept. Some layers of management will no longer be needed because teams will plan and control their work and do much of their own supervision. Leonard (1987) describes how one work activity, under traditional organization, involved 25 direct labor employees, 16 individual job descriptions, three supervisors, and a production manager. This changed to three working teams (and seven skill levels for individuals) that reported directly to the production manager, with no supervisors.

Thus, some middle managers will have a new job. That new job may be working with a self-managing team but perhaps now as a member, facilitator, or technical consultant instead of the hierarchical supervisor. Such a role change affects power, knowledge, rewards, and status and thus will be threatening. An organization has a responsibility to explain the new roles for managers clearly and to provide the training, understanding, and patience to achieve success.

Self-managing work teams are not always successful. For some managers, supervisors, and workers, the demands of the concept are more than they are willing to accept. But self-managing teams can be highly effective if they fit the technology, they are implemented carefully, and the people in the organization are comfortable with the concept.

7.10 ROLE OF THE QUALITY DIRECTOR

The quality director of the future will be likely to have two primary roles—administering the Quality Department and assisting upper management with strategic quality management (Gryna, 1991).

The Quality Department of the Future

What will the future role of a Quality Department be? The major activities are indicated in Table 7.5. The table indicates some traditional activities of the

TABLE 7.5
Functions of the quality department of the future

Companywide quality planning
Producing executive reports on quality
Auditing outgoing quality
Auditing quality practices
Coordinating and assisting with improvement projects
Training for quality
Consulting for quality
Developing new quality methodologies
Transferring activities to line departments

Quality Department but also some important departures from the current norm.

Note, for example, "transferring activities to line departments." In recent decades, it has become increasingly apparent that the best way by far to obtain *implementation* of quality methodologies is through line organizations rather than through a staff Quality Department. (Isn't it a shame that it took us so long to understand this point?) At a small number of organizations, this has been stressed for quite a few years, and some have been eminently successful in transferring many quality control activities to the line organization.

In order to achieve success in such a transfer, it is essential that the line departments clearly and fully understand the activities for which they are held responsible. In addition, the line departments must be trained to execute these newly acquired responsibilities.

Examples of such transfer include: shifting the sentinel (sorting) type inspection activity from a Quality Department to the work force itself, transfer of reliability engineering work from a Quality Department to the Design Engineering Department, and transfer of supplier quality activities from a Quality Department to the Purchasing Department.

Assisting Upper Management with Strategic Quality Management (SQM)

A wonderful opportunity exists for a quality director to assist upper management to plan and execute the many activities of SQM. This includes the activities shown in Table 7.6. (For elaboration, see Chapter 6.) Can a quality director achieve such an exalted role? It is useful to cite an analogy to the area of finance (see Table 7.7). Many organizations today have a "chief financial

TABLE 7.6
Assisting upper management with strategic quality management

Assessing quality
Formulating goals
Formulating policies
Developing strategies for selecting and implementing new directions for the three quality processes
Delegating organizational responsibilities
Carrying out reward and recognition
Reviewing progress
Determining personal roles for upper management
Integrating
Integrating quality during strategic business planning cycle

TABLE 7.7
A contrast of roles

Finance (today)	Quality (the future)
Chief Financial Officer	Quality director
Other "financial managers"	Other "quality managers"
Line managers	Line managers

officer." This officer is concerned with broad financial planning aspects addressing such questions as "Where should our company be going with respect to finance?" There are other financial managers who direct and manage detailed financial processes, such as accounts payable, accounts receivable, cash management, acquisitions, and budgeting. These roles are also vital in the organization but different from the broader role of the CFO. Finally, of course, line managers throughout the entire organization have specific activities that they must do in order to help meet the financial objectives of the company.

The quality director of the future could act as the right hand of upper management on quality in the same way that the chief financial officer acts as the right hand of upper management on finance. (Note that there are other essential quality activities such as inspection, audit, quality measurement, etc., which must be directed and managed by other quality managers.)

Some of the scars of experience that have been accumulated within financial circles apply also to the quality function. Years ago, there was no such role as chief financial officer. The detailed financial processes were handled by one or several managers. As time went on, the need for a person with a broader financial viewpoint became apparent. In some companies, the person who was then the "controller" was promoted to become the chief financial officer. In other companies, however, it was felt that the controller did not have the breadth of vision and scope to assist upper management on broad financial planning, even though the controller was excellent in administering some of the detailed financial processes. Thus, not every controller became a chief financial officer.

A similar issue arises in regard to the broad scope necessary for the quality director of the future. Is the present quality director prepared, or is that person willing to become prepared, for the broader business role with respect to quality? Those quality directors who wish to assume this broader role in the future need to learn from the lessons of the financial controllers.

Table 7.8 shows some of the ingredients for success as a quality director of the type indicated here. Clearly, this list goes far beyond the current scope of quality directors in many companies. In larger companies, quality managers, including those who will manage some of the technical quality activities, will be

TABLE 7.8
Ingredients for success as a quality director

Emphasis on business, not technology

Focus on customer needs, not just conformance to specifications

Attitude of service to upper management and line departments

Emphasis on company quality goals, not goals of Quality Department

Role as a catalyst/facilitator

Being a proponent for resources for other departments

needed at various levels. A quality director is likely to be involved in administering technical activities but will increasingly be called upon to assist upper management as upper management—not the quality director—*leads* the company on quality. For elaboration on the future role of the Quality Department, see Gryna (1991).

SUMMARY

- Coordination of quality activities throughout an organization requires two efforts: coordination for control and coordination for creating change.
- Coordination for control is often the focus of a quality department; coordination for creating change often involves "parallel organizations" such as a Quality Council and quality project teams.
- New forms of organization aim to remove the barriers, or "walls," between functional departments.
- To achieve quality excellence, upper management must lead the quality effort. The roles in this leadership can be identified.
- A Quality Council is a group of upper managers who develop quality strategy and guide and support its implementation.
- Middle management executes the quality strategy through a variety of roles.
- Inputs from the work force are essential.
- Quality teams create change. Four important types of teams are: quality project teams, Quality Circles, business process quality teams, and self-managing teams.
- The implementation of the quality strategy must occur through the line organization rather than through a staff Quality Department.
- The quality director of the future will have two roles: administering the Quality Department and assisting upper management with strategic quality management.

PROBLEMS

7.1. Conduct a research study and report on how any of the following institutions was organized for quality:
   (*a*) The Florentine Arte Della Lana (wool guild) of the twelfth, thirteenth, and fourteenth centuries
   (*b*) Venetian shipbuilding in the fourteenth century
   (*c*) Construction of cathedrals in medieval Europe
   (*d*) The Gobelin tapestry industry in the sixteenth and seventeenth centuries

7.2. Study the plan of organization for quality of any of the following institutions and report your conclusions:
   (*a*) a hospital,
   (*b*) a university,
   (*c*) a chain supermarket,
   (*d*) a chain of motels,
   (*e*) a restaurant,
   (*f*) a manufacturing company.

7.3. For any organization, make a list of the activities assigned to the Quality Department. Compare your list with Table 7.5 and explain what the reasons for the difference between the two lists might be.

7.4. For any organization, study the methods in use to attain
   (*a*) coordination for control and
   (*b*) coordination for change. Report your findings.

7.5. Review the three elements of self-control in Chapter 5. Explain how each of these elements can be helpful in setting up a self-managing team.

7.6. An often-asked question is "Who is responsible for quality?" As worded, the question is too vague. The question must be restated in terms of actions and decisions concerning quality. Choose one functional area of an organization. For this area, list in the rows of a table some key actions or decisions. Then set up a few columns showing organizational units that are candidates for responsibility. Fill in the table to show which unit should be responsible for each action or decision.

REFERENCES

Aubrey, Charles A. II and Derek S. Gryna (1991). "Revolution Through Effective Improvement Projects," *ASQC Quality Congress Transactions,* Milwaukee, pp. 8–13.

Baker, Edward M. (1988). "Managing Human Performance" in *Juran's Quality Control Handbook, Fourth Edition,* McGraw-Hill, Inc., New York, pp. 10.47, 10.48.

Business Week (1988). "Work Teams Can Rev Up Paper-Pushers, Too," November 28, pp. 64–72.

Dietch, Robert, Steve Tashjian, and Howard Green (1989). "Leadership Characteristics and Culture Change: An Exploratory Research Study," *Impro Conference Proceedings,* Juran Institute, Inc., Wilton, Connecticut, pp. 3C–21 to 3C–29.

Dronkers, John J. (1987). "Organizing for Quality: A Structural Perspective," *ASQC Quality Congress Transactions,* Milwaukee, pp. 746–754.

Gryna, Frank M. (1960). "Total Quality Control Through Reliability," *ASQC Convention Transactions,* pp. 295–301.

Gryna, Frank M. (1981). *Quality Circles,* Amacom, New York.

Gryna, Frank M. (1991). "The Quality Director of the 1990's, Parts 1 and 2," *Quality Progress,* April, pp. 37–40; May, pp. 51–54.

Kanter, Rosabeth Moss (1983). *The Change Masters,* Simon and Schuster, New York, Chapter 7.

Kilmann, Ralph H. (1989). "Tomorrow's Company Won't Have Walls," *The New York Times,* June 18.

Lawler, Edward E. III (1986). *Participative Strategies for Improving Organizational Performance,* Chapter 7. Jossey-Bass, San Francisco, California.

Leonard, James F. (1987). "Institutionalizing the Team Process," *Impro Conference Proceedings,* Juran Institute, Inc., Wilton, Connecticut, pp. 5B–17 to 5B–21.

Waite, Charles L., Jr. (1989). "Timing Is Everything," *Quality Progress,* April, pp. 22–23.

SUPPLEMENTARY READING

Organizing for quality: QCH4, Section 7.

Self-managing teams: Orsburn, Jack D., Linda Moran, Ed Musselwhite, and John H. Zenger (1990). *Self-Directed Work Teams,* Business One Irwin, Homewood, Ill.

CHAPTER
8

DEVELOPING
A QUALITY
CULTURE

8.1 TECHNOLOGY AND CULTURE

To become superior in quality, we must pursue two courses of action:

1. Develop technologies to create products and processes which meet customer needs. These technologies are discussed throughout this book.
2. Stimulate a "culture" throughout the organization that continually views quality as a primary goal. Wouldn't it be great if we could identify techniques for creating a quality culture? Culture is not a technocratic issue. There are, however, approaches that provide a path toward a quality culture. Such approaches are examined in this chapter.

We will define quality culture as the pattern of human habits, beliefs, and behavior concerning quality. Technology touches the head; culture touches the heart.

Recall that quality problems are mostly management-controllable. Thus, cultural issues apply to all levels—upper management, middle management, supervisors, technical specialists, business specialists, and the work force. We first examine some classic theories of motivation.

158

8.2 THEORIES OF MOTIVATION

The professionals in this field are behavioral scientists. (Managers are merely experienced amateurs.) Studies by the behavioral scientists provide useful theories which help us to understand how human behavior responds to various stimuli.

Hierarchy of Human Needs

Under this theory (Maslow, 1987), human needs fall into five fundamental categories in a predictable order of priorities. Table 8.1 shows this "hierarchy of human needs" together with the associated forms of motivation for quality.

Job Dissatisfaction and Satisfaction

Under this theory (Herzberg et al. 1959), job dissatisfaction and job satisfaction are not opposites. Job dissatisfaction is the result of specific dislikes—the pay is low, the working conditions are poor, the boss is unpleasant. It is possible to eliminate these dislikes—raise the pay, change the working conditions, reform the boss. The revised conditions are then accepted as normal but do not motivate behavior.

In contrast, job satisfaction depends on what the worker *does*. Satisfaction comes from doing—motivation comes from such factors as job challenges, opportunities for creativity, identification with groups, responsibility for planning, etc. To illustrate: At the end of the day, an assembly line worker is happy to leave that monotonous job and go home to something more

TABLE 8.1
Hierarchy of human needs and forms of quality motivation

Maslow's list of human needs	Usual forms of quality motivation
Physiological needs: i.e., need for food, shelter, basic survival. In an industrial economy, this translates into minimum subsistence earnings	Opportunity to increase earnings by bonus for good work
Safety needs: i.e., once a subsistence level is achieved, the need to remain employed at that level	Job security: e.g., quality makes sales; sales make jobs
Belongingness and love needs: i.e., the need to belong to a group and be accepted	Appeal to the employee as a member of the team—he or she must not let the team down
Esteem needs: i.e., the need for self-respect and for the respect of others	Appeal to pride of workmanship, to achieving a good score. Recognition through rewards, publicity, etc.
Self-actualization needs: i.e., the urge for creativity, for self-expression	Opportunity to propose creative ideas, to participate in creative planning

appealing. In the same company, a researcher may not leave precisely at closing time—the research project may be more fascinating than the outside hobby.

Theory X and Theory Y

Two theories bring us to a controversy about whether workers have lost their pride in their work. Is the change in the worker or in the work? These two alternatives have been given names—theory X and theory Y, respectively (McGregor, 1985).

Under theory X, the modern worker has become lazy, uncooperative, etc. Managers must combat this decline in worker motivation through skillful use of incentives and penalties.

Under theory Y, there has been no change in human nature. What has changed is the way in which work is organized. The solution is to create new job conditions which permit normal human drives to assert themselves.

Managers are not unanimous in adhering to one or the other of these theories. It is common to find, even within the same company, some managers who support theory X and others who support theory Y. This support is not merely philosophical—it is reflected in the operating conditions that prevail in different departments.

Both theory X and theory Y have their advocates. However, there seems to be no conclusive evidence that either can outperform the other in economic terms, i.e., productivity, cost, etc. There is some evidence to suggest that the theory Y approach makes for better human relations. Some studies have shown that certain workers regard repetitive, routine work as less stressful than a broader range of work with its demands for decision making and creativity.

A discussion of culture quickly moves into an examination of the actions necessary for *change*. Kilmann (1989) suggests that there are five tracks necessary for change: culture, management skills, team building, strategy-structure, and the reward system. Peters and Waterman (1982) believe that seven factors are essential for change: shared values, strategy, systems, staffing, style, structure, and skills (the "7S" model).

Differences in quality culture can have extreme illustrations, both negative and positive. Two examples:

- *Negative quality culture* ("*hide the scrap*" *scenario*). The culture in a paint manufacturing plant put pressure on supervisors to avoid reporting any batch of paint that did not meet specifications. One supervisor resorted to hiding some paint; he directed his workers to dig a hole in the yard and bury the paint.

- *Positive quality culture ("climb the ladders to delight the customer" scenario).* The culture in a hotel resulted in taking an extraordinary step to please a customer—on short notice. About an hour before a seminar was to be presented, the seminar leader heard a steady, clear tinkling sound. The cause—small glass prisms in two chandeliers colliding due to air movement from the air conditioning system. He mentioned this to the hotel management. Action was immediate—two work crews were assembled; ladders were set up; and every second prism was removed (about 100 in all).

Culture *can* be changed. We need to provide awareness of quality, evidence of upper management leadership, self-development and empowerment, participation, and recognition and rewards. These paths must be integrated with the methodologies and structure for quality (see Figure 8.1).

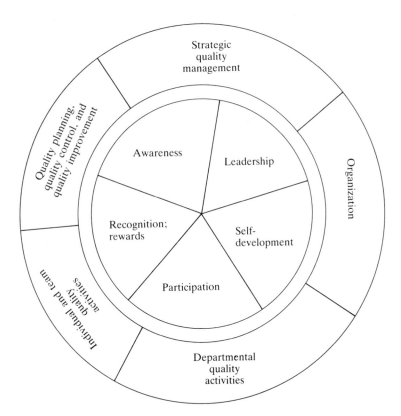

FIGURE 8.1
Technology and culture.

8.3 CREATE AND MAINTAIN AWARENESS OF QUALITY

To ensure action on quality, a starting point is to create and disseminate information on the current status of quality. Often this information provides dramatic evidence of a serious quality problem, provides "proof of the need," and prepares the way for presenting a program of action. Two important issues in presenting this evidence are the language used and the content of the information.

To create awareness, we need to present information in different "languages" for different populations in an organization. The pyramid in Figure 8.2 depicts these populations and the corresponding languages. At the apex is upper management, usually the general manager and the top management team; at the base are first-line supervisors and the work force; in between are middle managers and specialists.

These segments of the organization use different languages in everyday operations, and creating awareness of the need for quality must reflect this. Middle managers must not only understand their local dialects; they must also be fluent in the languages of the other levels (upper management and lower management and work force). Thus, middle managers must be "bilingual."

At the upper management level, creating an awareness of quality is best done in the language of money. Highlighting threats to sales income or opportunities for cost reduction are important. When quality can be related to either of these factors, an essential step in inspiring upper management action has been taken. The reader is urged to review Chapter 2, "Companywide Assessment of Quality," which describes three studies. A study on marketplace standing will identify threats to sales income; a study on the cost of poor quality will highlight opportunities for cost reduction; a study on quality culture will help to identify some of the obstacles to inspiring action.

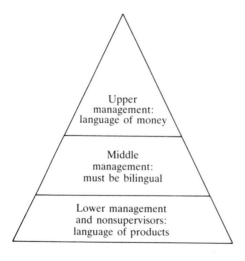

FIGURE 8.2
Common languages in the company.

Each of these three assessments can be made for the total organization or for individual areas such as product development or manufacturing. Note also that a presentation of the company's current status should be accompanied by an explanation of the *benefits* that can be expected from a new approach to quality. Demonstrations of these benefits are particularly useful (see Section 3.4 under "Use of a Bellwether Project"). Table 3.1 presents units of measure for both monetary and other languages to dramatize the importance of losses due to poor quality.

At middle management and lower levels, we sometimes can translate the impact of quality directly into the language of job security. When this can be done based on data, the result can be dramatic. A manufacturer of a consumer product was able to collect data on present customers who replaced the product made by the company. In one year, about 430,000 of these customers replaced the product by purchasing a competing brand—and thus were lost customers. About one-third of these lost customers stated that the main reason for switching to another brand was "poor quality" (four times as important as price and other factors). The sales income lost due to poor quality was then calculated as $1.3 billion. This sales income would have provided about 2,000 jobs—as many as were employed by one of the company's plants.

Maintain Awareness of Quality

The message on quality must be sustained through continuous reinforcement. One form of reinforcement is quality measurement.

Throughout this book, quality measurement will be proposed for major functional activities, i.e., product development, purchasing, manufacturing, marketing and customer service, and administrative and support operations. These measurements become the "vital signs" that provide people with data not only to perform their tasks but also to maintain a continuing awareness of quality. The reader is urged to review the discussions on measurement and on self-control in Chapter 5, "Control of Quality." In addition to continuous feedback to employees, some companies use a "chart room" to display key quality measurements as a dramatic way of showing the overall quality story.

Units of measure must be carefully defined to inspire a positive priority for quality. An example that does just the opposite is a poorly defined measure of productivity. Measures of productivity are usually a ratio of product output to input resources. Some companies calculate productivity using *total* output (instead of output meeting specifications) divided by input resources. Although total output must be measured, a single productivity measure based only on total output sends a clear message that meeting specifications is not important. Changing such deadly measures to count only good output provides continuing evidence that management sets a high priority on quality.

Reports and scoreboards of quality measurements can be highly effective, but caution must be exercised. Where the measurements show an unfavorable level of quality, the distinction between management-controllable and worker-controllable causes must be recognized. When the problem is mostly management-controllable (the typical case), management must make it clear that it is responsible for taking action. Otherwise, publication of the data implies that the low level of quality is the fault of the workers. Such an implication will be fiercely resented and will undermine a positive culture about quality (and even result in people hiding the defective output). In cases where the problems are mostly worker-controllable, then the publishing or posting of the data must be accompanied by showing the workers exactly what steps they must personally take to improve their quality of output.

Maintaining an awareness of quality can draw upon an array of ideas and techniques. These include quality newsletters, quality items on all meeting agendas, announcements on quality by key executives, company conferences on quality, and "interest arousers" (e.g., letters from customers).

Human ingenuity provides an unending array of possibilities. But ideas for maintaining a focus on quality can *never* be a substitute for real action by management. Some management groups expect clever posters and other media to improve quality when the management-controllable causes of poor quality have not been corrected. If they have this expectation, the posters should be placed high off the ground; otherwise, vulgar comments may appear on them.

8.4 PROVIDE EVIDENCE OF MANAGEMENT LEADERSHIP

Management commitment is necessary but not sufficient. To inspire action within a company, the single most important element is management leadership on quality—with the *evidence* to prove it.

The leadership role of upper management in strategic quality management was discussed in Section 7.4, "Role of Upper Management." Eight key tasks were identified:

1. Establish and serve on a Quality Council.
2. Establish quality policies.
3. Establish and deploy quality goals.
4. Provide the resources.
5. Provide problem-oriented training.
6. Serve on upper management quality improvement teams which address chronic problems of an upper management nature.
7. Stimulate improvement.
8. Provide for reward and recognition.

Such activities will take about 10 percent of the time of upper management—a heavy price to be paid for people who have many other demands on their time. (Establishing "proof of the need" is essential to convincing upper management to make the time investment.) When upper management spends time on these activities, it provides the evidence of leadership that inspires others to do their share.

Some upper management groups have chosen to be highly visible in the quality process by leading quality training. In such cases, managers at a variety of levels personally conduct some of the managerial training for their subordinates. With luck, the concepts presented are emphasized by the manager/instructor in everyday practice.

A further form of evidence is upper management quality improvement teams. Each team, consisting solely of upper management members, addresses a problem which requires attention at its level. Examples include the effectiveness of the product development process, the quality of decision making in selecting new product managers, and the administrative aspects of high warranty costs.

The visibility of upper management taking such training and then conducting such projects sets an example for other levels to follow.

Occasionally, there are opportunities for upper management to take dramatic action to demonstrate its commitment to quality. Here are some examples:

- A manufacturer of tires traditionally sold, at a discount, tires that had imperfections. (These imperfections had no impact on safety.) The sales income from these "seconds" made an important contribution to total sales income. A policy decision was made to discontinue all sales of tires with imperfections. The policy, one part of a broader company emphasis on quality, sent a strong message to all employees that quality was a top priority.
- A manufacturer of a small electronic product had always emphasized quality but found it necessary to rework about 8 percent of production. A potential customer objected to the rework concept, claiming that the rework might degrade the overall quality. (That customer was not satisfied that the product would be retested after rework.) The manufacturer announced that *no* rework would be permitted and that any nonconforming product would be discarded. In this case, the strong message proclaimed by the policy helped to uncover many hidden causes of defects that had previously been tolerated and corrected by rework.
- A plant manager wanted to demonstrate that he had faith in the employees' judgment in taking actions that would improve quality. He issued a directive authorizing everyone in the plant to spend up to $100, without approval, for any purpose that they believed would improve quality.
- At one major utility, department managers are required to submit and obtain approval each year on their departmental budget. This organization also requires that each manager prepare an annual quality plan. Each *quality plan* must first be approved before the annual budget is approved.

- A government agency had a reporting system on work output. Managers were evaluated on the quantity of output results versus goals. As the agency moved to a quality-oriented culture, the director took drastic action to demonstrate his feeling about the priority on quality. He discontinued the reports on output (even though he still had output goals from a higher level) and told his people that quality was the top priority. He explained that improvement in quality would contribute to meeting output goals by reducing the time spent on reprocessing activities due to poor quality.

Such dramatic actions, even though they are rare, are inspiring for a long time.

A corollary to these positive actions is the situation when management makes a decision that, on the surface, seems to suggest that quality has a low priority. The classical case is the shipment of product that does not meet specifications. In many cases, such product has been thoroughly reviewed (often with the customer) to evaluate the effect on the customer, and a logical decision has been made to ship. Unfortunately, the reasons for the decision are rarely explained to the work force, and thus they conclude that quality has been compromised. This and other cases in manufacturing can lead first-line supervisors and the work force to conclude that management does not regard quality to be as important as other standards. Communicating the reasons in such cases is essential to maintaining a strong emphasis on quality.

Providing evidence of leadership may involve changes in the manner in which management interacts with employees, i.e., the "style of leadership." A prerequisite to such change is understanding the present style. A division of the Rockwell Corporation decided that this was a key element in gaining employee support for quality. A survey was made to determine the management style of the president, his direct reports, and the people who reported to the direct reports (Warren, 1989). The management team exhibited six leadership styles: coercive, authoritative, affiliative, democratic, pace-setting, and coaching. Figure 8.3 summarizes the results. The predominant style was pace-setting ("The do-it-myself manager who performs many tasks personally, expects subordinates to follow his or her example, and motivates by setting high standards and letting subordinates work on their own"). Although the pace-setting style had advantages, it was concluded that it was not suitable for changing the organization or gaining employee support. (Pacesetters often take over a job themselves, have trouble delegating, are intolerant of mistakes, etc.) Further analysis revealed that a better management style is one where management provides a vision, sets clear standards and goals, shows individuals what is expected of them, lets employees do the job, and gives feedback along with rewards. A coaching process was developed to help managers to change their style.

Leadership style also applies to lower levels of management. The Southern California Edison Company conducted research to identify leadership characteristics associated with leaders of successful quality improvement

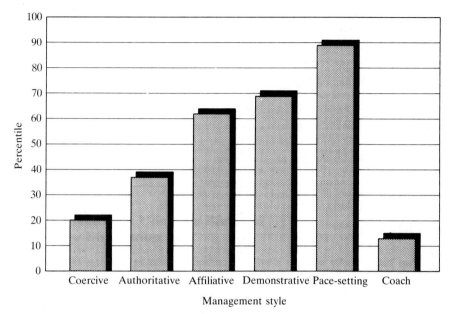

FIGURE 8.3
Composite of senior management. (*From Warren, 1989.*)

teams (Dietch et al., 1989). A questionnaire evaluated the following leadership characteristics:

Appropriate risk taking	Initiative
Confidence	Innovation
Creativity	Locus of control
Curiosity	Need for support
Excitement level	Pattern recognition
Flexibility	The right stuff
Handling setbacks	Tolerance of ambiguity
Independence/interdependence	

Successful team leaders exhibited a high tolerance for handling setbacks, an internal locus of control (they believe they have a great influence over what happens to them), a greater tolerance of ambiguity, flexibility, and a curiosity about the issues involved. The research also evaluated the characteristics of team members.

8.5 PROVIDE FOR SELF-DEVELOPMENT AND EMPOWERMENT

Inspiring people to take positive steps on quality is greatly influenced by the nature of the work performed by those people. We will address job content, empowerment, personal commitment, and selection and training.

The activities in any organization can be viewed as a set of interdependent functions that produce goods (e.g., parts) or services (e.g., information).

Whatever our job in an organization, all of us play three roles: supplier, processor, and customer (see Section 1.4, "The Quality Function"). These roles are executed by individuals at each stage of a process. Each stage is a supplier to subsequent stages and also a customer of previous stages. The components necessary for quality performance are illustrated in Figure 8.4 for a single supplier-customer interface (see Baker, 1988, for elaboration). The design of individual jobs is often based on function specialization, a key concept of the Taylor system.

The Taylor System

We now take a dip into history.

Frederick W. Taylor was a mechanical engineer who had worked as a machinist, foreman, and plant manager. He concluded from his experience that the supervisors and workers of his day (late nineteenth and early twentieth centuries) lacked the education needed to make various essential decisions, e.g., what work methods should be used, what constitutes a day's work, etc.

Taylor's remedy was to separate planning from execution. He assigned engineers and specialists to do the planning, and he left to the supervisor and workers the job of executing the plans.

Taylor's system achieved spectacular increases in productivity. The resulting publicity stimulated further application of his ideas. The outcome was

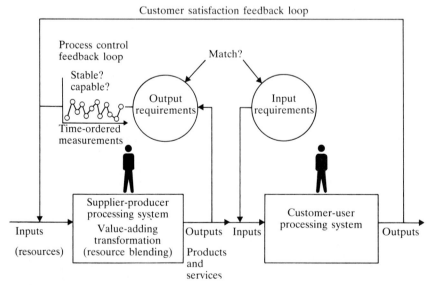

FIGURE 8.4
Processing system components necessary for quality performance. (*From QCH4, p. 10.24.*)

a widespread adoption of the concept of separating planning from execution. Through this adoption, the Taylor system (later called Scientific Management) became widely used and deeply rooted in the United States and, to a lesser degree, among the industrialized countries of the West.

Meanwhile, Taylor's major premise—lack of worker education—has been made obsolete by the remarkable rise in educational levels. As a consequence, the major *under*employed asset in the United States is the education, experience, and creativity of the work force. Other cultures, notably the Japanese, have found ways to employ this asset and have attained remarkable results.

The Taylor system is both a philosophy of management and an approach to worker motivation (through piecework incentives). The philosophy of separating planning from execution has endured, but motivation through piecework has been in a long-range decline.

The Taylor system, which is applied to both manufacturing and service industries, results in rigid definition and specialization of work for individuals, particularly at the work force level. The benefits have been offset by some negatives:

- Workers do not understand how their job contributes to the mission of the organization. Also, they often do not know their internal suppliers, their internal customers, and the associated needs.
- The work itself is often monotonous and meaningless and lacks a sense of accomplishment.
- Feedback to workers of the information they need to regulate the process is often inadequate or missing.
- Little opportunity is provided for workers to participate in quality improvement projects.

The time has come to reexamine the content and design of jobs. The concept of self-control provides a useful framework.

Self-Control and Job Design

Recall the concept of self-control (see Section 5.2, "Self-Control"). People must be provided with knowledge of what they are supposed to do, feedback on their performance, and the means of regulating their work in the event that they are failing to meet the goals. The lack of one or more of these three elements means that quality problems are management-controllable. (Generally, at least 80 percent of quality problems are management-controllable.) Placing workers in a state of self-control is a prerequisite to using behavioral approaches to motivate employees.

Some forms of job design will place workers in a greater degree of self-control. These are examined below.

Job Characteristics

Hackman and Oldham (1980) describe five characteristics of jobs that provide more meaningful and satisfying ("enriched") jobs for workers. These characteristics and the actions needed to enrich jobs are shown in Table 8.2. Approaches to the redesign of jobs include several forms of job enlargement. In horizontal job enlargement, the scope of a job is increased by having workers perform a larger variety of tasks. The extreme of horizontal job enlargement is for each worker to produce a complete product unit. In vertical job enlargement, the job is enlarged by having workers be responsible for tasks previously performed by others vertically higher in the organization (e.g., a supervisor).

Hackman and Oldham recommend caution on job redesign. They point out that most—but not all—people want a more demanding job. The opportunities are endless, but we must avoid placing employees in jobs to which they are not receptive or otherwise suited.

Self-Managing Teams

A special form of job enlargement is that applied to a group of workers, i.e., a self-managing team. Two elements are emphasized: (1) each worker is trained to have a variety of skills, thereby permitting rotation of tasks, and (2) the

TABLE 8.2
Job enrichment characteristics and management actions

Characteristic	Definition	Action
Skill variety	Degree to which the job has a sufficient variety of activities to require a diversity of employee skills and talents	Combine sequential tasks to produce larger work modules (horizontal enlargement)
Task identity	Extent to which work requires doing a job from beginning to end and results in a completed visible unit of output	Arrange work into meaningful groups, e.g., by customer, by product
Task significance	Extent to which the job impacts internal and external customers	Provide means of direct communication and personal contact with customer
Autonomy	Amount of employee self-control in planning and doing the work	Provide employee greater self-control for decision making (vertical enlargement)
Feedback	Degree to which direct knowledge of results is provided to employee	Create feedback systems to provide employees information directly from doing the job

Source: Adapted from Hackman and Oldham (1980).

team is given formal authority to execute certain job-planning and supervisory tasks (see Section 7.9, "Self-Managing Teams").

Empowerment

Empowerment is the process of delegating decision-making authority to lower levels within the organization. Particularly dramatic is empowerment of the work force. But empowerment goes far beyond delegating authority and providing additional training. It means encouraging people to take the initiative and broaden their scope; it also means being supportive if mistakes are made.

As employees became more empowered in their work, the feeling of ownership and responsibility becomes more meaningful. Further, the act of empowering employees provides evidence of management's trust. Additional evidence is provided when management shares confidential business information with employees. For many organizations, such steps are clearly a change in the culture.

The concept of empowerment applies both to individuals and to groups of workers. Self-managed teams (see Section 7.9, "Self-Managing Teams") provide an illustration of empowerment for groups of workers.

With empowerment comes the need to redefine the basic roles of upper management, middle management, and the work force. One model under consideration at a bank looks like this:

Upper management should act as shapers and coaches. As a shaper, it should create, communicate, and support the organization's mission. As a coach, it should help when asked but avoid entering into the day-to-day problems of middle management.

Middle management should not only run its area of responsibility but work as a group to integrate all parts of the organization. In addition, it must support the work force by eliminating obstacles to progress.

The *work force* is the primary producer of the output for customers. Its closeness and knowledge about its work means that it should use its empowerment to determine how the work can best be done.

Personal Commitment

Part of strategic quality management is establishing company quality goals and deploying them into subgoals and activities throughout the organization (see Section 6.5 under "Deployment of Goals"). Clear quality goals for individuals are important stimuli for inspiring superiority in quality. Odiorne (1987) presents a persuasive discussion on the importance of goal setting for individuals.

Selection and Training

Selection and training of personnel clearly have an important influence on people's development. Many of the principles are well known but are not always practiced with sufficient intensity. But this is changing in the United States. For example, some organizations are now making an annual investment in training of about 2 percent of sales income.

The Japanese have invested extensively in selection and training. Interviews and testing prior to employment assure compatibility of the candidate and the job. Rotational assignments then help to develop a broad base of technical skills, thus facilitating cooperation across departments. At the managerial level, rotational assignments help to develop the individual's concern for the company as a whole.

Sometimes the results of selection and training can have a dramatic effect on the customer. When McDonald's restaurants opened a site in Moscow, a Russian schoolteacher was so impressed with the workers that she remarked:

> What is killing us is that the average worker does not know how to work and so does not want to. Our enthusiasm has disappeared. But here my meal turned out to be just a supplement to the sincere smiles of the workers (Clines, 1990).

8.6 PROVIDE PARTICIPATION AS A MEANS OF INSPIRING ACTION

It is tempting to believe that, to inspire action on quality, we must start by changing the people's attitudes. A change in attitudes then should lead to a change in behavior. In reality, the opposite is true. If we first change people's behavior, then that will change their attitudes.

An age-old principle that helps to change behavior is the concept of participation. By personally participating in quality activities, people acquire new knowledge, see the benefits of the quality disciplines, and obtain a sense of accomplishment by solving problems. This participation leads to lasting changes in behavior.

Various forms of participation are described throughout this book. Table 8.3 summarizes these forms for levels from upper management to first-line supervisors and the work force.

Participation at *all* levels is decisive in inspiring action on quality. At the work force level, however, participation can have impacts that border on the dramatic. In conducting research on Quality Circles, some unforgettable events were observed (see Section 7.8, "Quality Circles").

Participation should include the officers of labor unions. Competitive economic challenges faced by most organizations require that management and unions find ways to work together for their mutual benefit. Important new forms of cooperation emerged during the 1980s (see Baker, 1988, for elaboration).

TABLE 8.3
Forms of participation

Form	Description	Upper management	Middle management	Specialists	First-line supervisors/ workers
Quality Council	Serve on the council	X			
Quality improvement teams	Serve as a leader or member of a cross-functional improvement team	X	X	X	X
Quality Circles	Serve as a leader or member of a circle within a department		X	X	X
Quality task forces	Serve on quality task forces appointed by the Quality Council	X	X	X	X
Process owner	Service as owner of a business process	X	X		
Design review	Participate in design review meetings		X	X	
Process review	Participate in process review meetings		X	X	X
Provide planning	Identify obstacles to self-control		X	X	X
Set quality goals	Provide input or set goals	X	X	X	X
Plan own work	Handle all aspects of planning	X	X	X	X
Customer visits	Hold discussions on quality with customers	X	X	X	X
Supplier visits	Hold discussions on quality with suppliers	X	X	X	X
Meetings with management	Make presentations on quality activities		X	X	X
Visit other companies	Learn about quality activities	X	X	X	X
Job rotation	Work in the Quality Department or other departments	X	X	X	X
Conferences	Make presentations or chair sessions	X	X	X	

8.7 PROVIDE RECOGNITION AND REWARDS

We define "recognition" as public acknowledgement of superior performance of specific activities. "Rewards" are benefits (such as salary increases, bonuses, and promotions) which are conferred for generally superior performance against goals.

Such expressions of esteem, which are discussed below, play an essential role in inspiring people on quality. An even more sustaining form is the positive feeling that people have internally when (1) their job has been designed to focus on self-development and (2) they are given opportunities to participate in planning and decision making. This tells employees that their skills, their judgment, and their integrity are trusted. Imagine their feeling when independent inspection is changed to self-inspection.

Recognition through public acknowledgement of superior activity can be provided at several levels—individuals, teams, and business units. In planning for recognition, here are some questions to address:

- What type of activity will receive formal recognition, e.g., normal *participation* in an activity such as Quality Circles, superior *effort,* or tangible *results*?
- Will recognition be given to individuals, to groups, or to both?
- Will selection of those to receive recognition be on a competitive or noncompetitive basis?
- What form will the recognition take, e.g., ceremonial, token award, or other?
- Who will decide on the form of recognition, e.g., a group of managers? Will others have input?
- Who will select the recipients, e.g., a management committee, peers of potential recipients, or someone else?
- How often will recognition be given? Many managers *overestimate* how often they provide recognition to employees.

As these questions apply to other activities (e.g., safety), experience is available in planning recognition.

Forms of Recognition

Forms of recognition range from a simple verbal message for a job well done (often overlooked in the rush of daily activities) to modest, or "token," awards. Token awards may be tangible (e.g., a savings bond, time off, a dinner) or intangible (a letter of praise, sending an employee to a seminar or conference, letting an employee be boss for a day).

Recognition must be genuine and must fit the local culture. Unfortunately, managers are sometimes naive about what best fits the culture. For example, each member of a quality team was given a shirt emblazoned with the name of the team. Some members, however, refused to accept the shirt—they viewed it as a "gimmick" that made a joke of their participation. In another case, a banquet was held for members of Quality Circles. The plant manager made some brief remarks thanking the employees for their efforts. An enjoyable evening was had by all. Employees were quite appreciative, but some of them remarked (constructively) that it was the first time they had ever seen the plant manager: "Wouldn't it be nice if he occasionally toured the production floor and spoke with everyone?" In deciding on forms of recognition, managers should ask for suggestions from respected work force employees. Not only will their ideas fit the culture better, but the act of asking for suggestions shows recognition of their judgment.

Sometimes, programs of recognition are more useful than monetary rewards. One organization reviewed the results of its suggestion system. About 800 suggestions were received each year; about 25 percent were accepted and received monetary rewards. But most people were dissatisfied—the winners said the decisions took too long and the monetary reward was too low; the others felt their suggestions should have been accepted. Under a new program, monetary awards were eliminated and replaced by a simple "thanks." Also, decisions on suggestions must be made within a short time interval. Under the new program, 7700 ideas are received annually and 60 percent are accepted.

Forms of Rewards

Rewards for quality-related activities are increasingly becoming part of the annual performance evaluation of middle managers, specialists, and first-line supervisors. One company has incorporated performance on improvement activities as a part of the annual appraisal of managers.

The highest rating for "improvement projects" requires a manager to demonstrate leadership of projects that achieved significant results and involved personnel who were from other organizational units of the company.

The concept of performance appraisal in general has come under scrutiny. Baird et al. (1988) analyze some of its weaknesses and provide recommendations for performance appraisal of quality activities. A key recommendation is the development of the employee (see Section 8.5).

The weakest area of quality motivation for managers is that of *improvement* of quality—for "breakthrough" to superior levels of performance. This weakness arises primarily because the problem of control—of meeting this year's goals—has a much higher priority.

Control sets its own priorities. When alarm bells ring, they demand corrective action then and there. The alarms must be heeded or the current goals will not be met. The manager wants to meet these current goals—managerial performance is judged mainly by measuring results against these goals. Fire fighters get the best rewards—they are the heroes. There may even be some arsonists.

In contrast, improvement of quality is not needed to meet this year's goals—it is needed to attain leadership in some future year, or at least to remain competitive. Hence, improvement can be deferred, whereas control cannot. Moreover, improvement to new levels requires special organizational machinery such as is described in Chapter 3. Such special machinery is not needed to maintain current control.

Upper management must change the reward system to inspire middle management to make breakthroughs to improved quality levels. A prerequisite, however, is for upper management to provide the infrastructure, resources, and training for such breakthroughs (see Chapters 3 and 7).

Texas Instruments measures the contribution to quality of every manager who has a profit-and-loss responsibility (Onnias, 1986). Managers are evaluated annually using four measures: leading indicators, concurrent indicators, lagging indicators, and the cost of quality. The first three refer to quality measures before, during, and after creation of a product or service. For example, the field complaint level is an example of a lagging indicator.

GTE California relates quality improvement to incentive compensation for both individuals and teams (Bowen, 1988). Team objectives which apply to "key performance units" and "companywide" have both quality and cost objectives. The weights assigned to the different levels and to cost and quality are shown in Figure 8.5.

The distribution of a monetary bonus may be related to quality. In one company, for each 1 percent increase in "customer satisfaction measure," a bonus is awarded.

Some organizations are developing "gain sharing" so that savings from improvement activities can be distributed. Typically, a formula defines the distribution to customers, employees, and the company. Gain sharing is a type of group incentive program. Ross and Hauck (1984) and Majerus (1984) are useful references. The latter provides a union leader's viewpoint.

8.8 TIME TO CHANGE THE CULTURE

Here are some words from the past: ". . . the really great problem involved in a change . . . consists in a complete revolution in the mental attitude and the habits of all of those engaged in the management, as well as the workmen . . . . The writer has over and over again warned those who contemplate making this change that it was a matter, even in a simple establishment, of from two to three years, and that in some cases it required from four to five years." That was Frederick Taylor in 1911, commenting on changing to a system of scientific management.

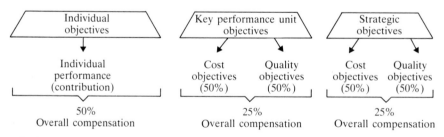

FIGURE 8.5
Incentive compensation. (*From Bowen, 1988.*)

SUMMARY

- To become superior in quality, we need to: (1) develop technologies to create products and processes which meet customer needs and (2) stimulate a culture that continually views quality as a primary goal.
- The culture for quality *can* be changed. We need to provide:
    Awareness of quality
    Evidence of upper management leadership
    Self-development and empowerment
    Participation
    Recognition and rewards
- These elements must be integrated with the methodologies and structure for quality.
- To change culture requires years, not months; to change quality requires trust, not techniques.

PROBLEMS

8.1. Consider an individual sport such as golf or racquetball. Apply the three principles of self-control to such a sport and decide if individuals are in a state of self-control. How does your conclusion relate to the design of jobs in an organization?

8.2. Prepare two lists to analyze the forces which have an impact on implementing quality improvement teams. One list should contain the restraining forces which are obstacles to implementing teams (e.g., lack of time); the other list should show the driving forces which can help (e.g., support by upper management). (This approach is part of a "force field analysis" or a "barriers and aids analysis.")

8.3. Look about your community to identify some of the ongoing drives or campaigns, such as for traffic safety, fund raising, political election, keep-your-city-clean, etc. For any campaign, analyze and report on:
(*a*) The methods used to secure attention
(*b*) The methods used to secure interest and identification with the program
(*c*) The methods used to secure action

8.4. For any organization known to you, study the prevailing continuing program of motivation for quality. Report your findings on (*a*) the ingredients of the program and (*b*) the organization's effectiveness in carrying out the various aspects of the program.

8.5. Develop three quality indicators for the performance of a buyer in a purchasing department: a lagging indicator, a concurrent indicator, and a leading indicator.

8.6. Tektronix, Inc. (1985) describes "people involvement" as moving through nine types of management (a "continuum"). These are: autocratic authoritarian management, directive command, selective information sharing, employee input, problem-solving groups, ad hoc task forces, participative decision making, work redesign and goal setting, and semiautonomous teams. For each of these types, describe in a few sentences the respective roles of managers and nonmanagers.

REFERENCES

Baird, Lloyd S., Richard W. Beatty, and Craig E. Schneier (1988). "What Performance Management Can Do for TQI," *Quality Progress*, March, pp. 28–32.

Baker, Edward M. (1988). "Managing Human Performance," in *Juran's Quality Control Handbook, Fourth Edition*, McGraw-Hill, Inc., New York, pp. 10.23–10.25.

Bowen, Michael D. (1988). "Quality Improvement Through Incentive Compensation," *Impro Conference Proceedings*, Juran Institute, Inc., Wilton, Connecticut, pp. 3A–21 to 3A–24.

Clines, Francis X. (1990). "Moscow McDonald's Opens: Milkshakes and Human Kindness," *The New York Times*, February 1.

Dietch, Robert, Steve Tashjian, and Howard Green (1989). "Leadership Characteristics and Culture Change: An Exploratory Research Study," *Impro Conference Proceedings*, Juran Institute, Inc., Wilton, Connecticut, pp. 3C–21 to 3C–29.

Hackman, J. R., and G. R. Oldham (1980). *Work Redesign*. Addison-Wesley, Reading, Massachusetts.

Herzberg, Frederick, Bernard Mausman, and B. Synderman (1959). *The Motivation to Work*, 2nd ed., John Wiley and Sons, New York.

Kilmann, Ralph H. (1989). *Managing Beyond the Quick Fix*, Jossey-Bass, San Francisco.

Majerus, R. E. (1984). "Workers Have a Right to Share Profits," *Harvard Business Review*, vol. 62, no. 5, pp. 42–50.

Maslow, A. H. (1987). *Motivation and Personality*, 3rd ed., Harper & Row, New York.

McGregor, Douglas (1985). *The Human Side of Enterprise*, McGraw-Hill, Inc., New York.

Odiorne, George S. (1987). *The Human Side of Management*, Lexington Books, Lexington, Massachusetts, Chapter 5.

Onnias, Arturo (1986). "The Quality Blue Book," *Juran Report Number Six*, Juran Institute, Inc., Wilton, Connecticut, pp. 127–131.

Peters, T. J., and R. A. Waterman, Jr. (1982). *In Search of Excellence*, Harper and Row, New York.

Ross, R. L., and W. C. Hauck (1984). "Gainsharing in the United States," *Industrial Management*, vol. 26, March–April, pp. 9–14.

Taylor, Frederick Winslow (1911). *Scientific Management*, Harper and Row, New York, p. 131.

Tektronix, Inc. (1985). "People Involvement: A Continuum," Tektronix, Inc., Beaverton, Oregon. All rights reserved. Reproduced with permission.

Warren, Jim (1989). "We Have Found the Enemy, It Is Us," *Annual Quality Congress Transactions*, American Society for Quality Control, Milwaukee, pp. 65–73.

SUPPLEMENTARY READING

Bringing about change:

Rybowiak, Joseph A. (1987). "The Role of Organizational and Cultural Change in Bringing about Quality Improvement," *Impro Conference Proceedings*, Juran Institute, Inc., Wilton, Connecticut, pp. 5B-11–5B-16.

Corporate culture: Miller, Lawrence M. (1984). *American Spirit*, William Morrow and Company, New York.

Leadership and goal setting: Stayer, Ralph (1990). "How I Learned to Let My Workers Lead," *Harvard Business Review*, November–December, pp. 66–69, 72–75, 80–83.

Managing human performance: QCH4, Section 10.

Herzberg, Frederick (1987). "One More Time—How Do You Motivate Employees?" *Harvard Business Review*, September–October, pp. 109–120.

CHAPTER
9

BASIC
PROBABILITY
CONCEPTS

9.1 STATISTICAL TOOLS IN QUALITY

Statistics is the collection, organization, analysis, interpretation, and presentation of data. The body of knowledge of statistical methods is an essential tool of the modern approach to quality. Without it, drawing conclusions about data becomes lucky at best and disastrous in some cases. The student is warned that statistics is just one of many *tools* necessary to solve quality problems.

9.2 THE CONCEPT OF VARIATION

The concept of *variation* states that no two items will be perfectly identical. Variation is a fact of nature and a fact of industrial life. For example, even "identical" twins vary slightly in height and weight at birth.

The dimensions of the contact window of a large-scale, integrated chip vary from chip to chip; cans of tomato soup vary slightly from can to can; the time required to assign a seat at an airline check-in counter varies from passenger to passenger. To disregard the existence of variation (or to rationalize falsely that it is small) can lead to incorrect decisions on major problems. Statistics helps to analyze data properly and draw conclusions, taking into account the existence of variation.

Data summarization can take several forms: tabular, graphical, and numerical. Sometimes, one form will provide a useful, complete summarization. In other cases, two or even three forms are needed for complete clarity.

9.3 TABULAR SUMMARIZATION OF DATA: FREQUENCY DISTRIBUTION

A *frequency distribution* is a tabulation of data arranged according to size. The raw data of the electrical resistance of 100 coils are given in Table 9.1. Table 9.2 shows the frequency distribution of these data with all measurements tabulated at their actual values. For examples, there were 14 coils each of which had a resistance of 3.35 ohms (Ω); there were 5 coils each of which had a resistance of 3.30 Ω. The frequency distribution spotlights where most of the data are grouped (the data are centered about a resistance of 3.35) and how much variation there is in the data (resistance runs from 3.27 to 3.44 Ω). Table 9.2 shows the conventional frequency distribution and the cumulative frequency distribution in which the frequency values are accumulated to show the number of coils with resistances equal to or less than a specific value. The particular problem determines whether the conventional or cumulative or both distributions are required.

When there are a large number of highly variable data, the frequency distribution can become too large to serve as a summary of the original data. The data may be grouped into *cells* to provide a better summary. Table 9.3 shows the frequency distribution for these data grouped into six cells, each 0.03 Ω wide. Grouping the data into cells condenses the original data, and therefore some detail is lost.

The following is a common procedure for constructing a frequency distribution:

1. Decide on the number of cells. Table 9.4 provides a guide.
2. Calculate the approximate cell interval i. The cell interval equals the largest observation minus the smallest observation divided by the number of cells. Round this result to some convenient number (preferably the nearest

TABLE 9.1
Resistance of 100 coils, Ω

3.37	3.34	3.38	3.32	3.33	3.28	3.34	3.31	3.33	3.34
3.29	3.36	3.30	3.31	3.33	3.34	3.34	3.36	3.39	3.34
3.35	3.36	3.30	3.32	3.33	3.35	3.35	3.34	3.32	3.38
3.32	3.37	3.34	3.38	3.36	3.37	3.36	3.31	3.33	3.30
3.35	3.33	3.38	3.37	3.44	3.32	3.36	3.32	3.29	3.35
3.38	3.39	3.34	3.32	3.30	3.39	3.36	3.40	3.32	3.33
3.29	3.41	3.27	3.36	3.41	3.37	3.36	3.37	3.33	3.36
3.31	3.33	3.35	3.34	3.35	3.34	3.31	3.36	3.37	3.35
3.40	3.35	3.37	3.35	3.32	3.36	3.38	3.35	3.31	3.34
3.35	3.36	3.39	3.31	3.31	3.30	3.35	3.33	3.35	3.31

TABLE 9.2
Tally of resistance values of 100 coils

Resistance, Ω	Tabulation	Frequency	Cumulative frequency
3.45			
3.44	|	1	1
3.43			
3.42			
3.41	||	2	3
3.40	||	2	5
3.39	||||	4	9
3.38	ЖІ	6	15
3.37	ЖІ |||	8	23
3.36	ЖІ ЖІ |||	13	36
3.35	ЖІ ЖІ ||||	14	50
3.34	ЖІ ЖІ ||	12	62
3.33	ЖІ ЖІ	10	72
3.32	ЖІ ||||	9	81
3.31	ЖІ ||||	9	90
3.30	ЖІ	5	95
3.29	|||	3	98
3.28	|	1	99
3.27	|	1	100
3.26			
Total		100	

uneven number with the same number of significant digits as the actual data).

3. Construct the cells by listing cell boundaries.

   (a) Each cell boundary should be to one more significant digit than the actual data and should end in a 5.

   (b) The cell interval should be constant throughout the entire frequency distribution.

TABLE 9.3
Frequency table of resistance values

Resistance, Ω	Frequency
3.415–3.445	1
3.385–3.415	8
3.355–3.385	27
3.325–3.355	36
3.295–3.325	23
3.265–3.295	5
Total	100

TABLE 9.4
Number of cells in frequency distribution

Number of observations	Recommended number of cells
20–50	6
51–100	7
101–200	8
201–500	9
501–1000	10
Over 1000	11–20

4. Tally each observation into the appropriate cell and then list the total frequency f for each cell.

This procedure should be adjusted when necessary to provide a clear summary of the data and to reveal the underlying pattern of variation.

9.4 GRAPHICAL SUMMARIZATION OF DATA: THE HISTOGRAM

A *histogram* is a vertical bar chart of a frequency distribution. Figure 9.1 shows the histogram for the electrical resistance data. Note that as in the frequency

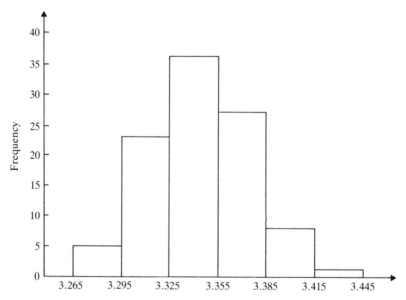

FIGURE 9.1
Histogram of resistance.

TABLE 9.5
Original data on wire break
strength

1. 346	6. 402	11. 368
2. 338	7. 635	12. 376
3. 323	8. 281	13. 311
4. 438	9. 431	14. 379
5. 398	10. 390	15. 216

distribution, the histogram highlights the center and amount of variation in the sample of data. The simplicity of construction and interpretation of the histogram makes it an effective tool in the elementary analysis of data.

Graphical methods are essential to effective data analysis and clear presentation of results. Many of these methods will be used throughout this book. More are available. Experienced practitioners are fascinated by the graphical tools, and rightly so. The vividness of a picture when compared to the cold logic of numbers has practical benefits, e.g. identifying subtle relationships and presenting results in clear form. Experience dictates that the first step in data analysis is: *Plot the data.*

An innovative variation of the histogram is the stem-and-leaf plot. Heyes (1985) presents data on wire break strength in grams (see Table 9.5) for supplier A. The corresponding stem-and-leaf plot is shown in Figure 9.2. Note that the stem is the first digit(s) of each value and the leaf is the remaining digits, e.g., for a value of 216, the stem is 2 and the leaf is 16. Note that this plot reveals the shape of the histogram but also makes it possible to regain the original values of the data.

9.5 BOX-AND-WHISKER PLOTS

A simple, clever, and effective way to summarize data is a box-and-whisker plot (usually called a boxplot). The boxplot is a graphical five-number

Stem	Leaf
2	16, 81
3	11, 23, 38, 46, 68, 76, 79, 90, 98
4	02, 31, 38
5	—
6	35

FIGURE 9.2
Stem-and-leaf plot. (*From Heyes, 1985.*)

TABLE 9.6
Ordered data on wire break strength

1. 216	6. 346	11. 398
2. 281	7. 368	12. 402
3. 311	8. 376	13. 431
4. 323	9. 379	14. 438
5. 338	10. 390	15. 635

summary of the data. In the basic (or "skeletal") boxplot, the five values are the median, maximum value, minimum value, first quartile, and third quartile. The quartiles are the values below which $^1\!/_4$ and $^3\!/_4$ of the observations lie.

Using the wire break strength data, the data are first arranged in rank order (see Table 9.6). The median is the middle value (the eighth rank, or 276). The extreme values are 216 and 635. The quartiles are 323 and 402 because those values divide the data into quarters. Figure 9.3 shows the resulting boxplot. The box, bounded by the two quartiles with the median inside the box, summarizes the middle part of the data. The lines extending out to the extreme values are the "whiskers." The longer whisker on the right suggests that the data include some values that are much larger than the other values. Also, the location of the median indicates that the values above the median are, as a group, closer to the median than the values below the median.

Innovative methods of graphical analysis and display of data are discussed in a now classic text by Tukey (1977). An excellent summary of graphical methods is presented in Wadsworth et al. (1986, Chapter 9).

9.6 QUANTITATIVE METHODS OF SUMMARIZING DATA: NUMERICAL INDICES

Data can also be summarized by computing (1) a measure of central tendency to indicate where most of the data are centered, and (2) the measure of

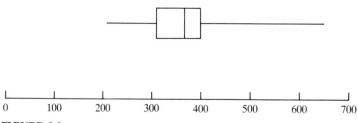

FIGURE 9.3
Boxplot. (*From Heyes, 1985.*)

dispersion to indicate the amount of scatter in the data. Often, these two measures provide an adequate summary.

The key measure of the central tendency is the arithmetic *mean*, or *average*. The definition of the average is

$$\bar{X} = \frac{\Sigma X}{n}$$

where $\bar{X}$ = sample mean
$\quad X$ = individual observations
$\quad n$ = number of observations
$\quad \Sigma$ = summation

Another measure of central tendency is the median—the middle value when the data are arranged according to size. The median is useful for reducing the effects of extreme values or for data that can be ranked but are not easily measurable, such as color or visual appearance.

Two measures of dispersion are commonly calculated. When the amount of data is small (ten or fewer observations), the *range* is useful. The range is the difference between the maximum value and the minimum value in the data. As the range is based on only two values, it is not as useful when the number of observations is large.

In general, the *standard deviation* is the most useful measure of dispersion. Like the mean, the definiton of the standard deviation is a formula:

$$s = \sqrt{\frac{\Sigma (X - \bar{X})^2}{n - 1}}$$

where s is the sample standard deviation. The square of the standard deviation, s^2, is called the *variance*.

There is usually difficulty in understanding the "meaning" of the standard deviation. The only definition is a formula. There is no hidden meaning to the standard deviation, and it is best viewed as an index which shows the amount of variation in a set of data. Later applications of the standard deviation to making predictions will help clarify its meaning.

With data in frequency distribution form, shortcut calculations can be employed to find the average and the standard deviation (see QCH4, pages 23.17, 23.18).

A problem that sometimes arises in the summarization of data is that one or more extreme values are far from the rest of the data. A simple (but not necessarily correct) solution is available. Drop such values. The reasoning is that a measurement error or some other unknown factor makes the values "unrepresentative." Unfortunately, this may be rationalizing to eliminate an annoying problem of data analysis. The decision to keep or discard extreme values rests with the investigator. However, statistical tests are available to help make the decision (see QCH4, pages 23.9–23.12).

9.7 PROBABILITY DISTRIBUTIONS: GENERAL

A distinction is made between a sample and a population. A *sample* is a limited number of items taken from a larger source. A *population* is a large source of items from which the sample is taken. Measurements are made on the items. Many problems are solved by taking the measurement results from a sample and, based on these results, making predictions about the defined *population* containing the sample. It is usually assumed that the sample is a random one; i.e., each possible sample of n items has an equal chance of being selected (or the items are selected systematically from material that is itself random due to mixing during processing).

Distribution	Form	Probability function	Comments on application
Normal	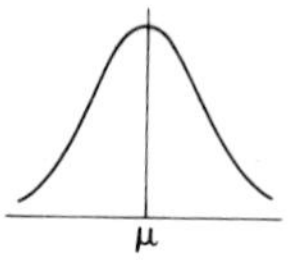	$y = \dfrac{1}{\sigma\sqrt{2\pi}} e^{-\frac{(X-\mu)^2}{2\sigma^2}}$ μ = Mean σ = Standard deviation	Applicable when there is a concentration of observations about the average and it is equally likely that observations will occur above and below the average. Variation in observations is usually the result of many small causes.
Exponential	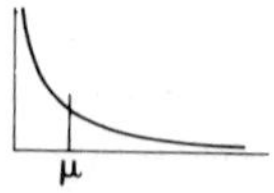	$y = \dfrac{1}{\mu} e^{-\frac{x}{\mu}}$	Applicable when it is likely that more observations will occur below the average than above.
Weibull	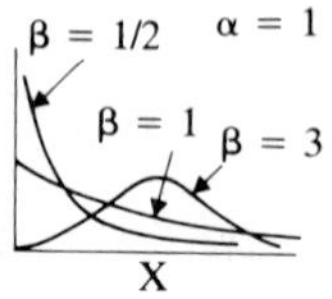	$y = \alpha\beta(X - \gamma)^{\beta-1} e^{-\alpha(X-\gamma)^\beta}$ α = Scale parameter β = Shape parameter γ = Location parameter	Applicable in describing a wide variety of patterns in variation, including departures from the normal and exponential.
Poisson*	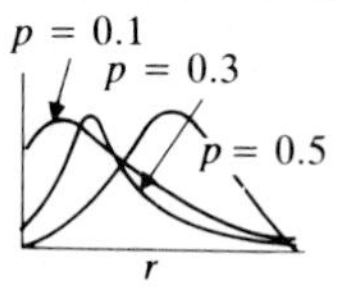	$y = \dfrac{(np)^r e^{-np}}{r!}$ n = Number of trials r = Number of occurrences p = Probability of occurrence	Same as binomial but particularly applicable when there are many opportunities for occurrence of an event, but a low probability (less than 0.10) on each trial.
Binomial*	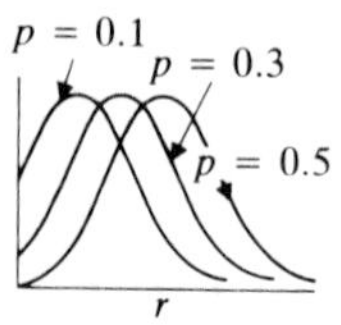	$y = \dfrac{n!}{r!(n-r)!} p^r q^{n-r}$ n = Number of trials r = Number of occurrences p = Probability of occurrence $q = 1-p$	Applicable in defining the probability of r occurrences in n trials of an event which has a constant probability of occurrence on each indepedent trial.

FIGURE 9.4
Summary of common probability distributions. (Asterisks indicate that these are discrete distributions, but the curves are shown as continuous for ease of comparison with the continuous distributions.)

A *probability distribution function* is a mathematical formula that relates the values of the characteristic with their probability of occurrence in the population. The collection of these probabilities is called a *probability distribution*. Some distributions and their functions are summarized in Figure 9.4. Distributions are of two types:

1. *Continuous* (for "variables" data). When the characteristic being measured can take on any value (subject to the fineness of the measuring process), its probability distribution is called a continuous probability distribution. For example, the probability distribution for the resistance data of Table 9.4 is an example of a continuous probability distribution because the resistance could have any value, limited only by the fineness of the measuring instrument. Experience has shown that most continuous characteristics follow one of several common probability distributions, i.e., the normal distribution, the exponential distribution, and the Weibull distribution. These distributions find the probabilities associated with occurrences of the *actual values* of the characteristic. Other continuous distributions (e.g., *t, F,* and chi square) are important in data analysis but are not helpful in directly predicting the probability of occurrence of actual values.
2. *Discrete* (for "attributes" data). When the characteristic being measured can take on only certain specific values (e.g., integers 0, 1, 2, 3, etc.), its probability distribution is called a discrete probability distribution. For example, the distribution for the number of defectives *r* in a sample of five items is a discrete probability distribution because *r* can only be 0, 1, 2, 3, 4, or 5. The common discrete distributions are the Poisson and binomial (see Figure 9.4).

The following paragraphs explain how probability distributions can be used with a sample of observations to make predictions about the larger population. Such predictions assume that the data come from a process that is stable over time. Sometimes this is not the case. Plotting the data points in order of production provides a rough test for stability; plotting the data on a statistical control chart provides a rigorous test (see Chapter 17, "Statistical Process Control").

9.8 THE NORMAL PROBABILITY DISTRIBUTION

Many engineering characteristics can be approximated by the *normal distribution function*:

$$y = \frac{1}{\sigma\sqrt{2\pi}} e^{-(X-\mu)^2/2\sigma^2}$$

where $e = 2.718$
$\pi = 3.141$
μ = population mean
σ = population standard deviation

Problems are solved with a table, but note that the distribution requires only the average μ and standard deviation σ of the population.[1] The curve for the normal probability distribution is related to a frequency distribution and its histogram. As the sample becomes larger and larger and the width of each cell becomes smaller and smaller, the histogram approaches a smooth curve. If the entire population were measured and if it were normally distributed, the result would be as shown in Figure 9.4. Thus the *shape* of a histogram of sample data provides some indication of the probability distribution for the population. If the histogram resembles[2] the "bell" shape shown in Figure 9.4, this is a basis for assuming that the population follows a normal probability distribution.

Making Predictions Using the Normal Probability Distribution

Predictions require just two estimates and a table. The estimates are:

$$\text{Estimate of } \mu = \bar{X} \qquad \text{Estimate of } \sigma = s$$

The calculations of the sample $\bar{X}$ and s are made by the methods previously discussed.

For example, from past experience, a manufacturer concludes that the burnout time of a particular light bulb follows a normal distribution. A sample of 50 bulbs has been tested and the average life found to be 60 days with a standard deviation of 20 days. How many bulbs in the entire population of light bulbs can be expected to be still working after 100 days of life?

The problem is to find the area under the curve beyond 100 days (see Figure 9.5). The area under a distribution curve between two stated limits represents the probability of occurrence. Therefore, the area beyond 100 days is the probability that a bulb will last more than 100 days. To find the area, calculate the difference Z between a particular value and the average of the curve in units of standard deviation:

$$Z = \frac{X - \mu}{\sigma}$$

---

[1] Unless otherwise indicated, Greek symbols will be used for population values and Roman symbols for sample values.

[2] It is *not* necessary that the sample histogram look as if it came from a normal population. The assumption of normality is applied only to the population. Small deviations from normality are expected in random samples.

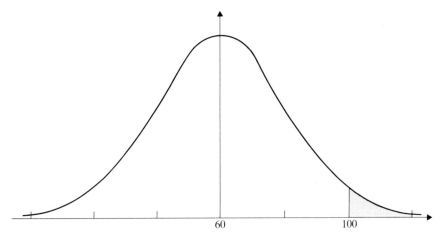

FIGURE 9.5
Distribution of light bulb life.

In this problem $Z = (100 - 60) \div 20 = +2.0$. Table A in the Appendix shows a probability of 0.9773 for $Z = 2$. The statistical distribution tables in this edition provide probabilities that cover the span from $-\infty$ up to and including the value of X included in the formula (i.e., cumulative probabilities). Thus 0.9773 is the probability that a bulb will last 100 days or less. The normal curve is symmetrical about the average and the total area is 1.000. The probability of a bulb lasting more than 100 days then is $1.0000 - 0.9773$, or 0.0227, or 2.27 percent of the bulbs in the population will still be working after 100 days.

Similarly, if a characteristic is normally distributed and if estimates of the average and standard deviation of the population are obtained, this method can estimate the total percentage of production that will fall within engineering specification limits.

Figure 9.6 shows representative areas under the normal distribution curve. Thus 68.26 percent of the *population* will fall between the average of the population plus or minus 1 standard deviation of the population, 95.46 percent of the population will fall between the average of $\pm 2\sigma$, and finally, $\pm 3\sigma$ will include 99.73 percent of the population. The percentage of a *sample* within a set of limits can be quite different from the percentage within the same limits in the population.

9.9 THE NORMAL CURVE AND HISTOGRAM ANALYSIS

As many manufacturing processes produce results which reasonably follow a normal distribution, it is useful to combine the histogram concept and the normal curve concept to yield a practical working tool known as *histogram analysis*.

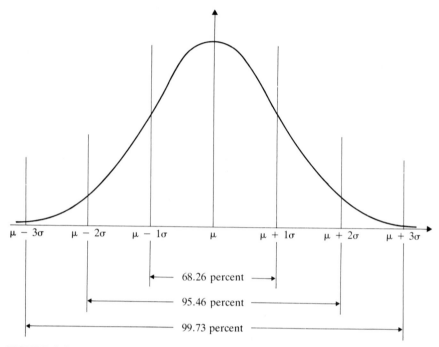

FIGURE 9.6
Areas of the normal curve (derived from Appendix, Table A).

A random sample is selected from the process and measurements are made for the selected quality characteristics. A histogram is prepared and specification limits are added. Knowledge of the manufacturing process is then combined with insights provided by the histogram to draw conclusions about the ability of the process to meet the specifications.

Figure 9.7 shows 16 typical histograms. The student is encouraged to interpret each of these pictures by asking two questions:

1. Does the process have the ability to meet the specification limits?
2. What action on the process, if any, is appropriate?

These questions can be answered by analyzing:

1. *The centering of the histogram.* This defines the aim of the process.
2. *The width of the histogram.* This defines the variability about the aim.
3. *The shape of the histogram.* When a normal or bell-shaped curve is expected, then any significant deviation or other aberration is usually caused by a manufacturing (or other) condition that may be the root of the quality problem. For example, histograms with two or more peaks may reveal that several "populations" have been mixed together.

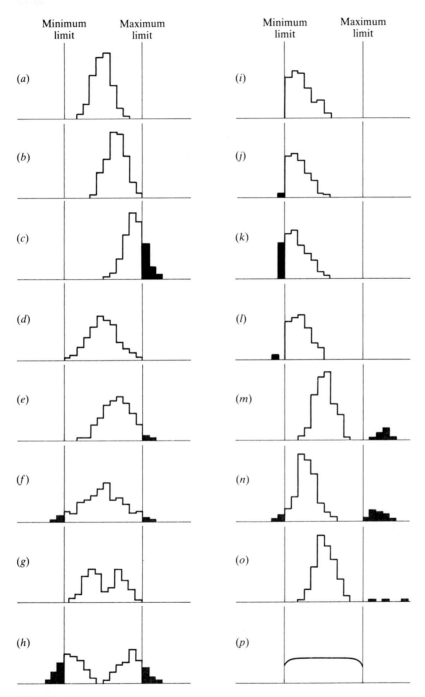

FIGURE 9.7
Distribution patterns related to tolerances. (*Adapted from Armstrong and Clarke, 1946.*)

Histograms illustrate how variables data provide much more information than do attributes data. For example, Figure 9.7*b, d, g,* and *i* warn of potential trouble even though all units in the sample are within the specification limits. With attributes measurement, all the units would simply be classified as acceptable and the inspection report would have stated "50 inspected, 0 defective"—therefore no problem. One customer had a dramatic experience based on a lot which yielded a sample histogram similar to Figure 9.7*i*. Although the sample indicated that the lot met quality requirements, the customer realized that the supplier must have made much scrap and screened it out before delivery. A rough calculation indicated that full production must have been about 25 percent defective. The histogram enabled the customer to deduce this *without ever having been inside the supplier's plant.* Note how the "product tells on the process." As the customer would eventually pay for this scrap (in the selling price), he wanted the situation corrected. The supplier was contacted and advice was offered in a constructive manner.

As a general rule, at least 50 measurements are needed for the histogram to reveal the basic pattern of variation. Histograms based on too few measurements can lead to incorrect conclusions, because the shape of the histogram may be incomplete without the observer realizing it. Note that the discussion here is based on the assumption of normality.

Histograms have limitations. Since the samples are taken at random rather than in the order of manufacture, the time-to-time process trends during manufacture are not disclosed. Hence the seeming central tendency of a histogram may be illusory—the process may have drifted substantially. In like manner, the histogram does not disclose whether the supplier's process was operating at its best, i.e., whether it was in a state of statistical control (see Chapter 17, "Statistical Process Control").

In spite of these shortcomings, the histogram is an effective analytical tool. The key to its usefulness is its simplicity. It speaks a language that everyone understands—comparison of product measurements against specification limits. To draw useful conclusions from this comparison requires little experience in interpreting frequency distributions and no formal training in statistics. The experience soon expands to include applications in development, manufacturing, supplier relations, and field data.

9.10   THE EXPONENTIAL PROBABILITY DISTRIBUTION

The *exponential probability function is*

$$y = \frac{1}{\mu} e^{-X/\mu}$$

Figure 9.4 shows the shape of an exponential distribution curve. Note that the normal and exponential distributions have distinctly different shapes. An examination of the tables of areas shows that 50 percent of a normally distributed population occurs above the mean value and 50 percent below. In an exponential population, 36.8 percent is above the mean and 63.2 percent below the mean. This refutes the intuitive idea that the mean is always associated with a 50 percent probability. The exponential describes the loading pattern for some structural members because smaller loads are more numerous than are larger loads. The exponential is also useful in describing the distribution of failure times of complex equipments. Note the ski jump shape of the curve.

Making Predictions Using the Exponential Probability Distribution

Predictions based on an exponentially distributed population require only an estimate of the population mean. For example, the time between successive failures of a complex piece of repairable equipment is measured and the resulting histogram is found to resemble the exponential probability curve. For the measurements made, the *mean time between failures* (commonly called MTBF) is 100 hours. What is the probability that the time between two successive failures of this equipment will be at least 20 hours?

The problem is one of finding the area under the curve beyond 20 hours (Figure 9.8). Table B in the Appendix gives the area under the curve beyond any particular value X that is substituted in the ratio X/μ. In this problem,

$$\frac{X}{\mu} = \frac{20}{100} = 0.20$$

From Table B the area under the curve beyond 20 hours is 0.8187. The probability that the time between two successive failures is greater than 20

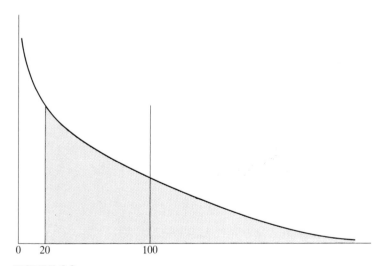

FIGURE 9.8
Distribution of time between failures.

hours is 0.8187; i.e., there is about an 82 percent chance that the equipment will operate without failure continuously for 20 or more hours. Similar calculations would give a probability of 0.9048 for 10 or more hours.

9.11   THE WEIBULL PROBABILITY DISTRIBUTION

The *Weibull distribution* is a family of distributions having the general function

$$y = \alpha\beta(X - \gamma)^{\beta-1}e^{-\alpha(X-\gamma)\beta}$$

where α = scale parameter
β = shape parameter
γ = location parameter

The curve of the function (Figure 9.4) varies greatly depending on the numerical values of the parameters. Most important is the shape parameter β, which reflects the pattern of the curve. Note that when β is 1.0, the Weibull function reduces to the exponential and that when β is about 3.5 (and $\alpha = 1$ and $\gamma = 0$), the Weibull closely approximates the normal distribution. In practice, β varies from about $\frac{1}{3}$ to 5. The scale parameter α is related to the peakedness of the curve; i.e., as α changes, the curve becomes flatter or more peaked. The location parameter γ is the smallest possible value of X. This is often assumed to be 0, thereby simplifying the equation. It is often unnecessary to determine the values of these parameters because predictions are made directly from Weibull probability paper, but King (1981) gives procedures for graphically finding α, β, and γ. Appendix, Table J provides a sample of Weibull paper. With this sample paper, β can be estimated by drawing a line parallel to the line of best fit and through the point circled on the vertical scale at 40.0. Then, the intersection with the arc gives an estimate of β. For an example, see Section 21.4, "Analyzing Field Data."

The Weibull covers many shapes of distributions. This makes it popular in practice because it reduces the problems of examining a set of data and deciding which of the common distributions (e.g., normal or exponential) fits best.

Making Predictions Using the Weibull Probability Distribution

An analytical approach for the Weibull distribution (even with tables) is cumbersome, and the predictions are usually made with Weibull probability paper. For example, seven heat-treated shafts were stress-tested until each of them failed. The fatigue life (in terms of number of cycles to failure) was as follows:

11,251	40,122
17,786	46,638
26,432	52,374
28,811	

The problem is to predict the percentage of failure of the population for various values of fatigue life. The solution is to plot the data on Weibull paper, observe if the points fall approximately in a straight line, and if so, read the probability predictions (percentage of failure) from the graph.

In a Weibull plot, the original data are usually[3] plotted against *mean ranks*. (Thus the mean rank for the *i*th value in a sample of *n* ranked observations refers to the mean value of the percentage of the population that would be less than the *i*th value in repeated experiments of size *n*.) The mean rank is calculated as $i/(n + 1)$. The mean ranks necessary for this example are based on a sample size of seven failures and are as shown in Table 9.7. The cycles to failure are now plotted on the Weibull graph paper against the corresponding values of the mean rank (see Figure 9.9). These points fall approximately in a straight line, so it is assumed that the Weibull distribution applies. The vertical axis gives the cumulative percentage of failures in the population corresponding to the fatigue life shown on the horizontal axis. For example, about 50 percent of the population of shafts will fail in fewer than 32,000 cycles. About 80 percent of the population will fail in fewer than 52,000 cycles. By appropriate subtractions, predictions can be made of the percentage of failures between any two fatigue life limits.

It is tempting to extrapolate on probability paper, particularly to predict life. For example, suppose that the minimum fatigue life were specified as 8000 cycles and the seven measurements displayed earlier were from tests conducted to evaluate the ability of the design to meet 8000 cycles. As all

TABLE 9.7
Table of mean ranks

Failure number (*i*)	Mean rank
1	0.125
2	0.250
3	0.375
4	0.500
5	9.625
6	0.750
7	0.875

---

[3] There are other plotting positions (see, e.g., QCH4, page 23.35).

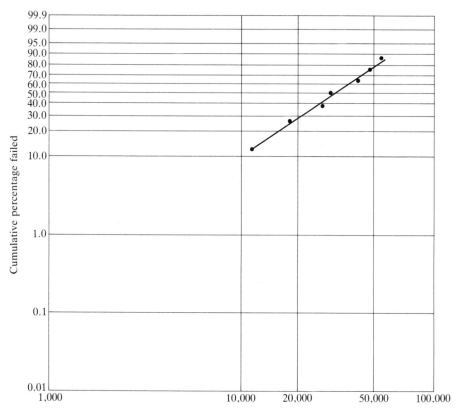

FIGURE 9.9
Distribution of fatigue life.

seven tests exceeded 8000 cycles, the design seems adequate and should therefore be released for production. However, extrapolation on the Weibull paper predicts that about 5 percent of the *population* of shafts would fail in less than 8000 cycles. This suggests a review of the design before release to production. Thus the small *sample* (all *within* specifications) gives a deceptive result, but the Weibull plot acts as an alarm signal by highlighting a potential problem.

Extrapolation can go in the other direction. Note that a probability plot of life-test data does *not* require that all tests be completed before the plotting starts. As each unit fails, the failure time can be plotted against the mean rank. If the early points appear to be following a straight line, it is tempting to draw in the line *before* all tests are finished. The line can then be extrapolated beyond the actual test data and life predictions can be made without accumulating a large amount of test time. The approach has been applied to predicting *early* in a warranty period the "vital few" components of a complex product that will be most troublesome. However, extrapolation has dangers. It requires the judicious melding of statistical theory and engineering experience and judgment.

To make a valid Weibull plot, at least seven points are needed. Any fewer casts doubt on the ability of the plot to reveal the underlying pattern of variation. When the plot is prepared, it is hoped that the points will approximate a straight line. This then implies a single stable population and the line can be used for predictions. However, non-straight-line plots are often extremely valuable (in the same way as nonnormal histograms) in suggesting that several populations have been mixed together.

Probability graph paper is available for the normal, exponential, Weibull, and other probability distributions.[4] Although the mathematical functions and tables provide the same information, the graph paper reveals *relationships* between probabilities and values of X that are not readily apparent from the calculations. For example, the reduction in percentage defective in a population as a function of wider and wider tolerance limits can be easily portrayed by the graph paper.

9.12 THE POISSON PROBABILITY DISTRIBUTION

If the probability of occurrence p of an event is constant on each of n independent trials of the event, the probability of r occurrences in n trials is

$$\frac{(np)^r e^{-np}}{r!}$$

where n = number of trials
p = probability of occurrence
r = number of occurrences

Making Predictions Using the Poisson Distribution

The Poisson is useful in calculating probabilities associated with sampling procedures. Appendix C directly gives cumulative Poisson probabilities, i.e., the probability of r or fewer occurrences in n trials of an event having probability p. For example, suppose that a lot of 300 units of product is submitted by a vendor whose past quality has been about 2 percent defective. A random sample of 40 units is selected from the lot. Table C in the Appendix provides the probability of r or fewer defectives in a sample of n units. Entering the table with a value of np equal to 40(0.02), or 0.8, for various values of r results in Table 9.8. Individual probabilities can be found by

---

[4] One source is Technical and Engineering Aids for Management, Box 25, Tamworth, NH 03886.

TABLE 9.8
Table of Poisson probabilities

r	Probability of r or fewer in sample
0	0.449
1	0.809
2	0.953
3	0.991
4	0.999
5	1.000

subtracting cumulative probabilities. Thus the probability of exactly 2 defectives is $0.953 - 0.809$, or 0.144. Of course, the probabilities in Table 9.8 could also be found by substituting into the formula six times ($r = 0, 1, 2, 3, 4, 5$).

The Poisson is an approximation to more exact distributions and applies when the sample size is at least 16, the population size is at least 10 times the sample size, and the probability of occurrence p on each trial is less than 0.1. These conditions are often met.

The Poisson is not just an approximation. It can be used as an exact distribution in cases where an event has many opportunities to occur but where the probability of occurrence of any opportunity is extremely unlikely.

9.13   THE BINOMIAL PROBABILITY DISTRIBUTION

If the conditions of the Poisson distribution are not met, the binomial distribution may be applicable. If the probability of occurrence p of an event is constant on each of n independent trials of the event, then the probability of r occurrences in n trials is:

$$\frac{n!}{r!(n-r)!}p^r q^{n-r}$$

where $q = 1 - p$.

In practice, the assumption of a constant probability of occurrence is considered reasonable when the population size is at least 10 times the sample size.[5] (Note that the binomial has fewer conditions than the Poisson.)

Tables for the binomial are available (QCH4, Appendix II, pp. 14–15).

---

[5] Under this condition, the change in probability from one trial to the next is negligible. If this condition is not met, the hypergeometric distribution should be used (QCH4, page 23.28).

TABLE 9.9
Table of binomial probabilities

r	P (exactly r defectives in 6) $= [6!/r!(6-r)!](0.05)^r(0.95)^{6-r}$
0	0.7351
1	0.2321
2	0.0306
3	0.0021
4	0.0001
5	0.0000
6	0.0000

Making Predictions Using the Binomial Probability Distribution

A lot of 100 units of product is submitted by a vendor whose past quality has been about 5 percent defective. A random sample of 6 units is selected from the lot. The probabilities of various sample results are given in Table 9.9.

In using the formula, note that $0! = 1$.

9.14 BASIC THEOREMS OF PROBABILITY

Probability is expressed as a number which lies between 1.0 (certainty that an event will occur) and 0.0 (impossibility of occurrence).

A convenient definition of probability is one based on a frequency interpretation: If an event A can occur in s cases out of a total of n possible and equally probable cases, the probability that the event will occur is

$$P(A) = \frac{s}{n} = \frac{\text{number of successful cases}}{\text{total number of possible cases}}$$

Example 9.1. A lot consists of 100 parts. A single part is selected at random, and thus each of the 100 parts has an equal chance of being selected. Suppose that a lot contains a total of 8 defectives. Then the probability of drawing a single part that is defective is then 8/100, or 0.08.

The following theorems are useful in solving problems:

Theorem 9.1. If $P(A)$ is the probability that an event A will occur, then the probability that A will not occur is $1 - P(A)$.

Theorem 9.2. If A and B are two events, then the probability that either A or B will occur is

$$P(A \text{ or } B) = P(A) + P(B) - P(A \text{ and } B)$$

A special case of this theorem occurs when A and B cannot occur simultaneously (i.e., A and B are *mutually exclusive*). Then the probability that either A or B will occur is

$$P(A \text{ or } B) = P(A) + P(B)$$

Example 9.2. The probability of r defectives in a sample of 6 units from a 5 percent defective lot was previously found by the binomial. The probability of 0 defectives was 0.7351; the probability of 1 defective was 0.2321. The probability of 0 or 1 defective is then $0.7351 + 0.2321$, or 0.9672.

Theorem 9.3. If A and B are two events, then the probability that events A and B occur together is

$$P(A \text{ and } B) = P(A) \times P(B \mid A)$$

where $P(B \mid A)$ = probability that B will occur assuming A has already occurred.

A special case of this theorem occurs when the two events are independent, i.e., when the occurrence of one event has no influence on the probability of the other event. If A and B are independent, then the probability of both A and B occurring is

$$P(A \text{ and } B) = P(A) \times P(B)$$

Example 9.3. A complex system consists of two major subsystems that operate independently. The probability of successful performance of the first subsystem is 0.95; the corresponding probability for the second subsystem is 0.90. Both subsystems must operate successfully in order to achieve total system success. The probability of the successful operation of the total system is therefore $0.95 \times 0.90 = 0.855$.

The theorems above have been stated in terms of two events but can be expanded for any number of events.

SUMMARY

- Statistical methods are essential in the modern approach to quality.
- Variation is a fact of nature and a fact of industrial life.
- In summarizing data, useful tabular and graphical tools include the frequency distribution, histogram, boxplot, and probability paper.
- In summarizing data, useful numerical indices include the average, median, range, and standard deviation.
- A sample is a limited number of items taken from a larger source called the population.
- A probability distribution function relates the values of a characteristic to their probability of occurrence in the population.

- The important continuous probability distributions are the normal, exponential, and Weibull; important discrete distributions are the Poisson and binomial.
- Three theorems of probability are basic in analyzing the probability of specific events.

PROBLEMS

Note: Many of the statistical problems in the book have intentionally been stated in industrial language. Thus the specific statistical technique required will often *not* be specified. Hopefully, the student will then gain some experience in translating the industrial problem into a statistical formulation and then choosing the appropriate statistical technique.

9.1. The following data consist of 80 potency measurements of the drug streptomycin.

4.1	5.0	2.0	2.6	4.5	8.1	5.7	2.5
3.5	6.3	5.5	1.6	6.1	5.9	9.3	4.2
4.9	5.6	3.8	4.4	7.1	4.6	7.4	3.5
4.9	5.1	4.6	6.3	8.3	6.3	8.8	1.0
5.3	5.4	4.4	2.9	7.5	5.7	5.3	3.0
4.2	5.2	7.0	3.7	6.7	5.8	6.9	2.8
6.0	8.2	6.1	7.3	8.2	6.2	4.3	2.2
5.2	5.5	3.5	7.1	7.9	5.6	5.4	3.9
6.8	8.2	4.2	4.2	5.5	6.2	3.5	3.4
6.8	4.7	4.6	4.1	4.7	5.0	3.4	7.1

(*a*) Summarize the data in tabular form.
(*b*) Summarize the data in graphical form.

9.2. Compute a measure of central tendency and two measures of variation for the data given in Problem 9.1. Calculate the following three sets of limits: $\bar{X} \pm 1s$, $\bar{X} \pm 2s$, $\bar{X} \pm 3s$. For each set, calculate the percentage of data values that fall within the limits. Compare these percentages to the theoretical percentages based on the normal distribution.

9.3. Examine the histograms in Figure 9.7. For each histogram, comment on (*a*) the ability of the process to meet specification limits and (*b*) what action, if any, on the process is appropriate.

9.4. Heyes (1985) presents the following data on the wire break strength for supplier *B*:

470	425	438	620	452
573	382	486	526	300
520	450	389	371	598

Prepare a boxplot for this data.

9.5. A company has a filling machine for low-pressure oxygen shells. Data collected over the past 2 months show an average weight after filling of 1.433 g with a standard deviation of 0.033 g. The specification for weight is 1.460 ± 0.085 g. Weight is normally distributed.

(*a*) What percentage will not meet the weight specification?

(*b*) Would you suggest a shift in the aim of the filling machine? Why or why not?

9.6. A company that makes fasteners has government specifications on a self-locking nut. The locking torque has both a maximum and a minimum specified. The offsetting machine used to make these nuts has been producing nuts with an average locking torque of 8.62 in-lb, and a variance σ^2 of 4.49 in-lb. Torque is normally distributed.

(*a*) If the upper specification is 13.0 in-lb and the lower specification is 2.25 in-lb, what percent of these nuts will meet the specification limits?

(*b*) Another machine in the offset department can turn out the nuts with an average of 8.91 in-lb and a standard deviation of 2.33 in–lb. In a lot of 1000 nuts, how many would have too high a torque?

Answer: (*a*) 97.95 percent.   (*b*) 40 nuts.

9.7. A power company defines service continuity as providing electric power within specified frequency and voltage limits to the customer's service entrance. Interruption of this service may be caused by equipment malfunctions or line outages due to planned maintenance or to unscheduled reasons. Records for the entire city indicate that there were 416 unscheduled interruptions in 1967 and 503 in 1966.

(*a*) Calculate the mean time between unscheduled interruptions, assuming that power is to be supplied continuously.

(*b*) What is the chance that power will be supplied to all users without interruption for at least 24 h? For at least 48 h? Assume an exponential distribution.

9.8. An analysis was made of repair time for an electrohydraulic servovalve used in fatigue test equipment. Discussions concluded that about 90 percent of all repairs could be made within 6 h.

(*a*) Assuming an exponential distribution of repair time, calculate the average repair time.

(*b*) What is the probability that a repair would take between 3 and 6 h?

Answer: (*a*) 2.6 h. (*b*) 0.217.

9.9. Three designs of a certain shaft are to be compared. The information on the designs is summarized as:

	Design I	Design II	Design III
Material	Medium-carbon alloy steel	Medium-carbon unalloyed steel	Low-carbon special analysis steel
Process	Fully machined before heat treatment, then furnace-heated, oil-quenched, and tempered	Fully machined before heat treatment, then induction-scan-heated, water-quenched, and tempered	Fully machined before heat treatment, then furnace-heated, water-quenched, and tempered

	Design I	Design II	Design III
Equipment cost	Already available	$125,000	$500
Cost of finished shaft	$57	$53	$55

Fatigue tests were run on six shafts of each design with the following results (in units of thousands of cycles to failure):

I	II	III
180	210	900
240	360	1400
100	575	1500
50	330	340
220	130	850
110	575	600

(a) Rearrange the data in ascending order and make a Weibull plot for each design.

(b) For each design, estimate the number of cycles at which 10 percent of the population will fail. (This is called the B_{10} life.) Do the same for 50 percent of the population.

(c) Calculate the average life for each design based on the test results. Then estimate the percentage of the population that will fail within this average life. Note that it is not 50 percent.

(d) Comment on replacing the current design I with II or III.

9.10. Life tests on a sample of 5 units were conducted to evaluate a component design before release to production. The units failed at the following times:

Unit number	Failure time, h
1	1200
2	1900
3	2800
4	3500
5	4500

Suppose that the component was guaranteed to last 1000 h. Any failures during this period must be replaced by the manufacturer at a cost of $200 for each component. Although the number of test data is small, management wants an estimate of the cost of replacements. If 4000 of these components are sold, provide a dollar estimate of the replacement cost.

REFERENCES

Armstrong, G. R., and P. C. Clarke (1946). "Frequency Distribution vs. Acceptance Table," *Industrial Quality Control*, vol. 3, no. 2, pp. 22–27.
Heyes, Gerald B. (1985). "The Box Plot," *Quality Progress*, December, pp. 12–17.
King, J. R. (1981). *Probability Charts for Decision Making*, rev. ed., TEAM, Tamworth, New Hampshire.
Tukey, John W. (1977). *Exploratory Data Analysis*, Addison-Wesley Publishing Company, Reading, Massachusetts.
Wadsworth, Harrison M., Kenneth S. Stephens, and A. Blanton Godfrey (1986). *Modern Methods for Quality Control and Improvement*, John Wiley and Sons, New York.

SUPPLEMENTARY READING

Graphical methods: Tufte, Edward R. (1983). *The Visual Display of Quantitative Information*, Graphics Press, Cheshire, Connecticut.
Plotting on probability paper: Nelson, Wayne (1979). *Volume 1: How to Analyze Data with Simple Plots*, ASQC Quality Press, Milwaukee, Wisconsin.
Role of the statistician: Snee, Ronald D. (1991). "Can Statisticians Meet the Challenge of Total quality," *Quality Progress*, January, pp. 60–64.

CHAPTER 10

STATISTICAL TOOLS FOR ANALYZING DATA

10.1 SCOPE OF DATA ANALYSIS

Here are some types of problems that can benefit from statistical analysis:

1. Determination of the usefulness of a limited number of test results in estimating the true value of a product characteristic.
2. Determination of the number of tests required to provide adequate data for evaluation.
3. Comparison of test data between two alternative designs, or comparison of test data from one design with the specification values.
4. Planning of experiments to determine the significant variable influencing a performance characteristic.
5. Determination of the quantitative relationship between two or more variables.

This chapter presents the statistical methods for handling these problems.

10.2 STATISTICAL INFERENCE

Drawing conclusions from a small number of data is notoriously unreliable. The "gossip" of a small sample size can be dangerous. Examine the following problems concerned with the evaluation of test data. For each, give a yes or no answer based on your intuitive analysis of the problem. (Write your answers on a piece of paper *now* and then check for the correct answers at the end of this chapter.) Some of the problems are solved in the chapter.

Examples of Engineering Problems That Can Be Solved Using the Concepts of Statistical Inference

1. A single-cavity molding process has been producing insulators with an average impact strength of 5.15 ft-lb [6.9834 Newton-meters (N-m)]. A group of 12 insulators from a new lot shows an average of 4.952 ft-lb (6.7149 N-m). Is this enough evidence to conclude that the new lot is lower in average strength?

2. Past data show the average hardness of brass parts to be 49.95. A new design is submitted and claimed to have higher hardness. A sample of 61 parts of the new design shows an average of 54.62. Does the new design actually have a different hardness?

3. Two types of spark plugs were tested for wear. A sample of 10 of design 1 showed an average wear of 0.0049 in (0.0124 cm) A sample of 8 of design 2 showed an average wear of 0.0064 in (0.0163 cm). Are these enough data to conclude that design 1 is better than design 2?

4. Only 11.7 percent of the 60 new-alloy blades on a turbine rotor failed on test in a gas turbine where 20 percent have shown failures in a series of similar tests in the past. Are the new blades better?

5. 1050 resistors supplied by one manufacturer were 3.71 percent defective. 1690 similar resistors from another manufacturer were 1.95 percent defective. Can one reasonably assert that the product of one plant is inferior to that of the other?

You probably had some incorrect answers. The statistical methods used to properly analyze these problems are called *statistical inference*. We shall start with the concept of sampling variation and sampling distributions.

10.3 SAMPLING VARIATION AND SAMPLING DISTRIBUTIONS

Suppose that a battery is to be evaluated to ensure that life requirements are met. A mean life of 30 hours is desired. Preliminary data indicate that life follows a normal distribution and that the standard deviation is equal to 10 hours. A sample of four batteries is selected at random from the process and tested. If the mean of the four is close to 30 hours, it is concluded that the battery meets the specification. Figure 10.1 plots the distribution of *individual* batteries from the population assuming that the true *mean* of the population is exactly 30 hours.

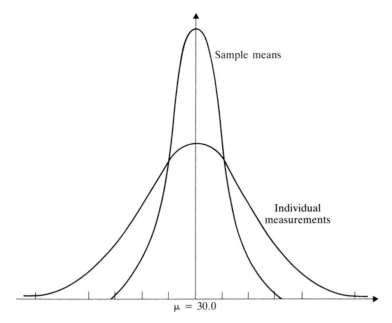

Sample means

Individual
measurements

$\mu = 30.0$

FIGURE 10.1
Distributions of individual measurements and sample means.

If a sample of four is life-tested, the following lifetimes might result: 34, 28, 38, and 24, giving a mean of 31.0. However, this is a random sample selected from the many batteries made by the same process. Suppose that another sample of four was taken. The second sample of four would likely be different from the first sample. Perhaps the results would be 40, 32, 18, and 29, giving a mean of 29.8. If the process of drawing many samples (with four in each sample) were repeated over and over, different results would be obtained in most samples. This is significant because *all* the samples were drawn from the *same* process. This outcome of different sample results illustrates the concept of sampling variation.

Returning to the problem of evaluating the battery, a dilemma exists. In the actual evaluation, only one sample of four can be drawn (because of time and cost limitations). Yet the experiment of drawing many samples indicates that samples vary. The question is: How reliable is that sample of four that will be the basis of the decision? The final decision can be influenced by the luck of which sample is chosen. The key point is that the existence of sampling variation means that any one sample cannot be relied upon to always give an adequate decision. The statistical approach analyzes the results of the sample, *taking into account the possible sampling variation that could occur.* Formulas have been developed defining the expected amount of sampling variation. Knowing this, a valid decision can be reached based on evaluating the one sample of data.

The problem, then, is to define how means of samples vary. If sampling were continued and for each sample of four the mean was calculated, these means could be compiled into a histogram. Figure 10.1 shows the resulting probability curve superimposed on the curve for the population. The narrow curve represents the distribution of life for the sample *means* (where each average includes four individual batteries). This is called the *sampling distribution of means*. The curve for means is narrower than the curve for individuals because in calculating means, extreme individual values are offset. The mathematical properties for the curve for averages have been studied and the following relationship developed:

$$\sigma_{\bar{x}} = \frac{\sigma}{\sqrt{n}}$$

where $\sigma_{\bar{x}}$ = standard deviation of means of samples (sometimes called the standard error of the mean)
σ = standard deviation of individual items
n = number of items in *each* sample

The relationship is significant because if an estimate of the standard deviation of *individual* items can be obtained, then the standard deviation of sample means can be calculated from the foregoing relationship instead of running an experiment to generate sample averages. The problems of evaluating the battery can now be portrayed graphically (Figure 10.2).
This concept of a sampling distribution is basic to the two major areas of statistical inference, i.e., estimation and tests of hypotheses, which will be discussed next.

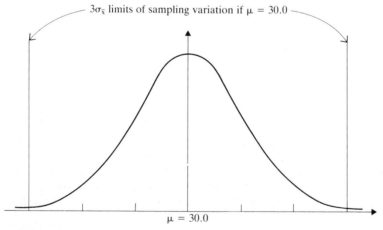

FIGURE 10.2
Distribution of sample means.

10.4 STATISTICAL ESTIMATION: CONFIDENCE LIMITS

Estimation is the process of analyzing a sample result in order to predict the corresponding value of the population parameter. For example, the sample of four batteries previously mentioned had a mean life of 31.0 hours. If this is a representative sample from the process, what estimate can be made of the true life of the entire population of batteries?

The estimation statement has two parts:

1. The *point estimate* is a single value used to estimate the population parameter. For example, 31.0 hours is the point estimate of the average life of the population.

2. The *confidence interval* is a range of values which includes (with a preassigned probability called a *confidence level*) the true value of a population parameter. *Confidence limits* are the upper and lower boundaries of the confidence interval. A confidence level is the probability that an assertion about the value of a population parameter is correct.[1]

Confidence limits should not be confused with other limits, e.g., control limits, statistical tolerance limits (see Chapter 13, "Designing for Quality-Statistical Tools," for a distinction among several types of limits).

Table 10.1 summarizes confidence limit formulas for common parameters. The following examples illustrate some of these formulas.

Example 10.1. Mean of a normal population. Twenty-five specimens of brass have a mean hardness of 54.62 and an estimated standard deviation of 5.34. Determine the 95 percent confidence limits on the mean.

Solution. Note that when the standard deviation is unknown and is estimated from the sample, the t distribution (Table D in the Appendix) must be used. The t value for 95 percent confidence is found by entering the table at 0.975 and $25 - 1$, or 24, degrees of freedom[2] and reading a t value of 2.064.

$$\text{Confidence limits} = \bar{X} \pm t\frac{s}{\sqrt{n}}$$

$$= 54.62 \pm (2.064)\frac{5.34}{\sqrt{25}}$$

$$= 52.42 \text{ and } 56.82$$

---

[1] Confidence levels of 90, 95, or 99 percent are usually assumed in practice.

[2] A mathematical derivation of degrees of freedom is beyond the scope of this book, but the underlying concept can be stated. *Degrees of freedom* (DF) is the parameter involved when, e.g., a sample standard deviation is used to estimate the true standard deviation of a universe. DF equals the number of measurements in the sample minus some number of constraints estimated from the data in order to compute the standard deviation. In this example, it was necessary to estimate only one constant (the population mean) in order to compute the standard deviation. Therefore, $DF = 25 - 1 = 24$.

TABLE 10.1
Summary of confidence limit formulas

Parameters	Formulas
Mean of a normal population (standard deviation known)	$\bar{X} \pm Z_{a/2} \dfrac{\sigma}{\sqrt{n}}$ where $\bar{X}$ = sample average Z = normal distribution coefficient σ = standard deviation of population n = sample size
Mean of a normal population (standard deviation unknown)	$\bar{X} \pm t_{a/2} \dfrac{s}{\sqrt{n}}$ where t = distribution coefficient (with $n-1$ degrees of freedom) s = estimated σ
Standard deviation of a normal population	Upper confidence limit $= s\sqrt{\dfrac{n-1}{\chi^2_{a/2}}}$ Lower confidence limit $= s\sqrt{\dfrac{n-1}{\chi^2_{1-a/2}}}$ where χ^2 = chi-square distribution coefficient with $n-1$ degrees of freedom $1-\alpha$ = confidence level
Population fraction defective	See Table F in the Appendix.
Difference between the means of two normal populations (standard deviations σ_1 and σ_2 known)	$(\bar{X}_1 - \bar{X}_2) \pm Z_{a/2}\sqrt{\dfrac{\sigma_1^2}{n_1} + \dfrac{\sigma_2^2}{n_2}}$
Difference between the means of two normal populations ($\sigma_1 = \sigma_2$ but unknown)	$(\bar{X}_1 - \bar{X}_2) \pm t_{a/2}\sqrt{\dfrac{1}{n_1} + \dfrac{1}{n_2}}$ $\times \sqrt{\dfrac{\Sigma(X - \bar{X}_1)^2 + \Sigma(X - \bar{X}_2)^2}{n_1 + n_2 - 2}}$
Mean time between failures based on an exponential population of time between failures	Upper confidence limit $= \dfrac{2rm}{\chi^2_{a/2}}$ Lower confidence limit $= \dfrac{2rm}{\chi^2_{1-a/2}}$ where r = number of occurrences in the sample (i.e., number of failures) m = sample mean time between failures DF $= 2r$

There is 95 percent confidence that the true mean hardness of the brass is between 52.42 and 56.82.

Example 10.2. Mean of an exponential population. A repairable radar system has been operated for 1200 hours, during which time eight failures occurred. What are the 90 percent confidence limits on the mean time between failures for the system?

Solution

$$\text{Estimated } m = \frac{1200}{8} = 150 \text{ h between failures}$$

$$\text{Upper confidence limit} = 2(1200)/7.962 = 301.4$$

$$\text{Lower confidence limit} = 2(1200)/26.296 = 91.3$$

The values 7.962 and 26.296 are obtained from the chi-square table (Table E in the Appendix). There is 90 percent confidence that the true mean time between failures is between 91.3 and 301.4 h.

Confusion has arisen on the application of the term "confidence level" to a reliability index such as mean time between failures. Using a different example, suppose that the numerical portion of a reliability requirement reads as follows:

"The MTBF shall be at least 100 hours at the 90 percent confidence level." This means that:

1. The minimum MTBF must be 100 hours.
2. Actual tests shall be conducted on the product to demonstrate with 90 percent confidence that the 100-hour MTBF has been met.
3. The test data shall be analyzed by calculating the observed MTBF and the lower one-sided 90 percent confidence limit on MTBF. The true MTBF lies above this limit with 90 percent of confidence.
4. The lower one-sided confidence limit must be ≥ 100 hours.

The term "confidence level" from a statistical viewpoint has great implications on a test program. The observed MTBF must be *greater* than 100 if the lower confidence limit is to be ≥ 100. Confidence level means that sufficient tests must be conducted to demonstrate, with statistical validity, that a requirement has been met. Confidence level does *not* refer to the qualitative opinion about meeting a requirement. Also, confidence level does *not* lower a requirement, i.e., a 100-hour MTBF at a 90 percent confidence level does *not* mean that 0.90×100, or 90 hours, is acceptable. Such serious misunderstandings have occurred. When the term "confidence level" is used, a clear understanding should be verified and not assumed.

10.5   IMPORTANCE OF CONFIDENCE LIMITS IN PLANNING TEST PROGRAMS

Additional tests will increase the accuracy of estimates. Accuracy here refers to the agreement between an estimate and the true value of the population parameter. The increase in accuracy does not vary linearly with the number of tests—doubling the number of tests usually does *not* double the precision. Examine the graph (Figure 10.3) of the confidence interval for the mean against sample size (a standard deviation of 50.0 was assumed): when the sample size is small, an increase has a great effect on the width of the confidence interval; after about 30 units, an increase has a much smaller effect. The inclusion of the cost parameter is vital here. The cost of additional tests must be evaluated against the value of the additional accuracy.

Further, if the sample is selected randomly and if the sample size is less than 10 percent of the population size, accuracy depends primarily on the absolute size of the sample rather than the sample size expressed as a percentage of the population size. Thus a sample size which is 1 percent of the population of 100,000 may be better than a 10 percent sample from a population of 1000.

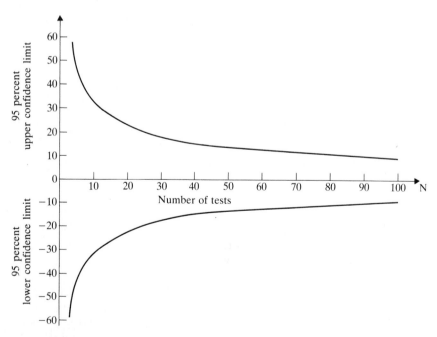

FIGURE 10.3
Width of confidence interval versus number of tests.

10.6 DETERMINATION OF THE SAMPLE SIZE REQUIRED TO ACHIEVE A SPECIFIED ACCURACY IN AN ESTIMATE

Confidence limits can help to determine the size of test program required to estimate a product characteristic within a specified accuracy. It is desired to estimate the true mean of the battery previously cited where $\sigma = 10$. The estimate must be within 2.0 hours of the true mean if the estimate is to be of any value. A 95 percent confidence level is desired on the confidence statement. The desired confidence interval is ± 2.0 hours, or

$$2.0 = \frac{(1.96)(10)}{\sqrt{n}} \qquad n = 96$$

A sample of 96 batteries will provide an average which is within 2.0 hours of the true mean (with 95 percent confidence). Notice the type of information required for estimating the mean of a normal population: (1) desired width of the confidence interval (the accuracy desired in the estimate), (2) confidence level desired, and (3) variability of the characteristic under investigation. The number of tests required cannot be determined until the engineer furnishes these items of information. Past information may also have a major role in designing a test program (see Section 10.11).

10.7 TESTS OF HYPOTHESIS

Basic Concepts

A *hypothesis,* as used here, is an assertion made about a population. Usually, the assertion concerns the numerical value of some parameter of the population. For example, a hypothesis might state that the mean life of a population of batteries equals 30.0 hours, written as $H : \mu_0 = 30.0$. This assertion may or may not be correct. A *test of hypothesis* is a test of the validity of the assertion, and is carried out by analysis of a sample of data.

There are two reasons why sample results must be carefully evaluated. First, there are many other samples which, by chance alone, could be drawn from the population. Second, the numerical results in the sample actually selected can easily be compatible with several different hypotheses. These points are handled by recognizing the two types of sampling error.

THE TWO TYPES OF SAMPLING ERROR. In evaluating a hypothesis, two errors can be made:

1. *Reject* the hypothesis when it is *true.* This is called the *type I error* or the *level of significance.* The probability of the type I error is denoted by α.

TABLE 10.2
Type I (α) error and type II (β) error

Suppose decision of analysis is:	Suppose the *H* is:	
	True	**False**
Accept *H*	Correct decision $P = 1 - \alpha$	Wrong decision $P = \beta$
Reject *H*	Wrong decision $P = \alpha$ $\Sigma P = 1.0$	Correct decision $P = 1 - \beta$ $\Sigma P = 1.0$

2. *Accept* the hypothesis when it is *false*. This is called the *type II error* and the probability is denoted by β.

These errors are defined in terms of probability numbers and can be controlled to desired values. The results possible in testing a hypothesis are summarized in Table 10.2.

The type I error is shown graphically in Figure 10.4 for the hypothesis $H_0 : \mu_0 = 30.0$. The interval on the horizontal axis between the vertical lines represents the *acceptance region* for the test of hypothesis. If the sample result (e.g., the mean) falls within the acceptance region, the hypothesis is accepted. Otherwise, it is rejected. The terms "accepted" and "rejected" require careful interpretation. The meanings are explained in a later section of this chapter.

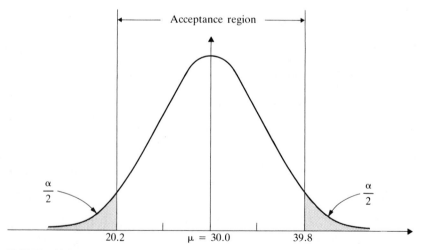

FIGURE 10.4
Acceptance region for $H : \mu = 30.0$.

Notice that there is a small portion of the curve which falls outside the acceptance region. This area (α) represents the maximum probability of obtaining a sample result outside the acceptance region, even though the hypothesis is correct.

Suppose it has been decided that the type I error must not exceed 5 percent. This is the probability of rejecting the hypothesis when, in truth, the true mean life is 30.0. The acceptance region can be obtained by locating values of mean life which have only a 5 percent chance of being exceeded when the true mean life is 30.0. Further, suppose a sample n of four measurements is taken and $\sigma = 10.0$.

Remember that the curve represents a population of sample means because the decision will be made on the basis of a sample mean. Sample means vary less than individual measurements according to the relationship $\sigma_{\bar{x}} = \sigma/\sqrt{n}$ (see Section 10.3, "Sampling Variation and Sampling Distributions").

Further, the distribution of sample means is approximately normal even if the distribution of the individual measurements (going into the means) is not normal. The approximation holds best for large values of n but is adequate for n as low as 4.

Table A in the Appendix shows that a 2.5 percent area in each tail is at a limit which is 1.96 standard deviations from 30.0. Then, under the hypothesis that $\mu_0 = 30.0$, 95 percent of sample means will fall within $\pm 1.96\sigma_{\bar{x}}$ of 30.0, or

$$\text{Upper limit} = 30.0 + 1.96\frac{10}{\sqrt{4}} = 39.8$$

$$\text{Lower limit} = 30.0 - 1.96\frac{10}{\sqrt{4}} = 20.2$$

The acceptance region is thereby defined as 20.2 to 39.8. If the mean of a random sample of four batteries is within this acceptance region, the hypothesis is accepted. If the mean falls outside the acceptance region, the hypothesis is rejected. This decision rule provides a type I error of 0.05.

The type II, or β, error, the probability of accepting a hypothesis when it is false, is shown in Figure 10.5 as the shaded area. Notice that it is possible to

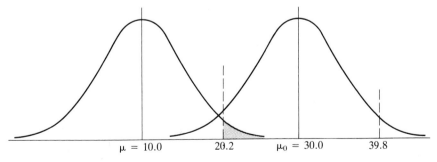

FIGURE 10.5
Type II, or β, error.

obtain a sample result within the acceptance region, even though the population has a true mean which is *not* equal to the mean stated in the hypothesis. The numerical value of β depends on the true value of the population mean (and also on n, σ, and α). The various probabilities are depicted by an *operating characteristic* (OC) *curve*.

The problem now is to construct an OC curve to define the magnitude of the type II (β) error. As β is the probability of *accepting* the original hypothesis ($\mu_0 = 30.0$) when it is *false*, the probability that a sample mean will fall between 20.2 and 39.8 must be found when the true mean of the population is something other than 30.0. This is done by finding the area under the normal curve for all possible values of the true mean of the population.

The results form the OC curve shown in Figure 10.6. The OC curve is a plot of the probability of accepting the original hypothesis as a function of the true value of the population parameter (and the given values of n, σ, and α). Note that for a mean equal to the hypothesis (30.0), the probability of acceptance is $1 - \alpha$. This curve should not be confused with that of a normal distribution of measurements. In some cases, the shape is similar, but the meanings of an OC curve and a distribution curve are entirely different.

The Use of the Operating Characteristic Curve in Selecting an Acceptance Region

The acceptance region was determined by dividing the 5 percent allowable α error into two equal parts (see Figure 10.4). This is called a *two-tail test*. The entire 5 percent error could also be placed at either the left or the right tail of the distribution curve. These are *one-tail tests*.

Operating characteristic curves for tests having these one-tail acceptance regions can be developed following the approach used for the two-tail region.

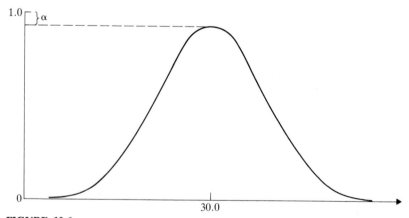

FIGURE 10.6
Operating characteristic curve.

Although the α-error is the same, the β error varies depending on whether a one-tail or two-tail test is used.

In some problems, knowledge is available to indicate that if the true mean of the population is *not* equal to the hypothesis value, then it is on one side of the hypothesis value. For example, a new material of supposedly higher mean strength will have a mean equal to or *greater than* that of the present material. Such information will help select a one-tail or two-tail test to make the β error as small as possible. The following guidelines are based on the analysis of OC curves:

Use a one-tail test with the entire α risk on the right tail if (1) it is suspected that (if μ_0 is not true) the true mean is $>\mu_0$ or (2) values of the population mean $<\mu_0$ are acceptable and we want to detect only a population mean $>\mu_0$.

Use a one tail test with the entire α risk on the left tail if (1) it is suspected that (if μ_0 is not true) the true mean is $<\mu_0$ or (2) values of the population mean $>\mu_0$ are acceptable and we want to detect only a population mean $<\mu_0$.

Use a two-tail test if (1) there is no prior knowledge on the location of the true population mean or (2) we want to detect a true population mean less than or more than the μ_0 stated in the original hypothesis.[3]

The selection of a one- or two-tail test will be illustrated by some examples in a later section. Every test of hypothesis has an OC curve. Duncan (1986) is a good source of OC curves. (Some references present "power" curves, but power is simply 1 minus the probability of acceptance, or $1 - \beta$.)

With this background, the discussion now proceeds to the steps for testing a hypothesis.

10.8 TESTING A HYPOTHESIS WHEN THE SAMPLE SIZE IS FIXED IN ADVANCE

Ideally, desired values for the type I and type II errors are defined in advance and the required sample size determined (see Section 10.10). If the sample size is fixed in advance because of cost or time limitations, then usually the desired type I error is defined and the following procedure is followed:

1. State the hypothesis.
2. Choose a value for the type I error. Common values are 0.01, 0.05, and 0.10.

---

[3] With a two-tail test, the hypothesis is sometimes stated as the original hypothesis $H_0 : \mu_0 = 30.0$ against the alternative hypothesis $H_1 : \mu_0 \neq 30.0$. With a one-tail test, $H_0 : \mu_0 = 30.0$ is used against the alternative $H_1 : \mu_1 < 30.0$ if α is placed in the left tail, or $H_1 : \mu_1 > 30.0$ is used if α is placed in the right tail.

3. Choose the test statistic for testing the hypothesis.
4. Determine the acceptance region for the test, i.e., the range of values of the test statistic which results in a decision to accept the hypothesis.
5. Obtain a sample of observations, compute the test statistic, and compare the value to the acceptance region to make a decision to accept or reject the hypothesis.
6. Draw an egineering conclusion.

TABLE 10.3
Summary of formulas on tests of hypotheses

Hypothesis	Test statistic and distribution
$H : \mu = \mu_0$ (the mean of a normal population is equal to a specified value μ_0; σ is known)	$Z = \dfrac{\bar{X} - \mu_0}{\sigma/\sqrt{n}}$ Normal distribution
$H : \mu = \mu_0$ (the mean of a normal population is equal to a specified value μ_0; σ is estimated by s)	$t = \dfrac{\bar{X} - \mu_0}{s/\sqrt{n}}$ t distribution with $n - 1$ degrees of freedom (DF)
$H : \mu_1 = \mu_2$ (the mean of population 1 is equal to the mean of population 2; assume that $\sigma_1 = \sigma_2$ and that both populations are normal)	$t = \dfrac{\bar{X}_1 - \bar{X}_2}{\sqrt{1/n_1 + 1/n_2} \, \sqrt{[(n_1 - 1)s_1^2 + (n_2 - 1)s_2^2]/(n_1 + n_2 - 2)}}$ t distribution with $\mathrm{DF} = n_1 + n_2 - 2$
$H : \sigma = \sigma_0$ (the standard deviation of a normal population is equal to a specified value σ_0)	$\chi^2 = \dfrac{(n - 1)s^2}{\sigma_0^2}$ Chi-square distribution with $\mathrm{DF} = n - 1$
$H : \sigma_1 = \sigma_2$ (the standard deviation of population 1 is equal to the standard deviation of population 2; assume that both populations are normal)	$F = \dfrac{s_1^2}{s_2^2}$ F distribution with $DF_1 = n_1 = 1$ and $DF_2 = n_2 - 1$
$H : p = p_0$ (the fraction defective in a population is equal to a specified value p_0; assume that $np_0 \geq 5$)	$Z = \dfrac{p - p_0}{\sqrt{p_0(1 - p_0)/n}}$ Normal distribution
$H : p_1 = p_2$ (the fraction defective in population 1 is equal to the fraction defective in population 2; assume that $n_1 p_1$ and $n_2 p_2$ are each ≥ 5)	$Z = \dfrac{X_1/n_1 - X_2/n_2}{\sqrt{\hat{p}(1 - \hat{p})(1/n_1 + 1/n_2)}} \qquad \hat{p} = \dfrac{X_1 + X_2}{n_1 + n_2}$ Normal distribution

Table 10.3 summarizes some common tests of hypotheses. The procedure is illustrated through the following examples. In these examples, a type I error of 0.05 will be assumed.

1. Test for a population mean, μ. (Standard deviation of the population is known.)

Example 10.3. A single-cavity molding press has been producing insulators with a mean impact strength of 5.15 ft-lb (6.98 N-m) and with a standard deviation of 0.25 ft-lb (0.34 N-m). A new lot shows the following data from 12 specimens:

Specimen	Strength
1	5.02
2	4.87
3	4.95
4	4.88
5	5.01
6	4.93
7	4.91
8	5.09
9	4.96
10	4.89
11	5.06
12	4.85
	$\bar{X} = 4.95$

Is the new lot from which the sample of 12 was taken different in mean impact strength from the past performance of the process?

Solution. $H_0: \mu_0 = 5.15$ ft-lb (6.98 N-m). (The mean of the population from which the sample was taken is the same as the past process average.)

Test statistic

$$Z = \frac{\bar{X} - \mu_0}{\sigma/\sqrt{n}}$$

Acceptance region. Assuming no prior information and that a deviation on either side of the hypothesis average is important to detect, a two-tail test (Figure 10.7) is applicable. From Table A in the Appendix, the acceptance region is Z between -1.96 and $+1.96$.

Analysis of sample data

$$Z = \frac{4.95 - 5.15}{0.25/\sqrt{12}} = -2.75$$

Conclusion. Since Z is outside the acceptance region, the hypothesis is rejected. Therefore, sufficient evidence is present to conclude that the mean impact strength of the new process is significantly different from the mean of the past process. The answer to the first question in Section 10.2 is yes.

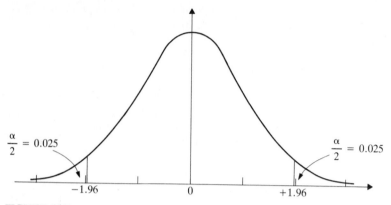

FIGURE 10.7
Distribution of Z (two-tail test).

2. Test for two population means, μ_1 and μ_2, when the standard deviation is unknown but believed to be the same for the two populations. (This assumption can be evaluated by test 4.)

Example 10.4. Two makes of spark plugs were operated in the alternate cylinders of an aircraft engine for 100 hours and the following data obtained:

	Make 1	Make 2
Number of spark plugs tested	10	8
Average wear per 100 h ($\bar{X}$), in	0.0049	0.0064
Variability (s), in	0.0005	0.0004

Can it be said that make 1 wears less than make 2?

Solution. $H: \mu_1 = \mu_2$.
Test statistic

$$t = \frac{\bar{X}_1 - \bar{X}_2}{\sqrt{1/n_1 + 1/n_2}\,\sqrt{[(n_1 - 1)s_1^2 + (n_2 - 1)s_2^2]/(n_1 + n_2 - 2)}}$$

with degrees of freedom $= n_1 + n_2 - 2$.

Acceptance region. We are concerned only with the possibility that make 1 wears less than make 2; therefore, use a one-tail test (Figure 10.8) with the entire α risk in the left tail. From Table D in the Appendix, the acceptance region is $t > -1.746$.

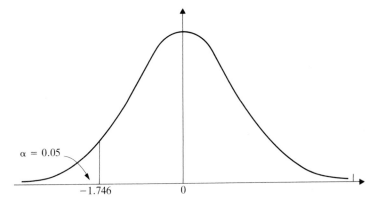

FIGURE 10.8
Distribution of t with α on left tail.

Analysis of sample data

$$t = \frac{0.0049 - 0.0064}{\sqrt{1/10 + 1/8}\ \sqrt{[(10-1)(0.0005)^2 + (8-1)(0.0004)^2]/(10+8-2)}} = -6.9$$

Conclusion. Since t is outside the acceptance region, the hypothesis is rejected. Therefore, sufficient evidence is present to conclude that make 1 wears less than make 2. The answer to the third question in Section 10.2 is yes.

3. Test for a population standard deviation, σ.

Example 10.5. For the insulator strengths tabulated in the first example, the sample standard deviation is 0.036 ft-lb (0.049 N-m). The previous variability, recorded over a period, has been established as a standard deviation of 0.25 ft-lb (0.34 N-m). Does the low value of 0.036 indicate that the new lot is significantly more uniform (i.e., standard deviation less than 0.25)?

Solution. $H : \sigma_0 = 0.25$ ft-lb (0.34 N-m).

Test statistic

$$\chi^2 = \frac{(n-1)s^2}{\sigma_0^2}$$

with degrees of freedom $= n - 1$.

Acceptance region. We believe that the standard deviation is smaller; therefore, we will use a one-tail test (Figure 10.9) with the entire risk on the left tail. From Table E in the Appendix the acceptance region is $\chi^2 \geq 4.57$.

Analysis of sample data

$$\chi^2 = \frac{(12-1)(0.078)^2}{(0.25)^2} = 1.08$$

Conclusion. Since χ^2 is outside the acceptance region, the hypothesis is rejected. Therefore, sufficient evidence is present to conclude that the new lot is more uniform.

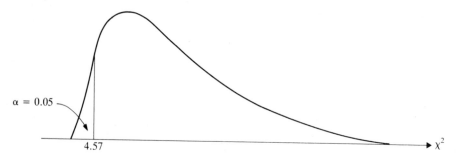

FIGURE 10.9
Distribution of χ^2 with α on left tail.

4. Test for the difference in variability (s_1 versus s_2) in two samples.

Example 10.6. A materials laboratory was studying the effect of aging on a metal alloy. They wanted to know if the parts were more consistent in strength after aging than before. The data obtained were:

	At start (1)	After 1 year (2)
Number of specimens (n)	9	7
Average strength ($\bar{X}$), psi	41,350	40,920
Variability (s), psi	934	659

Solution. $H : \sigma_1 = \sigma_2$.
Test statistic

$$F = \frac{s_1^2}{s_2^2} \quad \text{with} \quad DF_1 = n_1 - 1, \qquad DF_2 = n_2 - 1$$

Acceptance region. We are concerned with an improvement in variation; therefore, we will use a one-tail test (Figure 10.10) with the entire α risk in the right tail.

From Table G in the Appendix, the acceptance region is $F \leq 4.15$.
Analysis of sample data

$$F = \frac{(934)^2}{(659)^2} = 2.01$$

Conclusion. Since F is inside the acceptance region, the hypothesis is accepted. Therefore, there is not sufficient evidence to conclude that the parts were more consistent in strength after aging.

In this test and other tests that compare two samples, it is important that the samples be independent to ensure valid conclusions.

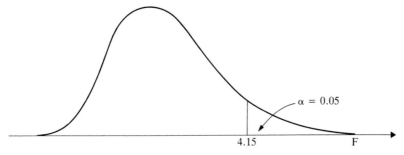

FIGURE 10.10
Distribution of F with α on right tail.

10.9 DRAWING CONCLUSIONS FROM TESTS OF HYPOTHESES

The payoff for these tests of hypotheses comes from reaching useful conclusions. The meaning of "reject the hypothesis" or "accept the hypothesis" is shown in Table 10.4, together with some analogies to explain the subtleties of the meanings.

When a hypothesis is rejected, the practical conclusion is: "the parameter value specified in the hypothesis is wrong." The conclusion is made with strong conviction—roughly speaking at a confidence level of $(1 - \alpha)$ percent. The key question then is: Just what is a good estimate of the value of the parameter for the population? Help can be provided on this question by calculating the confidence limits for the parameter. This was discussed in Section 10.4.

TABLE 10.4
The meaning of a conclusion from tests of hypotheses

	If hypothesis is rejected	If hypothesis is accepted
Adequacy of evidence in the sample of observations	Sufficient to conclude that hypothesis is false	Not sufficient to conclude that hypothesis is false; hypothesis is a reasonable one but has not been proved to be true
Difference between sample result (e.g., $\bar{X}$) and hypothesis value (e.g., μ_0)	Unlikely that difference was due to chance (sampling) variation	Difference could easily have been due to chance (sampling) variation
Analogy of guilt or innocence in a court of law	Guilt has been established beyond a reasonble doubt	Have not established guilt beyond a reasonble doubt
Analogy of a batting average in baseball	If player got 300 base hits out of 1000 times at bat, this is sufficient to conclude that his overall batting average is about 0.300	If player got 3 hits in 10 times, this is not sufficient to conclude that his overall average is about 0.300

When a hypothesis is accepted, the numerical value of the parameter stated in the hypothesis has not been proved, but it has not been disproved. It is not correct to say that the hypothesis has been proved as correct at the $(1 - \alpha)$ percent confidence level. Many other hypotheses could be accepted for the given sample of observations, and yet only one hypothesis can be true. Therefore, an acceptance does not mean a high probability of proof that a specific hypothesis is correct. (All other factors being equal, the smaller the sample size, the more likely it is that the hypothesis will be accepted. Less evidence certainly does not imply proof.)

With an acceptance of a hypothesis, a key question then is: What conclusion, if any, can be drawn about the parameter value in the hypothesis? Two approaches are suggested:

1. *Construct and review the operating characteristic curve for the test of hypothesis.* This defines the probability that other possible values of the population parameter could have been accepted by the test. Knowing these probabilities for values relatively close to the original hypothesis can help draw further conclusions about the acceptance of the original hypothesis. For example, Figure 10.6 shows the OC curve for a hypothesis which specified that the population mean is 30.0. Note that the probability of accepting the hypothesis when the population mean is 30.0 is 0.95 (or $1 - \alpha$). But also note that if μ really is 35.0, then the probability of accepting $\mu = 30.0$ is still high (about 0.83). If μ really is 42.0, the probability of accepting $\mu = 30.0$ is only about 0.33.

2. *Calculate confidence limits on the sample result.* These confidence limits define an interval within which the true population parameter lies. If this interval is small, an acceptance decision on the test of hypothesis means that the true population value is either equal to or close to the value stated in the hypothesis. Then it is reasonable to act as if the parameter value specified in the hypothesis is in fact correct. If the confidence interval is relatively wide, this is a stern warning that the true value of the population might be far different from that specified in the hypothesis. For example, the confidence limits of 21.2 and 40.8 on battery life in Section 10.4 would lead to an acceptance of the hypothesis of $\mu = 30.0$, but note that the confidence interval is relatively wide.

Care must always be taken in drawing engineering conclusions from the statistical conclusions, particularly when a hypothesis is accepted.

A test of hypothesis tests to see if there is a statistically significant difference between the sample result and the value of the population parameter stated in the hypothesis. A decision to reject the hypothesis means that there is a statistically significant difference. However, this does not mean that the difference has practical significance. Large sample sizes, although not generally available, can detect small differences that may not have practical importance. Conversely, "accept hypothesis" means that a statistically significant difference was not found, but this may have been due to a small sample size. A larger sample size could result in a "reject hypothesis" and thus detect a significant difference.

10.10 DETERMINING THE SAMPLE SIZE REQUIRED FOR TESTING A HYPOTHESIS

The previous sections assumed that the sample size was fixed by nonstatistical reasons and that the type I error only was predefined for the test. The ideal procedure is to predefine the desired type I and II errors and calculate the sample size required to cover both types of errors.

The sample size required will depend on (1) the sampling risks desired (α and β), (2) the size of the smallest true difference that is to be detected, and (3) the variation in characteristic being measured. The sample size can be determined by using the operating characteristic curve for the test (see QCH4, page 23.78).

The sample size can also be directly calculated:

$$n = \left[\frac{(Z_{\alpha/2} + Z_{\beta})\sigma}{\mu - \mu_0} \right]^2$$

Suppose that it was important to detect the fact that the mean life of the battery cited previously was 35.0 hours. Specifically, we want to be 80 percent sure of detecting this change ($\beta = 0.2$). Further, if the true mean was 30.0 hours (as stated in the hypothesis), we want to have only a 5 percent risk of rejecting the hypothesis ($\alpha = 0.05$). Then:

$$n = \left[\frac{(1.96 + 0.84)10}{35 - 30} \right]^2 = 31.4$$

The required sample size is 32.

10.11 THE DESIGN OF EXPERIMENTS

Experiments can have a wide variety of objectives, and the best strategy depends on the objective. In some experiments, the objective is to find the most important variables affecting a quality characteristic. The plan for conducting such experiments is called the *design of the experiment.* We will first cover an example that presents several alternative designs and defines the basic terminology and concepts.

Suppose that three detergents are to be compared for their ability in cleaning clothes in an automatic washing machine. The "whiteness" readings obtained by a special measuring procedure are called the *dependent,* or *response, variable.* The variable under investigation (detergent) is a *factor* and each variation of the factor is called a *level;* i.e., there are three levels. A factor may be qualitative (different detergents) or quantitative (water temperature). Finally, some experiments have a *fixed-effects model;* i.e., the levels investigated represent all levels of concern to the investigator (e.g., three brands of washing machines). Other experiments have a *random effects model*; i.e., the levels chosen are just a sample from a larger population (e.g., three operators of washing machines). A *mixed-effects model* has both fixed and random factors.

Figure 10.11 outlines six designs of experiments starting with the classical design in Figure 10.11*a*. Here all factors except detergent are held constant. Thus nine tests are run, i.e., three with each detergent with the washing time, make of machine, water temperature, and all other factors held constant. One drawback of this design is that the conclusions about detergent brands would apply only to the specific conditions run in the experiment.

Figure 10.11*b* recognizes a second factor at three levels, i.e., washing machines brands I, II, and III. However, in this design it would not be known whether an observed difference was due to detergents or washing times.

In Figure 10.11*c*, the nine tests are assigned completely at random; thus the name *completely randomized design*. However, detergent A is not used with machine brand III and detergent *B* is not used with machine brand I, thus complicating the conclusions.

(a)

A	B	C
–	–	–
–	–	–
–	–	–

(b)

I	II	III
A	B	C
A	B	C
A	B	C

(c)

I	II	III
C	B	B
A	C	B
A	A	C

(d)

I	II	III
B	A	C
C	C	A
A	B	B

(e)

	I	II	III
1	C	A	B
2	B	C	A
3	A	B	C

(f)

	I ABC	II ABC	III ABC
1	– – –	– – –	– – –
2	– – –	– – –	– – –
3	– – –	– – –	– – –

FIGURE 10.11
Some experimental designs.

Figure 10.11*d* shows the *randomized block design*. Here, each block is a machine brand and the detergents are run in random order within each block. This guards against any possible bias due to the order in which the detergents are used. This design has advantages in the subsequent data analysis and conclusions. First, a test of hypothesis can be run to compare detergents and a separate test run to compare machines and all nine observations are used in both tests of hypothesis. Second, the conclusions concerning detergents apply for the three machines and vice versa, thus providing conclusions over a wider range of conditions.

Now suppose that another factor such as water temperature was also to be studied. This could be done with the *Latin square design* shown in Figure 10.11*e*. Note that this design requires that each detergent be used only once with each machine and only once with each temperature. Thus three factors can be evaluated (by three separate tests of hypothesis) with only nine observations. However, there is a danger. This design assumes no "interaction" among the factors. No interaction between detergent and machine means that the effect of changing from detergent A to B to C does not depend on which machine is used, and similarly for the other combinations of factors. The concept of interaction is shown in Figure 10.12.

Finally, the main factors and possible interactions could be investigated by the *factorial design* in Figure 10.11*f*. "Factorial" means that at least one test is run at every combination of the main factors, in this case $3 \times 3 \times 3$ or 27 combinations. Separate tests of hypothesis can be run to evaluate the main factors and also the possible interactions. Again, all the observations contribute to each comparison.

Several key tools used in this example will now be explained.

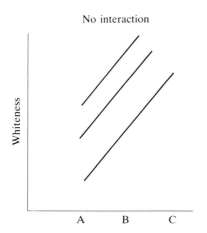
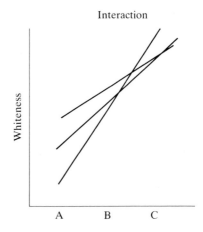

FIGURE 10.12
Interaction.

10.12 SOME TOOLS FOR SOUND EXPERIMENTATION

Planned Grouping or Blocking

Beyond the factors selected for study, there are other "background" variables which may affect the outcome of the experiments. Where the experimenter is aware of these variables, it is often possible to plan the experiment so that:

1. Possible effects due to background variables do not affect information obtained about the factors of primary interest.
2. Some information about the effects of the background variables can be obtained.

In designing experiments, wide use is made of the uniformity within blocks to minimize the effect of unwanted variables and to accentuate the effect of the variables under study. Designs that make use of this uniformity within blocks are called *block designs,* and the process is called *planned grouping.* It is useful that a specific design ensure that different effects can be directly estimated without any entanglement of unwanted variables. Designs that have this property are called "orthogonal" designs.

RANDOMIZATION. The assignment of specimens to treatments in a purely chance manner is called *randomization* in the design of experiments. Such assignment increases the likelihood that the effect of uncontrolled variables will balance out. It also improves the validity of estimates of experimental error and makes possible the application of statistical tests of significance and the construction of confidence intervals.

There are many famous examples of experiments where failure to randomize at a crucial stage led to completely misleading results. However, the beneficial effects of randomization are obtained in the long run, not in a single isolated experiment. Randomization may be thought of as insurance and, like insurance, may sometimes be too expensive. If a variable is thought unlikely to have an effect, and if it is difficult to randomize with respect to the variable, we may choose not to randomize.

REPLICATION. Replication is the repetition of an observation or measurement. It is done to increase precision and to provide the means of measuring precision. (In some kinds of experiments there is no outside source for measuring precision, so that the measure must come from the experiment itself.) In addition, replication provides an opportunity for the effects of uncontrolled factors to balance out and thus aids randomization as a bias-decreasing tool. (In successive replications, the randomization features must be independent.) Replication also helps to detect gross errors in the measurements.

In designing the experiment, some key questions that arise are:

1. How large a difference in the conditions being compared is considered significant from an engineering point of view? (How large a difference do we want the experiment to detect?)
2. How much variation has been experienced in the quality characteristics under investigation?
3. What risk do we want to take that the experiment incorrectly concludes that a significant difference exists when the correct conclusion is that no significant difference exists? (This is the type I error.)
4. What risk do we want to take that the experiment fails to detect the difference that really does exist? (This is the type II error.)
5. Do we have any knowledge about possible interactions of the factors? Do we wish to test for these interactions?

Many experimental problems can be handled with one of the standard experimental designs (see QCH4, Table 26.3).

10.13 CONTRAST BETWEEN THE CLASSICAL AND MODERN METHODS OF EXPERIMENTATION

The contrast between the classical method of experimentation (varying one factor at a time, holding everything else constant) and the modern approach is striking. Table 10.5 compares these two approaches for an experiment in which there are two factors (or variables) whose effects on a characteristic are being investigated. (The same conclusions hold for an experiment with more than two factors.)

This discussion has been restricted to the design or planning of the experiment. After the data are collected, the analysis phase begins. For simple experiments, some of the basic tests of hypotheses and confidence limits (previously discussed) provide the tools of analysis. For more complex experiments, we use additional tools such as the analytical analysis of variance (see QCH4, Section 26) and the graphical analysis of means (see Ryan, 1989).

10.14 REGRESSION ANALYSIS

Quality problems sometimes require a study of the relationship between two or more variables. This is called *regression analysis*. The uses of regression analysis include forecasting and prediction, determining the important variables influencing some result, and locating optimum operating conditions.

TABLE 10.5
Comparison of the classical and the modern methods of experimentation

Criteria	Classical	Modern
Basic procedure	Hold everything constant except the factor under investigation. Vary that factor and note the effect on the characteristic of concern. To investigate a second factor, conduct a separate experiment in the same manner	Plan the experiment to evaluate both factors in one main experiment. Include, in the design, measurements to evaluate the effect of varying both factors simultaneously
Experimental conditions	Care taken to have material, workers, and machine constant throughout the entire experiment	Realizes difficulty of holding conditions reasonably constant throughout an entire experiment. Instead, experiment is divided into several groups or blocks of measurements. Within each block, conditions must be reasonably constant (except for deliberate variation to investigate a factor)
Experimental error	Recognized but not stated in quantitative terms	Stated in quantitative terms
Basis of evaluation	Effect due to a factor is evaluated with only a vague knowledge of the amount of experimental error	Effect due to a factor is evaluated by comparing variation due to that factor with the quantitative measure of experimental error
Possible bias due to sequence of measurements	Often assumed that sequence has no effect	Guarded against by randomization
Effect of varying both factors simultaneously ("interaction")	Not adequately planned into experiment. Frequently assumed that the effect of varying factor 1 (when factor 2 is held constant at some value) would be the same for any value of factor 2	Experiment can be planned to include an investigation for interaction between factors
Validity of results	Misleading and erroneous if interaction exists and is not realized	Even if interaction exists, a valid evaluation of the main factors can be made
Number of measurements	For a given amount of useful and valid information, more measurements needed than in the modern approach	Fewer measurements needed for useful and valid information

TABLE 10.5 (*Continued*)

Criteria	Classical	Modern
Definition of problem	Objective of experiment frequently not defined as necessary	In order to design experiment, it is necessary to define the objective in detail (how large an effect do we want to determine, what numerical risks can be taken, etc.)
Application of conclusions	Sometimes disputed as applicable only to the controlled conditions under which the experiment was conducted	Broad conditions can be planned into the experiment, thereby making conclusions applicable to a wider range of actual conditions

The steps in a regression study are:

1. Clearly defining the objectives of the study. This must include a definition of the dependent or response variable and the independent variables that are thought to be related to the dependent variable.
2. Collecting pairs of data values.
3. Preparing scatter diagrams (plots of one variable versus another).
4. Calculating the regression equation.
5. Studying the equation to see how well it fits the data.
6. Providing measures of the precision of the equation.

These steps will be illustrated with an example.

Suppose it is thought that the life of a tool varies with the cutting speed of the tool and it is desired to predict life based on cutting speed. Thus life is the dependent variable (Y) and cutting speed is the independent variable (X). Data are collecting at four different cutting speeds (Table 10.6).

The plot of the data is called a *scatter diagram* (Figure 10.13). This plot should *always* be prepared before making any further analysis. The graph *alone* may provide sufficient information on the relationship between the variables to draw conclusions on the immediate problem, but the graph is also useful in suggesting possible forms of an estimating equation. Figure 10.13 suggests that life does vary with cutting speed (i.e., life decreases with an increase in speed) and that it varies in a linear manner (i.e., increases in speed result in a certain decrease in life that is the same over the range of the data). Note that the relationship is not perfect—the points scatter about the line.

Often it is valuable to determine a regression equation. For linear relationships, this can be done approximately by drawing a straight line by eye

TABLE 10.6
Cutting speed (X, in feet per minute) versus tool life (Y, in minutes)

X	Y	X	Y	X	Y	X	Y
90	41	100	22	105	21	110	15
90	43	100	35	105	13	110	11
90	35	100	29	105	18	110	6
90	32	100	18	105	20	110	10

and then graphically estimating the Y intercept and slope. The linear regression model is

$$Y = \beta_0 + \beta_1 X + \epsilon$$

where β_0 and β_1 are the unknown population intercept and slope and ϵ is a random-error term that may be due to measurement errors and/or the effects of other independent variables. This model is estimated from sample data by the form

$$\hat{Y} = b_0 + b_1 X$$

where $\hat{Y}$ is the predicted value of Y for a given value of X and b_0 and b_1 are the sample estimates of β_0 and β_1.

These estimates are usually found by the least-squares method, so named because it minimizes the sum of the squared deviations between the observed and predicted values of Y. The least-squares estimates are

$$b_1 = \frac{\sum (X_m - \bar{X})(Y_m - \bar{Y})}{\sum (X_m - \bar{X})^2} = \frac{\sum X_m Y_m - (\sum X_m \sum Y_m)/N}{\sum X_m^2 - (\sum X_m)^2/N}$$

$$b_0 = \bar{Y} - b_1 \bar{X}$$

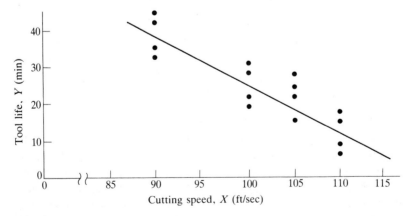

FIGURE 10.13
Tool life Y versus cutting speed X.

The summations range from $m = 1$ to $m = N$, where N is the total number of sets of values of X and Y.

The detailed calculations are easily handled by a regression software program. For this data:

$$b_1 = \frac{-1191.25}{875} = -1.3614$$

$$b_0 = 23.06 - (-1.3614)(101.25) = 160.9018$$

and hence the prediction equation is

$$\hat{Y} = 160.90 - 1.3614X$$

After estimating the coefficients of the prediction equation, the equation should be plotted over the data to check for gross calculation errors. Roughly half the data points should be above the line and half below it. In addition, the equation should pass exactly through the point $\bar{X}$, $\bar{Y}$.

A number of criteria exist for judging the adequacy of the prediction equation. One common measure of the adequacy of the prediction equation is R^2, the proportion of variation explained by the prediction equation. R^2 is called the *coefficient of determination*. This is the ratio of the variation due to the regression, $\sum (\hat{Y}_m - \bar{Y})$, to the total variation, $\sum (Y_m - \bar{Y})^2$. $\hat{Y}_m$ is the predicted Y value for X_m. The calculation formula is

$$R^2 = \frac{b_1 \sum (X_m - \bar{X})(Y_m - \bar{Y})}{\sum (Y_m - \bar{Y})^2}$$

$$= \frac{(-1.3614)(-1191.25)}{1958.94} = 0.828$$

Thus for this example the prediction equation explains 82.8 percent of the variation of the tool life. The coefficient of determinatin and *all* other measures of the precision of a regression relationship must be interpreted with great care. This is not an area for the amateur.

This brief treatment of regression is just an introduction to a complex subject. Further topics include confidence intervals and other measures of precision, multiple regression, and nonlinear regression. The literature provides more information (see QCH4, pages 23.96–23.116).

10.15 ENUMERATIVE AND ANALYTIC STUDIES

Deming (1982) provides an important distinction between two types of statistical studies—enumerative and analytic. In an enumerative study, we measure a *sample* and then estimate the characteristics of the *population*. For example, we draw a random sample of 20 units from a lot of 100 units. We measure the 20 units and then make predictions about the population of 100 units. All of this implies a defined, existing population. Typically in an enumerative study, we do not document information on the order of production—a pity.

In an analytic study, we measure periodic samples from a process which is continually manufacturing product, i.e., a changing population. Suppose we wish to predict the results for the next batch of product from the process. Such a prediction requires two assumptions: (1) the process has stabilized to a set of conditions that will repeat in the future and (2) any imbedded process changes with time such as trends or cyclical effects are known. To predict future process results, it is essential that data on the order of production be documented and used to analyze process stability and imbedded time effects. Techniques such as statistical control charts (see Chapter 17, "Statistical Process Control") are helpful in such analysis. In practice, the prediction of future process results predominates and thus makes the analytic type of study of great importance.

10.16   COMPUTER SOFTWARE FOR STATISTICAL ANALYSIS

With the advent of computer software, the practitioner can now use many statistical techniques that were not previously considered because of difficulty in understanding the techniques or doing the calculations. Now procedures define the input to a computer and the final result is then presented. Such accessibility has a danger. The practitioner must understand the assumptions behind the methods and what the final results do and do not mean. In the haste to obtain an answer and avoid tedious detail, there is a danger of wrong application of a technique or misunderstanding of a result. The serious consequences dictate a need for understanding.

QCH4, Section 27, presents a listing of statistical software packages. ASQC annually publishes in *Quality Progress* magazine a "Directory of Software for Quality Assurance and Quality Control."

The Journal of Quality Technology regularly publishes computer programs on specific statistical methods.

Answers to questions at the beginning of the chapter:
1. Yes   2. Yes   3. Yes   4. No   5. Yes

SUMMARY

- Estimation is the process of analyzing a sample result in order to predict the corresponding value of the population parameter.
- The point estimate is a single value used to estimate the population parameter. The confidence interval is a range of values which includes (with a preassigned probability called a confidence level) the true value of a population parameter.

- A hypothesis is an assertion made about a population. A test of hypothesis is a test of the validity of the assertion and is carried out by analysis of a sample of data.
- In evaluating a hypothesis, two types of errors can be made: type I error, reject the hypothesis when it is true, and type II error, accept the hypothesis when it is false.
- The statistical design of experiments provides plans for conducting experiments from which valid statistical analyses can be made.
- Randomization is the assignment of specimens to treatments in a purely chance manner.
- Replication is the repetition of an observation or measurement.
- Regression analysis is the study of the relationship between two or more variables.

PROBLEMS

Note: The specific questions have purposely been stated in nonstatistical language to provide the student with some practice in choosing techniques and making assumptions. When required, use a type I error of 0.05 and a confidence level of 95 percent. State any other assumptions needed.

10.1. In the casting industry, the pouring temperature of metal is important. For an aluminum alloy, past experience shows a standard deviation of 15°. During a particular day, five temperature tests were made during the pouring time.
   (a) If the average of these measurements was 1650°, make a statement about the average pouring temperature.
   (b) If you had taken 25 measurements and obtained the same results, what effect would this have on your statement? Make such a revised statement.

10.2. At the casting firm mentioned in problem 10.1, a new aluminum alloy is being poured. During the first day of pouring, five pouring temperature tests were made, with these results:

1705°   1725°   1685°   1690°   1715°

Make a statement about the average pouring temperature of this metal.

10.3. A manufacturer pressure-tests gaskets for leaks. The pressure at which this gasket leaked on nine trials was (in psi):

4000	3900	4500
4200	4400	4300
4800	4800	4300

Make a statement about the average "leak" pressure of this gasket.

10.4. In a test of 500 electronic tubes, 427 were found to be acceptable. Make a statement concerning the true proportion that would be acceptable.

10.5. In a meat packing firm, out of 600 pieces of beef, 420 were found to be Grade A. Make a statement about the true proportion of Grade A beef.

10.6. A specification requires that the average breaking strength of a certain material be at least 180 psi. Past data indicate the standard deviation of individual measurements to be 5 psi. How many tests are necessary to be 99 percent sure of detecting a lot that has an average strength of 170 psi?

10.7. Tests are to be run to estimate the average life of a product. Based on past data on similar products, it is assumed that the standard deviation of individual units is about 20 percent of the average life.

(a) How many units must be tested to be 90 percent sure that the sample estimate will be within 5 percent of the true average?

(b) Suppose funds were available to run only 25 tests. How sure would we be of obtaining an estimate within 5 percent?

Answer: (a) 44. (b) 78.8 percent.

10.8. A manufacturer of needles has a new method of controlling a diameter dimension. From many measurements of the present method, the average diameter is 0.076 cm with a standard deviation of 0.010 cm. A sample of 25 needles from the new process shows the average to be 0.071. If a smaller diameter is desirable, should the new method be adopted? (Assume that the standard deviation of the new method is the same as that for the present method.)

10.9. In the garment industry, the breaking strength of cloth is important. A heavy cotton cloth must have at least an average breaking strength of 200 psi. From one particular lot of this cloth, these five measurements of breaking strength (in psi) were obtained:

206
194
203
196
192

Does this lot of cloth meet the requirement of an average breaking strength of 200 psi?

Answer: $t = -0.67$.

10.10. In a drug firm, the variation in the weight of an antibiotic, from batch to batch, is important. With our present process, the standard deviation is 0.11 g. The research department has developed a new process that they believe will produce less variation. The following weight measurements (in grams) were obtained with the new process:

7.47
7.49
7.64
7.59
7.55

Does the new process have less variation?

10.11. A paper manufacturer has a new method of coating paper. The less variation in the weight of this coating, the more uniform and better the product. The following 10 sample coatings were obtained by the new method:

Coating weights (in weight/unit area × 100)	
223	234
215	229
220	223
238	235
230	227

If the standard deviation in the past was 9.3, is this proposed method any better? Should they switch to this method?

Answer: $\chi^2 = 5.43$.

10.12. A manufacturer of rubber products is trying to decide which "recipe" to use for a particular rubber compound. High tensile strength is desirable. Recipe 1 is cheaper to mix, but he is not sure if its strength is about the same as that of recipe 2. Five batches of rubber were made by each recipe and tested for tensile strength. These are the data collected (in psi):

Recipe 1	Recipe 2
3067	3200
2730	2777
2840	2623
2913	2044
2789	2834

Which recipe would you recommend that he use?

10.13. Test runs with five models of an experimental engine showed that they operated, respectively, for 20, 18, 22, 17, and 18 min with 1 gal of a certain kind of fuel. A proposed specification states that the engine must operate for a mean of at least 22 min.

(*a*) What can we conclude about the ability of the engine to meet the specification?

(*b*) What is the probability that the sample mean could have come from a process whose true mean is equal to the specification mean?

(*c*) How low would the mean operating minutes (of the engine population) have to be in order to have a 50 percent chance of concluding that the engine does not meet the specification?

Answer: (*a*) $t = -3.4$. (*b*) Approx. 0.03. (*c*) 20.1.

10.14. A manufacturer claims that the average length in a large lot of parts is 2.680 in. A large amount of past data indicates the standard deviation of individual lengths to be 0.002 in. A sample of 25 parts shows an average of 2.678 in. The manufacturer says that the result is still consistent with his claim because only a small sample was taken.

(a) State a hypothesis to evaluate his claim.
(b) Evaluate his claim using the standard hypothesis testing approach.
(c) Evaluate his claim using the confidence limit approach.

10.15. An engineer wants to determine if the type of test oven or temperature has a significant effect on the average life of a component. She proposes the following design of experiment:

	Oven 1	Oven 2	Oven 3
550°	1	0	1
575°	0	1	1
600°	1	1	0

The numbers in the body of the table represent the number of measurements to be made in the experiment. What are two reasons why interaction cannot be adequately evaluated in this design?

10.16. The molding department in a record manufacturing plant has been making too many defective records. There are many opinions about the reasons. One opinion states that the molding time per record has a cause-and-effect relationship with the number of defectives produced per 100 records. Several trial lots of 100 records each were made with various mold times. The results were:

Time, s	Number defective
2	16
4	13
5	8
7	8
10	4
11	6
13	5
17	3
17	5
20	3

Plot the data and graphically estimate the Y intercept and the slope.
Answer: The least-squares estimates are a Y intercept of 13.54 and a slope of -0.6076.

REFERENCES

Deming, W. Edwards (1982). *Out of the Crisis,* Massachusetts Institute of Technology, Cambridge, Massachusetts, p. 132.

Duncan, Acheson J. (1986). *Quality Control and Industrial Statistics,* 5th ed., Richard D. Irwin, Homewood, Illinois.

Ryan, T. P. (1989). *Statistical Methods for Quality Improvement,* John Wiley and Sons, New York.

SUPPLEMENTARY READING

Statistical methods: ASQC "How To" booklets (series of 13).

QCH4, Sections 23–26.

Siddhartha, R. Dalal, Edward B. Fowlkes, and Bruce Hoadley (1989). "Risk Analysis of the Space Shuttle: Pre-*Challenger* Prediction of Future," *Journal of the American Statistical Association,* December, pp. 945–957.

Wadsworth, Harrison M., Jr. (1990). *Handbook of Statistical Methods for Engineers and Scientists,* McGraw-Hill, Inc., New York.

CHAPTER
11

UNDERSTANDING CUSTOMER NEEDS

11.1 QUALITY AND COMPETITIVE ADVANTAGE

In the competitive world, all organizations aspire to have a unique competitive advantage. Such an advantage can be achieved by price, by ability to meet customer needs on short notice, and by quality. This chapter starts the journey to show how quality—both product features and freedom from deficiencies— can lead to a unique competitive advantage. By identifying customers, analyzing their needs, and understanding our quality status relative to competition, we can establish new product quality goals that will lead to a competitive advantage. We start with customers.

11.2 IDENTIFY THE CUSTOMERS

We define a customer as anyone who is impacted by the product or process. Three categories of customers then emerge:

1. *External customers, both current and potential.* A multiplicity of these customers gives rise to a variety of influences, depending on whether the customer is economically powerful or not and on its technological sophistication. For service organizations, the list of external customers may

extend far in scope. For example, customers of the Internal Revenue Service include not only taxpayers but the Treasury Department, Office of the President, Congress, accountants, lawyers, etc. Each customer has needs which must first be determined and then addressed in planning a product.

2. *Internal customers.* These include all functions impacted by the product at both the managerial and work force levels. Internal suppliers often view their internal customers as "captive" customers. Not so. Internal customers may have an alternative source, i.e., they may be able to purchase the product from an external supplier. For example, an Engineering Department procures research services from the company Research Department. The Engineering Department is an internal customer that may decide to use an external consultant to provide the services. An assembly plant purchases components from a sister plant within the company. That Assembly Department must be viewed as an internal customer that, in order to meet its own goals, could decide to go outside the company family to obtain the required quality on components.

3. *Suppliers as customers.* Suppliers should be viewed as extensions of internal customer departments such as Manufacturing. Thus, their needs must be understood and addressed during the planning for quality.

In identifying customers, some are obvious and some are not. An important tool for identifying all those who are impacted (i.e., customers) is the flow diagram. Figure 11.1 shows the flow diagram for the process of receiving, handling, and shipping "special customer orders" at Becton, Dickinson, a manufacturer of health care products (Engle and Ball, 1986). No one individual or department was able to describe the total process; a cross-functional quality improvement team created the diagram. Note that the diagram includes external customers (i.e., "consumer"), internal customers (e.g., "production inventory control"), and suppliers (e.g., "shipper").

Often, for external customers a "cast of characters" comprises the "customer." Thus, in selling products and services to a hospital, a supplier must understand the needs of the hospital purchasing manager, a quality assurance manager, heads of hospital departments, physicians, nurses, and (of no little consequence) the patient. One manufacturer learns the needs of four levels of customer: those who approve the purchase, those who influence the decision, those who sign the purchase order, and those who are users.

In practice, we must recognize that some customers are more important than others. It is typical that about 80 percent of the total sales volume comes from about 20 percent of the customers; these are the "vital few" customers who command priority. Within these key customer organizations, there is a distribution of individual customers which also may have a hierarchy of importance, e.g., a surgeon at a hospital is a key customer for surgical needles.

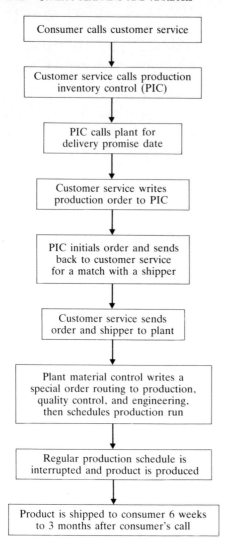

FIGURE 11.1
Special-order system (before remedial action).

11.3   SCOPE OF HUMAN NEEDS

In planning to collect information on customer needs, we must go beyond the search for obvious needs to the more subtle ones that present opportunities for innovative new-product designs.

First, let us focus on the distinction between stated needs and real needs. A consumer states a need for a "clothes dryer," but the real need is "to remove moisture"; a consumer wants a "lawn mower," but the real need is "to maintain height of lawn." In both cases, expressing the need in terms of a basic verb and noun can spawn new product ideas. One historical example is the replacement of hair nets by hair spray to satisfy the basic need of "secure hair."

Some needs are disguised or even unknown to the customer at the time of purchase. Such needs often lead to the customer using the product in a manner different from that intended by the supplier—a telephone number intended for emergencies is used for routine questions, a hair dryer is used in winter weather to thaw a lock, a tractor is used in unusual soil conditions. Designers view such applications as misuse of the product but might better view them as new applications for their products.

Some of these applications are misuse, but such needs must be understood and, in some cases, alternative design concepts considered. Then there are other needs that go far beyond the utilitarian. Some needs may be perceptional (e.g., the now classic example of Stew Leonard's supermarket customers, who believe that only unwrapped fish could be fresh); some needs may be cultural (e.g., a process such as computer-aided design threatens to reduce the need for a human expertise, and thus design engineers resist it).

The Hospital Corporation of America finds it useful to identify several levels of customer expectation, a concept suggested by Seraku Kano. Thus, at level I, a customer *assumes* that a basic need will be met; at level II, the customer will be *satisfied*; at level III, the customer will be *delighted* with the service. For example, suppose a patient must receive 33 radiation treatments. Waiting time in the therapy area is one attribute of this outpatient service. At level I, the patient *assumes* that the radiation equipment will be functioning each day for use; at level II, the patient will be *satisfied* if the waiting time in the area is moderate, say 15 minutes. At level III, the patient will be *delighted* if the waiting time is short, say 1 minute. To achieve a unique competitive advantage, we must focus on level III.

Customer needs may be clear or they may be disguised; they may be rational or less than rational. To create customers, those needs must be discovered and served.

11.4 SOURCES OF MARKET QUALITY INFORMATION

Market quality information includes quality alarm signals arising not only from a decline in sales but also from field failure reports, customer complaints, claims, lawsuits, etc.

Most alarm signals are poor measures of quality—rather, they are measures of expressed product dissatisfaction. A low level of alarm signals does not necessarily mean a high level of quality. Particularly for inexpensive products, complaint rates are a poor indicator of customer satisfaction. If customers are not satisfied, they simply switch brands—without submitting a complaint. Neither does the absence of product dissatisfaction mean that there is product satisfaction, since these two terms are not opposites. A product may be failure free and yet not be salable because a competitor's design is superior, has a lower price, etc.

A second source of market quality information is the vast array of published data available relative to quality. Some of these data are internal to the company. Many are published external to the company. Such "field intelligence" includes data bases on sales volume, price changes, success rate on bids, complaints, spare parts usage, salespersons' reports, ratings from customers and consumer journals, government reports, etc.

These two major sources of market quality information, while necessary, are not sufficient. A good deal of information is missing, and this can be provided only through special marketing research studies.

11.5 MARKETING RESEARCH IN QUALITY

In the broad sense, marketing research is the activity of studying those aspects of quality which influence or are influenced by the forces in the marketplace. In that sense, activities such as field complaint analysis or study of government research publications are a form of market research. In a narrower sense, marketing research involves exploring the unknown and creating data where none existed before. These newly created data come from such approaches as developing a new test device to simulate fitness for use, study of competitors' products, and, especially, making tests and securing feedbacks involving customers, users, and consumers. In the discussion that follows, the term "marketing research" will be used in its narrower sense. Gryna (1983) illustrates marketing research techniques as applied to quality.

Purposes of Marketing Research in Quality

The broad purposes are mainly to:

- Discover alarming situations for which existing alarm signals are silent
- Discover opportunities not disclosed by present information sources
- Test existing unsupported and even axiomatic beliefs

More specifically, marketing research in quality looks for answers to some cardinal questions:

- What is the relative importance of various product qualities as seen by the user? The answers provided by marketing research are typically different from the prior beliefs of the manufacturer. Sometimes the difference is dramatic.
- For the more important qualities, how does our product compare with competitors' products, as seen by users?
- What is the effect of these competing qualities (including our own) on users' costs, well-being, and other aspects of fitness for use?
- What are users' problems about which they do not complain but which we might nevertheless be able to remedy?
- What ideas do users have that we might be able to utilize for their benefit?

In the discussion below, the marketing research addresses customer needs for both components of quality—product features and freedom from deficiencies.

11.6 NEEDS RELATED TO PRODUCT FEATURES

To start, we need to identify the attributes that customers say are important in their purchasing decision. Table 11.1 shows the results of research in which customers (and potential customers) of floppy disks were asked to select important attributes. The relative importance was measured as the percent of customers who selected each attribute. Note that the list of attributes focuses both on the disks and on specific and general aspects of service.

An important next step is to learn how our product compares with the competition's. This can be accomplished by using a multiattribute study. Customers are asked to consider several product attributes and, for each attribute, to state the relative importance and a rating for our product and competitors' products. Section 2.9, "Standing in the Marketplace," presented three examples to illustrate customers' role in assessment. Additional examples of marketing research are given below.

The Shaving System Case

A leading manufacturer of razors and razor blades was confronted by a new competing model which featured an ingenious, improved blade-changing mechanism. When the competitor promoted the new model aggressively, the company marketing managers became apprehensive. They then succeeded in initiating a costly new product development to bring out a model that could

TABLE 11.1
Relative importance of attributes of floppy disks

Attribute	Relative importance, %
Quality of delivered products	98
Meeting delivery schedules	95
In-field reliability	95
Price	72
Provision of technical assistance	66
Handling large orders	64
Product sophistication	62
Meeting changing customer needs	51
Short delivery time	48
Capability of field service	45
Accessibility of suppliers' management	44
Specialization in floppy disk drive products	34

match the competition's. However, the top managers also authorized a field market research study to discover the reaction of consumers to the new development.

The planners of the research study identified the seven major quality characteristics of a shaving system. Next (through an intermediary market research company), they provided each of several hundred consumers with all three principal shaving systems then on the market. These users were asked to use each shaving system for a month and to report:

- The ranking of the seven qualities in their order of importance to the user.
- The ranking of the performance of each of the three systems for each of the seven qualities.

Table 11.2 shows the plan of the market research study. The resulting data showed that, as seen by the users:

1. Ease of blade changing was the least important quality.
2. The competitor's new blade-changing mechanism had failed to create a user preference over competing forms of blade changing.

    These findings denied the beliefs of the company marketing managers and came as a welcome surprise. They enabled the company to terminate the costly new product development then already in progress.

3. On one of the most critical qualities (product safety), the company's shaving system was inferior to both of the competing systems. This came as an unwelcome surprise and stimulated the company to take steps to eliminate this weakness. Note that *this inferiority could not have been discovered from field complaints*, since no normal user would conduct such a comparative study on his or her own initiative. It was "an alarming situation for which our present alarm signals are silent."

TABLE 11.2
Market research study—the shaving system case

Qualities	Users' rankings			
	Gillette	Gem	Schick	Importance
1. Remove beard				
2. Safety				
3. Ease of cleaning				
4. Ease of blade changing				
5. . . .				
6. . . .				
7. . . .				

Marketing Research for an Internal Customer

The central engineering staff of a large automotive manufacturer applied marketing research concepts to internal customers (Stevens, 1987). A survey questionnaire sent to internal customers first requested information about the frequency of contact with each of the seven staff areas. Respondents were then asked to state their degree of satisfaction with eight attributes of service: services meeting requirements, follow-up required, assistance available, competent people, cooperation, input requested, problem notification, and help in seeking contacts. An overall satisfaction rating was also requested. Finally, respondents were asked for details on any low ratings for the eight attributes and suggestions on how Engineering could improve its service to help achieve customer quality goals.

In generalizing about these examples, note that all were based on a study of customers who were experienced in using the product involved. Where possible, the studies determined both the relative importance of a number of attributes and a rating *relative to the competition* for each of those attributes. These studies can provide competitive benchmarks for the future.

Discovering Marketing Opportunities

Marketing research in the field provides access to realities that cannot be discovered in the laboratory. The conditions of use can involve environments, loads, user training levels, misapplication, etc., all of which may be different from the conditions prevailing in the laboratory. The laboratory does provide a relatively prompt, inexpensive simulation which is most helpful for making many decisions. However, this simulation cannot fully disclose the needs of fitness for use under the actual conditions of use.

Field studies can not only provide access to the realities of the conditions of use; they can also provide access to the users themselves. Through access to the user, it becomes possible to understand those user problems that are not a matter of poor quality but for which the manufacturer may nevertheless be able to provide a solution. For example, most users prefer to avoid disagreeable, time-consuming chores. Our food processors have successfully transferred many such chores from the household kitchen to the factory (e.g., soluble coffee, precooked foods) and have incidentally greatly increased their sales.

The study of the user's operation can be aided by dissecting the process of use. This is done by documenting all of the steps, analyzing them, and identifying opportunities for new-product development. Such information is valuable input to the product development function as that group embarks on a new design project.

Example 11.1. For a certain health care product, a clamp controlled the amount of flow of fluid from an external source to a patient during a dialysis process. An

TABLE 11.3
Opportunities for improving fitness for use of an industrial product

Stage	Opportunities
Receiving inspection	Provide data so incoming inspection can be eliminated
Material storage	Design product and packaging for ease of identification and handling
Processing	Do preprocessing of material (e.g., ready-mixed concrete); design product to maximize productivity when it is used in customer's manufacturing operation
Finished goods storage, warehouse and field	Design product and packaging for ease of identification and handling
Installation, alignment, and checkout	Use modular concepts and other means to facilitate setups by customer rather than manufacturer
Maintenance, preventive	Incorporate preventive maintenance in product (e.g., self-lubricated bearings)
Maintenance, corrective	Design product to permit self-diagnosis by user

analysis using a flow diagram showed that the proposed clamp was excellent in controlling the flow of fluid, but it was inconvenient in a later step that required the patient to wear the product under clothing. The original focus was on performance of the product, but the flow diagram pinpointed a later problem of inconvenience to the patient. See Section 12.3, "Designing for Basic Functional Requirements," for further discussion.

Opportunities for improvement span the full range of customer use from initial receipt through operation. The primary stages and examples of ideas for improving fitness for use are given in Table 11.3. (Also see Table 4.6 for examples of hidden customer needs that presented opportunities for improvement.) These opportunities must then be translated into specific product quality goals which, in turn, help to create a unique competitive advantage.

11.7   NEEDS RELATED TO PRODUCT DEFICIENCIES

Understanding customer needs must also include the deficiencies side of the quality definition. Clearly, the emphasis during planning must be on *prevention* of deficiencies (defects, failures, errors, etc.).

With respect to prevention of deficiencies, the following chapters discuss the concepts and tools necessary in various functional areas. An important input to such prevention effort are the data on field complaints. Most organizations have systems of collecting and analyzing information on customer complaints. (For a discussion of these systems, see Section 20.7, "Processing and Resolution of Customer Complaints.") A Pareto analysis of field failures, complaints, product returns, etc., serves to identify the "vital

TABLE 11.4
Pareto analysis of complaints on fuel nozzles

| Failure mode | Ranking based on various measures | | |
	Frequency	Warranty charges	Effect on user costs
G	1	4	3
A	2	1	6
D	3	2	1
F	4	5	4
N	5	7	8
L	6	3	2
P	7	6	5
R	8	8	7

few" quality problems to be addressed in both current and future product development. This type of analysis is in wide use. Table 11.4 shows a Pareto analysis of field complaints on fuel nozzles using several different indices. A conventional Pareto analysis would rank the various types of complaints according to the frequency of occurrence; but when those complaints are evaluated on an economic basis, the ranking changes. Note also that there are several possible economic indices such as warranty costs and effect on user costs. The priorities for future product development can be quite different depending on the measure used in the Pareto analysis. Similarly, data on defects found internally must be analyzed on the proper basis in order to prioritize prevention efforts, many of which must be addressed during product development.

To prevent recurrence of specific complaints in future products requires a careful analysis of the words and phrases used to describe complaints.

Example 11.2. An annual mail survey of automobile customers revealed a significant number of complaints on "fit of doors"; within the company, this term referred to the "margin" and "flushness." Margin is the space between the front door and fender or between the front and rear doors. Sometimes the margin was not uniform, e.g., a wider space at the top as compared to a narrower space at the bottom of the door. Flushness refers to the smoothness of fit of the door with the body of the car after the door is shut. Steps were taken (at a significant cost) during processing and assembly to correct the margin and flushness problems. But subsequent surveys again reported complaints on fit of doors.

Fortunately, other marketing research input became available. The company held periodic focus group meetings in which customers attended a meeting where they answered a questionnaire and discussed selected issues in more detail. Fit of doors again was proclaimed to be a problem by the customers. On the spot, they were asked, "What do you mean by fit of doors?" Their answer was *not* margin or flushness. First, fit meant the amount of effort required to close the door. They complained that they had to "slam the door hard in order to get it to close completely the first time." Second, fit meant sound. When they left the car and closed the door, they wanted to hear a solid, "businesslike" sound instead of "a metallic, loose sound" (that told them the door was not closed). The marketing research provided a correct understanding of the complaint, which subsequently required changes in the product design and the manufacturing process. Earlier, the company had acted on the complaint, but it had solved the wrong problem. It was a waste of resources—like spraying scrap with perfume.

11.8 SPECIAL SOURCES OF MARKETING RESEARCH INFORMATION

In addition to readily available published information and marketing research surveys, special sources of data and information are useful. These include employee use of company products, purchase of data, product monitoring, company maintained service centers, and continuing measurements. In one example, a national pizza chain gives several thousand customers $60 per year. In return, the customers purchase and consume one pizza per month and provide feedback in a detailed report. In another case, computer users are asked to install instruments in their computers as a means of collecting data on error rates. In a last example, Xerox uses a series of continuing measurements ("competitive benchmarks") that become the basis for quality, cost, and delivery targets (Pipp, 1983). See QCH4, pp. 12.10–12.12, for elaboration on special data sources.

SUMMARY

- A customer is anyone who is impacted by a product or process.
- Customers fall into three categories—external, internal, and suppliers.
- Customer needs may be clear or may be disguised; they may be rational or less than rational. But these needs must be discovered and served.
- A low level of customer dissatisfaction (e.g., complaints) does *not* necessarily mean that customers are satisfied.
- Marketing research for quality analyzes those aspects of quality which are impacted by forces in the marketplace.
- Customer satisfaction should be measured relative to the competition's and should address both product features and freedom from deficiencies.
- Marketing research can help to discover opportunities which can lead to achieving a unique competitive advantage.

PROBLEMS

11.1. For a specific output of your department in an organization, sketch a simple flow diagram of the journey of the output throughout the organization. Then prepare a list of the internal and external customers.

11.2. Identify your own customers and suppliers for a representative 24-hour day.

11.3. For any *consumer* product, prepare a plan of marketing research aimed at:

(*a*) Identification of the principal product qualities

(*b*) Ranking these qualities in their order of importance to users

(*c*) Discovering the relative performance of competing companies with respect to the principal product qualities

11.4. For any *industrial* product, prepare a plan of market research aimed at securing data similar to those set out in Problem 11.3.

11.5 Walk through a food supermarket and identify some of the products for which there has been an extensive transfer of work from the household kitchen to food-processing factories. In addition, identify some further potentialities for such transfer. Report your findings, with special emphasis on the quality problems involved.

11.6. You are participating in the preparation of a bid on a military optical system used for range finding. The military specification requires that the subsystems be interchangeable (so that in the event of damage, the failed subsystem can be unplugged and replaced with a spare). You know from experience that this is a wise provision. However, you are disturbed by the further requirement that the optical elements (lenses, prisms, etc.) within each subsystem should also be interchangeable. To your knowledge, this is a foolish requirement since the military has never had the special repair and test facilities needed to reassemble optical elements in the field. To your knowledge, the military also lacks the means of testing for this interchangeability.

There is a procedure available for proposing a change in such unrealistic specifications, but you once went through this procedure and found it to be shockingly long and difficult. In addition, your company has had poor success in securing military business because of being underbid in price by competitors. You have suspected for some time that one reason for this lack of success is that your company does its bidding on the basis of meeting all specification requirements (sensible or not), whereas the competitors may be doing their bidding on the basis of meeting only those requirements which make sense.

You are now faced with making a recommendation on how to structure the bid with respect to the requirement for the unneeded interchangeability. What do you propose? Why? If you propose to bid on the basis of not meeting the "foolish" requirement, what do you propose to do in the event the military later finds out what has happened?

REFERENCES

Engle, David, and David Ball (1986). "Improving Customer Service for Special Orders," *Juran Report Number Six,* pp. 106–110.

Gryna, Frank M. (1983). "Marketing Research and Product Quality," *ASQC Quality Congress Transactions,* Milwaukee, pp. 385–392.

Pipp, Frank J. (1983). "Management Commitment to Quality: Xerox Corporation," *Quality Progress,* August, pp. 12–17.

Stevens, Eric R. (1987). "Implementing an Internal—Customer Satisfaction Improvement Process," *Juran Report Number Eight,* pp. 140–145.

SUPPLEMENTARY READING

Marketing research for quality: QCH4, Section 12.

Plsek, Paul E. (1987). "Defining Quality at the Marketing/Development Interface," *Quality Progress*, June, pp. 28–36.
Marketing research: Barabba, Vincent P. (1990). "The Market Research Encyclopedia," *Harvard Business Review*, May–June, pp. 105–116.

CHAPTER
12

DESIGNING
FOR
QUALITY

12.1 OPPORTUNITIES FOR IMPROVEMENT IN PRODUCT DESIGN

In this step on the quality spiral, the needs of the user are translated into a set of product design requirements for manufacturing (or the operations function in a service organization). This activity is called product development, research and development, engineering, or product design.

There is dramatic evidence that many problems encountered by both external and internal customers can be traced to the design of the product.

> **Example 12.1.** In a classic study of 850 field failures of relatively simple electronic equipment, 43 percent of the failures were due to engineering design deficiencies.

> **Example 12.2.** In one chemical company, a startling 50 percent of the product shipped was out of specification. Fortunately, the product was fit for use. A review concluded that many of the specifications were obsolete and had to be changed.

253

Example 12.3. A study of health care products revealed that 34 percent of the product recalls were caused by faulty product or software design.

Example 12.4. A manufacturer of terminals, modems, and other computer products analyzed the reasons for design changes. Local "wisdom" said that (1) about 10 percent of the changes were due to errors in the design and (2) the remaining changes were related to cost reduction projects, requests from Manufacturing, and changing customer requirements. But an in-depth analysis of design changes on four product lines reached a surprising conclusion: 78 percent of the changes were due to design errors.

For mechanical and electronic products of at least moderate complexity, errors during product development cause about 40 percent of fitness-for-use problems. Where Product Development is responsible for both creating the formulation (design) of the product and developing the manufacturing process, as in chemicals, about 50 percent of the problems are due to development.

12.2 EARLY WARNING CONCEPT AND DESIGN ASSURANCE

The process of developing modern products involves an evolution through distinct phases of development (see Table 12.1 for an example of phases).

The frequency and severity of problems caused by design have stimulated companies to develop more and better forms of early warning on impending troubles. These early warnings are available in a variety of forms (Table 12.1). Much has been done to evolve special quality-oriented tools described in this chapter, to help evaluate designs, and to improve the design process itself. Collectively, these early warnings and quality-oriented tools provide added

TABLE 12.1
Forms of early warning of new-product problems

Phases of new-product progression	Forms of early warning of new-product troubles
Concept and feasibility study	Concept review
Prototype design	Design review, reliability and maintainability prediction, failure mode, effect, and criticality analysis, safety analyses, value engineering
Prototype construction	Prototype test, environmental test, overstressing
Preproduction	Pilot production lots, evaluation of tolerances
Early full-scale production	In-house testing (e.g., kitchen, road), consumer use panels, limited marketing area
Full-scale production, marketing and use	Employees as test panels, special provisions for prompt feedback
All phases	Failure analysis, data collection and analysis

assurance that the new designs will not create undue trouble as they progress around the spiral. Many of these forms of early warning are administered by specialists in reliability, maintainability, and other fields. The timing of their inputs is critical. Early timing can provide constructive help; late timing causes resistance to the warnings and often creates an atmosphere of blame. The cost of changes in a design can be huge, e.g., a design *change* during pilot production of a major electronics product can cost over a million dollars.

Next, we will examine some techniques that help to ensure overall design effectiveness. These design assurance techniques address functional performance, reliability, maintainability, safety, manufacturability, and other attributes.

12.3 DESIGNING FOR BASIC FUNCTIONAL REQUIREMENTS

Product development translates customer expectations for functional requirements into specific engineering and quality characteristics. For traditional products, this process is not complicated and can be achieved by experienced design engineers without using any special techniques. For modern products, it is useful to document and analyze the design logic. This means starting with the desired product attributes and then identifying the necessary characteristics for raw materials, parts, assemblies, and process steps. Such an approach goes under a variety of names, such as systems engineering, functional analysis systems technique, structured product/process analysis, and quality function deployment.

Quality Function Deployment

One technique for documenting overall design logic is quality function deployment (QFD). QFD is a technique consisting of a series of interlocking matrixes that translates customer needs into product and process characteristics (see Figure 12.1). Sometimes a matrix incorporates additional information or integrates information in an unusual and useful form. For example, Figure 12.2 is a matrix of customer needs ("customer requirements") and product features ("technical requirements") for paper being supplied to a commercial printer (Ernst and Young, 1990). Note the additional information on importance weighting, correlations between requirements, units of target values (e.g., millimeters for width and thickness), and competitive evaluations. The "roof" of the diagram showing the correlations leads to a name for the diagram, i.e., the "house of quality."

QFD helps to ensure that customer needs are translated into both the design of the product and the design of the process. The first two of four matrixes (Figure 12.2) become the starting point for detailed engineering design which leads to parameter design and product specifications. A dramatic

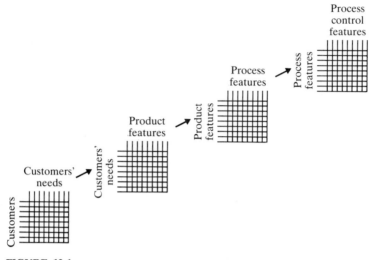

FIGURE 12.1
Generic planning spreadsheets. (*From Juran et al., 1990.*)

example of the deployment of an overall quality goal is the initial analysis for the Taurus automobile (see Section 4.10, "A Road Map for Planning of Products for Salability"). In that example, the overall goal of "best in class" was deployed into 429 parameters of the design. Akao (1990) provides many examples of various matrixes and charts that are useful in quality function deployment.

Parameter Design and Robust Design

The most basic product feature is performance, i.e., the output—the color density of a television set, the turning radius of an automobile. To create such output, engineers use engineering principles to combine inputs of materials, parts, components, assemblies, liquids, etc. For each of these inputs, the engineer identifies parameters and specifies numerical values to achieve the required output of the final product. For each parameter, the specifications state a target (or nominal) value and a tolerance range around the target. The process is called parameter and tolerance design.

In selecting these target values, it is useful to set values so that the performance of the product in the field is not affected by variability in manufacturing or field conditions. Then the design is said to be "robust." Robust designs provide optimum performance simultaneously with variation in manufacturing and field conditions.

Designers have always tried to create robust designs. But as products become more complex, with many factors affecting performance, it becomes difficult to know (1) what factors do affect performance and (2) what nominal

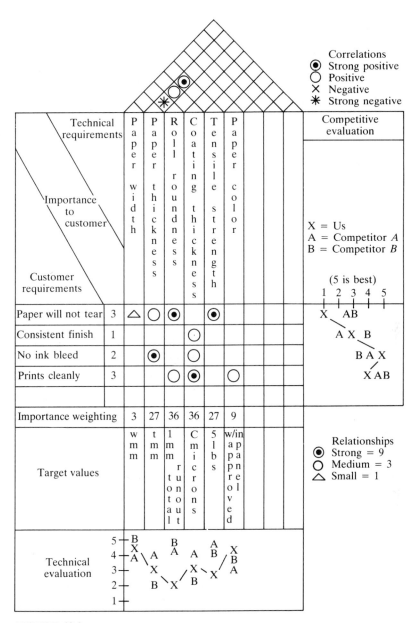

FIGURE 12.2
House of quality. (*From Ernst and Young, 1990.*)

values to set for each factor. Furthermore, some factors affect the mean value of an output parameter while others affect the variation about the mean. One of the purposes of development testing is to investigate these matters. A powerful aid to planning development testing is the statistical design of experiments (see Section 10.11, "The Design of Experiments").

Application of Experimental Design to Product and Process Design

Taguchi (1978) has developed a method for determining the optimum values of product and process parameters which will minimize variation while keeping the mean value on target. The emphasis of setting target values on design parameters in a way that minimizes variation is an important contribution of this technique.

Phadke et al. (1983) describe an application of this approach to integrated circuits in the Bell System. The example concerns the dimensions of the contact window of a large-scale integrated chip. Windows that are not open or are too small result in a loss of contact to the devices, while excessively large windows lead to shorted device features. The steps in window forming and the factors critical to each step are shown in Table 12.2.

Levels of each of the nine critical factors were selected. Six of the factors have three levels each; three of the factors have only two levels each. A full factorial experiment to explore all possible factor-level combinations would require $3^6 \times 2^3$, or 5832, observations. (Twelve experiments were originally planned.) Instead, a fractional factorial design was chosen to investigate 18 combinations with a total of 34 measurements. Three dimensions of each window were measured. Transformed variables instead of absolute values were used in the data analysis. The variables selected were the mean and the signal-to-noise ratio (s/n). The signal-to-noise ratio is defined as:

$$s/n = \log_{10}\left(\frac{\text{mean}}{\text{standard deviation}}\right)$$

TABLE 12.2
Fabrication steps and critical factors in window forming

Fabrication step	Critical factors
Applying photo resist	Photo-resist viscosity (B) and spin speed (C)
Baking	Baking temperature (D) and baking time (E)
Exposing	Mask dimension (A), aperture (F), and exposure time (G)
Developing	Developing time (H)
Plasma etching	Etching time (I)
Removing photo resist	Does not affect window size

The problem was to determine the factor levels that yield a maximum s/n while keeping the mean on target. Two steps were needed:

1. Determining the factors which have a significant effect on the s/n. These are the factors that control process variability and are referred to as control factors. For each control factor, the level chosen is that with the highest s/n, thus maximizing the overall ratio.

2. Selecting from the control factors one that has the smallest effect on the s/n. This factor is called a signal factor. The levels of the factors that are neither control factors nor signal factors are set at the nominal levels prior to the experiment. Finally, the level of the signal factor is set so that the mean response is on target.

The analysis of variance revealed the control factors to be factors *A, B, C, F, G,* and *H*. Based on an analysis of the data and engineering judgment, the signal factor was chosen to be the exposure time.

The levels selected for each of the factors are shown in Table 12.3. Using these levels, a sample of chips was manufactured. The resulting benefits were:

	Old conditions	Optimum conditions
Standard deviation	0.29	0.14
Visual defects (window per chip)	0.12	0.04

After observing these improvements, the process engineers eliminated a number of in-process checks, thereby reducing the overall time spent by the wafers in photolithography by a factor of two.

TABLE 12.3
Optimum factor levels

Label	Factors' names	Standard levels	Optimum levels
A	Mask dimension, μm	2.0	2.5
B	Viscosity	204	204
C	Spin speed, r/min	3000	4000
D	Bake temperature, °C	105	105
E	Bake time, min	30	30
F	Aperture	2	2
G	Exposure. PEP setting	Normal	Normal
H	Developing time, s	45	60
I	Plasma etch time, min	13.2	13.2

Source: Phadke et al. (1983, p. 1303).

The Taguchi methodology has spawned some controversy. For a rigorous and practical account of the "triumphs and tragedies" of the methodology, see Pignatiello and Ramberg (1992). See also the October 1985 issue of the *Journal of Quality Technology*; most of this issue is devoted to an examination of the Taguchi approach.

12.4 DESIGNING FOR TIME-ORIENTED PERFORMANCE (RELIABILITY)

Design engineers realize that a product should have a long service life with few failures. As products become more complex, failures increase with operating time. Traditional efforts of design, although necessary, are often not sufficient to achieve both the functional performance requirements and a low rate of failures with time. To prevent these failures, specialists have created a collection of tools called reliability engineering.

Reliability is the ability of a product to perform a required function under stated conditions for a stated period of time (ISO 8402-1986). (More simply, reliability is the chance that a product will work for the required time.) If this definition is dissected, four implications become apparent:

1. The quantification of reliability in terms of a probability.
2. A statement defining successful product performance.
3. A statement defining the environment in which the equipment must operate.
4. A statement of the required operating time between failures. (Otherwise, the probability is a meaningless number for time-oriented products.)

To achieve high reliability, it is necessary to define the specific tasks required. This task definition is called the *reliability program*. The early development of reliability programs emphasized the *design* phase of the product life cycle. However, it soon became apparent that the manufacturing and field-usage phases could not be handled separately. This resulted in reliability programs that spanned the full product life cycle, i.e., "cradle to grave."

A reliability program typically includes the following activities: setting overall reliability goals, apportionment of the reliability goals, stress analysis, identification of critical parts, failure mode and effect analysis, reliability prediction, design review, selection of suppliers (see Chapter 9), control of reliability during manufacturing (see Chapters 16 and 17), reliability testing, and failure reporting and corrective action system (see Chapter 20). Except as indicated, these activities will be discussed in this chapter and Chapter 13.

Some elements of a reliability program are *old* (e.g., stress analysis, part selection). The significant *new* aspect is the *quantification* of reliability. The act of quantification makes reliability a design parameter just like weight and tensile strength. Thus, reliability can be submitted to specification and verification. Quantification also helps to refine certain traditional design tasks such as stress analysis and part selection.

Before embarking on a discussion of reliability tasks, a remark on the application of the tasks is in order.

- These tasks are clearly not warranted for simple products. However, many products that were originally simple are now becoming more complex. When this is the case, the various reliability tasks should be examined to see which, if any, might be justified.
- Reliability techniques were originally developed for electronic and space products, but their adaptation to mechanical products has now achieved success.
- These techniques apply not only to products a company markets but also to capital equipment a company purchases, e.g., numerically controlled machines. A less obvious application is to chemical-processing equipment.

Setting Overall Reliability Goals

The original development of reliability quantification consisted of a probability and a mission time along with a definition of performance and usage conditions. This proved confusing to many people, so the index was abbreviated (using a mathematical relationship) to mean time between failures. Many people believe this to be the only reliability index. This is not so; no single index applies to most products. A summary of common indices (often called *figures of merit*) is presented in Table 12.4.

As experience is gained in quantifying reliability, many companies are learning that it is best to create an index that uniquely meets the needs of those who will use the index. Users of the index include not only internal technical personnel but also marketing personnel and users of the product. Examples of reliability indices and goals are:

- *For a telephone system.* The downtime of each switching center should be a maximum of 24 hours per 40 years.
- *For an engine manufacturer.* Seventy percent of the engines produced should pass through the warranty period without generating a claim. The number of failures per failed engine should not exceed one.

Note that both of these examples quantify reliability.

Setting overall reliability goals requires a meeting of the minds on (1) reliability as a number, (2) the environmental conditions to which the numbers apply, and (3) a definition of successful product performance. This is not easily

TABLE 12.4
Reliability figures of merit

Figure of merit	Meaning
Mean time between failures (MTBF)	Mean time between successive failures of a repairable product
Failure rate	Number of failures per unit time
Mean time to failure (MTTF)	Mean time to failure of a nonrepairable product or mean time to first failure of a repairable product
Mean life	Mean value of life ("life" may be related to major overhaul, wear-out time, etc.)
Mean time to first failure (MTFF)	Mean time to first failure of a repairable product
Mean time between maintenance (MTBM)	Mean time between a specified type of maintenance action
Longevity	Wear-out time for a product
Availability	Operating time expressed as a percentage of operating and repair time
System effectiveness	Extent to which a product achieves the requirements of the user
Probability of success	Same as reliability (but often used for "one-shot" or non-time-oriented products)
b_{10} life	Life during which 10% of the population would have failed
b_{50} life	Median life, or life during which 50% of the population would have failed
Repairs/100	Number of repairs per 100 operating hours

accomplished. However, the act of requiring designers to define both environmental conditions and successful product performance with precision forces the designer to understand the design in greater depth.

Reliability Apportionment, Prediction, and Analysis

The process of reliability quantification involves three phases:

1. *Apportionment (or budgeting):* the process of allocating reliability objectives among various elements which collectively make up a higher-level product.
2. *Prediction:* the use of prior performance data plus probability theory to calculate the expected failure rates for various circuits, configurations, etc.
3. *Analysis:* the identification of the strong and weak portions of the design to serve as a basis for improvements, trade-offs, and similar actions.

These phases are illustrated in Table 12.5, which shows reliability objectives of the Boeing Company.

In the top section of the table, an overall reliability requirement of 95 percent for 1.45 hours is apportioned to the six subsystems of a missile. The second section of the table apportions the budget for the explosive subsystem to the three units within the subsystem. The allocation for the fusing circuitry is 0.998 or, in terms of mean time between failures, 725 hours. In the final section of the table, the proposed design for the circuitry is analyzed and a reliability prediction made, using the method of adding failure rates. As the prediction indicates an MTBF of 1398 hours as compared to a budget of 725 hours, the proposed design is acceptable. The prediction technique not only provides a quantitative evaluation of a design or a design change but can also identify design areas having the largest potential for reliability improvement. Thus, the "vital few" will be obvious by noting the components with the highest failure rates. In this example, the transistors, diodes, and tantalum capacitors account for about 70 percent of all the unreliability.

The approach of adding failure rates to predict system reliability is analogous to the control of weight in aircraft structures, where a running record is kept of weight as various parts are added to the design.

Reliability prediction is a continuous process starting with paper *predictions* based on a design analysis, plus historical failure-rate information. The evaluation ends with reliability *measurement* based on data from customer use of the product. Table 12.6 lists some characteristics of the various phases.

While the visible result of the prediction procedure is to quantify the reliability numbers, the *process* of prediction is usually as important as the resulting numbers. This is so because the prediction cannot be made without obtaining rather detailed information on product missions, environments, critical component histories, etc. Acquiring this information often gives the designer knowledge previously unavailable. Even if the designer is unable to secure the needed information, this inability nevertheless identifies the areas of ignorance in which the designer is forced to work.

Reliability predictions and reliability analyses are made more effective by making use of computer software. Such software not only handles the detailed calculations but makes it feasible to identify and assess many alternatives before finalizing a design. The "Directory of Software" published periodically in *Quality Progress* includes a description of software for reliability.

Parts Selection and Control

In Table 12.5 we saw how system reliability rests on a base of reliability of the component parts.

The vital role played by parts reliability has resulted in programs for thorough selection, evaluation, and control of parts. These programs include parts application studies, approved parts lists, identification of critical components, and use of derating. For elaboration, see QCH4, pages 13.27–13.28.

TABLE 12.5
Establishment of reliability objectives*

		System breakdown			
Subsystem	**Type of operation**	**Reliability**	**Unreliability**	**Failure rate per hour**	**Reliability objective***
Air frame	Continuous	0.997	0.003	0.0021	483
Rocket motor	One-shot	0.995	0.005		1/200 operations
Transmitter	Continuous	0.982	0.018	0.0126	80.5 h
Receiver	Continuous	0.988	0.012	0.0084	121 h
Control system	Continuous	0.993	0.007	0.0049	207 h
Explosive system	One-shot	0.995	0.005		1/200 operations
System		0.95	0.05		

		Explosive subsystem breakdown		
Unit	**Operating mode**	**Reliability**	**Unreliability**	**Reliability objective**
Fusing circuitry	Continuous	0.998	0.002	725 h
Safety and arming mechanism	One-shot	0.999	0.001	1/1000 operations
Warhead	One-shot	0.998	0.002	2/1000 operations
Explosive subsystem		0.995	0.005	

	Unit breakdown		
Fusing circuitry component part classification	**Number used, n**	**Failure rate per part, λ (%/1000 h)**	**Total part failure rate, $n\lambda$ (%/1000 h)**
Transistors	93	0.30	27.90
Diodes	87	0.15	13.05
Film resistors	112	0.04	4.48
Wirewound resistors	29	0.20	5.80
Paper capacitors	63	0.04	2.52
Tantalum capacitors	17	0.50	8.50
Transformers	13	0.20	2.60
Inductors	11	0.14	1.54
Solder joints and wires	512	0.01	5.12
			71.51

$$\text{MTBF} = \frac{1}{\text{failure rate}} = \frac{1}{\sum n\lambda} = \frac{1}{0.0007151} = 1398 \text{ h}$$

Source: Adapted by F. M. Gryna, Jr., from Beaton (1959, p. 65).
* For a mission time of 1.45 hours.

TABLE 12.6
Stages of reliability prediction and measurement

	1. Start of design	2. During detailed design	3. At final design	4. From system tests	5. From customer usage
Basis	Prediction based on approximate part counts and part failure rates from previous product usage; little knowledge of stress levels, redundancy, etc.	Prediction based on quantities and types of parts, redundancies, stress levels, etc.	Prediction based on types and quantities of part failure rates for expected stress levels, redundancies, external environments, special maintenance practices, special effects of system complexity, cycling effects, etc.	Measurement based on the results of tests of the complete system; appropriate reliability indices are calculated from the number of failures and operating time	Same as step 4 except calculations are based on customer usage data
Primary uses	Evaluate feasibility of meeting a proposed numerical requirement Help in establishing a reliability goal for design	Evaluate overall reliability Define problem areas	Evaluate overall reliability Define problem areas	Evaluate overall reliability Define problem areas	Measure achieved reliability Define problem areas Obtain data for future designs

Note: System tests in steps 4 and/or 5 may reveal problems that result in a revision of the "final" design. Such changes can be evaluated by repeating steps 3, 4, and 5.

Critical Components List. A component part is considered "critical" if any of the following conditions apply:

• It has a high population in the equipment.
• It has a single source of supply.
• It must function to special, tight limits.
• It has not been proved to the reliability standard, i.e., there are no test data or usage data are insufficient.

The critical components list should be prepared early in the design effort. It is common practice to formalize these lists, showing, for each critical component, the nature of the critical features, the plan for quantifying reliability, the plan for improving reliability, etc. The list becomes the basic planning document for (1) test programs for qualifying parts, (2) design guidance in application studies and techniques, and (3) design guidance for application of redundant parts, circuits, or subsystems.

Derating Practice. Derating is the assignment of a product to operate at stress levels below its normal rating, e.g., a capacitor rated at 300 V is used in a 200-V application. For many components, data are available showing failure rate as a function of stress levels. The conservative designer will use such data to achieve reliability by using the parts at low power ratios and low ambient temperatures.

Some companies have established internal policies with respect to derating. Derating is also a form of quantifying the factor of safety and hence lends itself to setting guidelines as to the margins to be used. Derating may be considered a method of determining more scientifically the factor of safety which engineers have long provided on an empirical basis. For example, if the calculated load of a structure is 20 tons, engineers might design the structure to withstand 100 tons as a protection against unanticipated loads, misuse, hidden flaws, deterioration, etc.

Failure Mode, Effect, and Criticality Analysis

Two techniques provide a methodical way of examining a design for possible ways in which failures can occur. In the *failure mode, effect, and criticality analysis* (FMECA), a product is examined at the system and/or lower levels for all the ways in which a failure may occur. For each potential failure, an estimate is made of its effect on the total system and of its seriousness. In addition, a review is made of the action being taken (or planned) to minimize the probability of failure or to minimize the effect of failure. Figure 12.3 shows a portion of an FMECA for a traveling lawn sprinkler. Each hardware item is listed on a separate line. Note that the failure "mode" is the symptom of the failure, as distinct from the cause of failure, which consists of the proved reasons for the existence of the symptoms. The analysis can be elaborated to include such matters as:

- *Safety.* Injury is the most serious of all failure effects. In consequence, safety is handled through special programs.
- *Effect on downtime.* Must the system stop until repairs are made, or can repairs be made during an off-duty time?
- *Access.* What hardware items must be removed to get at the failed component?
- *Repair planning.* What is the anticipated repair time? What special repair tools are needed?
- *Recommendations.* What changes in designs or specifications should be made? What tests should be added? What instructions should be included in manuals of inspection, operation, or maintenance?

1 = Very low (<1 in 1000)
2 = Low (3 in 1000)
3 = Medium (5 in 1000)
4 = High (7 in 1000)
5 = Very high (>9 in 1000)

T = Type of failure
P = Probability of occurrence
S = Seriousness of failure to system
H = Hydraulic failure
M = Mechanical failure
W = Wear failure
C = Customer abuse

Product   HRC-1

Date   Jan. 14. 1991

By   S.M.

Component part number	Possible failure	Cause of failure	T	P	S	Effect of failure on product	Alternatives
Worm bearing 4224	Bearing worn	Not aligned with bottom housing	M	1	4	Spray head wobble or slowing down	Improve inspection
Zytel 101		Excessive spray head wobble	M	1	3	Ditto	Improve worm bearing
Bearing stem 4225	Excessive wear	Poor bearing/material combination	M	5	4	Spray head wobbles and loses power	Change stem material
Brass		Dirty water in bearing area	M	5	4	Ditto	Improve worm seal area
		Excessive spray head wobble	M	2	3	Ditto	Improve operating instructions
Thrust washer 4226	Excessive wear	High water pressure	M	2	5	Spray head will stall out	Inform customer in instructions
Fulton 404		Dirty water in washers	M	5	5	Ditto	Improve worm seal design
Worm 4527	Excessive wear in bearing area	Poor bearing/material combination	M	5	4	Spray head wobbles and loses power	Change bearing stem material
Brass		Dirty water in bearing area	M	5	4	Ditto	Improve worm seal design
		Excessive spray head wobble	M	2	3	Ditto	Improve operating instructions

FIGURE 12.3
Failure mode, effect, and criticality analysis.

267

In Figure 12.3, a ranking procedure has been applied in order to assign priorities to the failure modes for further study. The ranking is twofold: (1) the probability of occurrence of the failure mode, and (2) the severity of the effect. For each of these, a scale of 1 to 5 is used. If desired, a risk priority number can be calculated as the product of the ratings. Priority is then assigned to investigating failure modes with high risk priority numbers.

In this example, the analysis revealed that about 30 percent of the expected failures were in the worm-and-bearing-stem area and that a redesign could easily be justified.

For most products, it is not economical to conduct the analysis of failure mode and failure effect for each component. Instead, engineering judgment is used to single out items which are critical to the operation of the product. As the FMECA proceeds for these selected items, the designer will discover that ready answers for some of the failure modes are lacking and that further analysis is necessary.

Generally, FMECA on one item is helpful to designers of other items in the system. In addition, the analyses are useful in planning for inspection, assembly, maintainability, and safety.

Evaluating Designs by Testing

Although reliability prediction, design review, FMECA, and other techniques are valuable as early-warning devices, they cannot be a substitute for the ultimate proof, i.e., use of the product by the customer. However, field experience comes too late and must be preceded by a substitute—various forms of testing the product to simulate field use.

Long before reliability technology was developed, several types of tests (performance, environmental, stress, life) were made to evaluate a design. The advent of reliability, maintainability, and other parameters resulted in additional types of tests.

A summary of types of tests for evaluating a design is given in Table 12.7. It is often possible to plan a test program so that one type of test can serve more than one purpose, e.g., evaluating both performance and environmental capabilities.

All tests provide some degree of design assurance. They also involve a risk of leading one astray. The principal sources of risk are:

Intended use versus actual use. The designer typically aims to attain fitness for intended use. However, actual use can differ from the designer's concept due to variations in environment and other conditions of use. In addition, some users will misapply or misuse the product.

Model construction versus subsequent production. Models are usually built by skilled specialists under the supervision of designers. Subsequent production is carried out by less skilled factory workers under supervisors

TABLE 12.7
Summary of tests used to evaluate a design

Type of test	Purpose
Performance	Determine ability of product to meet basic performance requirements
Environmental	Evaluate ability of product to withstand defined environmental levels; determine interval environments generated by product operation; verify environmental levels specified
Stress	Determine levels of stress that a product can withstand in order to determine the safety margin inherent in the design; determine modes of failure that are not associated with time
Reliability	Determine product reliability and compare to requirements; monitor for trends
Maintainability	Determine time required to make repairs and compare to requirements
Life	Determine wear-out time for a product and failure modes associated with time
Pilot run	Determine if fabrication and assembly processes are capable of meeting design requirements; determine if reliability will be degraded

who must meet standards of productivity as well as quality. In addition, factory processes seldom possess the adaptive flexibility available in the model shop.

Variability due to small numbers. The number of models built is usually small. (Often there is only one.) Yet, tests on these small numbers are used to judge the adequacy of the design for making many production units, sometimes running into the thousands and even millions.

Evaluation of test results. Pressures to release a design for production can result in test plans and evaluations that do not objectively evaluate conformance to performance requirements, let alone complete fitness for use. One organization studied the process of qualifying a new design by having an independent review team analyze a sample of "qualification test" results on designs that had been approved for release. Two conclusions were that:

- Pressures to release designs caused design approvals that later resulted in field problems. The situation was traced to (1) inadequate initial testing or (2) lack of verification of design changes made to correct failures that surfaced on the initial test.
- Over 50 percent of the approved test results were rejected because the test procedure was unable to evaluate the requirements set by Product Development.

As a homework problem, the reader will be asked to recommend action to avoid these risks. O'Boyle (1990) describes a "chilling tale" of inadequate testing that resulted in the field replacement of over one million refrigerator compressors.

Methods for Improving Reliability during Design

The general approach to quality improvement (see Chapter 3) is widely applicable to reliability improvement as far as economic analysis and managerial tools are concerned. The differences are in the technological tools used for diagnosis and remedy. Projects can be identified through reliability prediction, design review, FMECA, or other reliability evaluation techniques.

Action to improve reliability during the design phase is best taken by the designer. The designer understands best the engineering principles involved in the design. The reliability engineer can help by defining areas needing improvement and by assisting in the development of alternatives. The following actions indicate some approaches to improving a design:

1. *Review the users' needs* to see if the *function* of the unreliable parts is really necessary to the user. If not, eliminate those parts from the design. Alternatively, look to see if the reliability index (figure of merit) correctly reflects the real needs of the user. For example, availability (see below) is sometimes more meaningful than reliability. If so, a good maintenance program might improve availability and hence ease the reliability problem.

2. *Consider trade-offs* of reliability for other parameters, e.g., functional performance, weight. Here again, it may be found that customers' real needs may be better served by such a trade-off.

3. *Use redundancy* to provide more than one means of accomplishing a given task in such a way that all the means must fail before the system fails. This is discussed in Section 13.4, "The Relationship between Part and System Reliability."

4. *Review the selection of any parts* that are relatively new and unproven. Use standard parts whose reliability has been proven by actual field usage. (However, be sure that the conditions of previous use are applicable to the new product.)

5. *Use derating* to ensure that the stresses applied to the parts are lower than the stresses the parts can normally withstand.

6. *Use "robust" design methods* that enable a product to handle unexpected environments.

7. *Control the operating environment* to provide conditions that yield lower failure rates. Common examples are potting electronic components to protect them against climate and shock and use of cooling systems to keep down ambient temperatures.

8. *Specify replacement schedules* to remove and replace low-reliability parts before they reach the wear-out stage. In many cases, the replacement is made contingent on the results of checkouts or tests which determine whether degradation has reached a prescribed limit.

9. *Prescribe screening tests* to detect "infant mortality" failures and to eliminate substandard components. The tests take various forms, e.g., bench tests, "burn-in," accelerated life tests.

10. *Conduct research and development* to attain an improvement in the basic reliability of those components which contribute most of the unreliability. While such improvements avoid the need for subsequent trade-offs, they may require advancing the state of the art and hence making an investment of an unpredictable size.

Although none of the foregoing actions provides a perfect solution, the range of choice is broad. In some instances, the designer can arrive at a solution single-handedly. More usually, collaboration with other company specialists will be necessary. In still other cases, the customer and/or company management will have to be adaptable because of the broader considerations involved.

12.5 AVAILABILITY

One of the major parameters of fitness for use is availability. Availability is the ability of a product, when used under given conditions, to perform satisfactorily when called upon. The total time in the operative state (also called uptime) is the sum of the time spent in active use and in the standby state. The total time in the nonoperative state (also called downtime) is the sum of the time spent under active repair and waiting for spare parts, paperwork, etc. The quantification of both availability and unavailability dramatizes the extent of the problems and areas for potential improvements. Formulas for quantifying availability are presented in Section 13.9, "Availability."

The proportion of time that a product is available for use depends on (1) freedom from failures, i.e., reliability, and (2) the ease with which service can be restored after a failure. The latter factor brings us to the subject of maintainability.

Designing for Maintainability

The tools for ensuring maintainability follow the same basic pattern as those for ensuring reliability; i.e., there are tools for specifying, predicting, analyzing, and measuring maintainability. The tools apply to both preventive maintenance (to reduce the number of failures) and corrective maintenance (to restore a product to operable condition). Some of the basic tools are discussed below. Quantitative tools are elaborated upon in QCH4, pages 13.40–13.48.

Maintainability is often specified in quantitative form, such as the mean time to repair (MTTR). MTTR is the mean time needed to perform repair work assuming a spare part and technician are available, e.g., a test set may have a specified MTTR of 2.5. As with reliability, there is no one maintainability index that applies to most products. Other examples of indices are percentage of downtime due to hardware failures, percentage of downtime due to software errors, mean time between preventive maintenance actions, etc.

Following the approach used in reliability, a maintainability goal for a product can be apportioned to the various components of the product. Also, maintainability can be predicted based on an analysis of the design. For elaboration, see QCH4, pages 13.44–13.47.

Approaches to improving maintainability of a design are both general and specific. General approaches include:

- *Reliability versus maintainability.* For example, given an availability requirement, should the response be an improvement in reliability or in maintainability?
- *Modular versus nonmodular construction.* Modular design requires added design effort but reduces the time required for diagnosis and remedy in the field. The fault need only be localized to the module level, after which the defective module is simply unplugged and replaced. This concept is being rapidly extended to consumer products such as television sets.
- *Repair versus throwaway.* For some products or modules, the cost of field repair exceeds the cost of making new units in the factory. In such cases, design for throwaway is an economic improvement in maintainability.
- *Built-in versus external test equipment.* Built-in test features reduce diagnostic time but usually at an added investment.
- *Person versus machine.* For example, should the operation/maintenance function be highly engineered with special instrumentation and repair facilities, or should it be left to skilled technicians with general-use equipment?

Specific approaches are based on detailed checklists that are used as a guide to good design for maintainability.

Maintainability can also be demonstrated by testing. The demonstration consists of measuring the time needed to locate and repair malfunctions or to perform selected maintenance tasks.

12.6 DESIGNING FOR SAFETY

Safety analysis tools include hazard quantification, designation of safety-oriented characteristics and components, fault tree analysis, fail-safe concepts, in-house and field testing, and publication of product ratings.

QUANTIFICATION OF SAFETY. Generally, quantification of safety has been time related. Industrial injury rates are quantified on the basis of lost-time accidents per million labor-hours of exposure. (Note that this expresses the frequency of occurrence but does not indicate the severity of the accidents.)

Motor vehicle injury rates are on the basis of injuries per 100 million miles. School injury rates are on the basis of injuries per 100,000 student days.

Product designers have tended to quantify safety in two ways:

1. *Hazard frequency.* A hazard is any combination of parts, components, conditions, or changing set of circumstances which present an injury potential. Hazard frequency takes the form of frequency of occurrence of an unsafe event and/or injuries per unit of time, e.g., per million hours of exposure. MIL-STD-882A (1984), has established categories of probability levels for hazards ranging from "frequent" to "improbable." Such probabilities are sometimes referred to as "risk."

2. *Hazard severity.* MIL-STD-882A recognizes four levels of severity:

- *Category I—catastrophic:* may cause death or system loss
- *Category II—critical:* may cause severe injury, severe occupational illness, or major system damage
- *Category III—marginal:* may cause minor injury, minor occupational illness, or minor system damage
- *Category IV—negligible:* will not result in injury, occupational illness, or system change

HAZARD ANALYSIS. Hazard analysis is similar to FMECA—but the failure event is one that causes an injury. Three forms of hazard analysis can be prepared: design concept, operating procedures, and hardware failures.

FAULT TREE ANALYSIS. This "top-down" approach starts by supposing that an accident takes place. It then considers the possible direct causes which could lead to this accident. Next, it looks for the origins of these causes. Finally, it looks for ways to avoid these origins and causes. The branching out of origins and causes is what gives the technique the name of "fault tree" analysis. The approach is the reverse of FMECA, which starts with origins and causes and looks for any resulting bad effects.

Hammer (1980) presents a fault tree analysis for an interlock safety circuit (Figure 12.4).

Based on field experience with specific products, detailed checklists are often developed to provide the designer with information on potential hazards, the injuries that can result, and specific types of design actions that can be taken to minimize the risk. See QCH4, pages 13.48–13.55, for further discussion.

As products have become more complex, the interaction of products with the human beings operating the product has assumed increasing importance. The evaluation of the design of a product to ensure compatibility with the capabilities of human beings is referred to as "ergonomics" or "human engineering." QCH4, page 13.55, provides a further discussion.

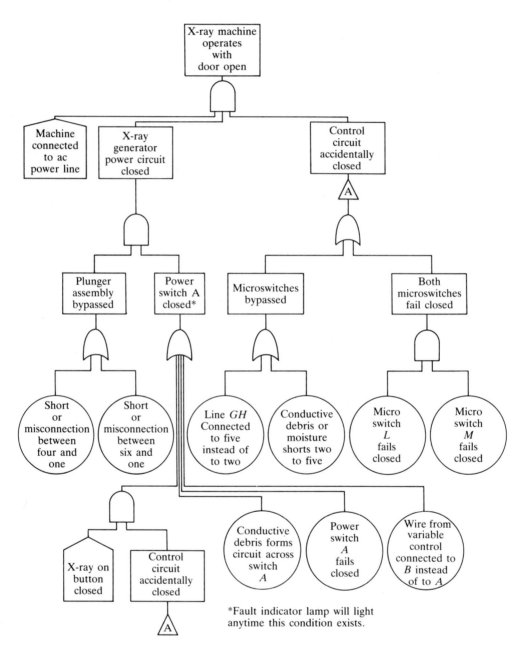

FIGURE 12.4
Fault tree analysis of an interlock safety circuit. (*From Hammer, 1980.*)

12.7 DESIGNING FOR MANUFACTURABILITY

Decisions made during design are the dominant influence on product costs, ability to meet specifications, and the time required to bring a new product to the marketplace. Furthermore, once these decisions are made, the cost of changes in the design can be huge, e.g., a design *change* during pilot production of a major electronics product can cost over a million dollars.

An important set of decisions is the selection of tolerances for product characteristics to be controlled during production. "Tolerance limits" specify the allowable limits of variability above and below the nominal value set by the designer.

The selection of tolerances has a dual effect on the economics of quality. The tolerance affects:

- Fitness for use and hence the salability of the product
- Costs of manufacture (facilities, tooling, productivity) and quality (equipment, inspection, scrap, rework, material review, etc.)

Chapter 13 explains some quantitative techniques for setting tolerances.

A technique called design for manufacturability focuses on simplifying a design to make it more producible. The emphasis is on reducing the total number of parts, the number of different parts, and the total number of manufacturing operations. This type of analysis is not new—"value engineering" tools have been useful in achieving design simplification (see Section 12.8). What is new, however, is the computer software available for analyzing a design and identifying opportunities for simplifying assembly products. Such software dissects the assembly step by step, poses questions concerning parts and subassemblies, and provides a summary of the number of parts, the assembly time, and the theoretical minimum number of parts or subassemblies. Use of such software enables designers to learn the principles for ease of manufacturing analogous to reliability, maintainability, and safety analyses. In one example, the proposed design of a new electronic cash register was analyzed with design for manufacturabilty (DFM) software. As a result, the number of parts was reduced by 65 percent. A person using no screws or bolts can assemble the register in less than two minutes—blindfolded. This simplified terminal was put onto the marketplace in 24 months—a record (*Newsweek,* 1989). Such design simplification reduces assembly errors and other sources of quality problems during manufacture.

Planning for inspection, packaging, transportation, and storage is discussed in Chapters 18 and 20. Some of this planning also has an impact on the product design.

12.8 COST AND PRODUCT PERFORMANCE

Designing for reliability, maintainability, safety, and other parameters must be done with a simultaneous objective of minimizing cost. Formal techniques of achieving an optimum balance between performance and cost include both quantitative and qualitative approaches.

The quantitative approach makes use of a ratio relating performance and cost. Such a ratio tells "what we get for each dollar we spend." The ratio is particularly useful in comparing alternative design approaches to accomplishing a desired function.

A cost-effectiveness comparison of four alternative designs is shown in Table 12.8. Note that design 3 is the optimum design, even though design 4 has higher availability.

Another approach to comparing several different designs over a number of attributes is shown in Table 12.9. A design for a food-waste disposer is compared to the designs of two competitor models for ten attributes describing fitness for use. For each combination of attribute and design, an effectiveness cost ratio is calculated. For example, for design G and the grinding time characteristic, the ratio is 6/2.14, or 2.8. The value of 6 is the product of a weighting factor of 3 for grinding time and a score of 2 for design G on grinding time. The value of \$2.14 is the estimated cost of achieving the grinding time of design G using the design G concept in production. The total of the ratios for each company provides a cost-effectiveness type of index.

Several approaches to achieving a balance between performance and cost have been developed. Value engineering is a technique for evaluating the design of a product to assure that the essential functions are provided at minimal overall cost to the manufacturer or user. A complementary technique is the "design-to-cost" approach. This starts with a definition of (1) a cost target for the product, and (2) the function desired. Alternative design

TABLE 12.8
Cost-effectiveness comparison of alternative designs

	Design			
	1	**2**	**3**	**4**
Mean time between failures (MTBF)	100	200	500	500
Mean downtime (MDT)	18	18	15	6
Availability*	0.847	0.917	0.971	0.988
Life-cycle cost (†)	51,000	49,000	50,000	52,000
Number of effective hours†	8,470	9,170	9,710	9,880
Cost/effective hour ($)	6.02	5.34	5.15	5.26

* Availability $= \dfrac{\text{MTBF}}{\text{MTBF} + \text{MDT}}$

† Number of effective hours $= 10{,}000$ h of life $\times$ availability

TABLE 12.9
Value comparison of food-waste disposers

	Company design	Competitor designs	
		B	G
Grinding time	9/1.73 = 5.2	9/0.87 = 10.3	6/2.14 = 2.8
Fineness of grind	4/9.18 = 0.4	4/7.82 = 0.5	4/11.88 = 0.3
Frequency of jamming	9/2.25 = 4.0	9/1.98 = 4.6	9/2.46 = 3.7
Noise	4/0.40 = 10.0	4/0.45 = 8.9	4/0.52 = 7.7
Self-cleaning ability	4/0.62 = 6.5	2/0.49 = 4.1	4/0.58 = 6.9
Electrical safety	16/0.58 = 27.6	16/0.52 = 30.8	16/0.43 = 37.2
Particle protection	6/0.29 = 20.7	6/0.30 = 20.0	2/0.37 = 5.4
Ease of servicing	6/0.70 = 8.6	4/0.52 = 7.7	6/0.98 = 6.1
Cutter life	9/0.96 = 9.4	9/0.83 = 10.8	9/1.32 = 6.8
Ease of installation	9/0.54 = 16.7	9/0.33 = 27.3	9/0.70 = 11.8
Total	76/17.25 = 4.4	72/14.11 = 5.1	69/21.44 = 3.2

Note: Value $= \dfrac{\text{Design score}}{\text{cost of achieving}}$.

concepts are then developed and evaluated. See QCH4, pages 13.63–13.66, for further discussion.

During the development cycle, the product undergoes several reviews. One form is a business review in which the results to date of the development effort are summarized and a decision is made whether or not to proceed further. Another type of review is technical in nature and is usually called design review.

12.9 DESIGN REVIEW

Design review is a formal, documented, comprehensive, and systematic examination of a design to evaluate the design requirements and the capability of the design to meet these requirements and to identify problems and propose solutions (ISO 8402-1986).

Design review is not new. However, in the past the term has referred to an informal evaluation of the design. Modern products often require a more formal program. A formal design review recognizes that many individual designers do not have specialized knowledge in reliability, maintainability, safety, producibility, and the other parameters that are important in achieving an optimum design. The design review aims to provide such knowledge.

For modern products, design reviews are based on the following concepts:

1. Design reviews are made mandatory because of either customer demand or upper management policy declaration.

2. The design reviews are conducted by a team consisting mainly of specialists who are not directly associated with the development of the design. These specialists must be highly experienced and must bring with them the reputation of being objective. The combination of competence, experience, and objectivity is present in some people, but these people are in great demand. The success of design reviews largely depends on the degree to which management supports the program by insisting that the best specialists be made available for design review work. The program deteriorates into superficial activity if (1) inexperienced people are assigned to design reviews or (2) those on the design review team are not given sufficient time to study product information prior to design review meetings.

3. Design reviews are formal. They are planned and scheduled like any other legitimized activity. The meetings are built around prepared agendas and documentation sent out in advance. Minutes of meetings are prepared and circulated. Follow-ups for action are likewise formalized.

4. Design reviews cover all quality-related parameters and others as well. The parameters can include reliability, maintainability, safety, producibility, weight, packaging, appearance, cost, etc.

5. As much as possible, design reviews are made based on defined criteria. Such criteria may include customer requirements, internal goals, and experience with previous products.

6. Design reviews are conducted at several phases of the progression of the design, such as design concept, prototype design and test, and final design. Reviews are made at several levels of the product hierarchy, such as system and subsystem.

7. The ultimate decision on inputs from the design review rests with the designer. The designer must listen to the inputs, but on matters of structural integrity and other creative aspects of the design, the designer retains the monopoly on decisions. The control and publication of the specification remain with the designer.

A universal obstacle to design review is the resistance of the Design Department. It has been common practice for this department to hold a virtual monopoly on design decisions, i.e., these decisions have historically been immune from challenge unless actual product trouble is encountered. With such a background, it is not surprising that designers have resisted the use of design reviews challenging their designs. Designers have contended that such challenges are based purely on grounds of theory and analysis (at which they regard themselves as the top experts) rather than on the traditional grounds of "failed hardware." This resistance is further aggravated in companies which permit reliability engineers to propose competing designs. Designers have resisted the idea of having competitors even more than they have resisted the idea of design review. An exciting concept that can overcome some of these cultural obstacles is concurrent engineering.

12.10 CONCURRENT ENGINEERING

Concurrent engineering, also called simultaneous engineering, is the process of designing a product using all inputs and evaluations *simultaneously and early* during design to ensure that internal and external customers' needs are met. The aim is to reduce the time from product concept to market, prevent quality and reliability problems, and reduce costs. An example is the approach used on the Taurus automobile (see Section 4.10, "A Road Map for Planning of Products for Salability").

Traditionally, activities during product development are handled sequentially, not concurrently. Thus, a Marketing or Research Department identifies a product idea; next, Design Engineering creates a design and builds a few prototype units; the Purchasing Department then calls for bids from suppliers; after that, the Manufacturing Department produces units, etc. At each step, the output of one department is "thrown over the wall" to the next department, i.e., there is little input during design from functions which are impacted by the design (Figure 12.5).

A further contrast of traditional and concurrent engineering is shown in Table 12.10. Concurrent engineering is not a set of techniques; it is a concept that enables all who are impacted by a design to (1) have *early access* to design information and (2) have the ability to influence the final design to identify and prevent future problems. All of the design parameters discussed in this chapter—basic functional requirements, reliability, maintainability, safety, human factors, manufacturability, inspection, packaging, transportation, and storage—can be addressed during concurrent engineering.

Dramatic benefits are reported from concurrent engineering, e.g., 75 percent fewer engineering changes, 55 percent less time from product concept to market. Vesey (1991) provides an overview with some examples.

12.11 IMPROVING THE EFFECTIVENESS OF PRODUCT DEVELOPMENT

Product development is a process which can be examined by the trilogy of quality processes, i.e., planning (see Chapter 4), control (see Chapter 5), and improvement (see Chapter 3). Gust (1985) describes the breakthrough sequence for improvement in the Films Division of Mobil Chemical.

A historical review of past product design changes can be a useful starting point for improvement. A study of 24 design changes revealed the following:

- Eleven of the changes were made to correct performance, reliability, or safety weaknesses; eight changes were made to correct administrative or

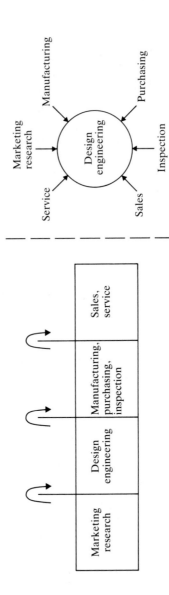

FIGURE 12.5

Walls of functional departments versus teamwork.

TABLE 12.10
Design engineering—contrast of traditional and concurrent

	Traditional	Concurrent
Organization	Engineering is separate from Manufacturing and other functions; emphasis is on functional objectives	Multifunctional team with emphasis on team objective
Timing of inputs from other functions and suppliers	Mostly after design has been finalized by Engineering	Simultaneous with creation of performance characteristics of design
Frequency and timing of design changes	Large number of changes, many of which occur after testing or during production	Smaller number of changes, most of which occur early, before the design is finalized
Information systems	Transfer of knowledge among functions and design changes are both subject to delays of paperwork systems	Computer systems interface so that all functions have immediate access to design changes and other information
Physical location of functions	Usually in separate locations	Often located in one area

paperwork errors; five changes were necessary to facilitate the manufacture of the product.

- Of the problems associated with these design changes, 23 were first found during production and one was found during field testing.
- In all 24 cases, notification of the change was given to the original designer but no one else.

Two conclusions emerged from the study: The process of product development was finding problems too late and feedback on problems was not shared with all designers.

The concept of self-control provides a framework for analyzing the work of designers. Universal in application, the concept holds that there are three criteria (see Section 5.2, "Self-Control") which must be met before a person can be held responsible for controlling the quality of his or her activities. The designer is said to be in a state of self-control only if all three criteria are fully met. A weakness in any of the three criteria requires that the *process of product development* be analyzed and corrected instead of looking to the individual designer for improvement. Homework Problem 12.14 asks the reader to identify questions for each of the criteria for self-control.

12.12 SOFTWARE DEVELOPMENT

For manufacturing industries, annual expenditures for computer-based data processing are about 0.5–1.5 percent of revenues; for service industries, the investment is about 3.0–7.0 percent (Fortune, 1988). Such staggering numbers make it worthwhile to study the effectiveness of the software development process.

The software development life cycle can be divided into six phases:

1. Requirements analysis
2. Preliminary design
3. Detailed design
4. Coding (programming)
5. Test and installation
6. Maintenance

Experience with software development provides some surprising statistics (Table 12.11). Note that 67 percent of the total effort is spent on *maintenance* which involves modifications to the software due to (1) changes in the initial requirements and (2) errors not previously detected. Thus, we have an opportunity for improvement.

Also note that 46 percent of the basic development effort goes for testing and installation. Sometimes the extent of testing (and review) during software development is great.

> **Example 12.4.** In one software development organization, the number of errors per thousand lines of code (KLOC) measured at the *final* stage was 2/KLOC. At the *first* stage of review/inspection during development, the number was 50/KLOC. The intermediate stages included various forms of inspection, review, and testing to weed out errors. There was an opportunity for improvement.

Fortune (1988), Gryna, D. (1988), and Schulmeyer and McManus (1987) elaborate on concepts and techniques for addressing quality during software development.

TABLE 12.11
Typical resource requirements for phases of a software development life cycle

	Total effort, %	Development effort, %
Requirements definition	3	9
Preliminary design	3	9
Detailed design	5	15
Coding	7	21
Testing and installation	15	46
Maintenance	67	

Source: QCH4, p. 14.7.

SUMMARY

- For complex products, errors during product development cause about 50 percent of fitness-for-use problems.
- Product development is a process having distinct phases which can incorporate forms of early warning of new-product troubles.
- Quality function deployment is a technique consisting of interlocking matrixes which translates customer needs into product and process characteristics.
- Robust designs provide optimum performance simultaneous with variation in manufacturing and field conditions.
- Taguchi methods determine optimum values of product and process parameters which minimize variation while keeping the mean on target.
- Reliability is the ability of an item to perform a required function under stated conditions for a stated period of time.
- Reliability quantification involves three phases: apportionment, prediction, and analysis. Maintainability quantification follows a similar approach.
- Failure mode, effect, and criticality analysis and fault tree analysis are helpful qualitative tools for design assurance.
- The design for manufacturability technique aims to simplify a product design to facilitate manufacture.
- Value engineering and design-to-cost techniques analyze designs to achieve an optimum balance between performance and cost.
- Design review is a systematic examination of design requirements and the capability of the design to meet the requirements.
- Concurrent engineering is the process of designing a product using all inputs and evaluations simultaneously and early during design to assure that both internal and external customers' needs are met.
- The process of product development can be examined using the elements of quality planning, control, and improvement.
- In software development, 67 percent of the effort involves making changes to the initial software—thus there is an opportunity for improvement.

PROBLEMS

12.1. Make a failure mode, effect, and criticality analysis for one of the following products:
   (*a*) a product acceptable to the instructor,
   (*b*) a flashlight,
   (*c*) a toaster,
   (*d*) a vacuum cleaner.

12.2. Make a fault tree analysis for one of the products mentioned in Problem 12.1.

12.3. Visit a local plant and determine whether any formal or informal numerical reliability and maintainability goals are issued to the design function for its guidance in designing new products.

12.4. Obtain a schematic diagram on a product for which you can also obtain a list of the components that fail most frequently. Show the diagram to a group of engineering students most closely associated with the product (e.g., a mechanical product would be shown to mechanical engineering students). Have the students *independently* write their opinion of the most likely components to fail by ranking the top three.

(*a*) Summarize the results and comment on the agreement, or lack thereof, among the students.

(*b*) Comment on the students' opinions versus actual product history.

12.5. A reliability prediction can be made by the designer of a product or by an engineer in a staff reliability department which might be a part of the design function. One advantage of the designer making the prediction is that his or her knowledge of the design will likely make possible a faster and more thorough job.

(*a*) What is one other advantage in having the designer make the prediction?

(*b*) Are there any disadvantages to having the designer make the prediction?

12.6. Prepare a formal presentation to gain adoption of one of the following:

(*a*) quantification of reliability goals, apportionment, and prediction,

(*b*) formal design reviews,

(*c*) failure mode, effect, and criticality analysis,

(*d*) critical components program.

You will make the presentation to one or more people who will be invited into the classroom by the instructor. These people may be from industry or may be other students or faculty. (The instructor will announce time and other limitations on your presentation.)

12.7. Outline a reliability test for one of the following products:

(*a*) a product acceptable to the instructor,

(*b*) a household clothes dryer,

(*c*) a motor for a windshield wiper,

(*d*) an electric food mixer,

(*e*) an automobile spark plug. The testing must cover performance, environmental, and time aspects.

12.8. Speak with some practicing design engineers and learn the extent of feedback of field information to them on their own design work.

12.9. You are the design engineering manager for a refrigerator. Most of your day is spent on administrative work. You do not have time to get into details on new or modified designs. However, you must approve (by sign-off) all new designs or changes. In reality, your sign-off consists of a brief review of the design, but you rely basically on the competence of your individual designers. You do not want to institute a formal reliability program for designers or set up a reliability group at this time. What action could you take to give yourself some assurance that a design presented to you has been adequately examined by the designer with respect to reliability? It is not possible to increase the testing, and any action you take must involve a minimum of additional costs.

12.10. You work for a public utility and your department employs outside contractors who design and build various equipment and building installations. You have just finished a value engineering seminar at a university, and you wonder if your utility should consider establishing such a function to evaluate contractor designs. Someone in your management group has heard that value engineering can reduce costs but "by lowering the performance or reliability of a design." Comment.

12.11. The chapter discusses a number of concepts (e.g., reliability prediction, design review, etc.). Select several concepts and outline a potential application of the concept to an actual problem on a specific product. The outline should state:
(a) the name of the concept,
(b) a brief statement of the problem,
(c) application of the concept to the problem,
(d) potential advantages,
(e) obstacles to actual implementation, and
(f) an approach to use to overcome each obstacle.
    The outline for each concept should be about one page.

12.12. The section on "Evaluating Designs by Tests" stated four risks. For each risk, recommend one or more preventive actions.

12.13. In designing the SX-70 camera system, the Polaroid Corporation first determined the top customer complaints on previous models. These included: customers had trouble getting the correct focus; customers forgot to change the batteries; customers did not like changing lenses; customers were not sure when to use the flash. For each of these complaints, propose a design feature to prevent the complaint.

12.14. Review the concept of self-control in Chapter 5. Apply the concept to design engineering by creating three questions for each of the three criteria of self-control.

REFERENCES

Akao, Yoji (1990). *Quality Function Deployment,* Productivity Press, Cambridge, Massachusetts.

Beaton, G. N. (1959). "Putting the R&D Reliability Dollar to Work,"*Proceedings of the Fifth National Symposium on Reliability and Quality Control,* Institute of Electrical and Electronics Engineers, New York, p. 65.

Ernst and Young Quality Improvement Consulting Group (1990). *Total Quality,* Dow Jones–Irwin, Homewood, Illinois, p. 121.

Fortune, Patrick J. (1988). QCH4, Section 14.

Gryna, Derek S. (1988). "Data Processing—A Software Quality Challenge," *ASQC Quality Congress Transactions,* Milwaukee, pp. 423–428.

Gust, Larry (1985). "Non-manufacturing Quality Improvement," *Juran Report Number Four,* Juran Institute, Inc., Wilton, Connecticut, pp. 112–120.

Hammer, Willie (1980). *Product Safety Management and Engineering,* Prentice-Hall, Englewood Cliffs, New Jersey.

Juran, J. M., et al. (1990). "Planning for Quality" course notes, 2nd ed., Juran Institute, Inc., Wilton, Connecticut.

MIL-STD-882A (1984). "System Safety Program Requirements," Department of Defense, Washington, D.C.

Newsweek (1989). "The Best Engineered Part Is No Part at All," May 8, p. 150.

O'Boyle, Thomas F. (1990). "Chilling Tale," *Wall Street Journal,* May 7, pp. 1, 5.

Phadke, M. S., R. R. Kackar, D. V. Speeny, and M. J. Grieco (1983). "Off-Line Quality Control in Integrated Circuit Fabrication Using Experimental Design," *The Bell System Technical Journal,* vol. 62, no. 5, pp. 1273–1309.

Pignatiello, Joseph J., and John S. Ramberg (1992). "Top Ten Triumphs and Tragedies of Genichi Taguchi," *Quality Engineering,* vol. 4, no. 2, pp. 211–225.

Schulmeyer, C. Gordon, and James I. McManus (1987). *Handbook of Software Quality Assurance,* Van Nostrand Reinhold, New York.

Taguchi, G. (1978). "Off-Line and On-Line Quality Control Systems," International Conference on Quality Control, Japanese Union of Scientists and Engineers, Tokyo, pp. B4-1 through B4-5.

Vesey, Joseph T. (1991). "The New Competitors: They Think In Terms of 'Speed to Market,'" *Executive,* May, pp. 23–33.

SUPPLEMENTARY READING

Customer-supplier relationship in design: Fouse, F. Edward, and John A. Matesich (1987). "Department Quality Analysis: A Case Study," *Quality Progress,* June, pp. 91–92.

Design assurance: Raheja, Dev G. (1991). *Assurance Technologies,* McGraw-Hill, Inc., New York.

Ireson, W. Grant, and Clyde F. Coombs, Jr. (1988). *Handbook of Reliability Engineering and Management,* McGraw-Hill, Inc., New York.

History of design problems: Mundel, August B. (1991). *Ethics in Quality,* ASQC Quality Press, Milwaukee, Chapter 6.

New-product introduction: Zurn, James T. (1988). "New Product Introduction and Quality Program Management," *Quality Engineering,* vol. 1, no. 1, pp. 29–43.

Product development: QCH4, Section 13.

DESIGNING FOR QUALITY-STATISTICAL TOOLS

13.1 QUALITY MEASUREMENT IN DESIGN

The management of quality-related activities in design—as in all functional activities—must include provision for measurement. A popular rallying cry is, "What gets measured, gets done."

We should carry out several activities when developing quality measurement for any activity:

1. Obtain input from customers (external and internal) to learn how they evaluate the quality of the output provided to them.
2. Design measurements not only for purposes of evaluation of performance but to provide feedback in a form useful to those performing the activity and thus help to place them in a state of self-control.
3. Design measurements to provide early indicators, concurrent indicators, and lagging indicators (final results). Thus, the number of design changes can be measured at design review, development testing, and after design release for steady-state production.

TABLE 13.1
Examples of quality measurement in design

Subject	Unit of measure
Overall design process	Cost of poor quality
	Number of months from first pilot unit to steady-state products
Design changes	Number of design changes (1) at design review, (2) at development testing, (3) after design release for steady-state production
	Number of design changes (1) to meet requirements, (2) to improve performance, (3) to facilitate manufacture
	Number of design changes requested by customer
	Number of waivers to specifications
	Number of drawing errors found by checkers on first check
Reliability, maintainability	Ratio of predicted reliability to actual reliability
	Ratio of actual reliability to reliability requirement
	Maintainability index compared to prior design
Software	Number of software errors per thousand lines of code (KLOC)—first internal review
	Number of software errors per KLOC—final internal review
	Number of software errors per KLOC—discovered by customer
	Average score given by customers on overall quality of software
Ease of manufacture	Ratio of number of parts to theoretical minimum number
	Total assembly time
	Total number of operations

Table 13.1 shows units of measure for various subject areas of product design.

We proceed to examine some statistical tools that are useful in design.

13.2 FAILURE PATTERNS
FOR COMPLEX PRODUCTS

Methodology for quantifying reliability was first developed for complex products. Suppose that a piece of equipment is placed on test and is run until it fails, and the failure time is recorded. The equipment is repaired and again placed on test, and the time of the next failure is recorded. The procedure is repeated to accumulate the data shown in Table 13.2. The failure rate is calculated, for equal time intervals, as the number of failures per unit of time. When the failure rate is plotted against time, the result (Figure 13.1) often follows a familiar pattern of failure known as the *bathtub curve*. Three periods

TABLE 13.2
Failure history for a unit of electronic ground support equipment

Time of failure, infant-mortality period		Time of failure, constant-failure- rate period		Time of failure, wear-out period	
1.0	7.2	28.1	60.2	100.8	125.8
1.2	7.9	28.2	63.7	102.6	126.6
1.3	8.3	29.0	64.6	103.2	127.7
2.0	8.7	29.9	65.3	104.0	128.4
2.4	9.2	30.6	66.2	104.3	129.2
2.9	9.8	32.4	70.1	105.0	129.5
3.0	10.2	33.0	71.0	105.8	129.9
3.1	10.4	35.3	75.1	106.5	
3.3	11.9	36.1	75.6	110.7	
3.5	13.8	40.1	78.4	112.6	
3.8	14.4	42.8	79.2	113.5	
4.3	15.6	43.7	84.1	114.8	
4.6	16.2	44.5	86.0	115.1	
4.7	17.0	50.4	87.9	117.4	
4.8	17.5	51.2	88.4	118.3	
5.2	19.2	52.0	89.9	119.7	
5.4		53.3	90.8	120.6	
5.9		54.2	91.1	121.0	
6.4		55.6	91.5	122.9	
6.8		56.4	92.1	123.3	
6.9		58.3	97.9	124.5	

are apparent. These periods differ in the frequency of failure and in the failure causation pattern:

1. *The infant mortality period.* This is characterized by high failure rates which show up early in use (see the lower half of Figure 13.1). Commonly, these failures are the result of blunders in design or manufacture, misuse, or misapplication. Usually, once corrected, these failures do not occur again, e.g., an oil hole that is not drilled. Sometimes it is possible to "debug" the product by a simulated use test or by overstressing (in electronics this is known as burn-in). The weak units still fail, but the failure takes place in the test rig rather than in service.

2. *The constant-failure-rate period.* Here the failures result from the limitations inherent in the design, changes in the environment, and accidents caused by use or maintenance. The accidents can be held down by good control on operating and maintenance procedures. However, a reduction in the failure rate requires a basic redesign.

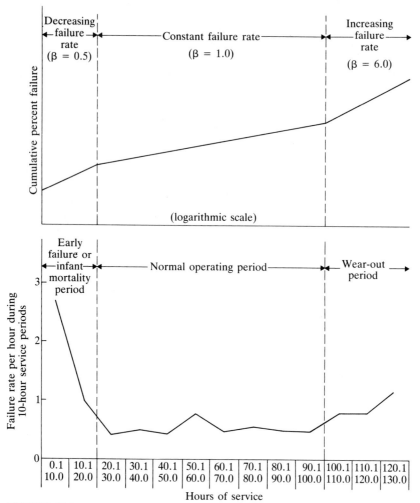

FIGURE 13.1
Failure rate versus time.

3. *The wear-out period.* These are failures due to old age; e.g., the metal becomes embrittled or the insulation dries out. A reduction in failure rates requires preventive replacement of these dying components before they result in catastrophic failure.

The top portion of Figure 13.1 shows the corresponding Weibull plot when $\alpha = 2.6$ was applied to the original data (see Section 9.11, "The Weibull Probability Distribution"). The values of the shape parameter, β, were approximately 0.5, 1.0, and 6.0, respectively. A shape parameter of less than 1.0 indicates a decreasing failure rate, a value of 1.0 a constant failure rate, and a value greater than 1.0 an increasing failure rate (see Figure 13.1).

The Distribution of Time between Failures

Together with low failure rates during the infant mortality period, users are concerned with the length of time that a product will run without failure. For repairable products, this means that the *time between failures* (TBF) is a critical characteristic. The variation in time between failures can be studied statistically. The corresponding characteristic for nonrepairable products is usually called the *time to failure*.

When the failure rate is constant, the distribution of time between failures is distributed exponentially. Consider the 42 failure times in the constant-failure-rate portion of Table 13.2. The time between failures for successive failures can be tallied, and the 41 resulting TBFs can be formed into the frequency distribution shown in Figure 13.2*a*. The distribution is roughly exponential in shape, indicating that when the failure rate is constant, the distribution of time between failures (not *mean time* between failures) is exponential. This is the basis of the *exponential formula for reliability*.

13.3   THE EXPONENTIAL FORMULA FOR RELIABILITY

The distribution of time between failures indicates the chance of failure-free operation for the specified time period. The chance of obtaining failure-free operation for a specified time period *or longer* can be shown by changing the TBF distribution to a distribution showing the number of intervals equal to or greater than a specified time length (Figure 13.2*b*). If the frequencies are expressed as relative frequencies, they become estimates of the probability of survival. When the failure rate is constant, the probability of survival (or reliability) is

$$P_s = R = e^{-t/\mu} = e^{-t\lambda}$$

where $P_s = R = $ probability of failure-free operation for a time period equal to
or greater than t
$e = 2.718$
$t = $ specified period of failure-free operation
$\mu = $ mean time between failures (the mean of TBF distribution)
$\lambda = $ failure rate (the reciprocal of μ)

Note that this formula is simply the exponential probability distribution rewritten in terms of reliability.

> **Example 13.1.** A washing machine requires 30 min to clean a load of clothes. The mean time between failures of the machine is 100 h. Assuming a constant failure rate, what is the chance of the machine completing a cycle without failure?
>
> $$R = e^{-t/\mu} = e^{-0.5/100} = 0.995$$
>
> There is a 99.5 percent chance of completing a washing cycle.

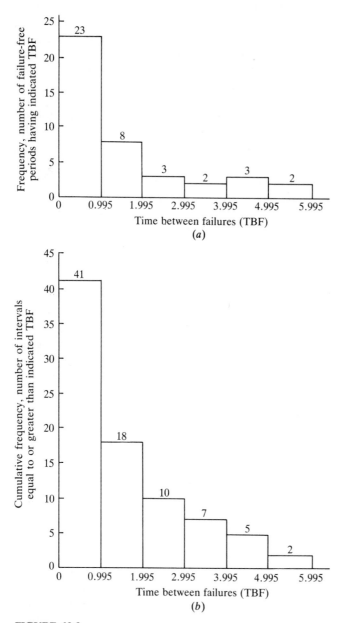

FIGURE 13.2
(*a*) Histogram of time between failures. (*b*) Cumulative histogram of time between failures.

How about the assumption of a constant failure rate? In practice, sufficient data are usually not available to evaluate the assumption. However, experience suggests that the assumption is often a fair one to make. This is particularly true when (1) infant mortality types of failures have been eliminated before delivery of the product to the user, and (2) the user replaces the product or specific components before the wear-out phase begins.

The Meaning of "Mean Time between Failures"

Confusion surrounds the meaning of "mean time between failures" (MTBF). Further explanation is warranted:

1. The MTBF is the mean (or average) time between successive failures of a product. This definition assumes that the product in question can be repaired and placed back into operation after each failure.
2. If the failure rate is constant, the probability that a product will operate without failure for a time equal to or greater than its MTBF is only 37 percent. This is based on the exponential distribution. (R is equal to 0.37 when t is equal to the MTBF.) This is contrary to the intuitive feeling that there is a 50–50 chance of exceeding an MTBF.
3. MTBF is not the same as "operating life," "service life," or other indices, which generally connote overhaul or replacement time.
4. An increase in an MTBF does not result in a proportional increase in reliability (the probability of survival). If $t = 1$ hour, the following table shows the mean time between failures required in order to obtain various reliabilities:

MTBF	R
5	0.82
10	0.90
20	0.95
100	0.99

A fivefold increase in MTBF from 20 to 100 hours is necessary to increase the reliability by 4 percentage points as compared with a doubling of the MTBF from 5 to 10 hours to get 8 percentage points' increase in reliability.

MTBF is a useful measure of reliability, but it is *not* correct for all applications. Section 12.4, "Designing for Time-Oriented Performance (Reliability)," includes a list of other reliability indices.

13.4 THE RELATIONSHIP BETWEEN PART AND SYSTEM RELIABILITY

It is often assumed that system reliability (i.e., the probability of survival P_s) is the product of the individual reliabilities of the n parts within the system:

$$P_s = P_1 P_2 \cdots P_n$$

For example, if a communications system has four subsystems with reliabilities of 0.970, 0.989, 0.995, and 0.996, the system reliability is 0.951. The formula assumes that (1) the failure of any part causes failure of the system, and (2) the reliabilities of the parts are independent of one another, i.e., the reliability of one part does not depend on the functioning of another part.

These assumptions are *not* always true, but in practice the formula serves two purposes. First, it shows the effect of increased complexity of equipment on overall reliability. As the number of parts in a system increases, the system reliability decreases dramatically (see Figure 13.3). Second, the formula is often a convenient approximation that can be refined as information on the interrelationships of the parts becomes available.

Sometimes designs are planned with redundancy so that the failure of one part will not cause system failure. Redundancy is an old design technique invented long before the advent of reliability prediction techniques. However, the designer can now predict in *quantitative* terms the effect of redundancy on system reliability.

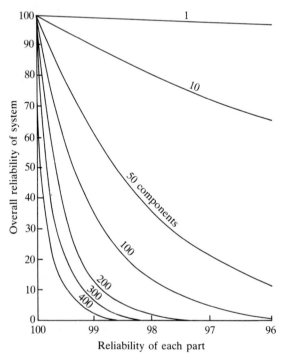

FIGURE 13.3
Relationship of part and system reliability.

Redundancy is the existence of more than one element for accomplishing a given task, where all elements must fail before there is an overall failure to the system. In *parallel redundancy* (one of several types of redundancy), two or more elements operate at the same time to accomplish the task, and any single element is capable of handling the job itself in case of failure of the other elements. When parallel redundancy is used, the overall reliability is calculated as follows:

$$P_s = 1 - (1 - P_1)^n$$

where P_s = reliability of the system

P_1 = reliability of the individual elements in the redundancy

n = number of identical redundant elements

Example 13.2. Suppose that a unit has a reliability of 99.0 percent for a specified mission time. If two identical units are used in parallel redundancy, what overall reliability will be obtained?

$$R = 1 - (1 - 0.99)(1 - 0.99) = 0.9999, \text{ or } 99.99 \text{ percent}$$

When it can be assumed that (1) the failure of any part causes system failure, (2) the parts are independent, and (3) each part follows an exponential distribution, then

$$P_s = e^{-t_1\lambda_1}e^{\lambda_1}e^{-t_2\lambda_2\cdots}e^{-t_n\lambda_n}$$

Further, if t is the same for each part,

$$P_s = e^{-t\Sigma\lambda}$$

Thus, when the failure rate is constant (and therefore the exponential distribution can be applied), a reliability prediction of a system can be made based on the addition of the part failure rates. This is illustrated below.

13.5 PREDICTING RELIABILITY DURING DESIGN

In Section 12.4 we introduced the reliability prediction method. Reliability prediction is still in the early stages of development. Several methods will be discussed in this chapter. Ireson and Coombs (1988) provide an extensive discussion of reliability prediction.

The following steps make up a reliability prediction method:

1. *Define the product and its functional operation.* The system, subsystems, and units must be precisely defined in terms of their functional configurations and boundaries. This precise definition is aided by preparation of a functional block diagram which shows the subsystems and lower-level products, their interrelationships and the interfaces with other systems.

Given a functional block diagram and a well-defined statement of the functional requirements of the product, the conditions that constitute failure or unsatisfactory performance can be defined.

2. *Prepare a reliability block diagram.* For systems in which there are redundancies or other special interrelationships among parts, a reliability block diagram is useful. This diagram is similar to a functional block diagram, but the reliability block diagram shows exactly what must function for successful operation of the system. The diagram shows redundancies and alternative modes of operation. The reliability block diagram is the foundation for developing the probability model for reliability. O'Connor (1991) provides further discussion.

3. *Develop the probability model for predicting reliability.* This may simply be the addition of failure rates or a complex model that accounts for redundancies and other conditions.

4. *Collect information relevant to parts reliability.* This includes information such as parts function, parts ratings, stresses, internal and external environments, and operating time. Many sources of failure-rate information state failure rates as a function of operating parameters. For example, MIL-HDBK-217 (1986) provides failure rates for fixed ceramic capacitors as a function of (1) expected operating temperature, and (2) the ratio of the operating voltage to the rated voltage. Such data show the effect of derating (see Section 12.4 under "Derating Practice") on reducing the failure rate.

5. *Select parts reliability data.* The required parts data consist of information on catastrophic failures and on tolerance variations with respect to time under known operating and environmental conditions. Acquiring these data is a major problem for the designer, since there is no single reliability data bank comparable to handbooks such as those that are available for physical properties of materials. Instead, the designer must build up a data bank by securing reliability data from a variety of sources:
   - Field performance studies conducted under controlled conditions.
   - Specified life tests.
   - Data from parts manufacturers or industry associations.
   - Customers' parts qualification and inspection tests.
   - Government publications such as MIL-HDBK-217 (1986), which contains a large amount of failure-rate data together with stress-analysis procedures essential to their use.
   - Government agency data banks such as the Government Industry Data Exchange Program (GIDEP).

6. *Combine all of the above to obtain the numerical reliability prediction.* An example of a relatively simple reliability prediction method is shown in Section 13.6. Other prediction methods are based on various statistical distributions, as explained in the following sections.

A technique for predicting future performance from tests and field data is the concept of reliability growth. The concept assumes that a product is undergoing continuous improvements in design and refinements in operating and maintenance procedures. Thus, the product performance will improve ("grow") with time. See Section 20.4, "Analyzing Field Data," for an example of a reliability growth model.

13.6 PREDICTING RELIABILITY BASED ON THE EXPONENTIAL DISTRIBUTION

When the failure rate is constant and when study of a functional block diagram reveals that all parts must function for system success, then reliability is predicted to be the simple total of failure rates. An example of a subsystem prediction, the prediction for a decoder board, is shown in Table 13.3. The prediction for the overall system is made by adding the failure rates of the subsystems; the mean time between failures (MTBF) is then calculated as the reciprocal of the failure rate.

13.7 PREDICTING RELIABILITY BASED ON THE WEIBULL DISTRIBUTION

Prediction of overall reliability based on the simple addition of component failure rates is valid only if the failure rate is constant. When this assumption cannot be made, an alternative approach based on the Weibull distribution can be used.

1. Graphically, use the Weibull distribution to predict the reliability R for the time period specified. $R = 100 - \%$ failure. Do this for each component. (See Section 9.8 under "Making Predictions Using the Weibull Probability Distribution.")
2. Combine the component reliabilities using the product rule and/or redundancy formulas to obtain the prediction of system reliability.

TABLE 13.3
Reliability prediction of decoder board

Parts	Number of parts	Failure rate per 10^6 h	Total failure rate
Composition resistors, fixed	108	0.0048	0.5184
Transistors	23	3.00	69.00
Diodes	50	1.00	50.00
Capacitors—paper	13	0.11	1.43
Button mica capacitor	1	0.054	0.054
			121.0024

Predictions of reliability using the exponential distribution or the Weibull distribution are based on reliability as a function of time. We next consider reliability as a function of stress and strength.

13.8 RELIABILITY AS A FUNCTION OF APPLIED STRESS AND STRENGTH

Failures are not always a function of time. In some cases, a part will function indefinitely if its strength is greater than the stress applied to it. The terms "strength" and "stress" here are used in the broad sense of inherent capability and operating conditions applied to a part, respectively.

For example, operating temperature is a critical parameter and the maximum expected temperature is 145°F (63°C). Further, capability is indicated by a strength distribution having a mean of 172°F/78°C and a standard deviation of 13°F (7°C) (see Figure 13.4). With knowledge of only the maximum temperatures, the *safety margin* is

$$\frac{172 - 145}{13} = 2.08$$

The safety margin says that the average strength is 2.08 standard deviations above the maximum expected temperature of 145°F (63°C). Table A in the Appendix can be used to calculate a reliability of 0.981 (the area beyond 145°F [63°C]).

This calculation illustrates the importance of *variation* in addition to the *average* value during design. Designers have always recognized the existence of variation by using a *safety factor* in design. However, the safety factor is often defined as the ratio of average strength to the worst stress expected.

Note that in Figure 13.5, all the designs have the same safety factor. Also note that the reliability (probability of a part having a strength greater than the stress) varies considerably. Thus the uncertainty often associated with this definition of safety factor is in part due to its failure to reflect the *variation* in

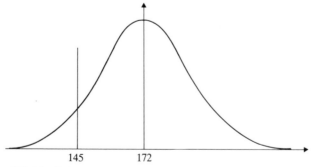

FIGURE 13.4
Distribution of strength.

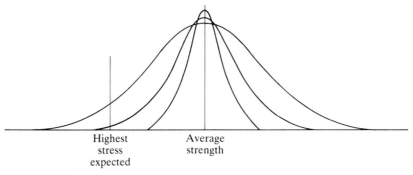

FIGURE 13.5
Variation and safety factor.

both strength and stress. Such variation is partially reflected in a safety margin, defined as

$$\frac{\text{average strength} - \text{worst stress}}{\text{standard deviation of strength}}$$

This recognizes the variation in strength but is conservative because it does not recognize a variation in stress.

13.9 AVAILABILITY

Availability has been defined as the probability that a product, when used under given conditions, will perform satisfactorily when called upon. Availability considers the operating time of the product and the time required for repairs. Idle time, during which the product is not needed, is excluded.

Availability is calculated as the ratio of operating time to operating time plus downtime. However, downtime can be viewed in two ways:

1. *Total downtime.* This includes the active repair (diagnosis and repair time), preventive maintenance time, and logistics time (time spent waiting for personnel, spare parts, etc.). When total downtime is used, the resulting ratio is called *operational availability* (A_0).
2. *Active repair time.* The resulting ratio is called *intrinsic availability* (A_i). Under certain conditions, availability can be calculated as

$$A_0 = \frac{\text{MTBF}}{\text{MTBF} + \text{MDT}} \quad \text{and} \quad A_i = \frac{\text{MTBF}}{\text{MTBF} + \text{MTTR}}$$

where MTBF = mean time between failures
MDT = mean downtime
MTTR = mean time to repair

This is known as the steady-state formula for availability.

TABLE 13.4
Availability data for mail system equipment

Equipment	MTBF, h	MTTR, h	Availability (%)
Sack sorter	90	1.620	98.2
Parcel sorter	160	0.8867	99.4
Conveyor, induction	17,900	1.920	100.0
Deflector, traveling	3,516	3.070	99.9

Garrick and Mulvihill (1974) present data on certain subsystems of a mechanized bulk mail system (see Table 13.4). If estimates of reliability and maintainability can be made during the design process, availability can be evaluated before the design is released for production.

The steady-state formula for availability has the virtue of simplicity. However, the formula has several assumptions that are not always met in the real world. The assumptions are:

- The product is operating in the constant-failure-rate period of the overall life. Thus, the failure-time distribution is exponential.
- The downtime or repair-time distribution is exponential.
- Attempts to locate system failures do not change the overall system failure rate.
- No reliability growth occurs. (Such growth might be due to design improvements or through debugging of bad parts.)
- Preventive maintenance is scheduled outside the time frame included in the availability calculation.

More precise formulas for calculating availability depend on operational conditions and statistical assumptions. These formulas are discussed by Ireson and Coombs (1988).

13.10 SETTING SPECIFICATION LIMITS

A major step in product development is the conversion of product *features* into dimensional, chemical, electrical, and other *characteristics* of the product. Thus, a heating system for an automobile will have many characteristics on the heater, air ducts, blower assembly, engine coolant, etc.

For each characteristic, the designer must specify (1) the desired average (or "nominal value") and (2) the specification limits (or "tolerance limits") above and below the nominal value which individual units of product must meet. The specification limits reflect the functional needs of the product and should also be realistic. Ideally, designers are provided with information on process capability, i.e., the expected amount of process variability.

Section 13.11 below provides methods for setting specification limits using data from the process.

13.11 ANALYZING PROCESS DATA TO SET LIMITS ON DISCRETE COMPONENTS OR PARTS

Generally, designers will not be provided with information on process capability. Their problem will be to obtain a sample of data from the process, calculate the limits that the process can meet, and compare these to the limits they were going to specify. (If they do not have any limits in mind, the capability limits calculated from process data provide them with a set of limits that are realistic from the viewpoint of producibility. These must then be evaluated against the functional needs of the product.)

Statistically, the problem is to predict the limits of variation of individual items in the total population based on a sample of data. For example, suppose that a product characteristic is normally distributed with a population average of 5.000 in (12.7 cm) and a population standard deviation of 0.001 in (0.00254 cm). Limits can then be calculated to include any given percentage of the population. Figure 13.6 shows the location of the 99 percent limits. Table A in the Appendix indicates that ±2.575 standard deviations will include 99 percent of the population. Thus, in this example, a realistic set of tolerance limits would be

$$5.000 \pm 2.575(0.001) = \frac{5.003}{4.997}$$

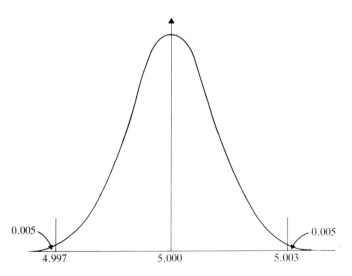

FIGURE 13.6
Distribution with 99 percent limits.

Ninety-nine percent of the individual pieces in the population will have values between 4.997 and 5.003.

In practice, the average and standard deviation of the population are *not* known but must be estimated from a sample of product from the process. As a first approximation, tolerance limits are sometimes set at

$$\bar{X} \pm 3s$$

Here the average $\bar{X}$ and standard deviation s of the sample are used directly as estimates of the population values. If the true average and standard deviation of the population happen to be equal to those of the sample, and if the characteristic is normally distributed, then 99.73 percent of the pieces in the population will fall within the limits calculated above. These limits are frequently called *natural tolerance limits* (limits that recognize the actual variation of the process and therefore are realistic). This approximation ignores the possible error in both the average and standard deviation as estimated from the sample.

Methodology has been developed for setting tolerance limits in a more precise manner. For example, formulas and tables are available for determining tolerance limits based on a normally distributed population. Table H in the Appendix provides factors for calculating tolerance limits that recognize the uncertainty in the sample mean and sample standard deviation. The tolerance limits are determined as

$$\bar{X} \pm Ks$$

The factor K is a function of the confidence level desired, the percentage of the population to be included within the tolerance limits, and the number of data values in the sample.

For example, suppose that a sample of 10 resistors from a process yielded an average and standard deviation of $5.04\,\Omega$ and $0.016\,\Omega$, respectively. The tolerance limits are to include 99 percent of the population, and the tolerance statement is to have a confidence level of 95 percent. Referring to Table H in the Appendix, the value of K is 4.433, and tolerance limits are then calculated as

$$5.04 \pm 4.433(0.016) = \frac{5.11}{4.97}$$

We are 95 percent confident that at least 99 percent of the resistors in the population will have a resistance between $4.97\,\Omega$ and $5.11\,\Omega$. Tolerance limits calculated in this manner are often called statistical tolerance limits. This approach is more rigorous than the $\pm 3s$ natural tolerance limits, but the two percentages in the statement are a mystery to those without a statistical background.

For products in some industries (e.g., electronics), the number of units outside of specification limits is stated in terms of parts per million (PPM). Thus, if limits are set at ± 3 standard deviations, 2700 PPM $(100\% - 99.73\%)$

TABLE 13.5
Standard deviations and PPM

Number of standard deviations	Parts per million (PPM)
$\pm 3\sigma$	2700
$\pm 4\sigma$	6.8
$\pm 5\sigma$	0.6

will fall outside the limits. For many applications (e.g., a personal computer with many logic gates), such a level is totally unacceptable. Table 13.5 shows the PPM for several standard deviations. These levels of PPM assume that the process average is constant at the nominal specification. A deviation from the nominal value will result in a higher PPM value. To allow for modest shifts in the process average, some manufacturers follow a guideline for setting specifiction limits at $\pm 6\sigma$. See Section 17.8 under "Six Sigma Concept of Process Capability."

Designers must often set tolerance limits with only a few measurements from the process (or more likely from the development tests conducted under laboratory conditions). In developing a paint formulation, the following values of gloss were obtained: 76.5, 75.2, 77.5, 78.9, 76.1, 78.3, and 77.7. A group of chemists was asked where they would set a minimum specification limit. Their answer was 75.0—a reasonable answer for those without statistical knowledge. Figure 13.7 shows a plot of the data on normal probability paper. If the line is extrapolated to 75.0, the plot predicts that about 11 percent of the population will fall below 75.0—even though all of the sample data exceed 75.0. Of course, a larger sample size is preferred and further statistical analyses could be made, but the plot provides a simple tool for evaluating a small sample of data.

All methods of setting tolerance limits based on process data assume that the sample of data represents a process that is sufficiently stable to be predictable. In practice, the assumption is often accepted without any formal evaluation. If sufficient data are available, the assumption can be checked with a control chart.

Statistical tolerance limits are sometimes confused with other limits used in engineering and statistics. Table 13.6 summarizes the distinctions among five types of limits (see also QCH4, pages 23.51–23.60).

13.12 SPECIFICATION LIMITS FOR INTERACTING DIMENSIONS

Interacting dimensions are those which mate or merge with other dimensions to create a final result. Consider the simple mechanical assembly shown in Figure 13.8. The lengths of components A, B, and C are interacting dimensions because they determine the overall assembly length.

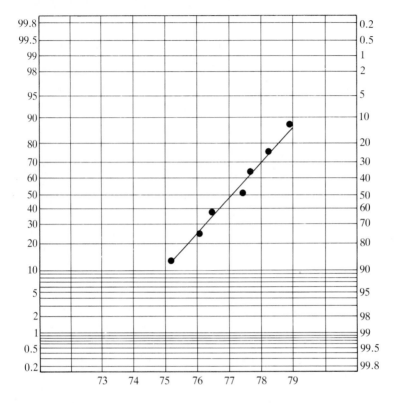

FIGURE 13.7
Probability plot of development data.

TABLE 13.6
Distinctions among limits

Name of limit	Meaning
Tolerance	Set by the engineering design function to define the minimum and maximum values allowable for the product to work properly
Statistical tolerance	Calculated from process data to define the amount of variation that the process exhibits; these limits will contain a specified proportion of the total population
Prediction	Calculated from process data to define the limits which will contain all of k future observations
Confidence	Calculated from data to define an interval within which a population parameter lies
Control	Calculated from process data to define the limits of chance (random) variation around some central value

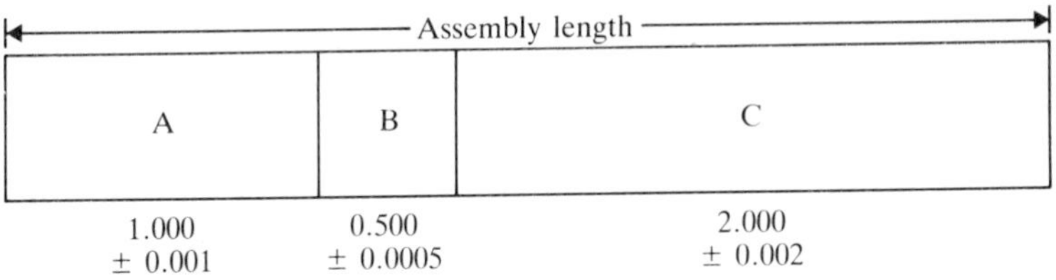

FIGURE 13.8
Mechanical assembly.

Suppose the components were manufactured to the specifications indicated in Figure 13.8. A logical specification on the assembly length would be 3.500 ± 0.0035, giving limits of 3.5035 and 3.4965. The logic of this may be verified from the two extreme assemblies:

Maximum	Minimum
1.001	0.999
0.5005	0.4995
2.002	1.998
3.5035	3.4965

The approach of adding component tolerances is mathematically correct but is often too conservative. Suppose that about 1 percent of the pieces of component A are expected to be below the lower tolerance limit for component A and suppose the same for components B and C. If a component A is selected at random, there is, on average, 1 chance in 100 that it will be on the low side, and similarly for components B and C. The key point is this: If assemblies are made at random and if the components are manufactured independently, then the chance that an assembly will have all *three* components simultaneously below the lower tolerance limit is

$$\frac{1}{100} \times \frac{1}{100} \times \frac{1}{100} = \frac{1}{1,000,000}$$

There is only about one chance in a million that all three components will be too small, resulting in a small assembly. Thus, setting component and assembly tolerances based on the simple addition formula is conservative in that it fails to recognize the extremely low probability of an assembly containing all low (or all high) components.

The statistical approach is based on the relationship between the variances of a number of independent causes and the variance of the dependent or overall result. This may be written as

$$\sigma_{result} = \sqrt{\sigma_{cause\ A}^2 + \sigma_{cause\ B}^2 + \sigma_{cause\ C}^2 + \cdots}$$

In terms of the assembly example, the formula is

$$\sigma_{\text{assembly}} = \sqrt{\sigma_A^2 + \sigma_B^2 + \sigma_C^2}$$

Now suppose that, for each component, the tolerance range is equal to ± 3 standard deviations (or any constant multiple of the standard deviation). As σ is equal to T divided by 3, the variance relationship may be rewritten as

$$\frac{T}{3} = \sqrt{\left(\frac{T_A}{3}\right)^2 + \left(\frac{T_B}{3}\right)^2 + \left(\frac{T_C}{3}\right)^2}$$

or

$$T_{\text{assembly}} = \sqrt{T_A^2 + T_B^2 + T_C^2}$$

Thus the squares of tolerances are added to determine the square of the tolerance for the overall result. This compares to the simple addition of tolerances commonly used.

The effect of the statistical approach is dramatic. Listed below are two possible sets of component tolerances which when used with the formula above will yield an assembly tolerance equal to ± 0.0035.

Component	Alternative 1	Alternative 2
A	± 0.002	± 0.001
B	± 0.002	± 0.001
C	± 0.002	± 0.003

With alternative 1, the tolerance for component A has been doubled, the tolerance for component B has been quadrupled, and the tolerance for component C has been kept the same as the original component tolerance based on the simple addition approach. If alternative 2 is chosen, similar significant increases in the component tolerances may be achieved. This formula, then, may result in a larger component tolerance with *no* change in the manufacturing processes and *no* change in the assembly tolerance.

A risk is involved with this approach. It is possible that an assembly will result which falls outside the assembly tolerance. However, the probability of this occurring can be calculated by expressing the component tolerances as standard deviations, calculating the standard deviation of the result, and finding the area under the normal curve outside the assembly tolerance limits. For example, if each of the component tolerances were equal to 3σ, then 99.73 percent of the assemblies would be within the assembly tolerance, i.e., 0.27 percent, or about 3 assemblies in 1000 taken at random, would fail to meet the assembly tolerance. The risk could be eliminated if components were changed for these few assemblies that did not meet the assembly tolerance.

The tolerance formula is not restricted to outside dimensions of assemblies. Generalizing, the left side of the equation contains the dependent variable or *physical result,* while the right side of the equation contains the independent variables of *physical causes.* If the result is placed on the left and the causes on the right, the formula always has *plus* signs under the square root—even if the result is an internal dimension (such as the clearance between a shaft and hole). The causes of variation are *additive* wherever the physical result happens to fall.

The formula has been applied to a variety of mechanical and electronic products. The concept may be applied to several interacting variables in an engineering relationship. The nature of the relationship need not be additive (assembly example) or subtractive (shaft-and-hole example). The tolerance formula can be adapted to predict the variation of results that are the product and/or the division of several variables.

Assumptions of the Formula

The formula is based on several assumptions:

- The component dimensions are independent and the components are assembled randomly. This assumption is usually met in practice.
- Each component dimension should be normally distributed. Some departure from this assumption is permissible.
- The actual average for each component is equal to the nominal value stated in the specification. For the original assembly example, the actual averages for components *A, B,* and *C* must be 1.000, 0.500, and 2,000, respectively. Otherwise, the nominal value of 3.500 will not be achieved for the assembly and tolerance limits set about 3.500 will not be realistic. Thus, it is important to control the average value for interacting dimensions. This means that process control techniques are needed using variables measurement.

Use caution if any of the assumptions is violated. Reasonable departures from the assumptions may still permit the concept of the formula to be applied. Notice that in the illustrative example the formula resulted in the doubling of certain tolerances. This much of an increase may not even be necessary from the viewpoint of process capability.

Bender (1975) has studied these assumptions for some complex assembly cases and concluded based on a "combination of probability and experience" that a factor of 1.5 should be included to account for the assumptions, i.e.,

$$T_{\text{result}} = 1.5\sqrt{T_A^2 + T_B^2 + T_C^2 + \cdots}$$

Finally, variation simulation analysis is a technique that uses computer simulation to analyze tolerances. This technique can handle product characteristics having either normal or nonnormal distributions. For further discussion, see Rowzee and Holmes (1986).

SUMMARY

- Quality measurements for the design process must be defined both for self-control and for evaluating design effectiveness.
- Complex products typically experience three periods of product life: infant mortality, constant-failure-rate, and wear-out.
- When the failure rate is constant, the distribution of time between failures is exponential. This is the basis of the exponential formula for reliability.
- If the failure of any part causes failure of the system and if the reliabilities of the parts are independent, then system reliability is the product of the parts reliabilities.
- Redundancy is the existence of more than one element for accomplishing a given task.
- For time-oriented products, reliability can be predicted during design using the exponential or Weibull distribution.
- For non-time-oriented products, reliability can be predicted as a function of stress and strength.
- Availability is the probability that a product, when used under given conditions, will perform satisfactorily when called upon.
- Specification limits must be based on the functional needs of the product and the variability of the manufacturing process. Statistical analysis quantifies process variability for the designer.
- Specification limits for interacting dimensions should recognize the probabilistic features of forming the final result.

PROBLEMS

13.1. A radar set has a mean time between failures of 240 h based on the exponential distribution. Suppose that a certain mission requires failure-free operation of the set for 24 h. What is the chance that the set will complete a mission without failure?
Answer: 0.91

13.2. A piece of ground support equipment for a missile has a specified mean time between failures of 100 h. What is the reliability for a mission time of 1 h? 10 h? 50 h? 100 h? 200 h? 300 h? Graph these answers by plotting mission time versus reliability. Assume an exponential distribution.

13.3. The average life of subassembly A is 2000 h. Data indicate that this life characteristic is exponentially distributed.
  (*a*) What percentage of the subassemblies in the population will last at least 200 h?
  (*b*) The average life of subassembly B is 1000 h and the life is exponentially distributed. What percentage of the subassemblies in the population will last at least 200 hours?

(c) These subassemblies are independently manufactured and then connected in series to form the total assembly. What percentage of assemblies in the population will last at least 200 hours?

Answer: (a) 90.5 percent. (b) 81.9 percent. (c) 74.1 percent.

13.4. It is expected that the average time to repair a failure on a certain product is 4 h. Assume that repair time is exponentially distributed. What is the chance that the time for a repair will between 3 and 5 h?

13.5. The following table summarizes basic failure-rate data on components in an electronic subsystem:

Component	Quantity	Failure rate per hour
Silicon transistor	40	74.0×10^{-6}
Film resistor	100	3.0×10^{-6}
Paper capacitor	50	10.0×10^{-6}

Estimate the mean time between failures. (Assume an exponential distribution. All components are critical for subsystem success.)

Answer: 267 h.

13.6 A system consists of subsystems A, B, and C. The system is primarily used on a certain mission that lasts 8 h. The following information has been collected:

Subsystem	Required operating time during mission, h	Type of failure distribution	Reliability information
A	8	Exponential	50% of subsystems will last at least 14 h
B	3	Normal	Average life is 6 h with a standard deviation of 1.5 h
C	4	Weibull with $\beta = 1.0$	Average life is 40 h

Assuming independence of the subsystems, calculate the reliability for a mission.

13.7. A hydraulic subsystem consists of two subsystems in parallel, each having the following components and characteristics:

Components	Failures/10^6 h	Number of components
Pump	23.4	1
Quick disconnect	2.4	3
Check valve	6.1	2
Shutoff valve	7.9	1
Lines and fittings	3.13	7

The components within each subsystem are all necessary for subsystem success. The two parallel subsystems operate simultaneously, and either can perform the mission. What is the mission reliability if the mission time is 300 h? (Assume an exponential distribution.)

13.8. The following estimates, based on field experience, are available on three subsystems:

Subsystem	Percent failed at 1000 mi	Weibull β value
A	0.1	2.0
B	0.2	1.8
C	0.5	1.0

If these estimates are assumed to be applicable for similar subsystems which will be used in a new system, predict the reliability (in terms of percentage successful) at the end of 3000 mi, 5000 mi, 8000 mi, and 10,000 mi.

13.9. It is desired that a power plant be in operating condition 95 percent of the time. The average time required for repairing a failure is about 24 h. What must be the mean time between failures in order for the power plant to meet the 95 percent objective?

Answer: 456 h.

13.10. A manufacturing process runs continuously 24 h per day and 7 days a week (except for planned shutdowns). Past data indicate a 50 percent probability that the time between successive failures is 100 h or more. The average repair time for failures is 6 h. Failure times and repair times are both exponentially distributed. Calculate the availability of the process.

13.11 The following table summarizes data on components in a hydraulic system:

Component	Quality	Failure rate per hour
Relief valve	1	200×10^{-6}
Check valve	1	150×10^{-6}
Filter	1	100×10^{-6}
Cylinder	1	50×10^{-6}

Assume that all components must operate for system success and that the system is used continuously throughout the 8760 h in a year with no shutdowns except for failures. Repair time varies with the type of failure but 50 percent of the repairs require 3 h or more. The following average cost estimates apply:

$$\text{Material cost/failure} = \$100.00$$

$$\text{Repair labor cost/hour} = \$5.00$$

Assume that failure time and repair time are exponentially distributed. Calculate the average cost of repairing failures per year.

Answer: $532.

13.12. Measurements were made on the bore dimension of an impeller. A sample of 20 from a pilot run production showed a mean value of 25.038 cm and a standard deviation of 0.000381 cm. All the units functioned properly, so it was decided to use the data to set specification limits for regular production.

(*a*) Suppose it was assumed that the sample estimates were exactly equal to the population mean and standard deviation. What specification limits should be set to include 99 percent of production?

(*b*) There is uncertainty that the sample and population values are equal. Based on the sample of 20, what limits should be set to be 95 percent sure of including 99 percent of production?

(*c*) Explain the meaning of the difference in (*a*) and (*b*).

(*d*) What assumptions were necessary to determine both sets of limits?

13.13. A circuit contains three resistors in series. Past data show these data on resistance:

Resistor	Mean, Ω	Standard deviation. Ω
1	125	3
2	200	4
3	600	12

(*a*) What percentage of circuits would meet the specification on total resistance of $930 \pm 30 \ \Omega$?

(*b*) Inquire from a local distributor if it is reasonable to assume that the resistance of a resistor is normally distributed.

13.14. A manufacturer of rotary lawn mowers received numerous complaints concerning the effort required to push its product. Studies soon found that the small clearance between the wheel bushing and shaft was the cause. Designers chose to make the clearance large enough for easy rotation of the wheel (or for a heavy grease coating), but still "tight enough" to prevent wobbling. Because of a large inventory of wheels and shafts, a decision was made to ream the bushings to a larger inside diameter (I.D.) and retain the shafts. The following specifications were proposed:

$$\text{Shaft diameter} = 0.800 \pm 0.002 \text{ in}$$

$$\text{New clearance} = 0.008 \pm 0.003 \text{ in}$$

$$\text{Bushing I.D.} = 0.808 \pm 0.001 \text{ in}$$

Production people claimed that they could not economically hold the tolerance on the bushing I.D. What comment would you make about this claim?

Answer: I.D. tolerance of ± 0.0022 could be allowed.

13.15. An assembly consists of two parts (*A* and *B*) which mate together "end to end" to form an overall length, *C*. It is desired that the overall length, *C*, meet a specification of 3.000 ± 0.005 cm. The nominal specification on *A* is 2.000, and on *B* it is 1.000. The manufacturing process for *B* has much more variability than the process for *A*. Specifically, the tolerance for part *B* should be twice as large as for part *A*. Assemblies are to be made at random, and parts *A* and *B* are independently manufactured. Assuming that we want only a small risk of not meeting the specification on *C*, what tolerances should be set on *A* and *B*?

13.16. A canning factory decided to set tolerance limits for filling cans of a new product by sampling a pilot run of 30 cans. The results of that run yielded an average of 446 g with a standard deviation of 1.25 g. What tolerance limits should be set which would be 95 percent certain of including 99 percent of production? The label on the can states that it contains 453 g of the product. How many grams of product should the average can contain if the company is to be 95 percent certain that 99 percent of production contains at least 453 g?

REFERENCES

Bender, Art (1975). "Statistical Tolerancing as it Relates to Quality Control and the Designer," *Automative Division Newsletter of ASQC,* April, p. 12.

Garrick, John B., and Robert J. Mulvihill (1974). "Reliability and Maintainability of Mechanized Bulk Mail Systems," *Proceedings of Annual Reliability and Maintainability Symposium,* Institute of Electrical and Electronics Engineers, New York.

Ireson, W. Grant, and Clyde F. Coombs Jr. (1988). *Handbook of Reliability Engineering and Management.* McGraw-Hill Book Company, New York, Chapter 15.

MIL-HDBK-217 (1986). "Reliability Prediction for Electronic Systems," Department of Defense, Washington, D.C.

O'Connor, Patrick, D. T. (1991). *Practical Reliability Engineering,* 3rd ed., John Wiley and Sons, New York, Chapter 5.

Rowzee, Mary R., and Richard K. Holmes (1986). "Optimizing Component and Assembly Tolerancing," *ASQC Quality Congress Transaction,* pp. 178–186.

SUPPLEMENTARY READING

Reliability, maintainability, and availability quantification: QCH4, pp. 13.19–13.27, 13.43–13.48, 23.81–23.90.

Raheja, Dev G. (1991). *Assurance Technologies,* McGraw-Hill Book Company, New York, Chapters 3, 4.

Statistical tolerance limits: QCH4, 23.51–23.60.

CHAPTER
14

SUPPLIER
RELATIONS

14.1 SUPPLIER RELATIONS— A REVOLUTION

This step on the spiral of quality concerns the purchase of goods or services from suppliers, or vendors.

For many companies, purchases account for 60 percent of the sales dollar and are the source of half of the quality problems (Burt, 1989). Poor quality of supplier items results in extra costs for the purchaser, e.g., for one appliance manufacturer, 75 percent of all warranty claims were traced to purchased components for the appliances.

Current emphasis on inventory reduction provides a further focus on quality. Under the "just-in-time" inventory concept, goods are received from suppliers only in the quantity and at the time that they are needed for production. The buyer stocks no inventories. If a portion of the purchased product is defective, production at the buyer's plant is disrupted because of the lack of a backup inventory. With conventional purchasing, supplier quality problems can be hidden by excess inventory; with the "just-in-time" concept, it is imperative that purchased product meet quality requirements.

The interdependence of buyers and suppliers has increased dramatically. Sometimes the interdependence takes the form of integrated facilities, e.g., a can manufacturer locates next door to a brewery; sometimes technological skills are involved, e.g., an automobile manufacturer asks a supplier to propose a design for a purchased item. The supplier becomes an extension of the buyer's organization.

These circumstances have led to a revolution in the relationship between buyers and suppliers. In the past, the parties were often adversaries; some purchasers viewed suppliers as potential criminals who might try to sneak some defective product past the purchaser's incoming inspection. Today, the key word is partnership, i.e., working closely together for the mutual benefit of both parties.

14.2 SCOPE OF ACTIVITIES FOR SUPPLIER QUALITY

A purchasing system includes three key activities: specification of requirements, selection of a supplier, and contract management. The overall quality objective is to meet the needs of the purchaser (and the ultimate user) with a minimum of incoming inspection or later corrective action; this in turn leads to minimizing overall cost.

To achieve this quality objective, certain primary activities must be identified and responsibilities assigned. Table 14.1 shows a typical list of responsibilities as assigned in one company. These activities are discussed in

TABLE 14.1
Responsibility matrix—supplier relations

Activity	Participating departments		
	Product Development	Purchasing	Quality
Defining product and program quality requirements	××		×
Evaluating alternative suppliers	×	×	××
Selecting suppliers		××	
Conducting joint quality planning	×		××
Cooperating with the supplier during the execution of the contract	×	×	××
Obtaining proof of conformance to requirements	×		××
Certifying qualified suppliers	×	×	××
Conducting quality improvement programs as required	×	×	××
Creating and utilizing supplier quality ratings		××	×

Note: ××, principal responsibility; ×, collateral responsibility.

this chapter and in Chapter 15. Further elaboration is provided in QCH4, Section 15.

The responsibility matrix shown in Table 14.1 shows the Quality Department as having the principal responsibility for many supplier quality activities. Under an alternative policy, the Purchasing Department has the principal responsibility for quality while others (e.g., Product Development and Quality) have collateral responsibility. Such a shift in responsibility places a stronger focus on quality in setting priorities on delivery schedules, price, and quality. To meet this responsibility, most Purchasing Departments would need to supplement their technical capabilities. Some organizations have met that need by transferring technical specialists into the Purchasing Department.

We proceed to examine how quality relates to the three key activities of a purchasing system: specification of requirements, selection of suppliers, and contract management.

14.3 SPECIFICATION OF QUALITY REQUIREMENTS FOR SUPPLIERS

For modern products, quality planning starts before a contract is signed. Such planning must recognize two issues:

1. The buyer must transmit to the supplier a full understanding of the use to be made of the product. Communicating usage requirements can be difficult even for a simple product.
2. The buyer must obtain information to be sure that the supplier has the capability to provide a product that meets all fitness-for-use requirements.

The complexity of many modern products makes it difficult to communicate usage needs to a supplier in a specification. Not only are the field usage conditions of a complex product sometimes poorly known, but the internal environments surrounding a particular component may not be known until the complete product is designed and tested. For example, specifying accurate temperature and vibration requirements to a supplier supplying an electric component may not be feasible until the complete system is developed. Such cases require, at the least, continuous cooperation between supplier and buyer. In special cases, it may be necessary to award separate development and production contracts to discover how to finalize requirements.

Circumstances may require two kinds of specifications:

1. Specifications defining the product requirements
2. Specifications defining what quality-related activities are expected of the supplier, i.e., the supplier's quality system

The second type of specification is a departure from the traditional practice of refraining from telling a supplier how to run his plant. Defining required activities within a supplier's plant is sometimes necessary to ensure that a supplier has the expertise to conduct the full program needed to result in a satisfactory product. For some products, government regulations require that a buyer impose certain processing requirements (e.g., sanitary conditions for manufacturing pharmaceutical products) on suppliers. For other products, such as a complex mechanical or electronic subsystem, the overall system requirements may result in a need for a supplier to meet a numerical reliability or maintainability requirement and to conduct certain activities to ensure that such requirements are met (see Chapter 12). For still other products, suppliers are required to use statistical process control techniques on selected product characteristics or process parameters. Documents such as the ISO 9000 series, which define the elements of quality programs can be cited as requirements in a contract with a supplier. QCH4, pages 15.9–15.12, provides further discussion of specifying quality activities in contracts.

> **Example 14.1.** Several suppliers were asked to submit bids on a battery needed in a space program. They were given a numerical reliability goal and asked to include in their bid proposal a description of the reliability activities that would be conducted to help meet the goal. Most of the prospective suppliers included a reliability program consisting of appropriate reliability activities for a battery. However, one supplier apparently had no expertise in formal reliability methodology and submitted a surprising write-up. That supplier made a word-for-word copy of a reliability program write-up previously published for a missile system (the word "battery" was substituted for "missile"). This led to a suspicion, later confirmed, that the supplier knew little about reliability programs.

For complex products for which a supplier is asked to design and manufacture a product, the supplier can be required to include in the proposal a preliminary reliability prediction, a failure mode, effect, and criticality analysis, a reliability test plan, or other reliability analyses (see Chapter 12). The supplier's response not only provides some assurance on the design concept but also shows that the supplier has the reliability expertise to conduct the program and has included the funds and schedule time in the proposal.

We proceed next to the selection of suppliers.

14.4 SUPPLIER SELECTION

Selection of suppliers starts with the decision as to whether to make or buy. This decision requires an analysis of factors such as the skills and facilities needed, plant capacity, ability to meet delivery schedules, expected costs of "making" or "buying," and other matters. With a decision to buy, the number of suppliers for each item must then be decided upon.

Multiple Suppliers versus Single Source

Multiple sources of supply have advantages: Competition can result in better quality, lower costs, better service, and minimum disruption of supply due to strikes or other catastrophes.

A single source of supply also has advantages: The size of the contract given to a single source will be larger than with multiple sources, and the supplier will attach more significance to the contract. With a single source, communications are simplified and more time is available for working closely with the supplier. The most dramatic examples of single sources are multi-divisional companies in which some divisions are suppliers to others.

A clear trend has emerged: Organizations are significantly reducing the number of multiple suppliers. Since about 1980, reductions of 50–70 percent in the supplier base have become common. This does *not* necessarily mean going to single source for all purchases; it *does* mean a single source for some purchases and fewer multiple suppliers for other purchases. Working with a smaller number of suppliers helps to achieve useful partnerships by providing the time and skills necessary to facilitate in-depth cooperation. The forms of cooperation are discussed later in this chapter.

Whether a single source or multiple suppliers, selection must be based on the reputation of the supplier, qualification tests of the supplier's design, survey of the supplier's manufacturing facility, and information from data banks and other sources on supplier quality.

14.5 ASSESSMENT OF SUPPLIER CAPABILITY

Evaluating supplier quality capability involves one or both of two actions:

1. Qualifying the supplier's design through the evaluation of product samples
2. Qualifying the supplier's capability to meet quality requirements on production lots

Qualifying the Supplier's Design

In some cases, the supplier is asked to create a new design to meet the functions desired by the purchaser. In these cases, the supplier makes samples based on the proposed design. (Such samples are often made in an engineering model shop because a manufacturing process for the new design has not yet been created.) The samples are tested (the "qualification test") either by the purchaser or by the supplier, who then submits the results to the purchaser. It is not unusual for qualification test results to be rejected. Two reasons are common: (1) The test results show that the design does not provide the product functions desired, or (2) the test procedure is not adequate to evaluate the performance of the product. Such rejections (and ensuing delays in shipments) can be prevented by starting with a rigorous definition of product requirements and by requiring an approval of the test procedure before the tests commence.

Qualification test results do show whether the supplier has created a design that meets the performance requirements; such test results do *not* show if the supplier is capable of manufacturing the item under production conditions.

Qualifying the Supplier's Manufacturing Process

Evaluation of the supplier's manufacturing capability can be done through three approaches: past data on similar products, process capability analysis, or an evaluation of the supplier's quality system through a quality survey.

The best approach makes use of data showing the supplier's past performance on the same or similar products. Such data may be available within the local buyer's organization, other divisions of the same corporation, government data banks, or industry data banks. See QCH4, page 15.13, for elaboration.

With the process capability analysis approach, data on key product characteristics are collected from the process and evaluated using statistical indices for process capability (see Chapter 17). All of this is done before the supplier is authorized to proceed with full production. Typically, process capability analysis of a supplier process is reserved for significant product characteristics, safety-related items, or products requiring compliance with government regulations.

The third approach, a quality survey, is explained below.

Supplier Quality Survey

A supplier quality survey is an evaluation of a supplier's ability to meet quality requirements on production lots. The results of the survey are used in the supplier selection process, or, if the supplier has already been chosen, the survey alerts the purchaser to areas where the supplier may need help in meeting requirements. The survey can vary from a simple questionnaire mailed to the supplier to a visit to the supplier's facility.

The questionnaire poses explicit questions such as these submitted to suppliers of a manufacturer of medical devices:

- Has your company received the quality requirements on the product and agreed that they can be fully met?
- Are your final inspection results documented?
- Do you agree to provide the purchaser with advance notice of any changes in your product design?

- What protective garments do your employees wear to reduce product contamination?
- Describe the air-filtration system in your manufacturing areas.

The more formal quality survey consists of a visit to the supplier's facility by a team of observers from departments such as Quality, Engineering, Manufacturing, and Purchasing. Such a visit may be part of a broader survey of the supplier covering financial, managerial, and technological competence. Depending on the product involved, the activities included in the quality portion of the survey can be chosen from the following list:

- *Management:* philosophy, quality policies, organization structure, indoctrination, commitment to quality
- *Design:* organization, systems in use, caliber of specifications, orientation to modern techniques, attention to reliability, engineering change control, development laboratories
- *Manufacture:* physical facilities, maintenance, special processes, process capability, production capacity, caliber of planning, lot identification and traceability
- *Purchasing:* specifications, supplier relations, procedures
- *Quality:* organization structure, availability of quality control and reliability engineers, quality planning (materials, in-process, finished goods, packing, storage, shipping, usage, field service), audit of adherence to plan
- *Inspection and test:* laboratories, special tests, instruments, measurement control
- *Quality coordination:* organization for coordination, order analysis, control over subcontractors, quality cost analysis, corrective action loop, disposition of nonconforming product
- *Data systems:* facilities, procedures, effective use reports
- *Personnel:* indoctrination, training motivation
- *Quality results:* performance attained, self-use of product, prestigious customers, prestigious subcontractors

An examination of quality practices of suppliers sometimes reveals a sobering picture. Table 14.2 shows the results for consumer products suppliers of Sears Canada, Inc. (Gordon, 1990) and electronic product suppliers of GTE Service Corporation (Johnson, 1989).

Following the survey, the team reports its findings. These consist of: (1) some objective findings as to facilities possessed or lacked by the supplier, (2) subjective judgments on the effectiveness of the supplier's operations, (3) a further judgment on the extent of assistance needed by the supplier, (4) a highly subjective prediction as to whether the supplier will deliver a good product if it is awarded a contract.

TABLE 14.2
Percentage of suppliers having specific quality practices

Suppliers of Sears Canada, Inc.		Suppliers of GTE Service Corporation	
Written quality procedures	20%	Computerized tracking of failures	50%
Control of nonconformances	25%	Use of bar code	26%
Corrective action procedures	29%	Process SPC	71%
Cost of nonconformance		Product SPC	9%
identified	29%	Design SPC	8%
Control of subsuppliers	42%	Component PPM program	43%
Quality commitment by CEO/		Solder PPM program	83%
President	46%		

An excellent discussion of the goals, planning and execution of supplier surveys is provided by Maass et al. (1990, Appendix 4).

Chapter 15 shows how the survey quality activities can be quantified by a scoring system.

Supplier quality surveys have both merits and limitations. On the positive side, such surveys can identify important weaknesses such as a lack of special test equipment or an absence of essential training programs. Further, the survey opens up lines of communication and can stimulate action on quality by the supplier's upper management. On the negative side, surveys that emphasize the supplier's organization, procedures, and documentation have had only limited success in predicting future supplier performance on the product.

In some industries, suppliers have been burdened with quality surveys from many different purchasers. These repeat surveys (called "multiple assessment") are time consuming for suppliers. In another approach, a standard specification of the elements of a quality system (e.g., the ISO 9000 series) is created and assessors are trained to evaluate supplier capability using the specification. The ISO 9000 series comprises separate assessment specifications for (1) a complete program from design through servicing, (2) production and installation, and (3) final inspection and test. A list of suppliers who have passed the assessment is published, and other purchasers are encouraged to use these results instead of making their own assessment of a supplier. The assessors are independent of the supplier or purchasing organization—thus the term "third-party assessment." In some countries, a national standards organization acts in this role.

Next, we proceed to the third phase of purchasing—contract management.

14.6 CONTRACT MANAGEMENT

The Bell Communications Research Company surveyed 30 major companies to gain information on their approaches to supplier quality (Pence and Saacke, 1988). Three categories of interacting with suppliers emerged:

- *Inspection.* This focuses on various forms of product inspection.
- *Prevention.* The premise here is that quality must be built in by the supplier, with the purchaser's help. But there is still an arm's-length relationship between purchaser and supplier.
- *Partnership.* Suppliers are offered the financial security of a long-term relationship in exchange for a supplier's commitment to quality which includes a strong teamwork relationship with the buyer.

Partnership—involving not just quality but also other business issues—is clearly the wave of the future. Teamwork actions vary greatly, e.g., training a supplier's staff in quality techniques, including suppliers in a design review meeting to gain ideas on how supplier parts can best be used, sharing confidential sales projections with suppliers to assist in supplier production scheduling. Such partnerships often lead to formation of supplier Quality Councils, which help provide new approaches for the benefits of both the buyer and suppliers. Various opportunities for teamwork are discussed below. But such teamwork depends on truly open communication between buyers and suppliers.

Such cooperation can best be achieved by setting up multiple channels of communication: designers must communicate directly with designers, quality specialists with quality specialists, etc. These multiple channels are a drastic departure from the single channel, which is the method in common use for purchase of traditional products. In the single-channel approach, a specialist in the buyer's organization must work through the purchasing agent, who in turn speaks with the salesperson in the supplier's organization, to obtain information. Of course, the concept of multiple channels seems sensible, but wouldn't it be useful to determine if multiple channels yield better results on quality? Carter and Miller (1989) did just that.

> **Example 14.2.** In an innovative research study, they compared quality levels for two communication structures: serial (single-channel) and parallel (multiple-channel). At a manufacturer of mechanical seals, one section of a plant followed the serial communication concept while a second area used parallel communication. Over a 19-month period, the section using parallel communication improved the average percentage of items rejected from 30.3 percent to 15.0 percent, a statistically significant difference; the section with serial communication had no such improvement—in fact, its percentage rejection increased slightly.

We next address how partnership can be achieved through joint economic planning, joint technological planning, and cooperation during contract execution.

Joint Economic Planning

The economic aspects of joint quality planning concentrate on two major approaches:

Buying value rather than conformance to specification. The technique used is to analyze the value of what is being bought and to try to effect an improvement. The organized approach is known as value engineering (see Section 12.8, "Cost and Product Performance"). Applied to supplier quality relations, value engineering looks for excessive costs due to: (1) overspecification for the use to which the product will be put, e.g., a special product ordered when a standard product would do, (2) emphasis on original price rather than on cost of use over the life of the product, and (3) emphasis on conformance to specification, not fitness for use. Suppliers are encouraged to make recommendations on design or other requirements that will improve or maintain quality at a lower cost.

Optimizing quality costs. To the purchase price, the buyer must add a whole array of quality-related costs: incoming inspection, materials review, production delays, downtime, extra inventories, etc. However, the supplier also has a set of costs it is trying to optimize. The buyer should put together the data needed to understand the life cycle costs or the cost of use and then press for a result that will optimize these.

> **Example 14.3.** A heavy-equipment manufacturer bought 11,000 castings per year from several suppliers. It was decided to calculate the total cost of the purchased casting as the original purchase price plus incoming inspection costs plus the costs of rejections detected later in assembly. The unit purchase price on a contract given to the lowest bidder was $19. The inspection and rejection costs amounted to an additional $2.11. The variation among bid prices was $2. Thus, the lowest bid does not always result in the lowest total cost.

Joint Technological Planning

The more usual elements of such planning include:

1. Agreement on the meaning of performance requirements in the specifications.
2. Quantification of quality, reliability, and maintainability requirements.

> **Example 14.4.** A supplier was given a contract to provide an air-conditioning system with a mean time between failures of at least 2000 hours. As part of joint planning, the supplier was required to submit a detailed reliability program early in the design phase. The program write-up was submitted and included a provision to impose the same 2000-hour requirement on each supplier of parts for the system. This revealed a complete lack of understanding by the supplier of the multiplication rule (see Section 13.4, "The Relationship between Part and System Reliability").

3. Definition of reliability and maintainability tasks to be conducted by the supplier.

4. Preparation of a process control plan for the manufacturing process. The supplier can be asked to submit a plan summarizing the specific activities which will be conducted during the manufacture of the product. Typically, the plan must include statistical process control techniques to prevent defects by detecting problems early.

5. Definition of special tasks required of the supplier. These may include activities to ensure that good manufacturing practices are met, special analyses are prepared for critical items, etc.

6. Seriousness classification of defects to help the supplier understand where to concentrate efforts.

7. Establishment of sensory standards for those qualities which require use of the human being as an instrument.

> **Example 14.5.** The federal government was faced with the problem of defining the limits of color on a military uniform. It was finally decided to prepare physical samples of the lightest and darkest acceptable colors. Such standards were then sent out with the provision that the standards would be replaced periodically because of color fading.

8. Standardization of test methods and test conditions between supplier and buyer to ensure their compatibility.

> **Example 14.6.** A carpet manufacturer repeatedly complained to a yarn supplier about yarn weight. Finally, the supplier visited the customer to verify the test methods. The mechanics of their test methods were alike. Next, an impartial testing lab was hired, and it verified the tests at the carpet plant. Finally, the mystery was solved. The supplier was spinning (and measuring) the yarn at bone-dry conditions, but the carpet manufacturer measured at standard conditions. During this period, $62,000 more was spent for yarn than if it had been purchased at standard weight.

9. Establishment of sampling plans and other criteria relative to inspection and test activity. From the supplier's viewpoint, the plan should accept lots having the usual process average. For the buyer, the critical factor is the amount of damage caused by one defect getting through the sampling screen. Balancing the cost of sorting versus sampling can be a useful input in designing a sampling plan (see Chapter 19). In addition to sampling criteria, error of measurement can also be a problem (see Section 18.9, "Errors of Measurement").

10. Establishment of quality levels. In the past, suppliers were often given "acceptable quality levels" (AQL). The AQL value was just one point on the "operating characteristic" curve that described the risks associated with sampling plans. A typical AQL value might be 2.0 percent. Many suppliers interpreted this to mean that product which included 2 percent defective was acceptable. It is best to make clear to the supplier through

the contract that *all* product submitted is expected to meet specifications and that any product which is nonconforming may be returned for replacement. In many industries, the unit of measurement is now defects per million (DPM).

11. Establishment of a system of lot identification and traceability. This concept has always been present in some degree, e.g., heat numbers of steel, lot numbers of pharmaceutical products. More recently, with intensified attention to product reliability, this procedure is more acutely needed to simplify the localization of trouble, to reduce the volume of product recall, and to fix responsibility. These traceability systems, while demanding some extra effort to preserve the order of manufacture and identify the product, make greater precision in sampling possible.

12. Establishment of a system of timely response to alarm signals resulting from defects. Under many contracts, the buyer and supplier are yoked to a common timetable for completion of the final product. Usually, a separate department (e.g., Materials Management) presides over major aspects of scheduling. However, upper management properly looks to the people associated with the quality function to set up alarm signals to detect quality failures and to act positively on these signals to avoid deterioration, whether in quality, cost, or delivery.

Such depth of joint technological planning bears no resemblance to the old approach of sending a supplier a blueprint with a fixed design and a schedule.

Cooperation during Contract Execution

This cooperation usually concentrates on the following activities.

Evaluation of initial samples of product. Under many circumstances, it is important that the supplier submit test results of a small initial sample produced from production tooling and a sample from the first production shipment before the full shipment is made. The latter evaluation can be accomplished by having a buyer's representative visit the supplier's plant and observe the inspection of a random sample selected from the first production lot. A review can also be made of process capability or process control type data from that lot.

Design information and changes. Design changes may take place at the initiative of either the buyer or the supplier. Either way, there is a need to treat the supplier like an in-house department when developing procedures for processing design changes. This need is especially acute for modern products, for which design changes can affect products, processes, tools, instruments, stored materials, procedures, etc. Some of these effects are obvious, but others are subtle, requiring a complete analysis to identify the effects. Failure to provide adequate design change information to suppliers has been a distinct obstacle to good supplier relations.

Surveillance of supplier quality. Quality surveillance is the continuing monitoring and verification of the status of procedures, methods, conditions, processes, products, services, and analysis of records in relation to stated references to ensure that specified requirements for quality are being met (ISO 8402-1986). Surveillance by the buyer can take several forms: inspection of product, meetings with suppliers to review quality status, audits of elements of the supplier quality program, monitoring of the manufacturing practices of the supplier, review of statistical process control data, and witnessing of specific operations or tests. Major or critical contracts require on-site presence or repeat visits.

Evaluating delivered product. Evaluation of supplier product can be achieved by using one of the methods listed in Table 14.3.

In previous decades, incoming inspection often consumed a large amount of time and effort. With the advent of modern complex products, many companies have found that they do not have the necessary inspection skills or equipment. This has forced them to rely more on the supplier's quality system or inspection and test data, as discussed later in this chapter.

TABLE 14.3
Methods of evaluating supplier product

Method	Approach	Application
100 percent inspection	Every item in a lot is evaluated for all or some of the characteristics in the specification	Critical items where the cost of inspection is justified by the cost of risk of defectives; also used to establish quality level of new suppliers
Sampling inspection	A sample of each lot is evaluated by a predefined sampling plan and a decision is made to accept or reject lot	Important items where the supplier has established an adequate quality record by the prior history of lots submitted
Identifying inspection	The product is examined to ensure that the supplier sent the correct product; no inspection of characteristics is made	Items of less importance where the reliability of the supplier laboratory has been established in addition to the quality level of the product
No inspection	The lot is sent directly to a storeroom or processing department	For purchase of standard materials or goods not used in the product, e.g., office supplies
Use of supplier data (supplier certification)	Data of the supplier inspection is used in place of incoming inspection	Items for which a supplier has established a strong quality record

The choice of evaluation method depends on a variety of factors:

- Prior quality history on the part and supplier.
- Criticality of the part on overall system performance.
- Criticality on later manufacturing operations.
- Warranty or use history.
- Supplier process capability information.
- The nature of the manufacturing process. For example, a press operation depends primarily on the adequacy of setup. Information on the first few pieces and last few pieces in a production run is usually sufficient to draw conclusions about the entire run.
- Product homogeneity. For example, fluid products are homogeneous and the need for large sample sizes is thus less.
- Availability of required inspection skills and equipment.

Action on nonconforming product. During the performance of the contract, there will arise instances of nonconformance. These may be on the product itself or on process requirements or procedural requirements. Priority effort should go to cases where a product is unfit for use.

Communications to the supplier on nonconformance must include a precise description of the symptoms of the defects. The best description is in the form of samples, but if this is not possible, the supplier should have the opportunity to visit the site of the trouble. There are numerous related questions: What disposition is to be made of the defective items? Who will sort or repair them? Who will pay the costs? What were the causes? What steps are needed to avoid a recurrence? These questions are outside the scope of pure defect detection; they require discussion among departments within each company and further discussions between buyer and supplier.

Improvement of supplier quality. The general approach to handling chronic supplier problems follows the step-by-step approach to improvement explained in Chapter 3, "Quality Improvement and Cost Reduction." This includes the early steps of establishing the "proof of the need" for the supplier to take action and the application of Pareto analysis to identify the "vital few" problems. Section 15.6, "Pareto Analysis of Suppliers," explains the form of such analyses of suppliers' problems.

Cooperation often requires that technical assistance be provided to suppliers. Miller and Kegaris (1986) describe how it may be necessary to share proprietary information on a "need-to-know" basis. This often represents a major breakthrough in communications.

Sometimes upper management must provide the leadership in obtaining action from suppliers. Amazing results can be achieved when the initial step in an improvement program is a meeting of both the buyer's and supplier's upper management teams, who plan the action steps for improvement together. Such discussions have much more impact than a meeting of the two quality managers do.

> **Example 14.7.** For an appliance manufacturer, 75 percent of the warranty costs were due to suppliers' items. The president and his staff met individually with the counterpart team from each of 10 key suppliers. Warranty data were presented to establish the "proof of the need." A goal was set for a 50 percent reduction in warranty costs over a 5-year period. Each supplier was asked to develop a quality improvement program. The purchaser provided an 8-hour training session for the president and staff members of the key suppliers. Follow-up meetings were held. A system of supplier recognition awards was set up and purchasing practices were changed to transfer business to the best suppliers. The result: a decline in service calls from 41 to 13 calls per 100 products and a saving of $16 per unit in warranty costs.

14.7 SUPPLIER CERTIFICATION

A "certified" supplier is one which, after extensive investigation, is found to supply material of such quality that it is not necessary to perform routine testing on each lot received (Bossert, 1988). Such a supplier is compared to an "approved" supplier which meets minimum requirements, and a "preferred" supplier, which produces better quality than the minimum. Certified suppliers are the ideal, but unfortunately they are in the minority.

ASQC recommends eight criteria for certification. These are summarized in Table 14.4.

Supplier certification provides a model for the low DPM levels necessary for just-in-time manufacture, drastically reduces buyer inspection costs, and

TABLE 14.4
Criteria for supplier certification

Criteria	Examples
No product-related lot rejections for at least 1 year	An alternative is volume related, e.g., no rejects in 20 consecutive lots
No non-product-related rejections for at least 6 months	The marking on a container or the timeliness of an analysis document
No production-related negative incidents for at least 6 months	Ease with which the supplier's product can be used in the buyer's process or product
Passed a recent on-site quality system evaluation	A supplier survey on defined criteria
Having a totally agreed on specification	No ambiguous phrases like "characteristic odor" or "clear of contamination"
Fully documented process and quality system	The system must include plans for continuous improvement
Timely copies of inspection and test data	Real-time availability of data
Process that is stable and in control	Statistical control and process capability studies

Source: Adapted from Maass et al. (1990).

identifies suppliers for partnerships. Certified suppliers receive preference in competitive bidding and also achieve industry recognition by their certified status.

SUMMARY

- A revolution in the relationship between buyers and suppliers has emerged in the form of supplier partnerships.
- Quality specifications often define requirements for both the product and for the quality system.
- Organizations are significantly reducing the number of multiple suppliers.
- Evaluating supplier quality capability involves qualifying the supplier's design and the manufacturing process.
- Supplier partnerships require joint economic planning, joint technological planning, and cooperation during contract execution.
- A certified supplier is one which, after extensive investigation, is found to supply material of such quality that it is not necessary to perform routine testing on each lot received.

PROBLEMS

14.1. Visit the purchasing agent of some local institution to learn the overall approach to supplier selection and the role of supplier quality performance in this selection process. Report your findings.

14.2. Visit a sampling of local suppliers (printer, merchant, repair shop, etc.) to learn the role of quality performance in their relationship with their clients. Report your findings.

14.3. Visit a local company and create a table similar to Table 14.2.

14.4. Outline a potential application of several concepts in this chapter. Follow the instructions given in Problem 12.11.

14.5. A government agency contracted with a company to design and build a satellite system. Months after the contract was signed, it was discovered that the design would not be immune to certain types of radar interference. The agency claimed that it had described the performance desired for the satellites. The company disagreed (with respect to the radar interference). If this need had been realized at the start of the project, it would have been relatively simple to create an appropriate design. The satellites are in an advanced stage of design and construction, and the necessary changes would cost $100 million. There was further confusion. The company had chosen a supplier to manufacture the satellites. This supplier had had previous experience on such products, and some people claimed that the supplier should have been aware of the radar interference problem. Comment on the actions that should be taken by three such organizations to prevent such a situation on a future project (*Business Week*, 1978).

14.6. During World War II, many manufacturers made products that were totally new to them. For example, the Ford Motor Company was asked to produce fuselage sections for B-24 aircraft. To do this, Ford had to work closely with the Consolidated Company, which was responsible for the manufacture of the entire aircraft. Thus Ford was a supplier for Consolidated. There was much friction between the companies. Lindbergh (1970, pp. 644–676) describes the background:

> In short, if the Consolidated men were carrying a chip on one shoulder, the Ford men arrived with a chip on each shoulder. Instead of taking the attitude that they had come to San Diego to learn how to build Consolidated bombers from the company that had developed those bombers, they took the attitude that they were there only as a preliminary to showing Consolidated how to build Consolidated bombers better and on mass production. The inevitable result was a deep-rooted antagonism which still exists.

The first article delivered by Ford was "not only as bad but considerably worse than the aviation people said it would be—rivets missing . . . badly formed skin . . . cracks *already* started . . . etc." However, this article had been passed both by Ford inspection and by the Army inspector stationed at Ford. Lindbergh concluded:

> What has happened is clear enough: under pressure, and encouraged by the desire to get production under way at Willow Run, and more than a little due to lack of experience, both Army and Ford inspection passed material that should have been rejected (and which was rejected by the more experienced and impartial inspectors at Tulsa).

Describe the *specific* actions that you would recommend to correct the immediate problem and prevent a recurrence in the future.

REFERENCES

Bossert, James L., ed. (1988). *Procurement Quality Control,* 4th ed., ASQC Customer-Supplier Technical Committee, ASQC Quality Press, Milwaukee.

Burt, David N. (1989). "Managing Product Quality Through Strategic Purchasing," *Sloan Management Review,* Spring, pp. 39–48.

Business Week (1978). "A $100 Million Satellite Error," August 7, p. 52.

Carter, Joseph R., and Jeffrey G. Miller (1989). "The Impact of Alternative Vendor/Buyer Communication Structures on the Quality of Purchased Materials," *Decision Sciences,* Fall, pp. 759–776.

Gordon, Niall (1990). "Supplier Quality Partnership Program," *ASQC Quality Congress Transactions,* pp. 39–49.

Johnson, Stanley G. (1989). "Continuous Vendor Improvement—A Proven Approach," *ASQC Annual Quality Congress Transactions,* Milwaukee, pp. 10–13.

Lindbergh, Charles A. (1970). *The Wartime Journals of Charles A. Lindbergh,* Harcourt Brace Jovanovich, New York.

Maass, Richard A., John O. Brown, and James L. Bossert (1990). *Supplier Certification—A Continuous Improvement Strategy,* ASQC Quality Press, Milwaukee, Wisconsin.

Miller, G. D., and Ronald J. Kegaris (1986). "An Alcoa-Kodak Joint Team," *Juran Report Number Six,* Juran Institute, Inc., Wilton, Connecticut, pp. 29–34.

Pence, John L., and P. Saacke (1988). "A Survey of Companies That Demand Supply Quality," *ASQC Quality Congress Transactions,* Milwaukee, pp. 715–722.

SUPPLEMENTARY READING

Purchasing and quality: QCH4, Section 15.

Johnson, Ross H., and Richard T. Weber (1985). *Buying Quality,* Watts Publications, New York.

Pyzdek, Thomas, and Roger W. Berger (1992). *Quality Engineering Handbook,* Marcel Dekker, ASQC Quality Press, New York, Chapter 7, "Supplier Quality Assurance."

CHAPTER
15

SUPPLIER
RELATIONS—
STATISTICAL
TOOLS

15.1 QUALITY MEASUREMENT IN SUPPLIER RELATIONS

The management of quality-related activities in supplier relations must include provision for measurement.

Recall the three guidelines for developing quality measurements for a functional activity (see Section 13.1, "Quality Measurement in Design"): obtain input from customers; design measurements for both evaluation of performance *and* feedback for self-control; provide early, concurrent, and lagging indicators of performance.

Table 15.1 shows units of measure for various subject areas of supplier relations.

We proceed to examine some statistical tools that are useful in supplier relations.

331

TABLE 15.1
Examples of quality measurement in supplier relations

Subject	Units of measure
Quality of submitted lots	Percentage of lots rejected
	Cost of poor quality
	Percentage of lots accepted on waiver
	Number of rejected lots classified "use as is"
	Special supplier rating metrics
Supplier relations program	Percentage of suppliers certified
	Percentage of suppliers classified acceptable as a result of a supplier survey
	Percentage of qualification test *procedures* approved on first submission
	Percentage of qualification test *results* approved on first submission
	Percentage of initial product samples approved on first submission
	Percentage of first production shipments approved on first submission
	Percentage of suppliers submitting data
	Average time to resolve problems
Business relationships	Average number of multiple suppliers per item
	Percentages of purchases as single source
	Percentage of purchases to lowest bidder
	Average time to secure bids
	Average time to secure answers to technical inquiries
Adequacy of inventory	Percentage of stockouts
Service to suppliers	Average number of days to pay supplier invoice
	Number of accounts payable beyond X days

15.2 DEFINITION OF NUMERICAL QUALITY AND RELIABILITY REQUIREMENTS FOR LOTS

Beyond the quality and reliability requirements imposed on individual units or products, there is usually a need for added numerical criteria to judge conformance of *lots* of products.

These criteria are typically needed in acceptance sampling procedures (see Chapter 19), which makes it possible to accept or reject an entire lot of product based on the inspection and test result of a random sample from the lot. The application of sampling procedures is facilitated if lot quality requirements are defined in numerical terms. Examples of numerical indices are shown in Table 15.2.

The selection of numerical values for these criteria depends on several factors and also on probability considerations. These matters are discussed in Chapter 19 and by Schilling (1988). These criteria are also a means of indexing sampling plans developed from statistical concepts. Unfortunately, many

TABLE 15.2
Forms of numerical sampling criteria

Quality index	Meaning	Typical values, %	Common misinterpretations
Part per million (PPM)	Number of defects per million items	20–1000	———
Acceptable quality level (AQL)*	Percentage defective which has a high probability (say ≥ 0.90) of being accepted by the sampling plan	0.01–10.0	All accepted lots are at least as good as the AQL; all rejected lots are worse than the AQL
Lot tolerance percentage defective (LTPD)	Percentage defective which has a low probability (say ≤ 0.10) of being accepted by the sampling plan	0.5–10.0	All lots better than the LTPD will be accepted; all lots worse than the LTPD will be rejected
Average outgoing quality limit (AOQL)	Worse average percentage defective over many lots after sampling inspection has been performed and rejected lots 100% inspected	0.1–10.0	All accepted lots are at least as good as the AOQL; all rejected lots are worse than the AOQL

* Some sampling tables and other sources define AQL as the maximum percentage defective considered satisfactory as a process average.

suppliers do not understand the statistical concepts and make incorrect interpretations of the quality level requirement and also the results of sampling inspection (see Table 15.2). Also, these criteria can be a source of confusion in product liability discussions. Suppliers must understand that *all* product submitted is expected to meet specifications.

For complex and/or time-oriented products, numerical reliability requirements can be defined in supplier purchasing documents. Sometimes such requirements are stated in terms of mean time between failures. Numerical reliability requirements can help to clarify what a customer means by "high reliability."

Example 15.1. A capacitor manufacturer requested bids on a unit of manufacturing equipment that was to perform several manufacturing operations. Reliability of the equipment was important to maintaining production schedules, so a numerical requirement on "mean time between jams" (MTBJ) was specified to prospective bidders. (Previously, reliability had not been treated quantitatively. Equipment manufacturers had always promised high reliability, but results had been disappointing.) After several rounds of discussion with bidders it was concluded that the desired level of reliability was unrealistic if the machine were to perform several operations. The capacitor manufacturer finally decided to revise the requirement for several operations and thereby reduce the complexity of the equipment. The effort to specify a numerical requirement in the procurement document forced a clear understanding of reliability. Suppliers can also be required to demonstrate, by test, specified levels of reliability (see Chapter 13).

15.3   QUANTIFICATION OF SUPPLIER SURVEYS

The quality survey is a technique for evaluating the supplier's ability to meet quality requirements on production lots (Section 14.5, "Assessment of Supplier Capability"). The evaluation of various quality activities can be quantified by a scoring system.

A scoring system that includes importance weights for activities is illustrated in Table 15.3. This system is used by a manufacturer of electronic assemblies. In this case, the importance weights (W) vary from 1 to 4 and must total to 25 for each of the three areas surveyed. The weights show the relative importance of the various activities in the overall index. The actual ratings (R) of the activities observed are assigned as follows:

10: The specific activity is satisfactory in every respect (or does not apply).
8: The activity meets minimum requirements but improvements could be made.
0: The activity is unsatisfactory.

TABLE 15.3
Scoring of a supplier quality survey

Activity	Receiving inspection			Manufacturing			Final inspection		
	R	W	$R \times W$	R	W	$R \times W$	R	W	$R \times W$
Quality management	8	3	24	8	3	24	8	3	24
Quality planning	8	4	32	8	4	32	10	4	40
Inspection equipment	10	3	30	10	3	30	10	3	30
Calibration	0	3	0	10	3	30	0	3	0
Drawing control	0	3	0	10	2	20	10	2	20
Corrective action	10	3	30	8	3	24	8	3	24
Handling rejects	10	2	20	8	2	16	10	3	30
Storage and shipping	10	1	10	10	1	10	10	1	10
Environment	8	1	8	8	1	8	8	1	8
Personnel experience	10	2	20	10	3	30	10	2	20
Area total			174			224			206

Note: R, rating; W, weight.
Interpretation of area totals:
  Fully approved: Each of the three area totals is 250.
  Approved: None of the three area totals is less than 200.
  Conditionally approved: No single area total is less than 180.
  Unapproved: One or more of the area totals is less than 180.

Scoring schemes can be made simpler or more complicated (see Bossert, 1988). Johnson (1987) describes how the Lotus 1–2–3 spreadsheet is used to record and evaluate supplier responses to a survey about the supplier quality systems. Each supplier receives a composite score, a comparison to the buyer standard score for suppliers, and a ranking relative to other suppliers.

15.4 USE OF HISTOGRAM ANALYSIS ON SUPPLIER DATA

A useful tool for learning about a supplier's process and comparing several suppliers' manufacturing product to the same specification is the histogram (see Section 9.9, "The Normal Curve and Histogram Analysis"). A random sample is selected from a lot and measurements are made on the selected quality characteristics. The data are charted as frequency histograms. The analysis consists of comparing the histograms to the specification limits.

An application of histograms to evaluating the hardenability of a particular grade of steel from four suppliers is shown in Figure 15.1. The specification was a maximum Rockwell C reading of 43 measured at Jominy position J8. Histograms were also prepared for carbon, manganese, nickel, and chromium content. Analysis revealed:

- Supplier 46 had a process without any strong central tendency. The histogram on nickel for this supplier was also rectangular in shape, indicating

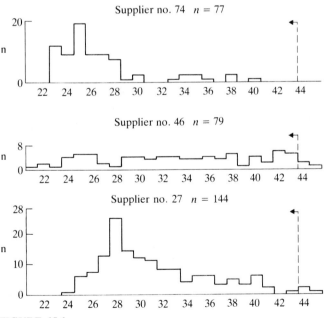

FIGURE 15.1
Histograms on hardenability.

a lack of control of the nickel content and resulting in several heats of steel with excessively high Rockwell values.

• Supplier 27 had several heats above the maximum, although the process had a central value of about 28. The histograms for manganese, nickel, and chromium showed several values above and apart from the main histogram.

• Supplier 74 showed much less variability than the others. Analysis of other histograms for this supplier suggested that about half of the original heats of steel had been screened out and used for other applications.

Note how these analyses can be made without visiting the supplier plants, i.e., "the product tells on the process." Histograms have limitations (see Chapter 9), but they are an effective tool for incoming inspection.

15.5   THE LOT PLOT PLAN

A lot plot is a sampling plan that uses histograms to make acceptance and rejection decisions on lots.

A minimum sample of 50 units is taken at random and is measured with a variables gage precise enough to subdivide product variability into about 10 cells. The data are recorded on a special form to form a histogram and calculations are made of $\bar{X}$ and σ. Then, under the assumption of a normal distribution and by using a graphic, "lot plot card," the percentage defective and other features of the lot can easily be computed. A decision to accept or reject the lot can then be made.

The simplified mechanics of predicting the percentage defective by making a lot plot of data should not overshadow the valuable information for quality improvement supplied by the histogram plot itself. Analysis of a plot (see Chapter 9) often helps to determine the corrective action needed. For this reason the plot should be discussed with the supplier. Comparisons of lot plots, e.g., the plots of several suppliers supplying the same part, the plots of one supplier supplying lots periodically, the plots from one supplier before and after material or other design changes, etc., are also revealing.

The plot plan was originally developed by Dorian Shainin. Grant and Leavenworth (1988) provide a more detailed discussion.

15.6   PARETO ANALYSIS OF SUPPLIERS

Supplier improvement programs can fail because the "vital few" problems are not identified and attacked. Instead, the programs consist of broad attempts to tighten up all procedures. The Pareto analysis (see Section 3.5 under "The Pareto Principle") can be used to identify the problem in a number of forms:

1. Analysis of losses (defects, lot rejections, etc.) by *material number* or *part number*. Such analysis serves a useful purpose as applied to catalog numbers involving substantial or frequent purchases.

2. Analysis of losses by *product family*. This identifies the vital few product families present in small but numerous purchases of common product families, e.g., fasteners, paints.
3. Analysis of losses by *process,* i.e., classification of the defects or lot rejections in terms of the processes to which they relate, e.g., plating, swaging, coil winding, etc.
4. Analyis by supplier across the entire spectrum of purchases. This can help to identify weaknesses in the supplier's managerial approach as contrasted to the technological, which is more usually correlated with products and processes. In one company there were 222 suppliers on the active list. Of these, 38 (or 17 percent) accounted for 53 percent of the lot rejections and 45 percent of the bad parts.
5. Analysis by *cost* of the parts. In one company, 37 percent of the part numbers purchased accounted for only 5 percent of the total dollar volume of purchases, but for a much higher percentage of the total incoming inspection cost. The conclusion was that these "useful many" parts should be purchased from the best suppliers, even at top prices. The alternative of relying on incoming inspection would be even more costly.
6. Analysis by *failure mode*. This technique is used to discover major defects in the management system. For example, suppose that studies disclose multiple instances of working to the wrong issue of the specification. In such cases, the system used for specification revision should be reexamined. If value analysis discovers multiple instances of overspecification, the design procedures for choosing components should be reexamined. These analyses by failure mode can reveal how the buyer is contributing to his own problems.

> **Example 15.2.** A manufacturer of industrial switches and controls had a significant quality problem with purchased printed circuit boards (Bowers, 1978). A study was made of 1092 lots received over 11 months from the five suppliers supplying the boards. Overall, 45.1 percent of the lots was rejected, and this varied, by supplier, from 39.0 percent to 68.8 percent. The cost of processing the rejected lots totaled $19.680. A Pareto analysis of the results at receiving inspection is shown in Table 15.4.
>   Of 27 requirements checked, 7 accounted for 70.4 percent of the defects. For many requirements (e.g., hole size and board dimensions), a large percentage of defects was finally accepted as a deviation to the specification. Based on an engineering review, certain specifications were changed. The study was instrumental in alerting management to the size of the problem, defining a main cause, and returning product to suppliers.

15.7 SUPPLIER QUALITY RATING

Supplier quality rating provides a quantitative summary of supplier quality over a period of time. This type of rating is useful in deciding how to allocate

TABLE 15.4
Pareto analysis of incoming inspection

Requirement	Pareto distribution			Defects accepted under deviation	
	Number of defects	Percentage defective	Cumulative percentage	Number accepted	Percentage accepted
Hole size	165	19.0	19.0	150	90.9
Board dimensions	110	12.7	31.7	96	87.3
Cond. defects	79	9.1	40.8	23	29.1
Cold thickness	69	8.0	48.8	31	44.9
Plating visual	66	7.6	56.4	31	50.8
Cold visual	61	7.0	63.4	27	44.3
PTH thickness	61	7.0	70.4	10	16.4
20 other	257	29.6	100.0	158	61.4
	868			526	60.6

Source: Bowers (1978).

purchases among suppliers. Rating furnishes both buyer and supplier with common factual information which becomes a key input for identification and tracking of improvement efforts and for allocating future purchases among suppliers.

To create a single numerical quality score is difficult because there are several units of measure, such as:

- The quality of multiple lots expressed as lots rejected versus lots inspected.
- The quality of multiple parts expressed as percentage nonconforming.
- The quality of specific characteristics expressed in numerous natural units, e.g., ohmic resistance, percentage of active ingredient, mean time between failures, etc.
- The economic consequences of bad quality, expressed in dollars.

Because these units of measure vary in importance among different companies, published rating schemes differ markedly in emphasis.

MEASURES IN USE. Supplier quality rating plans are based on one or more of the following measures:

Product percentage nonconforming. This is a ratio of the amount of defective items received to the total number of items received. On a lot-by-lot basis, the formula is number of lots rejected divided by number of lots received; on an individual piece basis, the formula is number of individual pieces rejected divided by the number of individual pieces received.

TABLE 15.5
AT&T quality performance rating

Rating element	Maximum points
Incoming inspection	
Visual mechanical PPM	10
Visual/mechanical—percentage of lot rejections	5
Testing PPM	10
Testing—lot rejections	5
Ship-to-stock credit	—
Production failures	
Shop complaints	20
Quality appraisal	10
Vendor response	
Response to problems	10
Failure analysis response	20
AT&T customer complaints	10
Total	100

Source: Nocera et al. (1989).

Overall product quality. This plan summarizes supplier performance at incoming inspection and later phases of product application. Points are assigned for each phase with the maximum number of points given when there are no problems encountered. Table 15.5 shows an example from AT&T. Note that the phases are incoming inspection, production, vendor response to problems, and AT&T customer complaints. Each rating element has further detailed criteria which are used to assign points for the element, e.g., if 3 percent of lots is rejected for "visual/mechanical" reasons in a rating period, then 1 point is deducted from the maximum of 5 for that element. Note that the overall rating evaluates the supplier response to problems, while detailed criteria include both timeliness and adequacy of the response.

Economic analysis. This type of plan compares suppliers on the total dollar cost for specific purchases. The total dollar cost includes the quoted price plus quality costs associated with defect prevention, detection, and correction.

Composite plan. Supplier performance is not limited to quality. It includes delivery against schedule, price, and other performance categories. These multiple needs suggest that supplier rating should include overall supplier performance rather than just supplied quality performance. The Purchasing Department is a strong advocate of this principle and has valid grounds for this advocacy. Table 15.6 illustrates this approach with an example from the Tecumseh Products Company. The overall rating of 92.46 is calculated by combining the four ratings using a weight of 40 percent for quality, 30 percent for delivery, 20 percent for cost, and 10 percent for responsiveness to problems.

TABLE 15.6
Supplier rating report

Overall combined rating	92.46
Total quality rating	99.05
Total delivery rating	95.58
Total cost rating	79.22
Total response rating	83.30
Total lots received	18
Total parts received	398,351
Total parts rejected	3,804

Source: Wind (1991).

Some organizations use periodic supplier rating to determine the share of future purchases given to each supplier. The rating system and effect on market share is fully explained to all suppliers. The approach has been used successfully by both automotive and appliance manufacturers to highlight the importance of quality to their suppliers.

SUMMARY

- Measurements for supplier relations should be based on input from customers, provide for both evaluation and feedback, and include early, concurrent, and lagging indicators of performance.
- Quality and reliability requirements should be stated in quantitative terms.
- Suppliers must understand that *all* product submitted is expected to meet specifications.
- The results of supplier surveys can be stated in quantitative terms.
- Histogram analyses of supplier data can reveal much information about the supplier's process.
- Pareto analysis of supplier data helps to establish priorities for improvement efforts.
- Supplier quality rating provides a quantitative summary of supplier quality over a period of time.

PROBLEMS

15.1. Apply the composite plan of supplier rating (Section 15.7) to compare three suppliers for one of the following: (*a*) any product acceptable to the instructor; (*b*) an automatic washing machine; (*c*) a new automobile; (*d*) a lawn mower.

15.2. Can you think of a situation other than 100 percent screening inspection that would result in the histogram shown in Figure 15.2?

15.3. Can you describe what caused the unusual histogram plots in Figure 15.3?

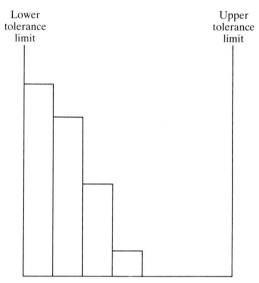

FIGURE 15.2.
Sample histogram.

15.4. You have been asked to propose a specific quality rating procedure for use in one of the following types of organizations: (*a*) a company acceptable to the instructor; (*b*) a large municipal government; (*c*) a manufacturer of plastic toys; (*d*) a bank; (*e*) a manufacturer of whisky. Research the literature for specific procedures and select (or create) a procedure for the organization.

15.5. Visit a local organization and learn how it determines the quality of purchased items. Define the specific procedures used and what use is made of the information compiled.

15.6. Outline a potential application of several concepts in this chapter. Follow the instructions given in Problem 12.11.

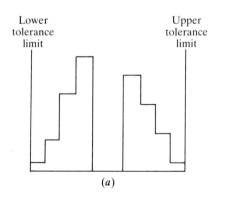

(*a*)

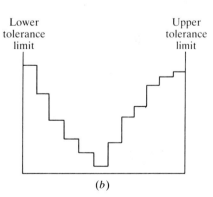

(*b*)

FIGURE 15.3.
Sample histograms.

REFERENCES

Bossert, James L., ed. (1988). *Procurement Quality Control,* 4th ed., ASQC Customer-Supplier Technical Committee, Quality Press, Milwaukee.
Bowers, Virgil L. (1978). "Procurement Quality Assurance of PC Boards," *ASQC Technical Conference Transactions,* pp. 69–72.
Grant, Eugene L., and Richard S. Leavenworth (1988). *Statistical Quality Control,* 6th ed., McGraw–Hill Book Company, New York, pp. 540–545.
Johnson, Stanley G. (1987). "Theory Y Vendor Evaluation Using Lotus 1–2–3," *ASQC Quality Congress Transactions,* pp. 702–709.
Nocera, C. D., M. K. Foliano, and R. E. Blalock (1989). "Vendor Rating and Certification," *Impro Conference Proceedings,* Juran Institute, Inc., Wilton, Connecticut, pp. 9A-29 to 9A-38.
Schilling, Edward G. (1988). QCH4, pp. 25.16–25.18, "Acceptance Sampling."
Wind, James F. (1991). "Revolutionize Supplier Rating by Computerization," *ASQC Quality Congress Transactions,* pp. 556–564.

SUPPLEMENTARY READING

Supplier measurement: QCH4, pp. 15.40–15.42 generally and pp. 30.18–30.21 for supplier measurement in the assembly industries.

CHAPTER
16

MANUFACTURE

16.1 IMPORTANCE OF MANUFACTURING PLANNING FOR QUALITY

Activities to integrate quality in manufacturing planning have two objectives: to *prevent* defects and to *minimize variability* in processes. Such objectives require an intensity of planning that goes beyond earlier types of planning only for inspection. The planning activities listed in Table 16.1 also show the usual end result of conducting such activities.

An emphasis on prevention is essential because of the increased complexity of products and processes, the lack of large buffer inventory to replace defective products under just-in-time (JIT) production systems, and the impact of computer-aided manufacturing (CAM).

The concepts and techniques for preventing defects and minimizing variability are discussed in this chapter and Chapter 17.

16.2 INITIAL PLANNING FOR QUALITY

This starts during the design review of the product. Section 12.9, "Design Review," emphasizes the evaluation of the product design for adequacy of *field*

TABLE 16.1
Manufacturing planning

Planning activity	Planning principally performed	End results of planning
Review design for clarity of specifications and for producibility; recommend changes	Manufacturing Engineering	Producible design; revised product specification
Choose process for manufacture: operations, sequences	Manufacturing Engineering	Economic, feasible process; process specification
Provide machines and tools capable of meeting tolerances	Manufacturing Engineering and Quality Engineering	Capable machines and tools
Provide instruments with accuracy adequate to control the process	Manufacturing Engineering	Capable instrumentation
Provide manufacturing information: methods, procedures, cautions	Manufacturing Engineering	Operation sheets
Provide system of quality controls: data collection, feedback, adjustment	Quality Engineering and Production	Control stations equipped to provide feedback
Define responsibilities for agreed pattern of quality	Production Supervision	Responsibilities
Select and train production personnel	Production Supervision	Qualified production workers
Prove adequacy of planning; tryouts, trial lots	Manufacturing Engineering	Proof of adequacy
Provide protection for material during handling and storage	Materials Control	Control of material
Provide proper environment	Plant Engineering	Controlled manufacturing conditions
Provide system for disposition of nonconforming product	Quality Engineering	Decision making at proper levels

performance. Design review must also include an evaluation of *producibility* to cover the following matters:

- Clarity of all requirements
- Relative importance of product characteristics (see below)
- Effect of tolerances on manufacturing economics (see below)
- Availability of processes to meet tolerances
- Tolerance buildup to create excess clearance or interference
- Ability to meet special requirements on surface finishes, fits, and other characteristics
- Identification of special needs for handling, transportation, and storage during manufacture

- Availability of measurement processes for evaluating requirements
- Ease of access for measurement
- Special skills required of manufacturing personnel

This review of the *product* design must be supplemented by a review of the *process* design, which is discussed below. These reviews are tools for preventing difficulties during manufacture.

Review of Process Design

A process design can be reviewed by laying out the overall process in a flow diagram. Several types are useful. One type shows the paths followed by materials through their progression into a finished product. An example for a coating process at the James River Graphics Company is shown in Figure 16.1. Planners use such a diagram to divide the flow into logical sections called workstations. For each workstation they prepare a formal document listing such items as operations to be performed, sequence of operations, facilities and instruments to be employed, and process conditions to be maintained. This formal document becomes the plan to be carried out by the production supervisors and work force. It serves as the basis for control activities by the inspectors. It also becomes the standard against which the process audits are conducted.

CORRELATION OF PROCESS VARIABLES WITH PRODUCT RESULTS. A critical aspect of planning during manufacture is to discover, by data collection and analysis, the relationships between process features or variables and product features or results. Such knowledge enables a planner to create process control features, including limits and regulating mechanisms on the variables, in order to keep the process in a steady state and achieve the specified product results. In Figure 16.1, each process variable is shown in a rectangle attached to the circle representing an operation; product results are listed in rectangles between operations, at the point where conformance can be verified. Some characteristics (e.g., coat weight) are both process variables and product results. Determining the optimal settings and tolerances for process variables sometimes requires much data collection and analysis. Eibl et al.(1992) discuss such planning and analysis for a paint coating process for which little information was available about the relationship between process variables and product results.

Many companies have not studied the relationships between process variables and product results. The consequences of this lack of knowledge can be severe. In the electronic component manufacturing industry, some yields are shockingly low and will likely remain that way until the process variables are studied in depth. In all industries the imposition of new quality demands (e.g., reduction in the weight of automotive components) can cause a sharp

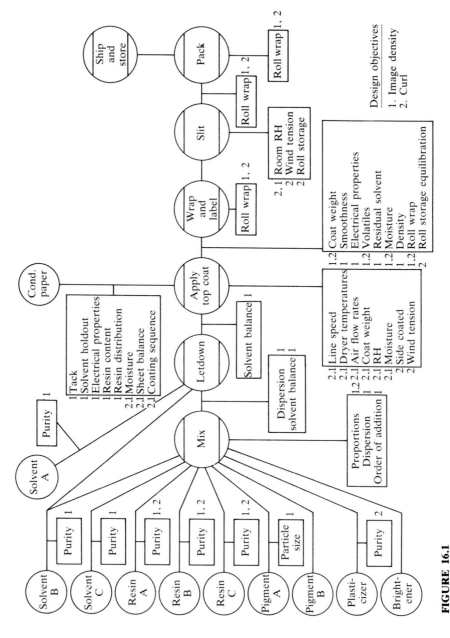

FIGURE 16.1
Product and process analysis chart. (*From Siff, 1984.*)

rise in scrap (and hence in costs) because not enough is known about the process variables to adapt promptly to the new demands.

To understand fully the relationship between process variables and product results, we often need to apply the concept of statistical design of experiments (see Section 10.11, "The Design of Experiments"). See also the discussion of the Taguchi approach (Section 12.3 "Parameter Design and Robust Design").

Error Proofing the Process

An important element of prevention is the concept of designing the process to be error free through "error proofing" (the Japanese call it *pokayoke* or *bakayoke*).

A widely used form of error proofing is the design (or redesign) of the machines and tools (the "hardware") so as to make human error improbable or even impossible. For example, components and tools may be designed with lugs and notches to achieve a lock-and-key effect, which makes it impossible to misassemble them. Tools may be designed to sense the presence and correctness of prior operations automatically or to stop the process on sensing depletion of the material supply. For example, in the textile industry a break in a thread releases a spring-loaded device which stops the machine. Protective systems, e.g., fire detection, can be designed to be "fail-safe" and to sound alarms as well as all-clear signals.

The second major form of error proofing is redundancy—requiring multiple improbable events to occur simultaneously before a defect can be created or can escape. Important process setups typically require multiple approvals. For example, the weighing out of the ingredients for a pharmaceutical batch must be done independently by each of two registered pharmacists. Look-alike products may bear multiple identity codes (numbers, colors, shapes, etc.). Automated 100 percent testing may be superimposed on the process controls. The "countdown" so well dramatized during the prelaunch phases of a space vehicle is also a form of redundancy.

A third approach helps human beings to reduce their own fallibility. Some of this involves magnifying normal human muscle strength and senses through programmed indexing of fixtures, optical magnification, viewing through closed-circuit television, simultaneous signals to multiple senses, etc. For example, ampoules of medicine may be dumped into a dye bath and left there overnight to simplify the discovery of cracks in the glass. Even in the review of documents there has recently emerged an awareness that there are two kinds of review—active and passive. The former requires so positive a participation, e.g., reading a number out loud, that full attention is indispensable. The passive review, e.g., silently looking or listening, does not make full attention indispensable.

TABLE 16.2
Summary of error-proofing principles

Principle	Objective	Example
Elimination	Eliminating the possibility of error	Redesigning the process or product so that the task is no longer necessary
Replacement	Substituting a more reliable process for the worker	Using robotics (e.g., in welding or painting)
Facilitation	Making the work easier to perform	Color-coding parts
Detection	Detecting the error before further processing	Developing computer software which notifies the worker when a wrong type of keyboard entry is made (e.g., alpha versus numeric)
Mitigation	Minimizing the effect of the error	Utilizing fuses for overloaded circuits

In a classic study, Nakajo and Kume (1985) discuss five fundamental principles of error proofing developed from an analysis of about 1000 examples collected mainly from assembly lines. These principles are elimination, replacement, facilitation, detection, and mitigation (see Table 16.2).

See QCH4, pages 16.35–16.37, for further examples of error proofing.

We will now apply the concept of self-control as a framework for planning for quality during manufacture.

16.3 CONCEPT OF CONTROLLABILITY; SELF-CONTROL

The concept of self-control was introduced in Section 5.2, "Self-Control." An ideal objective for manufacturing planning is to place human beings in a state of self-control. To do so, we must provide people with:

1. Knowledge of what they are supposed to do
2. Knowledge of what they are actually doing
3. A process that is capable of meeting specifications and can be regulated to meet specifications

The three basic criteria for self-control make possible a separation of defects into categories of "controllability," of which the most important are:

1. *Worker-controllable.* A defect or nonconformity is worker-controllable if all three criteria for self-control have been met.
2. *Management-controllable.* A defect or nonconformity is management-controllable if one or more of the criteria for self-control have not been met.

Only management can provide the means of meeting the criteria for self-control. Hence, any failure to meet these criteria is a failure of management, and the resulting defects are therefore beyond the control of the workers. This theory is not 100 percent sound. Workers commonly have a duty to call management's attention to deficiencies in the system of control, and sometimes they do not do so. (Sometimes they do, and it is management that fails to act.) However, the theory is much more right than wrong.

Whether the defects or nonconformities in a plant are mainly management-controllable or worker-controllable is of the highest order of importance. To reduce the former requires a program in which the main contributions must come from managers, supervisors, and technical specialists. To reduce the latter requires a different kind of program in which much of the contribution comes from workers. The great difference between these two kinds of programs suggests that managers should quantify their knowledge of the state of controllability before embarking on major programs.

An example of a controllability study is given in Table 16.3. A diagnostic team was set up to study scrap and rework reports in six machine shop departments for 17 working days. The defect cause was entered on each report by a quality engineer who was assigned to collect the data. When the cause was not apparent, the team reviewed the defect and, when necessary, contacted other specialists (who had been alerted by management about the priority of the project) to identify the cause. The purpose of the study was to resolve a lack of agreement on the causes of chronically high scrap and rework. It did

TABLE 16.3
Controllability study in a machine shop

Category	%
Management-controllable	
Inadequate training	15
Machine inadequate	8
Machine maintenance inadequate	8
Other process problems	8
Material handling inadequate	7
Tool, fixture, gage (TGF) maintenance inadequate	6
TFG inadequate	5
Wrong material	3
Operation run out of sequence	3
Miscellaneous	5
Total	68
Worker-controllable	
Failure to check work	11
Improper operation of machine	11
Other (e.g., piece mislocated)	10
Total	32

the job. The study was decisive in obtaining agreement on the focus of the improvement program. In less than 1 year over $2 million was saved and important strides were made in reducing production backlogs.

Controllability can also be evaluated by posing specific questions for each of the three criteria of self-control. (Typical questions that can be posed are presented below.) Although this approach does not yield a quantitative evaluation of management and worker-controllable defects, it does show whether the defects are primarily management- or worker-controllable.

In the experience of the authors, defects are about 80 percent management-controllable. This figure does not vary much from industry to industry, but it does vary greatly among processes. Other investigators in Japan, Sweden, the Netherlands, and Czechoslovakia have reached similar conclusions.

While the available quantitative studies make clear that defects are mainly management-controllable, many industrial managers do not know this or are unable to accept the data. Their long-standing beliefs are that most defects are the result of worker carelessness, indifference, and even sabotage. Such managers are easily persuaded to embark on worker-motivation schemes which, under the usual state of affairs, aim at a small minority of the problems and hence are doomed to achieve minor results at best. The issue is not whether quality problems *in an industry* are management-controllable. The need is to determine the answer *in a given plant.* This cannot be answered authoritatively by opinion but requires solid facts, preferably through a controllability study of actual defects, as shown in Table 16.3.

We now discuss the three main criteria for self-control.

Criterion 1: Knowledge of "Supposed to Do"

This knowledge commonly consists of the following:

1. The product standard, which may be a written specification, a product sample, or other definition of the end result to be attained
2. The process standard, which may be a written process specification, written process instructions, an oral instruction, or other definition of "means to an end"
3. A definition of responsibility, i.e., what decisions to make and what actions to take (discussed earlier in this section)

In developing product specifications, some essential precautions must be observed.

UNEQUIVOCAL INFORMATION MUST BE PROVIDED. Specifications should be quantitative. In cases where this is not possible, physical or photographic standards should be provided. But beyond the need for *clear* product specifications, there is also a need for *consistent* and *credible* specifications. In some organizations, production supervisors have a secret "black book" that contains the "real" specification limits used by inspectors for accepting product. A further problem is communicating changes to specifications, especially when there is a constant parade of changes.

INFORMATION ON SERIOUSNESS MUST BE PROVIDED. All specifications contain multiple characteristics, and these are not equally important. Production personnel must be guided and trained to meet all specification limits. But they must also be given information on the relative importance of each characteristic in order to focus on priorities. Section 18.5, "Seriousness Classification," explains methods of defining relative seriousness.

REASONS MUST BE EXPLAINED. Explanation of the purposes served by both the product and the specification helps workers to understand why both the nominal specification value and the limits must be met.

PROCESS SPECIFICATIONS MUST BE PROVIDED. Work methods and process conditions (e.g., temperature, pressure, time cycles) must be made unequivocally clear.

LTV, a steel manufacturer, uses a highly structured system of identifying key process variables, defining process control standards, communicating the information to the work force, monitoring performance, and accomplishing diagnosis when problems arise. The process specification is a collection of process control standard procedures (Figure 16.2). A procedure is developed for controlling each of the key process variables (variables that must be controlled in order to meet specification limits on the product). The procedure answers the following issues:

- What the process standards are
- Why control is needed
- Who is responsible for control
- What and how to measure
- When to measure
- How to report routine data
- Who is responsible for data reporting
- How to audit
- Who is responsible for audit
- What to do with product that is out of compliance
- Who developed the standard

Often, detailed process instructions are not known until workers have become experienced with the process. Updating of process instructions based

LTV Steel	INTEGRATED PROCESS CONTROL		
Plant __Indiana Harbor__	**Standard Procedures**	File No __716-2.2.2__	
Dept __No. 3 Sheet Mill__	**Process Control**	Date Orig Issue __3/83__	

Control Area	Control Point	Control Element	No	Revision No __1__
Tandem Mill	Rolling	Rolling Solutions	2.2.2	Date Revised __9/83__

Control Task To maintain rolling solution characteristics at the proper levels.	**Responsible for Control** Solution Attendant

Process Standard

- Oil concentration must be 2.5% to 3.5%
- Solution temperature must be 110°F - 120°F
- SAP value must be above 120
- Iron fines must be less that 600 ppm

Reason for Control

- To provide the correct lubricity between work rolls and strip for reduced roll wear and control of strip temperature. This helps control strip flatness and avoids friction scratches.

Measurement Tools Equipment - Standard chem. test set-up Frequency - Twice/turn By - Solution Attendant	**Routine Reporting of Data** Form Form No - Solution Attendant's Report By - Solution Attendant	**Control Chart** Yes/N [X] Type - X & Moving Range By - Solution Att.

Corrective Action
- Solution concentration approaching limits - add rolling oil or water.
- Solution temp. approaching limits - adjust temperature control.
- SAP reading between 100 & 120, skim solution tank and add new oil. SAP reading below 100, retest immediately and contact Operating Supervisor. If retest below 100, shutdown mill and switch to alternative solution tank.
- Iron fines approaching limit, skim tank for 2 hours and add 100 gallons oil. Retest after 30 minutes second time, repeat procedure if still near or above limit.

Operating Procedure

See attached sheet

Disposition of Non-Compliant Product

Identify coil(s) for special surface evaluation. Notify Metallurgical Supervisor.

Review Procedure

Once per turn the Operating Supervisor will:
- Check Solution Attendant's Report
- Visually check temperature of solution

Developed By: *Robert Goetken*	*Richard H. Berry*	
IPC Coordinator		
Approved: *DT Zid*	*Dale H. Dick Jr.*	*R. Voth*
Department Superintendent/Manager	Manager - Quality Control	General Superintendent/ Plant Manager

FIGURE 16.2
Process control standard procedure (*From LTV Steel.*)

on job experience can be conveniently accomplished by posting a cause-and-effect diagram in the production department and attaching index cards to the diagram (Fukuda, 1981). Each card states additional process instructions based on recent experience.

A CHECKLIST MUST BE CREATED. The above discussion covers the first criterion of self-control: People must have the means of knowing what they are supposed to do. To evaluate adherence to this criterion, a checklist of questions can be created, including the following:

1. Are there written product specifications, process specifications, and work instructions? If written down in more than one place, do they all agree? Are they legible? Are they conveniently accessible to the worker?
2. Does the specification define the relative importance of different quality characteristics? Are advisory tolerances on a process distinguished from mandatory tolerances on a product? If control charts or other control techniques are to be used, is it clear how these relate to product specifications?
3. Are standards for visual defects displayed in the work area?
4. Are the written specifications given to the worker the same as the criteria used by inspectors? Are deviations from the specification often allowed?
5. Does the worker know how the product is used?
6. Has the worker been adequately trained to understand the specification and perform the steps needed to meet the specification? Has the worker been evaluated by testing or other means to see if he or she is qualified?
7. Does the worker know the effect on future operations and product performance if the specification is not met?
8. Does the worker receive specification changes automatically and promptly?
9. Does the worker know what to do with defective raw material and defective finished product?
10. Have responsibilities in terms of decisions and actions been clearly defined?

Criterion 2: Knowledge of "Is Doing"

For self-control, people must have the means of knowing whether their performance conforms to standard. This conformance applies to:

- The product in the form of specifications on product characteristics
- The process in the form of specifications on process variables

This knowledge is secured from three primary sources: measurements inherent in the process, measurements by production workers, and measurements by inspectors.

CRITERIA FOR GOOD FEEDBACK TO WORKERS. The needs of production workers (as distinguished from supervisors or technical specialists) require that the data feedback can be read at a glance, deal only with the few important defects, deal only with worker-controllable defects, provide prompt information about symptom and cause, and provide enough information to guide corrective actions. Good feedback should:

- *Be readable at a glance.* The pace of events on the factory floor is swift. Workers should be able to review the feedback while in motion. Where a worker needs information about process performance over time, charts can provide an excellent form of feedback, provided they are designed to be consistent with the assigned responsibility of the worker (Table 16.4). It is useful to use visual displays to highlight recurrent problems. A problem described as "outer hopper switch installed backwards" displayed on a wall chart in large block letters has much more impact than the same message buried away as a marginal note in a work folder.
- *Deal only with the few important defects.* Overwhelming workers with data on all defects will result in diverting attention from the "vital few."
- *Deal only with worker-controllable defects.* Any other course provides a basis for argument which will be unfruitful.
- *Provide prompt information about symptoms and causes.* Timeliness is a basic test of good feedback; the closer the system is to "real-time" signaling, the better.
- *Provide enough information to guide corrective action.* The signal should be in terms which make it easy to decide on remedial action.

FEEDBACK RELATED TO WORKER ACTION. The worker needs to know what kind of *process* change to make to respond to a *product* deviation. Sources of this knowledge are:

- The process specifications (see Figure 16.2 under "Corrective Action")
- Cut-and-try experience by the worker
- The fact that the units of measure for both product and process are identical

TABLE 16.4
Worker responsibility versus chart design

Responsibility of the worker is to	Chart should be designed to show
Make individual units of product meet a product specification	Measurements of individual units of product compared to product specification limits
Hold process conditions to the requirements of a process specification	Measurements of the process conditions compared with the process specification limits
Hold averages and ranges to specified statistical control limits	Averages and ranges compared to the statistical control limits
Hold percentage nonconforming below some prescribed level	Actual percentage nonconforming compared to the limiting level

If lacking all of these, workers can only cut and try further or stop the process and sound the alarm.

Sometimes it is feasible for the data feedback to be converted into a form which makes easier the worker's decision about what action to take on the process.

For example, a copper cap had six critical dimensions. It was easy to measure the dimensions and to discover the nature of product deviation. However, it was difficult to translate the product data into process changes. To simplify this translation, use was made of a position-dimension (P–D) diagram. The six measurements were first "corrected" (i.e., coded) by subtracting the thinnest from all the others. These corrected data were then plotted on a P–D diagram as shown in Figure 16.3. Such diagrams provided a way of analyzing the tool setup.

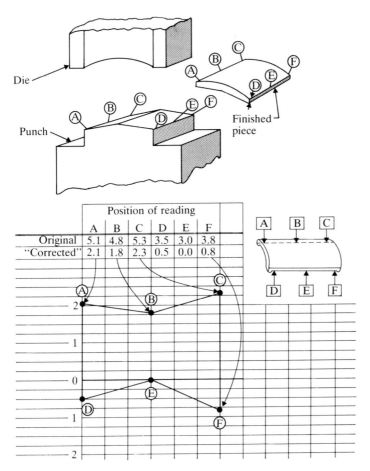

FIGURE 16.3
Method of drawing P–D diagram.

FEEDBACK TO SUPERVISORS. Beyond the need for feedback at workstations, there is a need to provide supervisors with short-term summaries. These take several forms.

Matrix summary. A common form of matrix is workers versus defects; i.e., the vertical columns are headed by worker names and the horizontal rows by the names of defect types. The matrix makes clear which defect types predominate, which workers have the most defects, and what the interaction is. Other matrixes include machine number versus defect type, defect type versus calendar week, etc. When the summary is published, it is usual to circle matrix cells to highlight the vital few situations which call for attention.

An elaboration of the matrix is to split the cell diagonally, thus permitting the entry of two numbers, e.g., number defective and number produced.

Pareto analysis. Some companies prefer to minimize detail and provide information on the total defects for each day plus a list of the top three (or so) defects encountered and how many there were of each. In some industries, a "chart room" displays performance against goals by product and by department.

Computer data analysis and reporting. Production volume and complexity are important factors in determining the role of the computer. Chapter 23, "Quality Information Systems," explains the role of computers in analyzing and reporting data during production and other phases of the product life cycle.

Automated quality information. Some situations justify the mechanization of both the recording and analysis of data. Direct feedback can even include printing of summaries at typewriters located in the offices of the supervisors involved. Fisher (1983) describes a system for using a mini-computer to control the net weight in a food-filling operation at the Gerber Company (Figure 16.4). The quality station has a cathode-ray tube (CRT) and a scale; the supervisor's office has a CRT and a hard copy machine; a modem connects corporate headquarters with each plant's computer setup.

As weight data are obtained and entered at the weight station, the computer forms the data into samples (five weights in each sample), and when the final net weight in each sample is obtained, the CRT instantly displays an average and range control chart. Touch another key and a histogram is the output. All graphs and charts are in real time and are updated automatically after each subgroup. Although the computer is graphing only subgroup averages and ranges, it is internally checking each individual reading against a minimum allowable value. If this value is not met, the CRT locks out until the worker acknowledges the low reading. In addition, a terminal in the

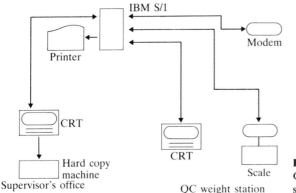

FIGURE 16.4
Gerber computerized net weight system. (*From Fisher, 1983.*)

Printer · IBM S/1 · Modem · CRT · Hard copy machine · Supervisor's office · CRT · QC weight station · Scale

supervisor's office beeps in response to an out-of-control situation. This beeping continues until the supervisor clears the terminal, signaling recognition of the problem. The system enables the supervisor to monitor the line without leaving the office.

Entry of data into computer terminals on production floors is now common. Many varieties of software are now available for analyzing, processing, and presenting quality information collected on the production floor. See Section 23.4, "Selection of Off-the-Shelf Software."

The term "quality information equipment" (QIE) designates the physical apparatus which makes measurements of products and processes, summarizes the information, and feeds the information back for decision making. Sometimes such equipment has its own product development cycle to meet various product effectiveness parameters for the QIE. For elaboration, see QCH4, page 16.52.

Checklist. A checklist to evaluate the second criterion of self-control includes questions such as:

1. Are gages provided to the worker? Do they provide numerical measurements rather than simply sorting good from bad? Are they precise enough? Are they regularly checked for accuracy?
2. Is the worker told how often to sample the work? Is sufficient time allowed?
3. Is the worker told how to evaluate measurements to decide when to adjust the process and when to leave it alone?
4. Is there a checking procedure to ensure that the worker does follow instructions on sampling work and making process adjustments?
5. Are inspection results provided to the worker, and are these results reviewed by the supervisor with the worker?

Criterion 3: Ability to Regulate

This is the third criterion for self-control. Regulating the process depends on a number of management-controllable factors, including:

The process must be capable of meeting the tolerances. This factor is of paramount importance. In some organizations, the credibility of specifications is a serious problem. Typically, a manufacturing process is created after release of the product design; a few trials are run; and full production commences. In cases where quality problems arise during full production, diagnosis sometimes reveals that the process is not capable of consistently meeting the design specifications. Costly delays to production then occur while the problem is resolved by changing the process or changing the specification. The capability of the manufacturing process should be verified during the product development cycle *before the product design is released for full production.* See Section 17.8, "Process Capability," for a full discussion.

The process must be responsive to regulatory action in a predictable cause-and-effect relationship in order to minimize variation around a target value.

Example 16.1. In a process for making polyethylene film, workers were required to meet multiple product parameters. The equipment had various regulatory devices, each of which could vary performance with respect to one or more parameters. However, the workers could not "dial in" a predetermined list of settings which would meet all parameters. Instead, it was necessary to cut and try in order to meet all parameters simultaneously. During the period of cut and try, the machine produced nonconforming product to an extent which interfered with meeting standards for productivity and delivery. The workers were unable to predict how long the cut-and-try process would go on before full conformance was achieved. In consequence it became the practice to stop "cut and try" after a reasonable amount of time and to let the process run, whether in conformance or not.

The worker must be trained in how to use the regulating mechanisms and procedures. This training should cover the entire spectrum of action—under what conditions to act, what kind and extent of changes to make, how to use the regulating devices, and why these things need to be done.

Example 16.2. Of three qualified workers on a food process, only one operated the process every week and became proficient. The other two workers were used only when the primary worker was on vacation or was ill, and thus they never became proficient. Continuous training of the relief people was considered uneconomical, and agreements with the union prohibited their use except under the situations cited above. This problem is management-controllable, i.e., additional training or a change in union agreements is necessary.

The act of adjustment should not be personally distasteful to the worker, e.g., should not require undue physical exertion.

Example 16.3. In a plant making glass bottles, one adjustment mechanism was located next to a furnace area. During the summer months, this area was so hot that workers tended to keep out of it as much as possible. When the regulation consists of varying the human component of the operation, the question of process capability arises in a new form: Does the worker have the capability to regulate? This important question is discussed in Section 3.10 "Technique Errors," which includes some examples of discovering worker "knack."

The process must be maintained sufficiently to retain its inherent capability. Without adequate maintenance, equipment breaks down and requires frequent adjustments—often with an increase in both defects and variability around a nominal value. Clearly, such maintenance must be both preventive and corrective. The importance of maintenance has given rise to the concept of total productive maintenance (TPM). Under this approach, teams are formed to identify, analyze, and solve maintenance problems for the purpose of maximizing the uptime of process equipment. These teams consist of production line workers, maintenance personnel, process engineers, and others as needed. Problems are kept narrow in scope in order to encourage a steady stream of small improvements. Examples of improvements include a reduction in the number of tools lost and simplification of process adjustments.

CONTROL SYSTEMS AND THE CONCEPT OF DOMINANCE. Specific systems for controlling characteristics can be related to the underlying factors that dominate a process. The main categories of dominance include the following:

- *Setup-dominant.* Such processes have high reproducibility and stability for the entire length of the batch to be made. Hence, the control system emphasizes verification of the setup before production proceeds. Examples of such processes are drilling, labeling, heat sealing, printing, and presswork.
- *Time-dominant.* Such a process is subject to progressive change with time (wearing of tools, depletion of reagent, heating up of machine). The associated control system will feature a schedule of process checks with feedback to enable the worker to make compensatory changes. Screw machining, volume filling, wood carding, and papermaking are examples of time-dominant processes.
- *Component-dominant.* Here the quality of the input materials and components is the most influential. The control system is strongly oriented toward supplier relations along with incoming inspection and sorting of inferior lots. Many assembly operations and food formulation processes are component dominant.

- *Worker-dominant.* For such processes quality depends mainly on the skill and knack possessed by the production worker. The control system emphasizes such features as training courses and certification for workers, error proofing, and rating of workers and quality. Workers are dominant in processes such as welding, painting, and order filling.
- *Information-dominant.* These are usually processes in which the job information undergoes frequent change. Hence, the control system places emphasis on the accuracy and up-to-dateness of the information provided to the worker (and everyone else). Examples include order editing and "travelers" used in job shops.

The different types of dominance differ also in the tools used for process control. Table 16.5 lists the forms of process dominance along with the usual tools used for process control.

CHECKLIST. A checklist for evaluating the third criterion of self-control typically includes such questions as the following:

1. Has the quality capability of the process been measured to include both inherent variability and variability due to time? Is the capability periodically checked?
2. Has the worker been told how often to reset the process or how to evaluate measurements to decide when the process should be reset?
3. Is there a process adjustment the worker can make to eliminate defects? Under what conditions should the worker adjust the process? When should the worker shut down the machine and seek more help? Whose help?
4. Have the worker actions which cause defects, and the necessary preventive action, been communicated to the worker, preferably in written form?
5. Is there an adequate preventive maintenance program on the process?
6. Is there a hidden "knack" possessed by some workers that needs to be discovered and transmitted to all workers?

16.4 DEFINING QUALITY RESPONSIBILITIES ON THE FACTORY FLOOR

In many organizations, the responsibility for product quality on the production floor is unclear. This becomes apparent from (1) the actions or lack of actions taken by various functions, and (2) the lack of agreement between functions (and even within a function) on current responsibilities for quality.

When the situation becomes serious enough, it gains attention because a question is raised: "Who is responsible for quality?" Discussion of this question is generally futile and a waste of time because it covers too broad a

TABLE 16.5
Control tools for forms of process dominance

Setup-dominant	Time-dominant	Component-dominant	Worker-dominant	Information-dominant
Inspection of process conditions	Periodic inspection	Supplier rating	Acceptance inspection	Computer-generated information
First-piece inspection	$\bar{X}$ chart	Incoming inspection	p chart	"Active" checking of
Lot plot	Median chart	Prior operation control	c chart	Documentation
Precontrol	$\bar{X}$ and R chart	Acceptance inspection	Operator scoring	Bar codes and electronic entry
Narrow-limit gaging	Precontrol	Mockup evaluation	Recertification of workers	Process audits
Attribute visual inspection	Narrow-limit gaging		Process audits	
	p chart			
	Process variables check			
	Automatic recording			
	Process audits			

361

scope. It is like asking "Who is responsible for cost?" or "Who is responsible for safety?" Such broad questions result in a haphazard discussion of many issues or conclude with a panacea that "everyone is responsible for quality."

The way toward constructive discussion of responsibility is to become specific. This can be done by defining the *decisions and actions* that collectively determine quality on the factory floor and then discussing the responsibility question *separately* for each decision and action.

Managers can quite readily work out an agreed-on pattern of decision making by using a responsibility matrix. Cognizant supervisors meet to discuss the problem. At this meeting a blank matrix is first drawn on the blackboard. The members then agree on what decisions and actions they will talk about. These are listed in the left-hand column and become the headings for the horizontal rows of the matrix. Next the members agree on who is available on the factory floor to make these decisions. These potential decision makers become the headings for the vertical columns of the matrix.

Next, the matrix is reproduced and a copy is given to each conferee to indicate who should make which decision and take which action. These filled-in copies (sometimes executed anonymously) are collected and all the marks are transferred to the blackboard to show the supervisors' composite opinion.

The summary enables the supervisors to identify their collective agreements and the extent of their differences. These differences can be talked out until agreement is complete. This agreement can then be reduced to a written procedure, formally approved, and published.

An example of the results of this approach is given in Table 16.6. Inputs were collected on five decisions—the four already mentioned and an additional decision on product sorting. The beliefs on current responsibility came from four plants (*A*, *B*, *C*, and *D*) within the company. That there was a lack of agreement on who was responsible for the decisions was a clear conclusion of the study. Disagreement existed within every plant on each of the five decisions. Clarification was essential.

Managers often ask, "Is there a right way to organize?" The answer is no. The pattern of responsibility must be designed to fit local conditions. In one department it may be convenient to assign the jobs of setup and operation to the same person; in another department setup is best done by a special setup person. In one department the process may be so stable that the original setup will endure for the length of the lot; in another department the setup requires checking and readjusting during the life of the lot. There are differences in the extent of training, the level of morale, etc., of the work force. The permutations of these and other differences make each department unique and require a made-to-measure design of responsibility for decision making.

The 1980s heralded the concept of teams as a means of (1) addressing specific problems and (2) conducting daily activities. See Section 3.6,

TABLE 16.6
Divergence of views on responsibility

Plant	W	S	I	E	W	S	I	E
	Setup acceptance				Running acceptance			
A	1	4	2	0	5	1	2	0
B	4	2	7	0	7	4	3	0
C	0	0	1	7	2	1	5	0
D	3	0	5	0	2	1	7	2
	Conformance				Fitness for use			
A	1	5	2	0	1	3	4	0
B	3	5	7	0	2	6	6	1
C	0	1	6	1	0	2	4	2
D	3	1	5	2	2	1	10	0
	Sorting							
A	0	4	3	0				
B	4	2	6	0				
C	0	1	4	0				
D	0	0	5	4				

Note: W, worker; S, supervisor; I, inspector; E, engineer.

"Organize Project Teams," and Sections 7.7 and 7.8, "Role of Teams" and "Quality Circles" on the role of teams in problem solving; see Section 7.9, "Self-Managing Teams," on the role of teams in executing daily work.

16.5 SELF-INSPECTION

In many organizations, decisions on whether the *process should run or stop* are made by the production department. Decisions on whether the *product conforms to specifications or not* are made by an Inspection Department. Sometimes it is possible to have production workers perform both of these functions.

In practice, many managers have the conviction that they dare not delegate the decision of product conformance to workers. The belief is that some or many of the workers will solve their production quota problems by accepting poor product. This belief is based on long-standing tradition buttressed by some experience, plus the contentions of the inspection and quality control specialists. All this has given rise to a sizable inspection function in many companies.

The point in question is whether production workers should make the conformance decisions on the product they make. What has evolved in some companies is the concept of self-inspection. Under this concept, all inspection and all conformance decisions, both on the process and on the product, are made by the production worker. (Decisions on the action to be taken on a nonconforming product are *not,* however, delegated to the worker.) However, an independent audit of these decisions is made. The Quality Department inspects a random sample periodically to ensure that the decision-making process used by workers to accept or reject a product is still valid. The audit verifies the *decision-making process.* Note that, under a pure audit concept, inspectors are not transferred to do inspection work in the production department. Except for those necessary to do audits, inspection positions are eliminated.

Self-inspection has decided advantages over the traditional delegation of inspection to a separate department:

- Production workers are made to feel more responsible for the quality of their work.
- Feedback on performance is immediate, thereby facilitating process adjustments. Traditional inspection also has the psychological disadvantage of an "outsider" reporting the defects to a worker.
- The costs of a separate Inspection Department can be reduced.
- The job enlargement that takes place by adding inspection to the production activity of the worker helps to reduce the monotony and boredom that are inherent in many jobs.
- Elimination of a specific station for inspecting all products reduces the total manufacturing cycle time.

Example 16.4. In a coning operation of textile yarn, the traditional method of inspection often resulted in finished cones sitting in the inspection department for several days, thereby delaying any feedback to production. Under self-inspection, workers received immediate feedback and could get machines repaired and setups improved more promptly. Overall, the program reduced nonconformities from 8 percent to 3 percent. An audit inspection of the products that were classified by the workers as "good" showed that virtually all of them were correctly classified. In this company workers can also classify product as "doubtful." In one analysis, worker inspections classified 3 percent of the product as doubtful, after which an independent inspector reviewed the doubtful product and classified 2 percent as acceptable and 1 percent as nonconforming.

Example 16.5. A pharmaceutical manufacturer employed a variety of tests and inspections before a capsule product was released for sale. These checks included chemical tests, weight checks, and visual inspections of the capsules. A 100 percent visual inspection had traditionally been conducted by an Inspection Department. Defects ranged from "critical" (e.g., an empty capsule) to "minor" (e.g., faulty print). This inspection was time consuming and frequently caused delays in production flow. A trial experiment of self-inspection by machine operators was instituted. Operators performed a visual inspection on a sample of 500 capsules. If the sample was acceptable, the operator shipped the full container to the warehouse; if the sample was not acceptable, the full container was sent to the Inspection Department for 100 percent inspection. During the experiment, both the samples and the full containers were sent to the Inspection Department for 100 percent inspection with reinspection of the sample recorded separately. The experiment reached two conclusions: (1) the sample inspection by the operators gave consistent results with the sample inspection by the inspectors and (2) the sample of 500 gave consistent results with the results of 100 percent inspection.

The experiment convinced all parties to switch to the sample inspection by operators. Under the new system, good product was released to the warehouse sooner and marginal product received a highly focused 100 percent inspection. In addition, the level of defects *decreased*. The improved quality level was attributed to the stronger sense of responsibility by operators (they themselves decided if product was ready for sale) and the immediate feedback received by operators from self-inspection. But there was another benefit—the inspection force was reduced by 50 people. These 50 people were shifted to other types of work, including experimentation and analysis activities on the various types of defects.

Sequence for Instituting Self-Inspection

If workers are to be given the product-conformance decision, it is necessary to decide whether the responsibility should be given to all workers or only to those who have demonstrated an ability to make good decisions. The latter approach is highly preferable and should proceed as follows:

1. Train workers in how to make product-conformance decisions.
2. Set up a system of product identification and order preservation to ensure that product decisions can readily be traced back to the worker who made them.
3. Institute a trial period during which workers make conformance decisions while duplicate decision making is done by inspectors. The purpose of this duplication is to discover, through data, which workers consistently make good product-conformance decisions.
4. Issue "licenses" (for making product-conformance decisions) only to those workers who demonstrate their competence. (This is analogous to qualification for certain manufacturing skills such as welding.)
5. For the licensed workers, institute an audit of decisions (see below). For the workers who do not qualify, retain the regular inspection.
6. Based on the results of the audits, continue or suspend the licenses.
7. Periodically conduct new trials in an effort to qualify the unlicensed workers.

If an audit reveals that wrong decisions have been made by the workers, the product evaluated since the last audit is reinspected—often by the workers themselves.

Worker response to such delegation of authority is generally favorable, the concept of job enlargement being a significant factor. However, workers who do qualify for the license commonly demand some form of compension for this achievement, e.g., a higher grade, more pay, etc. Companies invariably make a constructive response to these demands, since the economics of making the delegation are favorable. In addition, the resulting differential tends to act as a stimulus to the nonlicensed workers to qualify themselves.

Criteria for Self-Inspection

Before self-inspection can be adopted, some essential criteria must be met:

- Quality must be the number one priority within an organization. If this is not clear, a worker may succumb to schedule and cost pressures and classify products as acceptable that should be rejected.
- Mutual confidence is necessary. Managers must have sufficient confidence in the work force to be willing to entrust to them the responsibility of deciding whether the product conforms to specification. In turn, workers must have enough confidence in management to be willing to accept this responsibility.
- The criteria for self-control must be met. Failure to eliminate the management-controllable causes of defects suggests that management does not view quality as a high priority, and this may bias the workers during inspections. Workers must be trained to understand the specifications and perform the inspection.
- Specifications must be unequivocally clear. Workers should understand the use that will be made of their products (internally and externally) in order to grasp the importance of a conformance decision.
- The process must be of a nature which permits assignment of clear responsibility for decision making. An easy case for application is a worker running one machine, since there is clear responsibility for making both the product and the product-conformance decision. In contrast, a long assembly line or the numerous steps taken in a chemical process make it difficult to assign clear responsibility. Application of such multistep processes is best deferred until experience is gained with some processes.

QCH4, pages 17.23–17.26, provides further examples and cautions.

16.6 AUTOMATED MANUFACTURING

The march to automation proceeds unabated. Several terms have become important:

- *Computer-integrated manufacturing* (*CIM*). This is the process of applying a computer in a planned fashion from design through manufacturing and shipping of the product.
- *Computer-aided manufacturing* (*CAM*). This is the process in which a computer is used to plan and control the work of specific equipment.
- *Computer-aided design* (*CAD*). This is the process by which a computer assists in the creation or modification of a design.

This trio of concepts is producing huge increases in factory productivity. But automation, with proper planning, can also benefit product quality in several other ways:

- Automation can eliminate some of the monotony or fatigue tasks that causes errors by human beings. For example, when a manual seam-welding operation was turned over to a robot, the scrap rate plunged from 15 percent to zero (Kegg, 1985).
- Process variation can be reduced by the automatic monitoring and continuous adjustment of process variables.
- An important source of process troubles, i.e., the number of machine setups, can be reduced.
- Machines cannot only automatically measure product but can record, summarize, and display the data for line production operators and staff personnel. Feedback to the worker can be immediate, thus providing an early warning of impending troubles.
- With CAD, the quality engineer can provide inputs early in the design stage. When a design is placed into the computer, the quality engineer can review that design over and over again and thus keep abreast of design changes.

Achieving these benefits requires a spectrum of concepts and techniques. Three of these are discussed below: the key functions of CIM, group technology, and flexible manufacturing systems.

Key Functions of Computer-Integrated Manufacturing

To integrate the computer from design through shipping involves a network of functions and associated computer systems. Willis and Sullivan (1984, p. 32) describe this in terms of eight key functions: (1) design and drafting (CAD/CAM), (2) production scheduling and control, (3) process automation, (4) process control, (5) materials handling and storage, (6) maintenance scheduling and control, (7) distribution management, and (8) finance and accounting. Such a CIM system rests on a foundation of data bases covering both manufacturing data and product data.

Group Technology

Group technology is the process of examining all items manufactured by a company to identify those with sufficient similarity that a common design or manufacturing plan can be used. The aim is to reduce the number of new designs or new manufacturing plans. In addition to the savings in resources, group technology can improve both the quality of design and the quality of conformance by using proven designs and manufacturing plans. Gunn (1982, p. 121) reports that in many companies "only 20 percent of the parts initially thought to require new designs actually need them; of the remaining new parts, 40 percent could be built from an existing design and the other 40 percent could be created by modifying an existing design."

Each item is coded according to a variety of characteristics such as shape, material, tolerances, finish, and required production operations. After coding, parts with similar characteristics are sorted into groups. Phillipp (1982) shows an example of an 18-digit coding system:

Form	4 digits
Dimensions	4 digits
Tolerances	2 digits
Material	2 digits
Machine	2 digits
Process	2 digits
Inspection	2 digits

The process planner for a new part can retrieve a list of old parts that have some of the same characteristics. Planning for the new part can then simply specify the process for an old part with any differences noted.

Location of the production machines can also benefit from the group technology concept. Machines are grouped according to the parts they make and can be sorted into cells of machines, each cell producing one or several part families (thus "cellular manufacture").

Flexible Manufacturing System

A flexible manufacturing system (FMS) is a group of several computer-controlled machine tools linked by a materials handling system and a mainframe computer to process a group of parts completely. The FMS can be programmed to suit varying production requirements and can be reprogrammed to accommodate design changes or new parts. This is in contrast to a fixed automation system, which follows a preordained sequence.

Kegg (1984) summarizes the evolution of a flexible system in six steps:

1. The basic elements are a machine and an operator. Adjustments to the process are continually made by the operator.
2. Electronic intelligence is added in the form of computer control. This involves programming ("numerically controlling") the machine tools. A complicated series of operations can be repeated with the push of a single button.
3. Automatic devices for tool changing and workpiece loading and unloading are added.
4. Sensing devices that allow adjustments to be made automatically are added to the machine. Batch operations can then be performed continuously without human intervention.
5. The work cell is linked with other areas of the plant which supply workpieces, tooling, and other materials and information. The operator becomes a manager of a computer controlled system.
6. Finally, integration of all of the functions from design and manufacturing planning to inventory control, scheduling, and shop floor control is achieved by having all of the systems communicate with one another automatically.

Typically, the individual machines are robots or other types of numerically controlled machine tools, each of which is run by a microcomputer. Several of these numerically controlled tools are linked by a minicomputer, and then several of these minicomputers are tied into the mainframe computer.

Quality planning for automated processes requires some special precautions. These are identified and discussed in QCH4, page 16.56.

From the one extreme of the (typically) mass production in automated industries, we can shift to the other extreme of the (typically) low-volume production in job shop industries. Applying quality concepts in job shop industries is covered in QCH4, Section 32.

16.7 OVERALL REVIEW OF MANUFACTURING PLANNING

We incur great risk in going directly from a proposed manufacturing process plan into regular production. The time delays and extra costs involved in quality failures require a review of the proposed process, including software used with the process. Such a review is most effectively accomplished through preproduction trials and runs.

Ideally, product lots should be put through the entire system, with deficiencies found and corrected before full-scale production is begun. In practice, companies usually make some compromises with this ideal approach. "Preproduction" may be merely the first runs of regular production but with special provision for prompt feedback and correction of errors as found. Alternatively, the preproduction run may be limited to those features of product and process design which are so new that prior experience cannot reliably provide a basis for good risk taking. While some companies do adhere to a strict rule of proving in the product and process through preproduction lots, the more usual approach is one of flexibility, in which the use of preproduction lots depends on:

- The extent to which the product embodies new or untested quality features
- The extent to which the design of the manufacturing process embodies new or untried machines, tools, etc.
- The amount and value of product which will be out in the field before there is conclusive evidence of the extent of process, product, and use difficulties

These trials sometimes include "production validation tests" to ensure that the full-scale process can meet the design intent. See QCH4, page 16.43, for an example.

Preproduction trials and runs provide the ultimate evaluation—by manufacturing real product. Other techniques provide an even earlier warning before any product is made. For example, the failure mode, effect, and criticality analysis is useful in analyzing a proposed *product* design (see Section 12.4 "Failure Mode, Effect, and Criticality Analysis"). The same technique can dissect potential failure modes and their effects on a proposed *process* design. Another technique makes use of highly detailed checklists for the review of proposed processes. For elaboration, see QCH4, pages 16.42–16.48.

16.8 PROCESS QUALITY AUDITS

A quality audit is an independent evaluation of various aspects of quality performance for the purpose of providing information to those in need of assurance with respect to that performance. A full discussion of quality audits is given in Chapter 24, "Quality Assurance."

Application to manufacturing has been extensive and includes both audit of activities (systems audit) and audit of product (product audit).

Systems quality audit includes any activity that can affect final product quality. This audit (as contrasted to a broad survey) is usually made on a specific activity, such as the system for calibrating measuring equipment. The audit is made by one or more persons and consists of an on-site observation of the activity. Adherence to existing procedures is often emphasized, but audits often uncover situations of inadequate or nonexistent procedures. Audits must be based on a foundation of hard facts that are presented in the audit report in a way that will help those responsible to determine and execute the required corrective action.

Example 16.6. Dedhia (1985) describes an audit system for an electronics manufacturer. The audit consists of 14 subsystems, each having an audit checklist (see Table 16.7). Routine audits are performed by quality audit personnel on a scheduled basis. For selected activities, annual audits are conducted by a team from manufacturing, quality engineering, test engineering, purchasing, and other disciplines. The system includes a numerical audit rating based on classifying each discrepancy as major or minor. A rating below 90 percent requires an immediate corrective action response.

Example 16.7. A major airline uses audits to evaluate customer service in three areas:

- Airport arrival and departure
- Aircraft interior and exterior
- Airport facilities

Forty-seven specific activities are periodically audited, then performance measurements are made and compared to numerical goals. A few examples of goals are as follows:

- At least 95 percent of public contact transactions are positive overall. (The term "positive" is defined in terms of actions expected of agents when serving customers.)
- On ticketing, at least 80 percent of all passengers encounter line waits of not more than 5 minutes.
- At least 85 percent of the carpets inside the planes should be acceptable in appearance.
- At least 80 percent of the paint on planes should have acceptable adhesion.
- At airport security, at least 90 percent of all passengers should be processed within 3 minutes.
- At least 95 percent of agents should be acceptable in personal appearance and grooming. (Specific local guidelines are defined to reflect passenger perception of agent appearance.)
- Detailed reports are available to all station personnel, and a monthly summary is provided to several levels of management.

Product audit involves the reinspection of product to verify the adequacy of acceptance and rejection decisions made by inspection and testing personnel. In theory, such audits should not be needed. In practice, they can often be justified by field complaints. Such audits can take place at each inspection station for the product or after final assembly and packing. Sometimes an audit is required before a product may be moved to the next operation. For elaboration, see Section 24.11, "Product Audit."

TABLE 16.7
Audit checklist guidelines

Audit type	Audit type	Audit type

1. Equipment/tester/tools control
   Calibration/schedule
   Monitoring activity
   Certification status
   Maintenance status
   Data integrity/verification
   Standards check
   Availability of tools
   Startup/shutdown procedure
   Correlation verification
	4. Parts/assembly
	   Conformance to specification
	   EC level
	   Handling/packaging/storage/shipping
	   Data availability
	   Scrap/M.E. hold/MRB parts (nonconforming parts)
	   Traceability
	   In-process product
	   Finished product
	   Nonconforming product control and disposition
		9. Software system
		   Software control
		   Data integrity/verification

2. Operator
   Qualification status
   Compliance with procedure
   Output (quality) verification/operator capability
   Data recording verification
   Rework verification
   Observation for conformance to procedures
   Product handling
   Workmanship
	5. Process control status
	   Process control instructions/actions
	   Control chart status
	   Check corrective actions
	   Verify manufacturing data
		10. Q.A. self-audits
		   Inspection data verification
		   Housekeeping
		   Inspector training/qualification

	6. Environment
	   Cleanliness of the work area
	   Particle count verification
	   Humidity recording
	   Temperature recording
	   General housekeeping (safety, etc.)
		11. Production control crib
		  • Finished product control
		   Storage/handling
		   Receiving inspection status
		   EC level
		  • Raw material control
		   Storage/handling
		   Receiving inspection status
		   EC level

3. Documentation
  • Line documents (availability, readability, accessibility, document content, level)
   MPI
   PCN
  • Document adherence
   Quality documents
   Inspection instructions
   Inspection tools
   Applicable test procedures
  • Routings/flow chart/traveler
  • Maintenance documents
  • Training documents
  • Experimental procedures
  • Records/log books
  • Off-specs
	7. Calibration/standards audits
	   Calibration evidence
	   Overdue for calibration
	   Monitor standards
		12. Rework
		  • Procedures
		  • Product quality
		  • Product disposition

	8. Chemicals/matrix control
	   Shelf life labeling
	   Receiving inspection status
	   Handling/storage
	   Shelf life
	   Nonconforming chemicals/materials control and disposition
	   Relationship to work instructions
		13. System audit
		  • General administration
		  • Product development
		  • Product qualification
		  • Functional testing
		  • Field performance
		  • Personnel training

		14. MRB audit

Source: Adapted from Dedhia (1985).

16.9 QUALITY AND PRODUCTION FLOOR CULTURE

Meeting the criteria of self-control is necessary but not sufficient. Even if all three criteria are initially met, two problems remain:

1. Worker errors may occur. The causes of some of those errors can be corrected (see Section 3.10, "Test of Theories of Worker-Controllable Problems").
2. Conditions change and result in violations of the criteria of self-control, e.g., equipment deteriorates due to a reduction in preventive maintenance.

Production management and the work force must have a strong and positive quality ethic to correct these problems. Some companies have a strong—but negative—quality ethic. Examples are legion—hide the nonconforming product (e.g., bury the paint in the ground), finesse the inspector (e.g., keep producing defective product and wait until an inspector discovers the situation). Such negative actions are often taken in order to achieve other objectives such as production quotas.

To change a negative quality culture requires two steps: (1) collecting information to ascertain the present culture (see Section 2.10, "Company Culture on Quality") and (2) taking the steps necessary to change the culture (see Chapter 8, "Developing a Quality Culture").

SUMMARY

- Activities to integrate quality in manufacturing planning have two objectives: to prevent defects and to minimize variability.
- By creating a flow diagram, we can dissect a manufacturing process and plan for quality at each work station.
- To prevent defects and to minimize variability, we must discover the relationships between process variables and product results.
- Error proofing a process is an important element of prevention.
- For human beings to be in a state of self-control, we must provide them with knowledge of what they are supposed to do, knowledge of what they are actually doing, and a process that is capable of meeting specifications and can be regulated.
- Failure to meet all three of these criteria means that the quality problem is management-controllable. About 80 percent of quality problems are management-controllable.
- Quality responsibilities on the production floor are best defined in terms of specific decisions and actions.

- Under the self-inspection concept, conformance decisions are made by the production worker, with an independent audit by the Quality Department.
- Computer-integrated manufacturing is the process of applying a computer in a planned fashion from design through manufacturing and shipping; computer-aided manufacturing is the process in which a computer is used to plan and control the work of specific equipment; computer-aided design is the process by which a computer assists in the creation or modification of a design.
- In the group technology concept, all items are examined to identify those with sufficient similarity that a common design or manufacturing plan can be used.
- In a flexible manufacturing system, a group of several computer-controlled machine tools is linked by a materials handling system and a mainframe computer to process a group of parts completely.
- A systems quality audit is an independent evaluation of any activity that can affect final product quality.

PROBLEMS

16.1. Visit a local manufacturing company and identify the departments that have the principal and collateral responsibilities for carrying out the planning activities set out in Table 16.1.

16.2. For a specific manufacturing operation with which you are familiar, describe how you would conduct a controllability study.

16.3. Your plant has just conducted a controllability study by analyzing the causes of a large sample of defective parts. The results showed that 45 percent of the causes were worker-controllable and 55 percent management-controllable. One program (diagnosis of specific causes, determination of remedies, etc.) is planned for the management-controllable problems. For the worker-controllable problems, a motivation program for the workers producing poor work is planned. You are asked to comment on this approach.

16.4. Study the system of performance feedback available to any of the following categories of people and report your conclusions on the adequacy of this feedback for controlling quality of performance.
   (*a*) a motorist in city traffic
   (*b*) a student at school
   (*c*) a supermarket cashier

16.5. For any process to which you can gain access, determine the major form of "dominance" affecting attainment of quality.

16.6. In a certain operation involving the high-volume manufacture of discrete pieces from continuous lengths of material, the following is the system of controlling quality on the manufacturing floor:

- The *operator* makes initial roll adjustments for each new length of material by examining sample pieces and subsequently continues to make such examinations and adjustments while the machine is running.

- The *patrol inspector* (reporting to the chief inspector) also periodically examines sample pieces directly from the machine and, if he or she thinks it necessary, asks the operator to make adjustments.
- Usually the operator complies with such requests but on occasion remonstrates. If he or she feels strongly about it, appeal may be made to the *supervisor,* who may decide to let the machine run without making the requested adjustment.
- If this happens, the patrol inspector may appeal to the *chief inspector* (through his or her supervisor), who may then order the machine to be shut down. Such an order is complied with.
- All the pieces from the machine, in lots of 1000, go to a *bench inspector,* who samples them according to a prescribed plan. He or she passes some lots to the next operation on the basis of a good sample and sorts lots which fail the sampling plan if they contain particular types of defects (i.e., easily identifiable and removable). Other rejected lots (containing defects not so easily identifiable) are routed to the next operation, marked to indicate the nature of defects to be removed.
- The next operation is final inspection, where a *final inspector* reexamines all lots 100 percent (accepted, sorted, and rejected lots) and is supposed to remove all types of defects, including some attributable to operations preceding the one we have been considering.

Using the following form, place the necessary check marks to indicate who has authority to make the decisions indicated.

	Operator	Supervisor	Patrol inspector	Bench inspector	Final inspector	Chief inspector
Make setup						
Accept setup						
Operate process						
Accept process						
Correct process						
Accept lots						
Accept pieces						

Source: Course notes for Management of Quality Control, U.S. Air Force School of Logistics, 1959.

Are the responsibilities clear cut? Explain your answer.

16.7. The following example illustrates basic planning to meet a product result:

- *Product result:* hardness of a material
- *Process variable:* temperature in an oven
- *Regulating mechanism on the process variable:* input of energy into the oven to raise the temperature

For a manufacturing operation with which you are familiar, select a product result and identify one or more process variables and one or more regulating mechanisms.

REFERENCES

Dedhia, Navin S. (1985). "Process Audit System Effectiveness," *Annual Conference Proceedings, European Organization for Quality Control,* Berne, Switzerland, pp. 159–173.

Eibl, Siegfried, Ulrike Kess, and Friedrich Pukelsheim (1992). "Achieving a Target Value for a Manufacturing Process," *Journal of Quality Technology,* January, pp. 22–26.

Fisher, James R. (1983). "Computer Assisted Net Weight Control," *Quality Progress,* June, pp. 22–25.

Fukuda, Ryuji (1981). "Introduction to the CEDAC," *Quality Progress,* November, pp. 14–19.

Gunn, Thomas G. (1982). "The Mechanization of Design and Manufacturing," *Scientific American,* September, p. 121.

Kegg, Richard L. (1984). "Quality and Productivity in Manufacturing Systems," *Second Bi-Annual Machine Tool Technical Conference,* National Machine Tool Builders Association, Gaithersburg, Maryland, pp. 9–71 to 9–86.

Kegg, Richard L. (1985). "Quality and Productivity in Manufacturing Systems," *Annals of the CIRP* (International Association for Production Research), Paris, vol. 34, no. 2, pp. 531–534.

Nakajo, Takeshi, and Hitoshi, Kume (1985). "The Principles of Foolproofing and Their Application in Manufacturing," *Reports of Statistical Application Research,* Union of Japanese Scientists and Engineers, Tokyo, vol. 32, no. 2, June, pp. 10–29.

Phillipp, Thomas J. (1982). "Quality System Concepts in the CAD/CAM Era," *ASQC Quality Congress Transactions,* Milwaukee, pp. 569–573.

Siff, Walter C. (1984). "The Strategic Plan of Control—A Tool for Participative Management," *ASQC Quality Congress Transactions,* Milwaukee, pp. 384–390.

U.S. Air Force (1959). "Course Notes for Management of Quality Control," Washington, D.C.

Willis, Roger G., and Kevin H. Sullivan (1984). "CIMS in Perspective: Costs, Benefits, Timing, Payback Periods Are Outlined," *Industrial Engineering,* February, vol. 16, no. 2, pp. 23–36.

SUPPLEMENTARY READING

Manufacturing planning for quality: QCH4, Section 16.

Swift, Jill A., and Timothy J. Flynn (1989). "Methodology for Developing a Quality Plan Within a Manufacturing Company," *Quality Engineering,* vol. 1, no. 4, pp. 467–486, Marcel Dekker, New York.

Production of quality: QCH4, Section 17.

Quality information equipment: Feigenbaum, A. V. (1991). *Total Quality Control,* 3rd ed., McGraw-Hill Book Company, New York, Chapter 12.

Expert systems: Affisco, John F., and Mahesh Chandra (1991). "Quality Engineering and Expert Systems," *Quality Engineering,* vol. 3, no. 4, pp. 433–453, Marcel Dekker, New York.

CHAPTER
17

STATISTICAL
PROCESS
CONTROL

17.1 DEFINITION AND IMPORTANCE OF SPC

We define statistical process control (SPC) as the application of statistical methods to the measurement and analysis of variation in any process. A process is a unique combination of machines, tools, methods, materials, and people that attains an output in goods, software, or services. Let the reader be aware, however, that "SPC" has also assumed other definitions, even including some that involve little or no use of statistical analysis!

Methods of collecting, summarizing, and analyzing data are discussed in Chapter 9, "Basic Probability Concepts," and Chapter 10, "Statistical Tools for Analyzing Data." In the current chapter, we will examine the significance of variation, use of control charts in analyzing and minimizing variation, quantification of process capability, and the relation of these concepts to other techniques for process improvement.

The evidence is clear that these fascinating techniques can make an important contribution to achieving quality objectives. For most organizations, these techniques are essential. To help assure successful and continued application of these concepts in the reality of lean operating budgets, these techniques must not become an end in themselves. Pragmatic operating managers correctly demand that each potential application show a tangible opportunity for significant benefits.

17.2 QUALITY MEASUREMENT IN MANUFACTURING

The management of key work processes must include provision for measurement. In developing units of measure, the reader should review the basics of quality measurement discussed in Section 5.3, "The Quality Control Subject."

Table 17.1 shows examples for manufacturing activities. Note that many of the control subjects are forms of work output. In reviewing current units in use, a fruitful starting point is the measure of "productivity." Productivity is

TABLE 17.1
Examples of quality measurement in manufacturing

Subject	Unit of measure
Quality of manufacturing output	Percentage of output meeting specifications at inspection ("first-time yield")
	Percentage of output meeting specifications at intermediate and final inspection
	Amount of scrap (quantity, cost, percentage, etc.), amount of rework (quantity, cost, percentage, etc.)
	Percentage of output shipped under waiver of specifications
	Number of defects found in product audit (after inspection)
	Warranty costs due to manufacturing defects
	Overall measure of product quality (defects in parts per million, weighted defects per unit, variability for critical characteristics, etc.)
	Amount of downgraded output
Quality of input to manufacturing	Percentage of critical operations with certified workers
	Amount of downtime of manufacturing equipment
	Percentage of product input meeting specifications
	Percentage of instruments meeting calibration schedules
	Percentage of specifications requiring changes after release

usually defined as the amount of output related to input resources. Surprisingly, some organizations still mistakenly calculate only one measure of output, i.e., the total (acceptable *and* nonacceptable). Clearly, the pertinent output measure is that which is usable by customers (i.e., acceptable output).

The units in Table 17.1 become candidates for data analysis using statistical techniques such as control charts, discussed later in this chapter. But there is a more basic point—the selection of the unit of measure and the periodic collection and reporting of data demonstrate to operating personnel that management regards the subject as having priority importance. This sets the stage for improvement!

17.3 STATISTICAL CONTROL CHARTS— GENERAL

A statistical control chart is a graphic comparison of process performance data to computed "statistical control limits," drawn as limit lines on the chart. The process performance data usually consist of groups of measurements ("rational subgroups") that come from the regular sequence of production while preserving the order of the data.

A prime objective of a control chart is detecting *special* (or assignable) causes of variation in a process—by analyzing data from both the past and the future. Knowing the meaning of "special causes"is essential to understanding the control chart concept (see Table 5.6).

Process variations are traceable to two kinds of causes: (1) common (or random or chance), which are inherent in the process, and (2) special (or assignable), which cause excessive variation. Ideally, only common causes should be present in a process because these represent a stable and predictable process which leads to minimum variation. A process that is operating without special causes of variation is said to be "in a state of statistical control." The control chart for such a process has all of the data points within the statistical control limits. The objective of a control chart is not to achieve a state of statistical control as an end in itself but to reduce variation.

The control chart distinguishes between common and special causes of variation through its choice of control limits (Figure 17.1). These are calculated using the laws of probability in such a way that highly improbable causes of variation are presumed to be due not to random causes but to special causes. When the variation *exceeds* the statistical control limits, it is a signal that special causes have entered the process and the process should be investigated to identify these causes of excessive variation. Random variation *within* the control limits means that only common (random) causes are present; the amount of variation has stabilized, and minor process adjustments should be avoided. Note that a control chart detects the presence of a special cause but does not *find* the cause—that task must be handled by a subsequent investigation of the process.

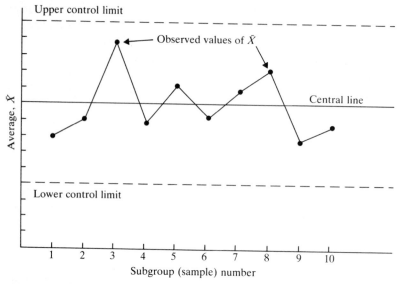

FIGURE 17.1
Generalized control chart for averages.

17.4 ADVANTAGES OF STATISTICAL CONTROL

A state of statistical control exists when only common causes of variation exist in the process. This condition provides several important advantages:

• The process has stability, which makes it possible to predict its behavior, at least in the near term.

• The process has an identity in terms of a given set of conditions that are necessary for making predictions. An analogy to baseball is useful. If we say that a player has a batting capability of about .250, we mean that on average he will get one hit in four times at bat. Of course, this assumes that the player is in a normal state of health, i.e., free of any assignable or special causes that would detract from the batting capability. Predictions of any kind must be related to an assumed set of conditions. For manufacturing and business processes, these conditions are represented by a state of statistical control. Ideally, drawing conclusions from any set of data should be preceded by an analysis to see if the data come from a process in statistical control.

• A process in statistical control operates with less variability than a process having special causes. Lower variability has become an important tool of competition (see Section 4.6, "Planning for Product Quality to Generate Sales Income").

- A process having special causes is unstable, and the excessive variation may hide the effect of changes being introduced to achieve improvement. Also, the removal of some special causes and subsequent replotting of the control chart may reveal that additional special causes exist which were masked earlier.
- Knowing that a process is in statistical control is helpful to the workers running a process. It says that when data fall within the statistical control limits, adjustments should *not* be made. Making such adjustments will add to the variability, not decrease it. Conversely, a control chart helps to avoid underadjustment as out-of-control points will signal the presence of special causes.
- Knowing that a process is in statistical control provides direction to those who are trying to make a long-term reduction in process variability. In order to reduce process variability, the process system must be analyzed and changed rather than management expecting the workers who run the process to reduce the variability by themselves.
- An analysis for statistical control, which includes the plotting of data in order of production, will easily identify trends over time that are hidden by other summarizations of data such as histograms.
- A stable process (as verified by statistical control) which also meets product specifications provides evidence that the process has conditions which, if maintained, will result in an acceptable product. Such evidence is needed *before* a process is transferred from the planning stage to full production.

All of these advantages of statistical control feed into the main objective, which is to reduce process variation. Process variation is much like the swing of a pendulum. Wouldn't it be nice if we could reduce the sweep of the arc?

17.5 STEPS IN SETTING UP A CONTROL CHART

Setting up a control chart requires the following steps:

1. Choosing the characteristic to be charted.
   - Giving high priority to characteristics which are currently running with a high defective rate. A Pareto analysis can establish priorities.
   - Identifying the process variables and conditions which contribute to the end-product characteristics, so as to define potential charting applications from raw materials through processing steps to final characteristics. For example, pH, salt concentration, and temperature of plating solution are process variables contributing to plating smoothness.

- Choosing measurement methods which will provide the kind of data needed for diagnosis of problems. Attribute data (e.g., percentage defective) provide summary information but may need to be supplemented by variables data (e.g., numerical diameter of individual pieces) to diagnose causes and determine action.
- Determining the earliest point in the production process at which testing can be done to get information on assignable causes so that the chart can serve as an effective early-warning device to prevent defectives.

2. Choosing the type of control chart. Table 17.2 compares three basic control charts.

TABLE 17.2
Comparison of some control charts

Statistical measure plotted	Average $\bar{X}$ and range R	Percentage nonconforming (p)	Number of nonconformities (c)
Type of data required	Variable data (measured values of a characteristic)	Attribute data (number of defective units of product)	Attribute data (number of defects per unit of product)
General field of application	Control of individual characteristics	Control of overall fraction defective of a process	Control of overall number of defects per unit
Significant advantages	Provides maximum utilization of information available from data	Data required are often already available from inspection records	Same advantages as p chart but also provides a measure of defectiveness
	Provides detailed information on process average and variation for control of individual dimensions	Easily understood by all personnel Provides an overall picture of quality	
Significant disadvantages	Not understood unless training is provided; can cause confusion between control limits and tolerance limits	Does not provide detailed information for control of individual characteristics	Does not provide detailed information for control of individual characteristics
	Cannot be used with go/no go type of data	Does not recognize different degrees of defectiveness in units of product	
Sample size	Usually 4 or 5	Use given inspection results or samples of 25, 50, or 100	Any convenient unit of product such as 100 ft of wire or one television set

3. Deciding the centerline to be used and the basis of calculating the limits. The centerline may be the average of past data, or it may be a desired average (i.e., a standard value). The limits are usually set at ±3 standard deviations, but other multiples may be chosen for different statistical risks.

4. Choosing the "rational subgroup." Each point on a control chart represents a subgroup (or sample) consisting of several units of product. For process control purposes, subgroups should be chosen so that the units *within* a subgroup have the greatest chance of being alike and the units *between* subgroups have the greatest chance of being different.

5. Providing a system for collecting the data. If the control chart is to serve as a day-to-day shop tool, it must be made simple and convenient for use. Measurement must be simplified and kept free of error. Indicating instruments must be designed to give prompt, reliable readings. Better yet, instruments should be designed which can record as well as indicate. Recording of data can be simplified by skillful design of data or tally sheets. Working conditions are also a factor. A machine department which abounds in cutting oil cannot keep respectable records with ordinary pencil and paper. Protective covers can be made and special paper and crayons provided. Copying of day-to-day data should be avoided.

6. Calculating the control limits and providing specific instructions on the interpretation of the results and the actions which are to be taken by various production personnel (see below). Control limit formulas for the three basic types of control charts are given in Table 17.3. These formulas are based on ±3 standard deviations and use a central line equal to the average of the data used in calculating the control limits. Values of the A_2, D_3, and D_4 factors used in the formulas are given in Table I in the Appendix. Each year, *Quality Progress* magazine publishes a directory which includes software for calculating sample parameters and control limits and also plotting the data.

7. Plotting the data and interpreting the results.

The control chart is a powerful statistical concept, but its use should be kept in perspective. The ultimate purpose of a manufacturing process is to

TABLE 17.3
Control chart limits—attaining a state of control

Chart for	Central line	Lower limit	Upper limit
Averages $\bar{X}$	$\bar{\bar{X}}$	$\bar{\bar{X}} - A_2\bar{R}$	$\bar{\bar{X}} + A_2\bar{R}$
Ranges R	$\bar{R}$	$D_3\bar{R}$	$D_4\bar{R}$
Percentage nonconforming p	$\bar{p}$	$\bar{p} - 3\sqrt{\dfrac{\bar{p}(1-\bar{p})}{n}}$	$\bar{p} + 3\sqrt{\dfrac{\bar{p}(1-\bar{p})}{n}}$
Number of nonconformities c	$\bar{c}$	$\bar{c} - 3\sqrt{\bar{c}}$	$\bar{c} + 3\sqrt{\bar{c}}$

TABLE 17.4
Life cycle of control chart applications

Stage	Step	Method
Preparatory	State purpose of investigation	Relate to quality system
	Determine state of control	Attributes chart
	Determine critical variables	Fishbone
	Determine candidates for control	Pareto
	Choose appropriate type of chart	Depends on data and purpose
	Decide how to sample	Rational subgroups
	Choose subgroup size and frequency	Sensitivity desired
Initiation	Ensure cooperation	Team approach
	Train user	Log actions
	Analyze results	Look for patterns
Operational	Assess effectiveness	Periodically check usage and relevance
	Keep up interest	Change chart, involve users
	Modify chart	Keep frequency and nature of chart current with results
Phase-out	Eliminate chart after purpose is accomplished	Go to spot checks, periodic sample inspection, overall p,c charts

Source: Schilling (1990).

make product that is fit for use—not to make product that simply meets statistical control limits. Once the charts have served their purpose, many should be taken down and the effort shifted to other characteristics needing improvement. Schilling (1990) traces the life cycle of control chart applications (Table 17.4). A given application might employ several types of control charts. Note that, in the "phase-out" stage, statistical control has been achieved, and some of the charts are replaced with spot checks.

17.6 CONTROL CHART FOR VARIABLES DATA

For variables data, the control chart for sample averages and sample ranges provides a powerful technique for analyzing process data.

A small sample (e.g., five units) is periodically taken from the process, and the average ($\bar{X}$) and range (R) are calculated for each sample. A total of at least 50 individual measurements (e.g., ten samples of five each) should be collected before the control limits are calculated. The control limits are set at $\pm 3\sigma$ for sample averages and sample ranges. The $\bar{X}$ and R values are plotted on separate charts against their $\pm 3\sigma$ limits.

Standard deviations are readily computed by modern calculators, but calculations can be avoided by using shortcuts.

The shortcut formulas for the control limits on sample averages are:

$$\text{Upper control limit} = \bar{\bar{X}} + A_2\bar{R}$$
$$\text{Lower control limit} = \bar{\bar{X}} - A_2\bar{R}$$

where $\bar{\bar{X}}$ = grand average = average of the sample averages
 $\bar{R}$ = average of the sample ranges
 A_2 = constant found from Table I in the Appendix

The shortcut consists of: (1) computing, for each sample, the range (difference between largest and smallest) of the individuals; (2) averaging the ranges thus obtained; and then (3) multiplying the average range by a conversion factor to get the distance from the expected average to the limit line. The central line is merely the average of all the individual observations.

The shortcut formulas for control limits on sample ranges are:

$$\text{Upper control limit} = D_4\bar{R}$$
$$\text{Lower control limit} = D_3\bar{R}$$

where D_3 and D_4 are constants found in Table I in the Appendix.

A partial tabulation of the A_2, D_3, and D_4 factors is reproduced in Table 17.5 for the convenience of the reader in following the text.

Consider the data for machines N-5 and N-7 in Figure 17.2. For each machine, the data consist of ten samples (with six units each) plotted in time order of production (sample number). Figure 17.2 shows the $\bar{X}$ and R charts for each machine. In the upper part of the figure, the display of individual observations on the vertical axis plotted against time is called a run chart.

TABLE 17.5
Constants for $\bar{X}$ and R chart

n	A_2	D_3	D_4	d_2
2	1.880	0	3.268	1.128
3	1.023	0	2.574	1.693
4	0.729	0	2.282	2.059
5	0.577	0	2.114	2.326
6	0.483	0	2.004	2.534
7	0.419	0.076	1.924	2.704
8	0.373	0.136	1.864	2.847
9	0.337	0.184	1.816	2.970
10	0.308	0.223	1.777	3.078

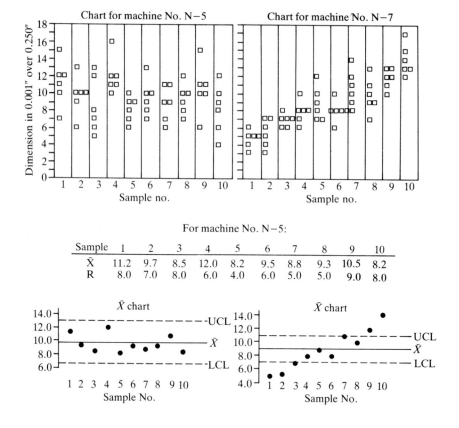

For machine No. N−5:

Sample	1	2	3	4	5	6	7	8	9	10
$\bar{X}$	11.2	9.7	8.5	12.0	8.2	9.5	8.8	9.3	10.5	8.2
R	8.0	7.0	8.0	6.0	4.0	6.0	5.0	5.0	9.0	8.0

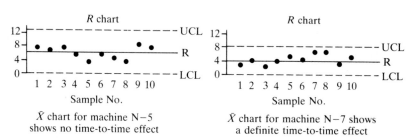

$\bar{X}$ chart for machine N−5
shows no time-to-time effect

$\bar{X}$ chart for machine N−7 shows
a definite time-to-time effect

FIGURE 17.2
$\bar{X}$ and R charts confirm suggested machine differences.

For machine N-5, the upper and lower control limits (UCL and LCL) are calculated as:

Averages:

$$UCL = \bar{\bar{X}} + A_2\bar{R} = 9.59 + 0.483(6.0) = 12.48$$
$$LCL = \bar{\bar{X}} - A_2\bar{R} = 9.59 - 0.483(6.0) = 6.68$$

Ranges:

$$\text{UCL} = D_4\bar{R} = 2.004(6.0) = 12.02$$

$$\text{LCL} = D_3\bar{R} = \quad 0(6.0) = 0$$

As all points fall within the control limits, it is concluded that the process is free of assignable causes of variation.

Control limits for a chart for averages represent three standard deviations of sample *averages* (not individual values). As specification limits usually apply to *individual* values, the control limits *cannot* be compared to specification limits, because averages inherently vary less than the individual measurements going into the averages (see Figure 10.1). Therefore, specification limits should *not* be placed on a control chart for averages. Sample averages, rather than individual values, are plotted because averages are more sensitive to detecting process changes than individual values are.

Another example is presented in Figure 17.2 for machine N-7. This machine has both within-sample variation shown by the range chart and between-sample variation as illustrated by the chart for sample averages. The $\bar{X}$ chart indicates that some factor such as tool wear is present that results in larger values of the characteristic with the passing of time (note the importance of preserving the order of the measurements). In such cases, measures of process capability should reflect both sources of variation. The inherent capability can be estimated in the usual way as 6σ (where $\sigma = \bar{R}/d_2$), and this will depict the variation about a given process aim. In addition, the time-to-time variation can be expressed separately as the difference in process aim over the time period covered by the averages plotted on the control chart.

Interpretation of Charts

Place the charts for $\bar{X}$ and R (or s) one above the other so the average and range for any one subgroup are on the same vertical line. Observe whether either or both indicate lack of control for that subgroup.

$\bar{X}$'s outside the control limits are evidence of a general change affecting all pieces after the first out-of-limits subgroup. The log kept during data collection, the operation of the process, and the worker's experience should be studied to discover a variable which could have caused the out-of-control subgroups. Typical causes are a change in material, personnel, machine setting, tool wear, temperature, or vibration.

R's outside control limits are evidence that the uniformity of the process has changed. Typical causes are a change in personnel, increased variability of material, or excessive wear in the process machinery. In one case a sudden increase in R warned of an impending machine accident.

A single out-of-control R can be caused by a shift in the process which occurred while the subgroup was being taken.

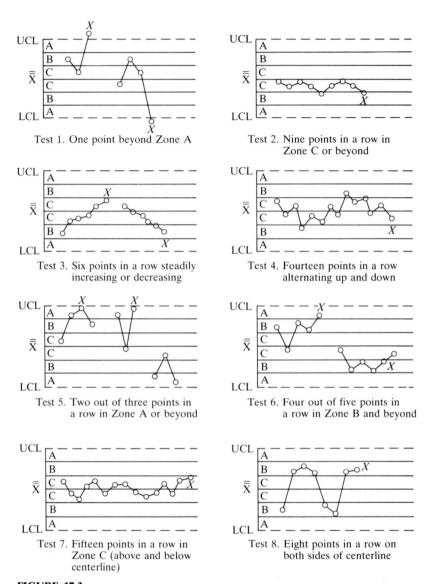

FIGURE 17.3
Illustrations of tests for special causes applied to $\bar{X}$ control charts. (*From Nelson, 1984.*)

Look for unusual patterns and nonrandomness. Nelson (1984, 1985) provides eight tests to detect such patterns on control charts using 3σ control limits (Figure 17.3). Each of the zones shown is 1σ wide. (Note that test 2 in Figure 17.3 requires nine points in a row; other authors suggest seven or eight points in a row; see Nelson, 1985, for elaboration.)

Flynn and Bolcar (1984) illustrate, in an entertaining and constructive

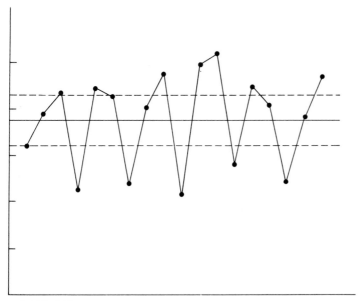

FIGURE 17.4
Coating film weights. (*From Flynn and Bolcar, 1984.*)

manner, the technical investigations that accompany control chart applications at the Coors Brewing Company along with the lessons learned from each:

> **Example 17.1.** Coating weights were a source of trouble on beer can coating lines. Control chart data indicated extreme variation on all coaters, requiring constant adjustment of the process (Figure 17.4).
>
> A controlled experiment was run on one coater. The technical expert thought the ranges, tho' "in control," were too high. A check on some historical data confirmed this. Some systematic cause had changed in the meantime, artificially inflating the range. This was traced to fluctuations in line pressure due to an overworked pump. When a second pump was activated, the range improved. Now a cycle was clearly evident. It was three samples long. This matched the procedure for using test cans. Test cans were weighed and reused three times before being replaced with fresh, uncoated cans. The procedure was changed so that fresh cans were used for each sample. The "necessary" adjustments dropped 80 percent and film weights became more uniform. It was then possible to reduce the number of checks. In the end, we had lower and more uniform film weights with fewer inspections and adjustments (Flynn and Bolcar, 1984, p. 195).

Ott and Schilling (1990) provide the definitive text on analysis after the initial control charts by presenting an extensive collection of cases with innovative statistical analysis clearly described.

Introducing Control Charts

To quality specialists, control charts serve as sensitive devices for detecting process changes; to operating forces, the charts represent a major change from the traditional "law of the shop," i.e., the specification limits. In introducing control charts, it is essential to prevent confusion about the role of control limits versus specification limits. Workers react to nonconforming product because specification limits have been the law of the shop; they do not react to control limits in the same way because the legitimacy of control limits may not have been fully established and clarified. For example, what is a worker to do if a control chart is frequently out of control but the product is well within specification limits? See QCH4, page 17.11, for elaboration. See also Section 17.15.

Chart for Individuals

An alternative to the $\bar{X}$ and R chart is the chart for individual X values. This chart, often called a run chart, is a plot of individual observations against time. In the simplest case, specification limits are added to the chart; in other cases, $\pm 3\sigma$ limits of individual values are added. A chart for individuals is not as sensitive as the $\bar{X}$ chart. See QCH4, pages 24.18–24.20, for further elaboration. See also Ryan (1989, Chapter 6).

Example 17.2. Edgeman and Athey (1990) present an innovative chart that combines a control chart for individuals with a stem-and-leaf plot of data (Figure 17.5).

From a process making contact lenses, 25 measurements are taken on the lens thickness. The measurements are recorded to four places, e.g., the first measurement was 0.3978. The first two digits (39) are the stem and the last two digits (78) are the leaf. The full measurements are plotted in order of production

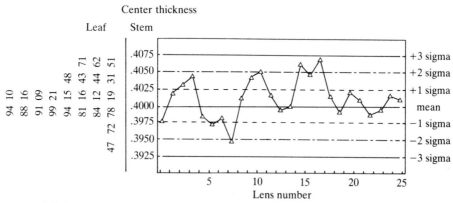

FIGURE 17.5
Contact lens center thickness. (*From Edgeman and Athey, 1990.*)

and the leaf values are recorded in order of occurrence within bands on the control chart. Thus, this "digidot" plot combines information on variation over time (the control chart) with a summary of the distribution pattern (the histogram).

17.7 PRE-CONTROL

PRE-Control is a statistical technique for detecting process conditions and changes which may cause defects (rather than changes which are statistically significant). PRE-Control focuses on controlling conformance to specifications, rather than statistical control. PRE-Control starts a process centered between specification limits and detects shifts that might result in making some of the parts outside a print limit. PRE-Control requires no plotting and no computations, and it needs only three measurements to give control information. The technique utilizes the normal distribution curve in the determination of significant changes in either the aim or the spread of a production process which could result in increased production of defective work.

The principle of PRE-Control is demonstrated by assuming the worst condition that can be accepted from a process capable of quality production, i.e., when the natural tolerance is the same as the print allows and when the process is precisely centered and any shift would result in some defective work.

If we draw in two PRE-Control (PC) lines, each one-fourth of the way in from each print-tolerance limit (Figure 17.6), it can be shown that 86 percent of the parts will be inside the PC lines, with seven percent in each of the outer sections. In other words, seven percent, or one part in 14, will occur outside a PC line under normal circumstances.

The chance that two measurements in a row will fall outside a PC line is $\frac{1}{14}$ times $\frac{1}{14}$, or $\frac{1}{196}$. This means that only once in about every 200 measurements should we expect to get two in a row in a given outer band. When two in a row

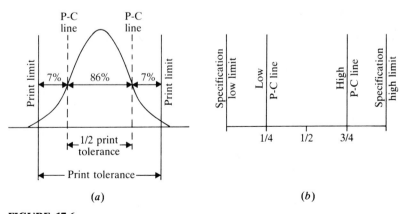

FIGURE 17.6
(*a*) Assumptions underlying PRE-Control. (*b*) Location of PRE-Control lines.

do occur, there is a much greater chance ($\frac{195}{196}$) that the process has shifted. It is therefore advisable to reset the process to the center. It is equally unlikely to get a measurement beyond one given PC line and the next outside the other PC line. In this case, the indication is not that the process has shifted but that some factor has been introduced which has widened the pattern to an extent that defective pieces are inevitable. An immediate remedy of the cause of the trouble must be made before the process can safely continue.

The zone within the PC lines is the "green zone"; between the PC lines and the specification limits is the "yellow zone"; outside the specification limits is the "red zone."

To qualify a process for PRE-Control:

1. Take consecutive individual measurements on a characteristic until five consecutive measurements fall within the green zone.

2. If one yellow occurs, restart the count.

3. If two consecutive yellows occur, adjust the process.

4. Anytime an adjustment or other process change occurs, requalify the process .

When the process is qualified, the following PRE-Control rules are applied to running the process:

1. Use a sample of two consecutive measurements, *A* and *B*. If *A* is green, continue running the process. If *A* is yellow, take a second measurement, *B*.

2. If *A* and *B* are both yellow, stop the process and investigate.

During either the qualification or running stages, if a red occurs, stop the process and investigate.

Most processes require periodic adjustments to remain within specifications. Six *A, B* pairs of measurements between adjustments are viewed as sufficient to provide virtually no out-of-specification product. Thus, if a process typically requires an adjustment about every two hours, than an *A, B* pair of measurements should be taken every 20 minutes.

PRE-Control is an example of a concept known as *narrow-limit gaging.* The broader concept provides sampling procedures (sample size, location of the narrow limits, and allowable number of units outside the narrow limits) to meet predefined risks of accepting bad product. Narrow-limit gaging is discussed by Ott and Schilling (1990, Chapter 7).

Further discussion of PRE-Control is provided by Shainin and Shainin in QCH4, Section 24.

For a comparison of PRE-Control versus control charts, see Mackertech (1990) and Shainin (1990).

17.8 PROCESS CAPABILITY

In planning the quality aspects of manufacture, nothing is more important than advance assurance that the processes will be able to hold the tolerances. In recent decades there has emerged a concept of *process capability* which provides a quantified prediction of process adequacy. This ability to predict quantitatively has resulted in widespread adoption of the concept as a major element of quality planning.

Process capability is the measured, inherent variation of the product turned out by a process.

Basic Definitions

Each key word in this definition must itself be clearly defined, since the concept of capability has an enormous extent of application and since nonscientific terms are inadequate for communication within the industrial community.

- *Process:* This refers to some unique combination of machine, tools, methods, materials, *and people* engaged in production. It is often feasible to separate and quantify the effect of the variables entering this combination. Such separation can be illuminating.
- *Capability:* This word is used in the sense of an ability, based on tested performance, to achieve measurable results.
- *Measured capability:* This refers to the fact that process capability is quantified from data which, in turn, are the results of measurement of work performed by the process.
- *Inherent capability:* This refers to the product uniformity resulting from a process which is in a state of statistical control, i.e., in the absence of time-to-time "drift" or other assignable causes of variation. "Instantaneous reproducibility" is a synonym.
- *Product:* The measurement is made on the product because it is product variation which is the end result.

Uses of Process Capability Information

Process capability information serves multiple purposes:

1. Predicting the extent of variability that processes will exhibit. Such capability information, when provided to designers, provides important information in setting realistic specification limits.
2. Choosing from among competing processes that which is most appropriate for the tolerances to be met.

3. Planning the interrelationship of sequential processes. For example, one process may distort the precision achieved by a predecessor process, as in hardening of gear teeth. Quantifying the respective process capabilities often points the way to a solution.

4. Providing a quantified basis for establishing a schedule of periodic process control checks and readjustments.

5. Assigning machines to classes of work for which they are best suited.

6. Testing theories of causes of defects during quality improvement programs.

7. Serving as a basis for specifying the quality performance requirements for purchased machines.

These purposes account for the growing use of the process capability concept.

Standardized Formula

The most widely adopted formula for process capability is

$$\text{Process capability} = \pm 3 \text{ (a total of } 6\sigma)$$

where σ = the standard deviation of the process under a state of statistical control, i.e., under no drift and no sudden changes.

If the process is centered at the nominal specification and follows a normal probability distribution, 99.73 percent of production will fall within $\pm 3\sigma$ of the nominal specification.

Some industrial processes operate under a state of statistical control. For such processes, the computed process capability of 6σ can be compared directly to specification tolerances, and judgments of adequacy can be made. However, the majority of industrial processes exhibit both drift and sudden changes. These departures from the ideal are a fact of life, and the practitioner must deal with them.

Nevertheless, there is great value in standardizing on a formula for process capability based on a state of statistical control. Under this state, product variations are the result of numerous small variables (rather than being the effect of a single large variable) and, hence, have the character of random variation. It is most helpful for planners to have such limits in quantified form.

Relationship to Product Tolerance

A major reason for quantifying process capability is to be able to compute the ability of the process to hold product tolerances. For processes which are in a state of statistical control, a comparison of the variation of 6σ to the tolerance limits permits ready calculation of percentage defective by conventional statistical theory.

Planners try to select processes with the 6σ process capability well within the tolerance width. A measure of this relationship is the capability ratio:

$$C_p = \text{Capability ratio} = \frac{\text{Specification range}}{\text{Process capability}} = \frac{\text{USL} - \text{LSL}}{6s}$$

where USL = upper specification limit
LSL = lower specification limit

Note that $6s$ is used as an estimate of 6σ.

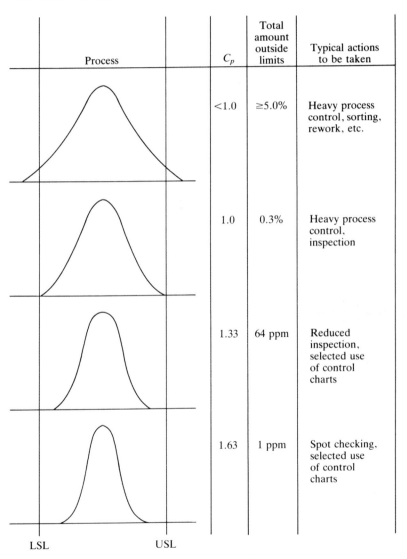

Process	C_p	Total amount outside limits	Typical actions to be taken
	<1.0	≥5.0%	Heavy process control, sorting, rework, etc.
	1.0	0.3%	Heavy process control, inspection
	1.33	64 ppm	Reduced inspection, selected use of control charts
	1.63	1 ppm	Spot checking, selected use of control charts

LSL   USL

FIGURE 17.7
Four examples of process variability.

Some companies define the ratio as the reciprocal. Some industries now express defect rates in terms of parts per million. A defect rate of one part per million requires a capability ratio (specification range over process capability) of about 1.63.

Figure 17.7 shows four of many possible relations between process variability and specification limits and the likely courses of action for each. Note that, in all of these cases, the average of the process is at the midpoint between the specification limits.

Table 17.6 shows selected capability ratios and the corresponding level of defects assuming the process average is midway between the specification limits. A process that is just meeting specification limits (specification range $= \pm 3\sigma$) has a C_p of 1.0. The criticality of many applications and the reality that the process average will not remain at the midpoint of the specification range suggest that C_p should be at least 1.33.

Six-Sigma Concept of Process Capability

For some processes, shifts in the process average are so common that such shifts should be recognized in setting acceptable values of C_p. In some industries, shifts in the process average of ± 1.5 standard deviations (of individual values) are not unusual. To allow for such shifts, high values of C_p are needed. For example, if specification limits are at $\pm 6\sigma$ (Figure 17.8) and if the mean shifts $\pm 1.5\sigma$, then 3.4 PPM will be beyond specification limits. The Motorola Company's "six-sigma" approach recognizes the likelihood of these shifts in the process average and makes use of a variety of quality engineering techniques to change the product, the process, or both in order to achieve a C_p of at least 2.0.

TABLE 17.6
Process capability index (C_p) and product outside specification limits

Process capability index (C_p)	Total product outside two-sided specification limits*
0.5	13.36%
0.67	4.55%
1.00	0.3%
1.33	64 PPM
1.63	1 PPM
2.00	0

* Assuming the process is centered midway between the specification limits.

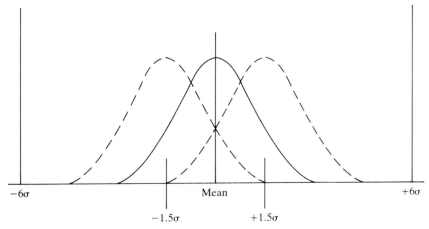

FIGURE 17.8
Six-sigma concept of process capability.

The C_{pk} Capability Index

Process capability, as measured by C_p, refers to the variation in a process about the average value. This is illustrated in Figure 17.9. The two processes have equal capabilities (C_p) because 6σ is the same for each distribution, as indicated by the widths of the distribution curves. The process aimed at μ_2 is producing defectives because the aim is off center, not because of the inherent variation about the aim (i.e., the capability).

Thus, the C_p index measures *potential* capability, assuming that the process average is equal to the midpoint of the specification limits and the process is operating in statistical control; as the average is often not at the midpoint, it is useful to have a capability index that reflects both variation and the location of the process average. Such an index is C_{pk}.

C_{pk} reflects the current process mean's proximity to either the upper specification limit (USL) or lower specification limit (LSL). C_{pk} is estimated by:

$$\hat{C}_{pk} = \min\left[\frac{\bar{X} - \text{LSL}}{3s}, \frac{\text{USL} - \bar{X}}{3s}\right]$$

In an example from Kane (1986):

$$\text{USL} = 20 \qquad \bar{X} = 16$$
$$\text{LSL} = 8 \qquad s = 2$$

the standard capability ratio is estimated as

$$\frac{\text{USL} - \text{LSL}}{6\sigma} = \frac{20 - 8}{12} = 1.0$$

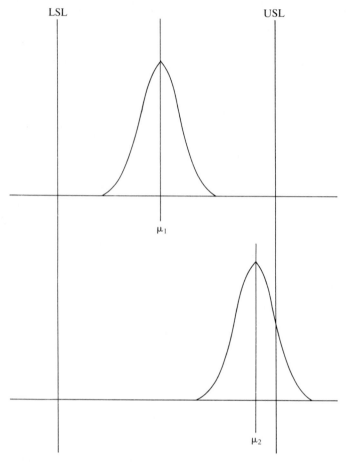

FIGURE 17.9
Process with equal process capability but different aim.

which implies that *if* the process were centered between the specification limits (at 14), then only a small proportion (about 0.27 percent) of product would be defective.

However, when we calculate C_{pk}, we obtain

$$\hat{C}_{pk} = \min\left[\frac{16-8}{6}, \frac{20-16}{6}\right] = 0.67$$

which alerts us that the process mean is *currently* nearer the USL. (Note that, if the process were centered at 14, the value of C_{pk} would be 1.0.) An acceptable process will require reducing the standard deviation and/or centering the mean.

Note that, if the *actual* average is equal to the midpoint of the specification range, then $C_{pk} = C_p$.

The higher the value of C_{pk}, the lower will be the amount of product which is outside specification limits. In certifying suppliers, some organizations use C_{pk} as one element of certification criteria. In these applications, the value of C_{pk} desired from suppliers can be a function of the type of commodity being purchased.

A capability index can also be calculated around a target value rather than the actual average. This index, called C_{pm} or the Taguchi index, focuses on reduction of variation from a target value rather than reduction of variability to meet specifications. See Boyles (1991) and Kane (1986) for discussion of the formulas and meaning.

Two types of process capability studies are as follows:

1. *Study of process potential.* In this study, an estimate is obtained of what the process *can* do under certain conditions, i.e., variability under short-run defined conditions for a process in a state of statistical control. The C_p index estimates the process capability.
2. Study of process performance. In this study, an estimate of capability provides a picture of what the process *is* doing over an extended period of time. A state of statistical control is also assumed. The C_{pk} index estimates the capability.

17.9 ESTIMATING INHERENT OR POTENTIAL CAPABILITY FROM A CONTROL-CHART ANALYSIS

In a process-potential study, data are collected from a process operating without changes in material batches, workers, tools, or process settings. This short-term evaluation uses consecutive production over one time period. Such an analysis should be preceded by a control chart analysis in which any assignable causes have been detected and eliminated from the process.

As specification limits usually apply to individual values, control limits for sample averages cannot be compared to specification limits. To make a comparison, we must first convert $\bar{R}$ to the standard deviation for individual values, calculate the $\pm 3\sigma$ limits, and compare them to the specification limits. This is explained below.

If a process is in statistical control, it is operating with the minimum amount of variation possible (the variation due to chance causes). If, and only if, a process is in statistical control, the following relationship holds for using s as an estimate of σ:

$$s = \frac{\bar{R}}{d_2}$$

Table I in the Appendix and Table 17.5 provide values of d_2. Knowing the standard deviation, process capability limits can be set at $\pm 3s$ and this used as an estimate of 3σ.

For the data of Figure 17.3 (machine N-5):

$$s = \frac{\bar{R}}{d_2} = \frac{6.0}{2.534} = 2.37$$

and $\pm 3s = \pm 3(2.37) = 7.11$

or $6s = 14.22$ (or 0.0l42 in the original data units)

The specification was 0.258 ± 0.005.

Thus,   USL $= 0.263$
LSL $= 0.253$

Then,

$$C_p = \frac{\text{USL} - \text{LSL}}{6s} = \frac{0.263 - 0.253}{0.0142} = 0.72$$

Even if the process is perfectly centered at 0.258 (and it was not), it is not capable.

The Assumption of Statistical Control and Its Effect on Process Capability

All statistical predictions assume a stable population. In a statistical sense, a stable population is one which is repeatable, that is, a population that is in a state of statistical control. The statistician rightfully insists that this be the case before predictions can be made. The manufacturing engineer also insists that the process conditions (feeds, speeds, etc.) be fully defined.

In practice, the original control chart analysis will often show the process to be out of statistical control. (It may or may not be meeting product specifications.) However, an investigation may show that the causes cannot be economically eliminated from the process. In theory, a process capability prediction should not be made until the process is in statistical control. However, in practice, some kind of comparison of capability to product tolerances is needed. The danger in delaying the comparison is that the assignable causes may never be eliminated from the process. The resulting indecision will thereby prolong interdepartmental bickering on whether "the tolerance is too tight" or "manufacturing is too careless."

A good way to start is by plotting individual measurements against specification limits. This may show that the process can meet the product specifications even with assignable causes present. If a process has assignable causes of variation but is able to meet the specifications, usually no economic problem exists. The statistician can properly point out that a process with assignable variation is unpredictable. This point is well taken, but in establishing priorities of quality improvement efforts, processes that are meeting tolerances are seldom given high priority.

If a process is out of control and the causes cannot be economically eliminated, the standard deviation and process capability limits can nevertheless be computed (with the out-of-control points included). These limits will be inflated because the process will not be operating at its best. In addition, the instability of the process means that the prediction is approximate.

It is important to distinguish between a process that is in a state of statistical control and a process that is meeting specifications. A state of statistical control does not necessarily mean that the product from the process conforms to specifications. Statistical control limits on sample averages *cannot* be directly compared to specification limits because the control limits refer to individual units. For some processes which are not in control, the specifications are being met and no action is required; other processes are in control but the specifications are not being met, and action is needed (see Section 17.5).

In summary, we need processes that are both stable (in statistical control) and capable (meeting product specifications).

17.10 MEASURING PROCESS PERFORMANCE

A process performance study collects data from a process that is operating under typical conditions but includes normal changes in material batches, workers, tools, or process settings. This study, which spans a longer term than the process potential study, also requires that the process be in statistical control.

The capability index for a process-performance study is:

$$C_{pk} = \min\left[\frac{\bar{X} - \text{LSL}}{3s}, \frac{\text{USL} - \bar{X}}{3s}\right]$$

Example 17.3. Consider a pump cassette used to deliver intravenous solutions (Baxter Travenol Laboratories, 1986). A key quality characteristic is the volume of solution delivered in a predefined time. The specification limits are:

$$\text{USL} = 103.5, \qquad \text{LSL} = 94.5$$

A control chart was run for 1 month and no out-of-control points were encountered. From the control chart data:

$$\bar{X} = 98.2 \qquad \text{and} \qquad s = 0.98$$

Figure 17.10 shows the process data and the specification limits.
The capability index is

$$C_{pk} = \min\left[\frac{98.2 - 94.5}{3(0.98)}, \frac{103.5 - 98.2}{3(0.98)}\right]$$

$$C_{pk} = 1.26$$

For many applications, this is an acceptable value of C_{pk}.

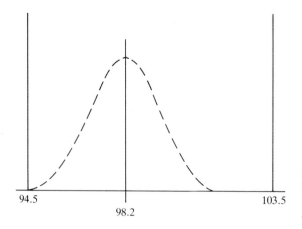

FIGURE 17.10
Delivered volume of solution. (*From Baxter Travenol Laboratories, 1986.*)

Interpretation of C_{pk}

In using C_{pk} to evaluate a process, we must recognize that C_{pk} is an abbreviation of two parameters—the average and the standard deviation. Such an abbreviation can inadvertently mask important detail on these parameters, e.g., Figure 17.11 shows that three extremely different processes can all have the same C_{pk} (in this case $C_{pk} = 1$).

Increasing the value of C_{pk} may require a change in the process average, the process standard deviation, or both. For some processes, it may be easier to increase the value of C_{pk} by changing the average value (perhaps by a simple adjustment of the process aim) than by reducing the standard deviation (by investigating the many causes of variability). The histogram of the process should always be reviewed to highlight both the average and the spread of the process.

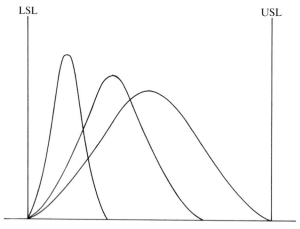

FIGURE 17.11
Three processes with $C_{pk} = 1$.

17.11 PROCESS CAPABILITY ANALYSIS
USING PROBABILITY PAPER

The use of probability paper was introduced in Chapter 9. Probability paper can also be used to determine process capability—without any calculation of the standard deviation.

For example, a sample of 100 measurements on total indicator reading (TIR) was grouped into a frequency distribution of ten cells. The frequencies were then plotted on normal probability paper (Figure 17.12). The measurements are plotted and are observed to follow a straight line (indicating that the population is normally distributed). The left-hand vertical scale shows the cumulative percent of the population under a value of TIR; the right-hand vertical scale shows the cumulative percentage over a value of TIR and also the number of standard deviations from the mean. The upper and lower horizontal grid lines represent $\pm 3\sigma$, respectively. When the plotted line is extended to intersect the grid lines for $\pm 3\sigma$, the values of 0.001 and 0.059 are

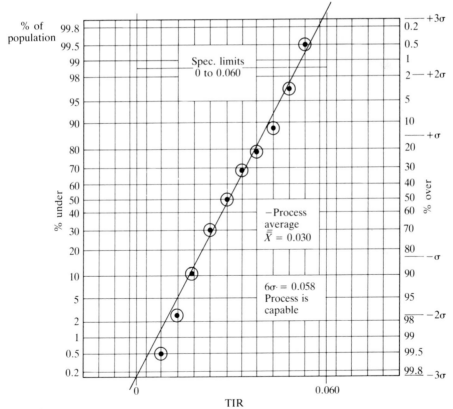

FIGURE 17.12
Capability analysis on probability paper. (*Adapted from Amsden et al., 1986.*)

read, indicating that 99.73 percent of the population will fall between 0.001 and 0.059. The $\pm 3\sigma$ capability is then calculated as $0.059 - 0.001$, or 0.058. As the C_{pk} specification range is 0.060, the value is $0.060/0.058 = 1.03$. As before, we are assuming that the process is in statistical control.

By extending the plotted line to intersect the specification limits (shown as vertical lines), the percentage of nonconforming product can be predicted. Essentially, zero percent will fall below the lower specification limit or above the upper specification limit.

The mean value can also be quickly estimated from the plot. Enter the vertical axis on the 50 percent line. This line intersects the diagonal at 0.030 on the horizontal scale.

The probability-paper approach has a few advantages. The term "standard deviation" (still a mystery to most people even after it is explained) is avoided. The plot provides an approximate test of normality. When data are limited, the probability-paper plot may be more valuable than comparing a histogram to the theoretical "bell shape" because small samples frequently yield histograms having many peaks and valleys, making it difficult to judge the underlying shape. Finally, Weibull probability paper could be used to allow for skewed or other unusual distributions.

17.12 THE ASSUMPTIONS UNDERLYING A PROCESS CAPABILITY STUDY

The interpretation of capability indices such as C_p and C_{pk} rests on a base of several assumptions:

1. The process is in a state of statistical control (see Section 17.9 "The Assumption of Statistical Control and Its Effect on Process Capability."
2. Sufficient data are collected during the capability study to minimize the sampling error for the capability indices. Lewis (1991) provides tables of 95 percent lower confidence limits for values of C_p and C_{pk}. If fewer than about 100 values make up the data, then the lower confidence limits should be calculated.
3. The data are collected over a sufficient period of time to ensure that the process conditions present during the study are representative of current and future conditions.
4. The parameter analyzed in the study follows a normal probability distribution. Otherwise, the percentages of product associated with values of C_p and C_{pk} are incorrect.

In the real world, assumptions are never fully met. *But the assumptions stated above should not be taken lightly.* See Gunter (1989) for a discussion of the effect on interpreting C_p and C_{pk} when these assumptions are not met.

17.13 ATTRIBUTES CONTROL CHARTS

Control charts for $\bar{X}$, R, and X require that actual numerical measurements be made, e.g., line width from a photoresist process. Control charts for attributes data require only a count of observations on a characteristic, e.g., the number of nonconforming items in a sample.

Examples of Attributes Charts

The fraction nonconforming (p) chart will be illustrated with data on magnets used in electrical relays. For each of 19 weeks, the number of magnets inspected and the number of nonconforming magnets were recorded. The total number of magnets tested was 14,091. The total number found to be nonconforming was 1030. The average sample size was

$$\bar{n} = \frac{14,091}{19} = 741.6$$

The average fraction nonconforming was

$$\bar{p} = \frac{1030}{14,091} = 0.073$$

Control limits for the chart were placed at

$$\bar{p} \pm 3\sigma_p = \bar{p} \pm 3\sqrt{\frac{\bar{p}(1-\bar{p})}{\bar{n}}} = 0.073 \pm 3\sqrt{\frac{0.073(1-0.073)}{741.6}}$$

$$= 0.073 \pm 0.0287 = 0.102 \quad \text{and} \quad 0.044$$

Note that these control limits are based on the *average* sample size.

The resulting control chart is shown in Figure 17.13. Note that the last sample is below the lower control limit, indicating a significantly low fraction

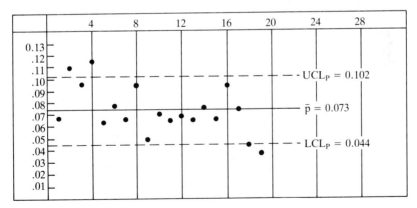

FIGURE 17.13
p chart for permanent magnets.

nonconforming. Although this might mean that there is some assignable cause resulting in better quality, such points can also be due to (1) an inspector's accepting some nonconforming units in error or (2) the sample size being quite different from the average used to calculate the limits. Note that three points are beyond the control limits even though the data were included in calculating the control limits. A fascinating and powerful feature of control limits is their ability to detect the presence of (at least some) special causes even though the control limits were influenced by those causes.

Leonard (1986) reports on the application of a p chart to recruiting new employees at the Rogers Corporation. Figure 17.14 shows a plot of the percentage of open job requisitions filled during calendar quarters. All of the

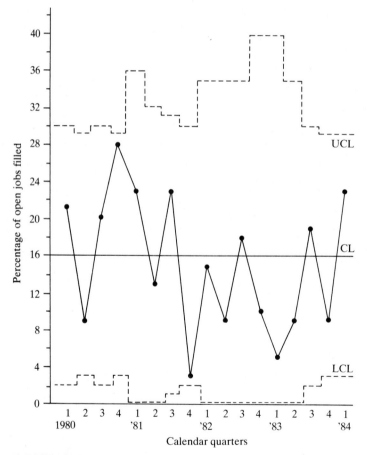

FIGURE 17.14
p chart of jobs filled as a percentage of jobs open by quarter (January 1, 1980–April 2, 1984). (*From Leonard, 1986.*)

points fall within the control limits, indicating that the variation is due to a system of common causes. Reducing that variation requires action "across the board" (as the team called it) rather than analyzing the cause of a low value such as three percent in the fourth quarter of 1981. Note that the control limits vary for each quarter. Instead of using an *average* sample size to calculate one set of control limits, the exact sample size is substituted in the formula to obtain the precise limits for each quarter. The price we pay for this precision is the difficulty in explaining why the control limits vary.

The c chart will be illustrated for nonconformities on paper sheets (Figure 17.15). Specimen sheets 11 by 17 inches in size were taken from production at intervals, and colored ink was applied to one side of the sheet. Each individual inkblot which appeared on the other side of the sheet within five minutes was counted as a nonconformity. Twenty-five sheets were inspected and a total of 200 nonconformities found.

The centerline of the chart is located at $\bar{c} = 200/25 = 8.0$ defects per sheet. Control limits were calculated as $8.0 \pm 3\sqrt{8.0}$, or 0 and 16.5. Again, note a point that is beyond the control limit even though the datum was included in calculating the limit.

Control charts can also be plotted for the number of nonconformities per unit of product, u. Such charts are useful when several independent nonconformities (they must be independent) may occur in one unit of product, as in complex assemblies.

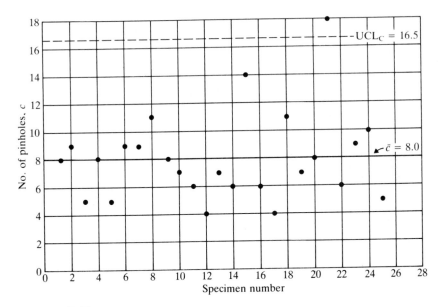

FIGURE 17.15
c chart for pinholes in paper.

The control chart lines for sample size n are:

$$\text{Central line} = \bar{u}$$
$$\text{Upper control limit} = \bar{u} + 3\sqrt{\bar{u}/n}$$
$$\text{Lower control limit} = \bar{u} - 3\sqrt{\bar{u}/n}$$

where $\bar{u}$ is the total number of nonconformities in all samples divided by the total number of units in all samples, that is, the nonconformities per unit in the complete set of test results. For samples of unequal size, control limits are computed for each size separately, using a pooled value of $\bar{u}$.

Control charts for p, c, or u are often plotted without statistical control limits. When such charts are installed on a process, a dramatic and quick improvement in quality may occur. There can be several reasons for such an improvement. First, the chart may provide tangible evidence that management is truly concerned with quality. Second, the chart may provide an operator with useful information that was not available before.

17.14   SPECIAL CONTROL CHARTS

The previous paragraphs presented the basic types of control charts for variables and attributes data—the ones needed for most applications. Sometimes other types of control charts are employed to address special needs. Such special control charts have ingenious aspects, and several types will be mentioned below to encourage the reader to explore further.

The *zone control chart* is a chronological plot of the cumulative sum of deviations of normally distributed observations from a target value (Jaehn, 1989). Divided into six zones corresponding to 1σ, 2σ, and 3σ intervals from the target, the chart provides a simple method of identifying shifts in the process average (Figure 17.16).

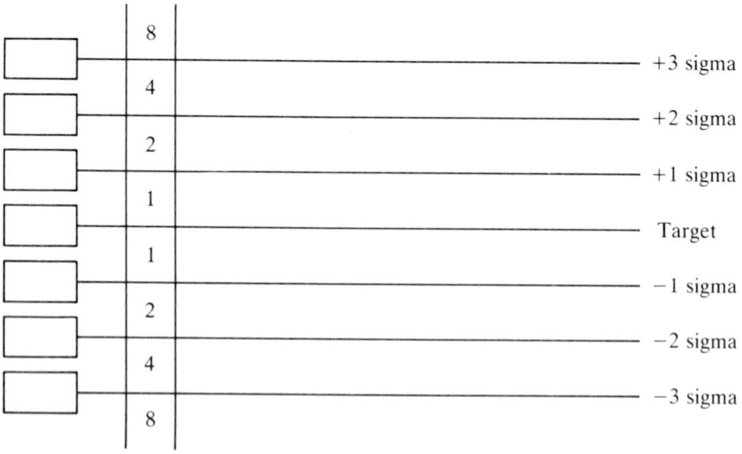

FIGURE 17.16
Basic zone control chart. (*From Jaehn, 1989.*)

This chart integrates four statistical tests for instability:

- A single point outside the 3σ limit
- Two of three successive points in the $2\sigma/3\sigma$ zones
- Four of five successive points in the $1\sigma/2\sigma$ zone
- Eight successive points in the 1σ zone or beyond

(Note the similarity to tests 1, 2, 5, and 6 in Figure 17.3.) Thus, the decision of when to take action depends not only on having a point outside the $\pm 3\sigma$ limits but also on the interpretation of unusual patterns within the $\pm 3\sigma$ limits.

To plot, we convert original test results to scores of 1, 2, 4, or 8 depending on the zone in which the result falls (see left-hand side of Figure 17.16). Figure 17.17 illustrates the procedure for a sample of seven test results from a process (at Consolidated Papers, Inc.) with a target of 50.0 and a standard deviation of 1.0. The first result of 50.2 is recorded in the zone between the target (50.0) and the $+1\sigma$ limit (51.0). The result is shown as a circle with a score of 1 based on the standard zone scoring system. The second result (51.8) is shown in the $+1\sigma$ to $+2\sigma$ zone as a circle with a cumulative score of 3, the sum of the previous score of 1 and the new score of 2. The procedure continues until a result falls on the opposite side of the target; then the score accumulation process ends and a new one begins, i.e., for a result of 49.3, a zone score of 1 is again assigned. If a result falls on the target, its zone score is 0; if a result falls exactly on one of the other zone lines, use the lower zone score.

A zone score of 8 or more is a signal for action—the process has shifted away from the established target. Following corrective action, the scoring process starts anew. Note the simplicity of plotting only circles, with scores, in a zone—this avoids the need to plot exact data values.

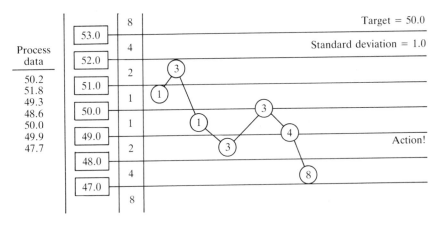

FIGURE 17.17
Illustration of zone control chart procedure. (*From Jaehn, 1989.*)

Application of the zone control chart has been particularly effective in the chemical and processing industries. Fang and Case (1990) provide further discussion of the zone control chart and offer suggestions for extending its effectiveness.

The *cumulative sum* (CUMSUM) *control chart* is a chronological plot of the cumulative sum of deviations of a sample statistic (e.g., $\bar{X}$, R, number of nonconformities) from a reference value (e.g., the nominal or target specification). By definition, the CUMSUM chart focuses on a target value rather than the actual average of process data. The control limits are neither parallel nor fixed; the limits are typically displayed in a V-shaped mask (Figure 17.18) which is constructed based on process data and which is placed onto the chart and moved as a new point is plotted. Each point plotted contains information from all observations (i.e., a *cumulative* sum). CUMSUM charts are particularly useful in detecting small shifts in the process average (say 0.5σ to 2.0σ). Calculations for constructing the chart shown in Figure 17.18 are given in QCH4, pages 24.26–24.29.

Another special chart is the *moving average chart*. This is a chronological plot of the moving average, which is calculated as the average value updated by dropping the oldest individual measurement and adding the newest individual measurement. Thus, a new average is calculated with each individual measurement. A further refinement is the *exponentially weighted moving average* (EWMA) *chart*. In the EWMA chart, the observations are weighted with the highest weight given to the most recent data. Moving average charts are effective in detecting small shifts, highlighting trends, and making use of data in processes in which it takes a long time to produce a single item.

Wadsworth et al. (1986, Chapter 8) present the details for these and other special control charts. *Multivariate control charts*, which plot a sample statistic

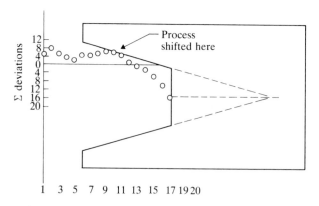

FIGURE 17.18
Cumulative sum control chart. (*From QCH4, p. 24.29.*)

that includes data from more than one variable, are discussed by Ryan (1989, Chapter 9).

17.15 STATISTICAL PROCESS CONTROL AND QUALITY IMPROVEMENT

In Chapter 1, "Basic Concepts," we distinguished between control and improvement. The control process detects and takes action on *sporadic* quality problems; the improvement process identifies and takes action on *chronic* quality problems.

In the control process, statistical control charts detect the existence of special causes of variation which result in sporadic problems. The charts show this in the form of sample data falling beyond statistical control limits, i.e., the process is "out of statistical control." Conversely, when a chart shows a process to be "in statistical control," the process is in a state of stability with variation due to a set of common causes inherent in the process. Statistical control means stability but stability does not always mean customer satisfaction with the result. Unfortunately, a process in statistical control can have serious quality problems. As the process is stable, the problems will continue (become chronic) unless a basic change in the system of common causes is made. Such a change, which typically affects the average or variation, is the job of improvement. "Removal of a special cause of variation, to move toward statistical control, important though it may be, is not improvement of the process" (Deming, 1986, p. 338).

Process improvement is directed at several different problems:

1. *The process average is misdirected:* Table 17.7 shows possible corrective action.
2. *The inherent variability of the process is too large:* Table 17.7 provides some of the arsenal of approaches available to reduce the variability.
3. *The instrumentation is inadequate:* See Section 18.9, "Errors of Measurement."
4. *There is a process drift:* Here the need is to quantify the amount of drift in a given period of time and to provide a means of resetting the process to compensate for this drift.
5. *There are cyclical changes in the process:* The need is to identify the underlying cause and either remove it or reduce the effect on the process.
6. *The process is erratic:* Sudden changes can take place in processes. As the capability studies quantify the size of these changes and help to discover the reasons for them, appropriate planning action can be taken:
   - *Temporary phenomena* (e.g., a cold machine coming up to operating temperature) can be dealt with by scheduling warming periods plus checks at the predicted time of stability.

TABLE 17.7
Approaches to process improvement

Changing the average	Reducing variability
Adjust settings on the process equipment.	Investigate work methods and equipment factors. This includes identifying the process variables that affect the product results.
Change selected product design parameters so that the design is more robust to manufacturing conditions.	Change selected product design parameters so that the design is more robust to manufacturing conditions.
Identify the process variables that affect the product results, determine the optimum values for the variables, and set the process to these values.	Identify and reduce the causes of variability due to human inputs. The concept of system versus worker-controllable input and the concept of self-control are useful guides.
Employ automated process controls to continually measure, analyze, and adjust process variables that affect the average.	Reduce the variability of inputs to the process through an improvement program with internal and external suppliers.
	Employ automated process controls to continually measure, analyze, and adjust process variables that affect variability.

- *More enduring phenomena* (e.g., changes due to new materials) can be dealt with by specifying setup reverification at the time of introducing such changes.

   The statistical design of experiments is an essential analytical tool for improvement that goes far beyond the investigation of out-of-control points on a statistical control chart. This tool, when combined with the knowledge of

TABLE 17.8
Action to be taken

	Product meets specifications	
	Process variation small relative to specifications*	Process variation large relative to specifications*
Process is in control	Consider value in marketplace of tighter specifications. Reduce inspection.	Continue tight controls on process average.
Process is out of control	Process is erratic and unpredictable and may be heading for trouble. Investigate causes of lack of control.	

* As a rule of thumb, a process variation (sometimes called natural tolerance $= 6\sigma$) less than a third of the specification range is small; more than two-thirds is large.

those who plan and run the processes, replaces intuitive decision making with a scientific basis. See Section 10.11, "The Design of Experiments," and Section 12.3, "Parameter Design and Robust Design."

Now, how does all of this relate to customer needs?

Clearly, in using statistical process control and taking subsequent actions of any sort, the focus must be on meeting customer needs. One definition— which is far from perfect—is given by the specification limits. Limits on statistical control charts are different from specification limits. In some situations, a process is not in statistical control but may not require action since the product specifications are easily being met; in other situations, a process is in statistical control, but the product specifications are not being met.

If a product *does not* meet specifications, then some type of action is needed—changing the average value, reducing the variability, doing both, changing the specifications, sorting the product, etc. If a product *does* meet the specifications, the alternatives are different—taking no action, using a less precise process, or reducing the variability further (see below for reasons why). Table 17.8 shows the more usual permutations encountered and provides suggestions on the type of action to be taken.

17.16 PURSUIT OF DECREASED PROCESS VARIABILITY

Suppose results on a product characteristic meet specification limits, the average value is equal to the target specification, and the process is in a state of statistical control (see Table 17.8). Should any action be taken to reduce the process variability further? Maybe. To decide, we need to analyze the benefits

TABLE 17.8 (*Continued*)

	Product meets specifications	
	Process variation small relative to specifications*	Process variation large relative to specifications*
Process is in control	Process is "misdirected" to wrong average. Generally easy to correct permanently.	Process may be misdirected and also too scattered. Correct misdirection. Consider economics of more precise process versus wider specifications versus sorting the product.
Process is out of control	Process is misdirected or erratic or both. Correct misdirection. Discover cause of lack of control. Consider economics of more precise process versus wider specifications versus sorting the product.	

of further reductions in variability on some characteristics versus the benefits of other improvement activities.

Lower variability mobilizes an army of marvelous advantages:

- Lower variability on a component characteristic may be the only way to compensate for high variability in other components and thereby meet performance requirements on an assembly or system. This may also require strict control of the average values of each component, as was the case in the design and manufacture of undersea cable.
- Lower variability may result in improved product performance that is discernible by the customer. Sullivan (1984) describes a case of two Sony plants making the same television set (Figure 17.19). The San Diego plant had no product outside specifications, but the distribution was virtually rectangular, with a large percentage of product close to the specification limits. In contrast, the plant in Japan did have some product outside of specification limits, but the distribution was normal and was concentrated around the target value. Field experience revealed that product near the specification limits generated complaints from customers. This and other reasons led to a higher loss per unit at San Diego even though that plant was superior in meeting the specification. The higher internal loss due to complaints would, of course, likely result in lower future sales.
- On some characteristics such as weight, lower variability may provide the opportunity to change the process average. Thus, reducing the standard deviation of fill content in a food package permits a reduction in the *average* fill, thereby resulting in cost reduction (Figure 17.20). Imagine the cumulative cost reduction over millions of packages!

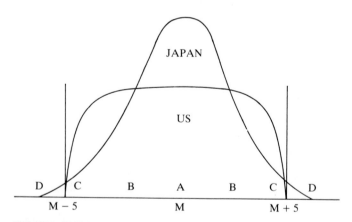

FIGURE 17.19
Uniformity and production quality of television sets produced in Japan and the United States, (*From Sullivan, 1984.*)

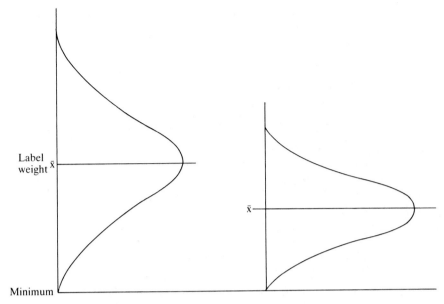

FIGURE 17.20
Reducing average overfill by reducing the standard deviation.

- Lower variability results in less need for inspection. In the extreme case, if there were *no* variability, inspection of only one unit of product would tell the whole story.
- Lower variability may command a premium price on a product. Some electronic components have traditionally been priced as a function of the amount of variability.
- Lower variability may be a competitive factor in determining market share. Increasingly, meeting specification limits is no longer sufficient. Industrial customers in particular realize that high variability of purchased material and components often requires that they make frequent (and costly) adjustments to their own processes in order to compensate for the variability of purchased products. The result is that these customers compare suppliers on variability of important product characteristics.

Example 17.4. The marketing manager of a commodity chemicals manufacturer describes two scenarios—old and new—between a customer and a salesperson.

Old scenario:
   Customer: "Your product quality is no good."
   Salesperson: "I'll lower the price."
   Customer: "Good, that's what I wanted to hear."

New scenario:

> Customer: "Your product quality is no good."
> Salesperson: "I'll lower the price."
> Customer: "The price is acceptable; I said your quality is no good."
> Salesperson: "Was some of the product out of specification?"
> Customer: "No."
> Salesperson: "I don't understand."
> Customer: "Look at these data." (Figure 17.21)
> Customer: "It's not enough to meet the specifications. Your competitor meets the same specification with less variability."

With a zeal for reducing variability, the Hughes Company has published a list of 219 "variability reduction specialists" who offer advice throughout the organization.

17.17 THE LOSS FUNCTION

The amount of variability can be related to economic loss through a *loss function*. Under this concept, *any* deviation from a target value results in a loss (Figure 17.22). With traditional thinking, a loss occurs only when a product exceeds specification limits.

The loss function is a formula that predicts loss as a function of deviation.

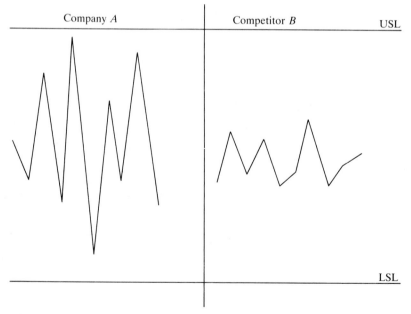

FIGURE 17.21
Variation and competition.

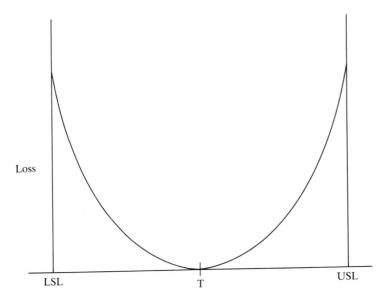

FIGURE 17.22
Loss function.

For example, a quadratic loss function is:

$$L = k(X - T)^2$$

where L = loss in monetary terms
k = cost coefficient
X = value of quality characteristic
T = target value

When the loss function is parabolic (Figure 17.22), then

$$k = \frac{c}{d^2}$$

where c = loss associated with a unit produced at a specification limit, assuming the loss for a unit at the target T is zero
d = distance from the target to the specification limit

Data collected for the television set production cited previously showed the following loss function:

$$L = \frac{4\sigma^2}{5^2} = 0.16\sigma^2$$

Then

$$\text{For San Diego:} \quad L = 0.16\left(\frac{10}{\sqrt{12}}\right)^2 = 1.33$$

$$\text{For Japan:} \quad L = 0.16\left(\frac{10}{6}\right)^2 = 0.44$$

San Diego had a higher loss per unit, even though that facility was producing a higher percentage of product within specification limits.

The concept of a loss function is intriguing (see Byrne and Taguchi, 1986, for elaboration). Certain assumptions are involved, e.g., the function is quadratic and cost and other data are available. Also, the matter of consumer insensitivity to "small" deviations from the target may mean that the loss function is more complicated—and determining the point of insensitivity may be difficult. Putting this all into perspective, the concept of a loss function is a healthy challenge to the conventional wisdom that the ultimate goal is to meet specification limits. Thus, a convincing case can be made that decreased variability (beyond meeting specification limits) can result in reduced costs and increased sales income. But are there situations in which a product meets specification limits and efforts to pursue a further reduction in variability are *not* worthwhile? To illustrate (an example provided by A. Blanton Godfrey), consider the drawing of wire through dies. The variability in wire dimension can be reduced by changing the die more frequently. But such changes will increase the cost of dies and result in disruptions in production. Industrial processes contain many similar examples. Conceptually, the need is to minimize *total* costs, not just minimize the cost of deviations from a target.

In summary, whether to pursue further reduction in variability on a product characteristic that meets specifications requires that the benefits that could be accrued be compared to the benefits by assigning improvement resources to other quality opportunities. In the simplest case, resources should not be assigned to a component that is functioning satisfactorily when there are other components with high failure rates or, even more basic, when there are customer needs that require a change in product features. Potential activities for reducing variability should be viewed as improvement project *nominations* which must face a priority test against other improvement nominations.

Note that this chapter focuses on the variability of product characteristics and its relationship to specification limits. A broader issue of improvement is the ability of existing product features to meet customer needs (see Chapter 11, "Understanding Customer Needs").

SUMMARY

Statistical process control (SPC) is the application of statistical methods to the measurement and analysis of variation of any process.

- Measurements for manufacturing and other operations should be based on input from customers, provide for both evaluation and feedback, and include early, concurrent, and lagging indicators of performance.
- A statistical control chart is a graphic comparison of process-performance data to computed statistical control limits drawn as limit lines on the chart.

- A control chart distinguishes between common causes and special causes of variation.
- A state of statistical control has important advantages for any process.
- Control charts come in many types for both variables data and attributes data.
- PRE-Control is a statistical technique for detecting process conditions and changes which may cause defects.
- Process capability is the measured, inherent reproducibility of a product turned out by a process.
- Capability ratios help to quantify process capability.
- Decreased process variability has important advantages. The amount of variability can be related to economic loss through a loss function.

PROBLEMS

17.1. A large manufacturer of watches makes some of its own parts and buys some other parts from a supplier. The supplier submits lots of parts that meet the specifications of the horologist. The supplier thus wishes to keep a continuous check on its production of watch parts. One gear has been a special problem. A check of 25 samples of five pieces gave the following data on a key dimension:

$$\bar{\bar{X}} = 0.3175 \text{ cm} \qquad \bar{R} = 0.00508 \text{ cm}$$

What criterion should be set up to determine when the process is out of control? How should this criterion compare with the specification? What are some alternatives if the criterion is not compatible with the specification?

17.2. A manufacturer of dustless chalk is concerned with the density of the product. Previous analysis has shown that the chalk has the required characteristics only if the density is between 4.4 g/cm^2 and 5.04 g/cm^2. If a sample of 100 pieces gives an average of 4.8 and a standard deviation of 0.2, is the process aimed at the proper density? If not, what should the aim be? Is the process capable of meeting the density requirements? Calculate C_p and C_{pk}.

17.3. The head of an automobile engine must be machined so that both the surface that meets the engine block and the surface that meets the valve covers are flat. These surfaces must also be 4.875 ± 0.001 in. apart. Presuming that the valve-cover side of the head is finished correctly, compare the capability of two processes for performing the finishing of the engine-block side of the head. A broach set up to do the job gave an average thickness of 4.877 in. with an average range of 0.0005 in. for 25 samples of four each. A milling machine gave an average of 4.875 in. and average range of 0.001 in. for 20 samples of four each. For each machine, calculate C_p and C_{pk}.

Answer: Broach $\pm 3s = \pm 0.00072$, milling machine $\pm 3s = 0.00144$.

17.4. A critical dimension on a double-armed armature has been causing trouble, and the designer has decided to change the specification from 0.033 ± 0.005 in. to 0.033 ± 0.001 in. To evaluate the proposed change, the Manufacturing Planning

Department has obtained the following coded data from the process:

Time	Left arm			Right arm			Comments
8:00	331	330	331	329	330	328	
8:30	332	331	329	327	331	329	
9:00	330	329	329	330	329	327	
9:30	332	330	331	331	332	328	
10:00	333	332	333	326	331	326	
10:30	332	331	332	329	330	331	
11:00	333	331	331	330	326	327	
11:30	332	332	333	327	326	329	
12:00	331	332	334	337	328	337	Adjustment
12:30	335	334	336	326	325	325	
1:00	333	332	332	329	332	330	
1:30	336	331	330	331	328	329	
2:00	332	334	329	332	330	329	
2:30	336	336	330	329	329	327	
3:00	329	335	338	333	330	331	Adjustment
3:30	341	333	330	329	331	332	

Comment on the proposal to change the specification.

17.5. A company manufactures an expensive chemical. The net package weight has a minimum specification value of 25.0 lb. Data from a control chart analysis show (based on 20 samples of five each):

$$\bar{\bar{X}} = 26.0 \qquad \bar{R} = 1.4$$

The points on both the average and range chart are all in control.
(a) Draw conclusions about the ability of the process to meet the specification.
(b) What action, if any, would you suggest on the process? If any action is suggested, are there any disadvantages to the action?

17.6. Samples of four units were taken from a manufacturing process at regular intervals. The width of a slot on a part was measured, and the average and range were computed for each sample. After 25 samples of four, the following coded results were obtained:

	Averages	Ranges
Upper control limit	UCL = 626	UCL = 37.5
Average value	$\bar{\bar{X}}$ = 614	$\bar{R}$ = 16.5
Lower control limit	LCL = 602	LCL = 0

All points on the $\bar{X}$ and R charts fell within control limits. The specification requirements are 610 ± 15. If the width is normally distributed and the distribution centered at $\bar{\bar{X}}$, what percentage of product would you expect to fall outside the specification limits?

Answer: 9.4 percent.

17.7. (*a*) What kind of conclusion about a process can be made from an average and range control chart that cannot be made from a histogram?

   (*b*) What kind of conclusion can be made from a histogram that cannot be made from an average and range control chart?

17.8. The percentage of water absorption is an important characteristic of common building brick. A certain company occasionally measured this characteristic of its product, but records were never kept. It was decided to analyze the process with a control chart. Twenty-five samples of four bricks each yielded these results:

Sample number	$\bar{X}$	R	Sample number	$\bar{X}$	R
1	15.1	9.1	14	9.8	17.5
2	12.3	9.9	15	8.8	10.5
3	7.4	9.7	16	8.1	4.4
4	8.7	6.7	17	6.3	4.1
5	8.8	7.1	18	10.5	5.7
6	11.7	9.1	19	9.7	6.4
7	10.2	12.1	20	11.7	4.6
8	11.5	10.8	21	13.2	7.2
9	11.2	13.5	22	12.5	8.3
10	10.2	6.9	23	7.5	6.4
11	9.6	5.0	24	8.8	6.9
12	7.6	8.2	25	8.0	6.4
13	7.6	5.4			

Plot the data on an average and range control chart with control limits. Comment.

   Answer: 15.8 and 3.97; 18.4 and 0.

17.9. The specification on a certain dimension is 3.000 ± 0.004 in. A large sample from the process indicates an average of 2.998 in and a standard deviation of 0.002 in. Suppose that controls are instituted to shift the process average to the nominal specification of 3.000. Each part outside specification limits results in a loss of $5. In a lot of 1000 parts, how much monetary saving would be achieved by shifting the average as compared to keeping it at 2.998?

   Answer: $573

17.10. A statistical control chart for averages and ranges has been used to help control a manufacturing process. The sample data are consistently within control limits and the control limits are inside the engineering tolerance limits. The supervisor is confused because a high percentage of product is outside the tolerance limits even though the process is within control limits. What is your explanation?

17.11. The following data represent the number of defects found on each sewing machine cabinet inspected:

Sample number	Number of defects	Sample number	Number of defects
1	8	14	6
2	10	15	4
3	7	16	7
4	7	17	5
5	8	18	8
6	6	19	6
7	9	20	4
8	8	21	5
9	4	22	7
10	7	23	4
11	9	24	5
12	6	25	5
13	5		

Plot a control chart with control limits. Comment on the chart.

17.12. A sample of 100 electrical connectors was inspected each shift. Three characteristics were inspected on each connector but each connector was classified simply as defective or acceptable. The results follow:

Sample number	Defective, %	Sample number	Defective, %
1	4	14	4
2	3	15	4
3	5	16	5
4	6	17	3
5	7	18	0
6	5	19	3
7	4	20	2
8	2	21	1
9	5	22	3
10	6	23	4
11	4	24	2
12	3	25	2
13	3		

(a) Plot a control chart with control limits. Comment on the chart.
(b) If the inspection results had been recorded in sufficient detail, what other type of chart could also have been plotted?

Answer: (a) 9.2 percent, 0.

17.13. An average and range chart based on a sample size of five has been run, with the following results:

	Averages	Ranges
Upper control limit	78.0	8.0
Average value	75.8	3.8
Lower control limit	73.6	0

How large an increase in the overall process average would have to occur in order to have a 30 percent chance that a sample average will exceed the upper control limit?

Answer: 1.83.

17.14. As part of a quality improvement program, a textile manufacturer decides to use a control chart to monitor the number of imperfections in bolts of cloth. The data from the last 25 inspections are recorded in the following table. From these data, compute control limits for an appropriate type of control chart. Plot the chart.

Bolt of cloth	Number of imperfections	Bolt of cloth	Number of imperfections
1	14	14	22
2	5	15	1
3	10	16	6
4	19	17	14
5	0	18	8
6	6	19	6
7	2	20	9
8	9	21	7
9	8	22	1
10	7	23	5
11	3	24	12
12	12	25	4
13	1	Total	191

Answer: Limits are 15.93 and 0.

17.15. Control chart data were collected for the softening point (in degrees) in a polymerization process. Based on 25 samples of four each, the following control limits were calculated:

	Averages	Ranges
Upper control limit	12.9	13.4
Average value	9.4	5.9
Lower control limit	5.9	0

Suppose that the population average shifts to 12.4. How large a sample would be necessary to have a 25 percent probability that the control chart for averages will signal out of control?

17.16. A p chart is to be used to analyze the September record for 100 percent inspection of certain radio components. The total number inspected during the month was 2196, and the total number of defectives was 158. Compute $\bar{p}$. Compute control limits for the following three days, and state whether the percentage defective falls within control limits for each day.

Date	Number inspected	Number of defectives
Sept. 14	54	8
Sept. 15	162	24
Sept. 16	213	3

REFERENCES

Amsden, R. T., H. E. Butler, and D. M. Amsden (1986). *SPC Simplified: Practical Steps to Quality,* UNIPUB, White Plains, New York.

Baxter Travenol Laboratories (1986). *Statistical Process Control Guideline,* Deerfield, Illinois, p. 17.

Boyles, Russell A. (1991). "The Taguchi Capability Index," *Journal of Quality Technology,* January, pp. 17–26.

Byrne, Diane M., and Shin Taguchi (1986). "The Taguchi Approach to Parameter Design," *ASQC Quality Congress Transactions,* Milwaukee, pp. 168–177.

Deming, W. E. (1986). *Out of the Crisis,* Massachusetts Institute of Technology, Center for Advanced Engineering Study, Cambridge, Massachusetts.

Edgeman, Rick L., and Susan B. Athey (1990). "Digidot Plots for Process Surveillance," *Quality Progress,* May, pp. 66–68.

Fang, Jengung, and Kenneth E. Case (1990). "Improving the Zone Control Chart.," *ASQC Quality Congress Transactions,* Milwaukee, pp. 494–500.

Flynn, Michael F., and John A. Bolcar, (1984). "The Road to Hell," *ASQC Quality Congress Transactions,* Milwaukee, pp. 192–196.

Gunter, Berton H. (1989). "The Use and Abuse of C_{pk}, Part 2." *Quality Progress,* March, pp. 108–109.

Jaehn, Alfred H. (1989). "Zone Control Charts Find New Applications," *ASQC Quality Congress Transactions,* Milwaukee, pp. 890–895.

Kane, Victor E. (1986). "Process Capability Indices," *Journal of Quality Technology,* vol. 18, no. 1, pp. 41–52.

Leonard, James F. (1986). "Quality Improvement in Recruiting and Employment," *Juran Report Number Six,* Winter, Juran Institute, Inc., Wilton, Connecticut, pp. 111–118.

Lewis, Sidney S. (1991). "Process Capability Estimates From Small Samples," *Quality Engineering,* vol. 3, no. 3, pp. 381–394.

Mackertech, N. A. (1990). "Precontrol vs. Control Charting: A Critical Comparison," *Quality Engineering,* vol. 2, no. 3, pp. 253–260.

Nelson, Lloyd S. (1984). "The Shewhart Control Chart-Tests for Special Causes," *Journal of Quality Technology,* vol. 16, no. 4, October, pp. 237–239.

Nelson, Lloyd S. (1985). "Interpreting Shewhart Charts," *Journal of Quality Technology,* vol. 17, no. 2, pp. 114–116.

Ott, Ellis R., and Edward G. Schilling (1990). *Process Quality Control,* McGraw-Hill, Inc., New York.

Ryan, Thomas P. (1989). *Statistical Methods for Quality Improvement,* John Wiley and Sons, New York.

Schilling, E. G. (1990). "Elements of Process Control," *Quality Engineering,* vol. 2, no. 2, p. 132. Reprinted by courtesy of Marcel Dekker, Inc.

Shainin, Dorian, and Peter D. Shainin (1988). "Section 24, Statistical Process Control," in *Juran's Quality Control Handbook,* 4th ed., McGraw-Hill Book Company, New York.

Shainin, D. (1990). "Comments on 'Precontrol versus Control Charting: A Critical Comparison' by Neil A. Mackertech," *Quality Engineering,* vol. 2, no. 3, pp. 261–268.

Sullivan, L. P. (1984). "Reducing Variability: A New Approach to Quality," *Quality Progress,* July, pp. 15–21.

Wadsworth, H. M., K. S. Stephens, and A. B. Godfrey (1986). *Modern Methods for Quality Control and Improvement,* John Wiley and Sons, New York.

SUPPLEMENTARY READING

Statistical process control, general: QCH4, Section 24

Krishnamoorthi, K. S. (1990). "On Assignable Causes That Can't Be Eliminated—An Example from a Foundry," *Quality Engineering,* vol. 3, no. 1, pp. 41–47.

Life cycle of statistical process control: Schilling, E. G. (1990). "Elements of Process Control," *Quality Engineering,* vol. 2, no. 2, pp. 121–136.

Roth, G. (1989). "The Statistical Process Control Life Cycle," *Quality Engineering,* vol. 1, no. 2, pp. 117–126.

Variation: *Quality Progress,* December 1990, includes nine papers on variation.

Process capability: Pyzdek, T. (1992). "Process Capability Analysis Using Personal Computers," *Quality Engineering,* vol. 4, no. 3, pp. 419–440.

CHAPTER
18

INSPECTION, TEST, AND MEASUREMENT

18.1 THE TERMINOLOGY OF INSPECTION

Inspection and test typically include measurement of an output and comparison to specified requirements to determine conformity. Inspection is performed for a wide variety of purposes, e.g., distinguishing between good and bad product, determining if a process is changing, measuring process capability, rating product quality, securing product design information, rating the inspectors' accuracy, and determining the precision of measuring instruments. Each of these purposes has its special influence on the nature of the inspection and on the manner of doing it.

The distinction between "inspection" and "test" has become blurred. Inspection, typically performed under static conditions on items such as components, can vary from simple visual examination to a series of complex measurements. The emphasis in inspection is to determine conformance to a standard. Test, on the other hand, is performed under either static or dynamic conditions and is typically performed on more complex items such as subassemblies or systems. Test results not only determine conformance but can also be input for other analyses such as evaluating a new design, diagnosing problems, or making physical adjustments on products. Some industries have their own terms for inspection or testing, e.g., "assay" is used in the mining and pharmaceutical industries.

Although the terms "inspection" and "test" usually refer to manufacturing industries, the concepts also apply to other industries. In service industries, different terms are used, e.g., review, checking, reconciliation, examination. The evaluation made of the correctness of an income tax return, of the cleanliness of a hotel room, or of the accuracy of a bank teller's closing balance are really all forms of inspection—a measurement, a comparison to a standard, and a decision.

18.2 CONFORMANCE TO SPECIFICATION AND FITNESS FOR USE

Of all the purposes of inspection, the most ancient and the most extensively used is product acceptance, i.e., determining whether product conforms to standard, and thereby whether the product should be accepted. "Product" can mean a discrete unit, a collection of discrete units (a "lot"), a bulk product (a tank car of chemicals), or a complex system. QCH4, Table 18.6, lists the criteria for judging conformance of product in units and lots.

"Product" can also mean a service, such as a transaction at a bank, an inquiry to an agency about tax regulations, or the performance of personnel before, during, and after an airline flight. In all of these examples, inspection characteristics can be identified, standards set, and a judgment made on conformance.

Product acceptance involves the disposition of product based on its quality. This disposition involves several important decisions:

1. *Conformance:* Judging whether the product conforms to specification
2. *Fitness for use:* Deciding whether nonconforming product is fit for use
3. *Communication:* Deciding what to communicate to insiders and outsiders

The Conformance Decision

Except in small companies, the number of conformance decisions made each year is huge. There is no possibility that the supervisory body can become involved in the details of so many decisions. Hence, the work is organized so that inspectors or production workers can make these decisions themselves. To this end, they are trained to understand the products, the standards, and the instruments. Once trained, they are given the jobs of making inspections and judging conformance. (In many cases, the delegation is to automated instruments.)

Associated with the conformance decision is the disposition of conforming product. The inspector is authorized to identify the product ("stamp it up") as acceptable product. This identification then serves to inform packers, shippers, etc., that the product should proceed to its next destination (further processing, storeroom, customer). Strictly speaking, this decision to "ship" is made not by inspectors but by management. With some exceptions, product that conforms to specification is also fit for use. Hence, company procedures (which are established by the managers) provide that conforming products should be shipped as a regular practice.

The Fitness-for-Use Decision

In the case of nonconforming products, a new question arises: Is this nonconforming product fit or unfit for use? In some cases, the answer is obvious—the nonconformance is so severe as to make the product clearly unfit. Hence, it is scrapped or, if economically repairable, brought to a state of conformance. However, in many cases the answer as to fitness for use is not obvious. In such cases, if enough is at stake, a study is made to determine fitness for use. This study involves securing inputs such as the following:

- *Who will the user be*? A technologically sophisticated user may be able to deal successfully with the nonconformance; a consumer may not. A nearby user may have easy access to field service; a distant or foreign user may lack such easy access.
- *How will this product be used*? For many materials and standard products, the specifications are broad enough to cover a variety of possible uses, and it is not known at the time of manufacture the actual use to which the product will be put. For example, sheet steel may be cut up to serve as decorative plates or as structural members; a television receiver may be stationed at a comfortable range or at an extreme range; chemical intermediates may be employed in numerous formulas.
- *Are there risks to human safety or to structural integrity*? Where such risks are significant, all else is academic.
- *What is the urgency*? For some applications, the client cannot wait, because the product in question is critical to putting some broader system into operation. Hence, it may demand delivery now and cause repairs in the field.
- *What are the company's and the users' economics*? For some nonconformances, the economics of repair are so forbidding that the product must be used as is, although at a price discount. In some industries, e.g., textiles, the price structure formalizes this concept by use of a separate grade—"seconds."
- *What are the users' measures of fitness for use*? These may differ significantly from those available to the manufacturer. For example, a manufacturer of abrasive cloth used a laboratory test to judge the *ability* of the cloth to polish metal; a major client evaluated the *cost* per 1000 pieces polished.

TABLE 18.1
Sources of information

Input	Usual sources
Who will the user be?	Marketing
How will this product be used?	Marketing; client
Are there risks to human safety or to structural integrity?	Product research and design
What is the urgency?	Marketing; client
What are the company's and the users' economics?	All departments; client
What are the users' measures of fitness for use?	Market research; marketing; client

These and other inputs may be needed at several levels of fitness for use, i.e., the effects on the economics of subsequent processors, the marketability requirements of the merchants, the qualities that determine fitness for the ultimate user, and the qualities that influence field maintenance.

The job of securing such inputs is often assigned to a staff specialist, e.g., a quality engineer who "makes the rounds," contacting the various departments which are able to provide pertinent information. There may be a need to contact the customer and even to conduct an actual tryout. A typical list of sources is shown in Table 18.1.

Once all the information has been collected and analyzed, the fitness-for-use decision can be made. If the amount of money at stake is small, this decision will be delegated to a staff specialist, to the quality manager, or to some continuing decision-making committee such as a Material Review Board. If the amount at stake is large, the decision will usually be made by a team of upper managers. For elaboration, see QCH4, pp. 18.31–18.35.

Deliberations on the fitness-for-use decision are often a dramatic blend of voices—some balanced and judicious, others bowing to the pressures of delivery deadlines even if it means tossing up gems of earnest nonsense.

The Communication Decision

The conformance and fitness-for-use decisions are a source of essential information, although some of this is not well communicated.

Data on nonconforming products are usually communicated to the producing departments to aid them in preventing a recurrence. In more elaborate data collection systems, there may be periodic summaries to identify "repeaters," which then become the subject of special studies.

When nonconforming products are sent out as fit for use, there arises a need for two additional categories of communication:

1. *Communication to "outsiders"* (usually customers) who have a right and a need to know. All too often manufacturing companies neglect or avoid informing their customers when shipping nonconforming products. Such avoidance can be the result of bad experience, i.e., some customers will seize on such nonconformances to secure a price discount despite the fact that use of the product will not add to their own costs. Neglect is more usually a failure even to face the question of what to communicate. A major factor here is the design of the forms used to record the decisions. With rare exceptions, these forms lack provisions which force those involved to make recommendations and decisions on (a) whether to inform the outsiders and (b) what to communicate to them.

2. *Communication to insiders.* When nonconforming goods are shipped as fit for use, the reasons why are not always communicated to inspectors and especially not to production workers. The resulting vacuum of knowledge has been known to breed some bad practices. When the same type of nonconformance has been shipped several times, an inspector may conclude (in the absence of knowing why) that it is a waste of time to report such nonconformances in the first place. Yet in some future case, the special reasons which were the basis of the decision to ship the nonconforming goods may not be present. In like manner, a production worker may conclude that it is a waste of time to exert all that effort to avoid some nonconformance which will be shipped anyway. Such reactions by well-meaning employees can be minimized if the company squarely faces the question, What shall we communicate to insiders?

18.3 DISPOSITION OF NONCONFORMING PRODUCT

Once an inspector finds a lot of product to be nonconforming, he or she prepares a report to that effect. Copies of this report are sent to the various cognizant departments. This sets a planned sequence of events into motion. The lot is marked "Hold" and is often sent to a special holding area to reduce the risk of mixups. The product is put into quarantine. Schedulers look into the possibility of shortages and the need for replacement. An investigator is assigned to collect the type of information needed as inputs for the fitness-for-use decision as discussed above.

Decision Not to Ship

The investigation may conclude that the lot should not be shipped as is. In that event, the economics are studied to find the best disposition: sorting, repairing, downgrading, scrapping, etc. There may be supplemental efforts of an accounting nature to charge the costs to the responsible source, especially where supplier responsibility is involved. There is also some degree of action to prevent a recurrence (see below).

Decision to Ship

This decision may come about in one of several ways:

- *Waiver by the designer.* Such a waiver is a change in specification as to the lot in question which thereby puts the lot into a state of conformance.
- *Waiver by the customer,* or by the Marketing Department on behalf of the customer. Such a waiver in effect supersedes the specification. (The waiver may have been "bought" by a change in warranty or by a discount in price.)
- *Waiver by the Quality Department* under its delegation to make fitness-for-use decisions on noncritical matters. The criteria for "noncritical" may be based on prior seriousness classification of characteristics, on the low cost of the product involved, or on still other bases. For minor categories of seriousness, the delegation may even be made by the quality engineers or by inspection supervisors. However, as to major and critical defects, the delegation is typically by the technical manager, the quality manager, or some team of managers.
- *Waiver by a formal Material Review Board.* This board concept was originally evolved by the military buyers of defense products as a means of expediting decisions on nonconforming lots. Membership on the board includes the military representative plus the cognizant designer and the quality specialist. A unanimous decision is required to ship nonconforming product. The board procedures provide for formal documentation of the facts and conclusions, thereby creating a data source of great potential value.
- *Waiver by upper managers.* This part of the procedure is restricted to cases of a critical nature involving risks to human safety, marketability of the product, or risk of loss of large sums of money. For such cases, the stakes are too high to warrant decision making by a single department. Hence, the managerial team takes over. Waivers, however, have an insidious way of becoming part of a culture. It is valuable to continuously track the amount of product shipped under waiver of specifications, e.g., the percentage of lots shipped each month under waiver.

Corrective Action

Aside from a need to dispose of the nonconforming lot, there is a need to prevent a recurrence. This prevention process is of two types, depending on the origin of the nonconformance.

1. Some nonconformances originate in some isolated, sporadic change which took place in an otherwise well-behaved process. Examples are a mixup in the materials used, an instrument that is out of calibration, a human mistake in turning a valve too soon, etc. For such cases the local supervision is often able to identify what went wrong and to restore the process to its normal good behavior. Sometimes this troubleshooting may require the assistance of a staff specialist. In any case, no changes of a fundamental nature are involved since manufacturing planning has already established an adequate process.

2. Other nonconformances are "repeaters." They arise over and over again, as evidenced from their recurring need for disposition by the Material Review Board or other such agency. Such recurrences point to a chronic condition which must be diagnosed and remedied if the problem is to be solved. The local supervision is seldom able to find the cause of these chronic nonconformances, mainly because the responsibility for diagnosis is vague. Lacking agreement on the cause, the problem goes on and on amid earnest debates about who or what is to blame—unrealistic design, incapable process, poor motivation, etc. The need is not for troubleshooting to restore the normal good behavior, since the normal behavior is bad. Instead, the need is to organize for an improvement project, as discussed in Chapter 3.

18.4 INSPECTION PLANNING

Inspection planning is the activity of (1) designating the "stations" at which inspection should take place and (2) providing those stations with the means for knowing what to do plus the facilities for doing it. For simple, routine quality characteristics, the planning is often done by the inspector. For complex products made in large multidepartmental companies, the planning is usually done by specialists such as quality engineers.

Locating the Inspection Stations

The basic tool for choosing the location of inspection stations is the flow chart (see, for example, Figure 16.1). The most usual locations are:

- At receipt of goods from suppliers, usually called "incoming inspection" or "supplier inspection."
- Following the setup of a production process to provide added assurance against producing a defective batch. In some cases this "setup approval" also becomes approval of the batch.
- During the running of critical or costly operations, usually called "process inspection."
- Prior to delivery of goods from one processing department to another, usually called "lot approval" or "toll gate inspection."

- Prior to shipping completed products to storage or to customers, usually called "finished-goods inspection."
- Before performing a costly, irreversible operation, e.g., pouring a melt of steel.
- At natural "peepholes" in the process.

The inspection station is not necessarily a fixed zone where the work comes to the inspector. In some cases the inspector goes to the work by patrolling a large area and performing inspections at numerous locations. The inspection station need not be located in or near the production area. Some inspection may be performed in the shipping area, at the supplier's plant, or on the customer's premises.

Choosing and Interpreting Quality Characteristics

The planner prepares a list of which quality characteristics are to be checked at which inspection stations. For some of these characteristics, the planner may find it necessary to provide information that supplements the specifications. Product specifications are prepared by comparatively few people, each generally aware of the needs of fitness for use. In contrast, these specifications must be used by numerous inspectors and operators, most of whom lack such awareness. The planner can help bridge this gap in a number of ways:

- By providing inspection and test environments which simulate the conditions of use. This principle is widely used, for example, in testing electrical appliances. It is also extended to such applications as the type of lighting used for inspecting textiles.
- By providing supplementary information which goes beyond the specifications as prepared by the product designers and process engineers. Some of this information is available in published standards—company, industry, and national. Other information is specially prepared to meet the specific needs of the product under consideration. For example, in an optical goods factory, the generic term "beauty defects" was used to describe several conditions which differed widely as to their effect on fitness for use. A scratch on a lens surface in the focal plane of a microscope made the lens unfit for use. A scratch on the large lens of a pair of binoculars, although not functionally serious, was visible to the user and hence was not acceptable. Two other species of scratches were neither adverse to fitness for use nor visible to the user and hence were unimportant. Through planning analysis these distinctions were clarified and woven into the procedures.
- By helping to train inspectors and supervisors to understand the conditions of use and the "why" of the specification requirements.
- By providing seriousness classification (see Section 15.4).

Detailed Inspection Planning

For each quality characteristic, the planner determines the detailed work to be done. This determination covers such matters as:

- The type of test to be done. This may require detailed description of testing environment, testing equipment, testing procedure, and associated tolerances for accuracy.
- The number of units to be tested (sample size).
- The method of selecting the samples to be tested.
- The type of measurement to be made (attributes, variables, other).
- Conformance criteria for the units, usually the specified product tolerance limits.

Beyond this detailed planning for the characteristics and units, there is further detailed planning applicable to the product, the process, and the data system:

- Conformance criteria for the lot, usually consisting of the allowable number of nonconforming units in the sample.
- The physical disposition to be made of the product—the conforming lots, the nonconforming lots, and the units tested.
- Criteria for decisions on the process—should it run or stop?
- Data to be recorded, forms to be used, reports to be prepared.

This planning is usually included in a formal document which must be approved by the planner and the inspection supervisor. For an example from Baxter Travenol, see Figure 18.1.

Sensory Characteristics

Sensory characteristics are those for which we lack measuring instruments and for which the senses of human beings must be used as measuring instruments. Sensory qualities may involve technological performance of a product (e.g., adhesion of a protective coating), aesthetic characteristics (e.g., odor of a perfume), taste (e.g., food), or human services characteristics (e.g., the spectrum of hotel services).

An important category of sensory characteristics is the visual quality characteristic. Typically, written specifications are not clear because of their

Part Number: XXXX **Part Name: YYYY**

Process	Characteristics	C_p[1] Index	C_{pk}[1] Index	Frequency[2]	Sample size[2]	Analysis methods	Out-of-control conditions are encountered[4]
Incoming inspection	Stock thickness	1.6	1.0	Every shipment	—	Review control charts provided with each lot	Impound lot — contact supplier for resolution
In-process inspection	Thickness	1.9	1.1	Every 1000 parts	2 pieces	Micrometers/$\bar{X}$ and s chart	Correct process
	Width	1.5	1.4	Every 10,000 parts	5 pieces	Micrometer/median chart	Correct process
	Length	1.6	1.2	Every 4 hours	75 pieces	Tapered ring gage/p chart	Correct process
Assembly area	Thickness	2.0	1.8	Hourly	30 pieces	Special gage/p chart	Correct process
	Width	2.2	1.9	Chart hourly	100%	Automatic tester/u chart	Repair by responsible operator
Outgoing[3]	Complete assembly	2.8	1.9	Hourly	20 pieces	Automatic tester/$\bar{X}$ and s chart	Correct process
	Complete assembly	NA	1500 DPM	Each lot	50 pieces	Complete visual inspection plus gage and test stand/c chart	Reject lot and sort for identified nonconformance

[1] Explanations and formulas are contained in the SPC Guideline.

[2] The frequencies and sample size are determined from the performance study of the stability of each process. They are periodically reviewed and updated as required.

[3] After 6 months production experience, the process control and inspection records will be reviewed to determine if outgoing inspection can be reduced.

[4] If any nonconforming products are found in the process samples, then there will be performed 100% inspection of all products produced since the last in control point.

FIGURE 18.1
Control plan. (*From Baxter Travenol Laboratories, 1986.*)

435

inability to quantify the characteristic. Several approaches are employed to describe the limits for the characteristics. These include:

1. Providing photographs to define the limits of acceptability of the product.

   Example 18.1. A fast food enterprise has the problem of defining quality standards for suppliers of hamburger buns. The solution is photographs showing the ideal and the maximum and minimum acceptable limits for "golden brown" color, symmetry of bun, and distribution of sesame seeds.

2. Providing physical standards to define the limits of acceptability.

   Example 18.2. A government agency needed to define the lightest and darkest acceptable shades of khaki for suppliers of uniforms. Color swatches of cloth were prepared for the limiting shades and issued to inspectors. Imagine the follow-up required to periodically replace the swatches when fading was imminent!

3. Specifying the *conditions* of inspection instead of trying to explicitly define the limits of acceptability.

   Example 18.3. Riley (1979) describes a special inspection procedure for cosmetic (appearance) defects of electronic calculators. Part drawings indicate the relative importance of different surfaces, using a system of category numbers and class letters. Three categories identify the surface being inspected:
   I.   Plastic window (critical areas only)
   II. External
   III. Internal
   Three classes indicate the frequency with which the surface will be viewed by the user:
   A. Usually seen by the user
   B. Seldom seen by the user
   C. Never seen by user (except during maintenance)
   For example, a sheet-metal part that will seldom be seen carries a grade of Coating IIB.
   The conditions of inspection are stated in terms of viewing distance, viewing time, and lighting conditions. The distance and time are specified for each combination of surface being inspected and the frequency of viewing by the user. Lighting conditions are required to be between 75 and 150 foot-candles from a nondirectional source.

   The guidelines help to establish cosmetic gradings on parts drawings. However, a judgment must still be made by the inspector as to whether or not the end user would consider the flaw(s) objectionable, using the specified time and distance.

   Elaboration on sensory characteristics is provided in QCH4, pp. 18.45–18.57.

18.5 SERIOUSNESS CLASSIFICATION

Quality characteristics are decidedly unequal in their effect on fitness for use. A relative few are "serious," i.e., of critical importance; many are of minor importance. Clearly, the more important the characteristic, the greater the attention it should receive in such matters as: extent of quality planning; precision of processes, tooling, and instruments; sizes of samples; strictness of criteria for conformance; etc. However, making such discrimination requires that the relative importance of the characteristics be made known to the various decision makers involved: process engineers, quality planners, inspection supervisors, etc. To this end, many companies utilize formal systems of seriousness classification. The resulting classification is used not only in inspection and quality planning but also in specification writing, supplier relations, product audits, executive reports on quality, etc. This multiple use of seriousness classification dictates that the system be prepared by an interdepartmental committee which then:

1. Decides how many classes or strata of seriousness to create (usually three or four)
2. Defines each class
3. Classifies each characteristic into its proper class of seriousness

Characteristics and Defects

There are actually two lists which need to be classified. One is the list of quality characteristics derived from the specifications. The other is the list of "defects," i.e., symptoms of nonconformance during manufacture and of field failure during use. There is a good deal of commonality between these two lists, but there are differences as well. (For example, the list of defects found on glass bottles has little resemblance to the list of characteristics.) In addition, the two lists do not behave alike. The design characteristic "diameter," for example, gives rise to two defects—oversize and undersize. The amount by which the diameter is oversize may be decisive as to seriousness classification.

Normally, it is feasible to make one system of classification applicable to both lists. However, the uses to which the resulting classifications are put are sufficiently varied to make it convenient to publish the lists separately.

Definitions for the Classes

Most sets of definitions show the influence of the pioneering work of the Bell System in the 1920s. Study of numerous such systems reveals an inner pattern which is a useful guide to any committee faced with applying the concept to its own company. Table 18.2 shows the nature of this inner pattern as applied to a company in the food industry.

TABLE 18.2
Composite definitions for seriousness classification in the food industry

Defect	Effect on consumer safety	Effect on usage	Consumer relations	Loss to company	Effect on conformance to government relations
Critical	Will surely cause personal injury or illness	Will render the product totally unfit for use	Will offend consumers' sensibilities due to odor, appearance, etc.	Will lose customers and will result in losses greater than value of product	Fails to conform to regulations for purity, toxicity, identification
Major A	Very unlikely to cause personal injury or illness	May render the product unfit for use and may cause rejection by the user	Will likely be noticed by consumers, and will likely reduce product salability	May lose customers and may result in losses greater than the value of the product; will substantially reduce production yields	Fails to conform to regulations on weight, volume, or batch control
Major B	Will not cause injury or illness	Will make the product more difficult to use, e.g., removal from package, or will require improvisation by the user; affects appearance, neatness	May be noticed by some consumers, and may be an annoyance if noticed	Unlikely to lose customers; may require product replacement; may result in loss equal to product value	Minor nonconformance to regulations on weight, volume, or batch control, e.g., completeness of documentation
Minor	Will not cause injury or illness	Will not affect usability of the product; may affect appearance, neatness	Unlikely to be noticed by consumers, and of little concern if noticed	Unlikely to result in loss	Conforms fully to regulations

Classification

This is a long and tedious but essential task. However, it yields some welcome by-products through pointing up misconceptions and confusion among departments and thereby opening the way to clear up vagueness and misunderstandings. Then, when the final seriousness classification is applied to several different purposes, it is subjected to several new challenges which provide still further clarification of vagueness.

A problem often encountered is the reluctance of the designers to become involved in seriousness classification of characteristics. They may offer plausible reasons: all characteristics are critical, the tightness of the tolerance is an index of seriousness, etc. Yet the real reasons may be unawareness of the benefits, a feeling that other matters have higher departmental priority, etc. In such cases it may be worthwhile to demonstrate the benefits of classification by working out a small-scale example. In one company the classification-of-characteristics program reduced the number of dimensions that had to be checked from 682 to 279, the effect being to reduce inspection time from 215 minutes to 120 minutes.

18.6 AUTOMATED INSPECTION

Automated inspection and testing are widely used to reduce inspection costs, reduce error rates, alleviate personnel shortages, shorten inspection time, avoid inspector monotony, and provide still other advantages. Applications of automation have successfully been made to mechanical gaging, electronic testing (for high volumes of components as well as system circuitry), nondestructive tests of many kinds, chemical analyses, color discrimination, visual inspection (e.g., of large-scale integrated circuits), etc. In addition, automated testing is extensively used as a part of scheduled maintenance programs for equipment in the field.

Examples in nonmanufacturing activities range from the spelling check provided within word processors to the checking of bank transactions for errors.

A company contemplating the use of automated inspection first identifies those few tests which dominate the inspection budgets and use of personnel. The economics of automation are computed, and trials are made on some likely candidates for a good return on investment. As experience is gained, the concept is extended further and further.

With the emphasis on defect levels in the parts-per-million range, many industries are increasingly accepting on-machine automated 100 percent inspection and testing. Orkin (1988) provides an extensive table which identifies seven categories of potential applications of automated inspection ranging from dimensional gaging to nondestructive testing.

A critical requirement for all automated test equipment is precision measurement, i.e., repeated measurements on the same unit of product should yield the "same" test results within some acceptable range of variation. This repeatability is inherent in the design of the equipment and can be quantified by the methods discussed in Section 16.6, "Automated Manufacturing." In addition, it is essential that means be provided to keep the equipment "accurate," i.e., in calibration with respect to standards for the units of measure involved.

Still another aspect of automated test equipment is the problem of processing the data which are generated by the tests. Modern systems of electronic data processing make it possible for these test data to be entered directly from the test equipment into the computer without the need for intermediate documents. Such direct entry makes possible the prompt preparation of data summaries, conformance calculations, comparisons with prior lots, etc. In turn, it is feasible to program the computer to issue instructions to the test equipment with respect to frequency of test, disposition of units tested, alarm signals relative to improbable results, etc.

18.7 HOW MUCH INSPECTION IS NECESSARY?

The amount of inspection to decide the acceptability of a lot can vary from no inspection to a sample to 100 percent inspection. The decision is governed mainly by the amount of prior knowledge available as to quality, the *homogeneity* of the lot, and the allowable degree of risk.

Prior knowledge that is helpful in deciding on the amount of inspection includes:

- Previous quality history on the product item and the supplier (internal or external).
- Criticality of the item on overall system performance.
- Criticality on later manufacturing or service operations.
- Warranty or use history.
- Process capability information. A process which is in statistical control with good uniformity around a target value will require minimum inspection.
- Measurement capability information, e.g., the availability of accurate and precise instruments.
- The nature of the manufacturing process. For example, some operations primarily depend on the adequacy of the setup.
- Inspection of the first few and the last few items in a production run. This is usually sufficient.
- Product homogeneity. For example, fluid product is homogeneous and reduces the need for large sample sizes.
- Data on process variables and process conditions, e.g., as provided by automatic recording charts.
- Degree of adherence to the three elements of self- control for the personnel operating the process (see Section 5.2, "Self-Control").

Competition to reduce costs has resulted in pressures to reduce the amount of inspection. The concept of inspection by the producers (self-inspection) has added to the focus of reducing inspection. Indeed, opportunities do exist for cost reduction in inspection activities. First, however, the causes of the high failure costs must be diagnosed and removed and the prerequisites for self-inspection must be met.

Example 18.4. The Datapoint Corporation manufactures office and computer products (Adams, 1987). Part of the operation was 100 percent in-line inspection of visual characteristics by the quality staff. A dramatic shift was planned—production personnel would do their own visual inspection; the quality staff would perform an audit inspection and do diagnostic work on the causes of nonconformities. But a number of steps were required: a quality education process for first-line management, supervisors, and line personnel; special training in workmanship standards to help people recognize nonconformances; an 18-month implementation plan to phase in the new approach; use of data from functional acceptance tests for process yield reports; analysis of process data; and a process audit system to review documentation, tools, materials, and people.

The results were dramatic: The staff of 35 in-line inspectors was reduced to five process auditors, while scrap and rework plunged from 15 percent to two percent.

18.8 INSPECTION ACCURACY

Inspection accuracy depends on: (1) the completeness of inspection planning (see above); (2) the bias and precision of the instruments (see later in this chapter); and the (3) level of human error.

High error rates are particularly prevalent in inspection tasks having a high degree of monotony, e.g., viewing jars of a food product for foreign particles, screening luggage at an airport security gate. Even with less monotony, the accuracy of inspection may be far from satisfactory. Some engineering organizations have "drawing checkers" who inspect drawings for adherence to drawing standards. In one experiment, several groups of documents having an average of 16 errors were submitted to the checkers. On the first check, an average of only eight errors was found; two additional checks were needed to find the remaining errors. Thus, 300 percent inspection was necessary to find all of the errors.

Human errors arise from multiple causes, of which four are most important: misinterpretation, technique errors, inadvertent errors, and conscious errors.

Misinterpretation

Errors due to misinterpretation can be concerned with the product itself, the inspection method, or both. Product quality characteristics that cannot be quantified are especially troublesome. Sensory characteristics such as scratches require clear definition of limits in the form of photographs, physical standards, or other means (see above under "Sensory Characteristics"). For all characteristics, it has become important to spell out in writing the steps in the inspection method to avoid a misunderstanding of what the inspector is to evaluate and the means to be used.

The nature of the other three errors (technique, inadvertent, and conscious) is similar to the same categories for other workers (see Section 3.10 under "Test of Theories of Worker-Controllable Problems"). For specific elaboration on inspection errors, see QCH4, pages 18.84–18.94.

Measure of Inspector Accuracy

Some companies carry out regular evaluations of inspector accuracy, either as part of the overall evaluation of inspection performance or as an essential part of an incentive pay plan for inspectors. Either way, the plans employ a check inspector who periodically reviews random samples of work previously inspected by the various inspectors. The check inspection findings are then summarized, weighted, and converted into some index of inspector performance. QCH4, pages 18.94–18.97, explains this procedure.

Harris and Chaney (1969) provided some early research on inspector accuracy. Among their findings were: inspection accuracy decreases with reductions in defect rates; inspection accuracy increases with repeated inspections (up to a total of six); inspection accuracy decreases with additional product complexity, and the effect cannot be overcome by increasing the allowable inspection time. These are sobering conclusions.

18.9   ERRORS OF MEASUREMENT

Even when correctly used, a measuring instrument may not give a true reading of a characteristic. The difference between the true value and the measured value can be due to problems of:

- *Precision.* The precision of an instrument is the extent to which the instrument repeats its results when making repeat measurements on the same unit of product. The scatter of these measurements may be designated as σ_E, meaning the standard deviation of measurement error. (The scatter is usually due to random error.) The lower the value of σ_E, the more precise the instrument (see Figure 18.2).
- *Bias.* The bias of an instrument is the extent to which the average of a long series of repeat measurements made by the instrument on a single unit of product differs from the true value. This difference is usually due to a systematic error in the measurement process. In this case the instrument is said to be "out of calibration."

There is much confusion as to terminology. This confusion extends to instrument catalogues. Table 18.3 shows the statements on error of measurement as listed in three catalogues. The confusion is compounded because none of these catalogues defines the word "accuracy."

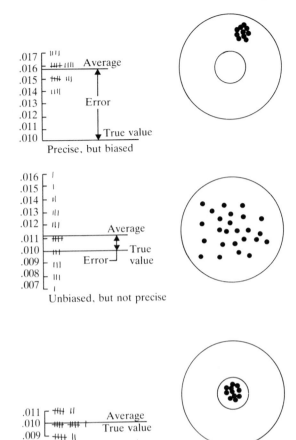

FIGURE 18.2
Distinction between bias and precision.

The American Society for Testing and Materials (ASTM) has long studied the issues of precision and bias in general and for applications to specific materials. We will be guided by their latest definitions of key terms and by their recommendations on expressing precision and bias.

ASTM (1986) uses the following definitions:

- *Accuracy* is a generic concept of exactness related to the closeness of agreement between the average of one or more test results and an accepted reference value. Accuracy depends on the imprecision and bias of the test method.

- *Precision* is a generic concept related to the closeness of agreement between test results obtained under prescribed like conditions from the measurement process being evaluated.

- *Bias* is a generic concept related to a consistent or systematic difference between a set of test results from the process and an accepted reference value of the property being measured.

TABLE 18.3
Comparison of catalogue statements

| Instrument | Manufacturer | | |
	A	B	C
Outside micrometer 0-1 in (0-2.54 cm)	Accuracy 0.0001 in (0.000254 cm)	Accuracy is maintained at 0.00005 in (0.000127 cm)	No statement
Dial caliper	Accuracy to 0.001 in (0.00254 cm) per 6 in (15.24 cm)	Accuracy guaranteed within 0.001 in (0.00254 cm)	No statement
Electronic comparator	Repeatable accuracies to 0.000004 in (0.0000101 cm)	Repeats to within 0.000002 in (0.00000508 cm)	Total error is less than $1\frac{1}{2}\%$ of full-scale reading

Note that accuracy depends on both the precision and the bias of the test method. Also, ASTM recommends that separate statements of precision and bias be presented instead of combining information on precision and bias into a single numerical value of accuracy.

Analytical Determination of Bias and Precision

Bias of measurement can be quantified by determining the difference between the true value of a characteristic and the average value of multiple measurements made on the characteristic. The question of "how many measurements" can be answered by confidence limit concepts (see Section 10.6). For example, suppose that σ_E is estimated as 2.0, and it is desired to estimate bias within 0.5 unit at the 95 percent confidence level. Then 62 repeat measurements should be taken on the same unit of product and the average of these calculated. The difference between the true value and the average of these repeat measurements is a measure of bias.

To determine the precision of a measuring process, we calculate the measurement variation that results if repeat measurements are made on one unit of product. The precision is calculated as a multiple of the standard deviation of these repeat measurements *about their own average*.

For both bias and precision, the number of measurements taken should be large enough to evaluate the *stability* of the measurement process. Ideally, this is done by using an average and range control chart with a minimum of 100 total measurements divided into small subgroups (see Section 17.6). However, it is often not practical to obtain this many readings for an error-of-measurement study. As a rough test of stability, the individual measurements can be evaluated against $\pm 3\sigma_E$ limits about the average. This is illustrated in the following example (ASTM, 1977).

Example 18.5. A micrometer was chosen at random from the half dozen available for use. Two operators were available, and one was chosen by the toss of a coin. The operator made 20 measurements on a standard 1.000-in (2.540-cm) steel cube with the following results:

$$\text{Average} = 1.00403 \text{ in } (2.55024 \text{ cm})$$

$$\text{Standard deviation} = 0.00024 \text{ in } (0.00061 \text{ cm})$$

All observed values fell within ± 3 standard deviations of the average. The estimate of the systematic error (bias) is $1.00000 - 1.00403$, or -0.00403 in (0.01024 cm). The single-operator-micrometer-day precision is ± 0.0005 in (0.0013 cm) (two standard deviations), as defined in ASTM Recommended Practice E177 (ASTM, 1977).

ASTM Methods of Expressing Bias and Precision

ASTM recommends several methods of expressing precision. These are:

1. The standard deviation, s, of a random set of individual test results taken in a laboratory.
2. Two standard deviation limits, $2s$, of a random set of individual test results taken in a laboratory. About 95 percent of individual test results can be expected to differ in absolute value from their average value by less than $1.96s$ (about $2.0s$).
3. Difference two standard deviation limits (called $d2s$ by ASTM). The basic data here come from *pairs* of test results taken in different laboratories. About 95 percent of pairs of test results from laboratories can be expected to differ in absolute value by less than $1.960\sqrt{2}\,s$, or $2.8s$. (The $\sqrt{2}$ reflects the two measurements in each pair.)

ASTM recommends that the "difference two standard deviation limits" be employed both for measuring the repeatability *within* a laboratory and for measuring the reproducibility *between* laboratories.

Also, ASTM recommends several methods of expressing bias. These are:

1. An estimate of the bias, based on a study of the average of repeat measurements compared to the "true value." This estimate may be supplemented by upper and lower bounds.
2. An adjustment procedure for applying corrections to the data.

Any statement of bias and precision must be preceded by three conditions:

1. *Definition of the test method.* This includes the step-by-step procedure, equipment to be used, preparation of test specimens, test conditions, etc.
2. *Definition of the system of causes of variability,* such as material, analysts, apparatus, laboratories, days, etc. ASTM recommends that modifiers of the word "precision" be used to clarify the scope of the precision measure. Examples of such modifiers are single-operator, single-analyst, single-laboratory-operator-material-day, and multilaboratory.
3. *Existence of a statistically controlled measurement process.* The measurement process must have stability in order for the statements on bias and precision to be valid. This stability can be verified by a control chart (see Section 17.6).

Effect of Measurement Error on Acceptance Decisions

Error of measurement can cause incorrect decisions on (1) individual units of product and (2) lots submitted to sampling plans.

In one example of measuring the softening point of a material, the standard deviation of the test precision is 2°, yielding two standard deviations of ±4°. The specification limits on the material are ±3°. Imagine the incorrect decisions that are made under these conditions.

Two types of errors can occur in the classification of a product: (1) a nonconforming unit can be accepted (the consumer's risk) and (2) a conforming unit can be rejected (the producer's risk). In a classic paper, Eagle (1954) showed the effect of precision on each of these errors.

The probability of accepting a nonconforming unit as a function of measurement error (called test error, σ_{TE}, by Eagle) is shown in Figure 18.3. The abscissa expresses the test error as the standard deviation divided by the plus-or-minus value of the specification range (assumed equal to two standard deviations of the product).

For example, if the measurement error is one-half of the tolerance range, the probability is about 1.65 percent that a nonconforming unit will be read as conforming (due to the measurement error) and therefore will be accepted.

Figure 18.4 shows the percentage of *conforming* units that will be *rejected* as a function of the measurement error. For example, if the measurement error is one-half of the plus-or-minus tolerance range, about 14 percent of the units that are really within specifications will be rejected because the measurement error will show these conforming units as being outside specification.

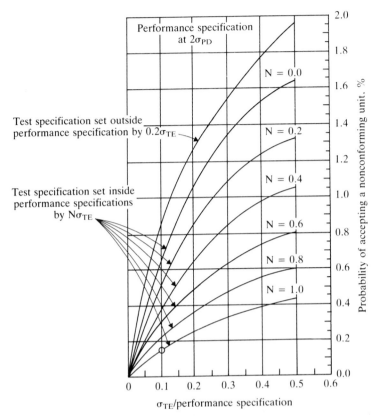

FIGURE 18.3
Probability of accepting a nonconforming unit. (*From Eagle, 1954.*)

The test specification can be adjusted with respect to the performance specification (see Figures 18.3 and 18.4). Moving the test specification inside the performance specification reduces the probability of accepting a nonconforming product but increases the probability of rejecting a conforming product. The reverse occurs if the test specification is moved outside the performance specification. Both risks can be reduced by increasing the precision of the test, i.e., by reducing the value of σ_E (see below under "Reducing and Controlling Errors of Measurement").

Hoag et al. (1975) studied the effect of inspector errors on the type I (α) and type II (β) risks of sampling plans. For a single sampling plan and an 80 percent probability of the inspector detecting a defect, the real value of β is two to three times that specified, and the real value of α is about one-fourth to one-half of that specified.

Case et al. (1975) investigated the effect of inspection error on the *average outgoing quality* (AOQ) of an attributes sampling procedure. They concluded that not only do the AOQ values change, but significant changes

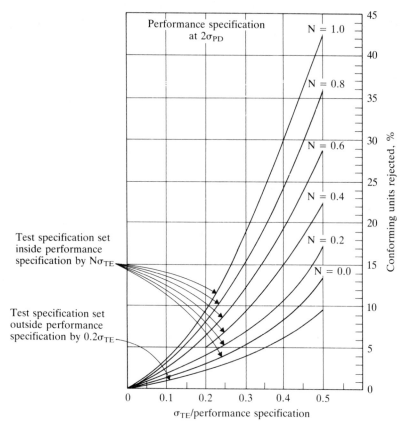

FIGURE 18.4
Conforming units rejected, %. (*From Eagle, 1954.*)

can occur in the shape of the AOQ curve. Case and Bennett (1976) investigated the effect of measurement error on the overall costs associated with variables sampling plans.

Suich (1990) analyzed the effect of inspection errors when one is inspecting for the number of nonconformities per item.

All these investigations concluded that measurement error can be a serious problem.

Components of Variation

In drawing conclusions about measurement error, it is worthwhile to study the causes of variation of observed values. The relationship is

$$\sigma_{observed} = \sqrt{\sigma^2_{cause\ A} + \sigma^2_{cause\ B} + \cdots + \sigma^2_{cause\ N}}$$

The formula assumes that the causes act independently.

It is valuable to find the numerical values of the components of observed variation, because the knowledge may suggest where effort should be concentrated to reduce the variation in the product. A separation of the observed variation into the product variation plus the other causes of variation may indicate important factors other than the manufacturing process. Thus, if the *measurement* error is found to be a large percentage of the total variation, this finding must be analyzed before proceeding with a quality improvement program. Finding the components (e.g., instrument, operator) of this error may help to reduce the measurement error, which in turn may completely eliminate a problem.

Observations from an instrument used to measure a series of different units of product can be viewed as a composite of (1) the variation due to the measuring method and (2) the variation in the product itself. This can be expressed as

$$\sigma_O = \sqrt{\sigma_P^2 + \sigma_E^2}$$

where $\sigma_O = \sigma$ of the observed data
$\sigma_P = \sigma$ of the product
$\sigma_E = \sigma$ of the measuring method

Solving for σ_P yields

$$\sigma_P = \sqrt{\sigma_O^2 - \sigma_E^2}$$

If σ_E is less than one-tenth of σ_O, the effect upon σ_P will be less than one percent. A common rule of thumb requires that the instrument should be able to divide the tolerance into about ten parts. As the effect is less than one percent, the rule of thumb seems uneconomically conservative for most applications.

Tsai (1988) shows a method of estimating the components of variation.

Reducing and Controlling Errors of Measurement

Steps can be taken to reduce and control errors in both bias and precision. The systematic errors that contribute to bias can sometimes be handled by applying a numerical correction to the measured data. If an instrument has a bias of −0.001, then, on the average, it reads 0.001 too low. The data can be adjusted by adding 0.001 to each value of the data. Of course, it is preferable to adjust the instrument as part of a calibration program.

In a calibration program the measurements made by an instrument are compared to a reference standard of known accuracy. If the instrument is found to be out of calibration, an adjustment is made.

A calibration program can become complex. This is due to:

1. The large number of measuring instruments
2. The need for periodic calibration of many instruments
3. The need for many reference standards
4. The increased technological complexity of new instruments
5. The variety of types of instruments, i.e., mechanical, electronic, chemical, etc.

A potentially enormous volume of work on a calibration program can be reduced by using a calibration interval based on the amount of actual use of an instrument rather than simply a specified calendar time since the last calibration. Scott (1976) reported that, in the first year of operation under the use concept, 10,000 fewer gages needed to be calibrated as compared to the previous system, which used a calendar-time interval.

A calibration program should include provisions for periodic audits. These follow the general approach for quality audits (see Section 22.5, "Business Process Quality Management").

Precision of measurement can be improved through:

- *Discovery of the causes of variation and remedy of these causes.* A useful step is to resolve the observed values into components of variation (see Section 16.7, "Overall Review of Manufacturing Planning"). This can lead to the discovery of inadequate training, perishable reagents, lack of sufficient detail in procedures, and other such problems. This fundamental approach also points to other causes for which the remedy is unknown or uneconomic, i.e., basic redesign of the test procedure. In such cases another approach is:
- *Multiple measurements and statistical methodology to control the error of measurement.* The use of multiple measurements is based on the following relationship (see Section 10.3, "Sampling Variation and Sampling Distributions"):

$$\sigma_{\bar{x}} = \frac{\sigma}{\sqrt{n}}$$

The formula states that halving the error of measurement requires quadrupling (not doubling) the number of measurements.

As the number of tests grows larger and larger, a significant reduction in the error of measurement can be achieved only by taking a still *larger* number of additional tests. This raises a question concerning the cost of the additional tests versus the value of the slight improvement in measurement error. The alternatives of reducing the causes of variation (by control charts or other techniques) must also be considered.

SUMMARY

- Product acceptance involves three decisions: conformance, fitness for use, and communication.
- In deciding whether nonconforming product is fit for use or not, inputs must be secured from several sources.
- The communication decision involves both outsiders (customers) and insiders.
- Inspection planning includes the designation of inspection stations and spelling out the instructions and facilities required.
- A classification of characteristics is a list of quality characteristics derived from the specifications; a classification of defects is a list of symptoms of nonconformance during manufacture and field use.
- The amount of inspection necessary depends mainly on the amount of prior knowledge about product quality, homogeneity of the lot, and the allowable risk.
- Human errors in inspection arise from misinterpretation, technique errors, inadvertent errors, and conscious errors.
- Errors of measurement have two parts: precision and bias. Both of these parts can be quantified.

PROBLEMS

18.1. Discuss the inspection of new homes with the appropriate municipal department. Determine the purpose of its inspection, the specification used, and how the inspection is conducted. Comment on this inspection from the viewpoint of the purchaser of a home.

18.2. In one large company making consumer durable products, the chief inspector operated on the principle that disposition of nonconforming lots of components must be done in only three ways: (1) by scrapping them, (2) by repairing them to bring them into conformance, or (3) by securing a waiver from the design department. What she did not permit was a tryout to see if the components were usable despite the nonconformance. Her stated reason was that if she authorized such tryouts, the production people would devote their energies to tryouts rather than to making the components right in the first place. What do you think of this philosophy?

18.3. Certain plates stamped out in a stamping press include holes for which there are close tolerances for diameter and for the distance between holes. In the discussion of how many pieces to gage for these dimensions, one proposal is to measure the first and the last piece for each lot and to accept the lot if both pieces conform to specification. A statistician objects to this proposal on the grounds that the sample is only two pieces and that, if the lot were 50 percent defective, it could easily be accepted due to statistical variation. What is your opinion?

18.4. A large manufacturer of minicomputers is incurring high costs due to the need for assembling and testing the computers to discover and eliminate defects before the computers are installed in clients' computer rooms. After this assembly, testing, and repair, the computers are disassembled, shipped to the clients' facilities, reassembled, and checked out. How would you go about reducing the cost of preassembly and pretest?

18.5. You are a quality manager engaged in a seminar to discuss common problems with other quality managers. A lively discussion has developed over some problems associated with pressures applied to quality managers. These pressures concern the shipment of nonconforming, unfit, or even unsafe products. In addition, the pressures concern the matter of the quality manager signing a test certificate or other document which puts him on record as having approved something when he was really against it.

Here are several of the problem categories identified by the group:

- A lot of product has been made with a nonconformance to specification. All company managers (including the quality manager) are convinced that the nonconforming product is fit for use. They are not agreed on whether to tell the client about the nonconformance. The marketing manager is against informing the client on the ground that some clients may use such information to wring a price concession out of the manufacturer.

- A product lot contains a small percentage of units which are clearly unfit for use. There is a debate on whether to sort the lot to remove the defective units or to ship the lot as is and pay any claims as they arise. The production manager (who wants to ship the product without sorting) contends that the problem is purely economic and that the quality considerations are secondary.

- A large electromechanical system has been made under a contract which includes a penalty clause for late delivery. The system has already met its test requirements and is being crated for shipment. At this point, it is discovered that the test equipment used to test one of the subsystems was out of calibration at the time of making the test. Under the accepted practice in the industry, such a discovery throws suspicion on the quality of the subsystem and hence on the quality of the system. Unfortunately, the subsystem is not easily accessible. It is buried deep within the system so that it would involve a serious delay as well as a large expense to take the system apart, test the subsystem, and then put it all back together again. The manufacturing people take the position that the subsystem is okay despite the condition of the test equipment. They note that another subsystem built by the same people using the same process has just tested okay. They urge that the system be shipped based on this evidence of a reliable process and work force.

- A product with a good safety record has resulted in a serious injury to a user. The injury involved a most unusual combination of unlikely events plus an obvious misuse by the user. The design manager defends the design on the record—the only known serious injury was associated with misuse.

What are your conclusions as to the position to be taken by the quality manager in the foregoing cases with respect to (*a*) shipping the product and (*b*) signing the documents?

18.6. An instrument has been used to measure the length of a part. The result was 6.70052 cm. An error-of-measurement study was made on the instrument with the following results:

Accuracy: +0.00254 cm (on the average, the instrument reads 0.00254 cm high)

Precision: 0.001016 cm (one standard deviation)

Make a statement concerning the true value of the part just measured. State all assumptions needed.

18.7. The precision of a certain mechanical gage is indicated by a standard deviation (of individual repeat measurements) of 0.00254 cm. Investigate the effect on precision of making multiple measurements. Consider two, three, four, five, ten, 20, and 30 as multiples. Graph the results.

18.8. One ball bearing was measured by one inspector 13 times with each of two vernier micrometers. The results are shown below:

Measurement number	Model A	Model B
1	0.6557	0.6559
2	0.6556	0.6559
3	0.6556	0.6559
4	0.6555	0.6559
5	0.6556	0.6559
6	0.6557	0.6559
7	0.6556	0.6559
8	0.6558	0.6559
9	0.6557	0.6559
10	0.6557	0.6559
11	0.6556	0.6559
12	0.6557	0.6560
13	0.6557	0.6560

Suppose that the true diameter is 0.65600. Calculate measures of bias and precision for each micrometer. What restrictions must be placed on the applicability of the numbers you determined?
  Answer: A: bias $= -0.00035$, precision $= 1\sigma$ of 0.000075; *B:* bias $= -0.000085$, precision $= 1\sigma$ of 0.000036.

18.9. A large sample of product has been measured. The mean was 2.506 in and the standard deviation was 0.002 in. A separate error-of-measurement study yielded the following results:
Bias $= +0.001$ in.
Precision: 0.0005 in (one standard deviation). The product has only a minimum tolerance limit. What should this limit be to take into account bias and precision and reject only five percent of the product?
  Answer: 2.502.

18.10. A sample of measurements shows a mean and standard deviation of 2.000 in and 0.004 in, respectively. These results are for the *observed* values. A separate error-of-measurement study indicates a precision of 0.002 in (one standard deviation). There is no bias error. The dimension has a specification of 2.000 ± 0.006 in. What percentage of the population has *true* dimensions outside the specification?

REFERENCES

Adams, Ray (1987). "Moving from Inspection to Audit," *Quality Progress*, January, pp. 30–31.

ASTM (1977). *ASTM Standards on Precision and Accuracy for Various Applications*, American Society for Testing and Materials, Philadelphia, pp. 132–133.

ASTM (1986). *ASTM Standards on Precision and Accuracy for Various Applications*, American Society for Testing and Materials, Philadelphia, pp. 282–293.

Baxter Travenol Laboratories (1986). "Statistical Process Control Guideline," Baxter Travenol Laboratories, Deerfield, Illinois, p. 23.

Case, Kenneth E., and G. Kemble Bennett (1976). "Measurement Error: The Economic Effect on Sampling Plan Design," *ASQC Annual Technical Conference Transactions*, Milwaukee, pp. 207–212.

Case, Kenneth E., G. Kemble Bennett, and J. W. Schmidt (1975). "The Effect of Inspection Error on Average Outgoing Quality." *Journal of Quality Technology*, vol. 7, no. 1, pp. 1–12.

Eagle, A. R. (1954). "A Method for Handling Errors in Testing and Measuring," *Industrial Quality Control*, March, pp. 10–14.

Harris, D. H., and F. B. Chaney (1969). *Human Factors in Quality Assurance*, John Wiley and Sons, New York, pp. 77–85.

Hoag, Laverne L., Bobbie L. Foote, and Clark Mount-Campbell (1975). "The Effect of Inspector Accuracy on Type I and Type II Errors of Common Sampling Techniques," *Journal of Quality Technology*, vol. 7, no. 4, pp. 157–164.

Orkin, Frederic I. (1988). In QCH4, Table 27.8.

Riley, Frederic D. (1979). "Visual Inspection—Time and Distance Method," *ASQC Annual Technical Conference Transactions*, Milwaukee, p. 483.

Scott, J. E. (1976). "Days Used Gage Program Drastically Reduces Wasted Calibration Time," *Quality*, February, pp. 22–24.

Suich, Ron (1990). "The Effects of Inspection Errors on Acceptance Sampling for Nonconformities," *Journal of Quality Technology*, vol. 22, no. 4, pp. 314–318.

Tsai, P. (1988). "Variable Gauge Repeatability and Reproducibility Study Using the Analysis of Variance Method," *Quality Engineering*, vol. 1, no. 1, pp. 107–115.

SUPPLEMENTARY READING

Inspection and testing, general: QCH4, Section 18.

Productivity in inspection and testing Wenske, Wayne J., and T. Godfrey Mackenzie (1988). "Quality Improvement in an Analytical Laboratory: A Case Study of Reducing Response Time," *Impro Conference Proceedings*, Juran Institute Inc., Wilton, Connecticut, pp. 5D–15 to 5D–24.

Pareto concept and testing errors: Gambino, Raymond, Peter Mallon, and George Woodrow, (1990). "Managing for Total Quality in a Large Laboratory," *Archives of Pathology and Laboratory Medicine*, November, pp. 1145–1148.

Measurement concepts in the automotive industry: Automotive Industry Action Group AIAG (1990). "Measurement Systems Analysis Reference Manual," AIAG, Southfield, Michigan.

Measurement error in batch processes: Basnet, Chuda, and Kenneth E. Case (1992). "The Effect of Measurement Error on Accept/Reject Probabilities for Homogeneous Products," *Quality Engineering*, vol. 4, no. 3, pp. 383–397.

CHAPTER
19

INSPECTION AND TEST— SAMPLING PLANS

19.1 THE CONCEPT OF ACCEPTANCE SAMPLING

Acceptance sampling is the process of evaluating a portion of the product in a lot for the purpose of accepting or rejecting the entire lot.

The main advantage of sampling is economy. Despite some added costs for designing and administering the sampling plans, the lower costs of inspecting only part of the lot result in an overall cost reduction.

In addition to this main advantage, there are others:

- The smaller inspection staff is less complex and less costly to administer.
- There is less damage to the product, i.e., handling incidental to inspection is itself a source of defects.
- The lot is disposed of in shorter (calendar) time so that scheduling and delivery are improved.
- The problem of monotony and inspector error induced by 100 percent inspection is minimized.

- Rejection (rather than sorting) of nonconforming lots tends to dramatize the quality deficiencies and to urge the organization to look for preventive measures.
- Proper design of the sampling plan commonly requires study of the actual level of quality required by the user. The resulting knowledge is a useful input to the overall quality planning.

The disadvantages are sampling risks, greater administrative costs, and less information about the product than is provided by 100 percent inspection.

Acceptance sampling is used when: (1) the cost of inspection is high in relation to the damage cost resulting from passing a defective product, (2) 100 percent inspection is monotonous and causes inspection errors, or (3) the inspection is destructive. Acceptance sampling is most effective when it is preceded by a prevention program that achieves an acceptable level of quality of conformance.

There is a need to emphasize what acceptance sampling does not do. It does not provide refined estimates of lot quality. (It does determine, with specified risks, an acceptance or rejection decision on each lot.) Also, acceptance sampling does not provide judgments on whether or not rejected product is fit for use. (It does give a decision on a lot with respect to the defined quality specification.)

In recent years, the emphasis on statistical process control has led some practitioners to conclude that acceptance sampling is no longer a valid concept. Their belief, stated here in oversimplified terms, is that only two levels of inspection are valid—no inspection or 100 percent inspection. In this text, our viewpoint is that the concept of prevention (using statistical process control and other statistical and managerial techniques) is the foundation for meeting product requirements. Acceptance sampling procedures are, however, important in a program of *acceptance control*. Under this latter approach, described at the end of this chapter, sampling procedures are continually matched to process history and quality results. This ultimately leads to phasing out acceptance sampling in favor of supplier certification and process control.

For some fascinating reading about the pros and cons of sampling, see *Quality Engineering* (1990) and Milligan (1991).

This chapter presents examples of specific acceptance sampling plans.

19.2 ECONOMICS OF INSPECTION

We have several alternatives for evaluating lots:

1. *No inspection.* This is appropriate in cases where prior inspections on the same lot have already been made by qualified laboratories, e.g., in other divisions of the same company or in supplier companies. Prior inspections by qualified production workers have the same effect.

2. *Small samples.* These can be adequate in cases where the process is inherently uniform and the order of production can be preserved. For example, in some punch press operations, the stamping dies are made to a high degree of stability. As a result, the successive pieces stamped out by such dies exhibit a high degree of uniformity for certain dimensional characteristics. For such characteristics, if the first and last pieces are correct, the remaining pieces are also correct, even for lot sizes running to many thousands of pieces. In its generalized form, the press example is one of a high degree of process capability combined with "stratified" sampling—sampling based on knowledge of the order of production.

Small samples can also be used when the product is homogeneous due to its fluidity (gases, liquids) or to prior mixing operations. This homogeneity need not be assumed—it can be verified by sampling. Even solid materials may be homogeneous due to *prior* fluidity. Once the fact of homogeneity has been established, the sampling needed is minimal.

3. *Large samples.* In the absence of prior knowledge, the information about lot quality must be derived solely from sampling, which means random sampling and hence relatively large samples. The actual sample sizes depend on two main variables: (a) the tolerable percentage of defects and (b) the risks that can be accepted. Once values have been assigned to these variables, the sample sizes can be determined scientifically in accordance with the laws of probability (see Section 10.10). However, the choice of defect levels and risks is largely based on empirical judgments.

Random sampling is clearly needed in cases where there is no ready access to prior knowledge, e.g., purchases from certain suppliers. However, there remain many, many cases in which random sampling is used despite the availability of inputs such as process capability, order of manufacture, fluidity, etc. A major obstacle is a lack of publications which show how to design sampling plans in ways which make use of these inputs. In the absence of such publications, quality planners are faced with creating their own designs. This means added work amid the absence of protection derived from use of recognized, authoritative published materials.

See QCH4, pp. 25.18–25.21, for a discussion of the formation of inspection lots and the selection of samples.

4. 100 *percent inspection.* This is used when the results of sampling show that the level of defects present is too high for the product to go on to the users. In critical cases, added provisions may be needed to guard against inspector fallibility, e.g., automated inspection or redundant 200 percent inspection.

An economic evaluation of these alternatives requires a comparison of *total* costs under each of the alternatives.

Let N = number of items in lot
       n = number of items in sample
       p = proportion defective in lot

A = damage cost incurred if a defective slips through inspection
I = inspection cost per item
P_a = probability that lot will be accepted by sampling plan

Consider the comparison of sampling inspection versus 100 percent inspection. Suppose it is assumed that no inspection errors occur and the cost to replace a defective found in inspection is borne by the producer or is small compared to the damage or inconvenience caused by a defective. The total costs are summarized in Table 19.1. These costs reflect both inspection costs and damage costs and recognize the probability of accepting or rejecting a lot under sampling inspection. The expressions can be equated to determine a break-even point. If the sample size is assumed to be small compared to the lot size, the break-even point, p_b, is

$$p_b = \frac{I}{A}$$

If it is thought that the lot quality (p) is less than p_b, the total cost will be lowest with sampling inspection or no inspection. If p is greater than p_b, 100 percent inspection is best.

For example, a microcomputer device costs \$.50 per unit to inspect. A damage cost of \$10.00 is incurred if a defective device is installed in the larger system. Therefore,

$$p_b = \frac{.50}{10.00} = .05 = 5.0\,\%$$

If it is expected that the percentage defective will be greater than five percent, then 100 percent inspection should be used. Otherwise, use sampling or no inspection.

The variability in quality from lot to lot is important. If past history shows that the quality level is much better than the break-even point and is stable from lot to lot, little if any inspection may be needed. If the level is much worse than the break-even point, and consistently so, it will usually be cheaper to use 100 percent inspection rather than sampling. If the quality is at neither of these extremes, a detailed economic comparison of no inspection,

TABLE 19.1
Economic comparison of inspection alternatives

Alternative	Total cost
No inspection	NpA
Sampling	$nI + (N-n)pAP_a + (N-n)(1-P_a)I$
100% inspection	NI

sampling, and 100 percent inspection should be made. Sampling is usually best when the product is a mixture of high-quality lots and low-quality lots, or when the producer's process is not in a state of statistical control.

The high costs associated with component failures in complex electronic equipment coupled with the development of automatic testing equipment for components has resulted in the economic justification of 100 percent inspection for some electronic components. The cost of finding and correcting a defective can increase by a ratio of ten for each major stage that the product moves to from production to the customer; i.e., if it costs $1.00 at incoming inspection, the cost increases to $10.00 at the printed circuit board stage, $100.00 at the system level, and $1,000.00 in the field (*Quality*, 1978).

19.3 SAMPLING RISKS: THE OPERATING CHARACTERISTIC CURVE

Neither sampling nor 100 percent inspection can guarantee that every defective item in a lot will be found. Sampling involves a risk that the sample will not adequately reflect the conditions in the lot; 100 percent inspection has the risk that monotony and other factors will result in inspectors missing some of the defectives (see Section 18.8). Both of these risks can be quantified.

Sampling risks are of two kinds:

1. Good lots can be rejected (the producer's risk). This risk corresponds to the α risk.
2. Bad lots can be accepted (the consumer's risk). This risk corresponds to the β risk.

The α and β risks are discussed in Section 10.7.

The operating characteristic (OC) *curve* for a sampling plan quantifies these risks. The OC curve for an attributes plan is a graph of the percentage defective in a lot versus the probability that the sampling plan will accept a lot. As p is unknown, the probability must be stated for all possible values of p. It is assumed that an infinite number of lots are produced. Figure 19.1 shows an "ideal" OC curve where it is desired to accept all lots 1.5 percent defective or less and reject all lots having a quality level greater than 1.5 percent defective. All lots less than 1.5 percent defective have a probability of acceptance of 1.0 (certainty); all lots greater than 1.5 percent defective have a probability of acceptance of zero. Actually, however, no sampling plan exists that can discriminate perfectly; there always remains some risk that a "good" lot will be rejected or that a "bad" lot will be accepted. The best that can be achieved is to make the acceptance of good lots more likely than the acceptance of bad lots.

An acceptance sampling plan basically consists of a sample size (n) and an acceptance criterion (c). For example, a sample of 125 units is to be

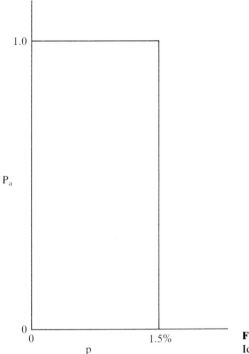

FIGURE 19.1
Ideal OC curve.

randomly selected from the lot. If five or fewer defectives are found, the lot is accepted. If six or more defectives are found, the lot is rejected.

The sample of 125 could, by the laws of chance, contain zero, one, two, three, even up to 125 defectives. It is this *sampling variation* that causes some good lots to be rejected and some bad lots to be accepted. The OC curve for $n = 125$ and $c = 5$ is curve A, Figure 19.2. (The other curves will be discussed later.) A 1.5 percent defective lot has about a 98 percent chance of being accepted. A much worse lot, say six percent defective, has a 23 percent chance of being accepted. With the risks stated in quantitative form, a judgment can be made on the adequacy of the sampling plan.

The OC curve for a specific plan states *only* the chance that a lot having p percent defective will be accepted by the sampling plan. The OC curve does *not:*

- Predict the quality of lots submitted for inspection. For example (Figure 19.2), it is incorrect to say that there is a 36 percent chance that the lot quality is five percent defective.
- State a "confidence level" in connection with a specific percentage defective.
- Predict the final quality achieved after all inspections are completed.

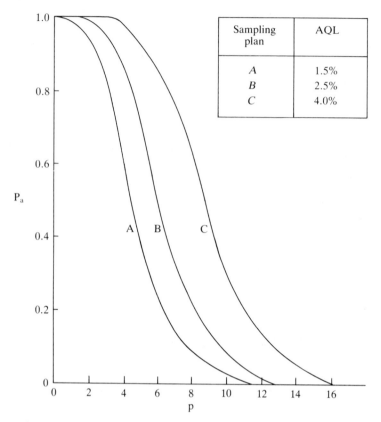

Sampling plan	AQL
A	1.5%
B	2.5%
C	4.0%

FIGURE 19.2
OC curves.

These and other myths about the OC curve require a careful explanation of the concept to those using it. (AQL is explained in Section 19.6)

Constructing the Operating Characteristic Curve

An OC curve can be developed by determining the probability of acceptance for several values of incoming quality, p. The probability of acceptance is the probability that the number of defectives in the sample is equal to or less than the acceptance number for the sampling plan. There are three distributions that can be used to find the probability of acceptance: the hypergeometric, binomial, and Poisson distributions. When its assumptions can be met, the Poisson distribution is preferable because of the ease of calculation.

Grant and Leavenworth (1988, pp. 199–209) describe the use of the hypergeometric and binomial distributions.

The Poisson distribution yields a good approximation for acceptance sampling when the sample size is at least 16, the lot size is at least ten times the sample size, and p is less than 0.1. The Poisson distribution function as applied to acceptance sampling is:

$$P\left(\begin{array}{c} \text{exactly} \\ r \text{ defectives} \\ \text{in sample of } n \end{array}\right) = \frac{e^{-np}(np)^r}{r!}$$

The equation can be solved using a calculator or by using Table C in the Appendix. This table gives the probability of r *or fewer* defectives in a sample of n from a lot having a fraction defective of p. To illustrate Table C, consider the sampling plan previously cited, i.e., $n = 125$ and $c = 5$. To find the probability of accepting a four percent defective lot, calculate np as $125(0.04) = 5.00$. Table C then gives the probability of five or fewer defectives as 0.616. Figure 19.2 (curve A) shows this as the value of P_a for four percent defective lot quality.

19.4 ANALYSIS OF SOME RULE-OF-THUMB SAMPLING PLANS

Rule-of-thumb sampling plans are frequently found to be inadequate when evaluated by an OC curve. The "ten percent sampling rule" is an example. For any lot size, a sample equal to ten percent of the lot is selected. If there are no defectives found in the sample, the lot is accepted. If any defectives are found in the sample, the lot is rejected. It is usually presumed that, with the sample always a constant percentage (ten percent) of the lot, the sampling risks will be constant. The ten percent rule, however does *not* provide equal risks. This is demonstrated by Problem 19.15.

Another rule-of-thumb plan is an extreme one that might be proposed for a destructive test. The plan is this: Test one unit and, if it is acceptable, pass the entire lot. If it is defective, test a second unit. If the second unit is acceptable, pass the lot. If the second unit is also defective, reject the lot. Figure 19.3 shows the operating characteristic curve. Destructive testing necessitates small sample sizes, but the OC curve shows that the sampling risks are so high for this plan that there is little protection against accepting bad quality. For example, if the lots submitted were about 70 percent defective, the probability of accepting such lots is 50 percent.

We show the inadequacy of these rule-of-thumb plans to emphasize that the intuitive approach can be so grossly in error as to seriously jeopardize the evaluation of a product. By deriving the OC curve the sampling risks become known. Even when these sampling risks are known, other considerations may dictate that a sampling plan be used which is inadequate from a statistical point of view. However, it is important that the size of the risk be known before a final judgment is made. No sampling plan should be adopted without first seeing its OC curve.

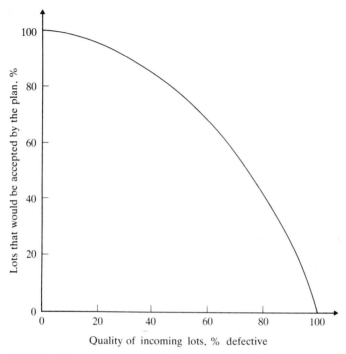

FIGURE 19.3
OC curve for a rule-of-thumb sampling plan.

19.5 EVALUATION OF PARAMETERS AFFECTING ACCEPTANCE SAMPLING PLANS

Sampling risks are affected by lot size, sample size, and the acceptance number (see Figure 19.4). In Figure 19.4a, the lot size is changed but the sample size and acceptance number are held constant. Notice that the lot size has little effect on the probability of acceptance. If the lot size is moderately large (at least ten times the sample size) and if the sample is selected randomly, the lot size has only a small effect on the probability of acceptance. It is tempting to conclude that lot size may be ignored in deriving a sampling plan. However, it is usually desired that larger lot sizes have a better operating characteristic curve in order to reduce the risk of error for costly amounts of product. The higher the amount at stake, the more precise should be the OC curve. Therefore, most sampling tables do show lot size as a parameter. (As the lot size increases, the absolute sample size increases but the ratio of sample size to lot size decreases.) The fact remains, however, that if all else is constant, the lot size has essentially no effect on the probability of acceptance.

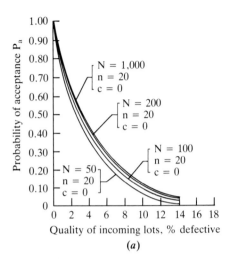

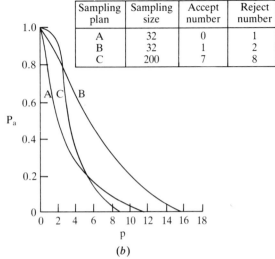

Sampling plan	Sampling size	Accept number	Reject number
A	32	0	1
B	32	1	2
C	200	7	8

FIGURE 19.4

(*a*) Effect of changing lot size on OC curve. (*b*) Effect of increasing sample size and acceptance number on OC curve.

The effect of other parameters is shown in Figure 19.4*b*.

1. When the acceptance number is zero, the OC curve is concave upward.

2. When the acceptance number is increased, the probability of acceptance, for low values of p, is increased.

3. Increasing the sample size and acceptance number together gives the closest approach to the ideal OC curve.

For safety-related products, we need sampling plans with a zero acceptance number (Schilling, 1978). This is important for product liability implications and regulatory requirements. The effect of sample size can then be shown by the OC curve. This is illustrated in Problem 19.15.

19.6 QUALITY INDICES FOR ACCEPTANCE SAMPLING PLANS

Many of the published plans can be categorized in terms of one of several quality indices:

1. *Acceptable quality level (AQL)*. The units of quality level can be selected to meet the particular needs of a product. Thus, ANSI/ASQC Z1.4 (1981) defines AQL as "the maximum percent nonconforming (or the maximum number of nonconformities per hundred units) that, for purposes of sampling inspection, can be considered satisfactory as a process average." If a unit of product can have a number of different defects of varying seriousness, then demerits can be assigned to each type and product quality measured in terms of demerits. As an AQL is an *acceptable* level, the probability of acceptance for an AQL lot should be high (see Figure 19.5).

2. *Limiting quality level (LQL).* This is a definition of *unsatisfactory* quality. Different titles are sometimes used to denote an LQL; for example, in the Dodge-Romig plans, the term "lot tolerance percentage defective (LTPD)" is used. As an LQL is an *unacceptable* level, the probability of acceptance for an LQL lot should be low (see Figure 19.5). In some tables, this probability is known as the consumer's risk, is designated as P_c, and has been standardized at 0.1. The consumer's risk is not the probability that the consumer will actually receive product at the LQL. The consumer will, in fact, not receive one lot in ten at LQL fraction defective. What the consumer actually gets depends on the actual quality in the lots *before* inspection and on the probability of acceptance.

3. *Indifference quality level (IQL).* This is a quality level somewhere between the AQL and LQL. It is frequently defined as the quality level having a probability of acceptance of 0.5 for a given sampling plan (see Figure 19.5).

It should be emphasized to both internal and external suppliers that *all* product submitted for inspection is expected to meet specifications. An

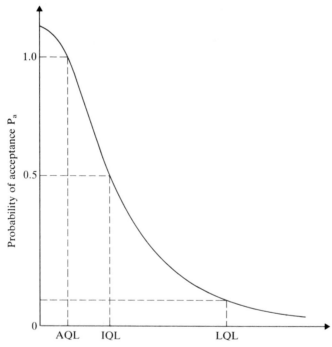

FIGURE 19.5
Quality indices for sampling plans.

acceptable quality level does not mean the submission of a certain amount of nonconforming product is approved. The AQL simply recognizes that, under sampling, some nonconforming product will pass through the sampling scheme.

4. *Average outgoing quality limit (AOQL)*. An approximate relationship exists between the fraction defective in the material before inspection (incoming quality p) and the fraction defective remaining after inspection (outgoing quality AOQ): $AOQ = pP_a$. When incoming quality is perfect, outgoing quality must also be perfect. However, when incoming quality is bad, outgoing quality will also be perfect (assuming no inspection errors) because the sampling plan will cause all lots to be rejected and detail-inspected. Thus, at either extreme—incoming quality excellent or terrible—the outgoing quality will tend to be good. Between these extremes is the point at which the percentage of defectives in the outgoing material will reach its maximum. This point is the average outgoing quality limit (AOQL). For a sample calculation, see QCH4, page 25.14.

These indices apply primarily when the production occurs in a continuing series of lots. For isolated lots, the LQL concept is recommended. The indices were originally developed by statisticians to help describe the characteristics of sampling plans. Misinterpretations (particularly of the AQL) are common and are similar to those mentioned in Section 15.2. For example, a sampling plan based on AQL *will* accept some lots having a quality level worse than the AQL.

19.7 TYPES OF SAMPLING PLANS

Sampling plans are of two types:

1. *Attributes plans*. A random sample is taken from the lot and each unit is classified as acceptable or defective. The number defective is then compared with the allowable number stated in the plan, and a decision is made to accept or reject the lot. This chapter will illustrate attributes plans based on AQL, LQL, and AOQL.

2. *Variables plans*. A sample is taken and a *measurement* of a specified quality characteristic is made on each unit. These measurements are then summarized into a simple statistic (e.g., sample average), and the observed value is compared with an allowable value defined in the plan. A decision is then made to accept or reject the lot. This chapter will describe an AQL variables plan.

The key advantage of a variables sampling plan is the additional information provided in each sample which, in turn, results in smaller sample sizes as compared with an attributes plan having the same risks. However, if a product has several important quality characteristics, each must be evaluated against a separate variables acceptance criterion (e.g., numerical values must be obtained and the average and standard deviation for each characteristic calculated). In a corresponding attributes plan, the sample size required may be higher, but the several characteristics can be treated as a group and evaluated against one set of acceptance criteria.

19.8 SINGLE SAMPLING, DOUBLE SAMPLING, AND MULTIPLE SAMPLING

Many published sampling tables give a choice among single, double, and multiple sampling. In single-sampling plans, a random sample of n items is drawn from the lot. If the number of defectives is less than or equal to the acceptance number (c), the lot is accepted. Otherwise, the lot is rejected. In double-sampling plans (Figure 19.6), a smaller initial sample is usually drawn,

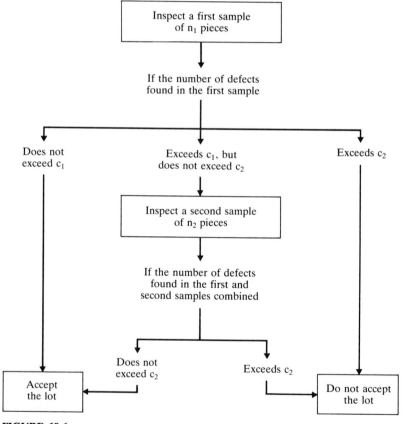

FIGURE 19.6
Schematic operation of double sampling.

and a decision to accept or reject is reached on the basis of this smaller first sample if the number of defectives is either quite large or quite small. A second sample is taken if the results of the first are not decisive. Since it is necessary to draw and inspect the second sample only in borderline cases, the average number of pieces inspected per lot is generally smaller with double sampling. In multiple-sampling plans, one or two or several still smaller samples are taken, usually continuing as needed until a decision to accept or reject is obtained. Thus, double- and multiple-sampling plans may mean less inspection but are more complicated to administer.

In general, it is possible to derive single-, double-, or multiple-sampling schemes with essentially identical OC curves (see QCH4, page 25.23 and Table 25.6).

19.9 CHARACTERISTICS OF A GOOD ACCEPTANCE PLAN

An acceptance sampling plan should have these characteristics:

- The index (AQL, AOQL, etc.) used to define "quality" should reflect the needs of the consumer and producer and not be chosen primarily for statistical convenience.
- The sampling risks should be known in quantitative terms (the OC curve). The producer should have adequate protection against the rejection of good lots; the consumer should be protected against the acceptance of bad lots.
- The plan should minimize the *total* cost of inspection of all products. This requires careful evaluation of the pros and cons of attributes and variables plans, as well as single, double, and multiple sampling. It should also reflect product priorities, particularly from the fitness-for-use viewpoint.
- The plan should make use of other knowledge, such as process capability, supplier data, and other information.
- The plan should have built-in flexibility to reflect changes in lot sizes, quality of product submitted, and any other pertinent factors.
- The measurements required by the plan should provide information useful in estimating individual lot quality and long-run quality.
- The plan should be simple to explain and administer.

See QCH4, Section 25, for elaboration of these characteristics. Fortunately, published tables are available which meet many of these characteristics. We now proceed to a discussion of three published plans. It will be seen that some published plans use the term "nonconformity" while others use the term "defective." We will follow the language of each plan.

19.10 ANSI/ASQC Z1.4

ANSI/ASQC Z1.4 (1981) is an attributes sampling system. Its quality index is the acceptable quality level (AQL). The AQL is the maximum percentage nonconforming (or the maximum number of nonconformities per 100 units) that, for purposes of sampling inspection, can be considered satisfactory as a process average. (The standard uses the term "nonconforming unit" rather than "defective unit.") The probability of accepting material of AQL quality is always high but not exactly the same for all plans. For lot quality just equal to the AQL, the "percentage of lots expected to be accepted" ranges from about 89 to 99. The choice may be made from 26 available AQL values ranging from 0.010 to 1000.0. (AQL values of 10.0 or less may be interpreted as percentage nonconforming or nonconformities per 100 units; values above 10.0 are interpreted as nonconformities per 100 units.)

The tables specify the relative amount of inspection to be used as "inspection level" I, II, or III; level II is regarded as normal. The inspection-level concept permits the user to balance the cost of inspection against the amount of protection required. The three levels involve inspection in amounts roughly in the ratio 0.4:1.0:1.6. (Four additional inspection levels are provided for situations requiring "small-sample inspection.")

A plan is chosen from the tables as follows:

1. The following information must be known:
   - Acceptable quality level (AQL)
   - Lot size
   - Type of sampling (single, double, or multiple)
   - Inspection level (usually level II)
2. Knowing the lot size and inspection level, a code letter is obtained from Table 19.2.
3. Knowing the code letter, AQL, and type of sampling, the sampling plan is read from Table 19.3. (Table 19.3 is for single sampling; the standard also provides tables for double and multiple sampling.)

For example, suppose a purchasing agency has contracted for a 1.5 percent AQL. Suppose also that the parts are bought in lots of 1500 pieces. From the table of sample-size code letters (Table 19.2), it is found that letter K plans are required for inspection level II. Table 19.3 states the sample size is 125. For AQL = 1.5, the acceptance number is given as five and the rejection number as six. This means that the entire lot of 1500 articles may be accepted if five or fewer nonconforming articles are found but must be rejected if six or more are found.

Sampling risks are defined by the OC curve published in the standard. The curve for this plan is shown in Figure 19.2 as curve A.

TABLE 19.2
Sample-size code letters

Lot or batch size	Special inspection levels				General inspection levels		
	S-1	S-2	S-3	S-4	I	II	III
2–8	A	A	A	A	A	A	B
9–15	A	A	A	A	A	B	C
16–25	A	A	B	B	B	C	D
26-50	A	B	B	C	C	D	E
51-90	B	B	C	C	C	E	F
91-150	B	B	C	D	D	F	G
151–280	B	C	D	E	E	G	H
281–500	B	C	D	E	F	H	J
501–1200	C	C	E	F	G	J	K
1201–3200	C	D	E	G	H	K	L
3201–10,000	C	D	F	G	J	L	M
10,001–35,000	C	D	F	H	K	M	N
35,001–150,000	D	E	G	J	L	N	P
150,001–500,000	D	E	G	J	M	P	Q
500,001 and over	D	E	H	K	N	Q	R

The standard provides single, double, and multiple plans for each code letter (i.e., lot-size category). The plans for code letter K are shown in Table 19.4. Thus, the three plans can be found under the AQL column of 1.5. For example, the double-sampling plan calls for a first sample of 80 units. If two or fewer nonconforming are found, the lot is accepted. If five or more nonconforming are found, the lot is rejected. If three or four nonconforming are found in the sample of 80, then a second sample of 80 is taken, giving a cumulative sample size of 160. If the total number of nonconforming in both samples is six or less, the lot is accepted; seven or more nonconforming means lot rejection.

Switching Procedures in ANSI/ASQC Z1.4

ANSI/ASQC Z1.4 includes provision for tightened inspection if quality deteriorates. If two out of five consecutive lots are rejected on original inspection, a tightened inspection plan is imposed. The sample size is usually the same as usual, but the acceptance number is reduced. (The tightened plans do require larger sample sizes if the probability of acceptance for an AQL lot is less than 0.75.) For the example previously cited, the tightened plan can be read from Table 19.4 as a sample size of 125 and an acceptance number of three.

TABLE 19.3
Master table for normal inspection (single sampling)

Acceptable quality (Ac Re), by AQL value:

Sample-size code letter	Sample size	0.010	0.015	0.025	0.040	0.065	0.10	0.15	0.25	0.40	0.65	1.0	1.5
A	2	↓	↓	↓	↓	↓	↓	↓	↓	↓	↓	↓	↓
B	3	↓	↓	↓	↓	↓	↓	↓	↓	↓	↓	↓	↓
C	5	↓	↓	↓	↓	↓	↓	↓	↓	↓	↓	↓	↓
D	8	↓	↓	↓	↓	↓	↓	↓	↓	↓	↓	↓	0 1
E	13	↓	↓	↓	↓	↓	↓	↓	↓	↓	↓	0 1	↑
F	20	↓	↓	↓	↓	↓	↓	↓	↓	↓	0 1	↑	↓
G	32	↓	↓	↓	↓	↓	↓	↓	↓	0 1	↑	↓	1 2
H	50	↓	↓	↓	↓	↓	↓	↓	0 1	↑	↓	1 2	2 3
J	80	↓	↓	↓	↓	↓	↓	0 1	↑	↓	1 2	2 3	3 4
K	125	↓	↓	↓	↓	↓	0 1	↑	↓	1 2	2 3	3 4	5 6
L	200	↓	↓	↓	↓	0 1	↑	↓	1 2	2 3	3 4	5 6	7 8
M	315	↓	↓	↓	0 1	↑	↓	1 2	2 3	3 4	5 6	7 8	10 11
N	500	↓	↓	0 1	↑	↓	1 2	2 3	3 4	5 6	7 8	10 11	14 15
P	800	↓	0 1	↑	↓	1 2	2 3	3 4	5 6	7 8	10 11	14 15	21 22
Q	1250	0 1	↑	↓	1 2	2 3	3 4	5 6	7 8	10 11	14 15	21 22	↑
R	2000	↑		1 2	2 3	3 4	5 6	7 8	10 11	14 15	21 22	↑	

Notes: ↓, use first sampling plan below arrow. If sample size equals, or exceeds, lot of batch size, do 100% inspection.

↑, use first sampling plan above arrow.

Ac, acceptance number.

Re, rejection number.

ANSI/ASQC Z1.4 also provides for reduced inspection where the supplier's record has been good. The preceding ten lots must have had a normal inspection with all lots accepted. A table of lower limits for the process average is provided to help decide if the supplier's record has been good enough to switch to reduced inspection. The plan does, however, provide an option of switching to reduced inspection without using the table of lower limits. Under reduced sampling, the sample size is usually 40 percent of the normal sample size.

These switching rules apply when production is submitted at a steady rate. The plan provides other rules concerning the use of normal, tightened, and reduced inspection.

Other Provisions of ANSI/ASQC Z1.4

The standard provides OC curves for most of the individual plans along with "limiting quality" values for a probability of acceptance of ten percent and five

levels (normal inspection)

2.5	4.0	6.5	10	15	25	40	65	100	150	250	400	650	1000
Ac Re	Ac Re	Ac Re	Ac Re	Ac Re	Ac Re	Ac Re	Ac Re	Ac Re	Ac Re	Ac Re	Ac Re	Ac Re	Ac Re
↓	↓	0 1	↓	↓	1 2	2 3	3 4	5 6	7 8	10 11	14 15	21 22	30 31
↑	0 1	↑	↓	1 2	2 3	3 4	5 6	7 8	10 11	14 15	21 22	30 31	44 45
0 1	↑	↓	1 2	2 3	3 4	5 6	7 8	10 11	14 15	21 22	30 31	44 45	↑
↑	↓	1 2	2 3	3 4	5 6	7 8	10 11	14 15	21 22	30 31	44 45		↑
↓	1 2	2 3	3 4	5 6	7 8	10 11	14 15	21 22	30 31	44 45		↑	
1 2	2 3	3 4	5 6	7 8	10 11	14 15	21 22		↑				
2 3	3 4	5 6	7 8	10 11	14 15	21 22	↑						
3 4	5 6	7 8	10 11	14 15	21 22	↑							
5 6	7 8	10 11	14 15	21 22	↑								
7 8	10 11	14 15	21 22	↑									
10 11	14 15	21 22	↑										
14 15	21 22	↑											
21 22	↑												

percent. Average sample-size curves for double and multiple sampling are also included. The latter curves show the average sample sizes expected as a function of the product quality submitted. Although the OC curves are roughly the same for single, double, and multiple sampling, the average sample-size curves vary considerably because of the inherent differences among the three types of sampling. The standard also states the AOQL that would result if all rejected lots were screened for nonconforming units.

In ANSI/ASQC Z1.4, a sampling scheme is defined as "a combination of sampling plans with switching rules and possibly a provision for discontinuance of inspection." For the sampling schemes associated with the individual plans, the standard provides OC curves and information on AOQL, limiting quality, and average sample sizes—all for single sampling.

The original ANSI/ASQC Z1.4 was a direct copy of a military standard, MIL-STD-105, "Sampling Procedures and Tables for Inspection by Attributes." Over the years, both standards have been revised but have retained

TABLE 19.4
Sampling plan for sample-size code letter: K

Acceptable quality levels (normal inspection)

Type of sampling plan	Cumulative sample size	Less than 0.10 (Ac/Re)	0.10 (Ac/Re)	0.15 (Ac/Re)	0.25 (Ac/Re)	1.0 (Ac/Re)	1.5 (Ac/Re)	2.5 (Ac/Re)	4.0 (Ac/Re)	6.5 (Ac/Re)	10 (Ac/Re)	Higher than 10 (Ac/Re)	Cumulative sample size
Single	125	▽	0 1	X	·	3 4	5 6	7 8	10 11	14 15	21 22	Δ	125
Double	80	▽	*	Use letter J	Use letter M	1 4	3 7	5 9	6 10	9 14	11 16	Δ	80
	160					4 5	11 12	12 13	15 16	23 24	26 27		160
Multiple	32	▽	*			# —	# 4	0 4	0 5	1 8	2 9	Δ	32
	64					0 3	1 5	2 7	3 8	6 12	7 14		64
	96					1 4	2 6	4 9	6 11	11 17	13 19		96
	128					2 5	3 7	6 11	8 13	16 22	19 25		128
	160					3 6	5 8	9 12	11 15	22 25	25 29		160
	192					4 7	7 9	12 14	14 17	27 29	31 33		192
	224					6 9	9 10	14 15	18 19	32 33	37 38		224

	Less than 0.15	0.15	X	0.25		1.5	2.5		4.0	6.5	10	Higher than 10	

Acceptable quality levels (tightened inspection)

Notes: ▽, Use next preceding sample-size code letter for which acceptance and rejection numbers are available.

▽, Use next subsequent sample-size code letter for which acceptance and rejection numbers are available.

Ac, Acceptance number.

Re, Rejection number.

*, Use single-sampling plan above (or alternatively use letter N).

#, Acceptance not permitted at this sample size.

474

their essential similarity. ANSI/ASQC Z1.4 issued a revision in 1981; MIL-STD-105E was issued in 1989. Mundel (1990) describes the subtle changes incorporated into MIL-STD-105E.

19.11 DODGE-ROMIG SAMPLING TABLES

Dodge and Romig (1959) provide four sets of attributes plans emphasizing either lot-by-lot quality (LTPD) or long-run quality (AOQL):

Lot tolerance percentage defective (LTPD):   single sampling
                                                double sampling
Average outgoing quality limit (AOQL):   single sampling
                                                double sampling

These plans differ from those in ANSI/ASQC Z1.4 in that they assume that all rejected lots are 100 percent inspected and the defectives replaced with acceptable items. Plans with this feature are called *rectifying inspection plans*. The tables provide protection against poor quality on either a lot-by-lot basis or average long-run quality. The LTPD plans assure that a lot having poor quality will have a low probability of acceptance, i.e., the probability of acceptance (or consumer's risk) is 0.1 for a lot with LTPD quality. The LTPD values range from 0.5 to 10.0 percent defective. The AOQL plans assure that, after all sampling and 100 percent inspection of rejected lots, the *average* quality over many lots will not exceed the AOQL. The AOQL values range from 0.1 to 10.0 percent. Each LTPD plan lists the corresponding AOQL, and each AOQL plan lists the LTPD.

Table 19.5 shows a Dodge-Romig table for single sampling on the lot tolerance basis. All the plans listed in this table have the same risk (0.10) of accepting submitted lots that contain exactly five percent of defective articles. For example, if the estimated process average percent defective is between 2.01 and 2.50 percent, the last column at the right gives the plans that will provide the minimum inspection per lot. However, the probability that a lot of quality p_t will be rejected is the same for all columns, so that an initial incorrect estimate of the process average would have little effect except to increase somewhat the total number of pieces inspected per lot. The selection of a plan thus requires only two items of information: the size of the lot to be sampled and the prevailing average quality of the supplier for the product in question. Process average is determined from past records, modified by any supplemental knowledge useful for predicting the expected quality level.

Table 19.6 shows a typical table of AOQL plans using double sampling. In contrast to the lot tolerance tables, this table gives plans which differ considerably as to lot tolerance but which have the same AOQL (one percent). (The corresponding lot tolerances are, however, given.)

TABLE 19.5
Single-sampling table for lot tolerance percentage defective (LTPD) = 5.0%

Lot size	Process average 0 to 0.05%			Process average 0.06 to 0.50%			. . . .	Process average 2.01 to 2.50%		
	n	c	AOQL %	n	c	AOQL %		n	c	AOQL %
1–30	All	0	0	All	0	0		All	0	0
31–50	30	0	0.49	30	0	0.49		30	0	0.49
51–100	37	0	0.63	37	0	0.63		37	0	0.63
101–200	40	0	0.74	40	0	0.74		40	0	0.74
201–300	43	0	0.74	43	0	0.74		95	2	0.99
301–400	44	0	0.74	44	0	0.74		145	4	1.1
401–500	45	0	0.75	75	1	0.95		150	4	1.2
501–600	45	0	0.76	75	1	0.98		175	5	1.3
601–800	45	0	0.77	75	1	1.0		200	6	1.4
801–1000	45	0	0.78	75	1	1.0		225	7	1.5
1001–2000	45	0	0.80	75	1	1.0		280	9	1.8
2001–3000	75	1	1.1	105	2	1.3		370	13	2.1
3001–4000	75	1	1.1	105	2	1.3		420	15	2.2
4001–5000	75	1	1.1	105	2	1.3		440	16	2.2
5001–7000	75	1	1.1	105	2	1.3		490	18	2.4
7001–10,000	75	1	1.1	105	2	1.3		535	20	2.5
10,001–20,000	75	1	1.1	135	3	1.4		610	23	2.6
20,001–50,000	75	1	1.1	135	3	1.4		700	27	2.7
50,001–100,000	75	1	1.1	160	4	1.6		770	30	2.8

Notes: n, sample size; *c*, acceptance number.
AOQL, average outgoing quality limit.
"All" indicates that each piece in the lot is to be inspected.
Source: Dodge and Romig (1959).

In terms of parts per million, the Dodge-Romig plans range from 1,000 PPM (AOQL of 0.1 percent) to 10,000 PPM (AOQL of 10.0 percent). Cross (1984) provides AOQL plans (single sampling, acceptance number of 0) for PPM values of 500, 250, 100, and 50. Be prepared for high sample sizes, e.g., for a lot size of 1000 and a PPM of 50, the sample size is 880.

AOQL plans are appropriate only when all rejected lots are 100 percent inspected. The averaging of the perfect quality of the 100 percent inspected lots with the poor quality of unsatisfactory lots occasionally accepted (owing to the unavoidable consumer's risk) determines the average outgoing quality and makes a limit possible. AOQL schemes are open to question where rejected

TABLE 19.6
Double-sampling table for average outgoing quality limit (AOQL) = 1.0%

	Process average 0 to 0.02%							Process average 0.21 to 0.40%					
	Trial 1		Trial 2			$p_t,$		Trial 1		Trial 2			$p_t,$
Lot size	n_1	c_1	n_2	n_1+n_2	c_2	%	· · · · · · ·	n_1	c_1	n_2	n_1+n_2	c_2	%
1–25	All	0	—	—	—	—		All	0				
26–50	22	0	—	—	—	7.7		22	0	—	—	—	7.7
51–100	33	0	17	50	1	6.9		33	0	17	50	1	6.9
101–200	43	0	22	65	1	5.8		43	0	22	65	1	5.8
201–300	47	0	28	75	1	5.5		47	0	28	75	1	5.5
301–400	49	0	31	80	1	5.4		55	0	60	115	2	4.8
401–500	50	0	30	80	1	5.4		55	0	65	120	2	4.7
501–600	50	0	30	80	1	5.4		60	0	65	125	2	4.6
601–800	50	0	35	85	1	5.3		60	0	70	130	2	4.5
801–1000	55	0	30	85	1	5.2		60	0	75	135	2	4.4
1001–2000	55	0	35	90	1	5.1		75	0	120	195	3	3.8
2001–3000	65	0	80	145	2	4.2		75	0	125	200	3	3.7
3001–4000	70	0	80	150	2	4.1		80	0	175	255	4	3.5
4001–5000	70	0	80	150	2	4.1		80	0	180	260	4	3.4
5001–7000	70	0	80	150	2	4.1		80	0	180	260	4	3.4
7001–10,000	70	0	80	150	2	4.1		85	0	180	265	4	3.3
10,001–20,000	70	0	80	150	2	4.1		90	0	230	320	5	3.2
20,001–50,000	75	0	80	155	2	4.0		95	0	300	395	6	2.9
50,00--100,000	75	0	80	155	2	4.0		170	1	380	550	8	2.6

Notes: Trial 1: first sample size; c_1, acceptance number for first sample.

Trial 2: n_2, second sample size; c_2, acceptance number for first and second samples combined.

p_t, lot tolerance percentage defective with a consumer's risk P_c of 0.10.

"All" indicates that each piece in the lot is to be inspected.

Source: Dodge and Romig (1959).

lots are returned to an outside supplier, since there is no assurance that they will be 100 percent inspected and returned.

Sampling is uneconomical if the average quality submitted is not considerably better than the AOQL specified. For this reason, the Dodge-Romig AOQL tables do not give any plans for process averages which exceed the AOQL. Similarly, lot tolerance plans are not given for process averages greater than one-half of the specified lot tolerance. Actually, 100 percent inspection is often less expensive than sampling if 40 percent or more of submitted lots are rejected, since the expenses of administration of the sampling plan and of double handling of rejected lots are eliminated.

Minimum Inspection per Lot

All Dodge-Romig plans are constructed to minimize the average total inspection (ATI) per lot for product of a given process average. This is an important feature of the Dodge-Romig plans and deserves further explanation.

Assume that a customer establishes acceptance criteria as follows:

$$\text{Lot tolerance fraction defective } p_t = 0.05$$

$$\text{Customer's risk } P_c = 0.1$$

A great many sampling plans meet these criteria; i.e., there are many combinations of sample size and acceptance number that would have an OC curve going through this point.

The total number of articles inspected is made up of two components: (1) the sample which is inspected for each lot, and (2) the remaining parts which must be inspected in those lots which fail to pass the sampling inspection.

For small acceptance numbers, the total number inspected is high because many lots need to be detailed. For large acceptance numbers, the total is again high, this time because of the large size of the samples. The minimum sum occurs at a point between these extremes. All Dodge-Romig plans minimize the average total inspection. For a sample calculation, see QCH4, page 25.16.

QCH4, Section 25, presents several other types of attributes sampling plans. See also Section 24.11 in this book for a discussion of sampling for product audit.

19.12 ACCEPTANCE SAMPLING BY VARIABLES

In *attributes* sampling plans, each item inspected is classified as either conforming or nonconforming. The total number of nonconforming items in the sample is then compared with the acceptance number and a decision made on the lot. In *variables* sampling plans, a *measurement* is taken and recorded for each item in the sample. An *index* is calculated from these measurements, compared with an "allowable" value, and a decision is made on the lot. The sample size and allowable value are a function of the desired sampling risks. This chapter explains one published plan. (Section 15.5 explains another variables plan known as the lot plot plan.)

An example of a variables plan is ANSI/ASQC Z1.9 (1980). The format and terminology are similar to those of ANSI/ASQC Z1.4; for example, the concepts of AQL, code letters, inspection levels, reduced and tightened inspection, and OC curves are all included. The military version of Z1.9 is MIL-STD-414.

ANSI/ASQC Z1.9 assumes a normal distribution and that information on variability is available or will be obtained in the sample. To provide flexibility in application, a number of alternative procedures are included.

Only one of the procedures will be described here. A plan is selected as follows:

1. An AQL is selected. Levels range from 0.04 to 15 percent.
2. A sample-size code letter based on the lot size and inspection level is selected. Five inspection levels are provided. Level IV is considered normal and is used unless another level is specified. Table 19.7 is used to determine the sample-size code letter.
3. Select the sampling plan from a master table in section B, C, or D in ANSI/ASQC Z1.9. Sections B and C contain plans for the case when the variability is unknown and is measured by the standard deviation or range, respectively. Section D provides the plans when the variability is known (in terms of standard deviation). A plan from section B will be selected for the following problem.

Example 19.1. The maximum temperature of operation for a device is specified as 209°F (98.3°C). A lot of 40 is submitted for inspection. Inspection level IV with an AQL of one percent is to be used. The standard deviation is unknown. Assuming that operating temperature follows a normal distribution, what variables sampling plan should be used to inspect the lot?

TABLE 19.7
Sample-size code letters

Lot size	Inspection level				
	I	II	III	IV	V
3–8	B	B	B	B	C
9–15	B	B	B	B	D
16–25	B	B	B	C	E
26–40	B	B	B	D	F
41–65	B	B	C	E	G
66–110	B	B	D	F	H
111–180	B	C	E	G	I
181–300	B	D	F	H	J
301–500	C	E	G	I	K
501–800	D	F	H	J	L
801–1300	E	G	I	K	L
1301–3200	F	H	J	L	M
3201–8000	G	I	L	M	N
8001–22,000	H	J	M	N	O
22,001–110,000	I	K	N	O	P
110,001–550,000	I	K	O	P	Q
550,001 and over	I	K	P	Q	Q

Note: Sample-size code letters given in body of table are applicable when the indicated inspection levels are to be used.

One type of plan in section B requires that n measurements be taken, the average and standard deviation calculated, and an evaluation made of the number of standard deviations between the sample average and the specification limit. More specifically,

1. The same average $\bar{X}$ and the estimate of the lot standard deviation s are computed. $(U - \bar{X})/s$ for an upper specification limit U, or $(\bar{X} - L)/s$ for a lower specification limit L, is also computed.
2. If the fraction computed in step one is equal to or greater than k, the lot is accepted; otherwise, the lot is rejected.

Table 19.7 provides the code letter as D, and Table 19.8 (Master Table B-1 in MIL-STD-414) provides the values of n and k as five and 1.53, respectively.

TABLE 19.8
Master table for normal and tightened inspection for means based on variability unknown, standard deviation method

		Single specification limit, form 1							
		Acceptability quality levels (normal inspection)							
Sample-size code letter	Sample size	0.04 k	· · · · · · ·	1.00 k	1.50 k	2.50 k	4.00 k	· ·	15.00 k
B	3			↓	↓	1.12	0.958		0.341
C	4			1.45	1.34	1.17	1.01		0.393
D	5			1.53	1.40	1.24	1.07		0.455
E	7			1.62	1.50	1.33	1.15		0.536
F	10			1.72	1.58	1.41	1.23		0.611
G	15	2.64		1.79	1.65	1.47	1.30		0.664
H	20	2.69		1.82	1.69	1.51	1.33		0.695
I	25	2.72		1.85	1.72	1.53	1.35		0.712
J	30	2.73		1.86	1.73	1.55	1.36		0.723
K	35	2.77		1.89	1.76	1.57	1.39		0.745
L	40	2.77		1.89	1.76	1.58	1.39		0.746
M	50	2.83		1.93	1.80	1.61	1.42		0.774
N	75	2.90		1.98	1.84	1.65	1.46		0.804
O	100	2.92		2.00	1.86	1.67	1.48		0.819
P	150	2.96		2.03	1.89	1.70	1.51		0.841
Q	200	2.97		2.04	1.89	1.70	1.51		0.845
		0.065		1.50	2.50	4.00	6.50		

Acceptable quality levels (tightened inspection)

Notes: All AQL values are in percentage defective.
↓, use first sampling plan below arrow, i.e., both sample size as well as k value. When sample size equals or exceeds lot size, every item in the lot must be inspected.

Now suppose the measurements were 197°F (91.7°C), 188°F (86.7°C), 184°F (84.4°C), 205°F (96.1°C), and 201°F (93.9°C). This yields an $\bar{X}$ of 195°F (90.6°C) and an s of 8.81°F (-12.9°C). Then $(U - \bar{X})/s = (209 - 195)/8.81 = 1.59$. As 1.59 is greater than 1.53, the lot is accepted. The OC curve for the plan is included in the standard.

The reader is referred to the standard itself for other procedures and tables.

QCH4, Table 25.16, summarizes nine types of variables sampling plans, including MIL-STD-414.

19.13 SAMPLING PROCEDURES BASED ON PRIOR QUALITY DATA

The plans discussed in this chapter make no assumption about the *distribution of percentage defective* of lots submitted to the plan. This implies that all possible values of percentage defective have an equal probability of occurrence. In practice, this is not true. As the plans provide protection against percentage defective that is unlikely to occur, the result is often excessive sample sizes.

Tables have been developed that incorporate data on the quality of previous lots into the sampling tables. We calculate certain parameters from past lots and define sampling parameters such as the AOQL, AQL, and LQL. The tables then provide sample size and acceptance criteria for single-sampling plans. These are called empirical *Bayesian sampling plans*.

The steps are:

1. Collecting quality data on previous lots of size N and sample size n. Calculate the fraction defective, p, in each sample.
2. Calculating the average fraction defective, $\bar{p}$, the total variance, and the sampling variance.
3. Defining values for parameters such as the AOQL, AQL, and LQL. The tables incorporate a producer's risk of five percent at the AQL and a consumer's risk of ten percent at the LQL.
4. Reading the plan from the tables.

Calvin (1984, 1990) provides procedures and tables for determining the sampling plans. A comparison of Bayesian single-sample sizes with the single-sample sizes in MIL-STD-105E shows that the Bayesian approach usually requires much smaller sample sizes, particularly when the variation in lot percentage defective is small.

In the Bayesian approach, the derivation of a sampling plan requires an assumption of a probability distribution for incoming quality.

The Bayesian approach to acceptance sampling has been slow in developing due to controversy about the likely probability distribution of lots.

Some people believe that such probabilities can be set based on subjective opinions about quality levels. Others believe that the probabilities must be based on actual data. In the opinion of the authors, these probabilities must be based on actual data. However, in many cases, such data are available, although not always in a convenient form. The challenge is to make use of all pertinent past data by developing ways to convert the data to probabilities of occurrence. If this is not done quantitatively, it *will* be done by default by practitioners, who must constantly use their past knowledge *intuitively* to arrive at compromise forms of action when sample sizes based on classical tables are larger than can be tolerated.

19.14 SELECTION OF A NUMERICAL VALUE OF THE QUALITY INDEX

The problem of selecting a value of the quality index (e.g., AQL, AOQL, or lot tolerance percentage defective) is one of balancing the cost of finding and correcting a defective against the loss incurred if a defective slips through an inspection procedure.

Enell (1954), in a classic paper, has suggested that the break-even point (see Section 19.2) be used in the selection of an AQL. The break-even point for inspection is defined as the cost to inspect one piece divided by the damage done by one defective. For the example cited, the break-even point was five percent defective.

As a five percent defective quality level is the break-even point between sorting and sampling, the appropriate sampling plan should provide for a lot to have a 50 percent probability of being sorted or sampled; i.e., the probability of acceptance for the plan should be 0.50 at a five percent defective quality level. The OC curves in a set of sampling tables such as ANSI/ASQC Z1.4 can now be examined to determine an AQL. For example, suppose that the device is inspected in lots of 3,000 pieces. The OC curves for this case (code letter K) are shown in ANSI/ASQC Z1.4 and Figure 19.2. The plan closest to having a P_a of 0.50 for a five percent level is the plan for an AQL of 1.5 percent. Therefore, this is the plan to adopt.

Some plans include a classification of defects to help determine the numerical value of the AQL. Defects are first classified as critical, major, or minor according to definitions provided in the standard. Different AQLs may be designated for groups of defects considered collectively or for individual defects. Critical defects may have a zero percent AQL while major defects may be assigned a low AQL, say one percent, and minor defects a higher AQL, say four percent. Some manufacturers of complex products specify quality in terms of number of defects per million parts.

In practice, the quantification of the quality index is a matter of judgment based on the following factors: past performance on quality, effect of nonconforming product on later production steps, effect of nonconforming product on fitness for use, urgency of delivery requirements, and cost of achieving the specified quality level.

A thorough discussion of this difficult issue is provided by Schilling (1982, pp. 571-586).

19.15 HOW TO SELECT THE PROPER SAMPLING PROCEDURES

Sampling procedures can serve different purposes. As itemized by Schilling (QCH4, pages 25.93–25.94), these include:

• Guaranteeing quality levels at stated risks
• Maintaining quality at AQL level or better
• Guaranteeing an AOQL
• Reducing inspection after good history
• Checking inspection
• Ensuring compliance to mandatory standards
• Reliability sampling
• Checking inspection accuracy

For each of the purposes, Schilling recommends specific attributes or variable sampling plans. Selection of a plan depends on the purpose, the quality history, and the extent of knowledge of the process. Listen to this simply stated wisdom from one of the early pioneers (Dodge, 1950, p. 8):

> A product with a history of consistently good quality requires less inspection than one with no history or a history of erratic quality. Accordingly, it is good practice to include in inspection procedures provisions for reducing or increasing the amount of inspection, depending on the character and quantity of evidence at hand regarding the level of quality and the degree of control shown.

The steps involved in the selection and application of a sampling procedure are shown in Figure 19.7. Emphasis is on the feedback of information necessary for the proper application, modification, and evolution of sampling in a manner that encourages continuous improvement and reduced inspection costs. This can be achieved by moving from a system of acceptance sampling to acceptance control.

Moving from Acceptance Sampling to Acceptance Control

Acceptance sampling is the process of evaluating a portion of the product in a lot for the purpose of accepting or rejecting the entire lot as either conforming or not conforming to a quality specification. Acceptance control is a "continu-

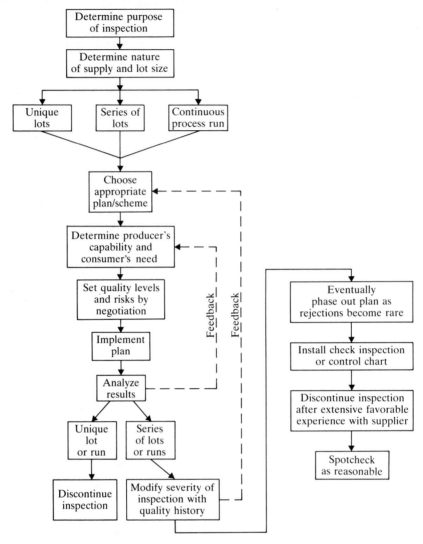

FIGURE 19.7
Check sequence for implementation of sampling procedure. (*From Schilling, 1982.*) Reprinted by courtesy of Marcel Dekker, Inc.

ing strategy of selection, application, and modification of acceptance sampling procedures to a changing inspection environment" (Schilling, 1982, p. 564). This evaluation of a sampling plan application is shown in the life cycle of acceptance control (Table 19.9). The cycle is applied over the lifetime of a product to achieve: (1) quality improvement (using process control and process capability concepts) and (2) reduction and elimination of inspection (using acceptance sampling).

TABLE 19.9
Life cycle of acceptance control application

Stage	Step	Method
Preparatory	Choose plan appropriate to purpose	Analysis of quality system to define the exact need for the procedure
	Determine producer capability	Process performance evaluation using control charts
	Determine consumer needs	Process capability study using control charts
	Set quality levels and risks	Economic analysis and negotiation
	Determine plans	Standard procedures if possible
Initiation	Train inspector	Include plan, procedure, records, and action
	Apply plan properly	Ensure random sampling
	Analyze results	Keep records and control charts
Operational	Assess protection	Periodically check quality history and OC curves
	Adjust plan	When possible change severity to reflect quality history and cost
	Decrease sample size if warranted	Modify to use appropriate sampling plans taking advantage of credibility of supplier with cumulative results
Phase out	Eliminate inspection effort where possible	Use demerit rating or check inspection procedures when quality is consistently good
		Keep control charts
Elimination	Spot check only	Remove all inspection when warranted by extensive favorable history

Source: Schilling (1982, p. 566). Reprinted by courtesy of Marcel Dekker, Inc.

SUMMARY

- Acceptance sampling is the process of evaluating a portion of the product in a lot for the purpose of accepting or rejecting the entire lot.
- We have four alternatives for evaluating lots: no inspection, small samples, large samples, or 100 percent inspection.
- Sampling risks are of two kinds: good lots can be rejected and bad lots can be accepted. An operating characteristic (OC) curve quantifies these risks.
- Published sampling plans categorize quality in terms of acceptable quality level (AQL), limiting quality level (LQL), indifference quality level (IQL), or average outgoing quality limit (AOQL).

- Attributes sampling plans evaluate each unit of product as simply acceptable or defective: ANSI/ASQC Z1.4 (1981) and the Dodge-Romig sampling tables are examples of attributes plans.
- Variables sampling plans involve measurements on product units. An example is ANSI/ASQC Z1.9 (1980).
- Bayesian sampling tables use data on the quality of previous lots to determine a probability distribution for incoming quality.

PROBLEMS

19.1. A large gray-iron foundry casts the base for precision grinders. These bases are produced at the rate of 18 per day and are 100 percent inspected at the foundry for flaws in the metal. The castings are then stored and subsequently shipped in lots of 300 to the grinder manufacturer. The grinder manufacturer has found these lots to be ten percent defective. Upon receiving a lot, the manufacturer inspects 12 of them and rejects the lot if two or more defectives are found. What is the chance that he will reject a given lot?

19.2. Verify the operating characteristic curve for a lot size of 200 in Figure 19.4a. Calculate at least three points by the Poisson method.

19.3. Using only the addition and multiplication rules for probability, verify the operating characteristic curve in Figure 19.3. Calculate at least three points.

19.4. The following double-sampling plan has been proposed for evaluating a lot of 50 pieces:

Sample	Sample Size	Acceptance number	Rejection number
1	3	0	3
2	3	2	3

Using only the addition and multiplication rules for probability, calculate the probability of accepting a lot which is ten percent defective.
    Answer: 0.984.

19.5. Prepare the operating characteristic curves for a single-sampling plan with an acceptance number of zero. Use sample sizes of two, five, ten, and 20.

19.6. Table 19.5 provides an LTPD plan for a lot size of 800 and process average of 0.50 percent. The plan calls for a sample size of 75 and an acceptance number of one. Prepare an operating characteristic curve by calculating at least three points. Also, calculate the average outgoing quality for each quality level.

19.7. A manufacturer wishes to sample a purchased component used in their assembly. They wish to reject lots that are five percent defective. The components are received in lots of 1,000 which average about 2.2 percent defective. From the past, they know the supplier usually submits lots two percent defective or less. The supplier has agreed to 100 percent inspect all rejected lots. Find a sampling plan to meet these conditions.

19.8. A double-sampling plan is desired that will assure long-run average quality of one percent defective or better. All rejected lots will be 100 percent inspected. The lot size is expected to vary between 1200 and 1800. Past data show the supplier to average about 0.30 percent defective.

  (*a*) Define the sampling plan.

  (*b*) What percent defective in a lot would have a ten percent chance of being accepted by this plan?

  (*c*) What is the probability that a lot which is four percent defective will be *rejected* on the *first* sample of the double-sampling procedure?

   Answer: (*b*) 3.8 percent, (*c*) 0.36.

19.9. You are quality manager for a company receiving large quantities of materials from a supplier in lots of 1000. The cost of inspecting the lots is $0.76/unit. The cost that is incurred if bad material is introduced into your product is $15.20/unit. A sampling plan of 75 with acceptance number equal to two has been submitted to you by one of your engineers. In the past, lots submitted by the supplier have averaged 3.4 percent defective.

  (*a*) Is a sampling plan economically justified?

  (*b*) Prepare an operating characteristic curve.

  (*c*) If you want to accept only lots of four percent defective or better, what do you think of the sampling plan submitted by the engineer?

  (*d*) Suppose that rejected lots are 100 percent inspected. If a supplier submits many four percent defective lots, what will be the average outgoing quality of these lots?

19.10. Refer to MIL-STD-105D with the following conditions:

  • Lot size = 10,000

  • Inspection level II

  • Acceptable quality level = four percent

  (*a*) Find a single-sampling plan for normal inspection.

  (*b*) Suppose that a lot is sampled and accepted. Someone makes the statement, "This means the lot has four percent or less defective." Comment on this statement. (Assume that the sample was randomly selected and no inspection errors were made.)

  (*c*) Calculate the probability of accepting a four percent defective lot under normal inspection.

   Answer: (*c*) 0.98.

19.11. A manufacturer sells his product in large lots to a customer who uses a sampling plan at incoming inspection. The plan calls for a sample of 200 units and an acceptance number of two. Rejected lots are returned to the manufacturer. If a lot is rejected and returned, the manufacturer has decided to gamble and send it right back to the customer without screening it (and without telling the customer it was a rejected lot). He hopes that another random sample will lead to an acceptance of the lot. What is the probability that a two percent defective lot will be accepted on either one or two submissions to the customer?

   Answer: 0.42.

19.12. A customer is furnished resistors to the government under MIL-STD-105D. Inspection level II has been specified with an AQL of 1.0 percent. Lot sizes vary from 900 to 1200.

(a) What single-sampling plan will be used?

(b) Calculate the quality (in terms of percentage defective) that has an equal chance of being accepted or rejected.

(c) What is the chance that a one percent defective lot will be accepted?

Answer: (b) 3.4 percent; (c) 0.95.

19.13. Refer to Problem 19.10. What sample size would be required by MIL-STD-414? (Assume inspection level IV, normal inspection, variability measured by the standard deviation, single specification limit, form 1.)

Answer: 75

19.14. Refer to Problem 19.12. What sample size would be required by MIL-STD-414? (Assume inspection level IV and Table 19.8 applies.)

Answer: 35

19.15. A rule-of-thumb sampling plan states that, for any lot size, the sample size should be ten percent of the lot and the acceptance number should be zero. It is believed that this procedure will hold the sampling risks constant. Prepare the operating characteristic curves using this plan for lot sizes of 100, 200, and 1000. Calculate points for quality levels of zero, two, four, six, ten, and 14 percent defective. Compare the three curves and draw conclusions about the sampling risks.

REFERENCES

ANSI/ASQC Z1.9 (1980). "Sampling Procedures and Tables for Inspection by Variables for Percent Nonconforming," American Society for Quality Control, Milwaukee.

ANSI/ASQC Z1.4 (1981). "Sampling Procedures and Tables for Inspection by Attributes," American Society for Quality Control, Milwaukee.

Calvin, Thomas W. (1984). *How and When to Perform Bayesian Acceptance Sampling,* American Society for Quality Control, Milwaukee.

Calvin, Thomas W. (1990). "Bayesian Analysis," in Harrison M. Wadsworth, ed., *Handbook of Statistical Methods for Engineers and Scientists,* McGraw-Hill, Inc., New York, pp. 10.15–10.18.

Cross, Robert (1984). "Parts per Million AOQL Sampling Plans," *Quality Progress,* November, pp. 28–30.

Dodge, H. F. (1950). "Inspection for Quality Assurance," *Industrial Quality Control,* vol. 7, no. 1, p. 8.

Dodge, H. F., and H. G. Romig (1959). *Sampling Inspection Tables,* 2nd ed., John Wiley and Sons, Inc., New York.

Enell, J. W. (1954). "What Sampling Plan Shall I Choose?" *Industrial Quality Control,* vol. 10, no. 6, pp. 96–100.

Grant, Eugene L., and Richard S. Leavenworth (1988). *Statistical Quality Control,* 6th ed., McGraw-Hill Book Company, New York.

Milligan, Glenn W. (1991). "Is Sampling Really Dead?" *Quality Progress,* April, pp. 77–81.

Mundel, August B. (1990). "MIL-STD-105E Sampling Procedures and Tables for Inspection by Attributes," *Quality Engineering,* vol. 2, no. 3, pp. 353–356.

Quality (1978). "Wescom Inc.—A Study in Telecommunications Quality," August, p. 30.

Quality Engineering (1990). "*Letters to the Editor,*" vol. 3, no. 2, pp. vii–xii.

Schilling, Edward G. (1978). "A Lot Sensitive Sampling Plan for Compliance Testing and Acceptance Inspection," *Journal of Quality Technology,* vol. 10, no. 2, pp. 47–51.

Schilling, E. G. (1982). *Acceptance Sampling in Quality Control,* Marcel Dekker, New York and Basel.

Schilling, E. G., and J. H. Sheesley (1978). "The Performance of MIL-STD-105D under the Switching Rules, Part I: Evaluation; Part II: Tables," *Journal of Quality Technology,* vol. 10, no. 2, pp. 76–83; vol. 10, no. 3, pp. 104–124.

SUPPLEMENTARY READING

Acceptance sampling—general: QCH4, Section 25.
Schilling, E. G. (1982). *Acceptance Sampling in Quality Control,* Marcel Dekker, New York and Basel.

Acceptance sampling—pros and cons: Papadakis, Emmanuel P. (1985). "The Deming Inspection Criterion for Choosing Zero or 100% Inspection," *Journal of Quality Technology,* vol. 17, no. 3, pp. 121–127.

CHAPTER
20

MARKETING, FIELD PERFORMANCE, AND CUSTOMER SERVICE

20.1 SCOPE OF THIS CHAPTER

This chapter discusses quality-related activities when the product is made available to potential customers. Included in the discussion are the quality-related activities in marketing, distribution, installation, use, product safety, customer service, processing of complaints, and field feedback. We start by discussing how customers perceive quality.

20.2 CUSTOMER PERCEPTION OF QUALITY

It is valuable to examine the factors that influence customer perception of quality. The insights gained can clearly help to market the product successfully. Research conducted by Takeuchi and Quelch (1983) concludes that the perception can be dissected into three phases—before purchase, at point of purchase, and after purchase (see Table 20.1). Note how perception is affected by the collection of quality-related activities from product design through customer use of the product.

490

TABLE 20.1
Factors influencing customer perception of quality*

Before purchase	At point of purchase	After purchase
Company's brand name and image	Performance specifications	Ease of installation and use
Previous experience	Comments of salespeople	Handling of repairs, claims, warranty
Opinions of friends	Warranty provisions	Spare parts availability
Store reputation	Service and repair policies	Service effectiveness
Published test results	Support programs	Reliability
Advertised price for performance	Quoted price for performance	Comparative performance

* Not necessarily in order of importance. *Source:* Takeuchi and Quelch (1983, p. 142).

Other research (American Management Association, 1987) asked companies what *their* perceptions were on six tactics of customer service. Companies were asked: (1) whether they used the tactic, (2) what rating (from a low of one to a high of five) they would give their own performance, and (3) which three tactics they felt were "most effective." The results are shown in Table 20.2.

Knowledge of these factors has led some organizations to focus on "customer-driven quality programs." Table 20.3 shows the elements of a program for a mail order apparel company (L. L. Bean) and an equipment manufacturer (Caterpillar, Inc.).

TABLE 20.2
Perceptions of companies on tactics of customer service

Tactic	Companies using tactic, %	Rating	Companies listing tactic as "most effective," %
Unconditional warranty/refund	65	3.86	26
Quality control and product assurance	89	4.00	60
On-time delivery	87	3.88	59
Postsale repair and replacement	69	3.90	28
Expedition of special customer requests	91	3.90	40
Special training for service personnel	82	3.60	36

Source: American Management Association (1987).

TABLE 20.3
Customer-driven quality programs

Mail order apparel company	Equipment manufacturer
Conducting regular customer satisfaction surveys and sample group interviews to track customer and noncustomer perceptions of the quality of its own and its competitors' products and services	Conducting two customer satisfaction surveys following each purchase, one after 300 h of product use and the second after 500 h of use
Tracking on its computer all customer inquiries and complaints and updating the file daily	Maintaining a centrally managed list of product problems as identified by customers from around the world
Guaranteeing all its products to be 100% satisfactory and providing a full cash refund, if requested, on any returns	Analyzing warranty and service reports submitted by dealers, as part of a product improvement program
Asking customers to fill out a short, coded questionnaire and explain their reasons for returning the merchandise	Asking dealers to conduct a quality audit as soon as the products are received and to attribute defects to either assembly errors or shipping damages
Performing extensive field tests on any new outdoor equipment before listing it in the company's catalogs	Guaranteeing 48-h delivery of any part to any customer in the world
Stocking extra buttons for most of the apparel items carried years ago, just in case a customer needs one	Encouraging dealers to establish side businesses in rebuilding parts to reduce costs and increase the speed of repairs

TABLE 20.4
Marketing and quality-related activities

Marketing activity	Quality-related activity
Launching new products	Conducting a "test market" to identify product weaknesses and weaknesses in the marketing plan
Labeling	Ensuring that products conform to label claims
	Ensuring that label information is accurate and complete
Advertising	Identifying the product features that will persuade customers to purchase a product
	Verifying the accuracy of quality claims included in advertising
Assistance to customers in product selection	Presenting quality-related data to help customers evaluate alternative products
Assistance to merchants	Providing merchants with quality-related information for use by salespeople
	Providing merchants with technical advice on product storage, handling, and sales demonstrating
Preparation of sales contract	Defining product requirements on performance, other technical requirements, and level of quality (e.g., defects per million)
	Defining requirements on execution of a contract, e.g., a quality plan, submission of specified documentation during contract
	Defining warranty provisions
	Defining incentive provisions on quality and reliability
Order entry and filling	Applying quality improvement concepts to reduce lead time or reduce errors

20.3 QUALITY CONCEPTS IN A MARKETING FUNCTION

As with all functions in an organization, activities within the marketing function can benefit from the application of quality concepts. Table 20.4 shows some marketing activities and their related quality activities. Further elaboration is provided in QCH4, Section 19. Golomski (1986) discusses some quality planning tools useful in marketing activities.

The marketing function has opportunities for identifying and acting upon chronic problems within marketing (see Chapter 2, "Companywide Assessment of Quality"). Nickell (1985) describes some pioneering efforts at IBM. The amount of product shipped that was canceled before installation is a dramatic example. Surprisingly, 13 percent of signed and shipped orders was canceled! This problem became a quality improvement project, and the team effort reduced the amount to three percent.

20.4 WARRANTY OF QUALITY

A warranty is a form of assurance that a product is fit for use or, failing this, that the user will receive some kind of compensation. In this sense, a warranty constitutes a system for reducing user costs of poor quality.

In most jurisdictions, a seller, by the mere act of sale, makes two *implied* warranties:

1. A *general* warranty of "merchantability," i.e., fitness for the customary use of such products.
2. An added *special* warranty of fitness for the specific use to which the product will be put. This warranty is implied only if the seller knows what that specific use is.

Beyond the warranties (which are implied by law), there are added *express* warranties made by the seller or negotiated between the parties. For consumer products, most such warranties are made unilaterally by the seller through oral representations about the product, display of samples, descriptions in catalogues, claims made in advertising, etc. In addition, there are specific statements of warranty published in documents which themselves are headed up by the word "warranty." In the case of sales made to industrial companies, warranties are sometimes specially negotiated, as are other aspects of the sales contract.

Traditionally, warranties as to quality were limited to replacement or repair of the product during the warranty period. With the proliferation of long-life products, there has been an extension of warranties into parameters such as reliability, downtime, maintenance costs, etc. This extension is squarely in line with the need to optimize users' costs. This trend can be expected to continue.

In the case of warranties to consumers, the complications associated with long-life products have led to much confusion as to their meaning, especially as to where the responsibility for action lies. This has given rise to national legislation which requires that warranties be clear and which sets out some criteria for clarity.

Consumer product warranties are either "full" or "limited." The term "full warranty" refers to the consumer's rights, not to the portion of the physical product that is covered by the warranty; i.e., it does not have to cover the entire product. A full warranty means that:

1. The manufacturer will fix or replace any defective product free of charge.
2. The warranty is not limited in time.
3. The warranty does not exclude or limit payment for consequential damages (see below).
4. If the manufacturer is unable to make an adequate repair, the consumer may choose between a refund and a replacement.
5. The manufacturer cannot impose unreasonable duties on the consumer. For example, the warranty cannot require the consumer to ship a piano to the factory (one manufacturer listed such a condition).
6. The manufacturer is not responsible if the damage to the product was caused by unreasonable use.

The full warranty also provides that not only the original purchaser but any subsequent owners of the product during the warranty period are entitled to make claims.

A limited warranty is a warranty that does not meet the requirements for a full warranty. Typically, a limited warranty may exclude labor costs, require the purchaser to pay for transportation charges, and be limited to the original purchaser of the product. As a practical matter, most warranties on consumer products are limited warranties and must be so labeled.

The duration and coverage of a warranty, for both industrial and consumer products, vary greatly. For example, for one industrial commodity product, the warranty may call only for compliance to specifications at the time of formal "acceptance"; another industrial product may have a warranty for a period of time and even provide for payment of consequential damage costs if the product fails. For a consumer product, the warranty covers normal performance during a limited period (usually about ten percent of the useful life); in a few cases (e.g., a pen), a lifetime warranty is provided for specified conditions.

Because the warranty period covers only a portion of the product life, users must contend with any service needs that arise during the remainder of the item's life. Recognizing this as a business opportunity, manufacturers have responded in several ways, including product redesign, competition in warranties, extended warranties, and reliability improvement warranties. See QCH4, pages 19.12–19.14, for further discussion.

20.5 FIELD PERFORMANCE

The act of final product acceptance may be regarded as terminating the manufacturing phase. Following this act and before customer use of the product, a number of preuse phases take place: packing, shipping, receiving, and storage. Finally, there are the use phases: installation, checkout, operation, and maintenance.

As product complexity grows, the extent of field problems increases. Field factors cause 20–30 percent of problems concerning fitness for use on long-life products of moderate to high complexity.

Those who do quality planning for service activities can learn much from the experience of formalizing quality planning in design and manufacturing. Those who perform service activities that affect quality often believe that their activities are sufficient to provide a quality service. In cases where service is in fact deficient, there is often a need to revise the service plan as it relates to the topics discussed below. Such planning must show—explicitly—what to do differently. Generalities are unacceptable.

Packaging, Transportation, and Storage

One major department store found that more customer complaints are caused by store activities in packaging, storing, and delivering the product than were caused by the original manufacturing.

The most critical aspect of the quality of packaging, transportation, and storage is the design and acquisition of effective packaging materials. Packaging requires a sequence of activities similar to those used to achieve fitness for use for the product itself. These activities include package design and the purchasing, manufacturing, and testing of packaging materials.

Package Design

Designing the package and the product simultaneously is the ideal approach. Sometimes a minor alteration in product design can strengthen the product and thereby eliminate the need for extensive packaging materials.

This simultaneous approach requires that packaging design start during the product design stage rather than after manufacture begins. If little or no product information is available to the packaging engineer, the result may be a package that either underprotects or overprotects the product. Design of packaging calls for laboratory testing (e.g., impact, vibration, compression, and drop tests) and field testing of materials.

Especially for products that undergo numerous or critical handlings, it becomes important to look at handling and packaging from a systems viewpoint as opposed to numerous department viewpoints. The extent of handling during production, packaging, and transportation can be surprising. Handling costs run about 20 percent of manufacturing costs, with some estimates as high as 60 percent. A system review can identify opportunities to improve the overall handling by methods such as:

- Modifying supplier packaging. Some electronic components are blister-packaged in a way that allows testing without unpacking.
- Starting unitized and other containerization at early operations or even at the supplier's location. For example, the drug industry has evolved unitized packaging of dosages in which the identity of the dose (and even its own environment) is designed into the unit package and carries through to the patient.
- Designing racks, trays, bins, tote boxes, etc., to provide optimal service to all companies and departments involved rather than to require added handling and repacking for some.

The systems concept includes the adaptation of the product and the package to each other. Fiedler (1978) described how a company that analyzed the interaction of its cartons (products) and cases (packages) determined the combined maximum compression resistance. The analysis led to a design that saved $50,000 annually in materials while increasing the compression resistance of the product/package system.

Purchasing, Manufacturing, and Testing of Packaging Materials

The techniques described in other sections of this book for manufacturing and testing of products apply equally to packaging materials. In many cases, packaging materials are obtained from a supplier, and thus the elements of a supplier quality program are applicable.

Transportation

Handling and transport introduce many perils to the product. Some of these are fully predictable: climatic temperature changes, humidity, vibration, and shock (during automated handling). Others are the result of ignorance, carelessness, blunder, and even sabotage. For some of these perils, the product is in greater danger from handling and transport than from usage.

Fiedler (1978) recommends a seven-step program for protecting a product during transportation:

1. Defining the packaging objectives.
2. Determining the method of shipment. Usually, about 80 percent of a manufacturer's products are handled by 20 percent of the available carriers and modes of shipment.
3. Determining the ability of the product to withstand the transportation hazards. Tests can be run which simulate shock, vibration, and other transport damage. The stresses are measured in terms of cycles per second, "g levels" of deceleration, pulse shapes, and still other quantified measures. The experience gained has found its way into specifications for packaging and vehicle loading.
4. Interpreting the test data to compare the product's resistance to the simulated environment with the predicted environmental hazard level.
5. Deciding on a course of action. This means deciding if a packaging material should be selected or some other course of action taken (e.g., modifying the product or changing the distribution method).
6. Selecting a packaging material.
7. Combining the package with the product and subjecting them to final testing together. This can be done by trial shipment or simulated laboratory testing.

A recent innovation is the use of small sensors physically placed into the transport containers. These sensors record—during the actual transportation of materials—data on shock, vibration, temperature, humidity, acceleration, container's drop height, etc. This provides a reading of what goes on during transportation of the item. The information is stored in a microprocessor-based digital data system inside the sensor and later is transferred to computers for processing and analysis (Hicks, 1991). The experience gained finds its way into later specifications for packaging and vehicle loading.

Storage

Immense quantities of raw materials, components, and finished products are constantly in storage, awaiting further processing, sale, or use. To minimize deterioration and degradation, various actions can be taken: establishing the shelf life of the product based on laboratory and field data, establishing standards to place limits on time in storage, dating the product conspicuously to make it easy to identify the age of the product in stock, and designing the package and controlling the environment to minimize both expected and unexpected degradation.

A common weakness of these programs is a failure to "date" the product conspicuously. Sometimes this failure is simply due to poor technique, e.g., iron in open storage rusts away because the color of the rust preservative is not changed annually. However, some failure to date conspicuously is the result of marketing decisions, e.g., the dates are put on the back of the product or on the front in tiny print because the advertising has priority; there is a fear of dating the product in a way which enables the consumer to know if he or she is getting out-of-date product. Such reasons, if they were ever valid, now have become obsolete. Conspicuous dating on outer cartons as well as on the unit package aids in traceability, stock rotation, and establishing age of inventories.

Some products such as drugs are made in batches that may be released only after tests are completed on a sample. While the batches are being held, special inventory procedures are needed to assure that unreleased product is not inadvertently sent to a customer.

Installation and Use

Before the packaged product is put into use, it undergoes additional processing during distribution, assembly, installation and checkout, etc. These operations are quite as much a part of the progression of the product as the design and manufacture are, and they demand corresponding controls.

PROCESSING DURING DISTRIBUTION. The distribution process carries out such operations as breaking bulk, readjusting, adding reagents, touching up finishes, repackaging, etc. The planning of these operations should be a part of the overall product planning. The results of this planning should then be embodied in specifications to be used by the distribution organizations. Compliance with these specifications should then be audited independently.

In some cases, it is found that the distribution process cannot be relied on to carry out these operations, e.g., there are international problems of language or culture or small retailers lack the technological skills to do so. In such cases, the need is for a systems redesign which eliminates the necessity for technological skills or even for the operations. These problems can be at their worst when the operations are to be performed by the ultimate user.

ON-SITE INSTALLATION BY SPECIALISTS. This is the assembly setup which is conducted at the user's premises to put the product into a state of readiness to operate plus installation "in place" at the site. For some products, installation requires the services of specialists; for others, users perform their own installation.

On-site installations may require:

- *Special facilities to house the product* (plus its auxiliary equipment), including means of controlling the environment.

- *Special tools and instruments.* All too often these are not as completely engineered as the corresponding facilities in the factory are because many marketing and service departments have lagged behind the factories in the use of formal quality planning and quality specialists.
- *Instructions for installing and checking out the product.* Written instructions for complex products are forever subject to omissions and mistakes because of their sheer complexity. One of the failures in an early space shot was traced to the omission in checkout procedures of a certain adjustment on the missile. The adjustment was not specified and hence was not made. The launch was a complete failure. Such problems are not, however, restricted to complex products.

INSTALLATION BY THE USER. Often a product is installed by a user—either a consumer or an employee of the client. Even with clear, well-illustrated instructions, a distressing number of users are seemingly unable to follow them. (A manufacturer of kitchen faucets provides an audio recording describing how the installation should be done.)

Richardson (1981) discusses some of the issues involved in designing for customer setup on computers and terminals:

- The setup must be simple enough to be accomplished by inexperienced people without using *any* tools.
- The instructions must be error-proof. Photographs and exploded drawings are superior to wordy descriptions. The design and manufacturing of the product should be such as to prevent connections from becoming loose during shipment.
- Customer education and telephone hotlines should be provided.
- Translations of written instructions into foreign languages must be verified to assure that the translations are clear.
- Each step of the instructions should contain only one task and, if possible, provide for positive feedback (e.g., an indicator light) upon successful completion of the task.
- When the product is available with options, instructions become more complicated to write because they must address the different combinations of features possible. One approach may be to modularize the instructions.
- Additional testing is needed to reduce susceptibility to shipping damage on customer setup products.

Use

Some field problems can be traced to improper operation of the product. LaSala and Siegel (1983) describe several studies done to quantify the extent and effect of human error on product reliability and maintainability. In one study, about 50 percent of the failures in major systems was due to human errors. The errors were sorted into five types: procedural, incorrect diagnosis, misinterpretation of communications, inadequate support of environment, and insufficient attention or caution.

As products become increasingly complex, the problem of human error during operation of the equipment becomes more critical to address. Manufacturers have done much to prepare operating manuals or other instructions for proper use and maintenance. These manuals are rudimentary for simple products and grow into elaborate handbooks for complex products. An intermediate example is the "owner's manual" for owners of automobiles.

While installation and use by specialists tend to be rather professional, use by consumers is characterized by much ignorance in several ways:

- *Failure to allow sufficient time for training and learning the operation of new and complex products.* The recent advances in word processing equipment provide an example. The amazing capabilities of such equipment can be realized only when personnel are thoroughly trained and given sufficient time to practice. The capabilities of the equipment have tended to overshadow the importance of learning time and practice.
- *Failure to use available information.* For example, a vacuum cleaner rotary brush encounters an obstruction and stops rotating. The owner's manual states clearly what to do: Remove the obstruction and reset the little red button. The user does not know this, because the owner's manual is lost or it is simpler to have the unit serviced.
- *Use under conditions that were never contemplated.* For example, a householder finds an automobile door lock frozen on a subzero day. A portable hair dryer is used in an attempt to thaw out the lock. The dryer fails because it was not designed to operate in subzero temperatures.
- *Application of stresses that were never contemplated.* For example, a householder stands on a washing machine to paint the ceiling overhead.
- *Failure to maintain.* Consumers are notoriously lax in following prescribed schedules for lubrication, cleaning, replacement of expendables, etc.

Of paramount importance is the need for the manufacturer to find out the actual use which takes place. As this knowledge becomes available—through field observations, complaint analysis, etc.—the manufacturer has a wide variety of options for improving use: consumer education, product redesign, systems redesign, etc.

In many cases, the prevention of human errors during use requires changes in the product design. In one study of a printing press (LaSala and

Siegel, 1983), the distribution of operating problems was as follows:

Difficulty in extracting a component	71 percent
Difficulty in positioning a component	14 percent
Extended inspection	6 percent
Difficulty in grasping a component	5 percent
Adjusting/greasing	4 percent

An analysis concluded that most of the problems could have been anticipated and prevented during product design.

Interaction of the worker and the product is important. Factors involved can be the anatomical dimensions of the worker; placement on products of push buttons and switches; physical loads imposed on the worker by the product; monotony or other psychological effects of product operation; environmental effects produced by the product, such as noise and vibration; and workplace design, such as lighting and space.

Collectively, such matters are called "ergonomics" and need to be considered during the product design.

Maintenance

One of the elements of fitness for use is availability. Availability is a function of reliability and maintainability (see Section 13.9, "Availability"). An adequate field maintenance program requires that product problems be fixed correctly and in a timely manner. For some consumer products, there are more complaints from customers on repair service than on the original product quality delivered. These complaints include both faulty repairs and long waits for the return of the product, resulting in lower availability of the product to the customer.

For simple products, a product malfunction can often be corrected by replacing the defective element. As products become more complex, the process of finding and correcting malfunctions becomes more difficult. The usual steps are shown in Figure 20.1. These steps often require more resources than originally anticipated. Trained personnel, technical data, and test equipment must be planned for far in advance to be completely ready when a product enters the field. In addition, spare parts must be planned for in sufficient quantity and quality. A failure mode, effect, and criticality analysis or a fault tree analysis (see Sections 12.4 and 12.5) can be helpful in planning both preventive and corrective maintenance programs.

ASSURING THE ADEQUACY OF MAINTENANCE SERVICES. Maintenance itself can be a cause of failures in the field. Horn and Hall (1983) discuss techniques for estimating the extent of the maintenance contribution to field failures as well as techniques for identifying maintenance-induced failures and their causes. On some Air Force activities, maintenance-induced failures

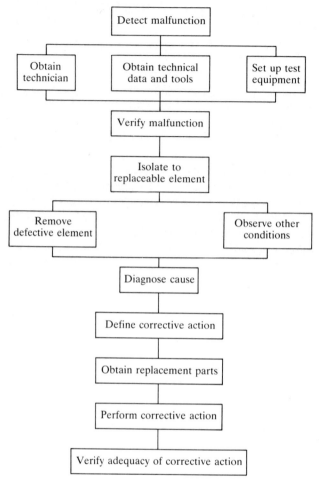

FIGURE 20.1.
Steps in correcting a malfunction.

varied from two to 48 percent of the total failures, depending on the type of equipment.

Quality control of repair work is troublesome for a service center. The great majority of shops are small, and the tradition has been self-inspection by the mechanic, with only sporadic review by the service manager. Some organizations establish standards of performance for service centers and provide audit and certification to assure that these standards are met. The Chevrolet Division of General Motors identifies 22 areas that are essential to total service satisfaction (e.g., quality, facilities, personnel, etc.). For each of these 22 areas, specific "evaluators" help to determine if a dealer conforms to the standards. The quality parameter has 15 evaluators, e.g., "inspection procedures are available." Technical assistance is provided by Chevrolet to enable dealers to achieve certification. Certification involves both a review of the dealer's procedures and facilities and formal feedback from customers on the performance of the dealer. The program also provides for periodic recertification of dealers.

Service Improvement

Good service is a moving target due to continuing changes in the marketplace. Keeping up with competition requires continuing improvement of service. Because improvement takes place project by project, it is necessary to agree on specific needed improvements and then to organize to carry out the resulting improvement projects.

An example of an approach to such improvement is seen in Lele and Karmarkar (1983). They use the term "support strategies" in the sense of nominations for service improvement projects. In their definition, the term "strategy" means a collection of activities used to satisfy customer service needs. A strategy can vary from one market segment to another and can change with conditions in the marketplace. A company must choose a strategy, evaluate its own and competitors' relative positions, and determine when customer needs or competitive pressures require that the strategy be changed. For example, Table 20.5 shows ten alternative strategies for an industrial tractor. These alternative strategies were identified after investigations revealed that customers were concerned about the downtime per product failure as well as the total downtime. A computer simulation was run to duplicate the effect of using a strategy (or combination of strategies) in terms of downtime

TABLE 20.5
Alternative strategies for a tractor

Key	Strategy
A	Improving fill rate for parts from 91% to 95%
B	Improving mean time between failures from 350 to 450 h
C	Developing and installing microprocessor-based diagnostic capability in each tractor
D	Providing faster parts service using parts vans
E	Redesigning tractor to permit faster modular exchange of electrical and hydraulic components
F	Providing users with tractors on loan during serious failures
G	Redesigning tractor for modular exchange of electrical, hydraulic, and engine-driven train components
H	Redesigning tractor as in strategy E and providing loaners
I	Redesigning tractor as in strategy G and providing loaners
J	Redesigning tractors as in strategy C; providing loaners and built-in diagnostics

Source: Lele and Karmarkar (1983, p. 130).

and operational availability. The life cycle cost of each alternative was also calculated. Additional information resulting from the simulation included the effects of improving parts availability, built-in diagnostics, making loans of equipment, and modular exchange. The simulation showed that there were three stages, each requiring different strategies: from 50 to 30 hours of downtime, from 30 to 20 hours, and from 20 to ten hours. Management decided to improve the reliability of the existing design, introduce equipment on loan (strategy F) if competitive pressures demanded it, change the design to allow progressive modularization of key components, and switch to a combination of modular exchange and loans (strategies H and I).

The simulation provided conclusions that ordinarily would not be available until many months of experience had been accumulated.

20.6 SAFETY AND PRODUCT LIABILITY

The responsibility of manufacturers to provide safe products is clear. "Product liability" refers to the legal obligation of a manufacturer or seller to compensate for injury or damage caused by a product.

The growth in both the number of lawsuits and the size of awards to victims has been dramatic. Awards in excess of a million dollars are no longer rare. The reasons are clear: More manufactured products are in the hands of amateurs, creating more opportunities for injury; some traditional legal defenses of manufacturers have become eroded, making it easier for a victim to sue a manufacturer successfully; the consumer movement has encouraged consumer action generally; the publicity given to large awards has stimulated more lawsuits.

The basic defense against liability is prevention—by eliminating the causes of the injuries or damage. All company functions contribute to this prevention activity, as shown in Table 20.6.

Most product liability lawsuits—"civil lawsuits"—are aimed at manufacturing companies because of their ability to pay, not at individuals such as design specialists.

But in a "criminal liability" case, the state is the plaintiff. In recent decades, public prosecutors have pursued individuals such as the head of a company or a manager of product development or quality. Criminal liability requires proof that the manager knowingly performed illegal actions or was grossly negligent in executing duties. As it is difficult to establish such proof, the likelihood that a manager will be found guilty of criminal liability is small.

Responsibility for investigating injuries varies but is typically divided among the insurance company, the legal department, and the appropriate technical departments. Irrespective of the allocation of responsibility, certain

TABLE 20.6
Activities for product safety

Upper management	Product design	Manufacturing inspection	Marketing	Advertising	Customer service
Creating a policy on product safety	Making product safety a formal design parameter	Emphasizing error proofing	Providing product labels with warnings, dangers, antidotes	Having advertising reviewed for technical and legal aspects	Providing service which minimizes likelihood of claims
Creating a companywide safety effort	Adopting fail-safe design practices	Providing documentation and traceability	Supplying safety information to distributors and dealers	Emphasizing safety through education	Providing feedback on how product is actually used
Directing that procedures be created for traceability and product recalls	Using design evaluation techniques for safety	Identifying safety-critical characteristics, operations, and tests	Training sales force in safety aspects of contracts		Ensuring that product repairs leave the product in safe condition
Establishing a safety scoreboard	Organizing formal design review for safety	Providing training on safety-related items	Training users in safety matters		
	Conforming to all safety standards	Assuring proper disposition of nonconforming products			
	Analyzing and providing feedback on injury data to designers				

505

precautions should be taken:

- Notifying the insurance company promptly.
- Assigning only qualified experts to make the investigation.
- Securing and retaining the product unit asserted to have caused the injury.
- Analyzing the injury environment and product thoroughly to identify the precise failure mode.
- Conducting laboratory tests with a view of reproducing the same failure mode. (If needed, verification from independent laboratories should be secured.)
- Making use of modern analysis techniques: high-speed cameras, scanning electron microscope, etc.

See QCH4, pages 34.19–34.22, for a discussion.

20.7 FRONTLINE CUSTOMER CONTACT IN SERVICE INDUSTRIES

A basic activity in the service industries is the service encounter, i.e., the contact made with the client when meeting a customer's need. Typical examples involve a bank teller processing deposits or withdrawals of money, a flight attendant providing services on an airplane, a hotel clerk registering a guest. In all cases, the quality of the transaction involves both the technical adequacy of the result and the social skills of the "frontline" person who conducts the transaction. Three factors emerge as important: selection of the frontline employee, training of that employee, and "empowerment" of the employee to act to meet customer needs. (The reader should compare these factors to the three elements of self-control; see Section 5.2, "Self-Control.")

In "person-to-person" type transactions, employee *selection* often has an immediate, direct, and lasting impact on customer perception. Some people have the necessary personal characteristics for frontline personnel; some people do *not* have these characteristics, even with training. Proper selection requires that we identify the personal characteristics required for a position (how about asking experienced employees?), use multiple interviews, train managers in interview procedures, identify nominees from among present employees, and ask for recommendations from present employees. As one example, Federal Express selects people using scientifically prepared profiles of successful performers.

Training, of course, is essential. Superior-quality service organizations devote from one to five percent of employee working hours to training. The content of the training depends on the job requirements, but often it stresses product knowledge. In addition, training involves such activities as role playing to handle situations when a transaction goes wrong, handling irate customers who have a complaint, etc. Such training takes time and special effort, e.g., at Lands' End, each mail order telephone representative spends time in a warehouse viewing the products. Isn't it impressive when such a person is able to describe what is meant by a "medium gray" pair of trousers? Basically, however, the training must enable the employee to provide customers with dependable and regular service. Customers are impressed when they know that they can depend on uniformly good service from an organization. When an extraordinary situation arises and it is handled well, we have a delighted customer.

Empowerment, a key step beyond training, involves giving a new degree of authority to frontline employees. The term usually means encouraging employees to handle unusual situations that standard procedures don't cover. In the past, the employee would check with a superior—while the customer waited—and waited. The concept minimizes the use of the rule book and maximizes the use of the frontline employee's knowledge, initiative, and judgment to take the action necessary to meet the need of a customer standing at a service counter. For example, the policy manual at Nordstrom's department store states: "Use your own best judgment at all times." Risky? Some people would think so, but the opportunities for customer satisfaction and the employee attitude toward "ownership" of his or her job are strongly convincing. Section 8.5, under "Empowerment," provides further discussion.

Zemke and Schaaf (1989) provide a wealth of additional examples on selection, training, and empowerment of frontline employees.

Banc One uses an extensive shopper survey to measure the performance of bank tellers. The survey queries customers on specific contact items such as a friendly greeting, employee identification, eye contact, a smile, use of the customer's name during the transaction, undivided employee attention, accurate processing of the transaction, ability to give clear explanations, a professional appearance, and a neatly organized work area.

The investment in selection, training, and empowerment of employees can lead to the fulfillment of a company's dream—delighted customers. Table 20.7 provides some categories of action and examples of remarkable exploits to generate delighted customers. Zemke and Schaaf (1989) present many examples.

20.8 PROCESSING AND RESOLUTION OF CUSTOMER COMPLAINTS

In small companies involved in few field complaints, there is little need for a systematic approach to complaint analysis. As the number of complaints increases, however, the need for a systematic approach also increases. However, in some companies the lack of an organized approach has been a serious obstacle to sound customer relations.

TABLE 20.7
Some action taken to achieve delighted customers

Action	Example
Providing a service far beyond the scope of the company service	An airline flight attendant accompanied a sick passenger and her daughter to a hospital
Providing a service beyond the call of a normal effort	To eliminate the sound of tinkling glass in a chandelier due to air conditioning, hotel employees removed every second piece of glass 30 minutes before the start of the meeting
Providing extraordinary recognition of customer inconvenience	An automobile manufacturer paid a customer $985 for "lost time" incurred by the customer on excessive and improperly made repairs
Providing a recognition of personal customer loss	A customer reported that she lost a pen, having sentimental value, in a grocery store. A clerk searched for the pen but with no success. The clerk presented the lady with three $20 gift certificates

Each quality complaint poses different problems requiring different programs of action:

- Satisfying the complainant. This program is oriented to the complainant and hence is needed in virtually every case of complaint. This involves prompt restoration of service, adequate claim adjustment, and restoration of goodwill.
- Preventing a recurrence of isolated complaints. It is common practice to bring isolated complaints to the attention of those who are suspected of having caused them and to ask them what they plan to do to prevent a recurrence.
- Identifying the "vital few" serious complaints which demand that in-depth studies be done to discover the basic causes and to remedy those causes. Usually, the decisive questions here are (1) whether the complaint is isolated or widespread, and (2) whether the complaint is on critical matters (e.g., safety, government regulations).
- In-depth analysis to discover the basic causes of the complaint. This action is oriented to the product and is normally needed only in those vital few cases which are responsible for the bulk of the failures.
- Further analysis to discover and apply remedies for the basic causes.

An approach to handling the vital few problems is shown in Figure 20.2. As the causes and remedies often involve many departments, a "corrective action group" is often formed with representatives from Design, Manufacturing, Purchasing, Quality, and Field Service. The group jointly analyzes the data to select the vital few problems, conducts an initial investigation to

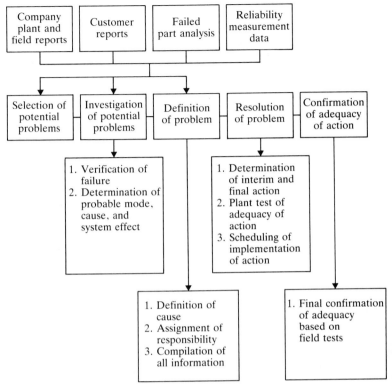

FIGURE 20.2
Corrective action system.

prepare a thorough problem statement, and assigns responsibility for determining a remedy.

The group meets regularly to review all new complaints and to review progress on current problems. A problem agenda is sent out by the chairperson several days ahead of the meeting date. Minutes of the meetings, including a problem-status log, are formally recorded, and actions to be taken are documented and distributed to all concerned. This log summarizes each problem before the committee. It also shows the scheduled start and completion of activity, assigns responsibility, and lists action taken. It gives project management an indication of major problems and the status of corrective efforts. Additional effort may then be placed on troublesome areas as deemed necessary.

The process of handling customer complaints has emerged as an important tool of competition in achieving sales. Data are now available showing how the level of customer satisfaction in handling complaints is related to lost sales (see Section 4.5, "Level of Satisfaction to Retain Present Customers").

TABLE 20.8
Collection and use of customer comments and complaints

Activity	Companies utilizing, %
Regular counts kept	72.6
Reports prepared and circulated	66.3
Response time tracked	64.8
Competition evaluated	34.1
Included in strategic planning	60.7
Part of performance appraisal	42.0

Source: American Management Association (1978).

Some organizations are superb at handling complaints. Other organizations are weak in even the most basic elements. Table 20.8 shows some results of a survey of 267 companies which were asked if they conducted certain activities related to complaints. Note that many companies did not regularly count, report, or track the response time on complaints.

The concepts of quality improvement can help to improve the process of handling complaints. In an application at the Mobil Chemical Company Films Division, the average response time on complaints was reduced from 92 to 30 days (Gust, 1985). The steps in the breakthrough sequence (see Chapter 3 generally), starting with proof of the need and ending with holding the gains, were the road to success.

20.9 OBTAINING FEEDBACK ON FIELD PERFORMANCE

Collecting, analyzing, and responding to customer complaints on a product are essential in order to minimize customer *dissatisfaction*. But activities on product complaints are not sufficient to increase customer *satisfaction*. Satisfaction involves a much broader scope of factors which relate to the need for an in-depth understanding of customer needs (see Chapter 11, "Understanding Customer Needs").

Customer needs can be more effectively addressed when field data are available. Such data have spawned the concept of customer-based (rather than company-based) measurement—obviously logical but *not* a reality for many companies.

An example of a customer-based measurement system comes from a manufacturer (Xerox) of reproduction equipment (Ekings, 1986). A monthly customer survey covers four categories: equipment, service, sales, and administrative support. The survey includes 25 questions covering equipment, service support, administrative support, and sales support (see Table 20.9).

TABLE 20.9
Customer satisfaction survey questions

Equipment	Service support	Administrative support	Sales support
Frequent equipment failure	Poor telephone service	Frequent billing errors	Sales do not meet needs
Frequent paper jams	Slow delivery service	Difficulty in correcting errors	Reps do not return calls
Copy quality not consistent	Failure to repair	Invoices difficult to understand	Reps are incompetent
	Too much downtime	Mishandling of multiple invoices	Reps are not interested
	No response in emergency	Problems with crediting delays	Difficulty in ordering supplies
	Service reps unprofessional	Problems with collections	Supply deliveries are late
	Poor key-op training	Phone message mishandling	Frequent supply failures
		Unprofessional administrators	

Each month, 40,000 survey forms are mailed, and the response rate is 45 percent. The results are used to take immediate action on customer problems, identify problems requiring generic corrective action, and provide a quantitative measurement of customer satisfaction. Similar information is obtained from users of competitor products, thus providing competitive benchmarking data.

Mail surveys are one component of an array of methods for collecting field information. See Section 2.9, "Standing in the Marketplace," for a discussion of some of these methods.

Most feedback of field performance emanates from company personnel. Historically, obtaining adequate feedback from personnel has been a continuing problem for many companies. Improving the quality and promptness of feedback requires a variety of actions to make the process as convenient and effective as possible. These include:

- Providing personnel with well-designed data sheets
- Providing incentives to encourage adequate feedback
- Providing a glossary of terms to improve communication and a mnemonic code number to simplify the data entry and analysis
- Providing training in the how and why
- Conducting audits of the data feedback process
- Making use of modern technology to collect the field information
- Making use of modern methods of analysis to provide managers with valid summaries for decision making
- Minimizing the number of data relay stations
- Making use of the sample concept

- Obtaining an operations log
- Buying the data.
- Making use of the concept of controlled usage.

See QCH4, pages 20.28–20.29, for elaboration of these actions.

20.10.   CUSTOMER DEFECTIONS

The longer a company keeps a customer, the larger the profit will be. For example, the co-owner of a Domino's Pizza store calculated that regular customers were worth more than $5,000 over the ten-year life of a franchise contract.

A *customer defection* occurs when a customer switches to another brand. When customers defect, the profit-making potential goes with them. Research conducted in service industries indicates that reducing the defection rate can have a dramatic impact on boosting the profits (Reichheld and Sasser, 1990).

Consider a defection rate of 20 percent at a credit card company, i.e., 20 percent of the current customers is lost each year, resulting in an average customer life span of five years. If the defection rate is cut to ten percent, the average life span doubles to ten years and the "value" of the customer to the credit card company jumps from $134 to $300. This value is the net present value of the profit streams for the average customer life. If the defection rate

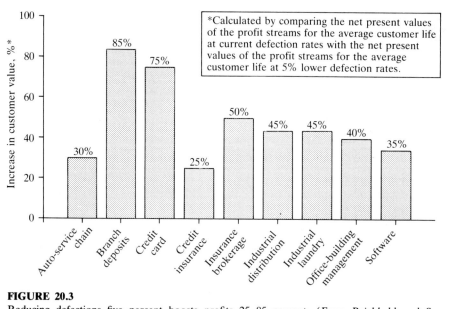

FIGURE 20.3
Reducing defections five percent boosts profits 25–85 percent. (*From Reichheld and Sasser, 1990.*)

drops another five percent, the value (profit) rises from \$300 to \$525 or 75 percent. Figure 20.3 shows, for a variety of service industries, the increase in the net present value of profits (over the average customer life) if defection rates are reduced by five percentage points from the current rate. Soliciting customer feedback is clearly important. But this must include measuring customer defections as an early-warning signal of dwindling profits. Such a signal then calls for in-depth discussions with defecting customers to identify weaknesses and decide on action.

SUMMARY

- Customers form perceptions of quality during three phases—before purchase, at point of purchase, and after purchase.
- A warranty is a form of assurance that a product is fit for use. Consumer product warranties are either "full" or "limited."
- Preuse phases of field performance include packing, shipping, receiving, and storage; use phases consist of installation, checkout, operation, and maintenance. Field factors cause about 20–30 percent of problems concerning fitness for use for complex products.
- Product liability refers to the legal obligation of a manufacturer or seller to compensate for injury or damage caused by a product.
- Three factors are important in achieving superior frontline customer contact in service industries: selection, training, and empowerment of the frontline employee.
- The process of handling customer complaints has become an important tool of competition in achieving sales.
- Feedback on field performance must use a customer-based measurement system.
- A customer defection occurs when a customer switches to another brand. When customers defect, the profit-making potential over many years goes with them.

PROBLEMS

20.1. Study the methods used for advertising quality for any of the following categories of products or services: beverages, cigarettes, automobiles, household appliances, airline travel, movies, electronic components, e.g., resistors, and mechanical components, e.g., bearings. Report on the extent to which the advertising: (*a*) identifies specific qualities; (*b*) quantifies the extent to which the product possesses these qualities; (*c*) engages in exaggeration; (*d*) appeals to various human traits, e.g., vanity, greed.

20.2. Visit a transportation service involving loading, storage, crating, unloading, transport, etc. Some possible examples: a trucking terminal, a steamship pier, an air freight terminal, a commercial warehouse, the shipping area of a factory, the parcel room of the post office, and a rail freight yard. Study the processes in use and their likely effect on the qualities of the products undergoing these processes. Report your findings and conclusions.

20.3. Visit a manager who is exposed to problems of installation and operation of consumers' hardware, e.g., the buyer in the home appliance department of a department store or the service manager of a factory making home appliances. Secure information on major troubles encountered by users in installation and operation, and also on what steps are being taken to minimize these troubles. Report your findings and conclusions.

20.4. Study the operating and/or maintenance instructions for a product. Report your findings and conclusions.

20.5. Select one of the field activities discussed in this chapter. Apply the concept of self-control (see Section 5.2) to evaluate whether the activity has been properly planned with respect to the effect on product quality. For each of the three criteria of self-control, list specific questions that can be asked to evaluate the planning.

20.6. Select a consumer product and make an ergonomics study to evaluate the adequacy of the design with respect to the operation of the product by a human being.

20.7. Prepare a plan of market research to secure data on the opinion of owners concerning repairs made on a specific product by a dealer or manufacturer.

20.8. For a specific product, list the misapplications and abuses of the product that occur during use.

20.9. Visit a repair facility and observe typical repairs made. Trace the steps taken and make a comparison to Figure 20.1.

REFERENCES

American Management Association (1987). "Close to the Customer," New York.

Ekings, J. Douglas (1986). "A Nine Step Quality Improvement Program to Increase Customer Satisfaction," *Proceedings of the 30th Annual Conference,* European Organization for Quality Control, Berne, Switzerland, pp. 399–408.

Fiedler, Robert M. (1978). "Portal to Portal Product Protection," *Quality,* May, pp. 12–14.

Golomski, William A. (1986). "Quality Improvement of Marketing," *Quality Progress,* June, pp. 24–26.

Gust, Lawrence J. (1985). "Non-Manufacturing Quality Improvement," *Juran Report Nunber Four,* Winter, Juran Institute, Inc., Wilton, Connecticut, pp. 112–120.

Hicks, Jonathan P. (1991). "Sensors That Tell Just How Good the Packaging Is," *New York Times,* September 15, p. F-7.

Horn, Roy L., and Fred M. Hall (1983). "Maintenance-Centered Reliability," *Proceedings, Annual Reliability and Maintainability Symposium,* IEEE, New York, pp. 197–204.

LaSala, Kenneth P., and Arthur I. Siegel (1983). "Improved R & M in Productivity by Designs for People," *Proceedings, Annual Reliability and Maintainability Symposium,* IEEE, New York, pp. 494–500.

Lele, Milind, and Uday S. Karmarkar (1983). "Good Product Support Is Smart Marketing," *Harvard Business Review,* November–December, pp. 124–132.

Nickell, Warren L. (1985). "Quality Improvement in a Marketing Organization," *Quality Progress,* June, pp. 46–51.

Reichheld, Frederick F., and W. Earl Sasser, Jr. (1990). "Zero Defections: Quality Comes to Services," *Harvard Business Review,* September–October, pp. 105–111.

Richardson, Hugh W. (1981). "Designing for Customer Setup." *Quality,* October, pp. 62–65.

Takeuchi, Hirotka, and John A. Quelch (1983). "Quality Is More Than Making a Good Product," *Harvard Business Review,* July–August, pp. 139–145.

Zemke, Ron, with Dick Schaaf (1989). *The Service Edge,* New American Library, New York, pp. 59–69.

SUPPLEMENTARY READING

Quality in marketing—general: QCH4, Section 19.
>   McGrath, Allan J. (1990). "What Marketing Can Learn from Manufacturing," *Across the Board,* The Conference Board, New York, April, pp. 37–42.

Quality in customer service—general: QCH4, Section 20.

Quality in consumer service industries: Berry, Thomas H. (1991). *Managing the Total Quality Transformation,* McGraw-Hill, Book Company, New York.
>   Zeithaml, Valarie A., A. Parasuraman, and Leonard L. Berry (1990). *Delivering Quality Service,* The Free Press, New York.
>   Zemke, Ron, and Dick Schaaf (1989). *The Service Edge,* New American Library, New York.

Ethics in quality: Mundel, August B. (1991). *Ethics in Quality,* Marcel Dekker, New York; ASQC Quality Press, Milwaukee.

CHAPTER
21

MARKETING, FIELD PERFORMANCE, AND CUSTOMER SERVICE— STATISTICAL TOOLS

21.1 QUALITY MEASUREMENT IN MARKETING, FIELD PERFORMANCE, AND CUSTOMER SERVICE

The management of quality-related activities in marketing, field performance, and customer service must include provision for measurement.

Recall the three guidelines for developing quality measurements for functional activities (see Section 13.1, "Measurement in Design"): obtaining input from customers; designing measurements for both evaluation of performance and feedback for self-control; providing early, concurrent, and lagging indicators of performance.

Table 21.1 shows control subjects for various subject areas of marketing, field performance, and customer service.

We now proceed to examine some statistical tools useful in these areas.

21.2 SIGNIFICANCE OF FIELD COMPLAINTS

Field complaints are a poor measure of product performance. Some users complain despite the fact that a product is fit for use; others do not complain

516

TABLE 21.1
Examples of quality measurement in marketing, field performance, and customer service

Subject	Unit of measure
Marketing	Percentage of orders canceled
	Percentage of bids that become contracts
	Order entry errors
	Number of misprocessed orders
Complaints	Total number of complaints
	Number of complaints per $1 million of sales
	Number of complaints per million units of product
	Value of material under complaint per $100 of sales for such products
Returns	Values of material returned per $100 of sales
Claims	Cost of claims paid
	Cost of claims per $1 million of sales
Failures	Mean time between failures (MTBF)
	Mean usage between failures, e.g., cycles, miles
	Mean time between repair calls
	Failure per 1000 units under warranty
Shipments	Amount of product shipped that did not meet specifications
Maintainability	Mean time to repair (MTTR)
	Mean downtime
	Number of repeat service calls for same complaint
Service cost	Ratio of maintenance hours to operating hours
	Repair cost per unit under warranty
	Cost per service call

despite the fact that a product is not fit for use. One research study estimated that for each complaint received at a company, there are at least six consumers with serious complaints and 20–50 consumers with less severe complaints (TARP, 1984). When complaints are made, how well they are acted upon has a decided effect on repeat sales (see below).

Whether or not a complaint is made depends on several factors:

- *Economic climate.* The number of complaints falls in a sellers' market and rises in a buyers' market, even for the same product.
- *Age, affluence, technological skills, etc., of users.* Individuals react differently to defects—the same product generates complaints from some customers but not from others.
- *Seriousness of the defect as seen by the user.* This is often influenced by the temperament of the user. For example, to a child a toy missing from a cereal box is a serious problem. In one company, complaint rates on cereals are about one per million packages compared to four per million packages on missing premiums.

- *Unit price of the product.* When the unit price of a product is low, the complaint rate can greatly understate field difficulties; the complaint rate may need to be inflated from 20 to more than 100 times to arrive at the actual defect rate.

Thus, a low complaint rate is not proof of customer satisfaction. However, a high complaint rate is proof of dissatisfaction, and therefore the rate should be measured and watched closely.

For elaboration on the significance of complaints, see QCH4, pages 20.16–20.19.

21.3   ESTIMATING LOST PROFIT DUE TO PRODUCT PROBLEMS

A model has been developed that estimates the profit lost annually because of problems that customers experience and the way those problems are handled by the company. We will use an example summarized from TARP (1988). The model uses company data and customer survey data (values for an illustrative example are shown in parentheses):

1. Company-provided data:
   - Average period of loyalty of the customer (five years)
   - Average number of purchases made by the customer over the period of loyalty (ten)
   - Size of the customer base (500,000)
   - Average profit per purchase ($20)
2. Data obtained from a survey of customers:
   - Percentage of customers who experience problems (70)
   - Percentage of customers who experience problems and request assistance (50)
   - Percentage of customers who don't experience problems but who, nevertheless, will not repurchase the product/service (12)
   - Percentage of customers who experience problems and do not request assistance who will not repurchase (45)
   - Percentages of customers who are satisfied, mollified, and dissatisfied by the contact handling system (40, 35, 25)
   - Percentages of customers who are satisfied, mollified, and dissatisfied by the contact handling system and who will not repurchase (5, 25, 70)
   - Word of mouth generated by customers who experience problems and don't request assistance (two)
   - Word of mouth generated by customers who are satisfied, mollified, and dissatisfied by the contact handling system (one, three, six)

Sales lost over the period of customer loyalty which are attributable to customers' problem experiences are estimated as sales lost due to problems less sales lost if no problems had been experienced.

The sales lost due to customers' problems have two components:

1. *Sales lost due to the way the company handles customer problems.* We start by calculating the number of sales lost over the period of loyalty as a result of *satisfied* contacters (customers) who will not recommend the company. This is:

$$(500,000 \times 0.70)(0.50)(0.40)(0.05)(10) = 35,000 \text{ sales.}$$

Similar calculations are made for customers who have problems but where the company action taken resulted in a "mollified" or "dissatisfied" customer rather than the "satisfied" customer assumed in the above calculation. Table 21.2 shows a summary.

But these calculations reflect only the 50 percent of customers who do contact the company about the problem; the other 50 percent who have a problem do not contact the company. The number of sales lost from this latter 50 percent are calculated as: $350,000(0.50)(0.45)(10) = 787,500$ sales (see Table 21.2.)

2. *Sales lost due to decreased brand loyalty and negative word of mouth.* We start by calculating the number of sales lost over the period of loyalty as a result of negative word of mouth from satisfied customers (with problems): $35,000(1.0)(0.02) = 700$ sales.

Similar calculations are made for the "mollified" and "dissatisfied" customers. Table 21.2 shows a summary.

But these calculations reflect only the 50 percent of customers who complain. For the 50 percent who do not complain, the number of sales lost is calculated as: $350,000(0.50)(0.45)(2)(10)(0.02) = 31,500$ (see Table 21.2.)

TABLE 21.2
Sales lost due to problems customers experience

Response of complainant	Sales lost due to company handling of problems	Sales lost due to negative word of mouth	
Satisfied	35,000	700	
Mollified	153,130	9,188	
Dissatisfied	306,250	36,750	
Total	494,380	46,638	541,018
Sales lost if customer does not complain	787,500	31,500	819,000
Sales lost due to problems customers experience			1,360,018

Thus, 1,360,018 is the estimated number of sales lost due to problems that customers experience. But some sales will be lost even if no problems are experienced. In this case, assume that 12 percent of sales will fall into this category. The sales lost are: $350,000(10)(0.12) = 420,000$ sales.

Thus, the total number of sales lost over the loyalty period which are attributable to customers' problem experience is: $1,360,018 - 420,000 = 940,018$.

The *annual* number of sales lost is $940,018/5$, or $188,004$. If profit is $20 per unit, the annual profit lost due to customer problems is estimated as $3,760,080.

21.4 ANALYZING FIELD DATA

For Problem Identification

The analysis of field data can have several objectives, including problem identification, measurement of actual performance, and prediction of future performance. Among the techniques for problem identification are:

1. *Defect matrices.* An example of this form is a table in which the horizontal lines list the principal defect types and the vertical columns list the product types. The cognizant managers and specialists are able to recognize significance in the patterns which emerge, e.g., defects which are restricted to certain product types or which affect all product types.
2. *Listing in order of importance.* This technique involves sorting and listing the basic data so that the resulting lists show the items in their order of importance. Typically, the listing appears in such forms as:
   - Failure rate by defect type
   - Unit repair cost by product type
   - Total repair cost by product type
   - Complaint rate by customer

Often these listings include columns for cumulative totals of all the elements under study. A principal purpose of these listings is to permit focus on the "vital few."

3. *Cost analyses.* "External failures" is a standard category of "quality costs" (see Chapter 2, "Companywide Assessment of Quality"). Most data systems provide for evaluating these costs using conventional subcategories such as repair labor, parts and supplies, travel costs, etc. These cost analyses are useful to the Quality Department in its role of using the quality cost figures to justify quality improvement programs.

4. *Spare-parts usage.* Two methods of analysis are available:

- The record of actual usage of products as derived from service reports. These records reflect the real consumption of these parts, but only if they are accurate and complete.
- The sale of spare parts to the distribution chain. This is also potentially unreliable and, to a greater degree, due to use of spare parts made by competitors and the fact that a sale to the distribution chain is not use—it is a transfer of inventory from one part of the chain to another.

Computer software can, of course, be extremely helpful in these data analyses.

For Problem Analysis

The basic analytical techniques mentioned in earlier chapters also apply to field data. Two such techniques are the Pareto analysis and a simple plot of frequency of failures over time. For example, because of the human contact–intensive nature of service industries, it is useful to perform a Pareto analysis to examine the distribution of service failures over a number of employees. Figure 21.1, which shows such an analysis, enables managers to determine whether faulty service is caused by a flaw in the process as a whole or by the work of just a few out of many employees.

Because of the cyclical nature of many service industries, trend analysis is performed to isolate "peak times," i.e., error-prone periods, in defective service performance. Figure 21.2 illustrates the month-by-month pattern of

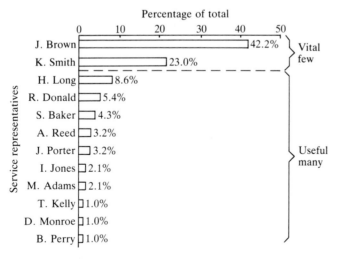

FIGURE 21.1
Pareto analysis of service follow-up failures. (*From QCH4, p. 33.19.*)

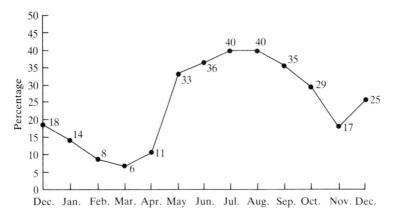

FIGURE 21.2
Trend analysis of service follow-up failures. (*From QCH4, p. 33.19.*)

certain service follow-up failures. Where measurements are recorded in sufficient detail, trend analysis can also reveal peak times of poor service on a daily or hourly basis.

- For example, First Tennessee Bank studied tellers and waiting lines and found regular, predictable patterns of bank traffic. These were accommodated by rearranging staffing patterns. Some part-time assignments were added, some full-time assignments were discontinued, and cross training was given to provide more flexibility for handling peaks. Without any layoffs, over $1 million a year was saved and the maximum waiting time was reduced by 80 percent.

- In another example, data on aircraft engine maintenance were analyzed. One important technique was plotting the probability of failure versus operating age. It had been assumed that the probability of failure would increase with operating age. This simple plot of probability of failure versus time revealed a surprise—for 89 % of the items, the probability did *not* increase with age. This eventually led to changing the traditional maintenance approach (replacing an item after it accumulated X hours of operation) to a different concept of maintenance.

See QCH4, pages 20.10–20.11, for elaboration.

For Measurement and Prediction

In the measurement and prediction of field performance, several techniques are useful. One is the cumulative complaint analysis. This requires that the product be "dated" to show when it was made, sold, or installed.

The various dates are useful not only in disposing of complaints and claims on product of a slow-perishable character (candy, photographic film, etc.); they can also help in predicting the failure rate of various product designs.

Example 21.1. Certain articles of women's clothing were tearing in service, and some were being returned. When the products made during one specific month were code dated, the cumulative returns reached two percent within two years after the date of manufacture. The resulting cumulative curve is shown in Figure 21.3. This two percent was regarded as tolerable. (At the unit price level of the product, it was likely that about 20 percent of the product was actually tearing in service.)

Meanwhile, the research department evolved a new product which went into full-scale production 14 months after the "specific month" noted above. The cumulative returns for the new product are also charted on Figure 21.3. Note that, by use of a horizontal time scale based on "months following manufacture," the two curves both start at the origin and hence can readily be compared with each other. By such analysis, the company could be informed *within the first few months* of the life of the new design that with regard to the problem of tearing, the new design had made the situation worse rather than better.

The concept of analyzing data using the cumulative graphing approach has broad application.

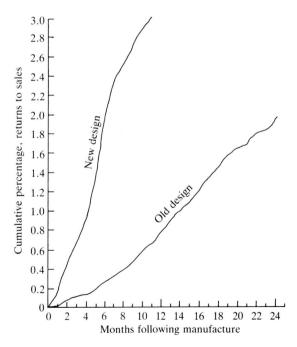

FIGURE 21.3
Comparison of cumulative returns based on number of months since month of manufacture.

Example 21.2. Nelson (1988) presents an example involving field repair data on residential heat pumps. Data were collected on both the cost and frequency of repairs over a life of ten years (in days). Figure 21.4a and b show plots of "mean cumulative cost" and "mean cumulative repair" functions. Note that the sample MCCF (Figure 21.4a) increases slowly up to 1000 days but increases faster and curves upward thereafter. This suggests that repairs get more expensive as the pumps age. But Figure 21.4b, MCRF versus age, increases linearly without curvature after 1000 days, suggesting (if repair costs and types were constant) that the MCCF should increase linearly instead of having an upward curvature. The explanation is that the curvature is due to inflation in repair costs. This example shows the value of expressing costs in constant dollars to compensate for inflation.

A technique for predicting future performance is the concept of *growth curves*. The concept assumes that the product involved is one that is undergoing continuous improvements in design and refinements in operating and maintenance procedure. Thus, the product performance will improve ("grow") with time. An early application was for predicting future reliability based on tests and early field data. One classic reliability growth model is that proposed by Duane (1964). He analyzed failure data for five different types of complex products. For these systems, the observed cumulative failure rate versus cumulative operating hours fell close to a straight line when plotted on log-log paper (see Figure 21.5). For his data, the slope of the lines was about −0.5. The fact that the lines are parallel indicates uniformity in the rate of reliability improvement.

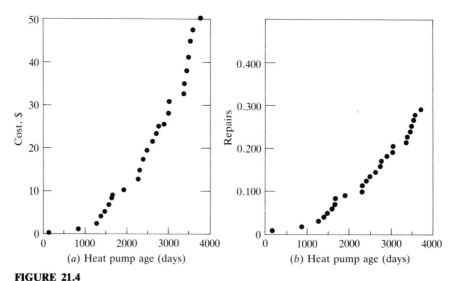

FIGURE 21.4
(a) Mean cumulative cost function (MCCF) and (b) mean cumulative repair function (MCRF) of fan motors. (*From Nelson, 1988.*)

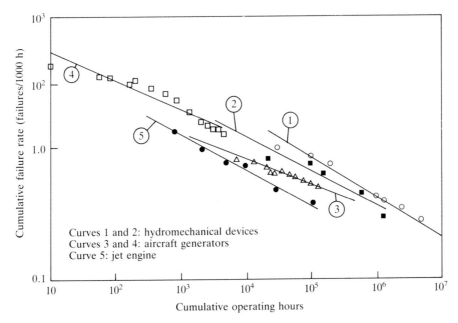

FIGURE 21.5
Example of reliability growth chart. (*From Duane, 1964.*)

When the model has been proven to apply to a class of products, early field data can be plotted on log-log paper and a line drawn using the slope based on previous similar products. The extrapolation of the line then provides a prediction of future performance. This has several uses, including the monitoring of actual progress toward meeting some requirement. Growth curves with dramatically different slopes mean that reliability improvement is taking place at different rates (see O'Connor, 1991).

The Duane model can be adapted for measures of use other than time. For example, a manufacturer of duplicating machines uses it to predict failure rates for new products by plotting failure rate versus cumulative number of copies run. Bentz and Hutchinson (1984) discuss reliability growth, including an application of the Duane model and an example showing how the rate of growth can vary with operating time.

Use of Probability Paper for Predicting Complaint Level

Weibull probability paper (see Section 9.11, "The Weibull Probability Distribution") can be used to analyze early field data on warranty claims. Through such analysis, it is possible to predict what the cumulative number of claims will be at the end of the warranty period.

TABLE 21.3
Repair information on electrical subassembly

Time in service, months	Repairs per 100 units ($R/100$)	Cumulative $R/100$
1	0.49	0.49
2	0.32	0.81
3	0.24	1.05
4	0.24	1.29
5	0.21	1.50
6	0.19	1.69
7	0.19	1.88
8	0.23	2.11

Source: Ford (1972).

Consider the repair information on an electrical subassembly listed in Table 21.3. The cumulative repairs per 100 units are interpreted as a cumulative failure rate in percentage. These data are summarized from a large number of warranty reports, and thus the data can be plotted directly without using the mean rank approach discussed in Chapter 9, "Basic Probability Concepts."

The Weibull plot is shown in Figure 21.6. The eight months of data have been plotted and a line drawn through the points. This line has been extended, and it predicts the repair rate at the end of the 12-month warranty period to be 2.6 repairs per 100 units. Extrapolation of the line beyond the plotted points is valid only on the assumption that the failure pattern does not change.

Note that this Weibull paper includes a scale for estimating the Weibull slope or shape parameter (see Section 9.11). The slope can be found by drawing a line parallel to the line of best fit and through the point circled on the vertical scale. Here, the slope is read as 0.7. This defines the shape of the failure distribution and can aid in problem definition. Table J in the Appendix shows a blank sheet of this same paper.

For slopes <1, the distribution is exponential in shape and generally means that the failures are early failures due to manufacturing or assembly deficiencies. When the slope is 1, the Weibull reduces to the exponential distribution (see Section 9.10, "The Exponential Probability Distribution").

For slopes >1, the distribution is skewed and generally means that the failures are due to wear-out or fatigue, especially for higher slopes. When the slope is about 3.5 (and $\alpha = 1$ and $\gamma = 0$), the Weibull approximates the normal distribution.

Extrapolation beyond the limits of actual data is always questionable. However, when extrapolated performance has been confirmed by actual performance on similar product lines, the approach may be justified. It should be stressed that decisions on the "vital few" warranty problems deserving major attention *must* and *will* be made by someone. Although the approach

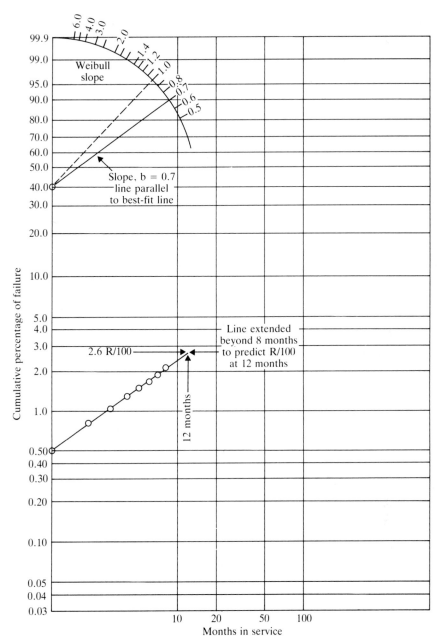

FIGURE 21.6
Warranty data plot. (*From Ford, 1972.*)

suggested here is not rigorous, it is a major step beyond intuitive decision making.

A special case of analysis involves the situation where the units in the field have been placed into service at different dates. Some of the units have failed at varying times, and the remainder are in operation again with varying accumulated operating times. This type of data can be handled with "hazard plotting paper" for the Weibull or other distributions. King (1981) describes the mechanics of analysis and the application to service and warranty problems.

Nelson (1982) provides a comprehensive reference on graphical and other forms of analysis of life data.

SUMMARY

- Measurements for marketing, field performance, and customer service should be based on input from customers, provide for both evaluation and feedback, and include early, concurrent, and lagging indicators of performance.
- The incidence of field complaints often underestimates field problems because many users do not complain (they simply go elsewhere to make their next purchase).
- Profit lost due to product problems can be estimated.
- Simple forms of data analysis serve three purposes: problem identification, problem analysis, and measurement and prediction.
- Reliability growth curves are useful in predicting future performance.
- Plotting data on Weibull probability paper can provide predictions on the level of complaints.

PROBLEMS

21.1. Propose one or more complaint indices for one of the following products: (*a*) checking and savings account services at a bank; (*b*) household refrigerators; (*c*) passenger automobiles; (*d*) corn processing by-products sold primarily to beer brewers and to pharmaceutical companies (for making medicine capsules); (*e*) the totality of products sold by a large department store; (*f*) jet engines for passenger planes.

21.2. Select a product which you or a friend owns and which has been tested and reported on in one of the consumer magazines.
    (*a*) Comment on the adequacy of the tests made to evaluate competing brands.
    (*b*) Compare the opinions of the user to the evaluation published in the magazine.

21.3. Visit a local organization and report on the procedures used to process complaints and to summarize complaint information for executive action.

21.4. Warranty data on an ignition switch show that 0.15 percent have failed by 3000 miles, 0.25 percent by 6000 miles, and 0.40 percent by 12,000 miles. Predict the percentage of failure at 24,000 miles and 50,000 miles. State the assumptions necessary.

   Answer: 0.7 percent, 1.2 percent.

21.5. Past data on a certain type of windshield wiper motor indicate a Weibull slope of about 0.5. A goal of no more than 0.5 percent failures by 24,000 miles has been set. What percentage of failure observed at 6000 miles would indicate that the goal would probably not be met? State the assumptions necessary.

   Answer: 0.22 percent.

21.6. Plants *A* and *B* are part of the same company and manufacture an identical product. The following data show the percent of returned product, by month, for each plant:

Month	A	B	Month	A	B
Jan.	0.4	0.2	July	0.5	0.2
Feb.	0.3	0.1	Aug.	0.2	0.1
Mar.	0.2	0.2	Sept.	0.3	0.2
Apr.	0.4	0.5	Oct.	0.3	0.2
May	0.3	0.3	Nov.	0.5	0.3
June	0.2	0.4	Dec.	0.4	0.1

Construct two plots using ordinary graph paper. One plot should compare the two plants using noncumulative data. The other plot should use cumulative data. Comment on the two methods of plotting.

21.7. Data on returned products are summarized weekly for each of three products (*A*, *B*, and *C*). For each return, the primary reason for the return is noted: V for visual defects, E for poor electrical performance, M for poor mechanical performance. Data are available for three weeks. For the first week, 26 units of product *A* were returned with a distribution of the reason as 5 V, 8 E, and 13 M. Eight units of product *B* were returned with 0 V, 3 E, and 5 M. Product *C* showed a tally of 34 units with 22 V, 10 E, and 2 M. For the second week, product *A* had 37 returns with 6 V, 11 E, and 20 M. Product *B* had 15 returns with 2 V, 9 E, and 4 M. Product *C* had 24 returns with 11 V, 8 E, and 5 M. Assuming that the data are representative of weekly returns, prepare a summary that indicates priorities for an improvement effort.

REFERENCES

Bentz, Richard W., and Leonard T. Hutchinson (1984). "An Approach to Reliability Growth Without Dedicated Testing: A Case History and Some Results," *Proceedings, Annual Reliability and Maintainability Symposium*, IEEE, New York, pp. 458–464.

Duane, J. T. (1964). "Learning Curve Approach to Reliability Monitoring," *IEEE Transactions on Aerospace*, vol. 2, no. 2, pp. 563–566.

Ford (1972). *Reliability Methods, Module No. XII*, Ford Motor Company, January, pp. 11–13.

King, James R. (1981). *Probability Charts for Decision Making,* rev ed., © James R. King, Tamworth, New Hampshire.

Nelson, Wayne (1982). *Applied Life Data Analysis,* John Wiley and Sons, New York.

Nelson, Wayne (1988). "Graphic Analysis of System Repair Data," *Journal of Quality Technology,* vol. 20, no. 1, January, pp. 24–35.

O'Connor, Patrick D. T. (1991). *Practical Reliability Engineering,* 3rd ed., John Wiley and Sons, New York.

TARP (Technical Assistance Research Programs) (1984). Summarized in *Juran Report, Number Three,* Juran Institute, Inc., Wilton, Connecticut, pp. 16–17.

TARP (Technical Assistance Research Programs) (1988). "Quantifying Market Impact: The TARP Market Damage Simulation Model," working paper, Technical Assistance Research Programs, Washington, D.C.

SUPPLEMENTARY READING

QCH4, pp. 20.16–20.18, 20.24–20.27.

CHAPTER
22

ADMINISTRATIVE AND SUPPORT OPERATIONS

22.1 DEFINITION AND SCOPE

Administrative operations are those required for the organization to complete its mission. Examples include accounting and finance, human resource tasks, training, security, data processing, plant engineering, legal activities, office services, and other activities. Support operations are those which have some effect on the product itself, e.g., shipping, receiving, storage, traffic, product publications, and order filling. Administrative and support activities are prevalent throughout manufacturing and service industries.

Traditionally, quality systems have focused on those activities which have a direct connection with the product or service provided to external customers, i.e., production activities in the manufacturing industries and customer-related activities in the service industries. Recent experience makes it clear that quality concepts apply equally to administrative and support activities, all of which have customers—some internal, some external.

In this chapter, we will describe applications of quality concepts, presented in earlier chapters, to administrative and support activities of manufacturing and service industries. In addition, the chapter will explain the concept of process management. Table 22.1 lists specific quality concepts that can be applied within individual administrative and support departments. The reader is urged to review earlier chapters and then identify applications, e.g.,

TABLE 22.1
Quality concepts for potential application in administrative and support operations

Concept	Reference in this book
Definition of quality	Chapter 1
Triple role	Chapter 1
Assessment	
Cost of poor quality	Chapter 2
Marketing research study	Chapter 2
Quality culture study	Chapter 2
Quality planning	Chapter 4
Quality control	Chapter 5
Quality improvement	Chapter 3

defining quality for employee benefit activities, explaining the triple roles in a shipping function, assessing quality performance in a data processing department, applying the three quality processes in an order-filling department.

22.2 QUALITY PLANNING

Section 4.10, "A Road Map for Planning of Products for Salability," presented a road map for quality planning. The steps are: establishing quality goals, identifying customers, determining customer needs, developing product features, developing process features, establishing process controls, and transferring to operations. This same road map and associated techniques apply to planning or revising products or processes for administrative and support activities. (Many of the techniques are helpful in all three of the quality processes, i.e., planning, control, improvement.)

> **Example 22.1.** Galvin (1991) describes how a team used a simple flow diagram to replan an employee separations process. Key transactions in the process included disposition of the employee's unused vacation time, disposition of retirement contributions, and issuance of the final paycheck. The primary goal was to improve process timeliness. Figure 22.1 is a simplified flow diagram developed by the team. At the start, boundaries on the study were set around the personnel and payroll departments because management believed that these were the primary sources of process variation. Team discussions of the flowchart concluded that client offices (where the separating employee worked) were the main suppliers and that measurement and analysis were needed to pinpoint the sources of process variation. As a result, project team boundaries were expanded to include client office functions. This boundary redefinition was instrumental in leading to process changes which increased on-time performance for the separation process from 62 percent to 88 percent.

Flow diagrams and other industrial engineering tools are useful in planning and replanning both for activities within a department and for

Client office	Personnel	Payroll	Process time flow
Employee gives notice			Two weeks before employee's last day
Supervisor and employee negotiate effective date		Receives notice and logs in	
Sends notice of separation →	Receives notice and logs in	Performs vacation time audit	Employee's last day
Employee leaves BLS			
	Issues official notice of separation		
	Receives audit ←	Sends audit	
	Sends paperwork package to Department of Labor		Three weeks after employee's last day

FIGURE 22.1
An employee separation process. (*From Galvin, 1991.*)

complete processes going across departments. One of the units of the IBM Corporation uses a "department activity analysis" to examine activities within a department. Three steps are involved:

1. Listing all major activities. For example, a finance department might have 12 activities such as payroll processing, supplier payment, etc.
2. For *each* activity:
   - Listing the inputs: What are they? From where do they come?
   - Analyzing the work: Why do it? What is its value? Suppose it is not done?
   - Listing the outputs: What are they? Who receives them?
3. For *each* activity:
   - Meeting with the supplier and agreeing on requirements.
   - Meeting with the customer and agreeing on requirements.
   - Defining the measurements that will evaluate output against requirements.

Suppliers and customers may be internal or external to the company.

Of particular importance is the "value-added" concept. This concept questions the need for doing a task at all ("What will the impact be if this task is not done?"). Over time, activities to satisfy a supposed customer need or to compensate for some process inadequacy can creep into processes and become imbedded. Sometimes, these added activities are justified, temporarily or permanently; sometimes they are justified temporarily but not permanently; sometimes they are not justified at all (no "value added"). For example, a department of 33 people was created to check the validity and accuracy of "transfer charges" to one division from other divisions of a utility. Experience had shown that the number of errors and the amount of money involved justified the checking activity. No action was taken on the causes of the errors ("Our job is to find the errors"). The annual budget of the department—well over a million dollars—thus represented a cost of poor quality, year after year.

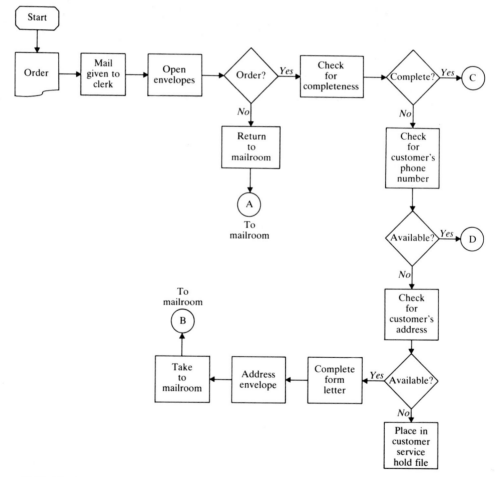

FIGURE 22.2
Segment of flow diagram for order receipt and entry. (*From Juran Institute, Inc., 1989.*)

Figure 22.2 shows a flow diagram for a segment of an order receipt and entry process. Note the use of some standard symbols: A rounded rectangle denotes the beginning or end of a process; a square or rectangle, a step in the process; a square with an irregular bottom, a document; a diamond, a decision or branch point; and a circle, a continuation of the diagram.

Another useful concept in planning a process is self-control. Self-control requires that the process planning provide personnel with the means of knowing what they are supposed to do, the means of knowing what they are doing, and the means of regulating their work.

The basic concept is described in Chapter 5; application to product development and manufacture is presented in Chapters 12 and 16, respectively. Typically, planning is weak in one or more of the three criteria.

> **Example 22.2.** At a bank, procedures for processing loans focus on financial criteria but exclude time standards for making a decision on a loan application (criterion one); many measurements are taken, but feedback is primarily to management and not to the line personnel (criterion two); a "proof operator" is not provided with any means of correcting a process in which a microencoding machine is unable to read a check because of handling of the check during previous process steps (criterion three).

Still another step in quality planning is to prove the capability of a process. The concept of process capability (see Section 17.8, "Process Capability") traditionally quantifies the amount of variability exhibited by a quality characteristic. Capability can also be evaluated in terms of the error rate of a process.

> **Example 22.3.** Dmytrow (1985) describes a study to measure the capability of a new "data-capture process" which used microcomputers to enter and edit data at the Bureau of Labor Statistics. Figure 22.3 shows control charts for the "keying" job. Figure 22.3a is for the first period of the test. Each point represents the error rate of one person. Many errors were made, both by the keyers and by the computer system. The charts for the keyers showed a capability that is much less than the standard of 99.5 percent perfect. Figure 22.3b shows the results after making changes to the process. The average error rate was reduced, but the process was not yet in a state of statistical control. Among the conclusions of the study: Errors were caused by lack of written procedures, inadequate instruction, and lack of feedback; some of the people, however, could perform the intensive keying at a computer terminal accurately for eight hours a day.

22.3 QUALITY CONTROL

Quality control, one of the trilogy of quality processes, is discussed in Chapter 5, "Control of Quality." Control involves a universal sequence of steps: choosing the control subject, choosing a unit of measure, setting a goal for the control subject, choosing a sensor, measuring actual performance, interpreting the difference between actual and standard, and taking action on the difference.

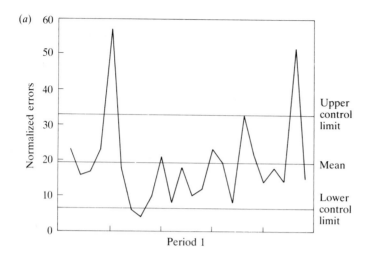

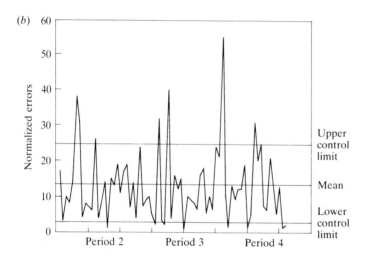

FIGURE 22.3
(*a*) Chart of data-capture errors, before changes. (*b*) Chart of data-capture errors, after changes.
(*From Dmytrow, 1985.*)

Basic to quality control of any activity is quality measurement. Recall the three guidelines for developing quality measurements for a functional activity (see Section 13.1, "Quality Measurement in Design"): obtaining input from customers; designing measurements for both evaluation of performance *and* feedback for self-control; providing early, concurrent, and lagging indicators.

Table 22.2 shows control subjects and units of measure for several areas of administrative and support activities.

TABLE 22.2
Quality measurement in administrative and support activities

Activity/control subject	Units of measure
Finance	
Payment of invoices	Monetary value of invoices paid late
Issuance of invoices	Average number of days to issue
Errors in invoices	Percentage of invoices returned due to errors
Accounts receivable	Monetary value of unrecoverable accounts receivable
Personnel	
Quality of candidates' résumés	Percentage of résumés received which result in interviews
Yield of recruitment process	Number of candidates interviewed before an offer is made and accepted
Time required	Average number of days from request for personnel to initial employment date
Qualification of skilled workers	Percentage of certified workers in critical activities
Duplicating services	
Reliability of equipment	Average number of copies between failures
Maintainability of equipment	Average number of office hours before a failure is corrected
Quality of output	Percentage of duplicating jobs requiring rework
Quality of input	Percentage of illegible input documents

Statistical Process Control

Control charts (see Chapter 17, "Statistical Process Control") can be a helpful tool for administrative and support activities.

> **Example 22.4.** Baker and Artinian (1985) describe the role of control charts in analyzing a system for auditing freight bills and making payments to an external carrier of freight for the Ford Motor Company. As one part of a study, data were collected on the time from receipt of a freight invoice to issuance of a check to the carrier. An average and range chart (Figure 22.4) showed the system to be in statistical control but at a level that was too high—an average of about 14 days. (When combined with mail delays and other factors, some carriers would wait at least 35 days for payment.)
>
> As the process was in statistical control, attention was directed to analyzing the system itself. Using a cause-and-effect diagram, the major reasons for rejection of freight bills were identified. Further analysis resulted in changes in the steps to audit bills and make payments. Results were dramatic: Bills rejected were reduced from 34 percent to under one percent; cycle time required to process bills dropped from an average of 15 days to six days with an associated reduction in variation.

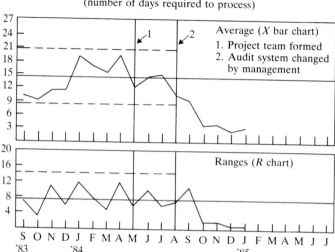

FIGURE 22.4
Control chart evaluation of time (days) taken to process invoices between stages two and five. (*From Baker and Artinian, 1985.*)

22.4 QUALITY IMPROVEMENT

The general approach to quality improvement is set out in Chapter 3, "Quality Improvement and Cost Reduction." The universal sequence of steps is: proving the need, identifying projects, organizing project teams, diagnosing the causes, providing remedies and proving their effectiveness, dealing with resistance to change, and instituting controls to hold the gains. The approach is fully applicable to administrative and support activities. Applications cover a spectrum of improvement projects: room turnover time in a hospital, inaccuracy of pricing information, errors in employee benefit plan transactions, computer programming errors, and office space utilization.

> **Example 22.5.** Engle and Ball (1986) describe a quality improvement project to "reduce the lead time from customer order to delivery on special orders" of medical products at the Becton Dickinson Company. (A special order is an order for a product that is not stocked in the warehouse, e.g., a standard syringe marked with the customer's logo.) The team used the breakthrough sequence, starting with confirmation of proof of the need. The proof was in two parts: A review of a random sample of 15 special orders showed that *all* of them were shipped late, even though the sales income from special orders was high.
> Next, the team started diagnosis by discussing the steps of handling a special order. Surprisingly, no one individual was able to describe the total process. An important step was for the project team to create a flow diagram. Nine steps were involved. Various data were collected and summarized, e.g., special orders were divided into market segments and ranked by number of

orders per year. A further analysis revealed that the top ten customers accounted for 88 percent of the special orders shipped in one year (the Pareto concept). This led to an analysis of the products involved in terms of types, quantities, and the features which made them nonstock. All of this newly found knowledge suggested a remedy that some of the "specials" should be manufactured for stock. Specifically, 42 new catalogue items were added and these accounted for 95 percent of the special order business. Under the old system, customers had waited an average of three months for a special order; under the new system, 85 percent of the special orders were processed with a cycle time of two days. Other benefits under the new system included monetary savings in administrative costs and fewer interruptions of high-volume production runs to fill low-volume special orders.

Diagnostic Tools

The diagnostic tools used in product-oriented quality improvement projects also apply to administrative and support activities.

> **Example 22.6.** In another example of histograms, data were plotted to analyze turnover time in rooms in a laboratory at Brigham and Women's Hospital (Laffel and Plsek, 1989). Turnover time was defined as the time between the moment all catheters and sheaths are removed from one patient and the time local anesthetic is injected into the next patient. Simply collecting data yielded some surprises: The mean time was 78 minutes (45 minutes had been the usual estimate); the variation ranged from 20 to 150 minutes. In one part of the analysis, data were stratified by room and histograms on turnover time were plotted by room (see Figure 22.5). Note what we learn when the total data are stratified by room, Room one had a shorter mean time and much less variation than room two. Further analysis showed that when a nurse called for the next patient before the previous case is completed, turnover time was relatively short. No one had been aware, until the data were recorded and the analysis made, that the timing of the call was a critical determinant of turnover time.

Another useful tool is the cause-and-effect diagram (see Section 3.10, "Diagnose the Causes").

> **Example 22.7.** An order entry department was running a 50 percent error rate on sales order documentation (yes, 50 percent). A project team created a cause-and-effect diagram (Figure 22.6). Analysis led to changes that, in a short time, cut the error rate in half.

The percentage of time spent by personnel in various types of work activities can be estimated by the work-sampling technique. Random observations are made on a process, and the activity taking place at each observation is recorded in predefined categories. The relative frequency of observations in each category then provides a statistically valid estimate of the percentage of time consumed in each category. See Salvendy (1992) for a discussion of the procedure.

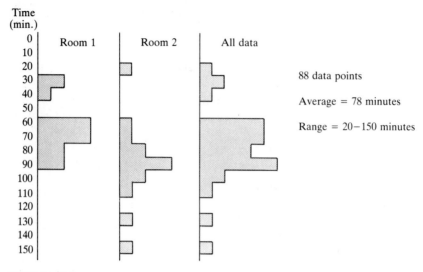

Time (min.)

88 data points

Average = 78 minutes

Range = 20-150 minutes

FIGURE 22.5
Room turnover times. (*From Laffel and Plsek, 1989.*)

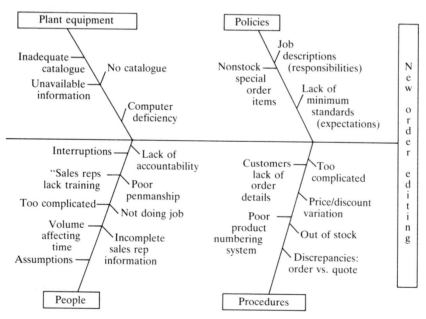

FIGURE 22.6
Cause-and-effect diagram. (*From Nader, 1989.*)

22.5 BUSINESS PROCESS QUALITY MANAGEMENT

We define a business process as any goods or non-goods-related cross-functional process of critical importance which will be managed by a permanent team. Typical examples include order entry, billing, payroll, accounts payable, and contract management. The concept can also be applied to still broader activities such as product and software development, customer service, and supplier relationships. A distinguishing feature is that the management of such critical processes typically requires a permanent team. Like all processes, a business process involves an organization of people, material, energy, equipment, and procedures designed into work activities to produce a specified result.

Although quality concepts had been applied to administrative areas for decades, the applications focused on relatively narrow *tasks* (e.g., a particular clerical operation) rather than on a complete *process* consisting of major activities, each having detailed tasks. As these matters were studied, one of the important concepts that emerged was that of managing quality for critical cross-functional processes. IBM was an important contributor to developing the concept and methodologies of business process quality management.

Fundamental to the concept is the distinction between functional and process management (Figure 22.7). Most enterprises organize along functional lines, with an emphasis on each function (the columns in Figure 22.7) meeting its own objectives. Thus, a development function has an objective as to the number of new products introduced, a sales function has an objective in terms of sales quotas, etc. The management of each function then emphasizes priorities that will help meet the functional objectives. An examination of the overall objectives of the enterprise, however, reveals that success depends on

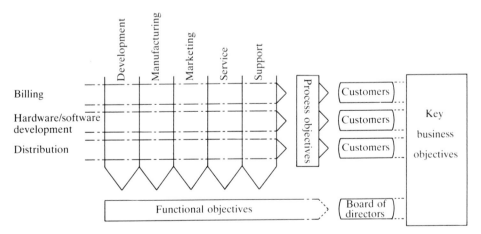

FIGURE 22.7
Functional versus process management system. (*From Juran Institute, Inc., 1990.*)

certain critical results that are the outcome of cross-functional processes (the rows in Figure 22.7). The traditional emphasis on functional (departmental) objectives can be a serious obstacle to achieving company business objectives which require cross-functional processes. Quality management for these critical processes provides a framework for meeting business objectives. Figure 22.7 shows a model and the application to three processes: billing, hardware and software development, and distribution.

Business process management and matrix or project management have similarities—but the former applies to a *process,* the latter to a *product.*

Methodology of Business Process Quality Management

This methodology builds on the customer-supplier relationship (see Section 1.4, "The Quality Function") and makes use of the processes of quality planning, quality control, and quality improvement (see Chapters 3, 4, and 5). Shaw et al. (1988) describe a model used at AT&T that has four stages: ownership, assessment, opportunity selection, and improvement (Figure 22.8). "Ownership" is the stage that ensures that an owner and a team have been appointed; "assessment" defines the process, customer expectations, and quality measurement; "opportunity selection" investigates the process and identifies, in priority order, the areas for improvement; "improvement" provides the follow-through to achieve a new level of performance.

Elements of cycle	Stages	Steps
Management	Ownership	1. Establish process management responsibilities
	Assessment	2. Define process and identify customer requirements 3. Define and establish measures 4. Assess conformance to customer requirements
	Opportunity selection	5. Investigate process to identify improvement opportunities 6. Rank improvement opportunities and set objectives
Improvement	Improvement	7. Improve process quality

FIGURE 22.8
The AT&T management and improvement cycle. (*From Shaw et al. 1988.*)

TABLE 22.3
AT&T Process quality management and improvement methodology

Steps	Activities	Tools
1. Establish process management responsibilities	Review owner selection criteria Identify owner and process members Establish/review responsibilities of owner and process members	Nominal group technique
2. Define process and identify customer requirements	Define process boundaries and major groups, outputs and customers, inputs and suppliers, and subprocesses and flows Conduct customer needs analysis Define customer requirements and communicate your own requirements to suppliers	Block diagram Survey Customer/supplier relations checklist Interview Benchmarking Affinity diagram Tree diagram
3. Define and establish measures	Decide on effective measures Review existing measures Install new measures and reporting system Establish customer satisfaction feedback system	Brainstorming Nominal group technique Survey Interview
4. Assess conformance to customer requirements	Collect and review data on process operations Identify and remove causes of abnormal variation Compare performance of stable process to requirements and determine chronic problem areas	Control chart Interview Survey Pareto diagram Cause-and-effect diagram Brainstorming Nominal group technique Trend chart
5. Investigate process to identify improvement opportunities	Gather data on process problems Identify potential process problem areas to pursue Document potential problem areas Gather data on subprocess problems Identify potential subprocess problems to pursue	Interview Flowcharting Brainstorming Pareto diagram Nominal group technique
6. Rank improvement opportunities and set objectives	Review improvement opportunities Establish priorities Negotiate objectives Decide on improvement projects	Pareto diagram Nominal group technique Trend chart
7. Improve process quality	Develop action plan Identify root causes Test and implement solution Follow through Perform periodic process review	Pareto digram Nominal group technique Brainstorming Cause-and-effect diagram Cause-and-effect/force-field analysis Control chart Survey

Source: Shaw et al. (1988).

Study of the AT&T seven steps in Table 22.3 reveals some similarities with and some differences from the concepts discussed earlier in this book. The similarities include an emphasis on the customer concept and the use of techniques from quality planning, quality control, and quality improvement. But important additions are provided by the process management concept:

1. Emphasis is placed on the overall effectiveness of a cross-functional *process,* rather than the output of individual functional departments.
2. The process is analyzed in an integrated manner not only for correcting defects, errors, or other problems but also for identifying and meeting customer needs.
3. Detailed tasks in the process are evaluated to assure that there is value added for each task (see Section 22.2).
4. Responsibility for the process is defined in terms of a process owner and a process team (see below). The owner and the team are permanent. The process team may set up quality teams that function temporarily to address specific problems within the total process.

Overall, these elements can help to (1) blast away the silos of functional departments and (2) move from an emphasis on departmental objectives to process objectives that are directly related to business objectives.

> **Example 22.8.** An example of process management is provided by a process which involves the preparation of price and delivery schedule of quotations for large customer orders that go beyond the quantities in standard price discount tables (Juran Institute, Inc., 1990). The process, called "contract management," required a review of the sales order, an analysis, and preparation of the final quotation. A process owner was selected and a process team appointed. The previously used process, a manual one, is depicted in Figure 22.9. Note that the customer's request for a quotation was received at a branch office, traveled through various offices at different locations, and required 28 sequential approvals before the decision was given to the branch office for notification to the customer. Typically, customers waited 14 weeks for a quotation and only 20 percent of these quotations resulted in a firm sales order.
>
> Analysis of the process revealed that much of the delay time was due to nonconformance to *internal* customer requirements on the format and content of the proposal for the *external* customer. Under a redesigned electronic process, many of the reasons for internal delays were eliminated. Also, separate procedures were created to handle the "vital few" and the "useful many" customer requests, with authority delegated to regional offices to make final decisions on the "useful many." Finally, two review boards were set up to break the bottleneck of the 28 sequential reviews. The cycle time required to respond to the customer was reduced to an average of 17 days (later refinements achieved further savings). This shortened response time was instrumental in raising the yield of firm sales orders from 20 percent to a solid 60 percent.

The Process Owner

The concept of a "process owner" deserves elaboration. We define a process owner as an individual who is responsible for the overall performance of a

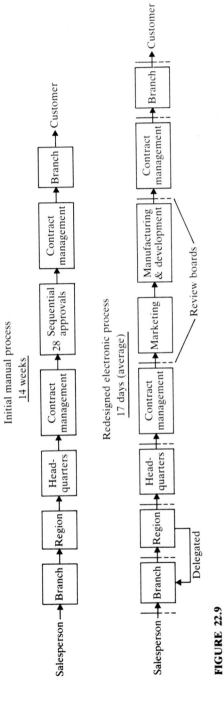

FIGURE 22.9
Contract management process. (*From Juran Institute, Inc., 1990.*)

Initial manual process
14 weeks

Salesperson → Branch → Region → Head- quarters → Contract management → 28 Sequential approvals → Contract management → Branch → Customer

Redesigned electronic process
17 days (average)

Salesperson → Branch → Region → Head- quarters → Contract management → Marketing → Manufacturing & development → Contract management → Branch → Customer

Delegated

Review boards

process. This responsibility includes:

- Effectiveness (often measured by level of defects)
- Efficiency (often measured by cost, including the cost of poor quality)
- Control (process documentation, measurement, clarification of duties, etc.)
- Adaptability (ability to handle future constraints and deficiencies)

McCabe (1986) discusses these elements.

For critical cross-functional processes, the responsibility is indeed a heavy one because the owner does *not* have line responsibility and authority for all of the component activities of the process. But the owner is responsible to upper management for the overall performance of the process. In practice, the owner focuses on establishing working relationships through a process team, installing quality concepts, resolving or escalating cross-functional issues, and driving for continuous progress. The typical owner is from a high level of management and is often the manager with the most resources in the process, or the one who is affected the most when problems occur. Thus, the purchasing manager is a good choice for the purchasing process. (Some processes have an "executive owner" serving as a champion and a "working owner" helping on the day-to-day activities.)

Extensive discussions of business process quality management are provided by Pall (1987), Ackerman et al. (1988), and Harrington (1991).

SUMMARY

- Administrative and support activities have both internal and external customers and can therefore benefit from the application of quality concepts.
- The quality planning road map (and associated techniques such as flow diagrams) is beneficial in planning or revising processes.
- The quality control road map (including techniques such as statistical quality control) helps to measure and regulate processes.
- The quality improvement road map (and techniques such as diagnosis) provides a means of addressing chronic problems in administrative and support processes.
- A business process is any goods or non-goods-related cross-functional process of critical importance. Typically, managing such processes requires a process owner and a permanent team.

PROBLEMS

22.1. Select one administrative or support department in an organization such as a business organization, a local government, a college, or a volunteer organization. Perform the "departmental activity analysis" described in the chapter. This includes: (*a*) listing all major activities; (b) for one of the major activities, listing the inputs, analyzing the work, and listing the outputs; (c) for the activity in (b), meeting with the supplier and customer and agreeing on requirements and defining measurements to evaluate the output.

22.2. Select one administrative or support department in an organization with which you are familiar. For that department, identify at least three chronic quality-related problems. For one of these problems, write a brief problem and mission statement for a project team. Follow the guidelines for these statements given in Section 3.5, "Identify Projects."

22.3. Prepare a flow diagram for one activity that takes place primarily within one administrative or support department.

22.4. For an organization with which you are familiar, identify three cross-functional business management processes that warrant appointing a process owner and a process team.

22.5. For one of the three processes in Problem 22.4, create a flow diagram.

REFERENCES

Ackerman, R. B., R. J. Coleman, E., Leger, and J. C. MacDorman (1988). *Process Quality Management and Improvement Guidelines*. Available through AT&T Customer Information Center, 1-800-432-6600, select Code 500-028.

Baker, Edward M., and Harry L. Artinian (1985). "The Deming Philosophy of Continuing Improvement in a Service Organization: The Case of Windsor Export Supply," *Quality Progress,* June, pp. 61–69.

Dmytrow, Eric D. (1985). "Process Capability in the Service Sector," *Juran Report Number Five,* Juran Institute, Inc., Wilton, Connecticut, pp. 31–37.

Engle, David, and David Ball (1986). "Improving Customer Service for Special Orders," *Juran Report Number Six,* Juran Institute, Inc., Wilton, Connecticut, pp. 106–110.

Galvin, John M. (1991). "Structural Problem-Solving for Administrative Processes: A Case Study," *ASQC Quality Congress Transactions,* Milwaukee, pp. 692–697.

Harrington, H. J. (1991). *Business Process Improvement,* McGraw-Hill, Inc., New York.

Juran Institute, Inc. (1989). "Quality Improvement Tools—Flow Diagrams," Wilton, Connecticut.

Juran Institute, Inc. (1990). "Management of Quality—Manufacturing Course Notes," Wilton, Connecticut.

Laffel, Glenn, and Paul E. Plsek (1989). "Preliminary Results from a Quality Improvement Demonstration Program at Brigham and Women's Hospital," *Impro Conference Proceedings,* Juran Institute, Inc., Wilton, Connecticut, pp. 8A–21 to 8A–27.

McCabe, William J. (1986). "Quality Methods Applied to the Business Process," *ASQC Quality Congress Transactions,* Milwaukee, pp. 429–436.

Nader, Gary J. (1989). "Applying Quality Methods: Non-Manufacturing Areas," *ASQC Quality Congress Transactions,* Milwaukee, pp. 14–21.

Pall, Gabriel A. (1987). *Quality Process Management,* Prentice-Hall, Englewood Cliffs, New Jersey.

Salvendy, Gavriel (1992). *Handbook of Industrial Engineering,* John Wiley and Sons, New York.

Shaw, Gregory T., Elias Leger, John C. MacDorman (1988). "Process Quality at AT&T," *Impro Conference Proceedings,* Juran Institute, Inc., Wilton, Connecticut, pp. 4D–5 to 4D–9.

SUPPLEMENTARY READING

Administrative and support operations: QCH4, Section 21.

CHAPTER
23

QUALITY
INFORMATION
SYSTEMS

23.1 SCOPE OF A QUALITY INFORMATION SYSTEM

A quality information system (QIS) is an organized method of collecting, storing, analyzing, and reporting information on quality to assist decision makers at all levels.

In the past, information on quality was concerned mainly with in-plant inspection data. However, products are now more complex, programs for controlling quality now span the spectrum of functional departments, and emphasis is now placed on fitness for use rather than conformance to specification. These changing conditions, coupled with the advent of the computer, have resulted in a broader viewpoint toward information on quality. Service industries report similar changes in the information environment.

This broader viewpoint requires inputs from a variety of functional areas. It also recognizes that "information" consists not only of data but also of other knowledge needed for decision making. Inputs for a quality information system include:

- *Market research information on quality*. Examples are (a) customer opinions on the product and service being provided and (b) results of customer experience that suggest opportunities for improving fitness for use.

- *Product design test data*. Examples are development test data, data on parts and components under consideration from various suppliers, and data on the environment that the product may encounter.

- *Information on design evaluation for quality.* Examples are minutes of design review meetings, reliability predictions, and failure mode, effect, and criticality analyses.
- *Information on purchased parts and materials.* Examples are inspection data, data on tests conducted by a supplier, data on tests conducted by an independent laboratory on a procured item, supplier survey information, and supplier rating data.
- *Process data.* These data cover the entire in-plant manufacturing inspection system from the beginning of manufacturing up to final inspection. Also included are process control data and process capability data. Many service industries now record, on a daily or weekly basis, corresponding data from key processes.
- *Final inspection data.* These data are the routine data at a final inspection.
- *Field performance data.* Examples are mean time between failures (MTBF) and other data from a company proving ground, and warranty and complaint information obtained from the customer.
- *Results of quality measurement.* This includes data from functional activities, product audits, systems audits, and management control data such as the cost of poor quality.

Thus, the scope of a quality information system may vary from a simple system covering in-process inspection data to a broad system covering all information on the overall effectiveness of both products and key processes.

The role of the computer in quality information systems seems to be without limit. We are moving toward the "paperless"—or at least "paperlite"—organization.

QCH4, Section 27, elaborates on this role. To cite just one example, consider a computer-assisted information system which captures, records, and retrieves data on performance of products. Data are entered using three categories: part name (e.g., semi-conductor), phenomenon (e.g., short circuit), and cause (e.g., excessive current). Key words are used with each category. Titles, abstracts, and key words of source documents are displayed on a computer screen. Documents are then supplied through a microfiche retrieval system. Imagine how helpful it is to be able to tap such history during the design of a product.

23.2 RELATIONSHIP OF A QUALITY INFORMATION SYSTEM TO A MANAGEMENT INFORMATION SYSTEM

A management information system (MIS) typically refers to a computer-based system which provides information for management decision making in financial, technological, marketing, and human resources activities. MIS attempts to provide all the information needs of management through one

TABLE 23.1
Impact of MIS on QIS

Impact	Examples
The MIS data base provides product information that can be useful as bases for quality data	Sales dollars, direct labor dollars, manufacturing cost, direct labor hours
Information on quality can be stored in the MIS and changes can be entered directly. The information can be drawn out as needed.	Information on quality costs, inspection and test data
Data analysis models can be incorporated in the MIS	Pareto analyses, statistical analyses, trend analyses
Recently developed hardware and methods for data collection and transmission can be applied to quality information	Special devices for data input, video display, computer graphics
Departments generating quality information can be required to submit it in the form required by the MIS data base	Inspection and test data, reliability data, supplier survey data

integrated system. The concept has several characteristics:

- Information input and output are planned from an overall company viewpoint rather than using separate departmental systems or handling each request for information on a case-by-case basis.
- Information that would ordinarily be maintained in separate departments is consolidated to form what is called a *data base.*
- There are several different uses for the same input data. (This justifies the integrated approach of a data base.)

When an organization does have an MIS, the system will impact on a quality information system. The impact can take various forms, as shown in Table 23.1. Such impact makes it imperative that those designing a quality information system work closely with those who are responsible for the MIS.

23.3 PLANNING A COMPUTER-BASED QUALITY INFORMATION SYSTEM

The planning of a computer-based QIS can be complex. The road starts with an analysis of customer needs, creation of a design specification for the system, and preparation of a proposal indicating costs and time required. When the proposal is approved by management, the system is developed, tested, and implemented. Finally, provisions are made for review of system performance.

A system must be tailored to meet the needs of both internal and external customers of an organization. The following principles are generally applicable.

- Plan the system to receive information in almost any form imaginable. Although most of the information will be received on special forms, the system should make it possible to receive and process information by means of a telephone call, letters, or other media.
- Provide flexibility for meeting new data needs. A cardinal example of this is the failure reporting form that must be revised periodically because someone suddenly discovers a critical need for an additional item of information to be recorded.
- Provide for collection of data on three time phases: (a) real time (continuous), (b) recent (minutes to hours) and (c) historical (extended time).
- Provide for eliminating collection of data that are no longer useful as well as reports that are no longer needed. This requires a periodic audit of the use (or lack of use) of the data and reports.
- Issue reports that are readable, timely, and have sufficient useful detail on current problems to facilitate investigations and corrective action and also provide early warning of potential problems.
- Prepare summary reports covering long periods of time to highlight potential problem areas and show progress on known problems.
- Keep track of the *cost* of collecting, processing, and reporting information and compare this cost to the *value* of the information.

Typically, the QIS becomes a reality through *software*. Software is the collection of computer programs, procedures, and associated documentation necessary for the operation of the information system. The computer software program is found either in existing computer software packages or by creating new software.

23.4   SELECTION OF OFF-THE-SHELF SOFTWARE

"Application software packages" are available for a wide variety of needs. Each year, *Quality Progress* magazine publishes a directory of software. In the March 1992 issue, packages were listed for the following categories: calibration, capability studies, data acquisition, design of experiments, gage repeatability and reproducibility, inspection, management, measurement, problem solving, quality assurance for software development, quality costs, reliability, sampling, simulation, statistical methods, statistical process control, supplier quality assurance, Taguchi techniques, training, and other. The *Journal of Quality Technology*, published by the American Society for Quality Control, regularly runs a column providing the detailed programming steps for statistical techniques. Such programs can be used as is or incorporated as part of a larger program created to meet the needs of a specific user.

Tables 23.2 and 23.3, respectively, show the steps in acquiring a software

TABLE 23.2
Steps in acquiring an application package

1. List present and future requirements of the application in detail
2. Survey all available packages for that application
3. Examine package documentation and user manuals
4. Check whether the package has sufficient application parameters
5. Check whether the package has adequate aids to maintenance
6. Draw up a short list of suitable packages
7. Try out each package with corporate data, if possible
8. Determine whether the package can link into the corporate data base plans
9. Conduct bencharks (comparison trials) if performance is critical
10. Allow end users to implement them on a temporary basis if the end user interface is critical
11. Negotiate and write an appropriate contract

Source: Adapted from Martin and McClure (1983).

application package and the pitfalls involved. In examining alternative software packages, it is useful to have a checklist of the attributes (often called "factors") of software along with a checklist of specific questions. Table 23.4 provides a listing of software quality factors. Berger (1986) has created a list of questions (for applications to quality) concerning the supplier, program design, technical features, third-party information, and pricing. A discussion of some of these issues is given in Espeillac (1987).

If one is fortunate enough to locate a satisfactory software package, work still remains to apply that package to local conditions of data input and output requirements. If an "off-the-shelf" software package is not available, then new software must be created.

23.5 CREATING NEW SOFTWARE

Experience makes it vividly clear that a primary issue in developing software is the lack of sufficient communication and understanding between the user and

TABLE 23.3
Pitfalls of application packages

1. The package does not fully adapt to changes in requirements
2. The data processing department must modify the package when it is installed, and subsequent maintenance becomes almost as expensive as in-house application programs
3. Expensive maintenance becomes necessary later when the hardware, operating system, terminals, network, or user requirements are changed
4. The package is hard to maintain owing to poor documentation, no provision for user-created code, poor structure, absence of source code, excessive complexity, low-level languages, or poor-quality coding
5. The package has been made difficult to maintain because it has been tinkered with inhouse and modificatons have been made that are ill documented and difficult for others to understand
6. The package does not fit with the corporate data base implementation and strategy
7. The software house that owns the package ceases operations

Source: Adapted from Martin and McClure (1983).

TABLE 23.4
Software quality factors

Factor	Definition
Correctness	Extent to which a program satisfies its specifications and fulfills the user's mission objectives
Reliability	Extent to which a program can be expected to perform its intended function with required precision
Efficiency	Amount of computing resources and code required by a program to perform a function
Integrity	Extent to which access to software or data by unauthorized persons can be controlled
Usability	Effort required to learn, operate, prepare input of, and interpret output of a program
Maintainability	Effort required to locate and fix an error in an operational program
Testability	Effort required to test a program to ensure that it performs its intended function
Flexibility	Effort required to modify an operational program.
Portability	Effort required to transfer a program from one hardware configuration and/or software system environment to another
Reusability	Extent to which a program can be used in other applications—related to the packaging and scope of the functions that programs perform
Interoperability	Effort required to couple one system with another

Source: Adapted from McCall et al. (1977).

the software developer. The software community addresses the issue from both a management and a technical viewpoint.

Consider the management dimension of software development. Depending on the scope and significance of the software desired, it is often desirable to form a project team to develop the software. Membership includes users, software developers, and others who will be affected by the software. A project manager is appointed and typically comes from either the user function or the software development function. A "project management" approach is adopted to plan and control the phases of software development. The broad phases are: defining the software requirements, designing the software system, implementing the system, and maintaining the system. See QCH4, pages 27.7–27.11, for elaboration of the project team concept and these four broad phases. Normally, a project management and control software system is used to organize, determine time-critical activities (the "critical path"), and monitor the progress of the project.

The technical dimension of the software development can involve many details of the four broad phases stated above. Table 23.5 tabulates eight steps with "deliverables" under each step (Gryna, D. 1988).

23.6 CREATING THE COMPUTER SOFTWARE PROGRAM

To process the input data, the computer must receive a series of instructions directing it to perform a sequence of operations. These instructions are called a *program.*

TABLE 23.5
System life cycle phases

Step	Deliverable/activity
1. Requirements analysis	System requirements specification
	Disaster recovery plan*
	Risk assessment*
	Resource requirements analysis*
	Requirements analysis review
2. External design	External design specifications
	User's manual
	Maintenance manual
	Preliminary test plan
	External design review
	System requirements specifications
3. Internal design	Internal design specifications
	Conversion/implementation plan
	System test plan
	Internal design review
	System requirements specifications
4. Detailed development	Code review
	Disaster recovery plan
	Security risk assessment
	Detailed development review
5. System test	Test report
	System test review
6. Data management	Software development file (SDF)
	User's manual
	Maintenance manual
7. Production/implementation	Implementation plan
	Maintenance manual
8. Maintenance	Scheduled activities
	Documentation of changes
	Maintenance manual

* May be excluded from system requirements specification.
Source: Gryna, D., (1988).

Computer programming spans the spectrum of complexity, depending on the processing that is desired for the information. The following steps are usually required to create a program:

1. *Studying the present system of information flow and the desired outputs for the future.* The present system should be thoroughly reviewed before proceeding with the development of a program. A system flowchart analysis and data flow diagrams are usually necessary. In this step, thorough communication between the programmer and the user of the information is essential.

Whitbeck (1989) explains how to create a "baseline description" of the current system for a process inspection function. Analysis of this baseline results in an improved process which then becomes the basis for developing the computer program.

2. *Developing a programming plan.* The programmer develops an approach for the project. This approach can include deciding on input and output media (with the user), deciding on what programming language to use, and deciding whether to use already prepared ("canned") programs.

3. *Detailing the processing operations.* The programmer prepares detailed flowcharts describing all elements of input, processing, and output of information. These charts are drawn with special programming symbols and they become the basis of writing the actual program. The step includes provision for coding the input data to prepare the data for the computer.

4. *Writing the program.* The program consists of a sequence of instructions written in a particular programming language and meeting the rules set up for that language. Examples of languages are "C," ADA, and COBOL (COmmon Business Oriented Language).

5. *Reviewing the program for errors.* This "desk check" (typically done by a programmer) and a "code walkthrough" (done by a programmer and peers) are necessary because of the difficulty of writing even a moderate-size program without making errors.

6. *Testing the program on the computer and making corrections as required.*

7. *Documenting the program.* The documentation is generated throughout the development phases and includes the flowcharts, the list of program steps, the output format, and special instructions (if needed) for the operator of the computer.

8. *Evaluating the program.* This starts with the adequacy, to the user, of the output. The evaluation also includes the degree of documentation, the utilization of prepared programs, and the utilization of the full capability of the computer.

9. *Providing for training.* New software is a mystery to many users, and training must be provided to encourage its use and make its application successful.

23.7 CONTROLLING THE QUALITY OF COMPUTER SOFTWARE

For many applications, it is virtually impossible to produce a program that is error-free. A complex program can contain several million lines of computer code. When there are that many lines, there will necessarily be errors, and the cost of software errors may be large.

Formal programs have been developed to attack this problem. The main elements of such programs draw upon some of the techniques used in controlling the quality and reliability of physical products. Emphasis is on both detection and prevention of errors. The elements usually include:

1. *Design review.* Several reviews are held. The purpose is to evaluate (a) the requirements for the software, (b) the software design approach, and (c) the detailed design. About 60 percent of all software errors are introduced during the requirements-definition and design phases. Dobbins (in Schulmeyer and McManus, 1987) identifies ten types of software defects (Table 23.6). Dudley (in Ireson and Coombs, 1988) provides a seriousness classification of software defects (Table 23.7). Eliminating errors *early* in the development process has the highest priority because the time and cost of removing them later in the process increases dramatically. Umbaugh (1991, p. 601) states the increases as ten times by the design phase, 1000 times by system acceptance, and 3000 times by actual systems production.

   Dobbins also cites three types of inspection as typical:

   • *High-level design inspection.* Here, inspection ensures that the performance requirements have been identified and translated into requirements for the computer program's mode of operation.

   • *Low-level design inspection.* This ensures that the key modules of the program are designed for accuracy, reliability and fault tolerance, flexibility, testability, and maintainability.

   • *Code inspection.* This inspection, made after there has been an error-free compilation, verifies that the design has been correctly converted to the

TABLE 23.6
Types of software defects

Type of defect	Definition
Design	Function description does not meet the requirements specification
Logic	Data is missing; wrong or extra information
Syntax	Does not adhere to the grammar of the design/code language defined
Standards	Does not meet the software standards requirements; this includes in-house standards, project standards, and military standards invoked in the contract
Data	Missing, extra, or wrong data definition or usage
Interface	Incompatible definition/format of information exchanged between two modules
Return code/message	Incorrect or missing values/messages sent
Prologue/comment	The explanation accompanying the design/code language is incorrect, inexplicit, or missing
Requirements	Change in the requirements specification which is the direct and proximate reason for the required change in the design or code
Performance improvement	Code will not perform in the amount of time/space/CPU allocated

Source: Dobbins in Schulmeyer and McManus (1987), p. 147.

TABLE 23.7
Classification of software defects

Type	Definition
Critical	Causes loss of data, interrupts operation, requires restart, requires manual intervention, destroys network connection, endangers operators, less workaround
Severe	Degrades performance significantly, produces inconsistent results, requires manual monitoring, forces user to use different approach, has difficult workaround
Average	Adequate workaround, software recovers automatically, can be avoided, results requires interpretation, performance is slowed somewhat, extra training is required, error message is difficult to interpret
Low	Cosmetic error, misspelling of error message, incorrectly linked user interface, inconvenient dialogue

Source: Dudley in Ireson and Coombs (1988).

appropriate language and that the module test plan is adequate to ensure compliance with the requirements.

For each of these levels, inspection would be made for each of the ten defect types listed in Table 23.6. Results would typically be reported in defects per thousand lines of code. (See Dobbins, 1987, for elaboration of the methods and illustrative results.)

2. *Documentation review.* The emphasis is on the plans and procedures that will be used to test the computer programs. Program packages are now available that test newly created computer programs. This documentation of test plans is one part of the total documentation of the project.

3. *Validation of software tests.* This consists of reviewing the results of the tests to evaluate the software. Dudley (in Ireson and Coombs, 1988) classifies software testing into two types: static and dynamic (Table 23.8). Static testing includes design review, various forms of inspection, etc.; dynamic testing runs the program on the computer, using test scenarios to find defects and weak points.

4. *Corrective action system.* This is similar to the system on physical products (see Section 20.8, "Processing and Resolution of Customer Complaints"). It includes documentation of all software problems and follow-up to assure resolution.

5. *Configuration management.* The collection of activities to implement design changes is called configuration management. For software, the objective is to identify different versions of the computer programs *accurately,* prevent unauthorized modifications, and ensure that approved modifications are executed.

23.8 REPORTS ON QUALITY

For those engaged in managing or regulating large enterprises, the bulk of quality information is derived from multiple sources of operational informa-

TABLE 23.8
Testing during development phases

Phase	Static testing	Dynamic testing
Investigation	Document inspection	
Specification	Document inspection Cross-reference check to investigation documents	
Design specification	Design inspection Cross-reference check to documents Design analysis tools	
Code	Code inspection Style analyzers Cross-reference check to design documents	Functional tests Reliability tests
System and user testing		Performance tests Configuration tests Installation tests
Release		Reliability tests Regression tests
Support	As above, by activity	As above, by activity

Source: Dudley in Ireson and Coombs (1988).

tion: laboratory tests, factory tests, field performance data, etc. This information is used in the first instance for operational controls, e.g., day-to-day regulation of factory and office process and field performance. The same information, when summarized and converted into suitable form, becomes a major input to the quality instrument panel—a system of information which enables busy managers to become adequately informed as to quality performance and trends without becoming heavily involved in day-to-day operations. Table 23.9 shows the interrelationship between operational and executive controls.

Operational Reports

Operational control reports are designed to assist in conducting day-to-day operations with particular emphasis on achieving improvement. Table 23.10 depicts an inspection reporting system for an electronics manufacturer. The system translates gross information into lower levels of detail so managers and engineers can isolate problems by product and by worker. Note that Pareto analysis is used extensively in this system.

Executive Reports

Early forms of executive reports on quality tended to be limited to summaries of factory quality information plus summaries of field complaints. In recent

TABLE 23.9
Operational quality controls versus executive quality controls

Aspects	Application to operational quality controls	Application to executive quality controls
Control subjects	Physical, chemical, specification requirements	Summarized performance for product lines, departments, etc.
Units of measure	Natural physical, chemical (ohms, kilograms, etc.)	Various: often in money
Sensing devices	Physical instruments, human senses	Summaries of data
Who collects the sensed information?	Operators, inspectors, clerks, automated in instruments	Various statistical departments
When is the sensing done?	During current operations	Days, weeks, or months after current operations
Standards used for comparison	Specification limits for materials, process, product	History, competitors, plan
Who acts on the information?	Servomechanisms, nonsupervisors, first-line supervisors	Managers
Action taken	Process regulation, repair, sorting	Replanning; quality improvement; motivation

TABLE 23.10
Summary of reports in an inspection information system

Name of summary	Description	Example
Part-operation accept/reject	Summarizes accept/reject information for each work area	In work area 5924, operation 85 on 40432 was highlighted as a poor performer; 46 inspections were made and 23 units were rejected
Part-operation listing	Summarizes fault categories for each part operation	For part operation 40432-85 there were 17 instances of "terminal solder missing" or 31 % of the total faults for operation 85
Fault listing	Summarizes fault categories for each work area	For work area 5924, there were 52 instances of terminal solder missing or 28% of the total; of these 52, 6 were charged to operator 37157
Operator listing	Summarizes faults charged to each operator	Operator 37157 was charged with 24 faults, 6 of which were terminal solder missing
Monthly inspection report	This is a graphical and tabular summary of overall performance; it also lists the major problem areas; a separate page is prepared for each work area	For work area 5924, a graph of percentage defective by month is plotted; for December, the major problem was on part operation 40432-85; 1693 units were inspected; 455 faults were found, of which 361 were due to operators; operator 37157 was a major contributor to defects, particularly missing and improper solder and wiring errors

TABLE 23.11
Revisions in executive reports on quality

Control subjects	Units of measure
Factory quality deficiencies	Cost of poor quality relative to sales
Finished goods quality	Parts (defective) per million; demerits per unit; demerits per $1000 of sales; demerits per 1000 possible errors
Field quality performance	Percentage uptime; maintenance hours per 1000 operating hours
Field quality deficiencies	Cost relative to sales; cost per 1000 units under warranty
Suppliers' quality	Cost of poor quality as a percent of purchases
Top 10 quality problems	Narrative listing
Significant events	Narrative listing

Source: QCH 4, p. 89.

years, refinements to these reports have included the use of monetary measures and identification of improvement areas (Table 23.11). As the performance of business systems has grown in importance, reports have included these additional control subjects (Table 23.12). Many chapters of this book present (under the subject of "quality measurement") control subjects for various functional areas. Some of these are candidates for inclusion in executive reports.

The information needed by managers for executive control varies widely from company to company, depending on the nature of the product, the extent to which the control problems have been solved, etc.

Example 23.1. General Dynamics Corporation, a defense contractor, undertook a form of corporate quality improvement. One element of the approach is a

TABLE 23.12
Influence of recent developments on executive reports on quality

Control subject	Unit of measure
Promptness of service	Days; percent of responses within target goals
Competitiveness in quality	Performance versus top three competitors
Avoidable changes in engineering drawings, purchase orders, etc.	Percentage of all changes
Document quality	Percentage of pages defective
Software quality	Errors per 1000 lines of code; cost to correct errors
Invoicing errors	Percentage in error; cost of correction
Quality improvement	Project data: undertaken, in progress, completed; results of project collectively; status of major projects individually; percentage of managers assigned to projects
Companywide quality management—progress against strategic quality goals	Various

Source: QCH 4, p. 8, 10.

report battery. The reports deal with numerous parameters, of which 12 are corporate, i.e., they are common to all divisions of the corporation. The corporate parameters are as follows:

- Avoidable engineering changes
- Deviations/waivers
- First-time yield
- Scrap (labor-hour content)
- Scrap (material value content)
- Repair and/or rework (labor-hour content)
- On-time delivery by production
- Purchased item acceptability
- Service report response time
- Material review actions
- Inspection escapes
- Overtime

For elaboration, see Talley (1986).

In many companies, these summarized executive reports are supplemented by independent audit reports. Such audits help to provide assurance that the report system correctly reflects what is actually going on with respect to quality.

Some organizations use phased indicators of quality performance.

Example 23.2. Texas Instruments designed its quality reporting system around three types of indicators: leading indicators, concurrent indicators, and lagging indicators (Onnias, 1986).

Figure 23.1 depicts this concept. Leading indicators include data on raw material or piece parts purchased from suppliers (e.g., parts per million defective material, purity level). Concurrent indicators include internal manufacturing data (e.g., dust count average, reliability of manufacturing equipment, warehouse errors). Lagging indicators are of two types: material rejected and returned by customers and customer feedback data. The Texas Instruments report battery is composed of these three types of indicators plus the cost of quality.

Some executive control subjects are lagging indicators because the reports appear weeks or even months after the operations have been performed. Such reports are nevertheless of great value in showing trends, identifying substantial failures in meeting goals, measuring performance of managers, and so forth.

In contrast, some subjects are leading indicators. Market research on quality may lead product development by months. Design review is a leading indicator of failure rates. Product audit lags behind date of manufacture but is a leading indicator of quality as received by the user.

A well-balanced system of executive reports makes use of leading indicators ("early warning signals") as well as summaries which lag behind operations.

TI's report (called the *Quality Blue Book*) is issued monthly and is the basis of annual performance appraisal of all managers for their contribution to quality.

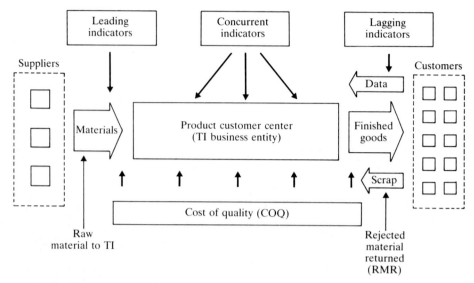

FIGURE 23.1
Content of the *Quality Blue Book*. (*From Onnias, 1986.*)

With the use of personal computers by managers, report systems are often "networked" to these personal computers. Smith (1990) describes a "quality network" system that enables manufacturing managers to select and receive real-time quality information on their personal computers.

SUMMARY

- A quality information system (QIS) is an organized method of collecting, storing, analyzing, and reporting information on quality to assist decision makers at all levels. Such a system should be designed to be compatible with a company management information system (MIS).
- We need to plan a QIS to meet the needs of internal and external customers.
- Application software packages are available for a wide variety of needs. Be alert to the lessons learned about acquiring software packages.
- In creating new software, the primary issue is the lack of sufficient communication between the user and the software developer. We should use a project management approach to plan and control software development.
- Controlling the quality of computer software involves both detection and prevention of errors.
- Reports on quality focus on both operational and executive matters. A useful framework is the concept of leading, concurrent, and lagging indicators of performance.

PROBLEMS

23.1. For any of the following, obtain the necessary information and draw up a flowchart for the data collection and analysis of: (*a*) final inspection results at a plant; (*b*) goods returned to a plant; (*c*) traffic fines; (*d*) complaints at a department store; (*e*) automobile accident insurance claims; (*f*) performance deficiencies by an athletic team; (*g*) loss of utility service to homes. Make recommendations for changes or additions.

23.2. For any institution, evaluate the usefulness of at least two reports on product quality by speaking with those who receive the report. Set up a scale of frequency of use and obtain opinions on use and on shortcomings of the present report.

23.3. For the computer system in an organization, define the characteristics in terms of input devices, means of external storage, and output devices.

23.4. For any institution, describe at least one area where manual processing of data could justifiably be replaced with automatic data processing using a computer.

23.5. Speak with people engaged in writing computer programs. Develop a list of common programming errors. For a sample of ten programs, tally the frequency of occurrence for each type of programming error.

23.6. Speak with people responsible for collecting information for a data base on quality or other subjects. Determine the steps taken, if any, to verify the quality of the input data and the output results, i.e., accuracy, completeness, and other criteria.

REFERENCES

Berger, Roger W. (1986). "Recent Advances in Computer Software for Quality," *ASQC Quality Congress Transactions*, Milwaukee, pp. 269–273.

Espeillac, Georgette (1987). "Selecting SQC/SPC Software," *Quality Progress*, March, pp. 28–31.

Gryna, Derek S. (1988). "Data Processing—A Software Quality Challenge," *ASQC Quality Congress Transactions*, Milwaukee, pp. 423–428.

Ireson, W. Grant, and Clyde F. Coombs (1988). *Handbook of Reliability Engineering and Management*, McGraw-Hill Book Company, New York, Chapter 16.

Martin, J., and C. McClure (1983). "Buying Software off the Rack," *Harvard Business Review*, November–December, p. 40.

McCall, J., P. Richards, and G. Walters (1977). "Factors in Software Quality," *Joint General Electric–U.S. Air Force Report No. RADC TR-77-369*, vol. 1, November, pp. 3–5.

Onnias, Arturo (1986). "The Quality Blue Book," *Juran Report Number Six*, Juran Institute, Inc., Wilton, Connecticut, pp. 127–131.

Schulmeyer, G. Gordon, and James I. McManus (1987). *Handbook of Software Quality Assurance*, Van Nostrand Reinhold, New York.

Smith, K. (1990). "Networking for Quality," *Quality Engineering*, vol. 3, no. 1, pp. 49–57.

Talley, D. J. (1986). "The Quest for Sustaining Quality Improvement," *Juran Report Number Six*, pp. 188–192.

Umbaugh, Robert E., ed. (1991). *Handbook of IS Management*, 3rd ed., Auerbach Publishers, Boston, Chapters XIV-1 to XIV-3.

Whitbeck, Craig W. (1989). "Designing Quality Information Systems," *ASQC Quality Congress Transactions*, Milwaukee, pp. 835–841.

SUPPLEMENTARY READING

Software quality: QCH4, Section 14 and pp. 27.1–27.11.

Dudley, Sally (1988). "Software Reliability" in W. Grant Ireson and Clyde F. Coombs, eds., *Handbook of Reliability Engineering and Management,* McGraw-Hill Book Company, New York, pp. 16.7–16.8.

Dobbins, James H. (1987). "Inspections as an Up Front Quality Technique," in G. Gordon Schulmeyer and James I. McManus, eds., *Handbook of Software Quality Assurance,* Van Nostrand Reinhold, New York, pp. 137–177.

Ireson, W. Grant, and Clyde F. Coombs (1988). *Handbook of Reliability Engineering and Management,* McGraw-Hill Book Company, New York, Chapter 16.

Schulmeyer, G. Gordon, and James I. McManus (1987). *Handbook of Software Quality Assurance,* Van Nostrand Reinhold, New York.

Reports on quality: QCH4: pp. 4.28–4.29, 8.8–8.19, 20.30–20.32, 30.40–30.44, 33.51–33.58

Data collection, storage, and retrieval: Bersbach, Peter L. (1992). "Quality Information Systems," in Thomas Pyzdek and Roger W. Berger, eds., *Quality Engineering Handbook,* Marcel Dekker, Inc., New York, pp. 61–83.

CHAPTER 24

QUALITY ASSURANCE

24.1 DEFINITIONS OF QUALITY ASSURANCE

In this book, "quality assurance" is the activity of providing the evidence needed to establish confidence, among all concerned, that the quality-related activities are being performed effectively. ISO 8402-1986 defines quality assurance as related to a product or service: All those planned or systematic actions necessary to provide adequate confidence that a product or service will satisfy given requirements for quality. The reader is warned that other meanings are common, e.g., "Quality Assurance" is often the title of a *department* which is concerned with many quality-related activities such as quality planning, quality control, quality improvement, quality audit, and reliability.

24.2 CONCEPT OF QUALITY ASSURANCE

Many quality assurance activities provide protection against quality problems through early warnings of trouble ahead. The assurance comes from evidence—a set of facts. For simple products, the evidence is usually some

TABLE 24.1
Examples of departmental assurance activities

Department	Assurance activity
Marketing	Product evaluation by a test market
	Controlled use of product
	Product monitoring
	Captive service activity
	Special surveys
	Competitive evaluations
Product development	Design review
	Reliability analysis
	Maintainability analysis
	Safety analysis
	Human factors analysis
	Manufacturing, inspection, and transportation analysis
	Value engineering
	Self-control analysis
Supplier relations	Qualification of supplier design
	Qualification of supplier process
	Evaluation of initial samples
	Evaluation of first shipments
Production	Design review
	Process capability analysis
	Preproduction trials
	Preproduction runs
	Failure mode, effect, and criticality analysis for processes
	Review of manufacturing planning (checklist)
	Evaluation of proposed process control tools
	Self-control analysis
	Audit of production quality
Inspection and test	Interlaboratory tests
	Measuring inspector accuracy
Customer service	Audit of packaging, transportation, and storage
	Evaluation of maintenance services

Source: QCH 4, p. 9.3.

form of inspection or testing of the product. For complex products, the evidence is not only inspection and test data but also reviews of plans and audits of the execution of plans. A family of assurance techniques is available to cover a wide variety of needs.

Quality assurance is similar to the concept of the financial audit, which provides assurance of financial integrity by establishing, through "independent" audit, that the plan of accounting is: (1) such that, if followed, it will correctly reflect the financial condition of the company and (2) actually being followed. Today, independent financial auditors (certified public accountants) have become an influential force in the field of finance.

Many forms of assurance previously discussed in this book are performed within functional departments (Table 24.1). This chapter discusses three forms of companywide quality assurance: quality audits, quality surveys, and product audit.

24.3 QUALITY AUDIT—THE CONCEPT

A quality audit is an independent review conducted to compare some aspect of quality performance with a standard for that performance. The term "independent" is critical and is used in the sense that the reviewer (called the "auditor") is neither the person responsible for the performance under review nor the immediate supervisor of that person. An independent audit provides an unbiased picture of performance.

The ISO 8402-1986 definition spells out some additional aspects: Quality audit is a systematic, independent examination and evaluation to determine whether quality activities and results comply with planned arrangements and whether these arrangements are implemented effectively and are suitable for achieving objectives. (Product audit, discussed later in this chapter, is a review of *physical product*; quality audit is a review of an *activity*.)

Quality audits are used by companies to evaluate their own quality performance and the performance of their suppliers, licensees, agents, and others and by regulatory agencies to evaluate the performance of organizations which they are assigned to regulate.

The specific purpose of quality audits is to provide independent assurance that:

- Plans for attaining quality are such that, if followed, the intended quality will, in fact, be attained
- Products are fit for use and safe for the user
- Standards and regulations defined by government agencies, industry associations, and professional societies are being followed
- There is conformance to specifications
- Procedures are adequate and are being followed
- The data system provides accurate and adequate information on quality to all concerned
- Deficiencies are identified and corrective action is taken
- Opportunities for improvement are identified and the appropriate personnel alerted

We will discuss the subject matter of audits, setting up and performing audits, and reporting the results.

24.4   SUBJECT MATTER OF AUDITS

For simple products, the range of audits is also simple and is dominated by product audits (see below). For complex products, the audit is far more complex. In large companies, even the division of the subject matter is a perplexing problem. For such companies, the programs of audit use one or more of the following approaches for dividing up the subject matter:

- *Organizational units.* In large companies, there are several layers of organization, each with specific assigned missions: corporate office, operating divisions, plants, etc. In such companies, it is common to use multiple teams of quality auditors, each reviewing its specialized subject matter and reporting the results to its own "clientele."
- *Product lines.* Here the audits evaluate the quality aspects of specific product lines (e.g., printed circuit boards, hydraulic pumps) all the way from design through field performance.
- *Quality systems.* Here the audits are directed at the quality aspects of various segments of the overall systematic approach to quality such as design, manufacturing, supplier quality, etc. A system-oriented audit reviews any such system over a whole range of products.
- *Specific activities.* Audits may also be designed to single out specific procedures which have special significance to the quality mission: disposition of nonconforming products, documentation, instrument calibration, etc. (see Table 24.2).

TABLE 24.2
Systems audits

Scope or activity	Examples of specific tasks audited
Engineering documentation	Use of latest issue of specifications by operators; time required for design changes to reach shop
Job instructions	Existence and adequacy of written job instructions
Machines and tools	Use of specified machines and tools; adequacy of preventive maintenance
Calibration of measuring equipment	Existence of calibration procedures and degree to which calibration intervals are met
Production and inspection	Adequacy of certification program for critical skills; adequacy of training
Production facilities	General cleanliness and control of critical environmental conditions
Inspection instructions	Existence and adequacy of written instructions
Documentation of inspection results	Adequacy of detail; feedback and use by production personnel
Material status	Identification of inspection status and product configuration; segregation of defective product
Materials handling and storage	Procedure for handling critical materials; protection from damage during handling; control of in-process storage environments

Audits of quality systems as well as specific activities may take the form of (1) audit of the plans or (2) audit of the execution versus the plans. Further, the subject matter may include internal activities or external activities such as those conducted by suppliers (see Section 14.6 under "Cooperation During Contract Execution").

Identifying Opportunities

An experienced, alert auditor is often able to discover opportunities for improvement as a by-product of his or her search for discrepancies. These opportunities may even be known to the operations personnel so that the auditor is only making a rediscovery. However, these personnel may have been unable to act due to any of a variety of handicaps: preoccupation with day-to-day control, inability to communicate through the layers of the hierarchy, lack of diagnostic support, etc.

The auditor, through his or her relatively independent status, may be able to prevail over these handicaps. He or she is not preoccupied with day-to-day control. In addition, the auditor's reports go to multiple layers of the hierarchy and thereby have a greater likelihood of reaching the ear of someone who has the power to act on the opportunity. For example, the auditor may find that the quality cost reports are seriously delayed owing to backlogs of work in the accounting department. His or her recommendation to computerize the reports may reach the person who can act, whereas the same proposal made by the operations personnel may never reach that level.

24.5 STRUCTURING THE AUDIT PROGRAM

Audits of individual tasks or systems of tasks are usually structured, e.g., they are designed to carry out agreed purposes and are conducted under agreed rules of conduct. Reaching agreement on these rules and purposes requires collaboration among three essential participating groups:

- The heads of the activities which are to be the subject of audit
- The heads of the auditing department(s)
- The upper management, which presides over both

Unless such collective agreements are reached, there are risks that the audit program will fail. The usual failure modes are: (1) an abrasive relationship between auditors and line managers, or (2) a failure of line managers to heed the audit reports.

Table 24.3 depicts the typical flow of events through which audit programs are agreed on and audits are carried out. A published statement of purposes, policies, and methods becomes the charter which legitimizes the audits and provides continuing guidelines for all concerned.

TABLE 24.3
Steps in structuring an audit program

	Audit department	Line department	Upper management
Discussion of purposes to be achieved by audits and general approach for conducting audits	×	×	×
Draft of policies, procedures, and other rules to be followed	×	×	
Final approval			×
Scheduling of audits	×	×	
Conduct of audits	×		
Verification of factual findings		×	
Publication of report with facts and recommendations	×		
Discussion of reports	×	×	×
Decisions on action to be taken		×	
Subsequent follow-up	×		

Audits are often done by full-time auditors who are skilled in both technical and human relations aspects. Audit teams of upper managers, middle managers, and specialists can also be effective. See QCH4, pages 8.20–8.24 and 9.27–9.28, for a discussion.

24.6 PLANNING AND PERFORMING AUDITS ON ACTIVITIES

ANSI/ASQC (1986) identifies the main steps in performing activity audits as initiation, planning, implementation, reporting, and completion. The reader is urged to study the flowchart in Figure 24.1, which describes these steps in some detail.

Behind the steps in Figure 24.1 are a number of important policy issues:

LEGITIMACY. The basic right to conduct audits is derived from the "charter" which has been approved by upper management, following participation by all concerned. Beyond this basic right, there are other questions of legitimacy: What shall the subject matter for audit be? Should the auditor be accompanied during the tour? Whom may the auditor interview? etc. The bulk of auditing practice provides for legitimacy—the auditor acts within the provisions of the charter plus supplemental agreements reached after discussion with all concerned.

SCHEDULED VERSUS UNANNOUNCED. Most auditing is done on a scheduled basis. "No surprises, no secrets." This enables all concerned to organize workloads, assign personnel, etc., in an orderly manner. It also minimizes the irritations which are inevitable when audits are unannounced. (There are,

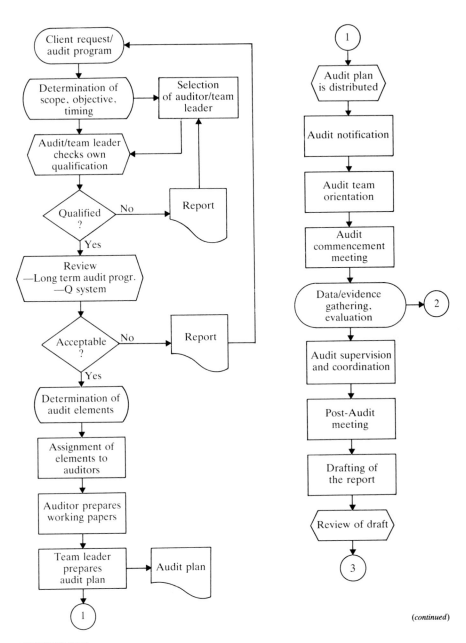

FIGURE 24.1
Flowchart for quality audit. (*Adapted from ANSI/ASQC, 1986, pp. 9–13.*)

(*continued*)

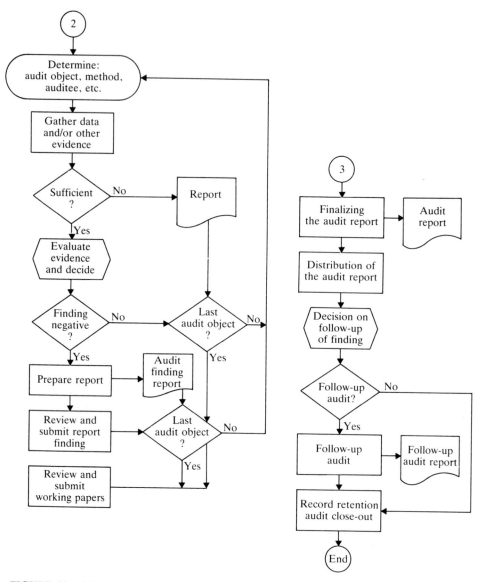

FIGURE 24.1 (*Continued*)

however, some situations, e.g., bank audits, where the need to avoid "cover-ups" may require surprise audits.)

USE OF REFERENCE STANDARDS AND CHECKLISTS. As far as possible, the auditor is expected to compare activities as they are with some objective standard of what they should be. Where such standards are available, there is less need for the auditor to make a subjective judgment and thereby less opportunity for wide differences of opinion. However, provision should be made for challenge of the standard itself. The reference standards normally available include:

- Written policies of the company as they apply to quality
- Stated objectives in the budgets, programs, contracts, etc.
- Customer and company quality specifications
- Pertinent government specifications and handbooks
- Company, industry, and other pertinent quality standards on products, processes, and computer software
- Published guides for conduct of quality audits
- Pertinent quality departmental instructions
- General literature on auditing

One type of checklist identifies areas of subject matter which are to be checked, leaving it to the auditor to supply the detailed checklist. Typical examples of such areas are maintenance of machines and tools or control of engineering change orders.

In some companies, the checklists go into great detail, requiring the auditor to check numerous items of operational performance (as well as recording the fact that such items were checked). For example, an auditor checking a test performed by an inspector would be required by the checklist to check the work of the inspector as to the correctness of the specification issue number used, the list of characteristics checked, the type of instruments employed, the sample size, data entries, etc. In a hospital, an audit checklist could include questions such as: "Are applicable intravenous solutions stored under refrigeration prior to delivery?" "Are all drugs, chemicals, and biologicals clearly, accurately, and appropriately labeled?" etc.

Section 16.8, "Process Quality Audits," presents additional examples, from both manufacturing and service industries of items checked during quality audits.

VERIFICATION OF FACTS. Auditors are universally expected to review with the line supervision the facts (outward symptoms) of any deficiencies discovered during the audit. The facts should be agreed on before the item enters a report that will go to higher management.

DISCOVERY OF CAUSES. In many companies, the auditor is expected to investigate major deficiencies in an effort to determine their causes. This investigation then becomes the basis of the auditor's recommendation. In other companies, the auditor is expected to leave such investigations to the line people; audit recommendations will then include proposals that such investigations be made.

RECOMMENDATIONS AND REMEDIES. Auditors are invariably expected to make recommendations with a view to reducing deficiencies and improving performance. In contrast, auditors are commonly told to avoid becoming involved in designing remedies and making them effective. However, auditors are expected to follow up recommendations to assure that something specific is done, i.e., that the recommendation is accepted or else considered and rejected.

Policy issues are often incorporated into a "Quality Audit Manual." Such a manual also includes details on the subject matter to be covered in audits, checklists of items to be checked and questions to be asked, classifying seriousness of deficiencies observed, use of software for entry, processing, storage and retrieval of audit data, and guidelines for audit reports.

24.7 HUMAN RELATIONS IN AUDITING

In theory, the audit is a sort of instrument plugged into operations to secure an independent source of information. Where it is a physical instrument, e.g., the propeller speed indicator on the bridge of a ship, there is no problem of clash of personalities. However, auditors are human beings and, in practice, their relationships with those whose work is being audited can become quite strained. Deficiencies turned up in the audit may be resented because of the implied criticism therein.

Recommendations in the audit may be resented as an invasion of responsibilities. In the reverse direction, auditors may regard slow responses to requests for information as a form of grudging collaboration. These and other human relations problems are sufficiently important to warrant extensive discussion plus indoctrination of both auditing personnel and operations personnel with respect to:

- *The reasons behind the audits.* These reasons may have been well discussed during the basic formulation of the audit program. However, that discussion was held among the managers. There is also a need to explain to both supervisors and nonsupervisors the "why" of the audits. (It is not enough to explain that upper management wants audits done.) Obviously, all employees are also customers, consumers, and concerned citizens, so it is easy to point out the benefits they derive from audits conducted in other companies. In addition, it can be made clear that the managers, customers, regulators, etc., of this company likewise require added assurance.
- *Avoiding an atmosphere of blame.* A sure way to cause a deterioration in human relations is to look for whom to blame rather than how to achieve improvement. Line managers as well as auditors can fall into this trap. An atmosphere of blame not only breeds resentment, it dries up the sources of information. Audit reports and recommendations should be problem-oriented rather than person-oriented.

- *Balance in reporting.* An audit which reports only deficiencies may be factual as far as it goes. Yet it will be resented because nothing is said about the far greater number of elements of performance which are done well. Some companies require the auditors to start their reports with "commendable observations." Others have evolved overall summaries or ratings which consider not only deficiencies but also the opportunities for deficiencies (see below).

- *Depersonalizing the report.* In many companies, the auditor derives much influence from the fact that his or her reports are reviewed by upper management. Auditing departments should be careful to avoid misusing this influence. The ideal is to depersonalize the reports and recommendations. The real basis of the recommendations should be the facts rather than the opinion of the auditor. Where there is room for a difference of opinion, the auditor has a right and a duty to give his or her opinion as an input to the decision-making process. However, any position of undue advocacy should be avoided, as this tends to reduce the auditor's credibility as an objective observer. (The ultimate responsibility for results rests on the line managers, not on the auditors.)

- *Postaudit meeting.* An important part of the implementation phase is the postaudit meeting that is held with the manager of the audited activity. At this meeting, the audit observations are presented so that the manager can plan for corrective action. In addition, the manager can point out to the auditor any mistakes with respect to the facts that have been collected.

A self-audit and an independent audit can be combined to a provide a "two-tier" audit. Goldstein (1983) describes how each of the two audits has an audit plan, execution, and report. The advantages include using the expertise of the person responsible for the function, assuring objectivity with an independent auditor, and minimizing some of the human relationship issues.

The aim of both the self-audit and the independent audit is to build an atmosphere of trust based on the prior reputation of the auditors, the approach used during the audit, and an emphasis on being helpful to the activity audited. Even such small matters as the title of the audit process should be carefully considered. Occasionally, people try to avoid the use of the term "audit" when, indeed, what will be done *is* an observation and evaluation. Also, audits may be hidden in a company education program. Such subterfuges detract from the trust that must be developed in order for audits to be effective and useful. Burr (1987) provides specific suggestions on overcoming resistance to audits.

For a discussion of some unique human relations aspects in a research and development activity, see Frank and Voigt (1988).

24.8 AUDIT REPORTING

Audit results should be documented in a report, and a draft should be reviewed (preferably at the postaudit meeting) with the management of the activity that was audited. The report may be jointly issued by the auditor and auditee.

The report should include the following items:

- Purpose and scope of the audit.
- Details of the audit plan, including audit personnel, dates, the activity that was audited (personnel contacted, material reviewed, number of observations made, etc.). Details should be placed in an appendix.
- Standards, checklist, or other reference documents that were used during the audit.
- Audit observations, including supporting evidence, conclusions, and recommendations.
- Recommendations for improvement opportunities.
- Recommendations for follow-up on the corrective action that is to be proposed and implemented by line management, along with subsequent audits if necessary.
- Distribution list for the audit report.

Bucella (1988) describes, for the Warner-Lambert pharmaceutical company, the audit approach used for "Ten Systems of Quality" (e.g., quality information). A histogram provides an overall picture of the effectiveness of each system. The histogram also shows the corrective action response time required for each system.

SUMMARIZING AUDIT DATA. In an audit, most elements of performance are found to be adequate, while some are found to be in a state of discrepancy. Reporting of these findings requires two different levels of communication:

1. Reports of each discrepancy to secure corrective action. These reports are made promptly to the responsible operating personnel, with copies to some of the managerial levels.
2. A report of the overall status of the subject matter under review. To meet these requirements, the report should:
   - Evaluate overall quality performance in ways which provide answers to the major questions raised by upper managers, for instance: Is the product safe? Are we complying with legal requirements? Is the product fit for use? Is the product marketable? Is the performance of the department under review adequate?
   - Provide evaluations of the status of the major subdivisions of the overall performance—the quality systems and subsystems, the divisions, the plants, the procedures, etc.
   - Provide some estimate of the frequency of inadequacies in relation to the number of opportunities for inadequacies (see below under "Units of Measure").

- Provide some estimate of the trend of this ratio (of inadequacies found to inadequacies possible) and of the effectiveness of programs to control the frequency of occurrence of inadequacies.

SERIOUSNESS CLASSIFICATION. Some audit programs make use of seriousness classification of inadequacies. This is quite common in the case of product audits, where defects found are classified in terms such as critical, major, and minor, each with some "weight" in the form of demerits. These systems of seriousness classification are highly standardized (see Section 18.5, "Seriousness Classification").

Some audit programs also apply seriousness classification to discrepancies found in planning, in procedures, in decision making, in data recording, and so on. The approach parallels that used for product audits. Definitions are established for such terms as "serious," "major," and "minor"; demerit values are assigned; and total demerits are computed (see, e.g., Thresh, 1984, pp. 3–18).

UNITS OF MEASURE. For audits of plans, procedures, documentation, and so forth, it is desirable to compare the inadequacies found against some estimate of the opportunities for inadequacies. Some companies provide for this by an actual count of the opportunities, such as the number of criteria or check points called out by the plans and procedures. Another form is to count the inadequacies per audit with a correction factor based on the length of time consumed by the audit. The obvious reason is that more time spent in auditing means more ground covered and more inadequacies found.

DISTRIBUTION OF AUDIT REPORT. Traditionally, copies of the audit report are sent to upper management for notification, review, and possible follow-up. Clearly, managers of activities which are audited are not happy with audit reports listing various deficiencies that are sent to their superiors. With a view to promoting harmony and a constructive viewpoint on audits, some organizations have adopted a different policy. The audit report is sent only to the manager whose activity is audited; a follow-up audit is scheduled; if the deficiencies are found to be corrected in the follow-up audit, the audit file is closed, otherwise a copy of both audit reports is sent to upper management.

24.9 ESSENTIAL INGREDIENTS OF A QUALITY AUDIT PROGRAM

Five ingredients are essential to a successful quality audit program:

1. An uncompromising emphasis on conclusions based on facts. Any conclusions lacking a factual base must be so labeled.
2. An attitude on the part of auditors that the audits not only serve to provide assurance to management but also must provide a useful *service* to line

managers in managing their departments. Thus, audit reports must provide sufficient detail on deficiencies to facilitate analysis and action by line managers.

3. An attitude on the part of auditors to identify opportunities for improvement. Such opportunities include highlighting good ideas used in practice that are not part of formal procedures. Sometimes, an audit can help to overcome deficiencies by communicating through the hierarchy the reasons for deficiencies that have a source in another department. For example, the auditor may find that the quality cost reports are seriously delayed owing to backlogs of work in the accounting department. An audit recommendation to computerize the reports may reach the person who can act, whereas the same proposal made by the operations personnel may never reach that level.

4. Addressing of the human relations issues discussed above.

5. Competence of auditors. The basic education and experience of the auditors should be sufficient to enable them to learn in short order the technological aspects of the operations they are to audit. Lacking this background, they will be unable to earn the respect of the operations personnel. In addition, they should receive special training in the human relations aspects of auditing. The American Society for Quality Control has embarked on a program for the certification of quality auditors.

These five essentials for a successful quality audit activity were responsible for a dramatic tribute to an audit activity within one company. Line managers voluntarily give up part of their own budget each year to provide funds for a quality audit group.

24.10 QUALITY SURVEYS

Audits, as described above, are concerned almost exclusively with conformance of various sorts: conformance of plans to standards of good planning and conformance of execution to plan. Such audits provide answers to some vital questions and must be regarded as an essential element of quality assurance. These audits are, however, not sufficient to provide full assurance to upper management that all is well with respect to quality since they commonly are not concerned with such matters as:

- Relative standing in the marketplace with regard to quality
- Analysis of users' situations with respect to cost, convenience, etc., over the life of the product
- Opportunities for reducing costs of poor quality
- Challenge to Product Development, Design Engineering, and other "monopolistic" departments on quality adequacy, perfectionism, cost, etc.
- Challenge to top management itself with respect to policies, goals, premises, and axiomatic beliefs
- Employee perceptions on quality

Providing such missing elements of quality assurance requires a broader view than the structured audit. The broader review is often called a "quality survey," a "quality assessment," or a "companywide audit." In this section, the word "audit" implies the existence of established criteria against which plans and their execution can be checked. In contrast, the word "survey" implies the inclusion of matters not covered by agreed criteria. (In a sense, the audit discovers discrepancies and alarm signals; the survey goes further and also discovers opportunities and unexpected threats.)

Such surveys can be accomplished in several ways:

1. Using an overall framework which includes an assessment of both quality results and the quality system. Chapter 2, "Companywide Assessment of Quality," presented such a framework consisting of four components: (a) cost of poor quality, (b) standing in the marketplace, (c) company culture on quality, and (d) assessment of current quality activities.

2. Assessing the quality system using published criteria which emphasizes quality *results*. An example of such criteria is the Malcolm Baldrige National Quality Award (see Section 2.11, "Assessment of Current Quality Activities").

3. Assessing the quality system using published criteria which emphasizes defined elements of the quality system. An example of such criteria is the ISO 9000 specification. Table 24.4 summarizes these elements as defined in Q91–Q93, the ASQC documents corresponding to the ISO 9001–9003 specification series for manufacturing industries. The scope is as follows:
   • *Q91 (ISO 9001):* design and development, production, installation, and service
   • *Q92 (ISO 9002):* production and installation
   • *Q93 (ISO 9003):* final inspection and testing

   A complete set of documents can be obtained from the American Society for Quality Control.

   Whereas ISO 9001, 9002, 9003 are used for contractual situations, ISO 9004, "Quality Management and Quality System Elements—Guidelines," describes elements for developing and implementing quality management systems. The elements include many of those listed in Table 24.4. ISO 9004-2, "Guidelines for Services," provides guidelines for service industries (see Table 24.5).

4. Assessing the quality system using criteria developed within a company for use in evaluating its own operations. Often, such criteria draw upon those contained in the National Quality Award or the ISO 9000 specification.

5. Assessing the quality system using criteria developed within a company for use in evaluating its suppliers (see Section 14.5, "Assessment of Supplier Capability"). This may involve a third-party audit or survey. Two parties are involved in the purchase of products; the purchaser and the supplier. In

TABLE 24.4
Summary of elements in Q91–Q93 (ISO 9001–9003)

Paragraph (or subsection) number in Q94	Title	Corresponding paragraph (or subsection) number in		
		Q91	Q92	Q93
4	Management Responsibility	4.1 ●	4.1 ◐	4.1 ○
5	Quality System Principles	4.2 ●	4.2 ●	4.2 ◐
5.4	Auditing the Quality System (Internal)	4.17 ●	4.16 ◐	—
6	Economics—Quality-Related Cost Considerations	—	—	—
7	Quality in Marketing (Contract Review)	4.3 ●	4.3 ●	—
8	Quality in Specification and Design (Design Control)	4.4 ●	—	—
9	Quality in Procurement (Purchasing)	4.6 ●	4.5 ●	—
10	Quality in Production (Process Control)	4.9 ●	4.8 ●	—
11	Control of Production	4.9 ●	4.8 ●	—
11.2	Material Control and Traceability (Product Identification and Traceability)	4.8 ●	4.7 ●	4.4 ◐
11.7	Control of Verification Status (Inspection and Test Status)	4.12 ●	4.11 ●	4.7 ◐
12	Product Verification (Inspection and Testing)	4.10 ●	4.9 ●	4.5 ◐
13	Control of Measuring and Test Equipment (Inspection, Measuring, and Test Equipment)	4.11 ●	4.10 ●	4.6 ◐
14	Nonconformity (Control of Nonconforming Product)	4.13 ●	4.12 ●	4.8 ◐
15	Corrective Action	4.14 ●	4.13 ●	—
16	Handling and Post-Production Functions (Handling, Storage, Packaging, and Delivery)	4.15 ●	4.14 ●	4.9 ◐
16.2	After-Sales Servicing	4.19 ●	—	—
17	Quality Documentation and Records (Document Control)	4.5 ●	4.4 ●	4.3 ◐
17.3	Quality Records	4.16 ●	4.15 ●	4.10 ◐
18	Personnel (Training)	4.18 ●	4.17 ◐	4.11 ○
19	Product Safety and Liability	—	—	—
20	Use of Statistical Methods (Statistical Techniques)	4.20 ●	4.18 ●	4.12 ◐
—	Purchaser Supplied Product	4.7 ●	4.6 ●	—

Notes: ●, full requirement.
◐, less stringent than ANSI/ASQC Q91.
○, less stringent than ANSI/ASQC Q92.
—, element not present.

Source: American Society for Quality Control (1987).

the past, the purchaser evaluated the quality from the supplier. Purchasers are now increasingly using the concept of a "third party" to evaluate supplier quality. The third party (a person or an organization) performs the evaluation service for the purchaser but is independent of the purchaser and the supplier. This relieves the purchaser of maintaining a staff with the necessary skills. A third party can inspect the product, evaluate the quality system, or both.

6. Assessing the quality system for a specific assessment purpose.

TABLE 24.5
Quality system elements listed in *ISO 9004-2*: 1991(*E*)

Characteristics of services
Quality system principles
  Key aspects of a quality system
  Management responsibility
  Personnel and material resources
  Quality system structure
  Interface with customers
Quality system operational elements
  Marketing process
  Design process
  Service process
  Service delivery process
  Service performance analysis and improvement

Source: Reproduced with the permission of the International Organization for Standardization (ISO). The complete standard can be obtained from the Central Secretariat, Case Postal 56, 1211 Geneva 20, Switzerland, or from its member body in the USA, ANSI.

In a different type of survey, a consultant was asked to define specific task responsibilities in the quality program for all major departments of a health care company. The consultant used five questions to interview the department managers:

1. What tasks in your department affect quality?
2. Should any additional quality-related tasks be performed in your department?
3. Should any additional quality-related tasks be performed anywhere else in the company?
4. What quality-related tasks have unclear responsibility?
5. What quality-related tasks currently done in your department require more definitive written procedures?

The consultant summarized the findings as follows: (1) the quality program consisted of 178 tasks performed in 26 functional areas, (2) responsibility for 19 tasks was not clearly defined, and (3) for 27 quality-related tasks, the managers expressed concern about the clarity of the task.

The report included detailed comments on the overall scope of the quality program, key tasks requiring improvement, organization for quality, and the role of upper management.

Sometimes these surveys are conducted by upper managers. See QCH4, pages 8.20–8.24, for elaboration.

Reference standards which provide criteria for quality systems are periodically revised. The "Standards Column" in *Quality Engineering* magazine provides the practitioner with updates on current standards and descriptions of new standards.

24.11 PRODUCT AUDIT

Product audit is an independent evaluation of product quality to determine its fitness for use and conformance to specification. Product auditing takes place after inspections have been completed. The purposes of product auditing include:

1. Estimating the quality level as delivered to customers
2. Evaluating the effectiveness of the inspection decisions in determining conformance to specifications
3. Providing information useful in improving the outgoing product quality level and improving the effectiveness of inspection
4. Providing additional assurance beyond routine inspection activities

There is a good deal of logic behind creating such product audits. In many cases, the inspection and testing department is subordinate to a manager who is also responsible for meeting other standards (schedules, costs, etc.). In addition, there is a value in reviewing the performance of the entire quality control function, which includes inspection and test planning as well as the conduct of the tests themselves. Finally, the more critical the product, the greater is the need for some redundancy as a form of assurance.

STAGE OF EVALUATION. Ideally, the product audit should compare actual service performance with users' service needs. This ideal is so difficult and costly to administer that most product auditing consists of an approximation (see Table 24.6).

For many simple, stable products, the approximation of test results versus specifications is a useful, economic way of conducting the product audit. Even for products not so simple, the majority of quality characteristics identifiable by the user are also completely identifiable while the product is still at the factory. Thus, product characteristics which are essential to use are properly evaluated at some appropriate stage, whether in the factory or in some more advanced stage of progression.

As products become increasingly complex, the product auditing is increasingly conducted at several of the stages shown in Table 24.6. The bulk of the characteristics may be evaluated at the most economical stage, that is, shortly after factory inspection. However, the remaining (and usually more sophisticated) characteristics may be evaluated at other stages.

SCOPE OF THE PRODUCT AUDIT. The scope of some product audits completely misses the mark in measuring customer reaction.

TABLE 24.6
Potential stages of product auditing

Stage at which product auditing is conducted	Pros and cons of using this stage
After acceptance by inspectors	Most economical, but does not reflect effect of packing, shipping, storage, or usage
After packing but before shipment to field	Requires unpacking and repacking, but evaluates effect of original packing
Upon receipt by dealers	Difficult to administer at such multiple locations, but reflects effect of shipping, storage
Upon receipt by users	Even more difficult to administer, but evaluates the added effects of dealer handling and storage plus effects of shipment to user and unpacking
Performance in service	The ideal, but also the most difficult to administer, owing to the number and variety of usages; can be simplified through sampling

As one example, the plant manager of an electronics manufacturing firm received a rating of 98 percent on a product audit from the plant. For this rating, the plant received an award for quality. When the mean time between failures of that same product was measured in the field, the value was only 200 hours. This was a known reason for customer complaints, but such matters had not been evaluated by the product audit.

In another case, a vehicle manufacturer had a system of taking a weekly product audit sample from production. A comparison of separate marketing research results with the internal product audit was devastating. Only 18 percent of the characteristics that customers claimed were important to them were being checked in the product audit.

For simple products, a representative sample of finished goods may be bought on the open market. These samples are then checked for fitness for use and conformance to specification. In some companies, such audits are conducted annually as part of the broad annual planning for the product line. Such audits may include a review of competitive product as well.

For complex consumer products, e.g., household appliances, it is feasible to secure product audit data at multiple stages of the product progression shown in Table 24.6. The most extensive product audit takes place immediately following factory inspection and testing. Additional audit data are then secured from selected distributors and dealers under a special joint "open and test" audit. Similar arrangements are made to secure data from selected servicing dealers. In addition, use is made of the data from consumer "arrival cards." When properly arranged with due regard to time lags, all of these data sources can be charted in a way which shows trends as well as levels.

Audit plans must spell out, or give guidance on, the selection of detailed product dimensions or properties that are to be checked. Provision should be made for two types of audit—random and focused. The former is based on a random selection of product characteristics in order to yield an unbiased picture of the quality status. A focused audit, on the other hand, concentrates on a specific area of the product that experience suggests needs to be studied. In many companies, audit manuals spell out the design of the audit for the auditor, almost to the last level of detail. For example, the manual may specify particular categories of dimensions to be audited (i.e., length) but may rely on the auditor to select which length dimension to audit.

24.12 SAMPLING FOR PRODUCT AUDIT

For products manufactured by mass production, sample sizes for product audit can often be determined using conventional statistical methods. These methods determine the sample size required for stated degrees of risk (see Section 10.4, "Statistical Estimation: Confidence Limits"). Thresh (1984, Section 7) applies these methods to quality audit. Sample sizes for product audit determined by these methods when applied to mass production still represent a small fraction of the product that needs to be sampled. In contrast, for products manufactured as large units or in small quantities, the conventional concepts of statistical sampling are prohibitively costly. In such cases, sample sizes are often arbitrary, and they seem small from the viewpoint of probability considerations. For example, a vehicle manufacturer uses a product audit sample consisting of two percent of production per shift with a minimum of five vehicles—whichever number is larger. Even though the number of vehicles sampled may be small, the total number of characteristics that is sampled may be quite large. For these vehicles, 380 items are checked on each vehicle and the product audit test includes a 17-mile (27.2 km) road test. In some cases of highly homogeneous production, a sample of one unit taken from batch production can be adequate for product audit. Thresh (1984) recommends a minimum of three units.

Hsiang and Gordon (1982) describe a method of determining the sample size that is based on the amount of production, the likelihood that current production is substandard, the cost of correcting problems in the field, the cost of audit sampling, the detection ability of the audit sampling, present quality standards, and overall budget constraints. Audit data for each period are converted into a quality rating and displayed in the form of a box-and-whisker plot (see Section 9.5, "Box-and-Whisker Plots").

24.13 REPORTING THE RESULTS OF PRODUCT AUDIT

The results of product audit appear in the form of the presence or absence of defects, failures, etc. A continuing score or "rating" of quality is then prepared based on the audit results.

Product audit programs often make use of seriousness classification of defects. Defects are classified in terms such as critical, major, minor A, minor B, each with some "weight" in the form of demerits. In product audits, the usual unit of measure is *demerits per unit of product.*

Example 24.1. A product audit system makes use of four classes of seriousness of defects. During one month, the product auditors inspected 1200 finished units of product, with the following results:

Type of defects	Number found	Demerits per defect	Total demerits
Critical	1	100	100
Major	5	25	125
Minor A	21	5	105
Minor B	64	1	64
Total	91		394

Although the 91 defects found represented many defect types and four classes of seriousness, the total of 394 demerits, when divided by the 1200 units inspected, gives a single number, i.e., 0.33 demerit per unit.

The actual number of demerits per unit for the current month is often compared against past history to observe trends. (Sometimes it is compared with competitors' products to judge a company's own quality versus market quality.) A major value of a measure such as demerits per unit is that it compares discrepancies found with the opportunity for discrepancies. Such an index appeals to operating personnel as being eminently fair.

The scoreboard in terms of demerits per unit is by no means universally accepted. Managers in some industries want ready access to the figures on critical and major defects, feeling that these are the real problems no matter what the figure of demerits per unit is.

It is often useful to summarize the product audit results in other languages. A manufacturer of consumer products classifies defects at a product audit as visual (V), electrical (E), and performance (P) and then predicts service costs on products in the field. This is done by first establishing classes for each type of defect in terms of the probability of receiving a field complaint (e.g., a class 2 visual defect has a 60 percent probability). Service call costs are then combined with the audit data. For example, Table 24.7 shows the results of an audit of 50 units. The expected cost is the product of the probability, the number of defects, and the cost per service call. The expected service cost per unit is then estimated as $269/50 = $5.38. Alternatively, as indicated in Table 24.7, the expected number of service calls is the product of the probability and the number of defects. The expected number of service calls per unit is then estimated as 10.8/50 = 0.22, or about 22 out of every 100 products delivered to the field can be expected to have a service call.

TABLE 24.7
Audit data

Class of defect	Probability	Number of defects revealed by audit	Cost per service call, $	Expected costs, $	Expected number of service calls
V1	1.00	1	15.00	15.00	1.00
V2	0.60	3	15.00	27.00	1.80
E1	1.00	3	30.00	90.00	3.00
E2	0.60	4	30.00	72.00	2.40
P1	1.00	1	25.00	25.00	1.00
P2	0.60	2	25.00	30.00	1.20
P3	0.20	2	25.00	10.00	0.40
Totals				269.00	10.80

In addition to summarizing the defects found (in both number and relative seriousness), the audit results can be tallied by functional responsibility (i.e., design, purchasing, production).

Audit results can also be summarized to show the effectiveness of the previous inspection activities. Typically, a simple ratio is used, such as the percentage of total defects which is detected by inspection. For example, if the previous inspection revealed a total of 45 defects in a sample of N pieces and if the product audit inspection revealed five additional defects, the inspection effectiveness would be (45/50)(100), or 90 percent.

Further elaboration on product audit may be found in QCH4, pages 9.22–9.27, 17.26–17.29, and 30.45–30.47. In addition, the January 1987 issue of *Quality Progress* is devoted to quality audit and includes 12 papers. Also a series of three papers describes how AT&T Microelectronics changed from a traditional audit approach of reinspection of product (product audit) to an approach which uses system audits and process audits combined with a reduced amount of product audit. During one period, inspection costs were reduced by 12 percent and the savings were then used to provide additional prevention activity, which resulted in a $2 saving in failure costs for each $1 added in prevention cost. The papers are Stravinskas (1989), Lane (1989), and Williams (1989).

SUMMARY

- Quality assurance is the activity of providing the evidence needed to establish confidence, among all concerned, that the quality-related activities are being performed effectively.
- Quality audit is an independent review conducted to compare some aspect of quality performance with a standard for that performance. We conduct quality audits on activities that have an impact on product quality.

- Five ingredients are essential for successful audits: emphasis on facts, attitude of service on the part of auditors, identification of opportunities for improvement, addressing human relations issues, and the competence of auditors.
- Quality surveys provide a broader review of quality activities than audits of specific activities.
- Product audit is an independent evaluation of product quality to determine its fitness for use and conformance to specifications.

PROBLEMS

24.1. Visit a supermarket and observe the extent to which shoppers make use of their senses in securing quality assurance of the raw and packaged food products they buy. Report your findings.

24.2. Visit a retail establishment which sells technological consumer products, e.g., audio and video equipment, and observe the extent to which customers make use of their senses in securing quality assurance of the products they buy. Report your findings.

24.3. Visit an apartment building and discuss with the superintendent the various means obtaining early warning of various potential dangers, e.g., burglary, fire. Report your findings.

24.4. List the early-warning devices in use in a dwelling house. Report your findings.

24.5. You are a quality manager. On one of your company's product lines, a report shows that power consumption has risen from the usual level of 35.5 W to a level of 35.9 W. This difference is, without a doubt, statistically significant. However, the line manager has taken no action to investigate the reason for the change on the grounds that (1) the product still conforms to the specification limit of maximum 36.4 W, and (2) he must give priority to several other products in which there are failures to comply with specification. What action do you take?

24.6. Visit a nearby facility which is a part of a chain of such facilities, e.g., food market, restaurant, motel, gasoline station, etc. You will most likely find that it is subject to periodic quality audits from some headquarters. Obtain a copy of the auditor's checklist, study it, and report on its contents with respect to the various aspects of quality audits discussed in this chapter.

24.7. For any manufacturing company to which you have access, secure a copy of the quality audit. Study it and report on its contents with respect to the various aspects of quality audits discussed in this chapter.

REFERENCES

American Society for Quality Control (1987). ANSI/ASQC Q90 "Quality Management and Quality Assurance Standards—Guidelines for Selection and Use," Milwaukee, p. 6.

ANSI/ASQC (1986). "Generic Guidelines for Auditing of Quality Systems." American Society for Quality Control, Milwaukee.

Bucella, Janit E. (1988). "Auditing—A New View." *ASQC Quality Congress Transactions,* Milwaukee, pp. 98–102.

Burr, John T. (1987). "Overcoming Resistance to Audits," *Quality Progress,* January, pp. 15–18.

Frank, Norman C., and James V. Voigt (1988). "Technical Auditors—A Positive Response for Auditing," *ASQC Quality Congress Transactions,* Milwaukee, pp. 94–97.

Goldstein, Raymond (1983). "The Two-Tier Audit System," *ASQC Quality Congress Transactions,* Milwaukee, pp. 14–16.

Hsiang, Thomas C., and John J. Gordon (1982). "New Statistical Methodologies in a QA Audit System," *ASQC Quality Congress Transactions,* Milwaukee, pp. 335–342.

Lane, Patricia A. (1989). "Continuous Improvement—AT&T QA Audits," *ASQC Quality Congress Transactions,* Milwaukee, pp. 772–775.

Stravinskas, J. M. (1989). "Manufacturing System and Process Audits," *ASQC Quality Congress Transactions,* Milwaukee, pp. 91–94.

Thresh, James L. (1984). *How to Conduct, Manage, and Benefit from Effective Quality Audits,* MGI Management Institute, Harrison, New York.

Williams, Catherine A. (1989). "Improving Your Quality Auditing Systems," *ASQC Quality Congress Transactions,* Milwaukee, pp. 797–799.

SUPPLEMENTARY READING

Quality assurance—general: QCH4, Section 9.

Quality audit: QCH4, pp. 9.4–9.14.
   Mills, Charles A. (1989). *The Quality Audit,* McGraw-Hill Book Company, New York.

Quality surveys: Arthur, William E., Domenick A. DeRosa, Robert J. Majerczyk, and Mary M. Radivoy (1989). "The Survey of Multi-Organizational Processes from Product Initiation to Product Delivery with Emphasis on Customer Satisfaction," *Impro Conference Proceedings,* Juran Institute, Inc., Wilton, Connecticut, pp. 4B–19 to 4B–25.

APPENDIX

I

EXAMPLES
OF EXAMINATION
QUESTIONS
AND ANSWERS

EXAMPLES OF EXAMINATION QUESTIONS USED IN FORMER ASQC QUALITY ENGINEER AND RELIABILITY ENGINEER CERTIFICATION EXAMINATIONS AS PUBLISHED IN *QUALITY PROGRESS* MAGAZINE (REFERENCES: *QUALITY PROGRESS*, FEBRUARY 1976, PP. 23–31; AUGUST 1978, PP. 17–26; SEPTEMBER 1980, PP. 24–32; JULY 1984, PP. 35–47)

Chapter 1

1. The most important measure of outgoing quality needed by managers is product performance as viewed by: (a) the customer; (b) the final inspector; (c) production; (d) marketing.

Chapter 2

1. When looking for existing sources of internal failure cost data, which of the following is usually the best source available? (a) operating budgets; (b) sales-personnel field reports; (c) labor and material cost documents; (d) returned material reports; (e) purchase orders.

2. Of the following, which are typically appraisal costs? (a) vendor surveys and vendor faults; (b) quality planning and quality reports; (c) drawing control centers and material dispositions; (d) quality audits and final inspection; (e) none of the above.

3. When analyzing quality cost data gathered during the *initial* stages of a new management emphasis on quality control and corrective action as part of a product improvement program, one normally expects to see: (a) increased prevention costs and decreased appraisal costs; (b) increased appraisal costs with little change in prevention costs; (c) decreased internal failure costs; (d) decreased total quality costs; (e) all of these.

4. Quality costs are best classified as: (a) cost of inspection and test, cost of quality engineering, cost of quality administration, and cost of quality equipment; (b) direct, indirect, and overhead; (c) cost of prevention, cost of appraisal, and cost of failure; (d) unnecessary; (e) none of the above.

5. Operating quality costs can be related to different volume bases. An example of volume base that could be used would be: (a) direct labor cost; (b) standard manufacturing cost; (c) processing cost; (d) sales; (e) all of the above.

6. When operating a quality cost system, excessive costs can be identified when: (a) appraisal costs exceed failure costs; (b) total quality costs exceed 10 percent of sales; (c) appraisal and failure costs are equal; (d) total quality costs exceed four percent of manufacturing costs; (e) there is no fixed rule—management experience must be used.

7. Analyze the following cost data:

$ 10,000	equipment design
150,000	scrap
180,000	reinspection and retest
45,000	loss or disposition of surplus stock
4,000	vendor quality surveys
40,000	repair

Considering only the quality costs shown above, we might conclude that: (a) prevention costs should be decreased; (b) internal failure costs can be decreased; (c) prevention costs are too low a proportion of the quality costs shown; (d) appraisal costs should be increased; (e) nothing can be concluded.

8. The percentages of total quality cost are distributed as follows:

Prevention	12%
Appraisal	28%
Internal failure	40%
External failure	20%

We conclude: (a) we should invest more money in prevention; (b) expenditures for failures are excessive; (c) the amount spent for appraisal seems about right; (d) nothing.

Chapter 3

1. McGregor's Theory X manager is typified as one who operates from the following basic assumption about subordinates (select the one best answer): (a) performance can be improved through tolerance and trust; (b) people have a basic need to produce; (c) status is more important than money; (d) self-actualization is the highest order of human need; (e) people are lazy and are motivated by reward and punishment.

2. Quality motivation in industry should be directed at: (a) manufacturing management; (b) procurement and engineering; (c) the quality assurance staff; (d) the work force; (e) all of the above.

3. To instill the quality control employee with the desire to perform to his or her utmost and optimum ability, which of the following recognition for sustaining motivation has been found most effective? (a) recognition by issuance of monetary award; (b) verbal recognition publicly; (c) private verbal recognition; (d) public recognition plus nonmonetary award; (e) no recognition; salary is sufficient motivation.

4. Which of the following methods used to improve employee efficiency and promote an atmosphere conducive to quality and profit is the most effective in the long run? (a) offering incentives such as bonus, praise, profit sharing, etc.; (b) strict discipline to reduce mistakes, idleness, and sloppiness; (c) combination of incentive and discipline to provide both reward for excellence and punishment for inferior performance; (d) building constructive attitudes through development of realistic quality goals relating to both company and employee success; (e) all of the above provided that emphasis is placed on attitude motivation, with incentive and discipline used with utmost caution.

5. The famous Hawthorne study provided which of the following clinical evidence regarding the factors that can increase work group productivity? (a) attention and recognition is more important than working conditions; (b) productivity did not change significantly under any of the test conditions; (c) informal group pressures set a production "goal"; (d) people with higher capabilities are bored with routine jobs; (e) work-station layout is critical to higher productivity.

Chapter 4

None.

Chapter 5

1. A quality control program is considered to be: (a) a collection of quality control procedures and guidelines; (b) a step-by-step list of all quality control check points; (c) a summary of company quality control policies; (d) a system of activities to provide quality of products and service.

Chapter 6

None.

Chapter 7

1. A quality program has the best foundation for success when it is initiated by: (a) a certified quality engineer; (b) contractual requirements; (c) the chief executive of company; (d) production management; (e) an experienced quality manager.
2. A fully developed position description for a quality engineer must contain clarification of: (a) responsibility; (b) accountability; (c) authority; (d) answers (a) and (c); (e) answers (a), (b), and (c).
3. When giving instructions to those who will perform a task, the communication process is completed: (a) when the worker goes to his work station to do the task; (b) when the person giving the instruction has finished talking; (c) when the worker acknowledges these instructions by describing how he or she will perform the task; (d) when the worker says that he or she understands the instructions.

Chapter 8

1. Which one of these human management approaches has led to the practice of job enrichment? (a) Skinner; (b) Maslow; (c) Herzberg's "Hygiene Theory"; (d) McGregor.
2. Extensive research into the results of quality motivation has shown that: (a) the supervisor's attitude toward his people is of little long-term consequence; (b) motivation is too nebulous to be correlated with results; (c) motivation is increased when employees set their own goals; (d) motivation is increased when management sets challenging goals slightly beyond the attainment of the better employees.
3. Select the nonhygienic motivator, as defined by Maslow: (a) salary increases; (b) longer vacations; (c) improved medical plan; (d) sales bonuses; (e) performance recognition.

Chapter 9

1. The sum of the squared deviations of a group of measurements from their mean divided by the number of measurements equals: (a) σ; (b) σ^2; (c) zero; (d) $\bar{X}$; (e) the mean deviation.
2. The mean of either a discrete or a continuous distribution can always be visualized as: (a) the point where 50 percent of the values are to the left side and 50 percent are to the right side; (b) its center of gravity; (c) the point where the most values in the distribution occur; (d) all of the above.
3. The lengths of a certain bushing are normally distributed with mean $\bar{X}'$. How many standard deviation units, symmetrical about $\bar{X}'$, will include 80 percent of the lengths? (a) ±1.04; (b) ±0.52; (c) ±1.28; (d) ±0.84.
4. An inspection plan is set up to randomly sample three feet of a 100 foot cable and accept the cable if no flaws are found in the three-foot length. What is the probability that a cable with an average of one flaw per foot will be rejected by the plan? (a) 0.05; (b) 0.95; (c) 0.72; (d) 0.03; (e) 0.10.
5. When using the Poisson as an approximation to the binomial, the following conditions apply for the best approximation: (a) larger sample size and larger fraction defective; (b) larger sample size and smaller fraction defective; (c) smaller sample size and larger fraction defective; (d) smaller sample size and smaller fraction defective.

6. A process is producing material which is 40 percent defective. Four pieces are selected at random for inspection. What is the probability of exactly one good piece being found in the sample? (a) 0.870; (b) 0.575; (c) 0.346; (d) 0.130; (e) 0.154.

7. The probability of observing at least one defective in a random sample of size ten drawn from a population that has been producing, on the average, ten percent defective units is: (a) $(0.10)^{10}$; (b) $(0.90)^{10}$; (c) $1 - (0.10)^{10}$; (d) $1 - (0.90)^{10}$; (e) $(0.10)(0.90)^9$.

8. A process is turning out end items that have defects of type A or type B or both in them. If the probability of a type A defect is 0.10 and of a type B defect is 0.20, the probability that an end item will have no defects is: (a) 0.02; (b) 0.28; (c) 0.30; (d) 0.72; (e) 0.68.

9. A trip is contemplated with an automobile equipped with four well-used tires on the wheels plus an equally well-used spare. Because of the poor condition of the five tires, the probability that any tire will experience a blowout during the trip is estimated to be 0.50. What is the expected probability of a successful trip (in the sense that no more than one blowout will occur, so that it would not be necessary to purchase a tire enroute)? (a) 0.0625; (b) 0.5000; (c) 0.0313; (d) 0.3125.

Chapter 10

1. In determining a process average fraction defective using inductive or inferential statistics, we use _____ computed from _____ to make inferences about _____.
(a) statistics, samples, populations; (b) populations, samples, populations; (c) samples, statistics, populations; (d) samples, populations, samples; (e) statistics, populations, statistics.

2. If in a t test, α is 0.01: (a) one percent of the time we will say that there is a real difference when there really is not a difference; (b) one percent of the time we will make a correct inference; (c) one percent of the time we will say that there is no real difference, but in reality there is a difference; (d) 99 percent of the time we will make an incorrect inference; (e) 99 percent of the time the null hypothesis will be correct.

3. Suppose that, given $\bar{X} = 50$ and $Z = \pm 1.96$, we established 95 percent confidence limits for μ of 30 and 70. This means that: (a) the probability that $\mu = 50$ is 0.05; (b) the probability that $\mu = 50$ is 0.95; (c) the probability that the interval contains μ is 0.05; (d) the probability that the interval contains μ is 0.95; (e) none of the above.

4. If it was known that a population of 30,000 parts had a standard deviation of $0.05s$, what size of sample would be required to maintain an error no greater than $0.01s$ with a confidence level of 95 percent? (a) 235; (b) 487; (c) 123; (d) 96; (e) 78.

5. Determine whether the following two types of rockets have significantly different variances at the five percent level.

Rocket 1	Rocket 2
61 readings	31 readings
1346.89 mi^2	2237.29 mi^2

(a) a significant difference because $F_{calc} < F_{table}$; (b) no significant difference because $F_{calc} < F_{table}$; (c) a significant difference because $F_{calc} > F_{table}$; (d) no significant difference because $F_{calc} < F_{table}$.

6. "A Latin square design is noted for its straightforward analysis of interaction effects." This statement is: (a) true in every case; (b) true sometimes, depending on the size of the square; (c) true only for Greco-Latin squares; (d) false in every case; (e) false except for Greco-Latin squares.

7. A factorial experiment has been performed to determine the effect of factor A and factor B on the strength of a part. An F test shows a significant interaction effect. This means that: (a) either factor A or factor B has a significant effect on strength; (b) both factor A and factor B affect strength; (c) the effect of changing factor B can be estimated only if the level of factor A is known; (d) neither factor A nor factor B affects strength; (e) strength will increase if factor A is increased while factor B is held at a low level.

8. If X and Y are distributed normally and independently, the variance of $X - Y$ is then equal to: (a) $\sigma_x^2 + \sigma_y^2$; (b) $\sigma_x - \sigma_y^2$; (c) $\sqrt{\sigma_x^2 + \sigma_y^2}$; (d) $\sqrt{\sigma_x^2 - \sigma_y^2}$.

Chapter 11

None.

Chapter 12

1. From the definition of reliability, it follows that in any reliability program there must be: (a) a quantification of reliability in terms of probability; (b) a clear statement defining successful performance; (c) a definition of the environment in which the equipment must operate; (d) a statement of the required operating times between failures; (e) all of the above.

2. When reliability people say they are breaking the monopoly of the designer, they mean: (a) they are relieving the designer of responsibility for the design; (b) they intend to review the design in conjunction with other experts; (c) they insist on having final approval of the design; (d) they intend to put the reliability engineer one level higher than the design engineer in the organization.

3. It is Reliability's job to see that all the tasks outlined in the reliability program are: (a) carried out by reliability engineers; (b) carried out by the department having the primary responsibility; (c) defined, making sure that quality control does its job; (d) done, including those jobs that the primary responsible departments are incapable of doing.

4. The process of dividing up or budgeting the final reliability goal among the subsystems is known as: (a) reliability estimation; (b) reliability prediction; (c) reliability apportionment; (d) all of the above.

5. Reliability prediction is: (a) a one-shot estimation process; (b) a continuous process starting with paper predictions; (c) a process to be viewed as an end in itself in fulfillment of a contract; (d) none of the above.

6. Reliability prediction and measurement is primarily useful in: (a) evaluating feasibility; (b) establishing reliability goals; (c) evaluating overall reliability; (d) defining problem areas; (e) all of the above.

7. Preventive maintenance is defined as: (a) actions performed as a result of failure; (b) repair of an item to a specified condition; (c) actions performed on a scheduled or routine basis to retain an item in a specified condition; (d) maintenance performed for detection and prevention of incipient failure.

8. Reliability testing of parts is performed to yield which of the following types of information? (a) application suitability; (b) environmental capability; (c) measurement of life characteristics; (d) all of the above.

9. Failure modes and effects analysis involves what activity? (a) the determination of the probability of failure in a specified period of time; (b) the expected number of failures in a given time interval; (c) the study of the physics of failure to determine exactly how a product fails and what causes the failure; (d) a study of the probability of success in a given time period; (e) none of the above.

Chapter 13

1. If the mean time between failure is 200 hours, what is the probability of surviving for 200 hours? (a) 0.20; (b) 0.90; (c) 0.10; (d) 0.63; (e) 0.37.

2. If a system reliability of 0.998 is required, what reliability of two components in series is required? (a) $R_c = 0.99$; (b) $R_c = 0.999$; (c) $R_c = 0.98$; (d) $R_c = 0.9999$; (e) $R_c = 0.998$.

3. Given mean time to failure of 200 hours for each of two components, what is the probability of failure if both components operate in series for one hour? (a) $P = 0.010$; (b) $P = 0.990$; (c) $P = 0.001$; (d) $P = 0.0025$; (e) $P = 0.000025$.

4. The reliability of a device comprised of various parts functionally in series is: (a) the sum of the probabilities of the unreliabilities; (b) the product of the unreliabilities; (c) the sum of the reliabilities; (d) the product of the reliabilities; (e) the sum of the combinations and permutations.

5. The flat portion of the bathtub curve is a region of chance failures; therefore, the reliability equation, $R = e^{-t\lambda}$: (a) does not apply to this region; (b) only applies to this region; (c) applies to the wear-out region as well as the flat region; (d) applies to the entire bathtub curve.

6. If a component has a known constant failure rate of 0.0037 failure per hour, the reliability of two of these components in a series arrangement would be: (a) less than 99 percent; (b) dependent on the wear-out rate of a mating subsystem; (c) insufficient information to solve the problem; (d) 99.63 percent.

7. Assuming an exponential failure distribution, the probability of surviving an operating time equal to twice the MTBF is: (a) practically zero; (b) about 14 percent; (c) about 36 percent; (d) none of the above.

8. Unless repair or maintenance action is taken, the probability of failure of a device which has progressed to the point of wear-out will: (a) decrease; (b) increase; (c) not change.

9. A practical method for accounting for all the tolerance spreads of devices in a unit is to: (a) add the tolerance percentages together and use as the unit tolerance spread; (b) divide the largest tolerance spread by six to obtain the approximate standard deviation for the unit; (c) statistically average the tolerances and use as the unit tolerance; (d) none of the above.

Chapter 14

1. Good housekeeping is an important quality factor in a supplier's plant because: (a) it promotes good working conditions; (b) it minimizes fire hazards; (c) it enhances safer operations; (d) it reflects favorably on the efficiency and management of a company; (e) all of the above.
2. A preaward survey of a potential supplier is best described as a _____ audit. (a) compliance; (b) assessment; (c) quantitative; (d) all of these; (e) none of these.
3. The most desirable method of evaluating a supplier is: (a) history evaluation; (b) survey evaluation; (c) questionnaire; (d) discuss with quality manager on phone; (e) all of the above.
4. The most important step in vendor certification is to: (a) obtain copies of vendor's handbook; (b) familiarize vendor with quality requirements; (c) analyze vendor's first shipment; (d) visit the vendor's plant.
5. During the preaward survey at a potential key supplier, you discover the existence of a quality control manual. This means: (a) that a quality system has been developed; (b) that a quality system has been implemented; (c) that the firm is quality conscious; (d) that the firm has a quality manager; (e) all of the above.
6. A vendor must perform tests on parts to determine which of the following? (a) functional capabilities under specified environmental conditions; (b) materials and processes; (c) configuration and size; (d) cost.

Chapter 15

1. Which of the following may be considered a justification for reinspection by the contractor of a lot which has been verified as nonconforming by the inspector? (a) belief by the contractor that the random samples did not constitute a true picture of the lot; (b) the fact that the contractor had not produced to these specifications before; (c) discovery that the scales used for inspection were out of adjustment; (d) none of the above.

Chapter 16

1. In recent months, several quality problems have resulted from apparent change in design specifications by engineering, including material substitutions. This has only come to light through Quality Engineering's failure-analysis system. You recommend which of the following quality system provisions as the best corrective action? (a) establishing a formal procedure for initial design review; (b) establishing a formal procedure for process control; (c) establishing a formal procedure for specification change control (sometimes called an ECO or SCO system); (d) establishing a formal system for drawing and print control; (e) establishing a formal material review (MRB) system.
2. When a quality engineer wants parts removed from a line which is operating for tolerance checking, he or she should: (a) request the operator and/or supervisor to get them while being observed; (b) request the operator and/or supervisor to sample the line and bring them to the engineer's office; (c) get the samples personally without notifying either the operator and/or supervisor; (d) go out to the line, stop it, take the part, start it, and leave as quickly as possible.

3. The quality engineer should be concerned with the human factors of a new piece of in-house manufacturing equipment as well as its operational effects because it: (a) may speed the line to the point where a visual operator inspection is impossible; (b) may require the operator's undivided attention at the controls so the product cannot be fully seen; (c) may remove an operator formerly devoting some portion of time to inspection; (d) all of the above.

Chapter 17

1. When used together for variables data, which of the following is the most useful pair of quantities in quality control? (a) $\bar{X}$, R; (b) $\bar{X}$, η; (c) R, σ; (d) $\bar{p}$, η; (e) AQL, p'.

2. An $\bar{X}$ and R chart was prepared for an operation using 20 samples with five pieces in each sample. $\bar{X}$ was found to be 33.6 and $\bar{R}$ was 6.2. During production, a sample of five was taken and the pieces measured 36, 43, 37, 34, and 38. At the time this sample was taken: (a) both average and range were within control limits; (b) neither average nor range was within control limits; (c) only the average was outside control limits; (d) only the range was outside control limits; (e) the information given is not sufficient to construct an $\bar{X}$ and R chart using tables usually available.

3. When an initial study is made of a repetitive industrial process for the purpose of setting up a Shewhart control chart, information on the following process characteristic is sought. (a) process capability; (b) process performance; (c) process reliability; (d) process conformance; (e) process tolerance.

4. A p chart is a type of control chart for: (a) plotting bar-stock lengths from receiving inspection samples; (b) plotting fraction-defective results from shipping inspection samples; (c) plotting defects per unit from in-process inspection samples; (d) answers (a), (b), and (c); (e) answers (a) and (c) only.

5. The sensitivity of a p chart to changes in quality is: (a) equal to that of a range chart; (b) equal to that of a chart for averages; (c) equal to that of a c chart; (d) equal to that of a u chart; (e) none of the above.

6. A p chart has exhibited statistical control over a period of time. However, the average fraction defective is too high to be satisfactory. Improvement can be obtained by: (a) a change in the basic design of the product; (b) instituting 100 percent inspection; (c) a change in the production process through substitution of new tooling or machinery; (d) all of the answers above are correct except (b); (e) all of the answers above are correct except (c).

7. In control-chart theory, the distribution of the number of defects per unit follows very closely the: (a) normal distribution; (b) binomial distribution; (c) chi-square distribution; (d) Poisson distribution.

8. You determine that it is sometimes economical to permit X to go out of control when: (a) the individual R's exceed R; (b) the cost of inspection is high; (c) 6σ is appreciably less than the difference between specification limits; (d) the $\bar{X}$ control limits are inside the drawing tolerance limits; (e) never.

9. An electronics firm was experiencing high rejections in their multiple connector manufacturing departments. p charts were introduced as part of a program to

reduce defectives. Control limits were based on prior history, using the formula

$$p' \pm 3\sqrt{\frac{p'(100-p')}{N}}$$

where p' is the historical value of percent defective and N is the number of pieces inspected each week. After six weeks, the following record was accumulated:

| | | | | Percent defective | | | |
Department number	p'	Week 1	Week 2	Week 3	Week 4	Week 5	Week 6
101	12	11	11	14	15	10	12
102	17	20	17	21	21	20	13
103	22	18	26	27	17	20	19
104	9	8	11	6	13	12	10
105	16	13	19	20	12	15	17
106	15	18	19	16	11	13	16

600 pieces were inspected each week in each department. Which department(s) exhibited a point or points out of control during the period? (a) dept. 101; (b) dept. 102; (c) dept. 103; (d) dept. 104; (e) dept. 105; (f) dept. 106.

10. You have just returned from a two-week vacation and are going over with your QC manager the control charts that have been maintained during your absence. The manager calls your attention to the fact that one of the X charts shows the last 50 points to be very near the centerline. In fact, they all seem to be within about 1σ of the centerline. What explanation would you offer? (a) "Somebody 'goofed' in the original calculation of the control limits"; (b) "The process standard deviation has decreased during the time the last 50 samples were taken and nobody thought to recompute the control limits"; (c) "This is a terrible situation. I'll get on it right away and see what the trouble is. I hope we haven't produced too much scrap"; (d) "This is fine. The closer the points are to the centerline, the better our control."

11. You look at a process and note that the chart for averages has been in control. If the range suddenly and significantly increases, the mean will: (a) always increase; (b) stay the same; (c) always decrease; (d) occasionally show out of control of either limit; (e) none of the above.

12. On the production floor, parts being produced measure 0.992 to 1.011. The specification requires the parts to be 0.995 to 1.005. Which of the following techniques would *not* be particularly useful in trying to improve and control the process? (a) PRE-Control; (b) MIL-STD-105 charts; (c) Multi-Vari charts; (d) $\bar{X}$ and R charts; (e) machine capability analysis.

Chapter 18

1. The inspection plan for a new product line may include: (a) detailed production schedule; (b) sampling procedures and techniques; (c) internal techniques for control and segregation of conforming or nonconforming product; (d) answers (a) and (b); (e) answers (a), (b), and (c).

2. Classification of defects is most essential as a prior step to a valid establishment of: (a) design characteristics to be inspected; (b) vendor specifications of critical parts; (c) process control points; (d) economical sampling inspection; (e) a product audit checklist.

3. When giving instructions to those who will perform a task, the communication process is completed: (a) when the worker goes to the work station to do the task; (b) when the person giving the instruction has finished talking; (c) when the worker acknowledges these instructions by describing how he or she will perform the task; (d) when the worker says that he or she understands the instructions.

4. The primary reason that nonconforming material should be identified and segregated is: (a) so that the cause of nonconformity can be determined; (b) to provide statistical information for the "zero defects" program; (c) so it cannot be used in production without proper authorization; (d) to obtain samples of poor workmanship for use in the company's training program; (e) so that responsibility can be determined and disciplinary action taken.

5. Sensory testing is used in a number of industries to evaluate their products. Which of the following is not a sensory test? (a) ferritic annial test; (b) triangle test; (c) duo-trio test; (d) ranking test; (e) paired-comparison test.

6. One of the major hazards in the material review board procedure is the tendency of the board to emphasize only the disposition function and to neglect the _____ function. (a) statistical analysis; (b) corrective action; (c) material evaluation; (d) tolerance review; (e) manufacturing methods.

7. A technique whereby various product features are graded and varying degrees of quality control applied is called: (a) zero defects; (b) quality engineering; (c) classification of characteristics; (d) feature grading; (e) nonsense—you cannot do it.

8. One method to control inspection costs even without a budget is by comparing _____ as a ratio to productive machine time to produce the product. (a) product cost; (b) company profit; (c) inspection hours; (d) scrap material.

9. In a visual inspection situation, one of the best ways to minimize deterioration of the quality level is to: (a) retrain the inspector frequently; (b) add variety to the task; (c) have a program of frequent eye exams; (d) have frequent breaks; (e) have a standard to compare against a part of the operation.

10. A variable measurement of a dimension should include: (a) an estimate of the accuracy of the measurement process; (b) a controlled measurement procedure; (c) a numerical value for the parameter being measured; (d) an estimate of the precision of the measurement process; (e) all of the above.

11. If not specifically required by the product drawing(s) or specification, a nondestructive test (NDT) may be required during production and/or during acceptance at the discretion of the quality engineer responsible for the inspection planning. This statement is: (a) false—because testing is limited to that specified by the design engineer; (b) true—because NDT is a form of inspection (with enhanced senses) not a functional test; (c) false—the quality engineer may impose NDT as he believes necessary but cannot delete it without design engineering permission; (d) true—because all acceptance testing and inspection requirements are up to quality engineering.

12. When specifying the "10:1 calibration principle," we are referring to what? (a) the ratio of operators to inspectors; (b) the ratio of quality engineers to metrology personnel; (c) the ratio of main-scale to vernier-scale calibration; (d) the ratio of calibration standard accuracy to calibrated instrument accuracy; (e) none of the above.

13. A qualification test is used to determine that design and selected production methods will yield a product that conforms to specification. An acceptance test is used to determine that a completed product conforms to design. On this basis, a destructive test can be used for: (a) qualification only; (b) qualification or acceptance; (c) acceptance only; (d) neither qualification nor acceptance.

14. Measuring and test equipment are calibrated to: (a) comply with federal regulations; (b) assure their precision; (c) determine and/or assure their accuracy; (d) check the validity of reference standards; (e) accomplish all of the above.

15. A basic requirement of most gage calibration system specifications is: (a) all inspection equipment must be calibrated with master gage blocks; (b) gages must be color-coded for identification; (c) equipment shall be labeled or coded to indicate date calibrated, by whom, and date due for next calibration; (d) gages must be identified with a tool number; (e) all of the above.

16. What four functions are necessary to have an acceptable calibration system covering measuring and test equipment in a written procedure? (a) calibration sources, calibration intervals, environmental conditions, and sensitivity required for use; (b) calibration sources, calibration intervals, humidity control, and utilization of published standards; (c) calibration sources, calibration intervals, environmental conditions under which equipment is calibrated, and controls for unsuitable equipment; (d) list of standards, identification report, certificate number, and recall records; (e) all of the above.

17. Quality information equipment: (a) is used only by the quality control function; (b) is used only for the purpose of accepting or rejecting product; (c) makes measurements of either products or processes and feeds the resulting data back for decision making; (d) includes automatic electronic instruments but not go/no go gages.

18. Calibration intervals should be adjusted when: (a) no defective product is reported as being erroneously accepted as a result of measurement errors; (b) few instruments are scrapped out during calibration; (c) the results of previous calibrations reflect few out-of-tolerance conditions during calibration; (d) a particular characteristic on a gage is consistently found out of tolerance.

19. A typical use for the optical comparator would be to measure: (a) surface finish; (b) contours; (c) depth of holes; (d) diameters of internal grooves; (e) all of the above.

Chapter 19

1. In MIL-STD-105D, the AQL is always determined at what P on the OC curve? (a) 0.05; (b) 0.10; (c) 0.90; (d) 0.95; (e) none of the above.

2. The steeper the OC curve: (a) the less protection for both producer and consumer; (b) the more protection for both producer and consumer; (c) the lower the AQL; (d) the smaller the sample size.

3. For an operation requiring shipments from your vendor of small lots of fixed size, the sampling plan used for receiving inspection should have its OC curve developed using: (a) the Poisson distribution; (b) the hypergeometric distribution; (c) the binomial distribution; (d) the log normal distribution; (e) the Gaussian (normal) distribution.

4. Two quantities which uniquely determine a single-sampling attributes plan are: (a) AOQL and LTPD; (b) sample size and rejection number; (c) AQL and producer's risk; (d) LTPD and consumer's risk; (e) AQL and LTPD.

5. Selection of a sampling plan from the Dodge-Romig AOQL sampling tables: (a) requires an estimate of the AOQ; (b) requires an estimate of the process average; (c) requires sorting of rejected lots; (d) requires larger samples than MIL-STD-105D for equivalent quality assurance; (e) requires that we assume a consumer's risk of 0.05.

6. The AQL for a given sampling plan is 1.0 percent. This means that: (a) the producer takes a small risk of rejecting product which is 1.0 percent defective or better; (b) all accepted lots are 1.0 percent defective or better; (c) the average quality limit of the plan is 1.0 percent; (d) the average quality level of the plan is 1.0 percent; (e) all lots are 1.0 percent defective or better.

7. Prior to the use of any sampling plan, one must consider: (a) the consumer's and producer's risks must be specified; (b) the method of selecting samples must be specified; (c) the characteristics to be inspected must be specified; (d) the conditions must be specified (material accumulated in lots or inspected by continuous sampling); (e) all of the above.

8. The probability of accepting material produced at an acceptable quality level is defined as: (a) α; (b) β; (c) AQL; (d) $1 - \alpha$; (e) $1 - \beta$.

9. A large lot of parts is rejected by your customer and found to be 20 percent defective. What is the probability that the lot would have been accepted by the following sampling plan: sample size = 10; accept if no defectives; reject if one or more defectives? (a) 0.89; (b) 0.63; (c) 0.01; (d) 0.80; (e) 0.11.

10. Your major product cannot be fully inspected without destruction. You have been requested to plan the inspection program, including some product testing, in the most cost-effective manner. You most probably will recommend that samples selected for the product verification be based upon: (a) MIL-STD-105D, latest issue; attribute sampling; (b) MIL-STD-414, latest issue; variables sampling; (c) either answer 1 or 2 will meet your criteria; (d) neither answer 1 nor 2 will meet your criteria.

Chapter 20

1. In product liability, the proper legal term for statements regarding the reliability of a product is: (a) advertisements; (b) warranties; (c) contracts; (d) representations; (e) obligations.

2. Analysis of data on all product returns is important because: (a) failure rates change with length of product usage; (b) changes in design and in customer use are often well reflected; (c) immediate feedback and analysis of product performance becomes available; (d) all of the above; (e) none of the above.

Chapter 21

1. In consumer products, the complaint rate is most directly a measure of: (a) product quality; (b) customer satisfaction; (c) market value; (d) rejection rate; (e) specification conformance.

2. Complaint indices should: (a) recognize the degree of dissatisfaction as viewed by the customer; (b) provide a direct input to corrective action; (c) not necessarily be based on field complaints or dollar values of claims paid or on service calls; (d) ignore life cycle costs.

Chapter 22

None.

Chapter 23

1. In today's world, quality information documentation is called: (a) end-item narrative; (b) hardware; (c) data pack; (d) software; (e) warrantee.
2. The quality needs for historical information in the areas of specifications, performance reporting, complaint analysis, or run records would fall into which of the following computer application categories? (a) data accumulation; (b) data-reduction analysis and reporting; (c) real-time process control; (d) statistical analysis; (e) information retrieval.
3. In establishing a quality reporting and information feedback system, primary consideration must be given to: (a) number of inspection stations; (b) management approval; (c) timely feedback and corrective action; (d) historical preservation of data; (e) routing copy list.
4. All quality information reports should be audited periodically to: (a) determine their continued validity; (b) reappraise the routing or copy list; (c) determine their current effectiveness; (d) all of the above; (e) none of the above.
5. The basic steps in any data processing system using computers generally are arranged in which of the following orders? (a) data input, storage and retrieval, processing, and output; (b) collection, analysis, input, and output; (c) evaluation, keypunch, processing, and output; (d) recording, input, calculation, and output; (e) keypunch, FORTRAN programming, and output.
6. When planning a system for processing quality data or for keeping inspection and other quality records, the first step should be to: (a) depict the system in a flowchart; (b) hire a statistician; (c) investigate applicable data processing equipment; (d) determine the cost of operating the system; (e) start coding your input data.
7. The management team is establishing priorities to attack a serious quality problem. You are requested to establish a data collection system to direct this attack. You use which of these general management rules to support your recommendations as to the quantity of data required? (a) you have compared the incremental cost of additional data with the value of the information obtained and stopped when they are equal; (b) your decision corresponds to the rules applicable to management decisions for other factors of production; (c) your decision is based upon the relationship between value and cost; (d) all of the above.
8. Computer information processing can become available to any quality engineer through the use of: (a) a terminal and time-sharing agreement; (b) a batch-

processing system in which data are brought to a central area for processing; (c) an in-house system with applicable software; (d) all of the above.

Chapter 24

1. Which of the following is not a legitimate audit function? (a) identify function responsible for primary control and corrective action; (b) provide no surprises; (c) provide data on worker performance to supervision for punitive action; (d) contribute to a reduction in quality cost; (e) none of the above.

2. In many programs, what is generally the weakest link in the quality auditing program? (a) lack of adequate audit checklists; (b) scheduling of audits (frequency); (c) audit reporting; (d) follow-up of corrective action implementation.

3. What item(s) should be included by management when establishing a quality audit function within their organization? (a) proper positioning of the audit function within the quality organization; (b) a planned audit approach, efficient and timely audit reporting, and a method for obtaining effective corrective action; (c) selection of capable audit personnel; (d) management objectivity toward the quality program audit concept; (e) all of the above.

4. Assurance bears the same relation to the quality function that _____ does to the accounting function. (a) vacation; (b) audit; (c) variable overhead; (d) control.

5. All quality information reports should be audited periodically to: (a) determine their continued validity; (b) reappraise the routing or copy list; (c) determine their current effectiveness; (d) all of the above; (e) none of the above.

6. Which of the following techniques would not be used in a quality audit? (a) select samples only from completed lots; (b) examine samples from viewpoint of critical customer; (c) audit only those items which have caused customer complaints; (d) use audit information in future design planning; (e) frequency of audit to depend on economic and quality requirements.

7. Which of the following quality system provisions is of the *least* concern when preparing an audit checklist for the upcoming branch operation quality system audit: (a) drawing and print control; (b) makeup of the MRB (material review board); (c) engineering design change control; (d) control of special processes; (e) calibration of test equipment.

8. You are requested by top management to establish an audit program of the quality systems in each branch plant of your firm. Which of the following schemes would you use in selecting the audit team to optimize continuity, direction, availability, and technology transfer? (a) full-time audit staff; (b) all-volunteer audit staff; (c) the boss's son and son-in-law; (d) hybrid audit staff [a proportion of answers (a) and (b)]; (e) any of the above will make an effective audit team.

9. An audit will be viewed as a constructive service to the function which is audited when it: (a) is conducted by nontechnical auditors; (b) proposes corrective action for each item uncovered; (c) furnishes enough detailed facts so the necessary action can be determined; (d) is general enough to permit managerial intervention.

10. Which of the following is not a responsibility of the auditor? (a) prepare a plan and checklist; (b) report results to those responsible; (c) investigate deficiencies for cause and define the corrective action that must be taken; (d) follow up to see if the corrective action was taken; (e) none of the above.

ANSWERS TO EXAMPLES OF EXAMINATION QUESTIONS USED IN FORMER ASQC QUALITY ENGINEER AND RELIABILITY ENGINEER CERTIFICATION EXAMINATIONS AS PUBLISHED IN *QUALITY PROGRESS*

Chapter 1:	**1** (a)					
Chapter 2:	**1** (c)	**2** (d)	**3** (b)	**4** (c)	**5** (e)	**6** (e)
	7 (c)	**8** (d)				
Chapter 3:	**1** (e)	**2** (e)	**3** (d)	**4** (e)	**5** (a)	
Chapter 4:	—					
Chapter 5:	**1** (d)					
Chapter 6:	—					
Chapter 7:	**1** (c)	**2** (e)	**3** (c)			
Chapter 8:	**1** (c)	**2** (c)	**3** (e)			
Chapter 9:	**1** (b)	**2** (b)	**3** (c)	**4** (b)	**5** (b)	**6** (e)
	7 (d)	**8** (d)	**9** (d)			
Chapter 10:	**1** (a)	**2** (a)	**3** (d)	**4** (d)	**5** (b)	**6** (d)
	7 (c)	**8** (a)				
Chapter 11:	—					
Chapter 12:	**1** (e)	**2** (b)	**3** (b)	**4** (c)	**5** (b)	**6** (e)
	7 (c)	**8** (d)	**9** (c)			
Chapter 13:	**1** (e)	**2** (b)	**3** (a)	**4** (d)	**5** (b)	**6** (c)
	7 (b)	**8** (b)	**9** (d)			
Chapter 14:	**1** (e)	**2** (b)	**3** (a)	**4** (b)	**5** (a)	**6** (a)
Chapter 15:	**1** (c)					
Chapter 16:	**1** (c)	**2** (a)	**3** (d)			
Chapter 17:	**1** (a)	**2** (c)	**3** (a)	**4** (b)	**5** (e)	**6** (d)
	7 (d)	**8** (c)	**9** (d)	**10** (b)	**11** (d)	**12** (b)
Chapter 18:	**1** (e)	**2** (d)	**3** (c)	**4** (c)	**5** (a)	**6** (b)
	7 (c)	**8** (c)	**9** (e)	**10** (c)	**11** (b)	**12** (d)
	13 (b)	**14** (c)	**15** (c)	**16** (c)	**17** (c)	**18** (d)
	19 (b)					
Chapter 19:	**1** (e)	**2** (b)	**3** (b)	**4** (b)	**5** (b)	**6** (a)
	7 (e)	**8** (d)	**9** (e)	**10** (b)		
Chapter 20:	**1** (d)	**2** (d)				
Chapter 21:	**1** (b)	**2** (a)				
Chapter 22:	—					
Chapter 23:	**1** (d)	**2** (e)	**3** (c)	**4** (d)	**5** (a)	**6** (a)
	7 (a)	**8** (d)				
Chapter 24:	**1** (c)	**2** (d)	**3** (e)	**4** (b)	**5** (d)	**6** (c)
	7 (b)	**8** (d)	**9** (c)	**10** (c)		

APPENDIX

II

TABLES

TABLE A
Normal distribution

Proportion of total area under the curve from $-\infty$ to $Z = \dfrac{X - \mu}{\sigma}$. To illustrate: when $Z = 2$, the probability is 0.9773 of obtaining a value equal to or less than X.

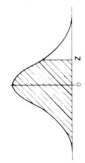

Z	0.00	0.01	0.02	0.03	0.04	0.05	0.06	0.07	0.08	0.09
-3.0	0.00135	0.00131	0.00126	0.00122	0.00118	0.00114	0.00111	0.00107	0.00104	0.00100
-2.9	0.0019	0.0018	0.0017	0.0017	0.0016	0.0016	0.0015	0.0015	0.0014	0.0014
-2.8	0.0026	0.0025	0.0024	0.0023	0.0023	0.0022	0.0021	0.0021	0.0020	0.0019
-2.7	0.0035	0.0034	0.0033	0.0032	0.0031	0.0030	0.0029	0.0028	0.0027	0.0026
-2.6	0.0047	0.0045	0.0044	0.0043	0.0041	0.0040	0.0039	0.0038	0.0037	0.0036
-2.5	0.0062	0.0060	0.0059	0.0057	0.0055	0.0054	0.0052	0.0051	0.0049	0.0048
-2.4	0.0082	0.0080	0.0078	0.0075	0.0073	0.0071	0.0069	0.0068	0.0066	0.0064
-2.3	0.0107	0.0104	0.0102	0.0099	0.0096	0.0094	0.0091	0.0089	0.0087	0.0084
-2.2	0.0139	0.0136	0.0132	0.0129	0.0125	0.0122	0.0119	0.0116	0.0113	0.0110
-2.1	0.0179	0.0174	0.0170	0.0166	0.0162	0.0158	0.0154	0.0150	0.0146	0.0143
-2.0	0.0228	0.0222	0.0217	0.0212	0.0207	0.0202	0.0197	0.0192	0.0188	0.0183
-1.9	0.0287	0.0281	0.0274	0.0268	0.0262	0.0256	0.0250	0.0244	0.0239	0.0233
-1.8	0.0359	0.0351	0.0344	0.0336	0.0329	0.0322	0.0314	0.0307	0.0301	0.0294
-1.7	0.0446	0.0436	0.0427	0.0418	0.0409	0.0401	0.0392	0.0384	0.0375	0.0367
-1.6	0.0548	0.0537	0.0526	0.0516	0.0505	0.0495	0.0485	0.0475	0.0465	0.0455
-1.5	0.0668	0.0655	0.0643	0.0630	0.0618	0.0606	0.0594	0.0582	0.0571	0.0559
-1.4	0.0808	0.0793	0.0778	0.0764	0.0749	0.0735	0.0721	0.0708	0.0694	0.0681
-1.3	0.0968	0.0951	0.0934	0.0918	0.0901	0.0885	0.0869	0.0853	0.0838	0.0823
-1.2	0.1151	0.1131	0.1112	0.1093	0.1075	0.1057	0.1038	0.1020	0.1003	0.0985
-1.1	0.1357	0.1335	0.1314	0.1292	0.1271	0.1251	0.1230	0.1210	0.1190	0.1170

Z	0.00	0.01	0.02	0.03	0.04	0.05	0.06	0.07	0.08	0.09
-1.0	0.1587	0.1562	0.1539	0.1515	0.1492	0.1469	0.1446	0.1423	0.1401	0.1379
-0.9	0.1841	0.1814	0.1788	0.1762	0.1736	0.1711	0.1685	0.1660	0.1635	0.1611
-0.8	0.2119	0.2090	0.2061	0.2033	0.2005	0.1977	0.1949	0.1922	0.1894	0.1867
-0.7	0.2420	0.2389	0.2358	0.2327	0.2297	0.2266	0.2236	0.2207	0.2177	0.2148
-0.6	0.2743	0.2709	0.2676	0.2643	0.2611	0.2578	0.2546	0.2514	0.2483	0.2451
-0.5	0.3085	0.3050	0.3015	0.2981	0.2946	0.2912	0.2877	0.2843	0.2810	0.2776
-0.4	0.3446	0.3409	0.3372	0.3336	0.3300	0.3264	0.3228	0.3192	0.3156	0.3121
-0.3	0.3821	0.3783	0.3745	0.3707	0.3669	0.3632	0.3594	0.3557	0.3520	0.3483
-0.2	0.4207	0.4168	0.4129	0.4090	0.4052	0.4013	0.3974	0.3936	0.3897	0.3859
-0.1	0.4602	0.4562	0.4522	0.4483	0.4443	0.4404	0.4364	0.4325	0.4286	0.4247
-0.0	0.5000	0.4960	0.4920	0.4880	0.4840	0.4801	0.4761	0.4721	0.4681	0.4641
Z	0.00	0.01	0.02	0.03	0.04	0.05	0.06	0.07	0.08	0.09
+0.0	0.5000	0.5040	0.5080	0.5120	0.5160	0.5199	0.5239	0.5279	0.5319	0.5359
+0.1	0.5398	0.5438	0.5478	0.5517	0.5557	0.5596	0.5636	0.5675	0.5714	0.5753
+0.2	0.5793	0.5832	0.5871	0.5910	0.5948	0.5987	0.6026	0.6064	0.6103	0.6141
+0.3	0.6179	0.6217	0.6255	0.6293	0.6331	0.6368	0.6406	0.6443	0.6480	0.6517
+0.4	0.6554	0.6591	0.6628	0.6664	0.6700	0.6736	0.6772	0.6808	0.6844	0.6879
+0.5	0.6915	0.6950	0.6985	0.7019	0.7054	0.7088	0.7123	0.7157	0.7190	0.7224
+0.6	0.7257	0.7291	0.7324	0.7357	0.7389	0.7422	0.7454	0.7486	0.7517	0.7549
+0.7	0.7580	0.7611	0.7642	0.7673	0.7704	0.7734	0.7764	0.7794	0.7823	0.7852
+0.8	0.7881	0.7910	0.7939	0.7967	0.7995	0.8023	0.8051	0.8079	0.8106	0.8133
+0.9	0.8159	0.8186	0.8212	0.8238	0.8264	0.8289	0.8315	0.8340	0.8365	0.8389
+1.0	0.8413	0.8438	0.8461	0.8485	0.8508	0.8531	0.8554	0.8577	0.8599	0.8621
+1.1	0.8643	0.8665	0.8686	0.8708	0.8729	0.8749	0.8770	0.8790	0.8810	0.8830
+1.2	0.8849	0.8869	0.8888	0.8907	0.8925	0.8944	0.8962	0.8980	0.8997	0.9015
+1.3	0.9032	0.9049	0.9066	0.9082	0.9099	0.9115	0.9131	0.9147	0.9162	0.9177
+1.4	0.9192	0.9207	0.9222	0.9236	0.9251	0.9265	0.9279	0.9292	0.9306	0.9319
+1.5	0.9332	0.9345	0.9357	0.9370	0.9382	0.9394	0.9406	0.9418	0.9429	0.9441

(continued)

TABLE A *(continued)*

Z	0.00	0.01	0.02	0.03	0.04	0.05	0.06	0.07	0.08	0.09
+1.6	0.9452	0.9463	0.9474	0.9484	0.9495	0.9505	0.9515	0.9525	0.9535	0.9545
+1.7	0.9554	0.9564	0.9573	0.9582	0.9591	0.9599	0.9608	0.9616	0.9625	0.9633
+1.8	0.9641	0.9649	0.9656	0.9664	0.9671	0.9678	0.9686	0.9693	0.9699	0.9706
+1.9	0.9713	0.9719	0.9726	0.9732	0.9738	0.9744	0.9750	0.9756	0.9761	0.9767
+2.0	0.9773	0.9778	0.9783	0.9788	0.9793	0.9798	0.9803	0.9808	0.9812	0.9817
+2.1	0.9821	0.9826	0.9830	0.9834	0.9838	0.9842	0.9846	0.9850	0.9854	0.9857
+2.2	0.9861	0.9864	0.9868	0.9871	0.9875	0.9878	0.9881	0.9884	0.9887	0.9890
+2.3	0.9893	0.9896	0.9898	0.9901	0.9904	0.9906	0.9909	0.9911	0.9913	0.9916
+2.4	0.9918	0.9920	0.9922	0.9925	0.9927	0.9929	0.9931	0.9932	0.9934	0.9936
+2.5	0.9938	0.9940	0.9941	0.9943	0.9945	0.9946	0.9948	0.9949	0.9951	0.9952
+2.6	0.9953	0.9955	0.9956	0.9957	0.9959	0.9960	0.9961	0.9962	0.9963	0.9964
+2.7	0.9965	0.9966	0.9967	0.9968	0.9969	0.9970	0.9971	0.9972	0.9973	0.9974
+2.8	0.9974	0.9975	0.9976	0.9977	0.9977	0.9978	0.9979	0.9979	0.9980	0.9981
+2.9	0.9981	0.9982	0.9983	0.9983	0.9984	0.9984	0.9985	0.9985	0.9986	0.9986
+3.0	0.99865	0.99869	0.99874	0.99878	0.99882	0.99886	0.99889	0.99893	0.99896	0.99900

Source: Adapted with permission from Eugene L. Grant and Richard S. Leavenworth, *Statistical Quality Control*, 4th ed., McGraw-Hill Book Company, New York, 1972, pp. 642–643.

And we can keep going:

Z	0.00
+4.0	0.9999683
+5.0	0.9999997133
+6.0	0.9999999990

TABLE B
Exponential distribution values of $e^{-X/\mu}$ for various values

Fractional parts of the total area (1.000) under the exponential curve greater than X. To illustrate: if X/μ is 0.45, the probability of occurrences for a value greater than X is 0.6376.

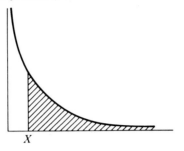

$\dfrac{X}{\mu}$	0.00	0.01	0.02	0.03	0.04	0.05	0.06	0.07	0.08	0.09
0.0	1.000	0.9900	0.9802	0.9704	0.9608	0.9512	0.9418	0.9324	0.9231	0.9139
0.1	0.9048	0.8958	0.8860	0.8781	0.8694	0.8607	0.8521	0.8437	0.8353	0.8270
0.2	0.8187	0.8106	0.8025	0.7945	0.7866	0.7788	0.7711	0.7634	0.7558	0.7483
0.3	0.7408	0.7334	0.7261	0.7189	0.7118	0.7047	0.6977	0.6907	0.6839	0.6771
0.4	0.6703	0.6637	0.6570	0.6505	0.6440	0.6376	0.6313	0.6250	0.6188	0.6126
0.5	0.6065	0.6005	0.5945	0.5886	0.5827	0.5769	0.5712	0.5655	0.5599	0.5543
0.6	0.5488	0.5434	0.5379	0.5326	0.5273	0.5220	0.5169	0.5117	0.5066	0.5016
0.7	0.4966	0.4916	0.4868	0.4819	0.4771	0.4724	0.4677	0.4630	0.4584	0.4538
0.8	0.4493	0.4449	0.4404	0.4360	0.4317	0.4274	0.4232	0.4190	0.4148	0.4107
0.9	0.4066	0.4025	0.3985	0.3946	0.3906	0.3867	0.3829	0.3791	0.3753	0.3716

$\dfrac{X}{\mu}$	0.0	0.1	0.2	0.3	0.4	0.5	0.6	0.7	0.8	0.9
1.0	0.3679	0.3329	0.3012	0.2725	0.2466	0.2231	0.2019	0.1827	0.1653	0.1496
2.0	0.1353	0.1225	0.1108	0.1003	0.0907	0.0821	0.0743	0.0672	0.0608	0.0550
3.0	0.0498	0.0450	0.0408	0.0369	0.0334	0.0302	0.0273	0.0247	0.0224	0.0202
4.0	0.0183	0.0166	0.0150	0.0130	0.0123	0.0111	0.0101	0.0091	0.0082	0.0074
5.0	0.0067	0.0061	0.0055	0.0050	0.0045	0.0041	0.0037	0.0033	0.0030	0.0027
6.0	0.0025	0.0022	0.0020	0.0018	0.0017	0.0015	0.0014	0.0012	0.0011	0.0010

Source: Adapted from S. M. Selby, ed., *CRC Standard Mathematical Tables*, 17th ed., CRC Press, Cleveland, Ohio, 1969, pp. 201–207.

TABLE C
Poisson distribution

1,000 × probability of r or fewer occurrences of event that has average number of occurrences equal to np.

np \ r	0	1	2	3	4	5	6	7	8	9
0.02	980	1,000								
0.04	961	999	1,000							
0.06	942	998	1,000							
0.08	923	997	1,000							
0.10	905	995	1,000							
0.15	861	990	999	1,000						
0.20	819	982	999	1,000						
0.25	779	974	998	1,000						
0.30	741	963	996	1,000						
0.35	705	951	994	1,000						
0.40	670	938	992	999	1,000					
0.45	638	925	989	999	1,000					
0.50	607	910	986	998	1,000					
0.55	577	894	982	998	1,000					
0.60	549	878	977	997	1,000					
0.65	522	861	972	996	999	1,000				
0.70	497	844	966	994	999	1,000				
0.75	472	827	959	993	999	1,000				
0.80	449	809	953	991	999	1,000				
0.85	427	791	945	989	998	1,000				
0.90	407	772	937	987	998	1,000				
0.95	387	754	929	984	997	1,000				
1.00	368	736	920	981	996	999	1,000			
1.1	333	699	900	974	995	999	1,000			
1.2	301	663	879	966	992	998	1,000			
1.3	273	627	857	957	989	998	1,000			
1.4	247	592	833	946	986	997	999	1,000		
1.5	223	558	809	934	981	996	999	1,000		
1.6	202	525	783	921	976	994	999	1,000		
1.7	183	493	757	907	970	992	998	1,000		
1.8	165	463	731	891	964	990	997	999	1,000	
1.9	150	434	704	875	956	987	997	999	1,000	
2.0	135	406	677	857	947	983	995	999	1,000	

TABLE C (*continued*)

np \ r	0	1	2	3	4	5	6	7	8	9
2.2	111	355	623	819	928	975	993	998	1,000	
2.4	091	308	570	779	904	964	988	997	999	1,000
2.6	074	267	518	736	877	951	983	995	999	1,000
2.8	061	231	469	692	848	935	976	992	998	999
3.0	050	199	423	647	815	916	966	988	996	999
3.2	041	171	380	603	781	895	955	983	994	998
3.4	033	147	340	558	744	871	942	977	992	997
3.6	027	126	303	515	706	844	927	969	988	996
3.8	022	107	269	473	668	816	909	960	984	994
4.0	018	092	238	433	629	785	889	949	979	992
4.2	015	078	210	395	590	753	867	936	972	989
4.4	012	066	185	359	551	720	844	921	964	985
4.6	010	056	163	326	513	686	818	905	955	980
4.8	008	048	143	294	476	651	791	887	944	975
5.0	007	040	125	265	440	616	762	867	932	968
5.2	006	034	109	238	406	581	732	845	918	960
5.4	005	029	095	213	373	546	702	822	903	951
5.6	004	024	082	191	342	512	670	797	886	941
5.8	003	021	072	170	313	478	638	771	867	929
6.0	002	017	062	151	285	446	606	744	847	916

np \ r	10	11	12	13	14	15	16
2.8	1,000						
3.0	1,000						
3.2	1,000						
3.4	999	1,000					
3.6	999	1,000					
3.8	998	999	1,000				
4.0	997	999	1,000				
4.2	996	999	1,000				
4.4	994	998	999	1,000			
4.6	992	997	999	1,000			
4.8	990	996	999	1,000			
5.0	986	995	998	999	1,000		
5.2	982	993	997	999	1,000		
5.4	977	990	996	999	1,000		
5.6	972	988	995	998	999	1,000	
5.8	965	984	993	997	999	1,000	
6.0	957	980	991	996	999	999	1,000

(*continued*)

TABLE C (*continued*)

np \ r	0	1	2	3	4	5	6	7	8	9
6.2	002	015	054	134	259	414	574	716	826	902
6.4	002	012	046	119	235	384	542	687	803	886
6.6	001	010	040	105	213	355	511	658	780	869
6.8	001	009	034	093	192	327	480	628	755	850
7.0	001	007	030	082	173	301	450	599	729	830
7.2	001	006	025	072	156	276	420	569	703	810
7.4	001	005	022	063	140	253	392	539	676	788
7.6	001	004	019	055	125	231	365	510	648	765
7.8	000	004	016	048	112	210	338	481	620	741
8.0	000	003	014	042	100	191	313	453	593	717
8.5	000	002	009	030	074	150	256	386	523	653
9.0	000	001	006	021	055	116	207	324	456	587
9.5	000	001	004	015	040	089	165	269	392	522
10.0	000	000	003	010	029	067	130	220	333	458

np \ r	10	11	12	13	14	15	16	17	18	19
6.2	949	975	989	995	998	999	1,000			
6.4	939	969	986	994	997	999	1,000			
6.6	927	963	982	992	997	999	999	1,000		
6.8	915	955	978	990	996	998	999	1,000		
7.0	901	947	973	987	994	998	999	1,000		
7.2	887	937	967	984	993	997	999	999	1,000	
7.4	871	926	961	980	991	996	998	999	1,000	
7.6	854	915	954	976	989	995	998	999	1,000	
7.8	835	902	945	971	986	993	997	999	1,000	
8.0	816	888	936	966	983	992	996	998	999	1,000
8.5	763	849	909	949	973	986	993	997	999	999
9.0	706	803	876	926	959	978	989	995	998	999
9.5	645	752	836	898	940	967	982	991	996	998
10.0	583	697	792	864	917	951	973	986	993	997

np \ r	20	21	22
8.5	1,000		
9.0	1,000		
9.5	999	1,000	
10.0	998	999	1,000

Source: Adapted with permission from E. L. Grant and Richard S. Leavenworth, *Statistical Quality Control,* 4th ed., McGraw-Hill Book Company, New York, 1972.

TABLE D
Distribution of *t*

Value of *t* corresponding to certain selected probabilities (i.e., tail areas under the curve). To illustrate: the probability is 0.95 that a sample with 20 degrees of freedom would have $t = +2.086$ or smaller.

DF	$t_{.60}$	$t_{.70}$	$t_{.80}$	$t_{.90}$	$t_{.95}$	$t_{.975}$	$t_{.99}$	$t_{.995}$
1	0.325	0.727	1.376	3.078	6.314	12.706	31.821	63.657
2	0.289	0.617	1.061	1.886	2.920	4.303	6.965	9.925
3	0.277	0.584	0.978	1.638	2.353	3.182	4.541	5.841
4	0.271	0.569	0.941	1.533	2.132	2.776	3.747	4.604
5	0.267	0.559	0.920	1.476	2.015	2.571	3.365	4.032
6	0.265	0.553	0.906	1.440	1.943	2.447	3.143	3.707
7	0.263	0.549	0.896	1.415	1.895	2.365	2.998	3.499
8	0.262	0.546	0.889	1.397	1.860	2.306	2.896	3.355
9	0.261	0.543	0.883	1.383	1.833	2.262	2.821	3.250
10	0.260	0.542	0.879	1.372	1.812	2.228	2.764	3.169
11	0.260	0.540	0.876	1.363	1.796	2.201	2.718	3.106
12	0.259	0.539	0.873	1.356	1.782	2.179	2.681	3.055
13	0.259	0.538	0.870	1.350	1.771	2.160	2.650	3.012
14	0.258	0.537	0.868	1.345	1.761	2.145	2.624	2.977
15	0.258	0.536	0.866	1.341	1.753	2.131	2.602	2.947
16	0.258	0.535	0.865	1.337	1.746	2.120	2.583	2.921
17	0.257	0.534	0.863	1.333	1.740	2.110	2.567	2.898
18	0.257	0.534	0.862	1.330	1.734	2.101	2.552	2.878
19	0.257	0.533	0.861	1.328	1.729	2.093	2.539	2.861
20	0.257	0.533	0.860	1.325	1.725	2.086	2.528	2.845
21	0.257	0.532	0.859	1.323	1.721	2.080	2.518	2.831
22	0.256	0.532	0.858	1.321	1.717	2.074	2.508	2.819
23	0.256	0.532	0.858	1.319	1.714	2.069	2.500	2.807
24	0.256	0.531	0.857	1.318	1.711	2.064	2.492	2.797
25	0.256	0.531	0.856	1.316	1.708	2.060	2.485	2.787
26	0.256	0.531	0.856	1.315	1.706	2.056	2.479	2.779
27	0.256	0.531	0.855	1.314	1.703	2.052	2.473	2.771
28	0.256	0.530	0.855	1.313	1.701	2.048	2.467	2.763
29	0.256	0.530	0.854	1.311	1.699	2.045	2.462	2.756
30	0.256	0.530	0.854	1.310	1.697	2.042	2.457	2.750
40	0.255	0.529	0.851	1.303	1.684	2.021	2.423	2.704
60	0.254	0.527	0.848	1.296	1.671	2.000	2.390	2.660
120	0.254	0.526	0.845	1.289	1.658	1.980	2.358	2.617
∞	0.253	0.524	0.842	1.282	1.645	1.960	2.326	2.576

Source: Adapted with permission from W. J. Dixon and F. J. Massey, Jr., *Introduction to Statistical Analysis*, 3rd ed., McGraw-Hill Book Company, New York, copyright © 1969. Entries originally from Table III of R. A. Fisher and F. Yates, *Statistical Tables*, Oliver & Boyd Ltd., London.

TABLE E
Distribution of χ^2

Values of χ^2 corresponding to certain selected probabilities (i.e., tail areas under the curve). To illustrate: the probability is 0.95 that a sample with 20 degrees of freedom, taken from a normal distribution, would have $\chi^2 = 31.41$ or smaller.

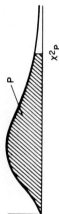

VALUES OF $x^2{}_P$ CORRESPONDING TO P

DF	$\chi^2_{.005}$	$\chi^2_{.01}$	$\chi^2_{.025}$	$\chi^2_{.05}$	$\chi^2_{.10}$	$\chi^2_{.90}$	$\chi^2_{.95}$	$\chi^2_{.975}$	$\chi^2_{.99}$	$\chi^2_{.995}$
1	0.000039	0.00016	0.00098	0.0039	0.0158	2.71	3.84	5.02	6.63	7.88
2	0.0100	0.0201	0.0506	0.1026	0.2107	4.61	5.99	7.38	9.21	10.60
3	0.0717	0.115	0.216	0.352	0.584	6.25	7.81	9.35	11.34	12.84
4	0.207	0.297	0.484	0.711	1.064	7.78	9.49	11.14	13.28	14.86
5	0.412	0.554	0.831	1.15	1.61	9.24	11.07	12.83	15.09	16.75
6	0.676	0.872	1.24	1.64	2.20	10.64	12.59	14.45	16.81	18.55
7	0.989	1.24	1.69	2.17	2.83	12.02	14.07	16.01	18.48	20.28
8	1.34	1.65	2.18	2.73	3.49	13.36	15.51	17.53	20.09	21.96
9	1.73	2.09	2.70	3.33	4.17	14.68	16.92	19.02	21.67	23.59
10	2.16	2.56	3.25	3.94	4.87	15.99	18.31	20.48	23.21	25.19
11	2.60	3.05	3.82	4.57	5.58	17.28	19.68	21.92	24.73	26.76
12	3.07	3.57	4.40	5.23	6.30	18.55	21.03	23.34	26.22	28.30
13	3.57	4.11	5.01	5.89	7.04	19.81	22.36	24.74	27.69	29.82
14	4.07	4.66	5.63	6.57	7.79	21.06	23.68	26.12	29.14	31.32
15	4.60	5.23	6.26	7.26	8.55	22.31	25.00	27.49	30.58	32.80
16	5.14	5.81	6.91	7.96	9.31	23.54	26.30	28.85	32.00	34.27
18	6.26	7.01	8.23	9.39	10.86	25.99	28.87	31.53	34.81	37.16
20	7.43	8.26	9.59	10.85	12.44	28.41	31.41	34.17	37.57	40.00
24	9.89	10.86	12.40	13.85	15.66	33.20	36.42	39.36	42.98	45.56
30	13.79	14.95	16.79	18.49	20.60	40.26	43.77	46.98	50.89	53.67
40	20.71	22.16	24.43	26.51	29.05	51.81	55.76	59.34	63.69	66.77
60	35.53	37.48	40.48	43.19	46.46	74.40	79.08	83.30	88.38	91.95
120	83.85	86.92	91.58	95.70	100.62	140.23	146.57	152.21	158.95	163.64

Source: Adapted with permission from W. J. Dixon and F. J. Massey, Jr., *Introduction to Statistical Analysis*, 3rd ed., McGraw-Hill Book Company, New York, copyright © 1969.

TABLE F
Ninety-five percent confidence belts for population proportion

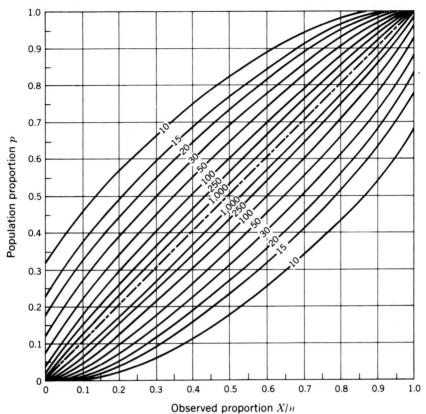

Example In a sample of 10 items, 8 were defective ($x/n = 8/10$). The 95% confidence limits on the population proportion defective are read from the two curves (for $n = 10$) as 0.43 and 0.98.

Source: C. Eisenhart, M. W. Hastay, and W. A. Wallis, *Selected Techniques of Statistical Analysis—OSRD*, McGraw-Hill Book Company, New York, 1947.

TABLE G
Distribution of F

Values of F corresponding to certain selected probabilities (i.e., tail areas under the curve). To illustrate: the probability is 0.05 that the ratio of two sample variances obtained with 20 and 10 degrees of freedom in numerator and denominator, respectively, would have $F = 2.77$ or larger. For a two-sided test, a lower limit is found by taking the reciprocal of the tabulated F value for the degrees of freedom in reverse. For the above example, with 10 and 20 degrees of freedom in numerator and denominator respectively, F is 2.35 and $1/F$ is $1/2.35$, or 0.43. The probability is 0.10 that F is 0.43 or smaller or 2.77 or larger.

n_2 \ n_1	1	2	3	4	5	6	7	8	9
					$F_{.95}(n_1, n_2)$				
1	161.4	199.5	215.7	224.6	230.2	234.0	236.8	238.9	240.5
2	18.51	19.00	19.16	19.25	19.30	19.33	19.35	19.37	19.38
3	10.13	9.55	9.28	9.12	9.01	8.94	8.89	8.85	8.81
4	7.71	6.94	6.59	6.39	6.26	6.16	6.09	6.04	6.00
5	6.61	5.79	5.41	5.19	5.05	4.95	4.88	4.82	4.77
6	5.99	5.14	4.76	4.53	4.39	4.28	4.21	4.15	4.10
7	5.59	4.74	4.35	4.12	3.97	3.87	3.79	3.73	3.68
8	5.32	4.46	4.07	3.84	3.69	3.58	3.50	3.44	3.39
9	5.12	4.26	3.86	3.63	3.48	3.37	3.29	3.23	3.18
10	4.96	4.10	3.71	3.48	3.33	3.22	3.14	3.07	3.02
11	4.84	3.98	3.59	3.36	3.20	3.09	3.01	2.95	2.90
12	4.75	3.89	3.49	3.26	3.11	3.00	2.91	2.85	2.80
13	4.67	3.81	3.41	3.18	3.03	2.92	2.83	2.77	2.71
14	4.60	3.74	3.34	3.11	2.96	2.85	2.76	2.70	2.65
15	4.54	3.68	3.29	3.06	2.90	2.79	2.71	2.64	2.59
16	4.49	3.63	3.24	3.01	2.85	2.74	2.66	2.59	2.54
17	4.45	3.59	3.20	2.96	2.81	2.70	2.61	2.55	2.49
18	4.41	3.55	3.16	2.93	2.77	2.66	2.58	2.51	2.46
19	4.38	3.52	3.13	2.90	2.74	2.63	2.54	2.48	2.42
20	4.35	3.49	3.10	2.87	2.71	2.60	2.51	2.45	2.39
21	4.32	3.47	3.07	2.84	2.68	2.57	2.49	2.42	2.37
22	4.30	3.44	3.05	2.82	2.66	2.55	2.46	2.40	2.34
23	4.28	3.42	3.03	2.80	2.64	2.53	2.44	2.37	2.32
24	4.26	3.40	3.01	2.78	2.62	2.51	2.42	2.36	2.30
25	4.24	3.39	2.99	2.76	2.60	2.49	2.40	2.34	2.28
26	4.23	3.37	2.98	2.74	2.59	2.47	2.39	2.32	2.27
27	4.21	3.35	2.96	2.73	2.57	2.46	2.37	2.31	2.25
28	4.20	3.34	2.95	2.71	2.56	2.45	2.36	2.29	2.24
29	4.18	3.33	2.93	2.70	2.55	2.43	2.35	2.28	2.22
30	4.17	3.32	2.92	2.69	2.53	2.42	2.33	2.27	2.21
40	4.08	3.23	2.84	2.61	2.45	2.34	2.25	2.18	2.12
60	4.00	3.15	2.76	2.53	2.37	2.25	2.17	2.10	2.04
120	3.92	3.07	2.68	2.45	2.29	2.17	2.09	2.02	1.96
∞	3.84	3.00	2.60	2.37	2.21	2.10	2.01	1.94	1.88

Note: n_1 = degrees of freedom for numerator; n_2 = degrees of freedom for denominator.

Source: Adapted with permission from E. S. Pearson and H. O. Hartley (eds.), *Biometrika Tables for Statisticians,* 2nd ed., vol. I, Cambridge University Press, New York, 1958.

10	12	15	20	24	30	40	60	120	∞
				$F_{.95}(n_1, n_2)$					
241.9	243.9	245.9	248.0	249.1	250.1	251.1	252.2	253.3	254.3
19.40	19.41	19.43	19.45	19.45	19.46	19.47	19.48	19.49	19.50
8.79	8.74	8.70	8.66	8.64	8.62	8.59	8.57	8.55	8.53
5.96	5.91	5.86	5.80	5.77	5.75	5.72	5.69	5.66	5.63
4.74	4.68	4.62	4.56	4.53	4.50	4.46	4.43	4.40	4.36
4.06	4.00	3.94	3.87	3.84	3.81	3.77	3.74	3.70	3.67
3.64	3.57	3.51	3.44	3.41	3.38	3.34	3.30	3.27	3.23
3.35	3.28	3.22	3.15	3.12	3.08	3.04	3.01	2.97	2.93
3.14	3.07	3.01	2.94	2.90	2.86	2.83	2.79	2.75	2.71
2.98	2.91	2.85	2.77	2.74	2.70	2.66	2.62	2.58	2.54
2.85	2.79	2.72	2.65	2.61	2.57	2.53	2.49	2.45	2.40
2.75	2.69	2.62	2.54	2.51	2.47	2.43	2.38	2.34	2.30
2.67	2.60	2.53	2.46	2.42	2.38	2.34	2.30	2.25	2.21
2.60	2.53	2.46	2.39	2.35	2.31	2.27	2.22	2.18	2.13
2.54	2.48	2.40	2.33	2.29	2.25	2.20	2.16	2.11	2.07
2.49	2.42	2.35	2.28	2.24	2.19	2.15	2.11	2.06	2.01
2.45	2.38	2.31	2.23	2.19	2.15	2.10	2.06	2.01	1.96
2.41	2.34	2.27	2.19	2.15	2.11	2.06	2.02	1.97	1.92
2.38	2.31	2.23	2.16	2.11	2.07	2.03	1.98	1.93	1.88
2.35	2.28	2.20	2.12	2.08	2.04	1.99	1.95	1.90	1.84
2.32	2.25	2.18	2.10	2.05	2.01	1.96	1.92	1.87	1.81
2.30	2.23	2.15	2.07	2.03	1.98	1.94	1.89	1.84	1.78
2.27	2.20	2.13	2.05	2.01	1.96	1.91	1.86	1.81	1.76
2.25	2.18	2.11	2.03	1.98	1.94	1.89	1.84	1.79	1.73
2.24	2.16	2.09	2.01	1.96	1.92	1.87	1.82	1.77	1.71
2.22	2.15	2.07	1.99	1.95	1.90	1.85	1.80	1.75	1.69
2.20	2.13	2.06	1.97	1.93	1.88	1.84	1.79	1.73	1.67
2.19	2.12	2.04	1.96	1.91	1.87	1.82	1.77	1.71	1.65
2.18	2.10	2.03	1.94	1.90	1.85	1.81	1.75	1.70	1.64
2.16	2.09	2.01	1.93	1.89	1.84	1.79	1.74	1.68	1.62
2.08	2.00	1.92	1.84	1.79	1.74	1.69	1.64	1.58	1.51
1.99	1.92	1.84	1.75	1.70	1.65	1.59	1.53	1.47	1.39
1.91	1.83	1.75	1.66	1.61	1.55	1.50	1.43	1.35	1.25
1.83	1.75	1.67	1.57	1.52	1.46	1.39	1.32	1.22	1.00

TABLE H
Tolerance factors for normal distributions (two-sided)

N	γ = 0.75					γ = 0.90					γ = 0.95					γ = 0.99				
P	0.75	0.90	0.95	0.99	0.999	0.75	0.90	0.95	0.99	0.999	0.75	0.90	0.95	0.99	0.999	0.75	0.90	0.95	0.99	0.999
2	4 498	6 301	7 414	9 531	11 920	11 407	15 978	18 800	24 167	30 227	22 858	32 019	37 674	48 430	60 573	114 363	160 193	188 491	242 300	303 054
3	2 501	3 538	4 187	5 431	6 844	4 132	5 847	6 919	8 974	11 309	5 922	8 380	9 916	12 861	16 208	13 378	18 930	22 401	29 055	36 616
4	2 035	2 892	3 431	4 471	5 657	2 932	4 166	4 943	6 440	8 149	3 779	5 369	6 370	8 299	10 502	6 614	9 398	11 150	14 527	18 383
5	1 825	2 599	3 088	4 033	5 117	2 454	3 494	4 152	5 423	6 879	3 002	4 275	5 079	6 634	8 415	4 643	6 612	7 855	10 260	13 015
6	1 704	2 429	2 889	3 779	4 802	2 196	3 131	3 723	4 870	6 188	2 604	3 712	4 414	5 775	7 337	3 743	5 337	6 345	8 301	10 548
7	1 624	2 318	2 757	3 611	4 593	2 034	2 902	3 452	4 521	5 750	2 361	3 369	4 007	5 248	6 676	3 233	4 613	5 488	7 187	9 142
8	1 568	2 238	2 663	3 491	4 444	1 921	2 743	3 264	4 278	5 446	2 197	3 136	3 732	4 891	6 226	2 905	4 147	4 936	6 468	8 234
9	1 525	2 178	2 593	3 400	4 330	1 839	2 626	3 125	4 098	5 220	2 078	2 967	3 532	4 631	5 899	2 677	3 822	4 550	5 966	7 600
10	1 492	2 131	2 537	3 328	4 241	1 775	2 535	3 018	3 959	5 046	1 987	2 839	3 379	4 433	5 649	2 508	3 582	4 265	5 594	7 129
11	1 465	2 093	2 493	3 271	4 169	1 724	2 463	2 933	3 849	4 906	1 916	2 737	3 259	4 277	5 452	2 378	3 397	4 045	5 308	6 766
12	1 443	2 062	2 456	3 223	4 110	1 683	2 404	2 863	3 758	4 792	1 858	2 655	3 162	4 150	5 291	2 274	3 250	3 870	5 079	6 477
13	1 425	2 036	2 424	3 183	4 059	1 648	2 355	2 805	3 682	4 697	1 810	2 587	3 081	4 044	5 158	2 190	3 130	3 727	4 893	6 240
14	1 409	2 013	2 398	3 148	4 016	1 619	2 314	2 756	3 618	4 615	1 770	2 529	3 012	3 955	5 045	2 120	3 029	3 608	4 737	6 043
15	1 395	1 994	2 375	3 118	3 979	1 594	2 278	2 713	3 562	4 545	1 735	2 480	2 954	3 878	4 949	2 060	2 945	3 507	4 605	5 876
16	1 383	1 977	2 355	3 092	3 946	1 572	2 246	2 676	3 514	4 484	1 705	2 437	2 903	3 812	4 865	2 009	2 872	3 421	4 492	5 732
17	1 372	1 962	2 337	3 069	3 917	1 552	2 219	2 643	3 471	4 430	1 679	2 400	2 858	3 754	4 791	1 965	2 808	3 345	4 393	5 607
18	1 363	1 948	2 321	3 048	3 891	1 535	2 194	2 614	3 433	4 382	1 655	2 366	2 819	3 702	4 725	1 926	2 753	3 279	4 307	5 497
19	1 355	1 936	2 307	3 030	3 867	1 520	2 172	2 588	3 399	4 339	1 635	2 337	2 784	3 656	4 667	1 891	2 703	3 221	4 230	5 399
20	1 347	1 925	2 294	3 013	3 846	1 506	2 152	2 564	3 368	4 300	1 616	2 310	2 752	3 615	4 614	1 860	2 659	3 168	4 161	5 312
21	1 340	1 915	2 282	2 998	3 827	1 493	2 135	2 543	3 340	4 264	1 599	2 286	2 723	3 577	4 567	1 833	2 620	3 121	4 100	5 234
22	1 334	1 906	2 271	2 984	3 809	1 482	2 118	2 524	3 315	4 232	1 584	2 264	2 697	3 543	4 523	1 808	2 584	3 078	4 044	5 163
23	1 328	1 898	2 261	2 971	3 793	1 471	2 103	2 506	3 292	4 203	1 570	2 244	2 673	3 512	4 484	1 785	2 551	3 040	3 993	5 098
24	1 322	1 891	2 252	2 950	3 778	1 462	2 089	2 480	3 270	4 176	1 557	2 225	2 651	3 483	4 447	1 764	2 522	3 004	3 947	5 039
25	1 317	1 883	2 244	2 948	3 764	1 453	2 077	2 474	3 251	4 151	1 545	2 208	2 631	3 457	4 413	1 745	2 494	2 972	3 904	4 985
26	1 313	1 877	2 236	2 938	3 751	1 444	2 065	2 460	3 232	4 127	1 534	2 193	2 612	3 432	4 382	1 727	2 460	2 941	3 865	4 935
27	1 309	1 871	2 229	2 929	3 740	1 437	2 054	2 447	3 215	4 106	1 523	2 178	2 595	3 409	4 353	1 711	2 446	2 914	3 828	4 888
30	1 297	1 855	2 210	2 904	3 708	1 417	2 025	2 413	3 170	4 049	1 497	2 140	2 549	3 350	4 278	1 668	2 385	2 841	3 733	4 768
35	1 283	1 834	2 185	2 871	3 667	1 390	1 988	2 368	3 112	3 974	1 462	2 090	2 490	3 272	4 179	1 613	2 306	2 748	3 611	4 611
40	1 271	1 818	2 166	2 846	3 635	1 370	1 959	2 334	3 066	3 917	1 435	2 052	2 445	3 213	4 104	1 571	2 247	2 677	3 518	4 493
100	1 218	1 742	2 075	2 727	3 484	1 275	1 822	2 172	2 854	3 646	1 311	1 874	2 233	2 934	3 748	1 383	1 977	2 355	3 096	3 954
500	1 177	1 683	2 006	2 636	3 368	1 201	1 717	2 046	2 689	3 434	1 215	1 737	2 070	2 721	3 475	1 243	1 777	2 117	2 783	3 555
1,000	1 169	1 671	1 992	2 617	3 344	1 185	1 695	2 019	2 654	3 390	1 195	1 709	2 036	2 676	3 418	1 214	1 736	2 068	2 718	3 472
∞	1 150	1 645	1 960	2 576	3 291	1 150	1 645	1 960	2 576	3 291	1 150	1 645	1 960	2 576	3 291	1 150	1 645	1 960	2 576	3 291

Source: From C. Eisenhart, M. W. Hastay, and W. A. Wallis, *Selected Techniques of Statistical Analysis,* McGraw-Hill Book Company, New York, 1947. Used by permission.

TABLE I
Factors for $\bar{X}$ and R control charts;* factors for estimating s from R†

$\begin{cases} \text{Upper control limit for } \bar{X} = \text{UCL}_{\bar{x}} = \bar{\bar{X}} + A_2\bar{R} \\ \text{Lower control limit for } \bar{X} = \text{LCL}_{\bar{x}} = \bar{\bar{X}} - A_2\bar{R} \end{cases}$

$\begin{cases} \text{Upper control limit for } R = \text{UCL}_R = D_4\bar{R} \\ \text{Lower control limit for } R = \text{LCL}_R = D_3\bar{R} \end{cases}$

$s = \bar{R}/d_2$

Number of observations in sample	A_2	D_3	D_4	Factor for estimate from $\bar{R}$: $d_2 = \bar{R}/s$
2	1.880	0	3.268	1.128
3	1.023	0	2.574	1.693
4	0.729	0	2.282	2.059
5	0.577	0	2.114	2.326
6	0.483	0	2.004	2.534
7	0.419	0.076	1.924	2.704
8	0.373	0.136	1.864	2.847
9	0.337	0.184	1.816	2.970
10	0.308	0.223	1.777	3.078
11	0.285	0.256	1.744	3.173
12	0.266	0.284	1.717	3.258
13	0.249	0.308	1.692	3.336
14	0.235	0.329	1.671	3.407
15	0.223	0.348	1.652	3.472

* Factors reproduced from *1950 ASTM Manual on Quality Control of Materials* by permission of the American Society for Testing and Materials, Philadelphia. All factors in Table I are based on a normal distribution.

† Reproduced by permission from *ASTM Manual on Presentation of Data*, American Society for Testing and Materials, Philadelphia, 1945.

TABLE J
Weibull Paper

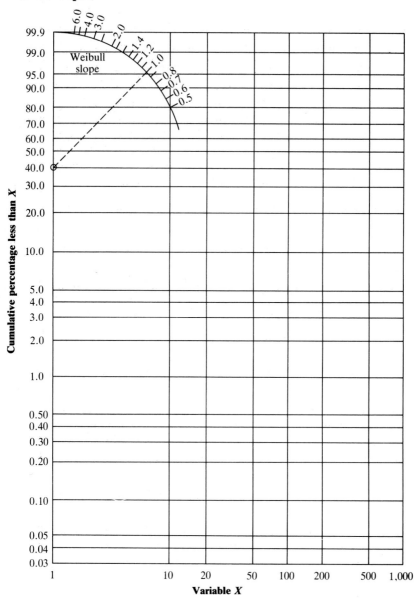

INDEX